不古不今不中不西之学

纪念陈寅恪西域与佛教语文学研究文集

PROCEEDINGS OF THE INTERNATIONAL SYMPOSIUM ON EURASIAN AND BUDDHIST PHILOLOGY IN MEMORIAM OF PROF. TSCHEN YIN-KOH

沈卫荣　侯浩然　主编

中西書局

图书在版编目(CIP)数据

不古不今不中不西之学 : 纪念陈寅恪西域与佛教语文学研究文集 / 沈卫荣, 侯浩然主编. -- 上海 : 中西书局, 2025. -- ISBN 978-7-5475-2397-1

Ⅰ. B948-53

中国国家版本馆CIP数据核字第20257ZN215号

BUGU-BUJIN-BUZHONG-BUXI ZHI XUE:
JINIAN CHENYINKE XIYU YU FOJIAO YUWENXUE YANJIU WENJI

不古不今不中不西之学:
纪念陈寅恪西域与佛教语文学研究文集

沈卫荣　侯浩然　主编

责任编辑　田　甜
助理编辑　杨小珊
装帧设计　王轶颀
责任印制　朱人杰

出版发行　上海世纪出版集团
　　　　　中西書局 (www.zxpress.com.cn)
地　　址　上海市闵行区号景路159弄B座（邮政编码：201101）
印　　刷　常熟市人民印刷有限公司
开　　本　787毫米×1092毫米　1/16
印　　张　36.5
字　　数　767 000
版　　次　2025年5月第1版 2025年5月第1次印刷
书　　号　ISBN 978-7-5475-2397-1/B·150
定　　价　198.00元

本书如有质量问题，请与承印厂联系。电话：0512-52601369

本书为国家社科基金重大项目“西域历史语言研究”

（项目批号 10&ZD086）的成果之一

目　录

中亚出土多语种佛教写本与残片

印藏佛教文本、叙事与互鉴

敦煌宗教与世俗文献

汉藏佛教文献与艺术

黑水城出土文献与西夏佛教

蒙藏文化交流

西藏民间信仰与仪式

文本翻译与跨文化传播

缅怀陈寅恪先生

代　序

何谓不古不今不中不西之学?

——再说汉学、虏学与中国学

沈卫荣
清华大学人文学院中文系

一

傅斯年（1896—1950）曾在其学术名篇《历史语言研究所工作之旨趣》一文中指出:“西洋人研究中国或牵连中国的事物，本来没有很多的成绩，因为他们读中国书不能亲切，认中国事实不能严辨，所以关于一切文字审求，文籍考订，史事辨别，等等，在他们永远一筹莫展。但他们却有些地方比我们范围来得宽些。我们中国人多是不会解决史籍上的四裔问题的，丁谦君的《诸史外国传考证》，远不如沙万君（Édouard Émmannuel Chavannes，沙畹，1865—1918）之译《外国传》、玉连（Stanislas Aignan Julien，儒莲，1797—1873）之解《大唐西域记》、高几耶（Henri Cordier，考狄，1849—1925）之注《马可·波罗行纪》、米勒（Friedrich W. K. Müller, 1863—1930）之发读回纥文书。……凡中国人所忽略，如匈奴、鲜卑、突厥、回纥、契丹、女真、蒙古、满洲等问题，在欧洲人却施格外的注意。说句笑话，假如中国学是汉学，为此学者是汉学家，则西洋治这些匈奴以来的问题岂不是虏学，治这学者岂不是虏学家吗？然而，也许汉学之发达有些地方正借重虏学呢！……西洋人作学问不是去读书，是动手动脚到处寻找新材料，随时扩大旧范围，所以，这学问才有四方的发展，向上的增高。”[①]

---

① 傅斯年:《历史语言研究所工作之旨趣》，载《国立中央研究院历史语言研究所集刊》第1本第1分，1928年，第5页。

于此，傅斯年以“汉学”与“虏学”之说，对中国人和西方人研究中国学问的差别做了一种十分形象和对比鲜明的区分。及至 1928 年傅斯年倡建中央研究院历史语言研究所之前，中国学者多半只通汉语文，只能阅读汉语文文献，并多以传统的经学和史学为主业，所以，他们是传统意义上的“汉学家”；而西方治中国学者，多半兼通汉语文以外的其他多种中国和欧亚地区的民族语文，并能利用这些民族语文的资料，借助比较语文学和历史语言学研究的科学方法，对“匈奴、鲜卑、突厥、回纥、契丹、女真、蒙古、满洲等问题”进行研究，从事的是“四裔之学”，是对中国境内其他众多民族的语文和文明的历史研究。

傅斯年的“汉学”“虏学”之说，在现代学术史上影响很大，对研究西方汉学史也具有启发意义，至今还常引起人们的讨论和思考。特别令人深思的是，“汉学”和“虏学”这样典型的中西学术差别今天依然存在，中西学术仍然各擅胜场，没有克服这种差别。譬如，中国的敦煌研究这几十年来成果卓著，推动中国敦煌研究蓬勃发展的一个重要动力是 20 世纪 80 年代初出现的一个以讹传讹的出自日本学者的说法，即“敦煌在中国，敦煌学在巴黎（或者敦煌学在日本）”，这促使几代中国学者众志成城、发心砥砺，要将敦煌学重镇转移到中国北京，就像当年傅斯年发愿“我们要科学的东方学之正统在中国”一样。遗憾的是，今天中国敦煌学的胜场依然只是其中的“汉学”，而敦煌研究中的“虏学”，依然是西方的“虏学家”占据上风。

还有，近几十年来中国的边疆民族研究取得了可喜的成就，但它多半不是从解读民族语文、文献的语文学出发的，故在利用非汉语文文献从事边疆民族历史文化研究方面，我们依旧相对落后。例如，这十余年来引发了激烈争议的有关北美“新清史”的讨论，其中一个争议的焦点是西方新清史家们爱拿满语文文献说事，批评和指责中国的清史学者不重视满语文文献资料的发现和利用，没有阅读和利用满文文献的能力，仅仅依靠汉语文文献来研究清朝和满族的历史，这样的清史研究当然是极不完美的。所以，清史研究必须有一个民族的转向，要将其学术关注点转向满族和满文文献。显然，中西方中国研究学者之间，依然还存在着“汉学”与“虏学”这种具有典型意义的差别，它还在阻碍着东西学术之交流、圆融和进步。

值得强调的是，傅斯年的“汉学”“虏学”之说只是形象地标示了中西中国学之间的典型差别，它既不是对西方汉学的否定，也不是要把“虏学”另立为一个独立于西方汉学，或者与西方汉学对立的新学科。以往论者习惯于将“虏学”界定为西方和日本学者对中国周边民族和边疆区域的研究，将“虏学家”认定为是那些专治突厥（回纥）学、蒙古学和满学的西方“东方学家”，这是一种显而易见的误解。被傅斯年点名的四位“虏学家”，即“沙万君之译《外国传》、玉连之解《大唐西域记》、高几耶之注《马可·波罗行纪》、米勒之发读回纥文书”①，其中只有米勒是德国柏林民俗博物馆的突厥 / 回纥语文学家，其他三人都是法国

① 傅斯年：《历史语言研究所工作之旨趣》，第 5 页。

的著名汉学家。即使米勒最初也是汉学家出身，他解读古回纥文《金光明经》之学术成就的取得，也是借助了《金光明经》的汉文原译本。[①]沙畹翻译《史记》中的《外国传》，儒莲译注《大唐西域记》，高儿耶注释《马可·波罗行纪》，这些都属于狭义汉学范畴。它们之所以值得称道，是因为它们得力于“虏学”，借助了对汉语文以外的其他民族语文的研究，故能更好地解读这些仅仅依靠汉学知识无法准确译解的汉语文文本。可见，傅斯年所说的“虏学”并非特指专门研究匈奴、回纥、蒙古和满洲的学问，而是西方“汉学”，更确切地说，是西方“中国学”研究的一个不可或缺的组成部分，它是西方中国学优胜于中国国学的一个学术长项。

其实，中学的“汉学”和西学的“虏学”，本可以取长补短，形成一个完整的世界“中国学”，“汉学”和“虏学”本来就是世界中国学这枚硬币的正反两面，二者结合起来，才是一个完整的中国学。当然，这并不是说，西方中国学中没有“汉学”，只有“虏学”，或者相反地说，中国的国学中只有“汉学”，没有“虏学”。傅斯年强调西方中国学以“虏学”见长的意义，在于说明中国之国学因过分专注“汉学”而有明显的不足和局限，“虏学”可为中国学研究扩张许多新的资料，“虏学家”从不满足于阅读那些间接的二手资料，他们“上穷碧落下黄泉，动手动脚找东西”[②]，利用一切有用的一手历史资料，研究中国古代各民族的历史和文化，材料愈扩充，学问愈进步。反观中国的国学家们只通“汉学”，不懂“虏学”，没有能力去扩充研究中国的新材料，对陆续出土的大量非汉语的多语种文献资料束手无策，只能一味地谈论什么整理国故，这样狭隘的汉学焉能取得进步呢？所以，傅斯年主张中国的国学研究，必须要突破传统国学或者“汉学”的范围，效法西方中国学的“虏学”传统，以在中国学界形成“汉学”和“虏学”两面一体的真正的“中国学”。[③]

以往亦有论者习惯于把“虏学”看作是西方学者对今日中国之周边诸民族和地区的研究，认为“虏学”的重要性体现在“自周边看中国”，研究周边是为了更好地看清和理解中国的核心。但是，从近代中西学术史的角度出发，并把“虏学”放在当时那个时代的政治和历史背景中来考察，将“虏学”理解为是一门“自周边看中国”的学问显然是不正确的。对于那个时代的西方和日本的“汉学家”而言，他们从事“虏学”研究，并没有要从周边来看中国的意趣，他们当时所面对的和要研究的那个中国不但本身就包括这些被纳入“虏学”研究范畴的地区和民族的语文和历史文化，而且从中国古代历史的视角来看，“如匈奴、鲜卑、突厥、回纥、契丹、女真、蒙古、满洲等”地区和民族，并非从来都是中国的“周边”，像蒙古人建立的元朝，满洲人建立的清朝，它们本来就是中国的核心，即使是突厥、回纥、契

① Desmond Durkin-Meisterernst, “Müller, Friedrich W. K,” *Encyclopædia Iranica*, July, 2004.
② 傅斯年：《历史语言研究所工作之旨趣》，第 9 页。
③ 傅斯年：《历史语言研究所工作之旨趣》，第 6—7 页。

丹、女真，和他们建立的政权，也不能说都是中国的周边。[①] 傅斯年说“汉学”和“虏学”之差别，并推崇“虏学”的学术意义，显然不是要把“虏学”的对象都看成是中国的周边，而是要把“虏学”像“汉学”一样作为中国学之不可分割的组成部分。从现实政治的角度来看，傅斯年重视“虏学”，正是为了要更好地界定中国，重构中华民族的身份认同。[②] 傅斯年主张“汉学”和“虏学”必须并举，就是要努力打破“国故”“国学”的旧规范，以建立现代的、新颖的“中国学”。兴“虏学”，意在扩展非汉语文献资料，将中国研究超越狭隘的“汉学”范畴，并研究中国与西域（欧亚），乃至世界交往、交流的历史，最终对“中国”和中华文明做出新的界定和定义。傅斯年主张“我们要科学的东方学之正统在中国！”[③] 这表明他不仅仅要争夺世界“汉学”的正统地位，而且还要争夺包括“虏学”在内的世界“东方学”的正统地位。傅斯年不无戏谑地使用了“虏学”这个名称，这或表明他自己曾经是一名“大汉族主义者”，但他将“虏学”和“汉学”并列，把它们当作“中国学”的一体两面，这无疑是对大汉族主义下的中国观的一种十分积极的破解。

二

傅斯年的“汉学”“虏学”之说，是在一个“世界中国学”的框架下提出来的，说的是中国国学以“汉学”为重点，而西方中国学的强项是“虏学”。不难看出，傅斯年此处所说的“汉学”与我们通常所理解的西方“汉学”或者“Sinology”并不是指同一个概念。傅斯年说：“原来‘国学’‘中国学’等等名词，说来都甚不详，西洋人造了支那学‘新诺逻辑’一个名词，本是和埃及脱逻辑、亚西里亚逻辑同等看的，难道我们自己也要如此看吗？”[④] 显然，他不同意把中国的“国学”“中国学”与西方的汉学、“支那学”、“Sinology”看成同一样东西。以往论者因习惯于将傅斯年说的“汉学”与西方汉学等而视之，故将“虏学”与“汉学”对立起来，把“虏学”看成是西方汉学之外的另一个特殊的学术领域，这是对西方汉学及其历史的误解所造成的错误认识，西方的“Sinology”，从一开始就不是狭义的“汉学”，而是一种原始的“中国学”。

从西方人文科学学术史的角度来看，西方汉学属于德国语文学传统中的“新语文学”（Neuphilologie）范畴，18 世纪末、19 世纪初，欧洲的比较语文学家们联合构建起了一个

---

① 傅斯年：《历史语言研究所工作之旨趣》，第 5 页。
② 傅斯年：《历史语言研究所工作之旨趣》，第 8 页。
③ 傅斯年：《历史语言研究所工作之旨趣》，第 10 页。
④ 傅斯年：《历史语言研究所工作之旨趣》，第 8 页。

超越单一民族语言的“印度日耳曼语系”（Indogermanische Sprachfamilie），形成了一个被称为“印度日耳曼（语文）学”的新学科。随之，欧洲语文学从对古典语文学（Classical Philology），即古典希腊语文学和古典拉丁语文学的专注中转移出来，开始了对古典时代之后的欧洲和其他地区诸民族的语言、文本和历史、文化的研究，出现了与古典语文学对应的“新语文学”。具体说来，脱离了古典语文学的“新语文学”，除了对“综比的系族语学，如“印度日耳曼族语学”，以及“赛米的系”（Semitic Languages）、“芬匈系”（Finnish and Hungarian Languages，亦称乌拉尔语系，Uralic Languages）的语文学之外，更催生了欧洲各国之“专语学”，亦即“民族语文学”（National Philology）的形成和成长。如日耳曼语文学（Germanistik）、芬兰语文学（Fennistik）、英语语文学（English Studies）、罗曼语语文学（Romanistik, Romance Philology）等学科的形成，都发生在印度日耳曼语学形成后的19世纪中叶前后。与此同时，与欧洲帝国主义、殖民主义积极对外扩张相应，欧洲的“东方学研究”（Orientalistik，Orientwissenschaft，Oriental Philology，Deutsche Morgenländische Gesellschaft）蓬勃兴起，他们对与西方（Occident）相对的东方（Orient）诸地区、国家、民族和族群的研究，形成了与西方新语文学对应的众多东方“民族语文学”新学科，如伊斯兰学、埃及学、亚述学、突厥学、伊朗学、印度学、中亚学、西藏学、蒙古学、日本学等，而汉学则是西方东方学体系中的一个重要的分支学科。汉学的成立时间与西方民族国家自己的“民族语文学”的创立几乎同时。

但是，必须强调的是，西方汉学从一开始就不是一门只从事汉语文、文本和历史文化之专门研究的学问。傅斯年称“Sinology”为“支那学‘新诺逻辑’”，以其与“国学”“中国学”对应，而不把它与“汉学”等同，这不是一种偶然和随意的表述，而表明他非常清楚“新诺逻辑”不等于“汉学”。尽管“Sinology”作为一门“民族语文学”的学问，它的研究对象应该是一个民族 / 国家的语言、文献、历史和文化。换言之，对于一个单一的民族 / 国家来说，“民族语文学”的研究对象必然就是这个民族的语文和历史文化，如“日耳曼语文学”（Germanistik）研究的是德意志民族的语文和历史文化。可是，西方“Sinology”形成于18世纪末、19世纪初，这个时代西方世界所面对的中国不是一个汉人统治下的传统中国，而是满族统治下的大清王朝。此即是说，“Sinology”诞生的时代与清朝统治下的中国同步，而清代中国不是一个单一的现代民族 / 国家，它的统治民族不是汉族，而是满族。所以，在那个时代形成的“民族语文学” / “汉学”，与它所对应的那个民族不是单一的“汉族”，而是清朝统治下的一个由众多个民族（族群）组成的“中国”，研究清代中国之语文和历史文化的“民族语文学”就不可能是单一的“汉学”。换言之，形成时的“Sinology”的研究对象是清代中国诸多民族语文之文献、历史和文化。所以，它更应该与“中国学”对应，而不是现在我们认知中的狭义的“汉学”。其实，将“Sinology”与“汉学”等而视之，是我们今天常常自以为是的一个错误认知，在很长一段时间内，于西方学界“汉学”这个名称并不常用。例如，早期的德国更经常使用的是“中国学”（Chinakunde，Chinaforschung，Chinawissenschaft），或者“东亚研究”（Ostasienforschung）、“东方语言”（Orientalische Sprache）等名称，甚至也会直接使用“东方学”（Orientalistik，Morgenlaendische Forschung）来指称“Sinologie”（Sinology）。在德国初期的学术语境中，“Sinologie”并不是指只研究汉语文文献和历史文化的“汉学”。

正因为最初与作为一种“民族语文学”的西方汉学相对应的是清朝统治下之中国的国学，而“清朝因兴起于东北，统治的地域达于北方、西北和西南诸边区，与正不断向亚洲内陆扩展的西方强国势力相遇。于是，朝野对边陲史地知识都很关注，除投入巨资，聘用西方传教士以先进仪器测量并编绘出蒙古地区、西北全境地图外，还编纂了大型方志或史地资料汇编，国人对边疆地区的了解比前代有很大增进。中叶以后，列强对我国边地的侵略日益严重，学者们更竞相讲求边陲（尤其是西北）史地之学，成为热门学问，‘如乾嘉间之竞言训诂音韵云’（梁启超语）”[①]。这就是清朝中国之“国学”最重视和关注的学问，它们显然多属于“虏学”，而不是狭义的“汉学”，是故，与它同时代的西方汉学，在其研究对象和内容上或当与清朝的“国学”基本同步。对于清代之中国学而言，“虏学”并不是“四裔之学”，而是它的学术核心。由此可见，“虏学”不是与当时代西方汉学相对立的东西，而正是后者最重要的组成部分，只是西方的“汉学”和“虏学”在研究手段和方法上与清代的国学有很大的不同，后者远远落后于前者。所以，傅斯年要借助西方中国学传统，特别是其“虏学”的学术视野和先进的学术方法，来改造中国传统的人文学术规范，实现中国人文学术的现代化。

于此，如果我们再来对法国和德国早期“汉学”的发展历史稍作回顾，或可更加清楚地认识到欧洲早期的“汉学”不是狭义的汉学，而是结合了“汉学”和“虏学”的典型的“中国学”。今日治西方汉学史者普遍认同法国最早的“汉学”教席是1814年法兰西学院设立的“汉语、鞑靼–满语语言和文献教席”（Chair of Chinese and Tartar Manchu Language and Literature），他的第一位拥有者，也是法国最早的汉学家，是雷慕沙（Jean-Pierre Abel-Rèmusat, 1788—1832）先生。显然，这个世界第一的汉学教席其实根本不能算是一个“汉学”的教席，而是一个“汉语、鞑靼–满语语言和文献”的教席，换言之，这是一个研究清朝之“中国学”的教席。雷慕沙除了汉语之外，还研究蒙古语、满语、藏语和其他多种东亚语言。法国早期的几位汉学大家没有一位是纯粹的、狭义的“汉学”家，而都是兼通多种中国之民族语文的大家。雷慕沙的接班人儒莲本来是一位古典语文学家，对希腊语、闪–含语有很深的研究，后来他专心于研究中国的小说、戏曲、科技史和道教、佛教资料等，他翻译

---

① 参见陈得芝：《王国维的学术进步观及其西域史蒙元史研究》，《蒙元史与中华多元文化论集》，上海古籍出版社2013年版，第220页。

的《大唐西域记》受到了傅斯年的激赏，因为他通过对《大唐西域记》的译注和解读，建构了中国与中亚、印度地区的宗教文化交流史。傅斯年称国人之“四裔之学”比不上“玉连之解《大唐西域记》”，这是因为《大唐西域记》里涉及大量非汉语的词汇，以及非汉族的宗教和文化的丰富内容，若非兼通汉语之外的其他多种欧亚语文，则绝无可能准确地解读《大唐西域记》。此即是说，能解读《大唐西域记》者，一定不只是纯粹的“汉学家”，而且还必须是兼通“虏学”的“中国学家”。雷慕沙之后法国另一位伟大的汉学家是沙畹，他把当时的“汉学”研究水准提高到了可与当时最优秀的希腊文、阿拉伯文和梵文学术研究相媲美的高度。他对圣山泰山的崇拜和宗教史研究，和一系列关于佛教和道教历史的出色著作，以及他对中国第一部信史《史记》之大部分内容的翻译和研究，都是当时代最出色的“中国学”学术著作，而傅斯年专门提到沙畹译《外国传》的水准超越了国人丁谦的《诸史外国传考证》，其中的原因同样是因为沙畹是“汉语、鞑靼–满语语言和文献”的教授，除了汉语以外，沙畹兼通多种欧亚民族语言，所以能对《史记》中的《外国传》做出纯粹的“汉学”家无法做到的精湛的解读。

当然，至今被认为是世界汉学“领头羊”的法国汉学大师伯希和（Paul Pelliot, 1878—1945）先生的学术经历和成就，也可以帮我们更好地理解法国的“汉学”“虏学”与“中国学”之间的关系。尽管伯希和是一位名满天下的天才汉学家，但他不是一位汉学教授，1911年伯希和被法兰西学院聘为“中亚语言、历史和考古学”的讲席教授，他最杰出的学术成就在于中亚和西域研究。他充分发掘和利用大量不同语种的东方语言文献，包括属于闪–含语、印度–伊朗语、阿尔泰语和汉语等不同语系的多种语言，来研究中国和西域的历史文化，可以说他是历史上最杰出的、最具典型意义的“虏学”家。“他有能力以一种史无前例的程度达到了对早期汉语文献的完全的理解，这些文献都程度不等地带上了受亚洲其他高等文化的语言和文献影响的烙印。他不把中国看成是一种自我封闭的、被孤立的文明，而是一种在整个亚洲的语境中形成的文明。”① 因此，伯希和无愧于世界最伟大的汉学家这个头衔，但仅此显然还不足以概括他的学术成就和贡献，他在狭义的“汉学”领域之外所做的“虏学”研究，甚至超越了他作为一名汉学家的成就，例如他在中国的藏学与蒙古学和中亚学（西域研究）等领域的成就同样出类拔萃，使他成为将“汉学”和“虏学”完美结合的“中国学家”。而伯希和的这份学术遗产，形成了欧洲“Sinology”研究中的一个伟大传统。②

像藏学、蒙古学等西方“东方学”的分支学科，尽管其称号很早就出现了，但它们作为一个独立的学科在欧洲大学等学术机构中建立的时间则相对较晚，在很长一段时间内，它们

① 薛爱华（Edward H. Schafer）著，沈卫荣译：《何为汉学，如何汉学？》，载沈卫荣、姚霜主编《何谓语文学：现代人文科学的方法和实践》，上海古籍出版社 2021 年版，第 186 页。

② 关于法国汉学史，参见薛爱华（Edward H. Schafer）著，沈卫荣译：《何为汉学，如何汉学？》，载沈卫荣、姚霜主编《何谓语文学：现代人文科学的方法和实践》，第 177—195 页。

都是被包括在广义的“Sinology”，即“中国学”之内。伯希和之后的多名法国汉学大家，也都在汉学之外，对藏学、蒙古学和中亚研究有非常出色的成就。例如，沙畹的弟子戴密微（Paul Demiéville, 1894—1979）先生，他最著名的学术著作是对藏学和佛学研究的进步有过重大推动意义的《吐蕃僧诤记》，研究的是发生在公元8世纪末的一场在汉地和尚摩诃衍和印度上师莲花戒之间的有关渐悟和顿悟的宗教辩论，他也是一位“中国学家”。[①] 而曾师从伯希和的石泰安（Ralf Stein, 1911—1999）先生，于1951—1975年出任法国高等研究应用学院的汉学教授，主持高地亚洲和中国宗教研究；于1966—1982年为法兰西学院的中国宗教研究教授。石泰安早年曾随巴考（Jacques Bacot, 1877—1965）、拉露（Marcelle Lalou, 1890—1967）学藏学，随葛兰言（Marcel Granet, 1884—1940）、马伯乐（Henri Maspero, 1883—1945）学汉学，随伯希和学习中亚语文学，他做学问能兼采这几位学术大家之长，成为他们之后法国最优秀的藏学家、蒙古学家和中亚语文学家。不得不说，石泰安虽然一直是汉学教授，但他显然更是一名好的藏学家，他把藏学置于整个中国学和亚洲文明研究的宏大背景之中，取得了纯粹的藏学家们无法企及的学术成就。他充分利用和发挥他汉学家的学术长处，对敦煌古藏文历史文献做出了无与伦比的精湛研究。将藏学、蒙古学等作为汉学、中国学研究的一个重要组成部分，这是欧洲学界的一个学术传统。最近，笔者十分惊讶地发现20世纪最伟大的西藏学家、世界藏学的“领头羊”、意大利最杰出的东方学家图齐（Giuseppe Tucci, 1894—1984）先生竟然从来没有担任过藏学教授，意大利似乎也从来没有设立过独立的藏学教席。1931年，图齐被任命为那不勒斯大学远东学院的汉语文讲席教授，但很快便转任罗马大学印度和远东之哲学和宗教学教授，直到1964年退休为止。图齐辉煌的学术生涯确实开始于汉学，他早年曾专注于对中国哲学的研究，翻译过孟子等汉文儒家经典文献。而图齐之后意大利最杰出的藏学家、西藏历史研究的权威人物伯戴克（Luciano Petech, 1914—2010）先生在罗马大学的教职是东亚历史教授（1955—1984），他曾担任过国际藏学研究协会的主席，但从来不是藏学教授。这些都充分说明欧洲早期的“汉学”其实是“中国学”，它不只是一个研究汉语文文献和历史、文化的学科，而是研究中国各民族语文和历史文化的一门学问。[②]

同样的情况亦见于德国早期汉学史中。被认为是德国历史上第一任汉学教授的是乔治·冯·伽贝伦茨（Georg von der Gabelentz, 1840—1893）先生，他于1878年被莱比锡大学任命为首任东亚语言特任教授（eine außerordentliche Professur für ostasiatische Sprachen），所以，他也不是汉学教授，而是“东亚语言”教授。除了教授汉语文外，他同时也教授藏

① Paul Demiéville, *Le Concile de Lhasa: Une controverse sur la quiétisme entre bouddhistes de l'inde et de le Chine au VIIIème siècle* (*The Council of Lhasa: A controversy on quietism between Buddhists of India and China in the 8th century*). Paris: Bibliothèque de l'Institut des Hautes Études chinoises, 1952.

② 参见沈卫荣：《世界藏学研究的回顾与展望》（待刊）。

语、蒙古语和满语等其他中国的民族语文，在汉学之外同时做着满学、蒙古学和藏学的学问。[①] 德国现代最著名的汉学大家是福兰阁（Otto Franke, 1863—1946）先生，他先后在汉堡大学和柏林大学建立起中国学的教席，有百余种著作传世，他的五卷本《中华帝国史》（*Geschichte des Chinesischen Reiches*）是那个时代欧洲中国研究的代表作品。但是，福兰阁的通史性的皇皇巨著却并没有得到欧洲学界的好评，甚至还遭到了曾在柏林大学留学的中国学生陈寅恪和傅斯年的诟病，因为他翻译《春秋》《左传》时犯了许多明显的语文学错误，他的作品"汉学"有余，"虏学"不足，在汉语文文献和历史之外，对中国其他民族语文和历史的关注不够。其实，与那个年代的大部分欧洲汉学家们一样，福兰阁原本也不是一个纯粹的"汉学家"，他最初是一位从事梵文研究的印度学家，后来才专注于中国研究，而且，他也不是只做汉语文文献研究，他在汉堡大学的教席是"东亚语言和历史"。他曾在柏林大学长期主持一个阅读清代四体文碑铭的读书班，同时关注汉文、蒙古文、满文和藏文文献的解读。

与伯希和同时代的德国汉学大家是海涅士（Erich Haenisch, 1880—1966）先生，虽然他曾经在莱比锡、柏林、哥廷根、慕尼黑等多所大学担任汉学教授，但他更是一位著名的蒙古学家和满学家。他的汉学成就自然比不上伯希和，但他的蒙古学和满学成就则超过了伯希和。他重新翻译、注释了著名蒙古文历史著作《蒙古源流》，后来还重构和翻译了蒙古文的《元朝秘史》，编写了蒙古文、满文字典，给德国的中国学研究打上了很深的蒙古学和满学的烙印。这个传统一直延续到当代。20 世纪德国最伟大的蒙古学家海西希（Walther Hessig, 1913—2005）先生原本也是一位汉学家，曾于 1936 年在柏林投归海涅士门下学习汉语和蒙古语，其后在奥地利维也纳大学获得博士学位。20 世纪 40 年代，海西希曾在中国的东北和蒙古地区做了多年的学术考察，收集了大量的蒙古文文献，从事蒙古学、满学研究。20 世纪 50 年代开始，海西希致力于在联邦德国建设一个新的蒙古学学科，他将中国的蒙古学与汉学、突厥学、乌拉尔–阿尔泰学、通古斯–满学、中国藏学和印度学紧密结合在一起，成为一个多学科互相支撑的学科。1964 年，海西希在波恩大学建立"中亚语言文化研究系"（Seminar für Sprach-und Kulturwissenschaft Zentralasiens），并将它发展成为当时世界上规模最大的从事中国蒙古学、藏学、满学和突厥学研究的专门学术机构，成就卓著。[②] 而战后德国汉学的领军人物傅海博（Herbert Franke, 1914—2011），可称是德国最后一位伟大的汉学家，也是一位世界著名的中亚学家。确切地说，他是一位中国边疆民族史研究的专家，是他那个

---

① Edward H. Schafer, "What and How is Sinology," *Tang Studies*, 8–9, 1990, pp.23–34；汉译文见薛爱华著，沈卫荣译：《何为汉学，如何汉学？》，载沈卫荣、姚霜主编《何谓语文学：现代人文科学的方法和实践》，第 177—195 页。Hans van Ess, "History of Pre-Modern Chinese Studies in Germany," *Journal of Chinese History*, 7, 2023, pp.491–524.

② 参见齐木德道尔吉：《德国著名蒙古学家海西西教授》，《蒙古学集刊》2005 年第 4 期。

时代最权威的辽、金、元史研究专家，是契丹、女真和蒙古民族历史研究的权威人士，同时他也曾为西夏和西藏研究作出了特殊的贡献，晚年专门从事元代西藏历史和宗教研究，并在巴伐利亚州科学院主持中亚研究委员会，编写古藏文词源字典。①

在20世纪前半叶，德国还曾出现过一批优秀的兼治“汉学”和“虏学”的中国学家，只是他们在中国藏学、蒙古学和突厥学（回鹘研究）研究等领域的学术成就远远超过了他们于汉学界的学术影响力。所以，他们不再作为汉学家而常被人提及。他们都是学习汉学或者中国学出身，于汉学研究都有不小的成就，但兼通中国藏语、蒙古语、满语和古回鹘文等，故在狭义的汉学之外，取得了更大的学术成就。傅斯年把德国早期的回鹘文研究专家米勒列为欧洲四大“虏学家”之一，其实米勒同样是汉学家出身，之后才专注于解读和研究吐鲁番出土的古回鹘文文献，成为当时最著名的突厥学家的。与米勒同样，欧洲现代最著名的突厥学家、古回鹘文研究专家冯·加班（Annemarie von Gabain，亦称“葛玛丽”，1901—1993）女士，最先也是汉学家，以陆贾之《新语》的德文译注本取得了汉学博士学位（*Ein Fürstenspiegel: Das Sin-yü des Lu Kia*, Tag der Promotion: 30.VII.1930），其后于1935年至1937年在土耳其安卡拉工作，开始从事吐鲁番出土回鹘文文献研究，成为世界上最著名的突厥学家。专门研究吐鲁番出土的古回鹘文文献，显然在冯·加班那个时代也被认为是广义的欧洲汉学或者中国学研究的一个组成部分。② 此外，著名的德国汉学家和“虏学”家还有如劳弗尔（Berthold Laufer, 1874—1934）、雷兴（Ferdinand Lessing, 1882—1961）、维勒（Friedrich Weller, 1889—1980）和霍夫曼（Helmut Hoffmann, 1912—1992）等一批优秀学者，他们都兼通汉学、藏学、蒙古学和佛学研究，但他们当时都未能在德国谋得教席，有的更是因为他们的犹太背景而受到政治迫害，被迫移居海外，如雷兴和劳弗尔后来成了美国最著名的汉学家和藏学家，有的则改任中亚学或者印度学的教职，如维勒和霍夫曼，前者是莱比锡大学的中亚学教授，后者是慕尼黑大学的印度学教授，霍夫曼最终于20世纪60年代末移居美国之后才于印第安纳大学的伯明顿分校出任藏学教授。③ 其中，劳弗尔是伯希和式的中国学研究大家，精通许多东亚和中亚民族语文，研究中国和中国西域地区的物质文明史，在汉学、藏学等领域都是那个时代最杰出的学者之一。④ 而雷兴早年曾在中国研究、工作很多年，曾是北京大学最早的梵文教授，参加过斯文赫定组织的中瑞西北科学考察，他研究汉学、佛学、

---

① 他晚年的代表作是 Herbert Franke, *Chinesischer und tibetischer Buddhismus im China der Yuanzeit: Drei Studien*, Kommision fur Zentralasiatische Studien, Bayerische Akademie der Wissenschaften, Muenchen, 1996。

② 参见苶默：《苶默谈突厥学》，载《上海书评》，澎湃新闻网，https://www.thepaper.cn/newsdetail_forward_4076792［2019-8-4］。

③ Martin Kern, “The Emigration of German Sinologists 1933-1945: Notes on the History and Historiography of Chinese Studies,” *Journal of the American Oriental Society* 118. 4 (1998): 507-529.

④ 参见王丁：《〈劳费尔著作集〉目录的汉译和其人其学》，澎湃新闻网，https://www.thepaper.cn/newsDetail_forward_22715328［2023-4-17］。

藏学和蒙古学，均多有建树，他的成名作《雍和宫》至今还是藏学、汉学的优秀作品。① 自20世纪50年代开始，雷兴担任美国加利福尼亚大学伯克利分校的汉学教授，将欧洲的汉学语文学传统引入美国大学。虽然，雷兴自己后期最主要的学术作品是他编写的蒙古文—英文词典，② 还曾和他的美国弟子 Alex Wayman 一起翻译、注释宗喀巴大师之弟子、第一世班禅喇嘛克主杰（mKhas grub rje dGe legs dpal bzang po）所造的一部关于密乘道次第的论著（*Mkhas grubrje's Fundamentals of the Buddhist Tantras*），③ 但雷兴和他的同事卜弼德（Peter Boodberg, 1903—1972），以及他的学生和学术继承人薛爱华等人在加州大学伯克利分校创立和坚持的汉学语文学传统，是当时美国中国研究的一朵奇葩。

至此，我们不难看出，欧洲早期的"汉学"与我们今天理解的主要以研究汉语文文献和历史为主体的狭义的"汉学"有很大的不同，它更是研究中国古代各种民族语文文献和历史文化的"中国学"研究。欧洲早期汉学家们所具备的这种兼擅"汉学"和"虏学"的学术素养，于今天看来，表明欧洲汉学从一开始就具备了"中国学"的学术性质。如前所述，欧洲汉学形成和发展的初期，面对的是满族统治下的清朝，他们所要了解和研究的"Sinology"，不只是以汉语文和汉族文明为主体的"汉学"。他们对中国古代文明的研究并不局限于对汉语文文献和经典的研究，他们充分认识到他们所研究的这些汉语文献都程度不等地带上了受亚洲其他高等文化的语言和文献影响的烙印。所以，他们不把中国看成一种纯粹汉族的、自我封闭的、被孤立的文明，而是一种在整个亚洲，甚至在整个欧亚文明不断互动、交流的语境中形成的一种高度发达的文明。不得不说，这是一种相当进步的中国古代文明观，而早期西方汉学之所以能够取得如此巨大的学术成就，无疑与这种先进的中国观有密切的关联。

比较而言，近二十年来备受中国学界瞩目和批评的北美新清史家们，却反其道而行之，他们不像欧洲早期的汉学家们那样，把清代中国看成一个多民族和多种语文、文化组成的有机的整体，而坚持要把它拆分成一个"汉人的帝国"和一个"内亚的帝国"，一方面不把满族统治下的清朝作为当时中国的核心，另一方面又过分强调清朝统治之有别于汉族统治王朝的"内亚特性"，不承认清代汉、满、蒙古、藏等各民族之间于宗教、文化上有着很深的交流和融合的历史事实，把"汉化"与"内亚性"作为理解清代历史的两个截然对立的层面，过分地强调汉、满、蒙古、藏等民族之间于政治和宗教方面的冲突，这样的中国观显然远远

---

① Ferdinand D. Lessing, *Yung-ho-kung: An Iconography of the Lamaist Cathedral in Peking. With Notes on Lamaist Mythology and Cult*. Vol. I (Reports from the Scientific Expedition to the North-Western Provinces of China under the Leadership of Dr. Sven Hedin - The Sino-Swedish Expedition-Publication 18. VIII. Ethnography 1.) Stockholm 1942, XX, p.179.

② Ferdinand D. Lessing, *Mongolian-English Dictionary*, London: Routledge, 1960.

③ Ferdinand D. Lessing and Alex Wayman (ed. and tr.) , *Mkhas-grubrje's Fundamentals of the Buddhist Tantras: Rgyud sde spyiḥi rnam par gźag pa rgyas par brjod* (Indo-Iranian Monographs, Vol. VIII.), The Hague, Paris: Mouton, 1968, p.382, Guilders 64.

落后于早期欧洲汉学家们对中国古代文明和历史的认识。于清代历史的学术研究上，作为当代北美中国研究（区域研究）之代表人物的新清史家们，不但早已经缺乏伯希和等欧洲学术前辈学者们那样兼具“汉学”和“虏学”的优秀学术能力，而且不再把“汉学”与“虏学”看成中国研究这枚硬币的正反两面，而坚持要把以利用汉文史料为主的清史研究和必须依靠满文文献的满学研究人为地对立起来，不惜夸大其词地宣传它们之间的不同，并在二者之间制造矛盾和冲突，严重违背了早期欧洲“汉学”与“虏学”相辅相成、圆融无碍的学术传统。是故，这样的“新清史”其实并无多少新意，它是无法推动清史研究的真正进步的。[①]

三

中国现代人文科学研究起步较晚，它的建立或可以傅斯年先生于1928年在中央研究院建立历史语言研究所为标志。以往多有论者认为傅斯年借助法国汉学模式，倡导以历史学和语文学研究为核心，开展对中国各民族语文、文献、历史和文化的研究，以改造中国旧式的“国学”和经学传统，建构理想的中国现代人文科学研究，实现了对中国人文学术的现代化。

傅斯年自称他建立历史语言研究所的目的之一是“我们要科学的东方学之正统在中国！”，他所说的“科学的东方学”指的或是以汉学为主体，兼带其他中国古代民族之语文学学科的中国学研究。西方的“东方学”（Orientalistik）或者“东方语文学”（Oriental Philology），其具体的学术定位随时空的改变而变化，很难明确界定。在今天欧洲的学术语境中，它多指对中东、近东的伊朗、波斯、阿拉伯学和伊斯兰学的研究，但在19世纪、20世纪初，它经常与东亚、远东、中国的语言和古典文明研究相关。所以，傅斯年这里说的“科学的东方学”当是以中国为核心的东亚语文和文明研究。傅斯年不仅倡导和引进法国汉学扎实的语文学和历史学传统，而且也十分推崇法国汉学独具一格的“虏学”传统，即除了对汉语文文献、经典的研究之外，也重视汉语文之外的中国古代其他民族、地区之语文和文献的研究，并善于借助“虏学”来改进和解决“汉学”中仅仅依靠汉学难以解决的问题。这或即是傅斯年理想中的“科学的东方学”。傅斯年没有把西方的“Sinology”与中国学术语境当中的“汉学”等而视之，他把纯粹的汉语文研究的汉学看作中国学者的强项，而西方汉学家专擅的则是中国学中的“虏学”。西洋人最擅长解决的是那些与中国边疆民族语文相关的问题。[②] 中国学者对汉语文以外的其他民族语文的知识极其有限，且缺乏从事“虏学”研究

① 沈卫荣：《我看“新清史”的热闹和门道》，《大元史与新清史——以元代和清代西藏和藏传佛教研究为中心》，上海古籍出版社2019年版，第195—268页。

② 傅斯年：《历史语言研究所工作之旨趣》，第5页。

的语文学，特别是历史语言学研究的比较方法，所以，他们在中国的“四裔之学”方面大大地落后于西方的中国学家。如果中国学者能把西方学者的“虏学”本事学到手，“师夷之长技以制夷”，那么，我们将拥有对汉学和中国学的学术主导地位，“科学的东方学之正统”也就一定会转移到我们中国了。

傅斯年于1928年建立中央研究院历史语言研究所时，距清朝败亡已经十又七年，于中华民国统治下的中国的国学，已与满族统治下的清代中国的国学发生了翻天覆地的变化。不管是西方的汉学，还是中国的国学，此时都处在一个相应地向更传统的汉语文和汉族传统文化转变的过程之中。此外，中国学术当时还纠结于如何于中西两种人文学术传统中找到一条圆融并举的道路，而傅斯年则坚定不移地站在西方汉学和中国学一边，反对中国的国学回归旧式之经学和汉学的道路。王国维曾预言：“异日发明广大我国之学术者，必在兼通世界学术之人，而不在一孔之陋儒。”[①]而既能“兼通世界学术”，又能“发明广大我国之学术者”，当首推傅斯年无疑。傅斯年完全接受了欧洲早期汉学家们从与清朝的交往中所得出的这种今天看来相对先进的中国古代文明观，自然地把它作为其构建中国现代人文科学学术传统的基调和模板，还把它用于他为建构中国和中华民族之身份认同的积极努力之中。傅斯年是最早提出“中国学”这个名称的现代中国人文学术的先驱之一，他明确表示中国古代文明不只是狭义汉学的研究对象，它同时也是“虏学”的研究对象，汉学和“虏学”兼修圆融，才是“中国学”应有的面貌。今日，当我们回顾民国时代中国人文科学研究之辉煌历史的时候，不得不惊叹当时灿烂的学术成就正是傅斯年所推动的这种兼融汉学与“虏学”之学术风气结出的累累硕果。[②]

傅斯年强调现代人文科学之中国古代文明研究，不是一种以注疏四书五经为主的传统的经学和哲学研究，也不是文章家、伦理家所做的那种官样文章式的历史研究，而应该是对中国古代精神文化和物质文明进行历史学的和语文学的研究。傅斯年强调，“汉学”和“虏学”都是一种语文学的研究，“汉学之发达有些地方正借重虏学”[③]。傅斯年推崇“虏学”的目的之一是要纠正中国学者只懂“汉学”的偏差，批评他们不能扩张汉语文文献以外的新材料，不能和西方学者一样“上穷碧落下黄泉，动手动脚找东西”[④]，对到手的出土文献资料也束手无策，甚至干脆抹杀。“不特不因和西洋人接触，能够借用新工具，扩张新材料，反要坐看修元史、修清史的做那样官样形式的文章。又坐看章炳麟君一流人尸学问上的大权威，章氏在文字学以外是个文人，在文字学以内做了一部《文始》，一步倒退过孙诒让，再步倒退过吴

---

① 王国维：《奏定经学科大学文学科大学章程书后》，《东方杂志》1906年第3卷第6期，第113页。

② 参见沈卫荣：《何谓“历史语言研究”？——重读傅斯年〈历史语言研究所工作之旨趣〉》，《北京大学学报》（哲学社会科学版）2024年第5期。

③ 傅斯年：《历史语言研究所工作之旨趣》，第5页。

④ 傅斯年：《历史语言研究所工作之旨趣》，第9页。

大澂，三步倒退过阮元，不特自己不能用新材料，即是别人已经开头用了的新材料，他还抹杀着。至于那部《新方言》，东西南北的猜去，何尝寻扬雄就一字因地变异作观察？这么竟倒退过二千多年了。”①

傅斯年没有把国人修元史、修清史归入“虏学”范畴，而是批评像柯劭忞（1850—1933）这样只通汉学、不通“虏学”的旧式史家，不能扩张新材料、借用新工具，所以，他自修的《新元史》和参编的《清史稿》都只是官样形式的文章，没有什么学术价值。“材料愈扩充，学问愈进步，利用了档案，然后可以订史，利用了别国的记载，然后可以考四裔史事。”② 不懂“虏学”，一定做不好“汉学”。不利用“别国的记载”，又怎么能够写好元史、清史呢？今日北美新清史家批评中国清史学者不重视发现和利用满文档案文献，这是中国当代历史学家没有继承傅斯年倡导的“虏学”传统所造成的后果。但是，美国的清史研究同样从一开始就脱离了“虏学”传统，费正清（John King Fairbank, 1907—1991）、列文森（Joseph R. Levenson, 1920—1969）等美国晚清史学者所做的清史研究都是地道的“汉学”式的研究，他们的中国历史观落后于当年的傅斯年。傅斯年旗帜鲜明地称颂王国维、陈寅恪所做的历史语言研究，特别是他们所从事的属于“虏学”性质的蒙古、西藏研究和西北舆地之学。一方面，他将王国维的《殷卜辞中所见先公先王考》和陈寅恪的《吐蕃彝泰赞普名号年代考》树立为历史研究的新经典、新典范，而另一方面却把“一代宗师”章太炎先生贬称为“一流人尸学术上的大权威”，对他所做的旧式的语言、古文字和经学研究予以彻底的否定，这表明傅斯年与旧式国学决绝的态度，亦表明他贬抑“汉学”和推崇“虏学”的鲜明立场。

清华大学国学研究院（1925—1929）是人们津津乐道的民国时代中国人文学术的一个传奇，四大导师及他们的学术成就是后人不可超越的历史丰碑。但是，很少人注意到这样一个显而易见的事实，即清华国学院和四大导师身体力行的学术研究与中国旧传统中理想的“国学”毫无关系，国学院名不符实！虽然清华国学院的四大导师都是那个时代最杰出的学者，但他们中没有一人是传统国学的经学或者儒学大师，相反他们都是反传统和反“国学”的历史学和语文学大师，王国维和陈寅恪在清华国学院任职期间所做的学问基本上都是“虏学”。陈寅恪倡导的“独立之精神、自由之思想”是典型的现代语文学精神，其学术实践突出他对中国古代文明的理性的和批判性的研究。陈寅恪所说的“不中不西、不古不今之学”是傅斯年所说“虏学”的另一种称呼，它亦古亦今，亦中亦西，是将中国之“汉学”与西方之“虏学”完美结合的典范。陈寅恪留学欧美时的学习经历，都属于西域和佛教语文学范畴，他学习了梵文、藏文、西夏文、蒙古文和满文等多种非汉语的中国古代民族语文，为他今后从事“虏学”研究打下了扎实的语文学基础。陈寅恪于清华十年的学术研究重心在于佛教和西

① 傅斯年：《历史语言研究所工作之旨趣》，第5页。
② 傅斯年：《历史语言研究所工作之旨趣》，第6页。

域语文学，都属于“虏学”范畴，他虽没有专业地从事藏学、蒙古学和满学研究，而是学习伯希和，将他的“虏学”知识和技能，运用于他的“汉学”研究，取得了传统的中国的“汉学”家们难以企及的学术成就。[①]

王国维一向盛赞伯希和为“东方语文学家并史学大家”，“于亚洲诸国古今语无不深造”，他自己也是一位杰出的“中国学”大家，除了释读甲骨文、金文文献取得重大成就以外，进入清华国学院后他专注于对中国西北史地的研究，其中对蒙古史的研究用力最勤，而这与他和伯希和的学术交往，受其影响有很深的关联。1919 年，王国维在为沈曾植七十寿庆写的寿序中这样说道：“道咸以降，途辙稍变，言经者及今文，考史者兼辽金元，治地理者逮四裔，务为前人所不为。虽承乾嘉专门之学，然亦逆睹世变，有国初诸老经世之志。”[②] 同年，王国维翻译了伯希和于法兰西学院的就职演讲稿，深知西方学者“言语学之发明”对于史学研究的功效，并深切体会到掌握多种语言对于西域史地研究的重要意义，急切地希望能培养具有这种能从事“虏学”研究的优秀学者。[③] 1925 年，王国维就任清华国学院导师，开始专注于元史研究，两年多的时间内取得了极其丰硕的成果，使得中国的元史研究一改屠寄之《蒙兀儿史记》和柯劭忞的《新元史》的旧面貌，一跃而占据世界领先的地位。他用力为早期元史研究的重要汉文一手史料作注，出版了《长春真人西游记注》《黑鞑事略笺证》《蒙鞑备略笺证》和《皇元圣武亲征录校注》等，引用极其丰富的各类文献为这些一手的元史资料作注，其“注释之丰富，足以压倒前人”，受到了伯希和的高度赞扬。晚年的王国维无疑是世界上最优秀的“虏学”家之一。[④]

清华国学院的另一位导师赵元任（1892—1982）先生则是中国现代语言学研究的创始人，他对中国各民族语言和地方方言的田野调查，是傅斯年所倡导的历史语言研究的一个重要分支。被人称为中国藏学之父的于道泉（1901—1992）先生曾在陈寅恪的推荐下入职新成立的历史语言研究所，他所做的一项重要工作便是协助赵元任先生用国际音标来记录藏语文文本，而他们当年所选用的藏语文文本就是今日风靡世界的六世达赖喇嘛仓央嘉措的情歌。与此同时，于道泉还将仓央嘉措的六十首情歌分别翻译成了汉文和英文，并做了注释，成为于先生留下的极少的藏学著作中的具有重大影响的一种。[⑤] 国学院四大导师中与传统国学最为接近的是梁启超（1873—1929）先生，但他同样接受了西方语文学、历史学研究方法，他

---

① 参见沈卫荣：《陈寅恪与语文学》，《北京大学学报》（哲学社会科学版）2020 年第 4 期，第 99—108 页。沈卫荣：《陈寅恪与佛教和西域语文学研究》，《清华大学学报》（哲学社会科学版）2021 年第 1 期，第 1—14 页。

② 王国维：《沈乙庵先生七十寿序》，《王国维全集》第八卷，浙江教育出版社、广东教育出版社 2010 年版，第 618 页。

③ 伯希和著，王国维译：《近日东方古言语学上之发明与其结论》，《王国维全集》第十九卷，第 658—672 页。

④ 关于王国维于西域元史研究的成就，参见陈得芝先生上揭文。

⑤ 仓央嘉措著，于道泉译：《第六世达赖喇嘛仓央嘉措情歌》，中央研究院历史语言研究所，1930 年。

从日本引进中国的“文献学”其实就是“语文学”，他所倡导的“新史学”也正是对中国传统历史研究的批评和改革，具有明确的现代人文学术性质。[①] 值得一提的是，曾经流亡于北平二十余年的爱沙尼亚男爵钢和泰（Baron Alexander von Stael-Holstein, 1877—1937）先生，是将欧洲印度学、汉印、汉藏佛教语文学介绍进当时代中国人文学界的重要学术人物，而最初在北平欣赏、支持钢和泰在中国从事这样的“虏学”研究的中国学术大佬就是梁启超先生，梁先生曾为钢和泰在中国出版梵藏汉六种版本对勘的《大宝积经迦叶品梵藏汉六种合刊》而积极奔走，还专门为这本书作序予以推荐。[②] 曾经担任过台湾“中研院历史语言研究所”所长的王汎森先生曾经由衷地感叹“天才为何总是成群结队而来”，民国时期之所以会一下子出现如此众多的学术大家，特别是历史语言研究所成立以后，短时间内能够集结如此众多的学术天才，毫无疑问，这与傅斯年借鉴法国汉学传统，以实现中国人文学术现代化的努力有十分密切的关联。[③]

四

与所有“民族语文学”或者“东方学”的分支学科一样，不管是“汉学”，还是“虏学”，它们首先是一门语文学（philology）的学科，分别是对汉语和民族语言和文献的语文学研究。后人有直接称“汉学”为“汉学语文学”（Sinological Philology）者，就像欧洲早期的“东方学”常常被人与“东方语文学”（Oriental Philology, 陈寅恪等常将它译作“东方古文字学”）等而视之一样。狭义的汉学即是对汉语语言、词义、文献和经典的研究，包括字源学、语法、批评、文化史、文学史和语言史等，而广义的汉学就是中国学研究，它是以中国古代多民族语文的经典、思想和历史为中心的中国古典文明研究，是以研究中国古代各民族的文学、历史和哲学思想为核心的人文科学研究。

对由“汉学”和“虏学”组成的“中国学”或者“中国古典学”的构建和设计，即是傅斯年《历史语言研究所工作之旨趣》的主题，傅斯年理想中的“中国学”就是对中国古代文明的“历史语言研究”。西方现代人文科学一再强调它们是一种历史的和语文学的研究，而不是一种神学的和哲学的研究。在现代科学的人文主义学术语境中，所有人文科学学科，包括哲学和神学，都必须是一种历史的和语文学的研究，否则，它们就是不科学的和不学术

---

① 详见张伯伟：《文献学与 Philologie：旧领域的新认识及其可能的新未来》，《文献》2023 年第 6 期。

② 梁启超：《大宝积经迦叶品梵藏汉六种合刊 · 序》，见 Stael-Holstein，*The Kāçyapaparivarta: a Mahāyānasūtra of the Ratnakūṭa class, edited in the original Sanskrit, in Tibetan and in Chinese*，上海商务印书馆 1926 年版。

③ 王汎森：《天才为何成群地来》，社会科学文献出版社 2019 年版。

的。从这个视角来看，傅斯年建立的历史语言研究所是中国第一个现代人文科学研究所，他主张的将“汉学”和“虏学”合二而一的中国学研究，就是现代中国人文学术研究的核心。对此，我们可以通过对他提出的“史学即史料学”和“语学即史学”这两个概念的解读，来理解他所主张的中国学研究的基本学术理念和指导方针。

20世纪20年代末，傅斯年提出了“史学即史料学”的主张，认为只要用现代科学的手段把史料整理好，历史就跃然纸上了，而这就是史学的全部。他说“历史学不是著史，著史每多多少少带点古世、中世的意味，且每取伦理家的手段，作文章家的本事。近代的历史学只是史料学，利用自然科学供给我们的一切工具，整理一切可逢着的史料”[①]。对此，后人多有挑战和质疑，近百年来历史学发展日新月异，今天很难让人信服历史研究不过是一种史料学的功夫。但我们不应忘记的是，在傅斯年的那个时代，人文学术中对文、史、哲等学科的划分还远没有像今天一样如此壁垒分明。当时的文史哲研究在很大程度上还是互不分家的。傅斯年所说的“历史研究”更接近于西方现代人文科学强调的任何人文学科都必须是历史的和语文学的研究中的那个笼统的“历史研究”，而不是今天被界定为区别于文学和哲学的历史学学科。正因为人文科学的任何学科都必须是一种历史学的学科，都是对一个文本的历史的和语文学的研究，所以，历史学和语文学二者是不可分的，对一个文本（史料）的研究必须采用语文学的方法，而语文学家本身就是一个职业的历史学家。今天很少有人记得傅斯年当年提出“史学即史料学”的同时还提出了“语学即史学”的观念，而这两个概念是相辅相成的，史料之所以可以是史学，即是因为有语学的缘故。“语学即史学”是人文科学研究的核心，傅斯年建立历史语言研究所的学理基础就是“语学即史学”。它与西方的人文学术研究必须是历史的和语文学的研究的准则同出一辙。

“史学即史料学”的历史观并不是傅斯年的创造，而是19世纪欧洲史学主流兰克学派的核心主张。兰克把客观地重现历史作为史学之最崇高和最核心的任务，他拒绝一切历史哲学，反对对历史做概念化、理论化和一般化的处理。兰克史学的基本方法就是尽可能全面和彻底地发现和利用一切可能的历史资料，并对它们做专业的文本整理、编辑、翻译和比较研究，进而能全面、准确和客观地重现历史。傅斯年“史学即史料学”的历史观与兰克史学一脉相承，他指出“史的观念之进步，在于由主观的哲学及伦理价值论变作客观的史料学”，“著史的事业之进步，在于由人文的手段，变做如生物学、地质学的等一般的事业”。[②]“史学即史料学”的宗旨是用自然科学的手段来做“客观的史料学”，将历史研究做成生物学、地质学一般的自然科学的事业。

但是，史料何以能够成为史学呢？傅斯年强调整理史料的方法是“比较不同的史料”，

---

① 傅斯年：《历史语言研究所工作之旨趣》，第3页。
② 傅斯年：《史学方法导论》，载欧阳哲生主编《傅斯年全集》（第二卷），湖南教育出版社2003年版，第308页。

由于“史料是不同的，有来源的不同，有先后的不同，有价值的不同，有一切花样的不同。比较方法之使用，每每是‘因时制宜’的”。“历史的事件虽然一件事只有一次，但一个事件既不尽止有一个记载，所以，这个事件在或种情形下，可以比较而得其近真；好几件的事情又每每有相关联的地方，更可以比较而得其头绪。”① 而史家进行不同史料的比较，并将历史研究做成自然科学一般的事业的手段和工具，就是傅斯年心心念念的“语学”。在《史学方法导论》中，傅斯年说：“其实史学、语学是全不能分者”，像王国维的《殷卜辞中所见先公先王考》和陈寅恪的《吐蕃彝泰赞普名号年代考》这样看似“古文字学”或者“语学”的论文，其实都是史学的典范之作。② 傅斯年这里所说的“语学”“古文字学”指的都是“语文学”，他竭力倡导的“历史语言研究”就是一种将历史学和语文学合二而一的学术方法，它的研究对象不只是狭义的历史，而是包括文学、历史、哲学、艺术和思想在内的整个人文科学。“历史语言研究”是人文科学最基本、最核心的学术方法。既然史学是比较不同史料的语文学，历史研究是对不同史料的文本语文学研究，那么，推而广之，文学、哲学、艺术和思想研究也都是一种文本语文学的研究，要在其本来的历史的和语文的语境中来准确地还原其历史的、文学的和思想的意义。它们与纯粹的历史研究的差别仅在于其所处理的文本的类型不同。

《历史语言研究所工作之旨趣》对傅斯年理想中的“历史语言研究”提出了三个宗旨，这是对“语学即史学”这个概念的具体说明。他提出的第一个宗旨是“凡能直接研究材料便进步，凡间接的研究前人所研究或前人所创造之系统，而不繁丰细密的参照所包含的事实，便退步；上项正是所谓科学的研究，下项正是所谓书院学究的研究，在自然科学是这样，在语言学和历史学亦何尝不然？”③ 此即是说，语学的关键是要研究直接史料，而不是经中间人改动过的间接史料。直接的材料虽然最可信，但它往往又是孤立的、偏重的、例外的，而间接的史料虽然已辗转百千年若干人之手，故多有错乱、改动和不足，但有时它或是前人精密地归纳直接材料所得，故或更加全面、更有系统。科学的历史研究是要充分利用直接的史料来订正间接的史料，而其手段即是语学，比较不同的文本是传统文本语文学的经典做派，所以，“语学即史学”。面对众多不同的文本，文本语文学通常会选择一个现存的或者流传的文本作为基础，充分发掘和利用与这个文本相关的一切更早的、不同来源、不同传承的文本，从语言的和历史的角度对它们做细致的比较文本研究，以对前者做厘定、改正和补充，从而形成一种更可靠、更正确的文本。文本研究是如此，历史研究也是如此，后者无非就是比较各种不同的直接的和间接的史料，以准确地重现历史，达到对它的一种更可靠和合理的理解。用语文学的方法来处理史料，研究历史，这就是傅斯年倡导的“历史语言研究”。

---

① 傅斯年：《史学方法导论》，第 308 页。
② 傅斯年：《史学方法导论》，第 321 页。
③ 傅斯年：《历史语言研究所工作之旨趣》，第 4 页。

傅斯年还提出："凡一种学问能扩充他做研究时应用的工具的，则进步，不能的，则退步。实验学家之相竞如斗宝一般，不得其器，不成其事，语言学和历史学亦复如此。中国历来的音韵学者审不了音，所以把一部切韵始终弄不甚明白，一切古音研究仅仅以统计的方法分类，因为几个字的牵连，使得分类上各家不同，即令这些分类有的对了，也不过能举其数，不能举其实，知其然不知其所以然。"于此，傅斯年提出了要"将来以（西方）比较言语学的方法来建设中国古代言语学"的号召。[①]此之所谓"比较言语学"就是西方学术中的"比较语文学"（comparative philology），即是马克斯·缪勒（Friedrich Max Müeller, 1823—1900）等欧洲学者借以构建"印欧语系"的新的学术工具。与着重于研究某一种语言之发展变化规律的历史语言学不同，它更关注于比较研究世界各种语言间的历史关联，以构建超越单一语言的语族、语系的发展历史。傅斯年提倡的历史语言研究非常重视中国除汉语文以外的其他民族语文的研究，试图构建起中国众多民族语文之间的历史联系，以便更好地理解中国各民族语文的历史发展轨迹和语言体系。

以往我们习惯于将伯希和最擅长的一套比较语文学方法指称为"虏学"，这是历史语言学和比较语文学在汉学和中国学研究中的具体运用，是一套对汉语文文献中出现的其他语文词汇和名物制度名称的"审音与勘同"的方法。这套比较语文学方法对于研究中国古代汉语文献和古代历史非常重要，凸显"语学即史学"的学术意义。[②]但是，伯希和的这套属于历史语言学范畴的"审音与勘同"的学术方法，并不是"虏学"的全部，后者更多是指西方汉学家利用其掌握的非汉语语文能力，尽可能多地扩展和利用与中国历史研究相关的非汉语文献资料，而"审音勘同"则主要是用于解决古汉语文献中出现的非汉语词汇和名物制度名称的还音和释义问题。伯希和精通汉学，同时还是杰出的中亚语文学家（Central Asian Philologist），能利用大量非汉语的文献和考古资料来研究汉学，把汉学置于整个亚洲，乃至世界人文学术研究的高度，所以，他是当之无愧的一流"汉学家"和"虏学家"。同时，伯希和更在汉学研究中将"比较言语学"和"历史语言学"这两门工具运用到了出神入化的地步，故被认为是世界上唯一能完全读懂古代汉语文献的汉学家，其成就超越了只懂得汉语文的乾嘉大师钱大昕。傅斯年要借助伯希和使用的这两门工具，"来处治些新获见的材料，所以才有这个历史语言研究所之设置"[③]。在傅斯年看来，只有掌握了"审音勘同"这门工具，我们才能够像西方汉学家一样来讨论"希拉艺术如何影响中国佛教艺术，中央亚细亚的文化

① 傅斯年：《历史语言研究所工作之旨趣》，第 6 页。

② 参见韩儒林：《关于西北民族史中的审音与勘同》，《南京大学学报（哲学社会科学）》1978 年第 3 期。亦参见陈得芝：《浅论边疆民族历史文献学的建设》，载吴春梅主编《安大史学·第一辑》，安徽大学出版社 2004 年版；陈得芝：《蒙元史研究中的历史语言学问题》，《西域研究》2012 年第 4 期。当下从事"审音与勘同"之最优秀的作品是卓鸿泽：《还音杂录》，上海古籍出版社 2023 年版。

③ 傅斯年：《历史语言研究所工作之旨趣》，第 7 页。

成分如何影响到中国的物事，中国文化成分如何于安西西去，等等”[①]有关中国与世界交互影响和作用之历史的重大问题。

总而言之，傅斯年主张的“史学即史料学”秉承的是兰克史学的科学史观，而“语学即史学”是他倡导的“历史语言研究”的核心，遵循的是现代西方人文学术的主流思想，它融合“汉学”和“虏学”，是现代中国学研究的核心。近百年来，世界人文科学研究发生了翻天覆地的变化，语文学不再是人文科学的主流，人文科学内部学科的划分越来越细致，不同学科间的学术壁垒越来越分明，而历史学的学科性则越来越模糊，古典的中国学与当代的中国研究完全是两个不同性质的学科，傅斯年当年倡导的“历史语言研究”已经成为陈年往事，人们不复理解他所谓“史学即史料学”和“语学即史学”的学术意义。可是，语文学基础训练的普遍缺失显然是影响今天中国人文科学事业发展的一个重要障碍，“虏学”依然是中国学者至今无法克服的学术短板，这严重影响了我们当下建构和实践一种超越西方汉学和东方学的、属于我们自己的中国学的学术研究。我们今天重新讨论傅斯年的“史学即史料学”和“语学即史学”的历史观和方法论，重新审视和理解他所说的“汉学”“虏学”与中国学的关系和意义，对于我们今天倡导和建设新时代的世界中国学，具有特别重大的现实意义。

---

① 傅斯年：《历史语言研究所工作之旨趣》，第 7 页。

中亚出土多语种佛教写本与残片

Divisions and Chapter Titles of the *Lotus Sūtra* in Central Asia

Peter Zieme
Berlin-Brandenburg Academy of Sciences and Humanities

1. General survey

Given the immense number of more than 5 000 manuscripts or prints of the *Saddharmapuṇḍarīka-sūtra* (*Lotus sūtra*) in the main languages of Sanskrit, Chinese, and Tibetan, the attestation of the text in the local Central Asian languages is rather limited. Versions in Tocharian and Sogdian are missing. The sparse attestation of the sūtra in Khotanese is justified by the fact that it was probably recited rather in Sanskrit[①] by the Khotanese because a great many Sanskrit manuscripts come from this region. In Khotan, the *Saddharmapuṇḍarīkasūtra* was part of the Buddhists' regular repertoire, only an abridged version of the sūtra[②] is preserved in their own language. Moreover, in *Zambasta* chapter 6 there are among the quotations from different sūtras[③] two short passages from the *Saddharmapuṇḍarīkasūtra*. In the Tangut language (Xixia), more than 30 manuscripts are known alone in the treasure house of St. Petersburg.[④]

---

① Cp. Von Hinüber 2014.
② Katayama 2014.
③ Chen & Sanclemente 2018; Katayama 2014.
④ Kyčanov 1999.

2. Old Uyghur Buddhism

In Old Uyghur Buddhism the *Lotus sūtra* is richly attested, mainly its chapter 25[①], while other parts are less known.[②] So far all Uyghur fragments seem to be translated from Kumārajīva's Chinese version which was most widespread, but further research may reveal other results, especially as there are copies in different scripts. All in all, the *Lotus sūtra* is known in Old Uyghur Buddhism from the 10th century to the end of the Yuan Dynasty. Although the Old Uyghur material is very heterogeneous, it can be stated without exaggeration that the sūtra was held in high esteem by Uyghur Buddhists. A temple banner is of particular importance. It has already been described in detail by Albert Grünwedel[③]. The central part shows Avalokiteśvara handing over the jewel chain to the Two Buddhas. In cartouches accompanying the individual scenes, the quotations from the *Lotus Sūtra* are inscribed in Old Uyghur translation.[④] There is evidence of manuscripts fed by the Indian tradition, other copies written in Sogdian script are rather bound to the local Central Asian Buddhism and can be attributed to the early period of Old Uyghur culture. The largest group of manuscripts based on Kumārajīva's version (T 262) are the Uyghur manuscripts in the classical Uyghur Sūtra script. The Old Uyghur translation of the influential lotus commentary *Miao Fa Lianhua Jing Xuanzan* (妙法蓮華經玄贊) is preserved in at least five manuscripts.[⑤]

3. Old Uyghur concertina booklet

Among the Uyghur block-printed books of the Turfan collection in Berlin there are so far only two pieces of a booklet which are related to the *Lotus sūtra*. These two fragments of the Berlin Turfan Collection bear witness to a special concertina book: U 4780 (TM 31)[⑥] and Mainz 490 (T III D)[⑦]. These are block-printed sheets whose "pages" have 6 lines. Pagination numbers are not preserved. Only a few lines are complete.

---

① Known in about 25 copies, latest edition Özcan Devrez 2020.
② Survey in Zieme 2005.
③ Grünwedel 1905: 68–70.
④ Zieme 2021.
⑤ Kudara 1980; Kudara 1988.
⑥ VOHD 13,23 # 286.
⑦ VOHD 13,23 # 332.

4. Structure of the booklet

This previously unidentified text is structured as follows. The ordinal number of a given chapter is followed by its chapter title and concludes with a word meaning "chapter": *bölök* or *bölmäk*①. After that, the author quotes a verse taken from the respective chapters. Whether this quotation is meant to represent an essential aspect of the chapter, however, remains rather doubtful. Probably, it serves to identify the given chapter within the sūtra. The booklet thus proves to be a kind of guide in the form of an overview of the *Saddharmapuṇḍarīkasūtra*. Whether this Old Uyghur concertina book is an original version is not certain, but it is highly probable. The chapter names from the 11th to the 24th chapter have been preserved.② Whether this booklet is a translation or not, remains dubious, at any rate, it shows to what extent Uyghur Buddhists have studied the *Lotus Sūtra*. Perhaps the work served as a bibliographical medium to arrange Buddhist scriptures, because with the listing of chapter names and distinctive sentences it was possible to get a quick overview. However, at this point, to give a definite determination is nearly impossible.

Chinese fragments of chapter titles of the *Fahua jing* are known from Turfan: Ch/U 7727 recto③, but more from Dunhuang,④ mainly Or.8210/S.189v and Or.8210/S.2092v. Manuscripts of this kind may well have been models for the Old Uyghur print, which, however, not only lists the chapters but also adds quotations.⑤ Another field is represented by numerous lists of sūtras known

---

① For both terms, cf. Wilkens 2021.

② In my (then preliminary) comment on these fragments in Zieme 2011: 228, I included Mainz 805 (VOHD 143, 23 # 334). However, this block print does not belong to the text group discussed here, since its "pages" have 5 lines.

③ G. Kara, P. Zieme & L. Tugusheva, *Avalokitesvara-Sutras* (*Berliner Turfantexte L*), Turnhout 2022, p.240.

④ At this point I express my gratitude for the information I received via H-Buddhism and emails (May 2021). Both texts are transcribed in the *Dunhuang Fojiao Jinglu Jijiao* 敦煌佛教經録輯校 [An Annotated Transcript of Buddhist Catalogues from the Dunhuang Corpus] (Nanjing: Jiangsu guji, 1997) by Fang Guangchang 方廣錩. Both texts follow Kumārajīva's translation, but p.2092 also include the captions of the so-called chapter 29 and chapter 30, two apocryphal chapters that mostly circulated separately. Although Fang thinks that both texts were copied in the Guiyijun era (848–1006) (Fang 1997: 411–417), it seems doubtful that one can easily date several lines written on the verso of two manuscripts that may possibly date from before the mid-8th century.

⑤ In this context, Allan Ding reminds me (via the same email as mentioned in the preceding footnote) of the manuscript Pelliot chinois 3150 (Fang 1997: 377–401), which contains the table of contents of the *Mahāyāna Mahānirvāṇa Sūtra*, and each chapter caption is accompanied with the incipit (and sometimes the explicit) of the chapter in question. (I guess this may represent some kind of notes for the librarian and/or amanuensis).

from Dunhuang which were intended for libraries of certain schools or for cataloguing Buddhist books.[1]

5. Edition and interpretation according to the chapter names

Chapter Eleven[2]

Mainz 490b

01 01 biry(e)g[(i)rminč[3] ärdini üzäki stup]

02 02 körmäk[4] böl[ök]

03 03 ıdok-lar-nıŋ [edisi atı kötrül]

04 04 -miš nirvan-ka kirü[5] [ ]

05 05 kečti ärsär ymä ʾ[ ]

06 06 ärdini üzäki stu[p ičintä ärür]

The Seeing [of the Jewel Stūpas]. El[eventh] chap[ter].

[The Lord] of the saints, [Whose name is exalted]—though [a long time] has passed since he entered the nirvāṇa—[dwells in] the jewel stūpa.

T.IX.262.32b16 見寶塔品第十一	The appearance of the Jewel Stūpa. Chapter 11.
T.IX.262.33c17 聖主世尊	The holy ruler, the world revered,
雖久滅度在寶塔中	though long extinguished, already dwells in the jewel stūpa.

Chapter Twelve

Mainz 490a

The chapter title in Old Uyghur is missing. Only the last verse of the quotation is preserved.

07 00 [küsä]

① Giles 1957, No. 7887–7912.

② The Sanskrit title is *stūpasaṃdarśanaparivartaḥ*.

③ Written as one word.

④ It would be expected *közünmäk* "appearance", for the stūpa magically rises from the earth and so appears.

⑤ Chin. *miedu* 滅度 : "complete extiction of all physical and emotional suffering"; "death of the Buddha" (DDB).

08 01 -mädim[①] beš törlüg [kü]s[änčig]

09 02 mäŋi-lär-kä[②]

I have not [desired] after the fivefold [wonder]ful bliss.

T.IX.262.34b23 提婆達多品第十二	Devadatta. Chapter 12.
T.IX.262.34c10–11 我念過去劫	I remember ages past,
爲求大法故	when I, in pursuit of the Great Law,
雖作世國王	I was king of a worldly kingdom,
不貪五欲樂	but felt no desire for the five desires.

Chapter Thirteen

10 03[③] üč y(e)g(i)rminč tutgalı üt

11 04 -lämäk bölök:

12 05 küsüš-ümüz täginür adı kötrül

13 06 -miš-ä näŋ bo nom ugurınta

The instructing to hold (fast). Thirteenth chapter.

Our desire[④] is: O Thou whose name is exalted, [may] by no means [worry about teaching!]

T.IX.262.35c27 勸持品第十三	Perseverance. Chapter 13.
c29 皆于佛前作是誓 36a01 言	and in front of the Buddha they made the following vow:
唯願世尊	May the World Honoured One
不以爲慮	not worry about this any further!
我等于佛滅後	We will - after the Buddha has passed away -
36a02 當奉持讀誦説此經典	preserve, read, recite and expound this Sūtra

Chapter Fourteen or Fifteen

U 4780a

① The emendation to *[küsä]mädim* follows Chin. *butan* 不貪 [*tan* 貪: "craving greed; sensual attachment, covetousness; to hanker after. To crave, to want (Skt. *rāga, lobha*; Tib. *chags pa, 'dod chags*)"].

② After that the line has remained empty. This shows that the chapter name was marked as a heading.

③ Continuation of Mainz 490a.

④ *shi shi* 是誓 .

14 01 ʾwqw[ ]
15 02 ywr[ ]
16 03 ʾʾs [ ]
17 04 pwsʾ[ ]
18 05 ülgüsü[z]
19 06 [ ]kʾrq lʾr [ ]

The preserved word remains are not clear enough for a localization.

Chapter Sixteen

20 07 [al]tı y[egirminč burhannıŋ yašı]
21 08 bölmäk [ ]
22 09 adı [kötrülmiš]
23 10 ülgü[ ]

[Lifespan of the Buddha]. Six[teenth] chapter.
He whose name [is exalted] measure [ ].

These two words are insufficient for locating the exact passage, but the word *ülgü* "measure" can be regarded as a hint for a possible quotation from the 16th chapter.

T.IX.262.42a29 如來壽量品第十六　　The Life Span of the Tathāgata. Chapter 16.

Chapter Seventeen

24 11 yetiy(e)g[irminč]
25 12 bar bolu täg[ ]
U 4780b
26 01 tägin[ ]
27 02 učsuz [ ]

Seve[nteenth chapter]: [Merit is] accessible(?).
[ ] boundless [ ].

The localization of the quotation is not possible.

T.IX.262.44a05 分别功德品第十七	The discernment of merit. Chapter 17.

Chapter Eighteen

28 03 säkiz [y(e)g(i)rminč]

29 04 eyin [ögirmäk atlıg bölök]

30 05 kamag kiši-lär [ ]

31 06 äšidip alku-gun [ ]

U 4780c

32 01 -lar arhant kut[ın]

33 02 bulsar-lar [ ]

34 03 -kä : üč [törlüg]

35 04 bilig [ ]

With [joy]. Eight[eenth chapter]

All men hear [this law and] all attain arhatship, (endowed) with [the six supernatural faculties], the three[fold knowledge and the eight liberations].

T.IX.262.46b21 隨喜功德品第十八	Merit of Compassionate Joy. Chapter 18.
T.IX.262.47b07–08 諸人聞是法	All who hear this law,
皆得阿羅漢	attain arhatship,
具足六神通	endowed with the six supernatural faculties,
三明八解脱	the threefold knowledge, and the eight deliverances.

Chapter Nineteen

36 05 tokuz y(e)g[irminč]

37 06 ädgüs[i]

38 07 bi[rök]

39 08 atl(ı)g ya[ ]

40 09 kiši-nin[g ätözi arıg süz]

41 10 -ök bolur inčä [ ]

42 11 vaituri ärd[ini]

Good [for the teachers]. Nine[teenth Chapter].

If [someone keeps the teaching, then the body] of the person [becomes pure] like the *vaiḍūrya* jew[el...].

T.IX.262.47c02 法師功德品第十九	Merits for the Teachers of the Law. Chapter 19.
50a03–04 若持法花者	If there is one who keeps the lotus of the law,
其身甚清浄	his body will be pure
如彼浄琉璃	as pure lapis lazuli,
衆生皆憙見	and living creatures will rejoice at the sight of him.

Chapter Twenty

43 12 y(e)g(i)rminč suda ta[ ]

[Bodhisattva Sadāprarudita]. Twentieth [Chapter].

T.IX.262.50b23 常不輕菩薩品第二十 The Bodhisattva Never Despising. Chapter 20.

The preserved letters let us suppose a form of the bodhisattva name: swdʾ[....]. The Sanskrit form of the bodhisattva's name Chang bujing 常不輕 is translated from Sadāparibhūta or Sadāprarudita. The Chinese transcription for this is Satuobolun 薩埵波倫, but this cannot be the template for the Uyghur transcription unless there has been an erroneous transcription.

Chapter Twenty-three

U 4780d

44 01 üč [otuzunč]

45 02 bodis(a)t(a)v [bölök]

46 03 m(ä)n čankram[it]

47 04 ulug oron [ ]

48 05 bultum s[ ]

Bodhisattva [Bhaiṣajyarāja]. [Twenty]-third [chapter:]

I, wandering① [ ] great place [ ] I obtained.

① The Uyghur text has the special term *caṅkramita* which is mostly used in in connection with *kıl-* "to make", i.e., to make circumambulation, to go around during a meditation practice.

[T.IX.262.53a04] 藥王菩薩本事	The former matters of the Bodhisattva Bhaiṣajyarāja.
品第二十三	Chapter 23.

I estimate that the quotation from this chapter can be seen in the following passage.

[T.IX.262.53a26] 得此三昧已	After he (i.e. the Buddha) obtained this samādhi,
心大 [a27] 歡喜	the heart was (with) great joy.
即作念言	And he said:
我得現	I obtained the samādhi
一切色身三昧	by which one can appear in all kinds of bodies
皆 [a28] 是得聞法華經力	only through the power of listening to the *Fahua jing*.

Unfortunately, there is no direct equivalent to *ulug oron* "great place" so that the equation remains uncertain.

Chapter Twenty-four

The short remainder of Mainz 490c can be related to chapter 24 (Gadgadasvara *Miaoyin pusa* 妙音菩薩) of the sūtra[1].

49 01 bo nom ärdini üčün kälü [ya]rlıka[dı]

50 02 [ ]r [ ]

For this sūtra jewel he deigned to come.

This sentence is a condensed form of the following passage of the chapter in question:

[T.IX.262.55b24] 爾時釋迦牟 [b25] 尼佛	At that time Śākyamuni Buddha
告文殊師利	spoke to Mañjuśrī:
是妙音菩薩摩訶薩	This Bodhisattva-Mahāsattva Gadgadasvara
欲 [b26] 从净華宿王智佛國	wishes to leave the realm of the Buddha
净華宿王智	
與八萬四千菩薩圍繞	— together with 84000 Bodhisattva circumambulating —
[b27] 而來至此娑婆世界	to come to this Sahā world

① Here, I express my gratitude to S.-Chr. Raschmann for checking my contribution and especially for this important observation.

供養親近禮拜于我	to make offerings to me, to become familiar and to worship
b28 亦欲供養聽法華經	also to make offerings to the *Fahua jing* for listening to it.

Abbreviations

DDB = Digital Dictionary of Buddhism (Charles Muller, Tokyo).

VOHD 13, 23 = Yakup, Abdurishid (2009). *Alttürkische Handschriften Teil 15: Die Uigurischen Blockdrucke der Berliner Turfansammlung Teil 3: Stabreimdichtungen, Kalendarisches, Bilder, Unbestimmte Fragmente und Nachträge*. Stuttgart.

References

Chen, Ruixuan & Sanclemente, Diego Loukota. 2018. "Mahāyāna Sūtras in Khotan. Quotations in Chapter 6 of the Book of Zambasta (I)." In: *Indo-Iranian Journal* 61: 131–175.

Fang, Guangchang 方廣錩. 1997. *Dunhuang Fojiao Jinglu Jijiao* 敦煌佛教經録輯校 [An Annotated Transcript of Buddhist Catalogues from the Dunhuang Corpus]. Nanjing: Jiangsu guji.

Giles, Lionel. 1957. *Descriptive catalogue of the Chinese manuscripts from Tunhuang in the British Museum*. London: The Trustees of the British Museum.

Grünwedel, Albert.1905. *Bericht über archäologische Arbeiten in Idikutschari and Umgebung. Abhandlungen der I. Klasse der Königlichen Akademie der Wissenschaften 24*. München.

von Hinüber, Oskar. 2014. "A Saddharmapuṇḍarīkasūtra Manuscript from Khotan: The Gift of a Pious Khotanese Family." In: *Journal of Oriental Studies* 24: 134–156.

Katayama, Yumi. 2014. "The Khotanese Summary of the Saddharmapuṇḍarīkasūtra and the Saddharmapuṇḍarīkopadeśa." In: *Acta Tibetica et Buddhica* 7, 82–102.

Kudara, Kōgi.1980.「ウイグル訳『妙法蓮華経玄賛』(1)」,『佛教學研究』36: 45–65.

Kudara, Kōgi. 1988. "Uigurische Fragmente eines Kommentars zum Saddharmapuṇḍarīka-Sūtra." In: J. P. Laut & K. Röhrborn (eds.), *Der türkische Buddhismus in der japanischen Forschung*. Wiesbaden, 34–55, 102–106.

Kychanov, E. I. 1999. *Katalog tangutskich buddijskich pamjatnikov Instituta vostokovedenija Rossijskoj akademii nauk*. Kioto: Universitet Kioto.

Özcan Devrez, Ceyda. 2020. *Eski Uygurca Kuanşi İm Pusar İncelemesi*. Ankara: Türk Dil Kurumu Yayınları Yazar.

Wilkens, Jens. 2021. *Handwörterbuch des Altuigurischen*. Göttingen: Universitätsverlag Göttingen.

Yakup, Abdurishid. 2011. "An Old Uyghur Fragment of the *Lotus Sūtra* from the Krotkov Collection in St. Petersburg." In: *Acta Orientalia Academiae Scientiarum Hungaricae* 64: 411–426.

Zieme, Peter. 2005. "Uighur Version of the Lotus Sutra with Special Reference to Avalokiteśvara's transformation bodies." In: ユーラシア古語文献の文献学的研究 NEWSLETTER No. 13 2005–9–22.

Zieme, Peter. 2011. Review of Yakup, Abdurishid/Knüppel, Michael, *Die uigurischen Blockdrucke der Berliner Turfansammlung Teil 1: Tantrische Texte*. Stuttgart 2007 [*Alttürkische Handschriften Teil 11*, VOHD XIII, 19]; Yakup, Abdurishid, *Die uigurischen Blockdrucke der Berliner Turfansammlung Teil 2: Apokryphen, Ma-hāyāna-Sūtren, Erzählungen, Magische Texte, Kommentare und Kolophone*. Stuttgart 2008 [Alttürkische Handschriften Teil 12, VOHD XIII, 20]; Yakup, Abdurishid, *Die uigurischen Blockdrucke der Berliner Turfansammlung Teil 3: Stabreimdichtungen, Kalendarisches, Bilder, Unbestimmte Fragmente und Nachträge*. Stuttgart 2009 [*Alttürkische Handschriften Teil 15*, VOHD XIII, 23] In: *Orientalistische Literaturzeitung* 106 (3): 224–228.

Zieme, Peter. 2021. "Scenes from the Lotus Sūtra. An Old Uygur Temple Banner with Cartouche Inscriptions." In: *Manuscripta Orientalia* 27: 3–19.

Appendix

For conservation purposes the original block printed fragments were pasted on paper in a combined way as one can see from the digital images in the Digital Turfan Archive of the Berlin Brandenburg Academy of Sciences and Humanities, Berlin: http://turfan.bbaw.de/dta/.

Here they are separated according to the "pages" à six lines and given in a reconstructed manner according to the contents:

pict. 1. **01–06** (Mainz 490b 01–06)
pict. **2. 07–13** (Mainz 490a 01–06)
pict. 3. **14–19** (U 4780a 01–06)
pict. 4. **20–25** (U 4780a 07–12)
pict. 5. **26–31** (U 4780b 01–06)
pict. 6. **32–37** (U 4780c 01–06)
pict. 7. **38–43** (U 4780c 07–12)
pict. 8. **44–48** (U 4780d 01–05)
pict. 9. **49–50** (Mainz 490c 01–02)

pict. 1. 01–06 (Mainz 490b 01–06)

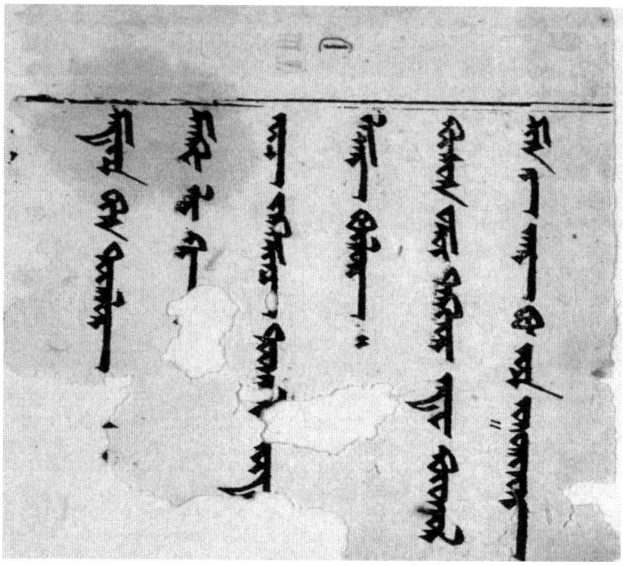

pict. 2. 07–13 (Mainz 490a 01–06)

pict. 3. 14–19 (U 4780a 01–06)

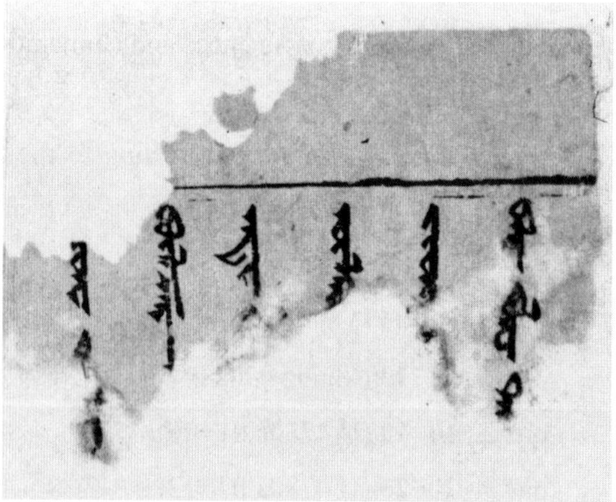

pict. 4. 20–25 (U 4780a 07–12)

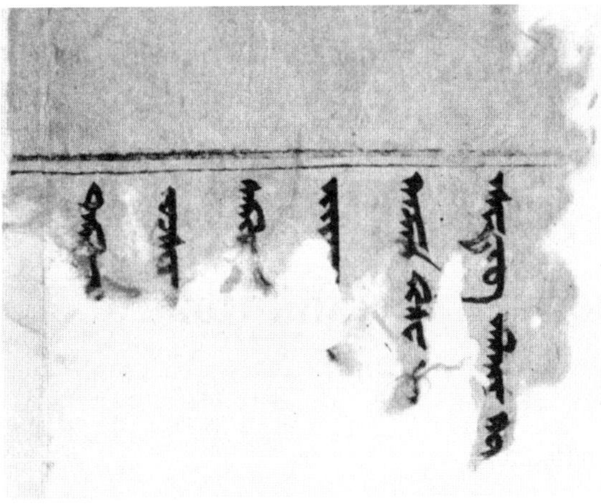

pict. 5. 26–31 (U 4780b 01–06)

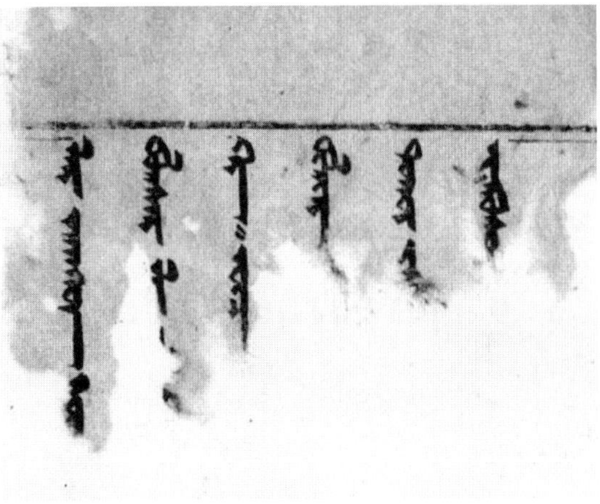

pict. 6. 32–37 (U 4780c 01–06)

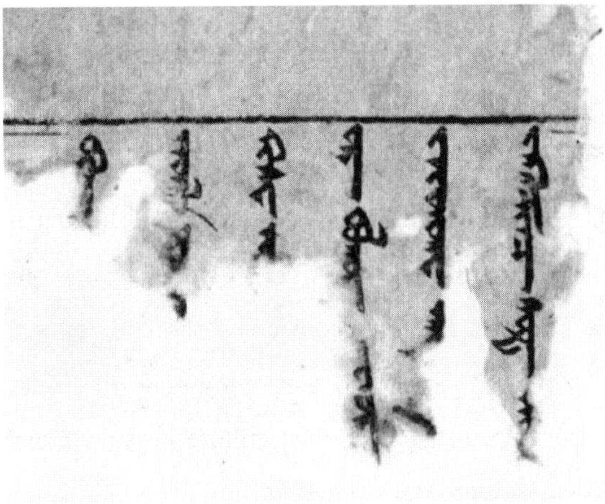

pict. 7. 38–43 (U 4780c 07–12)

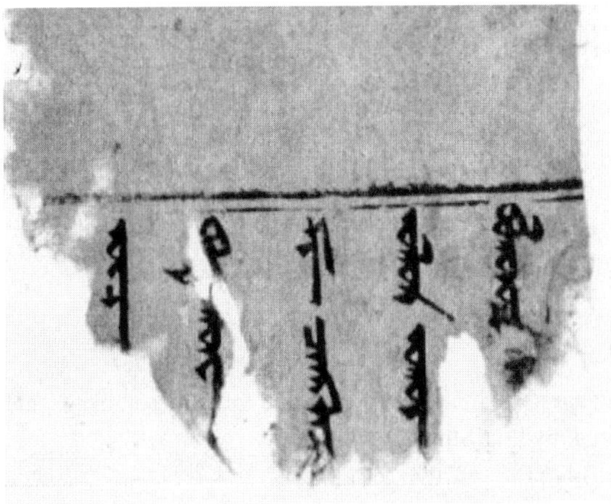

pict. 8. 44–48 (U 4780d 01–05)

pict. 9. 49–50 (Mainz 490c 01–02)

New Traces of Aśvaghoṣa on the Silk Road *

Jens-Uwe Hartmann
Munich University

It is hardly an exaggeration to call Aśvaghoṣa the greatest Buddhist poet in classical India. If our dating—probably 2nd century CE—and the ascription of a play and two epics to him are correct, he is the first author—at least the first one known to us— to have composed works within the genres of Nāṭaka and Mahākāvya in the Sanskrit tradition. Although both genres existed before him, it is conceivable that he not only appropriated these forms for his religious purposes, but also became one of the pioneers in early Sanskrit poetry.① Among the Buddhists he was considered the embodiment of the masterful poet, and, as was usually the case in ancient India, had a growing body of poetry attributed to him over the centuries. With the diffusion of Sanskrit Buddhist culture beyond India, his fame spread throughout large parts of Asia. His works were transmitted and imitated, and some of them translated, despite forbidding language barriers, which made it difficult, if not impossible, to preserve the intricacies of refined Sanskrit poetry. This is also the most plausible reason for the greater success of his works outside of India wherever Sanskrit was continued to be used as a church language, to employ the term coined by Jan Nattier (1990). This is evident in the civilizations along the ancient Silk Road, most notably those of the Tocharians and the Uigurs, which adopted Buddhism in the first millennium CE. Manuscript finds at the beginning of the 20th century brought to light many traces of Aśvaghoṣa's works; this paper will review the traces known so far and add some new ones.②

---

* It is my pleasant duty to thank Péter-Dániel Szántó (Budapest) and Klaus Wille† (Leer) for their comments and corrections, and Grace Ramswick (Stanford) for correcting my English.

① Cf. Salomon 2015, Tubb 2014: 75–85 and Warder 1974: 144–181 (§§709–768).

② For an earlier detailed survey and a study of the readings in the Central Asian fragments see Salomon 2012 (1999).

The finds contain fragments of at least four works directly connected with Aśvaghoṣa's name: the two epics, one play, and a poem on the consolation of grief. The famous epics, *Buddhacarita* and *Saundarananda*, and the poem are also attested in Indian manuscripts and/or translations into Chinese and Tibetan, but the play is known only from two Central Asian manuscripts brought to Germany by the third so-called Prussian Turfan Expedition.① The older of the two manuscripts contains fragments of two more plays,② which its editor, Heinrich Lüders, considered also to stem from Aśvaghoṣa's pen.③ This older manuscript, made of palm-leaf, was an import from India; a hundred and ten years ago, for palaeographical reasons it seemed not only the earliest Buddhist Sanskrit manuscript, but the oldest Indic manuscript in general.④ Lüders' ascription of the plays to Aśvaghoṣa was based on the fact that the second manuscript preserved not only the end of one of the plays, but also a colophon that mentions its title and author: *śāriputraprakaraṇe navamo 'ṅkaḥ 9 āryyasuvarṇṇākṣiputrasyāryyāśvaghoṣasya kṛtiś śāradvatīputrapprakaraṇaṃ samāptaṃ [sa]-māptāni cāṅkāni nava*,⑤ "(This is) the ninth act in the play on Śāriputra, a work of the noble Aśvaghoṣa, son of Suvarṇākṣi. The *Śāradvatīputraprakaraṇa* is finished, and finished are the nine acts." This was sensational: The *Śāriputraprakaraṇa*, as it is commonly known, is the earliest Indian play that has come down to us; it presents a Buddhist story, it is written by a Buddhist author, and without the manuscripts from the Silk Road would never have been known to us.

Since I am not familiar with the work of Tschen Yin-Koh 陳寅恪 , I cannot say if this great Chinese scholar ever referred to Aśvaghoṣa, but his biography strongly suggests that he knew something about him, and probably quite a lot. In 1921 Tschen went to Berlin, at that time the stronghold of Oriental Studies in Germany, and there studied with many great scholars, among them Heinrich Lüders, who was the towering figure in the realm of Sanskrit philology. Lüders had edited the plays in 1911, exactly ten years before Tschen Yin-Koh arrived in Berlin. To this day, Lüders' work is considered a masterpiece among the editions of Buddhist Sanskrit manuscripts from Central Asia. Therefore, it seems impossible that Tschen Yin-Koh, while studying with Lüders, did not learn about, and perhaps even read, some of those fragments during his time in Berlin. If he did, he would have been surprised and pleased to see what I am going to present here, since there will be a

---

① SHT I, catalogue nos. 16 and 57.

② On the question whether the manuscript contains three plays or only two and an interlude that could belong to either one of them see Tieken 2010.

③ Lüders 1911a.

④ Now we have a radiocarbon dating, which gives 254–409 CE as the most likely dates, see Allon/Salomon/Jacobson/Zoppi 2006: 280.

⑤ Lüders 1911b: 392 (= 1940: 195), C 4 verso, line 4, and SHT I: 37–38.

connection with the *Śāriputraprakaraṇa*.

However, before I turn to this play and Aśvaghoṣa's other works attested in the Tarim basin, I have to introduce another text with an unusual title, the *Tridaṇḍamālā*. It has nothing to do with Central Asia; so far, it is only known from a unique Sanskrit manuscript found in Xizang. Ninety years ago the Indian scholar Rāhula Sāṃkṛtyāyana went to Xizang searching for Sanskrit manuscripts. He found the manuscript of the *Tridaṇḍamālā* in sPos-khang Monastery, and described it in a report on his findings, published in 1938.① The colophon attributes this work to Aśvaghoṣa; if true, this would have been an amazing find. However, only one year later, in 1939, Edward Hamilton Johnston questioned the ascription and concluded that Aśvaghoṣa had to be ruled out as the author of the text.② Since Johnston was considered the leading expert on everything connected with Aśvaghoṣa and his works, the *Tridaṇḍamālā* remained unstudied.

Six years ago my Japanese colleague Kazunobu Matsuda from Kyoto invited me to study this text with him, and when we took a closer look, an amazing number of connections with Aśvaghoṣa came to light. There is no room here to describe all our finds,③ but among other results, they have led to the identification of several fragments of Central Asian Sanskrit manuscripts. However, before I introduce these new identifications, a brief survey of all the manuscripts from Central Asia connected with Aśvaghoṣa will be helpful.

Until recently, three works of Aśvaghoṣa had been attested along the Silk Road: First, the *Buddhacarita* (Bc): This is an epic, a poetical description of the life of the Buddha in 28 cantos. Only half of it is preserved in the Sanskrit manuscripts edited by Johnston;④ the second half (cantos 14.32–28.74) is lost. Up to now, seven fragments belonging to four different manuscripts were known from Central Asia. One is in the Hoernle Collection of the British Library, while the others are in the German Turfan Collection.⑤ One fragment (SHT I 432 b) preserves text of canto 16; this was a first glimpse into the original Sanskrit text of the lost second half. Two fragments contain glosses in Tocharian—a highly interesting addition since it suggests that Tocharian scholars indeed read and studied the poem.

---

① Sāṇkṛtyāyana 1938; cf. Hartmann forthcoming for details on this manuscript and the available photographs.

② Johnston 1939.

③ See Hartmann/Matsuda 2024 for an overview of the present state.

④ Johnston 1936.

⑤ *Buddhacarita*:

1. SHT I, catalogue nos. 432 a and b: Bc 3.16–29 and 16.20–36 (Weller 1953);
2. SHT IX, catalogue nos. 2054+2250 a and b (Hartmann 1988: 57–60): Bc 13.66–14.1 and 2.48a–54d; to fragment a belongs SHT XII, catalogue no. 7367, containing Bc 13.69c–70c (all fragments with Tocharian glosses);
3. SHT XII, catalogue no. 7191: Bc 2.8c–15c (with Tocharian glosses);
4. Or.15009/45 (H.149/122): Bc 10.12–17 (ed. Hartmann 2006).

An early palm-leaf manuscript, SHT 24, contains a remarkable continuation of canto 13 of the Bc, which includes a number of original verses (see also below, imitations).①

The second work is another epic, the *Saundarananda* ("Handsome Nanda"; Saund), which describes the conversion and the way to awakening of Nanda, the half-brother of the Buddha. Four fragments from four different manuscripts, three in the German collection and one in the Hoernle Collection in London, contain stanzas of the Saund.② Two of them appear to be manuscripts of the epic; in the other two, single verses are cited within an unidentified context.

The third work is the *Śāriputraprakaraṇa*, a play in nine acts, apparently a dramatic adaptation of the well-known story describing the conversion of the Buddha's two main disciples, Śāriputra and Maudgalyāyana. As mentioned before, it is attested in two very fragmentary manuscripts,③ one of which contains the remains of two more dramatic works, probably also from Aśvaghoṣa.

All the fragments above reproduce original works of Aśvaghoṣa. Beyond that, there are imitations or adaptations ("Nachdichtungen") of his works found in Central Asia, which underline the fame and importance of the originals. It is quite difficult to deal with this phenomenon, since it is something not regarded highly in Western poetics and, as far as I am aware, not studied extensively in classical Indian literature. Apparently there is no specific term for it in Indian poetics, but it appears that in the Indian context an imitator would not have to be ashamed of his work. On the contrary, he expresses his admiration for the imitated work or its author.④ Richard Salomon has

---

① SHT I, catalogue no. 24, fragments p, w, ii, y1–3 (Hartmann 1988: 60–66): Bc 13.28–29, 58b–59, 66b–68, 70–72, but sometimes only partial.

② *Saundarananda*:

1. SHT I, catalogue no. 515: Saund 4.37–5.06 (ed. Weller 1953);
2. SHT III, catalogue no. 921: Saund 16.21–33 (ed. Hartmann 1988); cf. Salomon 2012: 91–96 and 102–103 (1999: 231–241 and 254–259), and Tanaka 2020 for the doctrinal implications and especially for the connection with the *Tridaṇḍamālā*, where these verses also occur.
3. SHT X, catalogue no. 4221, A3–5: Saund 10.19 and 22 (identified by Gudrun Melzer).
4. IOL Toch 59 (H.149.205), a Sanskrit/Tocharian bilingual: the lines r1–3 preserve remains of Saund 7.48b–49d (identified by Klaus Wille).

③ *Śāriputraprakaraṇa*:

1. SHT I, catalogue no. 16; see also SHT X and XI, Nachträge.
2. SHT I, catalogue no. 57.

④ In this context mention should be made of another case from Central Asia, a folio containing the text of a stotra clearly making use of Mātṛceṭa's *Prasādapratibhodbhava* (PPU), s. Hartmann 1988: 88–92 and Salomon/Cox 1988: 141–145. This is not an imitation in the strict sense of the word; it is difficult to assess the exact relation between the PPU and the unknown stotra, but it is evident that its author knew the PPU. Speaking of the PPU, another form of imitation comes to mind, the *samasyāpūraṇa*; here, a second author adds a verse of his own to each verse of the original work. For the PPU, such a supplementation is preserved, although only in a Tibetan translation: this is the *Miśrakastotra*, which the colophon ascribes to Dignāga, see Shackleton Bailey 1951: 5, 16, 26–27 and 182ff.

discussed this phenomenon in a paper with the telling title "The Sincerest Form of Flattery: On Imitations of Aśvaghoṣa's Mahākāvyas".[①] There he also refers to examples from Central Asia; at present we know of three, two in Sanskrit and one in Tocharian:

1. The composite manuscript SHT 24 of the German Turfan Collection, which contains an imitation of the Māravijaya, the "Defeat of Māra". This is canto 13 of the *Buddhacarita*. The text in SHT 24 is, first, a mixture of verse and prose (Campū style), and second, a mixture of verses taken from the *Buddhacarita* and prose sentences which paraphrase the verses in the Bc, but with many similarities in the wording.[②]

2. The second example—two fragments of the same folio—is in the Stein Collection.[③] It was found by Marc Aurel Stein at Khadaliq (near Khotan) and published by Louis de La Vallée Poussin.[④] The text covers part of a ninth *sarga* or chapter, an incomplete chapter colophon, and the first akṣaras of the tenth chapter. La Vallée Poussin proposed to reconstruct the chapter title in the colophon as *(Tapovanapraveś)o*, "Entry into the Penance Grove"; the preceding verses contain a dialogue between a prince and some ascetic brahmans, which "is essentially parallel to BC VII.37–58".[⑤]

3. The third example concerns a Tocharian work: Here Salomon refers to Hiromi Habata, who had pointed out that fragments of a Tocharian text concerning the life of the Buddha are clearly based on *Buddhacarita* 12.108 and 111 and show specific parallels with it in their phrasing.[⑥] Besides the Tocharian glosses mentioned above, this is a further indication that local scholars received and appreciated the works of Aśvaghoṣa.

All of this is well-known. For new insights, it is necessary to come back to the *Tridaṇḍamālā* (TDM), because only the study of this text has made it possible to identify more fragments of Aśvaghoṣa's works on the Silk Road. The TDM is an extremely interesting text. It consists of forty chapters; each chapter is tripartite, which explains its name, the "Garland of Tripartite (Sections)". A canonical sūtra, quoted in full, forms the core of each chapter. The remainder of the text consists exclusively of verses, which frame the sūtra. Each chapter begins with a triad of verses of homage to the Three Jewels, followed by a set of verses related to the dogmatic contents of the embedded sūtra. Next comes the sūtra quotation, and after that another set of verses, again related to the contents of the sūtra. Except for the homage at the beginning of each chapter, most, and perhaps even all, of the

---

① Salomon 2019; cf. also the remarks in Salomon 2012: 100 (1999: 251–252).

② Edited in Hartmann 1988: 60–66; see Salomon 2019: 333–334.

③ The present number is IOL San 1233+1234.

④ La Vallée Poussin 1911: 770–772; see Salomon 2019: 334–336.

⑤ Salomon 2019: 334.

⑥ Salomon 2019: 336; Habata 2015: 226–227.

verses are taken from other poetical works, and here one observes a decided preference for sources connected with Aśvaghoṣa's name.

There are extensive quotations from the *Buddhacarita* and the *Saundarananda*, which presently amount to over 330 stanzas. It is especially welcome that nearly 140 of them come from the latter half of the *Buddhacarita*, the Sanskrit original of which is lost. This means that presently about 13% of the lost half have been recovered from the quotations in the TDM, and more may be added once the whole manuscript has been scrutinized.[①]

What was the purpose of this unusual work? The formal setting—each chapter starting anew with veneration of the Three Jewels—points in a certain direction, and there are further indications which, taken together, strongly suggest that the *Tridaṇḍamālā* was something like a collection of texts for recitation in rituals that were needed for the community of monastics and possibly also for the laity. It is very probable that each of the forty chapters served a specific ritual purpose.[②]

If this understanding of the function of the TDM as a ritual textbook is correct—and I am quite sure that it is—, it means that not only the sūtras, but also the verses, serve a specific ritual function. One example may illustrate this. In the middle part of chapter 16 of the TDM, the **Sumanārājakumārī-sūtra* (cf. *Aṅguttaranikāya* III 32) is quoted, which deals with the five advantages of alms-giving. In the first part of this chapter, some verses are quoted from canto 18 of the *Buddhacarita*. This canto describes a particularly important event: the donation of the Jetavana, the former park or garden of prince Jeta, by the rich merchant Anāthapiṇḍada to the Buddha. It is verses 62–78 of this canto that are cited in the TDM. Since canto 18 belongs to the second half of the *Buddhacarita*, the Sanskrit original of which is lost, the verses quoted in the TDM recover the Sanskrit text of this passage. When these "new" verses were searched for among the Central Asian fragments, the quotation made it possible to identify previously unknown verses in altogether three Sanskrit manuscripts. Five verses, namely 18.62–66, are also preserved in SHT 141, a manuscript in the German Turfan Collection, which had already been identified as a collection of donation formulas.[③] The *Buddhacarita* verses confirm not only the assumed purpose of the manuscript, but also the probable function of the TDM as a recitation text book for rituals, in this case for a donation. The same five verses are found in a fragment preserved in the Pelliot Collection in Paris, also

① An extremely difficult and sometimes even impossible task due to the fact that very often a part of a photograph is out of focus, cf. Hartmann forthcoming.

② Cf. Hartmann forthcoming.

③ SHT I: 81; ed. Lüders 1930: 5 (Blatt 4, r3–v3) and 11, note 2, with a reference to SHT 191h. Lüders still had complete folios at his disposal and therefore could read more; cf. SHT X: 287–288, catalogue nos. 4158 and 4161, which contain many small fragments, among them also some belonging to Blatt 4.

previously identified as a donation formula;[①] this is a further corroboration. Finally, the same five are again found in SHT 191h, a manuscript previously identified as a Sammelhandschrift, a composite manuscript, that contains a variety of different texts.[②]

This latter manuscript is noteworthy also for another text that it contains. But again, first it is necessary to go back to the *Tridaṇḍamālā*. A colleague, Péter-Dániel Szántó, succeeded in identifying another work connected with Aśvaghoṣa in the *Tridaṇḍamālā*. This is the *Śokavinodana*, a text hardly ever studied so far despite its connection with Aśvaghoṣa. It consists of forty verses, and was known only from its Tibetan translation, the *Mya ngan bsal ba*. Szántó detected that chapter 14 of the TDM contained the Sanskrit original of all forty verses.[③] Again, the Sanskrit original allowed a search for parallels in the Central Asian manuscripts and again, the search was not in vain. It turned out that SHT 191 did not only contain verses of the Bc, but also an incomplete folio, consisting of two fragments (k and m), which preserves verses of the *Śokavinodana*.[④] Sanskrit manuscripts from the Silk Road are distinguished by a convenient feature: Very often they contain verse numbers. The incomplete folio preserves the numbers 19, 23 and 31, and these numbers agree perfectly well with the respective verses in the TDM and the Tibetan translation of the *Śokavinodana*. Therefore, it is almost certain that the Central Asian manuscript contained the whole text of the poem. Actually, this is an interesting little work full of expressive images; as usual in such cases, we have no means whatsoever to decide if it is a genuine work of Aśvagoṣa, but it is definitely a fine poem with real quality. This assessment is supported by the large number of verses from it quoted anonymously in a wide range of Sanskrit works, very few of which display a specific Buddhist orientation.[⑤]

To come back once more to its possible purpose in a ritual context: *Śokavinodana* means "Consolation of Grief", and the topic of this poem is the instability of human life and the inevitability of death with all its consequences. Thus, it is not difficult to imagine that it was used in connection with deathbed rituals, but we have no means to verify this assumption, since

---

① PK NS 14; edited in Couvreur 1970: 179–180.

② SHT I: 107 "Sammelhandschrift mit Buddhastotras, Lehrversen, Versen erzählenden Inhalts, Versen über das Geben"; edited in Schlingloff 1955: 38, no. 38; for Bc 18.65 cf. also Tripāṭhī 1966: 216, note 11, where he connects its wording with a stanza on the benefits of giving in the *Mahāparinirvāṇasūtra* (ed. Waldschmidt 1950–1951: 188 [§12.7]).

③ For a first survey see Hartmann/Matsuda/Szántó 2022.

④ Schlingloff 1955: 39–40, fragments 41–42 and 45–46.

⑤ A complete list will be published in the forthcoming edition of the *Śokavinodana* by Péter-Dániel Szántó, Kazunobu Matsuda, and myself.

neither the TDM nor the Central Asian manuscript provide instruction for how and when to use it. Both, however, facilitated another finding: based on the Sanskrit text and the Tibetan translation, Kazunobu Matsuda was able to identify a Chinese translation, the *Jiěyōu Jīng* 解忧经 (Taishō 804), a late translation by Fǎtiān 法天 in the 10th century; it is not identical, but closely corresponds to the 14th chapter of the TDM, and it also contains the *Śokavinodana*.

There are three more points, and the first brings us back to the *Śāriputraprakaraṇa*, the play which must have been known to Tschen Yin-Koh. Kazunobu Matsuda and I found two verses in the TDM that are also attested in the fragments of the *Śāriputraprakaraṇa*. This was a real surprise; so far, remains of that play were known exclusively from Central Asia. One of the two verses is contained in chapter 19 of the TDM, the other in chapter 27. The Śikhariṇī verse beginning with *parikleśais tais taiḥ svajanagatam ākṛṣya ca mano* occurs as the second verse in section 19.3 of the TDM (fol. 72r4–5) and on fragments 26 b2 and 64 a3 of SHT 16.[①] Another Śikhariṇī verse beginning with *yathā niṣṭaptānāṃ trapumadhughṛtāmedhyapayasāṃ*, is found in section 19.1 of the TDM (fol. 44v2–3) and in SHT 16 no 68[②] and SHT 57b r4.[③] Since the state of preservation of the Central Asian fragments is somewhat problematic, a more detailed treatment will be reserved for another occasion.[④] Of course it is difficult to assess these findings. Did the compilers of the TDM have a manuscript of the play at their disposal? This seems unlikely. It is more probable that they quoted from another source, which also contained these verses. One possibility to be reckoned with—and this possibility is strongly favored by Kazunobu Matsuda—could be Aśvaghoṣa's lost **Sūtrālaṃkāra*.[⑤]

There is no room to discuss a second point, the rather complicated question of whether this **Sūtrālaṃkāra* ever existed. However, a growing number of indications suggest the possibility that there was a commentary on canonical sūtras which consisted mainly of verses, and which was also composed by Aśvaghoṣa. In fact there are several Central Asian manuscripts that seem to represent a commentary of this kind. Here mention will be made of only one, SHT 378,[⑥] because it connects once more with the TDM. Only three folios are preserved, which contain poetical verses on Buddhist dogmatics, interspersed with brief references in prose which introduce a new topic, for

---

① Lüders 1911a: 74 and 81.

② Lüders 1911a: 82.

③ Lüders 1911b: 391 (= 1940: 193), C 2 recto, line 4.

④ Hartmann/Matsuda forthcoming (2024).

⑤ Cf. Matsuda 2020b.

⑥ SHT I: 169–170 entitled „Kāvya-Anthologie"; cf. Schlingloff 1966: 421–422 and SHT IV: 310–314. For a new comparative edition of SHT 378 and the corresponding passages in the TDM see Hartmann/Matsuda 2023.

instance *pañcasūpādānaskandheṣu* "about the five groups of clinging ...", or *atha bhadraghaṭam upākhyāyāha* "now referring to the vase of fortune, it says ...". None of these prose phrases, but all the verses in two of the three folios, are found in the same order in two chapters of the TDM. What does this mean? Could SHT 378 be a version of the lost **Sūtrālaṃkāra*? Again this is difficult to answer, but one possibility is highly suggested. Given the evidence now available, it appears almost certain that the editors of the TDM knew or believed that these verses were connected with Aśvaghoṣa, since the overwhelming majority of identified verses in the TDM comes from Aśvaghoṣa's works or—to put it more carefully—from works that at one point in history became connected with his name.

Finally, a most recent finding has to be added. As shown above, glosses and a Tocharian imitation indicate that Tocharian-speaking scholars read at least the *Buddhacarita*, but there was no evidence for a reception of the Sanskrit originals of Aśvaghoṣa's works in other language communities along the Silk Road. This picture has to be modified now, again with regard to the Bc: recently we found three Sanskrit-Uigur bilingual manuscripts containing passages of the Bc.① All three share the same feature: not only the Sanskrit, but also the Uigur text is written in a form of Indian Brāhmī and not in the usual Uigur script. Two of them (AtüHs I 25 and AtüHs II 115) belong to the German Turfan Collection.② For only of them is the find spot, Murtuq, known. The third fragment (80 TBI 774b) was found in Bezeklik; it belongs to the collection of the Academia Turfanica.③ All three preserve passages of the Bc not preserved in Sanskrit. The two German fragments overlap, and there are strong indications that both are derived from a common ancestor. First of all, both excerpt the Sanskrit very unevenly. Sometimes several words of a verse are excerpted and then several verses are skipped. The reason for this extremely elective procedure remains obscure. The first fragment, AtüHs I 25, contains words of verses from Bc 16.36 to at least 17.17, while the second, AtüHs II 115, covers words from the verse 16.61 to at least 17.5. The fragment from Bezeklik, on the other hand, quotes more or less every word of the Sanskrit text, but usually reduces it to its first akṣara. It preserves the text of Bc 15.27–38. Again, the three fragments could only be identified because parts of these passages are quoted in the TDM (Bc 16.76, 80–87, 88–89 in chapter 8.1, 16.90–93 in 8.3 and the complete text of Bc 15.1–58④ in chapter 34.1).

---

① Hartmann/Wille/Zieme 2022.

② The first was already published by Annemarie von Gabain (1954: 45–47) and described in AtüHs I: 34. The second is published in AtüHs II: 265–269.

③ Published in Maue/Niu 2012.

④ For an edition of this chapter see Matsuda 2020a and for an English translation of this edition see Jones 2021.

Summing up, several points become evident. First, there are manuscripts which comprise exclusively works of Aśvaghoṣa, and there are others which contain quotations from his works combined with various other texts. In all cases of the latter category one observes an intersection with verses in the *Tridaṇḍamālā*. This holds true for SHT 141, 191h and PK NS 14 (Bc 18.62–66), IOL Toch 59 (Saund 7.48b–49d, with the second verse also attested in chapter 23.1 of the TDM), SHT 4221 (Saund 10.19 and 22, both verses in chapter 18.1 of the TDM) and for SHT 191 k+m (*Śokavinodana*). The old palm-leaf manuscript SHT 921 (Saund 16.21–33) probably belongs to the first category, but it is at least noteworthy that the verses of Saund 16.4–41 are quoted in the TDM (chapter 34.3). The case of the three Uigur bilinguals cannot be finally decided, since the surviving parts contain only verses of the *Buddhacarita* and nothing else. In the case of quotations, which fully or partly coincide with those in the TDM, it is at least plausible to assume a ritual use for the respective manuscript.

Second, despite the long history of research on the Sanskrit manuscripts from the Silk Road, there are still many amazing discoveries waiting to be made through further study. Third, such discoveries usually require new material with which to compare them, and here the TDM provides first-rate material. Fourth, and last, the new findings should have made it exceedingly clear: Aśvaghoṣa is a central figure in the *Tridaṇḍamālā*, but no less so in the Sanskrit literature from the Silk Road.

Abbreviations

AtüHs I see Maue 1996.

AtüHs II see Maue 2015.

Bc see Johnston 1936.

PPU Prasādapratibhodbhava.

Saund E. H. Johnston (ed. and transl.), *The Saundarananda of Aśvaghoṣa*. Lahore: Oxford University Press, 1928.

SHT I–XII Ernst Waldschmidt, Lore Sander, Klaus Wille (eds.), *Sanskrithandschriften aus den Turfanfunden*, Teil 1–12. Wiesbaden, Stuttgart: Franz Steiner 1965–2017.

TDM *Tridaṇḍamālā*.

References

Allon, Mark, Richard Salomon, Geraldine Jacobson, Ugo Zoppi. 2006. "Radiocarbon Dating of Kharoṣṭhī Fragments from the Schøyen and Senior Manuscript Collections." In: Jens Braarvig *et al.* (eds.), *Buddhist Manuscripts*, Vol. III. Oslo: Hermes Publishing, 279–291.

Couvreur, Walter. 1970. "Boeddhistische Sanskritfragmenten in Koetsjische handschriftenverzamelingen." *Anamnhcic. Gedenkboek Prof. Dr. E. A. Leemans*. Brugge: De Tempel, 175–184.

Gabain, Annemarie von. 1954. *Türkische Turfan-Texte VIII, Texte in Brāhmīschrift*. Berlin: Akademie-Verlag.

Habata, Hiromi. 2015. "The Legends of the Buddha in Tocharian Texts." *Journal of the International Association of Buddhist Studies* 38: 223–243.

Hartmann, Jens-Uwe. 1988. "Neue Aśvaghoṣa- und Mātṛceṭa-Fragmente aus Ostturkistan." *Nachrichten der Akademie der Wissenschaften in Göttingen, Phil.-hist. Klasse*: 55–92.

Hartmann, Jens-Uwe. 2006. "Ein weiteres zentralasiatisches Fragment aus dem Buddhacarita." In: Ute Hüsken, Petra Kieffer-Pülz und Anne Peters (eds.), *Jaina-itihāsa-ratna. Festschrift für Gustav Roth zum 90. Geburtstag*. Marburg: Indica et Tibetica, 259–264.

Hartmann, Jens-Uwe. Forthcoming. "Forms of Intertextuality and Lost Sanskrit Verses of the Buddhacarita: the Tridaṇḍaka and the Tridaṇḍamālā." In: Daniel Boucher and Shayne Clarke (eds.), *Minding the Buddha's Business: Essays in Honor of Gregory Schopen* (*Studies in Indian and Tibetan Buddhism*). Somerville: Wisdom.

Hartmann, Jens-Uwe, Kazunobu Matsuda. 2023. "Possible Fragments of Aśvaghoṣa's Lost Sūtrālaṃkāra from the 'Manuscript Cave' in Šorčuq." In: Hiroko Matsuoka, Shinya Moriyama, and Tyler Neill (eds.), *To the Heart of Truth. Felicitation Volume for Eli Franco on the Occasion of His Seventieth Birthday*. Wien: Arbeitskreis für Tibetische und Buddhistische Studien Universität Wien, 111–130.

Hartmann, Jens-Uwe, Kazunobu Matsuda. 2024. "(Re)discovering Aśvaghoṣa in the Tridaṇḍamālā." In: Charles DiSimone and Nicholas Witkowski (eds.), *Buddhakṣetrapariśodhana: a Festschrift for Paul Harrison*. Marburg: Indica et Tibetica, 229–260.

Hartmann, Jens-Uwe, Kazunobu Matsuda, Péter-Dániel Szántó. 2022. "The Benefit of Cooperation: Recovering the Śokavinodana Ascribed to Aśvaghoṣa." In: Mahīnda Deegalle (ed.), *Dharmayātrā. Felicitation Volume in Honour of Venerable Tampalawela Dhammaratana*. Paris: Nuvis Press, 173–180.

Hartmann, Jens-Uwe, Klaus Wille, Peter Zieme. 2022. "Aśvaghoṣa's *Buddhacarita* in the Old Uigur Literature." *Annual Report of the International Research Institute of Advanced Buddhology at Soka University* 25.

Johnston, E. H. 1936. *The Buddhacarita or Acts of the Buddha*, Calcutta: Baptist Mission Press.

Johnston, E. H. 1939. "The Tridaṇḍamālā of Aśvaghoṣa." *Journal of the Bihar and Orissa Research Society* 25.1: 11–14.

Jones, Dhivan Thomas. 2021. "'Turning the Wheel of the Teaching': A translation of Aśvaghoṣa's *Buddhacarita* Canto 15 from a recently rediscovered Sanskrit manuscript." *Asian Literature and Translation* 8.1: 47–62.

La Vallée Poussin, Louis de. 1911. "Documents sanscrits de la seconde collection M. A. Stein." *Journal of the Royal Asiatic Society*: 759–777.

Lüders, Heinrich. 1911a. *Bruchstücke buddhistischer Dramen*. Berlin: Georg Reimer.

Lüders, Heinrich. 1911b. "Das Śāriputraprakaraṇa, ein Drama des Aśvaghoṣa." *Sitzungsberichte der Königlich Preussischen Akademie der Wissenschaften* 17, 388–411 [= H. Lüders: *Philologica Indica, Ausgewählte kleine Schriften, Festgabe zum 70. Geburtstage*, Göttingen: Vandenhoeck & Ruprecht, 1940: 190–213].

Lüders, Heinrich. 1930. "Weitere Beiträge zur Geschichte und Geographie von Ostturkestan." *Sitzungsberichte der Preussischen Akademie der Wissenschaften*: 7–64 [= H. Lüders: *Philologica Indica, Ausgewählte kleine Schriften, Festgabe zum 70. Geburtstage*, Göttingen: Vandenhoeck & Ruprecht, 1940: 595–658].

Matsuda, Kazunobu 松田和信. 2020a. "ブッダチャリタ第 15 章「初転法輪」— 梵文テキストと和訳 —Buddacharita dai15shō 'Shotenpōrin'—Bonbun tekisuto to wayaku— (Sanskrit Text and Japanese Translation of the Buddhacarita Canto 15 'The First Dharmacakrapravartana')." 佛教大学仏教学会紀要 (*The Bulletin of the Association of Buddhist Studies, Bukkyo University*), No. 25: 81–98.

Matsuda, Kazunobu 松田和信. 2020b. "大智度論におけるアシュヴァゴーシャ — 如来十号論に埋め込まれた荘厳経論 — (Aśvaghoṣa's Lost Stanzas Included in the *Mahāprajñāpāramitopadeśa')." 印度学佛教学研究 (*Journal of Indian and Buddhist Studies*) 69.1: 53–61.

Maue, Dieter. 1996. *Alttürkische Handschriften. Teil 1: Dokumente in Brāhmī und tibetischer Schrift*. Stuttgart: Franz Steiner (Verzeichnis der orientalischen Handschriften in Deutschland XIII, 9).

Maue, Dieter. 2015. *Alttürkische Handschriften, Teil 19: Dokumente in Brāhmī und tibetischer Schrift*. Teil 2. Stuttgart: Franz Steiner (Verzeichnis der orientalischen Handschriften in Deutschland XIII, 27).

Maue, Dieter, Niu Ruji. 2012. "80 TBI 774 b: A Sanskrit-Uigur Bilingual Text from Bezeklik." *Studies on the Inner Asian Languages* 27: 43–91.

Nattier, Jan. 1990. "Church Language and Vernacular Language in Central Asian Buddhism." *Numen* 37: 195–219.

Salomon, Richard. 2012. "Aśvaghoṣa in Central Asia: Some Comments on the Recensional

History of His Works in Light of Recent Manuscript Discoveries." In: John R. McRae and Jan Nattier, Philadelphia (eds.), *Buddhism Across Boundaries* (Sino-Platonic Papers, 222), 86–105 [= revised version of a paper originally published in *Buddhism Across Boundaries: Chinese Buddhism and the Western Regions. Collection of Essays 1993*. Sanchung: Foguang Cultural Enterprise 1999, 219–263].

Salomon, Richard. 2015. "Narratives and Long Poetry: Aśvaghoṣa." In: Jonathan A. Silk, Oskar von Hinüber, Vincent Eltschinger (eds.), *Brill's Encyclopedia of Buddhism, Vol. 1: Literature and Languages*. Leiden/Boston: Brill, 507–514.

Salomon, Richard. 2019. "The Sincerest Form of Flattery: On Imitations of Aśvaghoṣa's Mahākāvyas." *Journal of Indian Philosophy* 47: 327–340.

Salomon, Richard, Collett Cox. 1988. "Two New Fragments of Buddhist Sanskrit Manuscripts from Central Asia." *Journal of the International Association of Buddhist Studies* 11.1: 141–153.

Sāṅkṛtyāyana, Rāhula. 1938. "Search for Mss. in Tibet." *Journal of the Bihar and Orissa Research Society* 24: 137–163.

Schlingloff, Dieter. 1955. *Buddhistische Stotras aus ostturkistanischen Sanskrittexten*, Berlin: Akademie-Verlag.

Schlingloff, Dieter. 1966. Review of *Sanskrithandschriften aus den Turfanfunden*, Teil I, ed. Ernst Waldschmidt, Walter Clawiter, Lore Holzmann, Wiesbaden: Franz Steiner 1965, *ZDMG* 116: 419–425.

Shackleton Bailey, D. R. 1951. *The Śatapañcāśatka of Mātṛceṭa*, Cambridge: Cambridge University Press.

Tanaka, Hironori 田中裕成. 2020. 三啓集に収められたサウンダラナンダの異読について ("Variant Readings of the *Saundarananda* as Presented in the *Tridaṇḍamālā*"), 佛教大学仏教学会紀要 (*The Bulletin of the Association of Buddhist Studies, Bukkyo University*) 25: 91–109.

Tieken, Herman. 2010. "Aśvaghoṣa and the History of Allegorical Literature in India." In: Eli Franco, Monika Zin (eds.), *From Turfan to Ajanta. Festschrift for Dieter Schlingloff on the Occasion of his Eightieth Birthday*, 2 vols., Lumbini International Research Institute, 993–997.

Tripāṭhī, C. B. 1966. "Karmavibhaṅgopadeśa und Berliner Texte." *Wiener Zeitschrift für die Kunde Süd- und Ostasiens* 10: 208–219.

Tubb, Gary. 2014. "Baking Umā." In: Yigal Bronner, David Shulman, Gary Tubb (eds.), *Innovations and Turning Points: Towards a History of* Kāvya *Literature*. New Delhi: Oxford University Press, 71–85.

Waldschmidt, Ernst. 1950–1951. *Das Mahāparinirvāṇasūtra. Text in Sanskrit und Tibetisch, verglichen mit dem Pāli nebst einer Übersetzung der chinesischen Entsprechung im Vinaya der*

Mūlasarvāstivādins, parts I–III. Berlin: Akademie-Verlag.

Warder, A. K. 1974. *Indian Kāvya Literature*, Vol. II, *Origins and Formation of the Classical Kāvya*. Delhi: Motilal Banarsidass.

Weller Friedrich. 1953. "Zwei zentralasiatische Fragmente des Buddhacarita." *Abhandlungen der Sächsischen Akademie der Wissenschaften, Philologisch-historische Klasse*, Band 46, Heft 4. Berlin: Akademie Verlag.

Reading between the Characters: Notes on the *Dhūta-sūtra* and Its Reception*

Chen Ruixuan 陈瑞翾
School of Foreign Languages, Peking University

The so-called *Dhūta-sūtra* is a Chinese Buddhist apocryphal text① whose complete title is *Fo wei Xinwang pusa shuo toutuo jing* 佛爲心王菩薩説頭陀經 ("Sūtra on *Dhūta* Expounded by the Buddha to the Bodhisattva Mind-King"), sometimes abbreviated as *Xinwang jing* 心王經 ("Sūtra of Mind-King").

The text, at one time, caught the attention of Chen Yinke 陳寅恪 (aka Tschen Yin-Koh), the honorand of the present volume, due to obscure references to its title in two poems by the renowned mid-Tang literatus Bai Juyi 白居易 (772–846), each presented in response to his lifelong friend Yuan Zhen 元稹 (779–831).② According to Bai, Yuan held the *Dhūta-sūtra*, among others, in such high esteem that he constantly showed it to Bai as a token of his religious aspirations. Despite the popularity of Bai's poems, the apocryphal text had long been considered lost, and did not resurface

---

* The present contribution may be seen as the first installment of a series of studies concerning the cross-cultural reception of Buddhist *sūtra*s composed in China that I am planning to undertake. For useful comments on an earlier draft of the notes, thanks go to my teachers and friends Jonathan A. Silk (Munich/Leiden), Helmut Tauscher (Vienna), and Benedikt Peschl (Berlin). The usual disclaimers apply.

① The term "apocrypha" is borrowed into the field of Buddhist Studies from that of Biblical Studies, not without problems. For the potential problems of the use of this and similar terms (e.ge. pseudepigrapha) in the context of Chinese Buddhism, see Buswell 1990: 3–7. With the caveats outlined by Buswell in mind, I use this term as a heuristic device to render Chin. *yi/wei jing* 疑 / 僞經 (Jap. *gi/gikyō* 疑 / 僞経) "doubtful/spurious sūtras", referring to texts which were composed in China, but were presented in such a form as if they were genuine translations from Indic originals, and as such were accorded the status of authoritative texts at least in some milieux.

② For a study of the poetic exchange between these two mid-Tang literati, who were towering figures of a literary circle, with special focus on their nostalgic poems, see Shields 2006: 321–361.

until the discovery of several manuscripts in the Library Cave in Dunhuang. Probably in the mid-1930s, Chen Yinke read a Japanese edition of the *Dhūta-sūtra* based on one of the Dunhuang manuscripts (Or.8210/S.2474),① and wrote an epilogue to this manuscript:②

寅恪取閱之，了無精義，蓋僞經之下品也。[……] 寅恪昔日讀白詩至此，以未能得其確詁爲憾。今日見此佚籍，始知白詩之心王頭陀經即敦煌寫本之佛爲心王菩薩説投陀經 [……] 特爲記之，以告同讀香山詩者，此或亦今日老嫗之所不能解者歟？

I read it, [and find] it without any essential doctrines [of Buddhism], since it is an apocryphal sūtra of the poorest quality. [...] Previously, when reading the poem by Bai [Juyi] up to this point, I regretted having been unable to pin down its exact references (i.e., to what texts Bai referred). It is not until now that, seeing these [allegedly] lost books, I have known that the "Sūtra of Mind-King" [or] *Dhūta-sūtra*, mentioned in Bai's poem, is none other than the "Sūtra on *Dhūta* Expounded by the Buddha to the Bodhisattva Mind-King", known from Dunhuang manuscripts; [...] Hereby I jot it down, in order to inform my fellow readers of the poetry of "[Retired Scholar on] Mount of Fragrance" (i.e., alias of Bai) [about the finds]; this is perhaps also something incomprehensible to an old lady③ nowadays?

About a decade later, Chen Yinke reiterated and elaborated on the remarks in his monographic disquisition on the poetry of Yuan and Bai:④

寅恪少讀樂天此詩，遍檢佛藏，不見所謂心王頭陀經者，頗以爲恨。近歲始見倫敦博物院藏斯坦因號貳肆柒肆，佛爲心王菩薩説投陀經卷上，五陰山室寺惠辨禪師注殘本

---

① See T. 2886: vol. 85, 1401c–1403b. A photograph of the Dunhuang manuscript was reproduced in *Meisha yoin* 鳴沙餘韻 ; see Yabuki 1930: pl. 74.V. Actually, Chen Yinke purchased a copy of *Meisha yoin* from Japan through the good offices of Qian Daosun 錢稻孫 (1887–1966) in 1931, as evinced in a handwritten letter from Hu Shih 胡適 to Chen Yinke, dated 31 May 1931, which later came into the possession of Lo Hsiang-lin 羅香林 (1906–1978); see the University of Hong Kong–Main Library, Lo 110–60–S76. It seems that Chen had possibly gained access to the photograph reproduced by Yabuki before he saw the Japanese edition in the Taishō canon. For the channels by which Chen accessed and utilized Dunhuang manuscripts in general, see Nagata 2012: 215–237 (esp. 221–226 for Chen's debts to the Taishō canon and Japanese publications).

② See Chen 1939: 9, reprinted in Chen 2001a: 201–202.

③ This is an allusion to an anecdote that can be traced back to the 11th century: Bai Juyi used an old lady, presumably of plebeian origin, as a sounding board for his new poems, and removed those which she could not understand. See Huihong 惠洪 (1071–1128), Poems Understood by an Old Lady (*laoyu jieshi* 老嫗解詩), in *Night Talks from the Chilly Studio* (*Lengzhai yehua* 冷齋夜話), reprinted in Zhang 2002: 18.

④ See Chen 2001b: 102–103.

（大正續藏貳捌捌陸號），乃一至淺俗之書，爲中土所僞造者。[……] 夫元白二公自許禪梵之學，叮嚀反復于此二經。今日得見此二書，其淺陋鄙俚如此，則二公之佛學造詣，可以推知矣。

In my youth, when reading this poem by Letian (i.e., courtesy name of Bai), I searched high and low in the Buddhist canon for the so-called "Sūtra of Mind-King" [or] *Dhūta-sūtra*, but to no avail; I deeply regretted it. It is not until recent years that I have seen the Stein manuscript no. 2474 preserved at the [British] Museum in London, [which carries] the first fascicle of "Sūtra on *Dhūta* Expounded by the Buddha to the Bodhisattva Mind-King", [coupled with] a fragmentary commentary by Huibian, the Chan Master of the "cella" monastery on Mount of Five Aggregates① (no. 2886 in the Taishō canon) －[this] is a very shallow and indelicate book, forged in China. [...] [Ironically,] both Yuan and Bai took pride in their learning in Chan and Sanskrit, giving instructions repeatedly on the two sūtras (i.e., the *Dhūta-sūtra* and another apocryphal text). Now we have access to the two books, which are so ill-informed and unrefined; from thence it can be extrapolated what their "accomplishments" in Buddhist learning would have been like.

Apparently, the *Dhūta-sūtra* failed to impress Chen Yinke, who considered it a shoddy Chinese product lacking doctrinal sophistication. At first glance, his remarks appear to be impressionistic and may raise a few eyebrows; but we must bear in mind that Chen was not primarily interested in the text *per se*, but rather in Yuan's predilection for this type of Buddhist apocrypha and how that reflects the entanglement of mid-Tang literati of his ilk in the ethos of the early 9th century.

A nuanced understanding and reappraisal of Chen Yinke's thesis would prove a worthwhile endeavor in its own right, and should best be undertaken by an expert of Tang history. As a scholar of Buddhist philology, I set myself the perhaps thankless task of taking a close look at the *Dhūta-sūtra*, a sample of which will be dealt with and commented upon in the present paper. In doing so, I have no intention to claim that a philological approach is superior to a historical one; neither should the paper be read as a correction to the observations cited above, which must be interpreted with due

① The name of the mountain (i.e., *wu yin* 五陰 "Five Aggregates") looks quite artificial, and the character *shi* 室 "cella, room" has a variant reading *kong* 空 "empty", which might be superior in some respects. The so-called Mount of Five Aggregates is mentioned in the *Dhūta-sūtra* as the place where the Buddha lived in seclusion before his enlightenment, a context in which its symbolism is transparent; see Fang 1995: vol.1, 306. This symbolic mountain is otherwise mentioned in other apocryphal texts. Thus it is not impossible that the purported commentator Huibian is a complete fabrication and his monastic affiliation a sheer figment; see Fang 1995: vol. 1, 327.

charity. The following pages should rather be conceived of as a pedantic attempt to keep Chen Yinke company in a "garden of forking paths", to use a hackneyed metaphor for a (hyper)text, which fascinates both him and me, despite the different paths we take.

Before entering the labyrinthine text, a few introductory remarks on the primary sources may be helpful to get one's bearings. The Chinese text of the *Dhūta-sūtra* has come down to us in six manuscripts from Dunhuang① and three fragments from Turfan, which are newly identified and currently preserved at the Lüshun Museum.② Therefore, there are good reasons to reckon with a certain degree of popularity enjoyed by this text among Chinese-speaking Buddhists in both Dunhuang and Turfan. A commentary attributed to an enigmatic monk named Huibian 惠辨 / 辯 ③ (lit. "Wisdom-Discernment/Eloquence") was known from Dunhuang, where it is written in small characters and embedded in the root text in some of the extant manuscripts.④ According to Ibuki Atsushi 伊吹敦 , the root text was composed at the end of the 6th century, while the version with the embedded commentary probably did not come into being until the first half of the 8th century.⑤ Ibuki's dating, albeit hypothetical, provides a chronological framework within which to tentatively accommodate all the Dunhuang manuscripts discovered so far. It is presumably within the same framework that the newly identified Turfan fragments, which show no trace of the embedded commentary, are to be dated. In addition, quotations from this text are found in a number of Buddhist and non-Buddhist works,⑥ the oldest of which, dating from the early to mid-7th century,⑦ set the

① Apart from Or.8210/S.2474 (incomplete, with Huibian's commentary) known to Chen Yinke, BD15369 (complete, with commentary), TY171 (complete, without commentary) at the Tianjin Arts Museum, Pelliot chinois 2052 (incomplete, with commentary), Дx. 16997 (incomplete, without commentary), and an unnumbered manuscript (complete, with commentary) in the Mitsui Bunko 三井文庫 (Tōkyō) are identified as the text in question; see Fang 1995: vol.1, 323–325. In addition, there are two fragments preserved at the National Library of China, i.e., BD09746 *verso* and BD09779 *verso*, which can be joined together as part of possibly an unfinished copy (incomplete, with commentary); see Cao 2011: 344–345. See also Tanaka & Tei 2014: 228–233, for further bibliographical information.

② The find-spot of the fragments is unclear: LM20–1454–07–06, LM20–1457–25–08, and LM20–1521–18–04; see Rong 2019: 36. On close scrutiny, LM20–1454–07–06 and LM20–1521–18–04 can be joined together and thus are taken from the same sheet of paper. Given the similar hand-writing, it is conceivable that all the three fragments originally belonged to one and the same manuscript, which merely contains the text without Huibian's commentary.

③ On the identity of the commentator, see fn. 7 above.

④ On Huibian's commentary, see Ibuki 1993a: 285–288.

⑤ See Ibuki 2003: 186–187; Ibuki has also proposed a relative chronology for the extant manuscripts with commentary: Mitsui Bunko ms. > BD15369 > Or.8210/S.2474, Pelliot chinois 2052; see Tanaka & Tei 2014: 232.

⑥ For the quotations see Cao 2011: 345–349.

⑦ The text is quoted in the *Dasheng si lun xuanyi* 大乘四論玄義 by Huijun 慧均 , probably composed at some point between 623 and 658; and in Li Shan's 李善 commentary to the *Wenxuan* 文選 , finalized and presented to the imperial court in 658 CE. For the dates of the two works, see Itō 1972: 790–792; and Jao 1998: 56–57.

terminus ante quem for its composition.

Its Chinese origin notwithstanding, the *Dhūta-sūtra* seems to have had a sphere of influence extending well beyond the confines of the Chinese-speaking Buddhist milieu. This is testified to, first and foremost, by a Sogdian translation whose *codex unicus*, possibly written in the 8th century,① was brought by Marc Aurel Stein from Dunhuang to London, where it is now preserved in the British Library under the shelf-number Or.8212/160. The Sogdian text was first edited in 1928 by Hans Reichelt, who coined the nickname *Dhūta-sūtra* but was unaware of the text's Chinese background.② The identification of the Chinese original should be accredited to Paul Demiéville, who was in a position to utilize the aforementioned Chinese manuscript (i.e., S.2474) from Dunhuang, published at the beginning of the 1930s.③ Reichelt's *editio princeps* is by and large superseded by a new, revised edition, published in 1976 by D.N. MacKenzie,④ which remains the standard work on this body of materials. A thorough comparison of the Sogdian text with its Chinese parallel is still a desideratum.⑤

No Tibetan translation of the *Dhūta-sūtra* is known to have existed. It is well known that Chan exerted a significant influence on Tibetan Buddhism in its incipient phase,⑥ and that a number of Chinese apocrypha, particularly some Chan-related texts, were translated into Tibetan during the first period of Buddhist dissemination (*snga dar*) and/or quoted in Tibetan works known from

---

① On the date of the Sogdian version, see Ibuki 2003: 187, who proposed the first half of the 8th century. This is in conformity with the dating of the Sogdian *Dhūta-sūtra* on account of linguistic criteria by Xavier Tremblay, who assigned it to a "sub-standard" stratum (ca. 8th century); see Tremblay 2001: 76–77.

② See Reichelt 1928: 15–32; and the review by Benveniste 1933: 33–44; reprinted in Benveniste 1979: 33–44.

③ Since the only Chinese manuscript known at that time contains only the first fascicle and since the opening section of the Sogdian text is missing, Demiéville proposed the identification without pinpointing any direct parallelism between the extant Chinese and Sogdian texts at his disposal; see Benveniste & Demiéville 1933: 194, 239–241; reprinted in Benveniste 1979: 68 and 113–115. This identification is now corroborated by the close parallels to the remaining Sogdian text found in the three complete Chinese manuscripts (i.e., BD15369, TY171, and Mitsui Bunko ms.). It is of some interest that Paul Demiéville and Chen Yinke, two prominent Sinologists of the 20th century, paid attention to the *Dhūta-sūtra* almost around the same time. The fact that Demiéville's findings were published as an appendix of a paper by an Iranist might be one of the reasons that Chen was not informed about the Sogdian text or Demiéville's identification.

④ See MacKenzie 1976: 33–51; and the review by Sims-Williams 1978: 260.

⑤ A pioneering attempt was made by Ibuki 1993b: 12–39 (173–146). But his achievements are compromised by his limited proficiency in Sogdian on the one hand, and by the erstwhile inaccessibility of the complete Chinese text on the other. A genuine comparative philological study has been undertaken by Yoshida Yutaka 吉田豊, who published some notes on selected passages of the Sogdian text about two decades ago; see Yoshida 1998: 167–173.

⑥ For an overview of the history and legacy of Chan Buddhism in the Tibetan cultural sphere, see most recently van Schaik 2015.

Dunhuang.[①] In this regard, the *Dhūta-sūtra* is ostensibly an exception. Be that as it may, I have identified a quotation from this apocryphal text (cf. Appendix I) in a Tibetan catechetical anthology of sūtra quotations, attributed to sPug Ye shes dbyangs, about whom we know next to nothing.[②] The anthology, alternatively titled *mDo sde brgyad bcu khungs* "Quotes from Eighty Sūtras" or *rNal 'byor chen po bsgom pa'i don* "Essentials for the Practice of Mahāyoga", was presumably compiled in the second half of the 8th century,[③] and survives in manuscripts from both Dunhuang and the Western Himalayas (i.e., Tabo and Gondhla).[④] Therefore, knowledge about part of the *Dhūta-sūtra*, if not the text in its entirety, was available to Tibetan-speaking Buddhists from the 9th century onward. This finding sheds light on a less known chapter in the history of the text's cross-cultural reception.

Structurally speaking, the *Dhūta-sūtra* consists of several rounds of teaching delivered by the Buddha in dialogue with two Bodhisattva-interlocutors, named Mind-King (Xinwang 心王) and Illuminator (Zhaoming 照明), respectively.[⑤] The apocryphal text was composed prior to the emergence of the so-called East Mountain community of Daoxin 道信 (580–651), so it would be a bit anachronistic to describe it as a "Chan-related" text, for a fully-fledged Chan identity based on a lineage descending from Bodhidharma did not appear until the late 7th century.[⑥] It is, however, fair to say that the *Dhūta-sūtra* probably took root in a milieu of meditation practitioners deeply imbued with Tathāgatagarbha doctrine and the notion of a self-reliant path towards liberation.[⑦] The persona of Mind-King, explicitly identified as a good friend (*shan zhishi* 善知識← Skt. Kalyāṇamitra) to be sought after by all, is a symbol personifying the innately pure mind inherent in every sentient being. The encounter with the good friend, symbolic of the awakening to the innate purity of the mind, is made possible through the cultivation of *dhūta* (or *dhuta*), i.e.,

---

① See Hironobu 1975: 170–171 (667–668); Kimura 1986: 55–77. See also Silk 2019: 232, 236–238.

② See van Schaik 2015: 167.

③ Okimoto 1993: 16–17, dated the *floruit* of the compiler to 771–850. Tauscher 2007: 83, n. 13, considers Okimoto's date "problematic and possibly too late." Tauscher himself proposes 735–814 for the life of the compiler and 775–779 for the compilation of the anthology, while admitting the hypothetical nature of his own proposal; see Tauscher 2021: 16–18.

④ For a comprehensive list of manuscripts and their dating, see Tauscher, *mDo sde brgyad bcu khungs* (2021), pp. 35–39. The manuscripts from Tabo and Gondhla probably date from the 14th or early 15th century, while the Dunhuang manuscript (Pelliot tibétain 818 + IOL Tib J 705) is likely to have been produced at the turn of the 11th century at the latest.

⑤ For a useful synoptic table of the text's content, see Ibuki 2006: 209–211.

⑥ See Greene 2008: 49–114.

⑦ See Ibuki 2006: 212–217.

a set of ascetic practices of purification originating in Indian Buddhism,① which, in the context of the *Dhūta-sūtra*, is reinterpreted in rather idealized and abstract terms.② The idealization and abstraction might indicate that the text was composed by metropolitan monk(s) at pains "to appropriate the prestige and legitimacy previously associated with mountain-dwelling [meditation] practitioners." ③

What has not been sufficiently discussed by previous scholars is, to my mind, the stylistic peculiarities of the *Dhūta-sūtra*. The text is pervaded by symbolism; hence its interpretation is, more often than not, based on semiotics. On the other hand, the way certain concepts are reinterpreted strikes me as creative. A case in point is *dhūta*, a term of utmost significance for this text:④

> 1) 頭者，行人初破煩惱，擊大法鼓，吼煩腦賊，得其頭主。賊民無主[a]，無所依止。即求出家，爲我弟子，攝心學道，身心清净，悟無生忍。故言頭也。2) 陀者，後心行人，善巧方便，雖得[b]前心，後念多失。既失其後，即是漏心，名爲煩惱。行人勤加精進，前心注後，後心注前，前後不二，名爲正法。即是阿難受持佛語，無有遺漏。是故言陀。3) 又復陀者，陀汰煩惱。如陀[c]金沙，先除粗者，真金始現。
>
> a. 主] 王 TY171　b. 得] TY171; 念 BD15369, Mitsui Bunko ms.　c. 陀] 地 TY171
>
> 1) As for *tou* (MChin. *dəw) "head, chief," the practitioner initially smashes defilements, beats the great *Dharma* drum, roars at the enemy defilements, and takes their chief captive. [Thus] the enemy subjects, without a chief, are at a loss as to whom to rely on. Then he seeks to go forth from the household [into homelessness and] becomes my disciple; with his mind concentrated [on] studying the Way, he becomes purified in body and mind, awakened to the intellectual tolerance [of the fact that *dharma*s] have no origination. Therefore, it is called *tou*. 2) As for *tuo* (~ *tuo* 馱, MChin. *da) "to carry," though the practitioner of the posterior mind, skilled in means, obtained the anterior mind, his remembrance [thereof] gets lost afterwards for the most part. Having lost its posterior [counterpart], [the anterior] then becomes a mind under evil influence, [which] is named defilements. The practitioner exerts himself with diligence, infusing the posterior mind with the anterior and the anterior mind with the posterior; the

---

① There is too much scholarly literature published on this topic to quote here. For an imperfect overview, the reader is referred to Dantinne 1991 and Abe 2001.

② See Ibuki 2006: 217–224.

③ See Greene 2008: 103, for coeval attempts to the same end, made in a different context. The hypothesis that the composer(s) of the *Dhūta-sūtra* may have led a life that entailed entering metropoles has also been suggested by Ibuki 2006: 224.

④ See Fang 1995: vol. 1, 298–299.

non-duality of the anterior and posterior mind is named the true *Dharma*. Precisely this is the Buddha's words, which were carried and passed on by Ānanda, without any omission. On that account it is called *tuo*. [3)] Again, as for *tuo* (~ *tao* 淘, MChin. **daw*) "to pan," [it] also [means] the panning and sifting of defilements. [It is] like panning sand [for] gold: First coarse [gravel] is removed, [then] pure gold begins to appear.①

In this passage, extant both in Chinese and Sogdian (cf. Appendix II), each of the two syllables of the Chinese transcription of *dhūta* (i.e., *tou* 頭 and *tuo* 陀) is glossed with a word in which it is embedded (e.g., *touzhu* 頭主 "head, chief" and *tuotai* 陀汰 ~ *taotai* 淘汰 "to pan and sift"). In each case, the word is further explicated in association with "defilements" (*fannao* 煩惱), i.e., the Chinese counterpart of Skt. *kleśa* "id." The defilements, in the context of the *Dhūta-sūtra*, are none other than so-called incidental or adventitious defilements (Skt. *āgantukakleśa*, Chin. *kechen fannao* 客塵煩惱), by which the innate purity and luminosity of the mind is obscured.

This idiosyncratic explanation was quoted and critiqued by the renowned Tiantai monk Zhanran 湛然 (711–782), who referred to it as one of the misconceptions of of *dhūta* prevalent to the south of the Yangtze River (*jiangbiao* 江表).② As a matter of fact, whoever composed the *Dhūta-sūtra* was not ignorant of what Zhanran believed to be the orthodox meaning of *dhūta*, namely "shaking off" (*dousou* 抖擻),③ but felt it insufficient to abide by the received interpretation that needed amplifying. In this respect, the approach of the *Dhūta-sūtra* is, as it were, not so much *exegetic* as *eisegetic*. That is to say, what is at issue here is not an arbitrary, unsophisticated pareidolia of a shadowy technical term, but an informed, deliberate attempt at reading into the concept of *dhūta* ideas related to Tathāgatagarbha doctrine, which are almost entirely absent in Indian Buddhist discourses on *dhūta*

---

① The simile of gold fallen into impurities is a trope for the germ covered with defilements, well attested in Tathāgatagarbha literature of Indian origin; e.g., *Tathāgatagarbhasūtra* §4, see Zimmermann 2002: 37, 117–119, 278–283. But the notion of gold panning seems to be an innovation in the *Dhūta-sūtra*.

② This is dealt with in a section of his magnum opus, the *Zhiguan fuxing chuanhong jue* 止觀輔行傳弘决 "A Resolution to Assist and Promote the Practice of Concentration and Insight"; see T. 1912: vol. 46, 263c10–12. Zhanran attributed the *Dhūta-sūtra* to a certain Chan master Ren from what is present-day Haining, Zhejiang (*Yanguan Ren chanshi* 鹽官忍禪師), whose identity is disputed; see Fang 1995: vol. 1, 326–327.

③ See Zhanran, *Zhiguan fuxing chuanhong jue*, in T. 1912: vol. 46, 263c5: 頭陀此云抖擻 "*Dhūta* is what is called 'shaking off' here (i.e., in Chinese)". Virtually the same gloss occurs at the very beginning of the *Dhūta-sūtra*; see Fang 1995): vol.1, 253: 頭陀者，西國之語，此土往翻名爲抖擻 "*Dhūta* is [from] the languages of the western countries (i.e., India and Central Asia), formerly translated as 'shaking off' in this land." This is in line with the tradition of glossing *dhūta* or *dhuta* with *dhutakleśa* (Pāli *dhutakilesa*) or *(vi)dhutarajas* "with defilements/impurities shaken (off)," "purified from defilements/impurities" that can be traced back to Indic sources; see Tournier 2014: 27–28.

(or *dhutaguṇa*). Zhanran apparently missed this point.

This method of syllable-for-syllable analysis and synthesis is well established in the Chinese tradition of semantic glossing (*xungu* 訓詁) and applies especially well to disyllabic hendiadys, i.e., compounds expressing one idea by means of the joining of two synonymous characters, in which Chinese abounds.① By glossing each of the two characters of a given compound in their own right and then merging the resultant meanings into a coherent whole, one is capable of broadening the range of applications of the two characters, which are thereby liberated from their specific context, and coming up with a more profound interpretation of the compound itself. It is conceivable that this method came in handy for glossing hendiadys and was thence generalized to disyllabic words of other types. In early Medieval China, the extended use of this method found its way into the circle of Buddhist scholiasts who applied it first and foremost to opaque renditions of non-Chinese technical terms. In a recent article, Funayama Tōru 船山徹 showcases the application of more or less the same method to *zhenru* 真如, a coinage in Buddhist Hybrid Chinese translating Skt. *tathatā* "Thusness, truth." By explicating *zhen* 真 "true" and *ru* 如 "as [usual]" "← changeless" in separate, yet interrelated meanings, Chinese Buddhist thinkers experimented with a theological synthesis of multiple aspects of what they subsumed under the connotations of *tathatā*, which unfolds in tantalizing relation to a nexus of concepts and doctrines in vogue, such as *tathāgata, tathāgatagarbha* (or Buddha-Nature), and *dharmadhātu*.② This is possibly inspired by semantic etymologizing (*nirvacana*) known from the Indian tradition,③ but is essentially distinct from the latter, insofar as it is not based on a series of similar-sounding—(even, in some cases, etymologically related—)roots, but operates on the polysemy and interpretative potentials of each and every syllable. To wit, we have to do here with a way of thinking and interpretation peculiar to the so-called Sinosphere dominated by the use of Chinese characters.

By way of a final remark on this issue, let me go a step further and argue that the aforesaid method can be developed to its full potential only in isolating languages, such as Chinese, with

① Among Chinese scholars, this type of compounds is known as "compounded words consisting of synonymous characters" (*tongyi fuci* 同義複詞). In some cases, the meanings of the two originally synonymous characters had changed over time; therefore, they were no longer perceived by later scholiasts as synonyms, but were separately glossed as semantically divergent words. See Guo 2005: 13–14, with examples.

② See Funayama 2017: 22–37, 53–60. The case of *zhenru* is not an isolated example: Funayama has pinpointed a half-dozen terms which were explicated in similar ways in early Medieval Chinese Buddhist works (Funayama 2017: 38–52). The deployment of this kind of analysis can be a shibboleth to locate Chinese texts for which a claim of Indianness is made.

③ For the appropriation and deployment of *nirvacana* in Indian Buddhist literature, see most recently Apple 2009: 161–173 (= 80–68); Apple 2019: 171–192; and Visigalli 2017: 1143–1190; Visigalli 2019: 162–180.

the lowest possible morpheme-per-word ratio. In such languages, each word contains a single morpheme which is, in most cases, monosyllabic; hence every single syllable can potentially become an independent word, the smallest unit of sense-making. In Chinese, given the productivity of homonyms and loan characters, a single syllable, in some cases, can be interpreted as several different words, opening up a wide field of interpretive possibilities. As is demonstrated above, a disyllabic Indic loanword (Chin. *toutuo* 頭陀 ← Skt. *dhūta*), from which three Chinese words are extracted, affords three intersecting layers of reading. The composer(s) of the *Dhūta-sūtra* not only had a sound grasp of, but also deliberately capitalized on this structural characteristic of the Chinese language in order to create an intricate and multi-layered discourse put in the golden mouth of the Buddha. This distinguishes the *Dhūta-sūtra* from the textual products of the "western countries" (*xiguo* 西國), where, in overall terms, fusional Indo-European languages were spoken. In this light, it comes as no surprise that the two ingenious Chinese poets of the early 9th century were enthralled by this text. Chen Yinke might have been justified in frowning upon their Buddhological learning, but there should be no questioning their literary taste and sensitivity to the rhythm and structure of the Chinese language.

Appendix I: Quotation in the *mDo sde brgyad bcu khungs*

The aforementioned quotation from the *Dhūta-sūtra* occurs in the 74th section of the Tibetan anthology, which addresses the question: How does one rise from the generation of the initial aspiration [towards Buddhahood] to [higher] stages [of a Bodhisattva] through non-referential meditative practice (*dang po sems bskyed pa nas myi dmyigs pa bsgom pa las sar ci ltar 'phar zhe na*)? In this context, the *Dhūta-sūtra* is quoted along with a handful of Mahāyāna sūtras as the scriptural foundation for the relativity of the distinction of the successive stages (*bhūmi*) of the Bodhisattva practice:①

Seṃs kyi rgyal po'i mdo' las/dbang po mchog dang ldan pas/dang po sems bskyed pa nyid kyis dang po[a] *tshor ba rdzogs te/rim par bya ba myed do //*

a. *dang po*] read *dag po*; cf. Chin. 正

[Quote] from the "Sūtra of Mind-King": One [who is] endowed with superb faculties

① See Tauscher 2021: 118, §74, no. 376. Helmut Tauscher (p.c.) has drawn my attention to the likelihood that the Tibetan passage can potentially be read as a verse of four lines, each having six syllables, if a small modification is made to it (*dang po sems bskyed pa nyid kyis* → *dang po sems bskyed nyid kyis /*). This might be understood as an attempt at emulating the Chinese passage's four-character rhythm.

attains the perfect enlightenment① just as generating the initial aspiration [towards Buddhahood]; it does not have to be done gradually.

This is a slightly abridged quotation from the following Chinese passage:②

直[a]是最上利根菩薩，聞一悟解，初發心時，便成正覺，不由次第。

a. 直] TY171; 真 BD15369, Mitsui Bunko ms.

It is the foremost Bodhisattva of sharp faculties [who], fully awakening [to reality] after hearing but one point, attains the perfect enlightenment as soon as [he] generates the initial aspiration [towards Buddhahood], without following the sequence.

Unfortunately, the Sogdian manuscript breaks off right before this passage. It is unclear whether sPug Ye shes dbyangs gleaned this passage from a Tibetan translation lost to history, or excerpted it from a Chinese source himself. It is quite possible that he knew this quotation from an anthology,③ similar to his own work, rather than from a complete version of the *Dhūta-sūtra*. But the details remain nebulous. This passage is also quoted by Huijun 慧均, a 7th-century Chinese Mādhyamika, in his *Dasheng si lun xuanyi* 大乘四論玄義, one of the oldest witnesses to the *Dhūta-sūtra*, among the scriptural discourses on the ten stages of a Bodhisattva (*shi di yi* 十地義).④

Appendix II: The Sogdian Version of the Passage on *Dhūta*

The passage explicating *dhūta*, discussed above, survives in its entirety in the presumably 8th-century Sogdian manuscript of the *Dhūta-sūtra* from Dunhuang. Previous scholars of Iranian philology, particularly Hans Reichelt and D.N. MacKenzie, have made admirable contributions to a proper understanding of the fragmentary Sogdian text. Nevertheless, due to the inaccessibility of the complete Chinese text, their trail-blazing work can now be improved. In the following, I quote

① For the use of Tib. *tshor* (lit. 'feeling, awareness') in the sense of "enlightenment" (cf. Chin. *jue* 覺 'id.'), peculiar to early translations from Chinese, see Gomez 1983: 153.

② See Fang 1995: vol.1, 300.

③ It has been well established by previous scholarship that sPug Ye shes dbyangs appropriated a number of sūtra quotations from the *Sūtrasamuccaya* attributed to Nāgārjuna as well as from the *Zhujing yao chao* 諸經要抄 (T.2819), a Chinese anthology known from a fragmentary Dunhuang manuscript; see Otokawa 1999: 112–117; and Tauscher 2021: 24–26.

④ The quotation is missing from the *Zokuzōkyō* 続蔵経 edition of this work (no. 784), in which the section on the ten stages is incomplete, but can be retrieved on the basis of a second-hand quotation in the *Sanron gensho mongi yō* 三論玄疏文義要 by a Japanese monk named Chinkai 珍海 (1091/2–1152); see T. 2209: vol. 70, 315b27–c2. See also Itō 1974: 75. It is noteworthy that Huijun consistently refers to the text's title as the '*Dhūta-sūtra* for Bodhisattvas' (*Pusa toutuo jing* 菩薩頭陀經).

the transliteration and translation by MacKenzie, while furnishing a sample of my commentary in footnotes to facilitate future research:①

1) rty nwkr ZK δ'w w'γ'wn'k 'γw 'PZY ZNH **δynδ'r mrtγm'k** cnn ''γ'zy ZKw wytγwy 't ZKw sryβt'm 'nγ'wyt, rty ZKw mz'γyh δrm'yk' kws ''**k'wct**, ZY ZKw wytγwy sryβt'm s'n **syδt**, rty 'myn s'n sry ZKw 'βš'yws βyrt. pr'w 'PZY kδ ZK s'n pw **γwt'w** βwt, nwkr pw'nwth βwt. rty② ywn'yδ δynδ'r k'mt nyẓy'y ZKZY mn' δrγwšky βwt, rty ZKw p'zn '**nš'ypt** ZKw '**rt'wspy** {ZKw 'rt'wspy} ywγsty wβyw, pr CWRH 'PZY pr p'zn 'ws'wγtk 't zp'rt βwt, ZY ZKw n' ''z'yt wyn βyrt. rty cym'yδ pyδ'r δ'w wγsty. || 2) 'PZY ms ZK t' w'γwn'k 'γw 'PZY ZK pyštr'yck' p'zn'k δynδ'r prw šyr'k γwp prγ'npy, styw ZKw pyrnm'yck p'zn βyrt, **pyštrw** šm''rt, rty βr'yštr βr'wšcy wnty. rty šw kδ pn'yšt γyδ prw''r p'zn βwt, ZKZY wytγwy sryβt'm γwynty. rty nwkr ZK δynδ'r prtr 'nt'wγst, rty ZKw pyrnm'yck' p'zn pšycyk wnty, 'PZY 'w pš'yck p'zn pyrnmcyk, rty ZK pyrnm pyštrw dw' wkry L' wnty, rty γyδ wyzrh δrm βwt. c'γwn'k 'tšy ZK ''**n't** ptγrβty, ZKw pwt'n'k δrm ZKZY nyδcw, L' pr'yct L' βr'wcy wnty. cym'yδ pyδ'r t' γwynty. || 3) 'PZY ms w'γwn'k 'γw ZKZY wytγwy sryβt'm **βδ'yštk** βwt. m'yδ 'YKZY ZKw zyrn šykth **βδ'yẓ'** k'm, pyrnm ZKw st'npyr'k pγ'rš, rty ZK kr''n zyrn 'prw wyn'ncy βwt. ||

"1) Now the *dh*[*ū*] is such that the pious man③ breaks the passions from the beginning and hangs up④ the great *Dharma* drum and destroys⑤ the enemy passions and takes the head of the

---

① See MacKenzie 1976: 48–49, ll. 270–287. The parts commented upon are highlighted with boldface in the Romanized transliteration.

② This conjunction was overlooked by MacKenzie, and is added by Sims-Williams in his review; see Sims-Williams 1978: 260.

③ Sogd. *δynδ'r mrtym'k* "pious man" translates Chin. *xingren* 行人 "practitioner". This is not a perfect match: Sogd. *δynδ'r* literally means "holder of the religion, religious", thus referring to a "priest" in Christian texts, to a "monk" in a Buddhist context, and to an "elect" in the case of Manicheism. However, the Chinese term, as is clear from the present passage, applies also to a lay practitioner before going forth. Whether monastic or lay is irrelevant to the use of *xingren* in the *Dhūta-sūtra*. In Manicheism, *δynδ'r* has its next of kin *δyn''βr* 'elect', possibly a loanword from Parthian, which became significant later on in a schism among Manicheism (cf. *Dēnāwar*); see Tremblay 2001: 123–126. See also Colditz 1992: 322–341.

④ In translating "hangs up", MacKenzie probably derived Sogd. *''k'wct* from the Iranian verb **kauč-* "to bend, draw into, contract", to which also belongs Sogd. *ptkwc-* "to angle, fish"; see Cheung 2007: 248–249 with further references. While this etymology is not in doubt, Chin. *ji* 擊 "to strike" suggests that Sogd. *''k'wc-* also means "to strike" (< **ā-kauč-*), a meaning which is well attested in its cognates: Khot. *paṣkūj-* "to strike" < **pati-(s)kauč-*, and Shughni *angaxs-* "to strike against" < **ham-kuxsa-*. See Emmerick 1968: 77; and Sims-Williams 1979: 135.

⑤ MacKenzie followed Benveniste 1933: 42 = Benveniste 1979: 42, in rendering Sogd. *syδt* as "destroys". However, in the light of Chin. *hou* 吼 "to roar, shout", it would be more plausible to associate it with **said-*² "to call" (cf. Sogd. *'ns'yδ* "to exhort") rather than **said-*¹ "to break, split, destroy"; see Cheung 2007: 327.

enemy, the master, so that when the enemy becomes without a lord① it becomes unsupported. Immediately the pious man wishes to go out (from his home) to become my disciple, and he envelops② the mind and learns the righteous < ? >,③ and both in body and mind becomes

---

① Sogd. *γwt'w* (~ *MLK'*) in most cases, translates Chin. *wang* 王 "king". To my knowledge, only in one exceptional case does it seem to be the counterpart of Chin. *zhu* 主 "master"; see Weller 1937: 48–49. Given the similarity between the two characters, it is quite frequently the case that they get mixed up by scribes. But the present case is clear-cut: *zhu* "master" occurs in the preceding sentence where it clearly corresponds to Sogd. *'βš'yws* (cf. Av. *fšuiiaṇt-* "possessing cattle; cattle-breeder"); therefore, it is more likely that *γwt'w* translates *wang* "king" here. If that is the case, the Sogdian translation seems to be based on a *Vorlage* sharing the same variant reading as TY171.

② Sogd. *'nš'ypt* does not mean "envelops", as MacKenzie suggested, but means "collects, buries", and thus "concentrates" when construed with the mind (cf. Chin. *shexin* 攝心); see Yakubovich 2002: 544–545.

③ MacKenzie was uncertain regarding this set phrase. Sogd. *'rt'wspy ywys-* should translate Chin. *xuedao* 學道 "to learn the Way", while Chin. *dao* 道 "Way, i.e., enlightenment (*bodhi*)" is normally translated by Sogd. *r'δ(h)* "road, path"; see Weller 1937: 44, and MacKenzie 1976: 199.

In a Manichean context, Sogd. *(δyn) 'rtwspy'* is used as a technical term for "community (of the [Mainchean] Church)", the collective meaning of which Gershevitch traced back to its putative Iranian forebear, i.e., Av. *aṣ̌auuasta-* "ownership of Truth"; see Gershevitch 1959: 77, 89, and 163 [*ad* 5^2]. For the assumption of a sound change *-st* > *-sp*, see Gershevitch 1954: 70, §470.

Gershevitch's interpretation of the Avestan term was impugned by Jean Kellens, who rendered it as "sainteté" and remarked that "toutes les attestations d'*aṣ̌auuasta-* font penser à un nom abstrait plutôt qu'à un nom collectif"; see Kellens 1974: 219. Benedikt Peschl (p.c.) suggests the scenario of its derivation, as follows: **artāu a(n)t-* "associated with True-Order" → **artāu at-ta-* > **artāu asta-* "the state of being associated with True-Order"; the collective meaning (i.e., "the collective body of those in the state of being associated with True-Order" → "the ecclesiastical community") could have blended in with the abstract noun through the secondary addition of the denominal abstract suffix /-yā/ (Sims-Williams 1981: 14–17) in Sogdian or its forebear.

MacKenzie made a distinction between an adjective *'rt'wsp(')y* "righteous", which he considered a light stem, and an abstract noun *'rt'wspy'(h)* "righteousness" (MacKenzie 1976: 85–86). In an unpublished note, Peschl refutes MacKenzie's theory by pointing out that (1) all spellings of *'rt'wsp(')y* in fact belong to the abstract noun in /-yā/, showing the development of /-yē/ to /-ē/ (Sims-Williams 1981: 15); that (2) Sogd. /*artawasp/ is a heavy stem rather than a light stem; and that (3) no adjectival reading of Sogd. *'rt'wsp(')y* is unequivocally borne out by textual evidence. Therefore, it is likely that the present occurrence of *'rt'wspy* is nothing but the obl. sg. of the abstract noun in /-yā/. As far as the *Dhūta-sūtra* is concerned, no distinction between *'rt'wspy* and *'rt'wspy'* is discernible in light of the Chinese parallels. All the other occurrences of *'rt'wspy(')* can be tentatively divided into two groups (the Sogdian text is cited from MacKenzie 1976, and the Chinese text from Fang 1995):

[A1] p.42, ll. 174–175: *'PZY šy ZK CWRH 't ZK p'zn 'ws'wγtk 'PZY zp'rt 'myn* ***'rt'wspy*** *'M 'ns''ky* (read *'ns'ky*) 'His body and mind [are] cleansed and pure, fitting with this /artǎ̄waspyā/' = p.292: 身心清净，與道相應 "[His] body and mind [are] cleansed and pure, in accordance with the Way."

[A2] p.48, ll. 265–266: *'PZY kδ ZK δynδ'r mrtγm'k prw* ***'rt'wspy'*** *šwt rty pr 10 wkkry' šm'r'yck' 'spt'k βwt* 'And if the religious man goes in /artǎ̄waspyā/, he becomes perfect in the ten conceptual [items]' = p.298: 行人修道，十念成就 "The practitioner cultivates the way, [and becomes] accomplished in the ten recollections."

[A3] p.50, ll. 294–296: *rty ywn'k wyspw 'myn pwty šyr'y 't z[']ry m'n ''γδ'k z'wr 'γw ZKZY m'γw k'w* ***'rt'wspy*** *r'δh ZKw 'šyh βyrt* (read *βrt*) "And this is all the power of the wish of the good and compassionate mind of these Buddhas, which brings our intellect to /artǎ̄waspyā/, the Way" = p.300: 并是如來慈悲願力，使我悟道 "[This] is all the power of vows, loving kindness, and compassion of the Tathāgatas, making us awakened to the Way." （转下页）

purified and acquires the view of non-birth. Therefore, it is said *dh*[*ū*]. [2)] And the *ta* is such that the future-minded pious one with good means, although he acquires the former mind, thinks of the future and forgets more. When he loses it, then he has a mind of the discharge which is called the passions. Now the pious one strives more and makes the former mind the later (?) and the later mind the former, and makes no duality of former and later. That is the true *Dharma*, as

---

（接上页）**[B1]** p.40, ll. 110–111: *kδʾwty ZNH pwtystβt prw δʾw-tʾ* ***ʾrtʾwspy*** *šwʾnt rty cw škšʾpt δʾrʾnt* "If the Bodhisattvas go in the *dhūta*, /artăwaspyā/, what precepts do they uphold?" = p.288: 諸菩薩行頭陀時，受持何戒? "When all the Bodhisattvas etc. practice the *dhūta*, what precepts should they undertake?"

[B2] p.40, ll. 116–117: *kδ prw δʾw-tʾ* ***ʾrtʾwspy*** *šwʾ rty pyrnm sʾct ZK pryʾnpy ʾkrty* "If you would go in the *dhūta*, /artăwaspyā/, you must first make the means" = p.288: 行頭陀時，前作方便 "When [one] practices the *dhūta*, [one must] initially make (i.e., prepare) the expedient."

[B3] p.40, ll. 137–138: *rty cnn cymʾyδ pyδʾr ZKw δʾw-tʾ* ***ʾrtʾwspy****ʾ ʾnywʾyt* 'And on this account he breaks the *dhūta*, /artăwaspyā/' = p.290: 破頭陀戒 'He breaks the precepts of the *dhūta*' (Chin. *jie* 戒 "precept" is otherwise translated by Sogd. *škšʾpt* [Skt. *śikṣāpada*] "id."; it is not impossible that the *Vorlage* of the Sogdian version testifies to a variant reading such as 破頭陀行).

[B4] p.42, ll. 151–152: *rty ʾYKʾ prʾymʾyδ wkry kβnw kβnw prw* ***ʾrtʾwspy*** *pδkh ʾwšt* "And when, in this way, little by little, he stands in /artăwaspyā/, *dharma* [...]" = pp.290–291: 如是念念，行法成時 "When he, [exerting himself] in this way every moment, has accomplished the practice of *dharma* [...]".

[B5] p.46, ll. 222–223: *γw δʾw-tʾ zpʾrt δrm γwyzʾkw nyx ʾγw ʾt pyʾstk ZY pʾrʾγʾz wyspyʾ* ***ʾrtʾwspy****ʾ myδʾny sry* "The pure *dharma* of *dhūta* is very profound and adorned and excellent, the foremost among all /artăwaspyā/" = p.296: 頭陀净法，是法微妙，甚深玄奥，諸行中上 "The *dhūta* [is] a pure *dharma*; this *dharma* is subtle, very profound and abstruse, the foremost among all the practices."

To sum up, Sogd. *ʾrtʾwspy(ʾ)* corresponds with Chin. *dao* 道 "way" on the one hand (→ Group A), and with Chin. *xing* 行 "practice" on the other (→ Group B). In the latter case, it seems to be a generic term in apposition to the concept of *dhūta*, which is said to be the foremost in the group or class designated by this term (cf. **[B5]**). A collocation *prw ʾrtʾwspy(ʾ) šw-/wytr-* "to go in /artăwaspyā/" → "to be engaged in practice" seems to be well established in the translation idiom of Buddhist Sogdian. The same use of this term is known from other Sogdian Buddhist texts translated from Chinese, usually as the counterpart of Chin. *xiu/xing* 修 / 行 "practice; to practice, cultivate;" see Annemarie von Gabain *apud* Weller 1937: 27–29.

The case of Group A, to which the occurrence in question belongs, is a bit more complex. Sogd. *prw ʾrtʾwspy šw-* (cf. **[A2]**) and *ʾrtʾwspy ywys-*, translating Chin. *xiudao* 修道 and *xuedao* 學道 , respectively, are semantically close to Group B. In this case, *dao* 道 "way" should be construed in the sense of a "religious way of life", which is not substantially different from *xing* 行 "practice, engagement". Both of the concepts were expounded to a Sogdian audience through the inherited Iranian notion of the state of being associated with True-Order. If the collective meaning, inferred by Gershevitch from the Manichean evidence, is to be taken seriously, it might be conceivable to assume a communal aspect inherent in Sogd. *ʾrtʾwspy(ʾ)*, which, in a Buddhist context, implies that the act of learning the way of life or practice was interpreted by Sogdian translators as partaking in a truthful state pertaining to the religious community rather than as a lone undertaking. In addition, the parallelism between Sogd. *ʾrtʾwspy(ʾ)* and *dao* 道 "way [of life] " seems to have triggered a secondary extension of the denotation of the term, which has come to be used also in the sense of "Way, i.e., enlightenment (*bodhi*)" (cf. **[A1][A3]**). This is all the more transparent, as Sogd. *ʾrtʾwspy(ʾ)* occurs in apposition to Sogd. *rʾδh* (cf. **[A3]**), which, as mentioned above, is the most common Sogdian expression of this Buddhist doctrinal idea.

he clearly[①] understands it, the *Buddhadharma*, which he does not abandon or forget. Therefore it is called *ta*. [3)] Also, [*ta*] is such as is wrapped[②] in the passions, as you would cover[52] gold in gravel. First remove the coarse (matter) and the pure gold then becomes visible."

Abbreviations

BD	Beijing Dunhuang. Dunhuang manuscripts preserved at the National Library in Beijing.
Дх.	Dunhuang. Dunhuang manuscripts preserved at the Institute of Oriental Manuscripts, Russian Academy of Sciences, in St. Petersburg.
IOL Tib	Tibetan manuscripts and wooden tablets preserved at the British Library and of the joint British Library Oriental Collection/India Office Library in London.
LM	Lüshun Museum. Collection of manuscripts preserved at Lüshun Museum in Dalian.
Or.	Manuscripts of the Department of Oriental Manuscripts and Printed Books of the British Library and of the joint British Library Oriental Collection/India Office Library in London.
Pelliot chinois	Pelliot Collection of Chinese Dunhuang manuscripts preserved at the Bibliothèque nationale de France in Paris.
Pelliot tibétain	Pelliot Collection of Tibetan Dunhuang manuscripts preserved at the Bibliothèque nationale de France in Paris.

---

① Chin. Anan 阿難 suggests *ʾʾnʾt* to be a scribal error for *ʾʾnʾnt* "Ānanda".

② On this verb, see Yoshida 1998: 168. "Here *βδʾyẓ/βδʾyšt* translating 陀（汰）'destroying and (washing out)' can hardly be identified with the verb discussed above (i.e., *βδʾyẓ* 'to load') and one may be induced to postulate two verbs: [1]*βδʾyẓ* 'to load' and [2]*βδʾyẓ* 'to destroy, grind' (possibly homographs coming from **abi-darzaya-* and **fra-darzaya-*). However, since 陀 is a rare and difficult character, one must also envisage the possibility that the Sogdian translator totally misunderstood the Chinese original, and that we have one and the same verb meaning 'to load, fasten' here." Some of the comments by Yoshida are justified, but his proposal "to destroy" is, to my mind, a bit far-fetched. The verb **darz-* "to attach, fasten, load" is well established in the Iranian languages; see Cheung 2007: 62–63. There is no reason to assume a misunderstanding in the present case, and the Sogdian translator(s) may well have comprehended the tenor of the panning metaphor, but rendered it in a way comprehensible to Sogdian speakers. One must reckon with the likelihood that the panning of gold was practiced in Sogdiana differently from in China; for instance, the ancient tradition of using sheepskins to extract alluvial gold is well known through the Greek myth of the Golden Fleece, which may have been a mature sheepskin laden with gold particles. A similar tradition was probably continued among Iranian peoples; see Ross & Allan 2003: 72. In that context, the meaning "to load" could possibly make good sense.

T. Takakusu Junjirō 高楠順次郎 & Watanabe Kaikyoku 渡辺海旭 (eds.), *Taishō shinshū daizōkyō* 大正新脩大蔵経. Tōkyō: Taishō issaikyō kankōkai 大正一切経刊行会, 1924–1932.

TY Tianjin Yishu. Dunhuang manuscripts preserved at Tianjin Arts Museum in Tianjin.

References

Abe, Jion 阿部慈園. 2001. *Zuda no kenkyū: Pāri bukkyō wo chūshin to shite* 頭陀の研究：パーリ仏教を中心として. Tōkyō: Shunjūsha.

Apple, James. 2009. "'Wordplay': Emergent Ideology through Semantic Elucidation, A Rhetorical Technique in Mahāyāna Buddhist Formulations." *Bulletin of the Institute of Oriental Philosophy* 25: 161–173 (80–68).

Apple, James. 2019. "The Semantic Elucidation (*nirukta*) of Bodhisattva Spiritual Attainment: A Rhetorical Technique in Early Mahāyāna Sūtras." *Annual Report of the International Research Institute for Advanced Buddhology at Soka University* 22: 171–192.

Benveniste, Émile. 1933. "Notes sur les texts sogdiens bouddhiques du British Museum." *Journal of the Royal Asiatic Society*: Issue 1, 9–68.

Benveniste, Émile. 1979. *Études sogdiennes*. Wiesbaden: Reichert.

Benveniste, Émile and Paul Demiéville. 1933. "Notes sur le fragment sogdien du Buddhadhyān asamādhisāgarasūtra." *Journal Asiatique* 223: 193–245.

Buswell, Robert E., Jr. 1990. "Introduction." In: Robert E. Buswell, Jr. (eds.), *Chinese Buddhist Apocrypha*. Honolulu: University of Hawai'i Press, 1–30.

Cao, Ling 曹凌. 2011. *Zhongguo fojiao yiweijing zonglu* 中國佛教疑僞經綜錄. Shanghai: Shanghai guji chubanshe.

Chen,Yinke 陳寅恪. 1939. "Dunhuang ben Xinwang toutuo jing ji Faju jing bawei" 敦煌本心王投陀經及法句經跋尾. *Bulletin of the Institute of History and Philosophy Academia Sinica* 中央研究院歷史語言研究所集刊 8.1: 19.

Chen, Yinke 陳寅恪. 2001a. *Jinming guan conggao er bian* 金明館叢稿二編. Beijing: SDX Joint Publishing.

Chen, Yinke 陳寅恪. 2001b. *Yuan Bai shi jianzheng gao* 元白詩箋証稿. Beijing: SDX Joint Publishing.

Cheung, Johnny. 2007. *Etymological Dictionary of the Iranian Verb*. Leiden/Boston: Brill.

Colditz, Iris. 1992. "Hymnen an Šād-Ohrmezd: Ein Beitrag zur frühen Geschichte der

Dīnāwarīya in Transoxanien." *Altorientalische Forschungen* 19.2: 322–341.

Dantinne, Jean. 1991. *Les qualités de l'ascète (Dhutaguṇa): Étude sémantique et doctrinale*. Bruxelles: Thanh-Long.

Emmerick, R.E. 1968. *Saka Grammatical Studies*. London: Oxford University Press.

Fang, Guangchang 方廣錩.1995. *Zangwai fojiao wenxian* 藏外佛教文獻. Beijing: Zongjiao wenhua chubanshe.

Funayama, Tōru 船山徹. 2017. "Shinnyo no sho kaishaku: Bongo *tathatā* to kango 'honmu' 'nyo''nyonyo''shinnyo'" 真如の諸解釈：梵語 tathatā と漢語「本無」「如」「如如」「真如」. *Tōhō gakuhō* 東方學報 92: 1–75.

Gershevitch, Ilya. 1954. *A Grammar of Manichean Sogdian*. Oxford: Blackwell.

Gershevitch, Ilya. 1959. *The Avestan Hymn to Mithra*. Cambridge: Cambridge University Press.

Gomez, Luis O. 1983. "The Direct and the Gradual Approaches of Zen Master Mahāyāna: Fragments of the Teachings of Mo-ho-yen." In: *Studies in Ch'an and Hua-yen*. Honolulu: University of Hawai'i Press.

Greene, Eric. 2008. "Another Look at Early Chan: Daoxuan, Bodhidharma, and the Three Levels Movement." *T'oung Pao*, Second Series, 94.1/3: 49–114.

Guo, Zaiyi 郭在貽. 2005. *Xungu xue* 訓詁學. Beijing: Zhonghua shuju.

Ibuki, Atsushi 伊吹敦. 1993a. "'Shin'ō kyō chū' no seiritsu ni tsuite"『心王経註』の成立について. *Indogaku bukkyōgaku kenkyū* 印度學佛教學研究 42.1: 285–288.

Ibuki, Atsushi 伊吹敦. 1993b. "'Shin'ō kyō' ni tsuite: Sogudo go yaku sareta zenshūkei gikyō"『心王経』について：ソグド語譯された禅宗系偽経. *Komazawa daigaku zen kenkyūjo nenpō* 駒澤大學禅研究所年報 4: 12–39 (= 173–146).

Ibuki, Atsushi 伊吹敦. 2003."'Shin'ō kyō' no shohon ni tsuite"『心王経』の諸本について. *Indogaku bukkyōgaku kenkyū* 印度學佛教學研究 52.1: 180–187.

Ibuki, Atsushi 伊吹敦. 2006. "'Shin'ō kyō' no shisō to seisakusha no seikaku"『心王経』の思想と制作者の性格." In: *Nihon Tonkōgaku ronshū* 日本敦煌学論叢 1: 205–241.

Itō, Ryūju 伊藤隆寿. 1972. "Ekin 'Daijō shiron gengi' ni tsuite (2)" 慧均『大乗四論玄義』について（二）. *Indogaku bukkyōgaku kenkyū* 印度學佛教學研究 20.2: 790–792.

Itō, Ryūju 伊藤隆寿. 1974. "Daijō shiron gengi" itsubun no seiri"『大乗四論玄義』逸文の整理. *Komazawa daigaku bukkyōgaku bu ronshū* 駒澤大学仏教学部論集 5: 64–90.

Jao, Tsung-i 饒宗頤. 1998. "Tang dai wenxuan xue lüeshu" 唐代文選學略述. *Tang Studies* 唐研究 4: 47–66.

Kellens, Jean. 1974. *Les noms-racines de l'Avesta*. Wiesbaden: Dr. Ludwig Reichert Verlag.

Kimura, Ryūtoku 木村隆德. 1986. "Tonkō Chibetto go zen bunken ni okeru in'yō kyōmon" 敦煌チベット語禅文献に於ける引用経文. In: *Chibetto no bukkyō to shakai* チベットの仏教と社会. Tōkyō: Shunjūsha, 55–77.

Obata, Hironobu 小畠宏允. 1975. "Chibetto no zenshū to zōyaku gikyō ni tsuite" チベットの禅宗と蔵訳偽経について. *Indogaku bukkyōgaku kenkyū* 印度學佛教學研究 23.2:170–171 (667–668).

Okimoto, Katsumi 沖本克己. 1993. "Daijō mufunbetsu shūjūgi jobun (Pelliot 996) ni tsuite" 大乗無分別修習義・序文 (Pelliot 996) について. *Hanazono daigaku kenkyū kiyō* 花園大学研究紀要 25: 1–23.

Otokawa, Bun'ei. 1999. "New Fragments of the *rNal 'byor chen por bsgom pa'i don* from Tabo." In: C.A. Scherrer-Schaub and E. Steinkellner (eds.), *Tabo Studies II: Manuscripts, Texts, Inscriptions, and the Arts*. Rome: Istituto Italiano per l'Africa e l'Oriente, 99–162.

Reichelt, Hans. 1928. *Die sogdischen Handschriftenreste des Britischen Museums*, vol. 1: *Die Buddhistischen Texte*. Heidelberg: Carl Winter Universitätsbuchhandlung.

Rong, Xinjiang 榮新江. 2019. "Lüshun bowuguan cang Xinjiang chutu fodian de xueshu jiazhi" 旅順博物館藏新疆出土佛典的學術價值. In: *Sichou zhi lu yu Xinjiang chutu wenxian: Lüshun bowuguan bai nian jinian guoji xueshu yantao hui lunwen ji* 絲綢之路與新疆出土文獻：旅順博物館百年紀念國際學術研討會論文集. Beijing: Zhonghua shuju, 24–40.

Ross, Jennifer C. & James W. Allan. 2003. "Gold." In: Ehsan Yarshater (ed.), *Encyclopaedia Iranica* 11.1. Encyclopaedia Iranica Foundation, 68–75.

Schaik, Sam van. 2015. *Tibetan Zen: Discovering a Lost Tradition*. Boston: Snow Lion.

Shields, Anna. 2006. "Remembering When: The Uses of Nostalgia in the Poetry of Bai Juyi and Yuan Zhen." *Harvard Journal of Asiatic Studies* 66.2: 321–361.

Silk, Jonathan. 2019. "Chinese Sūtras in Tibetan Translation: A Preliminary Survey." *Annual Report of the International Research Institute for Advanced Buddhology at Soka University* 22: 228–246.

Sims-Williams, Nicholas. 1978. "Book Review of *The Buddhist Sogdian Texts of the British Library* (*Acta Iranica*, 10. Troisième Série, Textes et Mémoires, 3) by D. N. MacKenzie." *Indo-Iranian Journal* 20.3/4: 256–260.

Sims-Williams, Nicholas. 1979. "Notes and Communications: A Parthian Sound Change." *Bulletin of the School of Oriental and African Studies* 42.1: 133–136.

Sims-Williams, Nicholas. 1981. "Some Sogdian Denominal Abstract Suffixes." *Acta Orientalia* 42: 11–19.

Tanaka, Ryōshō 田中良昭 & Tei Sei 程正. 2014. *Tonkō zenshū bunken bunrui mokuroku* 敦煌

禅宗文献分類目録. Tōkyō: Daitō shuppansha.

Tauscher, Helmut. 2007. "The rNal 'byor chen po bsgom pa'i don Manuscript of the 'Gondhla Kanjur'." In: Deborah Klimburg-Salter, Kurt Tropper and Christian Jahoda (eds.), *Text, Image and Song in Transdisciplinary Dialogue: PIATS 2003*. Leiden/Boston: Brill, 79–103.

Tauscher, Helmut. 2021. *mDo sde brgyad bcu khungs: An Early Tibetan Sūtra Anthology*. Vienna: Arbeitskreis für Tibetische und Buddhistische Studien Universität Wien.

Tournier, Vincent. 2014. "Mahākāśyapa, His Lineage, and the Wish for Buddhahood: Reading Anew the Bodhgayā Inscriptions of Mahānāman." *Indo-Iranian Journal* 57.1/2: 1–60.

Tremblay, Xavier. 2001. *Pour une histoire de la Sérinde: Le manichéisme parmi les peuples et religions d'Asie Centrale d'après les sources primaires*. Vienna: Verlag der Österreichischen Akademie der Wissenschaften.

MacKenzie, D. N. 1976. *The Buddhist Sogdian Texts of the British Library*. Tehran/Liège: Bibliothèque Pahlavi.

Nagata, Tomoyuki 永田知之. 2012. "Chin Inkaku ronkyū Tonkō bunken zakki: Riyō keiro wo chūshin ni" 陳寅恪論及敦煌文献雑記：利用経路を中心に. *Tonkō shahon kenkyū nenpō* 敦煌写本研究年報 6: 215–237.

Visigalli, Paolo. 2017. "Words in and out of History: Indian Semantic Derivation (*nirvacana*) and Modern Etymology in Dialog." *Philosophy East and West* 67.4: 1143–1190.

Visigalli, Paolo. 2019. "Charting 'Wilderness' (*araṇya*) in Brahmanical and Buddhist Texts." *Indo-Iranian Journal* 62.2: 162–180.

Weller, Friedrich. 1937. *Zum sogdischen Vimalakīrtinirdeśasūtra*. Leipzig: Deutsche Morgenländische Gesellschaft.

Yabuki, Keiki 矢吹慶輝. 1930. *Meisha yoin: Tonkō shutsudo miden koitsu butten kaihō* 鳴沙餘韻：燉煌出土未傳古逸佛典開寶. Tōkyō: Iwanami shoten.

Yakubovich, Ilya. 2002. "Nugae Sogdicae." *Bulletin of the School of Oriental and African Studies* 65.3: 544–549.

Yoshida, Yutaka. 1998. "The Sogdian Dhūta Text and Its Chinese Original." *Bulletin of the Asia Institute*, New Series 10: 167–173.

Zhang, Bowei. 張伯偉. 2002. *Xijian ben Song ren shihua si zhong* 稀見本宋人詩話四種. Nanjing: Jiangsu guji chubanshe.

Zimmermann, Michael. 2002. *A Buddha Within: The Tathāgatagarbhasūtra, the Earliest Exposition of the Buddha-Nature Teaching in India*. Tōkyō: The International Research Institute for Advanced Buddhology, Soka University.

印藏佛教文本、叙事与互鉴

Three *Nayatraya* Texts: Path Hierarchization within Indian Buddhism*

Kazuo Kano
Komazawa University

In the long course of the history of Indian Buddhism there are several transformations that sent it leaping and bounding forward. Among the most important are the emergence of Mahāyāna and Tantric Buddhism. The background to the formation of these two currents is still a matter of debate, but there is no doubt that their influence was enormous. Their influence, for example, led to a turning point in the activities of Indian Buddhist monasteries in terms of vows and doctrine/practice. In terms of vows, we can find traces of this in the word **saṃvaratraya* ("Three Sets of Restraints"), and in terms of doctrine and practice, in the word *nayatraya* ("Three Methods"). The former relates to official aspects of monastic life its members commit themselves to, and the latter to individual aspects. To put it simply, with the advent of Mahāyāna and Tantric Buddhism, the monks at the monasteries were able to choose between the three paths (courses) of *śrāvaka* (i.e. non-Mahāyāna), Mahāyāna, and Tantric Mahāyāna. Modern scholars speculate that monks and nuns who adhered to one or more of these three sets of restraints and methods[①]—in other words, both non-Mahāyāna and Mahāyāna Buddhists—were very probably active alongside each other in the same monastic communities (I do not believe that any *saṃgha* of *bodhisattva*/Mahāyāna monks existed independently of the traditional *saṃgha*s of *śrāvaka*/non-Mahāyāna monks, but premise rather that

* I would like to thank Dr. Li Xuezhu for his generous collaboration in carrying out the research, and with whom the full text of the Sanskrit edition of the three *nayatraya* works will be published. I thank Philip Pierce for his careful English proofreading and Prof. Harunaga Isaacson for his very valuable suggestions on Sanskrit texts. This research was financially supported by the Japan Society for the Promotion of Science KAKENHI [grant numbers JP17K02222, JP18K00074, JP18H03569, and JP22H00002, JP24K04479].

① See Table 1, below.

monks of non-Mahāyāna and Mahāyāna dwelled together in common *saṃgha*s).

It is important to realize that Mahāyāna and Tantric Buddhism did not drive out the *śrāvaka*s' tradition, which was maintained until the end of Indian Buddhism.① Although there were some trends, such as the *ekayāna*, that attempted to unify the separate courses, it appears that all three courses were accommodated in the majority of Indian Buddhist monasteries.

1. **Saṃvaratraya*

The Three Sets of Restraints are a triple-layered group of guidelines for the lives of all monks, consisting of the *prātimokṣasaṃvara*, the *bodhisattvasaṃvara*, and the *vajrasattvasaṃvara* (or **vidyādharasaṃvara*). They are respectively the basic monastic codes for every fully ordained Buddhist (no matter which course), the additional guideline for every *bodhisattva* (of non-Tantric Mahāyāna), and the further additional guideline for every *vajrasattva* (of Tantric Mahāyāna). First of all, all ordained Buddhists must formally accept the Vinaya/monastic code (i.e. *prātimokṣasaṃvara*). In the case of Mahāyāna monks, they go on to accept the *bodhisattvasaṃvara* in addition to the *prātimokṣasaṃvara*②; and of Tantric monks, the *vajrasattvasaṃvara* in addition to the two previous sets of restraints (See Table 1, below).

The following description from the *Vajraśekharatantra* is one of the earliest examples of the Three Sets of Restraints (*sdom pa gsum*) being taught together.③ The unordained are said to be able to perfect the Tantric practice by observing the lay practitioner's set of restraints (*khyim pa'i sdom pa*), namely to keep *bodhicitta*, devote themselves to the Three Jewels, and observe the five moral disciplines. This tantra then teaches that ordained practitioners should abide by the three sets of restraints: the *prātimokṣasaṃvara*, the *bodhisattvasaṃvara*, and the supreme **vidyādharasaṃvara*.

---

① It is not easy to determine, given the insufficient pool of witnesses, who constituted the majority in Indic monasteries in the final phase of Indian Buddhism, whether non-Mahāyana or Mahāyana monks.

② According to the Bodhisattvabhūmi, a bodhisattva without the *bodhisattvasaṃvara* is not a true (*bhūta*) bodhisattva but a "fake bodhisattva" (*bodhisattvapratirūpaka*). See *Bodhisattvabhūmi* (ed. Dutt) 203.14–17 and Ōtake 2020: 251.

③ Other early examples of monks who practised the Tantric teachings are found, for instance, in the *Subhāhuparipṛcchā* (see Ōtsuka 2013: 925), *Mahāpratisarā* (*bhikṣuṃ vajradharaṃ kuryād duṣṭatarjanatatparam*, see Sakurai 1996: 286), and Dīpaṅkarabhadra's *Guhyasamājamaṇḍalavidhi* (a.k.a. *Lokālokakārikā*), verse 184 (*caturṇām apy anujñātaḥ parṣadāṃ maṇḍale vidhiḥ | śikṣāsu svāsu yuktānāṃ mahāyānaratātmanām* ||, see Sakurai 1996: 287).

If one is ordained, one [should] stabilize oneself in the three sets of restraints (*sdom pa gsum*), i.e. the *prātimokṣasaṃvara*, the *bodhisattvasaṃvara*, and the supreme **vidyādharasaṃvara*.①

The system of the Three Sets of Restraints was expounded by Buddhists down to the final phase of the monastic tradition in Indian Buddhism in such treatises as the *Sarvasamayasaṃgraha* ascribed to Atiśa (or Adhīśa), Abhayākaragupta's *Munimatālaṃkāra* (Skt. Ms. fols. 2r4–13v3), and Vibhūticandra's **Trisaṃvaraprabhāmālā*.

In any event, further studies are required in order to clarify the extent to which this system of Three Sets of Restraints spread geographically and temporally and to determine the degree to which they were strictly adhered to.②

2. *Nayatraya*

On the other hand, the ideological and soteriological aspects of the traditions of *śrāvaka*, Mahāyāna, and Tantric Mahāyāna are summarized in the term *nayatraya*, which denotes the Three Methods: the *śrāvakanaya* (the method followed by "auditors"), *pāramitānaya* (the method of observing the six perfections), and *mantranaya* (the method of using mantras). For example, according to the *Nayatrayabheda*, the method associated with *śrāvaka*s is the teaching of dependent origination and the Noble Ones' Four Truths, the method associated with perfections is the teaching of the selflessness of dharmas (phenomena), and the method associated with mantras is the teaching of mantras (see below). These three methods are not mutually exclusive, but can be understood as inclusive, with latter ones successively encompassing former ones. Such an inclusive relationship is also compatible with the Three Sets of Restraints (see Table 1).③

---

① *Vajraśekhara*, D480, 199b4–5: *gal te de ni rab byung gyur || sdom pa gsum la yang dag gnas || so sor thar dang byang chub sems || rig 'dzin sdom pa mchog yin no ||*. This verse is quoted in the *Vajrayānamūlāpattiṭīkā*, D2488, 222b3; *Tantrārthāvatāra*, D2501, 36b5; *Prathamakarmasamayasūtrasaṃgraha*, D3726, 49b6–7; *Trisaṃvaraprabhāmālā*, D3727, 55a6, etc. See also Sobisch 2002: 106–107. **Vidyādharasaṃvara* is later called *vajrasattvasaṃvara*.

② For example, Vāgīśvarakīrti refutes an opponent's objection that points out the contradiction between the Tantric practice of sexual yoga and the monastic code of sexual misconduct. See Sakurai 1996: 283–293, 419–421.

③ When, however, the superiority of individual *naya*s is discussed, a hierarchical relationship is sometimes explicitly stated. For example, in the *Nayatrayapradīpa* it is explained that the practice of detachment by *śrāvaka*s is inferior to the practice of compassion by *bodhisattva*s. See Kano 2021.

In Indian Buddhism, there is a realm of literature that explains these three methods, but it has not been fully elucidated by modern scholarship.① Three texts that I will discuss in this paper, namely the *Nayatrayapradīpa* ("A Lamp for the Three Methods"), *Nayatrayabheda* ("The Distinction among the Three Methods"), and *Nayatrayahṛdaya* ("The Essence of the Three Methods") can serve as a starting point for such research.

3. The actual state of affairs

There are still many unknowns about the extent to which the *saṃvara*s or *naya*s were applied in actual practice, but their actual existence in the monastic life of Indian Buddhism can be traced, for instance, thanks to descriptions in colophons of Sanskrit manuscripts and inscriptions. Those who chose the Mahāyāna course called themselves, for instance, *mahāyānānuyāyin*s, while those who chose the Tantric Mahāyāna course called themselves *mantranayānuyāyin*s.② Since the *śrāvaka* course is the default state for every ordained practitioner, it is conceivable that *śrāvaka*s may have referred to themselves only as *śākyabhikṣu*,③ which probably denotes anyone ordained under the *prātimokṣasaṃvara*. There are many examples in which the two titles *śākyabhikṣu* and *mahāyānānuyāyin* are applied to a single person,④ suggesting that such a person was first ordained under the *prātimokṣasaṃvara* (*bhikṣusaṃvara*), and then under the *bodhisattvasaṃvara*, though this requires further investigation.

---

① There are scholastic Indic treatises which provide overviews of Indian Buddhism as a whole by way of the *nayatraya* concepts or the corresponding concepts in Tanjurs (e.g. D3710–3720). For previous studies on relevant literatures, see, for instance, Takada 1965, Isoda 1979, Onians 2002, Tanemura 2008, Kyuma 2009, Szántó 2015 and 2020, van der Kuijp 2020, and Kano 2021.

② See the colophon of the birchbark manuscript dating from A.D. 1057 preserved in the Xizang Museum, Lhasa: *deyadharmo 'yam* ***mantranayānuyāyina*** *ācāryaratnaśrībhadrasya*. See Kano 2014. Ratnaśrībhadra was probably a monk, to judge by his name (the name closely resembles Rin chen bzang po's (958–1055), but the year 1057 does not fit). As another term for Tantric practitioners, Tsukamoto (2001: 206) notes the word *tāntrakabodhisattvagaṇa* (with reference to members of the Nālandā monastic institution) found in a 9th-century inscription which he labels "Nālandā No. 10".

③ For one instance of the application of the term *śākyabhikṣu* to a non-Mahāyana monk, see the colophon of the *Tridaṇḍamālā* (fol. 116r3–4): *samāptā ceyaṃ tridaṇḍamālā. kṛtir ācāryasthavirāśvaghoṣasya śākyabhikṣoḥ sarvāstivādino mahāvādinaḥ* (cf. Matsuda 2021: 65).

④ See, for instance, Tsukamoto 2001: 202–203 and Schopen 2005: 223–246.

[Table 1: *Nayatraya*-holders in the case of monks]

Holders:	*śrāvakanaya*	*pāramitānaya*	*mantranaya*
Vow:	*prātimokṣasaṃvara*		
		+ *bodhisattvasaṃvara*	
			+**vidyādharasaṃvara*
Status:	*śākyabhikṣu*		
		+ *mahāyānānuyāyin*	
			+ *mantranayānuyāyin*

Although it is not yet possible to determine when the set notions of the Three Sets of Restraints and the Three Methods first appeared in Indian Buddhism, the Three Methods probably appeared at around the same time as the *Vairocanābhisaṃbodhi*, in which the word *mantramukhacaryācārin bodhisattva* appears,① while the Three Sets of Restraints appeared around the time of the aforementioned *Vajraśekharatantra*. Both set notions probably emerged in connection with each other.

4. Three *nayatraya* Works

A reassessment and ordering of the status of various doctrines and practices came about in the 8th and 9th centuries in order to gain a view of Buddhism as a whole. The tradition of explaining Buddhism in terms of the *nayatraya* is a typical example of what was being aimed at. At about the same time in Japan, Kōbō-Daishi Kūkai 弘法大師空海 (774–835) surveyed the whole of Buddhism from the standpoint of Tantric Buddhism (密教) of the *jūjūshin* (十住心). In Indian Buddhism, on the other hand, it was the *nayatraya* system that was spread, with a series of works being written on the subject.

Since the works on the *nayatraya* are mostly known only in Tibetan translation, and since the Sanskrit originals of the works have not been available, there has been a lack of sufficient research on them. However, in collaboration with Dr. Li Xuezhu (CTRC), we have now discovered the Sanskrit texts of three works on the *nayatraya*: (1) the *Nayatrayapradīpa* by Trivikrama, (2) the *Nayatrayabheda* by Kuśalaśrī, and (3) the *Nayatrayahṛdaya* by an unknown author. Of these, (1) was known only in Tibetan translation, and (2) and (3) were not even known to exist. The *Nayatrayapradīpa* consists of 20 verses and a prose commentary on them (in total 23 palm-leaf

① See Namai 1996 and 1998.

folios), the *Nayatrayabheda* consists of 88 verses (4 folios), and the *Nayatrayahṛdaya* consists of 18 verses (1 folio). The three works differ in style and size, and each has its own unique characteristics in content. In this paper, I shall give an overview and a preliminary report on what these three works are trying to teach about the *nayatraya*.

5. The Manuscript

The three works are contained in a palm-leaf manuscript preserved at the Norbulingka palace in Lhasa consisting of 190 leaves (31.8 x 5.9 cm) and written in the Nepalese script of the 12th and 13th centuries. A microfilm of this manuscript is preserved in box no. 63 of the CTRC. The manuscript contains 62 minor works in total, mostly Tantric ones. The 62 works divide up into 31 in the first half (= Part I) and 31 in the second half (= Part II), with a page containing a table of contents at the beginning of each half. The three *nayatraya* works in question are included in Part I.

According to Luo Xiao, the first part (containing the first 31 works up to fol. 118) consists of works dealing with "various kinds of Tantric doctrinal works" (密宗的各類義理), and the second part (containing the second 31 works after fol. 118) consists of works dealing with "various kinds of Tantric mantras and rituals." (多種密宗咒語和修法儀軌)① The titles of the works in Part I are listed in the following table (when the author's name is attested in the text itself, on the page containing the table of contents, or in other relevant sources, it is written in parentheses).②

[Table 2: Works contained in Part I of the bundle]

1. Svapnanirukti (Advayavajra)	12. Subhadrā nāma Saṃkṣiptasārasaṃgraha (*ibid.*)
2. Māyānirukti (*ibid.*)	**13. Nayatrayapradīpa (Trivikrama)**
3. Yuganaddhaprakāśa (*ibid.*)	14. Paralokasaṃkṣepa
4. Nirvedhapañcaka (*ibid.*)	15. Tattvopadeśa (Dautkaṭīpāda)
5. Apratisthānaprakāśa (*ibid.*)	**16. Nayatrayahṛdaya**
6. Tattvaprakāśa (*ibid.*)	17. Gocarapariśuddhi (Rāhulaśrī)②
7. Tattvadaśaka (*ibid.*)	**18. Nayatrayabheda (Kuśalaśrī)**
8. Pañcatathāgatamudrāvivaraṇa (*ibid.*)	19. Caturthāloka (Vāgīśvarakīrti) =Tattvaratnāvaloka
9. Sekatātparyasaṃgraha (*ibid.*)	20. Sahajasadyogaḥ (Ratnākaraśānti)
10. Sekakrama (*ibid.*)	21. Sampradāyikakārikā
11. Sekatātparyasaṃgraha (*ibid.*)	

(Continued)

① See Kano 2019.
② This title is listed on the page containing the table of contents, but has yet to be found in the manuscript itself.

22. Olicatuṣṭaya (Kṛṣṇācārya) 23. Tattvopadeśakārikā 24. Ye-dharmā-gāthāyā upacārasaṃgr (Rāhulaśrībhadra) 25. Olicatuṣtaya (fols. 68–70 are misssing)	26. Madhupāvadāna 27. Kapphiṇāvadāna (Abhayamitra)① 28. Lokatattvāvatāra (Mātṛceṭa)② 29. Sahakāropadeśa (Gopadatta) (The titles of nos. 30–31 have yet to be determined.)

Nos. 13, 16, and 18 are the three *nayatraya* works which will be elucidated in this paper. The first twelve works (Nos. 1–12) are attributed to Advayavajra. The majority of his works in Sanskrit have been published four times as his collected works.③ Nos. 1–9 and 11 in this manuscript are known works in that collection (nos. 9 and 11 are the same text); nos. 10 and 12 are not contained in the collected works.

No. 10, entitled *Sekakrama*, is a hitherto unknown work of Advayavajra,④ being a brief initiation manual consisting of the following sections: Maṇḍalapraveśa (fols. 4v1–5r5), Pañcākārābhiṣekavidhi (fols. 5r5–v2), Vidyābhiṣeka (fol. 5v2), Ācāryābhiṣeka (fols. 5v3–6r1), Guhyābhiṣeka (fol. 6r1–6), and Prajñābhiṣeka (fols. 6r6–v2).

No. 12, entitled in the colophon as *Subhadrā nāma Saṃkṣiptasārasaṃgraha*, is an anthology of 112 verses from various works.⑤

No. 15, the *Tattvopadeśa*,⑥ is a work consisting of 55 verses, which discusses four kinds of objective supports, i.e. *vastvālambana, vijñānālambana, tathatālambana*, and *advayālambana*.

Sanskrit editions of no. 19, the *Caturthāloka* (a.k.a. *Tattvaratnāvaloka*) by Vāgīśvarakīrti, and no. 20, the *Sahajasadyoga* by Ratnākaraśānti, were published on the basis of other manuscripts.⑦

No. 22, the *Olicatuṣṭaya* by Kṛṣṇācārya (≈ D1451), is a work dealing with four procedures

---

① The colophon in fol. 21v2 runs: *kapphiṇāvadānaṃ samāptaṃ. kṛtir iyaṃ abhayamitrasya*. There is another incomplete Ms. of the same work included in a Bhaikṣukī Ms. See Kano 2025.

② The colophon in fol. 12v3 runs: *samāpto 'yaṃ lokatattvāvatāraḥ kṛtir āryabhadantamātṛceṭapādānām.*

③ Isaacson and Sferra (2014: 73) list 23 of his works in the collected works. For more on his other works, see Isaacson and Sferra 2014: 71–82.

④ The colophon in fol. 6v6 reads: *sekakramaḥ samāptaḥ. kṛtir iyam ācāryaśrīmadadvayavajrapādānām.*

⑤ The colophon in fol. 6v7 runs: *iti subhadrā nāma saṃkṣiptasārasaṃgrahaḥ samāptaḥ. kṛtir iyam avadhūtaśrī-advayavajrasyeti*. Works quoted in the *Subhadrā* include the *Cittaviśuddhiprakaraṇa, Vajrapañjara, Laghukālacakra, Pañcakrama, Guhyāvalī, Hevajra, Bodhicittavivaraṇa, Sūtakamelāpaka, Guhyasamāja, Hevajrapiṇḍārthaṭīkā, Sekoddeśa, Paramārthastava*, etc. For details of this work and problems relating to its authorship, see Kano 2019.

⑥ The colophon in fol. 2v7–8 runs: *tattvopadeśaḥ samāptaḥ. kṛtir iyaṃ śrīdhautkaṭīpādānām*. I am not sure if this figure is identical with Dauḍīpāda, the author of the *Guhyāvalī* (see Kuranishi 2014).

⑦ The colophons of these two works run: *caturthalokaḥ* (read: *caturthālokaḥ*) *samāptaḥ*; *samāptaḥ sahajasadyogaḥ*. For published editions of the two works, see Isaacson 2001 and Dhīḥ 1997.

within the Cakrasaṃvara practice.[①]

No. 23, the *Tattvopadeśakārikā* (≈ D1632), is a work in the Cakrasaṃvara cycle consisting of 27 verses in total. Verses 1–5 and 6–25 parallel verses in the *Abhidhānottarottara*, chapter 1 (Kāyasaṃvaravidhipaṭala) and chapter 65 (Ātmabhāvapūjāpaṭala), respectively.[②]

No. 24, the *Ye-dharmā-gāthāyā upacārasaṃgraha* by Rāhulaśrībhadra, is a ritual manual using the well-known formula beginning with "*ye dharmā hetuprabhavā*." [③]

A Sanskrit edition of no. 29, the *Sahakāropadeśa* (a.k.a. *Ajātaśatrvavadāna*) by Gopadatta, was published by Hahn 1981 on the basis of another manuscript.[④]

The palm leaves of this manuscript are uniform in size, but the handwriting and number of lines in folia vary from work to work; and in many cases the numbering of folios is unique to each work. It is still unclear what criteria were used by the compiler of this collection to select the works to be included, but overall the collection contains many works related to doctrinal aspects of Tantric Buddhism. The above is a preliminary report; a detailed report on the works in this manuscript will be left for another occasion.

6. The *Nayatrayapradīpa*

The *Nayatrayapradīpa* is a well-known work that has been cited in more than nineteen other works, all approximately datable to between the 10th and 13th centuries.[⑤] Since the influence of Kamalaśīla (ca. 740–795) can be seen in this work, and since it was translated into Tibetan by Rin chen bzang po (958–1055), it can be dated to around the 9th or 10th century.[⑥] The identity of the author, Trivikrama, is still nebulous. Although it is clear that his work is based on the *Guhyasamāja* maṇḍala system of the Jñānapāda school, some of the Tantric doctrines and

---

① The colophon in fol. 10r4–5 runs: *ācāryacaryāvratinaḥ kṛṣṇācāryasyeti. samāptom* (read: *samāptam*) *olicatuṣṭayaṃ* ||. For details of the work, see Sugiki 1999.

② I owe the identification of Ātmabhāvapūjāpaṭala to Shiori Ijūin. A prose commentary on this work is preserved in a Sanskrit manuscript and in Tibetan translation (D1633). According to the Sanskrit manuscript, the author of the commentary is Sujanaśrībhadra, and according to the Tibetan translation, Blo bzang snying po. Dr. Li Xuezhu is currently preparing a Sanskrit edition of this commentary.

③ The colophon in fol. 13r5–6 runs: *ye-dharmā-gāthāyā upacārasaṃgrahaḥ samāptaḥ. kṛtir ācāryarāhulaśrībhadrasyeti śubhaṃ*.

④ Deokar 2021: 131–132 identifies the *Sahakāropadeśa* quoted in Subhuticandra's *Kavikamadhenu* with the *Ajātaśatrvavadāna*.

⑤ See Isaacson 2015.

⑥ See Kano and Li 2019, 2020.

practices he mentions have not been traced. The name Trivikrama suggests some link to Viṣṇu, whose epithet it is. We do not know if he was a monk or a lay practitioner. The colophon (*kṛtir ācāryabhaṭṭatrivikramapādānāṃ*) merely states the name.

In this work, the author mentions an unknown work called *Paramārthapradīpa*, which he himself seems to have written.① In Abhayākaragupta's *Upadeśamañjarī*, Trivikrama is described as a teacher who embraced the three-body theory of the Buddha.②

The author's purpose in composing the *Nayatrayapradīpa* is declared in the opening and concluding verses: The opening three verses run (fol. 1v1–2):

> *namaḥ prajñākṛpālokajagadadhyakṣacakṣuṣe*③ |
> *jināya jñānatejobhir dhvastadhvāntāya tāyine* ||
> *yathāgamaṃ yathānyāyaṃ yathāprajñābalaṃ mayā* |
> *nayatrayapra*$_{(1v2)}$*dīpo 'yaṃ tattvasiddhyai nigadyate* ||
> *yadi nainaṃ janaḥ kaścid bhāgyahīnaḥ prapatsyate* |
> *svamanaḥśodhanopāyo mamaivāyaṃ bhaviṣyati* ||

(Transl.) I bow to the Victorious One, the Protector, whose eyes directly perceive the world (*jagat*) with the eyesight (*āloka*) of wisdom and compassion, and who has destroyed darkness by means of the fire of gnosis.

This Lamp of Three Methods will be told by me in accordance with scriptures, with logic, and with [my own] power of wisdom, in order to establish the truth.

If people, for lack of fortune, do not understand it, then it will become a means of purifying only my own mind.

The concluding three verses (fols. 22v5–23r1) run:

> *ciram amalagurum upāsya bhaktyā*
> *sphuṭam adhigamya nayatrayaṃ*④ *niruktyā* |
> *kṛśamatibhir a*$_{(22v6)}$*niścitaṃ mayaitat*

---

① See Kano and Li 2021: 197 (Skt. Ms. fol. 6r4).

② *Upadeśamañjarī* (Peking no. 5024), 207b7–208a1. This work is not contaned in the Derge Tanjur. See Kano 2021: 134–135 n. 8.

③ -kṛpā-] em. ($\approx$ Tib.), -kṛtā- Ms.

④ -trayaṃ] em., -traya Ms.

kathitam anākulam āgamārthasāram ||[①]

satyatattvanaye[②] *yo 'rtho yo 'rthaḥ pāramitānaye* |
mahāmantranayārthaś ca saṅkṣepeṇeha darśitaḥ ||

yad avagāhya nayatrayasāga$_{(23r1)}$*raṃ*
gurukathānuguṇena pathā mayā |
adhigataṃ jagato 'stu samṛddhaye
atanudīdhiti[③] *ratnam ihādvayam* ||

(Transl.) After serving the stainless master (*guru*) with devotion for a long time, and then having clearly understood the Three Methods with the help of [his] explanation (*nirukti*), I have explained them without any confusion—the essence of the meaning of scriptures, which had not been ascertained by those of poor understanding [before].

In this [work], the meaning of the method that takes [the Noble Ones' Four] Truths as the reality (i.e. *śrāvakanaya*), the meaning of the *pāramitānaya*, and the meaning of the great *mantranaya* are concisely presented.

The non-dual jewel of great radiance that has been obtained/realized here by me after entering the ocean of the Three Methods along a path that conforms to the teaching (*kathā*) of the masters—may it be for the prosperity of the world!

The following is an outline of the *Nayatrayapradīpa*[④]:

vv. 1–5: The superiority of the Mahāyāna to the *śrāvaka* path (wisdom of the Noble Ones' Four Truths vs. non-dual wisdom of *bodhisattva*s)

vv. 6–9: The compassion of the Mahāyāna (*śrāvaka*s' detachment vs. *bodhisattva*s' compassion)

vv. 10–15: Five respects in which the Mahāyāna is superior to the *śrāvaka* and non-Buddhist paths

vv. 16–20: Four respects in which Tantric Mahāyāna is superior to non-Tantric Mahāyāna.

① Metre: Puṣpitāgrā.
② -naye] em., -nayo Ms.
③ atanu-] conj., danuta- Ms.
④ In addition, there are two opening verses and three closing verses; the verse numbers have been partially revised from Kano and Li 2019 and 2020.

Verse 10 in particular lists five examples of the *pāramitānaya*'s superiority:①

praṇidhānāt pravṛtteś ca gāmbhīryaudāryayos tathā |

anivṛtteḥ phalāptes ca mahāyānaṃ viśiṣyate ||

(Transl.) The Mahāyāna is superior [to the Śrāvakayāna] because of the (1) vow/ resolve, (2) practice [of offering, etc.], (3) profundity and extensiveness [of compassion], (4) unstoppable nature, and (5) attainment of the fruit [associated with it].

Verse 16 teaches four aspects of the *mantranaya*'s superiority:

ekārthatve 'py asaṃmohād bahūpāyād aduṣkarāt |

tīkṣṇendriyādhikārāc ca mantraśāstraṃ viśiṣyate ||

(Transl.) Even though its goal is the same, the *mantra*-teaching (*śāstra*) is superior [to the *pāramitānaya*] because (1) it is free of confusion (*asammoha*), (2) offers many methods (*bahūpāya*), (3) presents no difficulties (*aduṣkara*), (4) and is for [practitioners] with sharp facultiy (*tīkṣṇendriyādhikāra*).

The order of the three *naya*s can be summarized as follows②:

(nayatraya)	(indriya)	(practitioner)	(tattva)	(upāya)
Śrāvakanaya	mṛdvindriya	satyatattvayogin	—	—
Pāramitānaya	madhyendriya	pāramitātattvayogin	○	—
Mantranaya	tīkṣṇendriya	mantramukhacaryācārin	○	○

	(indriya)	(mudrā)	(practice)
Mantranaya	adhimātrādhimātrendriya	Mahāmudrā	practice without proliferation
	adhimātramadhyendriya	Jñānamudrā	practice of visualization
	adhimātramṛdvindriya	Samayamudrā	practice of sexual yoga
	others	Karmamudrā	an alternative practice

① This verse is quoted in the *Yogānuttaratantrārthāvatārasaṃgraha* (D3713, 105a5–6), *Bodhimārgapradīpapañjikā* (D3948, 286b1–2), *Sūtrasamuccayabhāṣya* (D3935, 243a6), *Tattvasārasaṃgraha* (D3711, 83a7–b1).

② The first table is based on verse 19 and the prose commentary on it, and the second table on verse 18 and the prose commentary on it. *Tattva* and *upāya* in the table refer to whether or not the truth (*tattva*) can be proven by the *naya* in question, and whether or not the latter supplies the means (*upāya*) of reaching the truth.

Parts of the Sanskrit text of the *Nayatrayapradīpa* have been published (Kano and Li 2020, 2021, 2022, 2023, 2024). As mentioned above, this work is dedicated to presenting the hierarchy of methods and arguing for the superiority of the *pāramitānaya* over the *śrāvakanaya*, and that of the *mantranaya* over the first two.

In the *Nayatrayapradīpa*, in addition to the superiority mentioned above, there is also a description of the daily behaviour of *bodhisattva*s toward *śrāvaka*s.

> *tatra tatra ca bhagavatā bodhisattvānāṃ śrāvakasaṃvāsālāpaśikṣādipratiṣedha ādiṣṭa iti.*①
>
> (Transl.) The prohibition of dwelling with, chatting with, and learning from *śrāvaka*s, etc., was everywhere declared to *bodhisattva*s by the Buddha.

Similar statements can be found, for example, in the Vajrasattvasaṃvara, the vow for Tantric Buddhists. In the *Sthūlāpatti* ascribed to one Aśvaghoṣa, for instance, there is a prohibition against "dwelling among/with *śrāvaka*s for more than seven days." (*śrāvakānāṃ madhye saptāham upavāsataḥ*)② Why were such prohibitions that kept *bodhisattva*s from associating too freely with *śrāvaka*s created? Based on the Vinaya's principle that a new rule is enacted only after a corresponding transgression occurs (随犯随制) for the first time, it is obvious that these prohibitions were enacted because at that time *bodhisattva* monks were interacting too frequently with *śrāvaka* monks. The conclusion to be drawn is that both types cohabited the same monastic institutions.

The *Nayatrayapradīpa* thus describes the *bodhisattva*s' way of behaving towards *śrāvaka*s, while remaining silent on how *śrāvaka*s should behave towards *bodhisattva*s, on which point we need to look into other texts (see **Appendix III**).

7. The *Nayatrayabheda*

The *Nayatrayabheda* is a hitherto unknown work (for a critical edition, see Kano and Li 2023a, 2024a, 2025a). From the colophon (*iti nayatrayabhedaḥ samāptaḥ. kṛtir ācāryakuśalaśriya iti śubhaṃ*), we know only the title (*Nayatrayabheda*) and the author's name (Kuśalaśrī). The career of Kuśalaśrī is unknown, but he can probably be dated to sometime between the 10th and

---

① *Nayatrayapradīpa*, fol. 5v5–6; Kano and Li 2021: 106.

② This is the sixth of eight *sthūlāpatti*s (ordinary sins and transgressions). See Yoritomi 1990: 448, 456.

13th centuries. The following is a synoptic overview of the work:

vv. 1–3: Opening verses

vv. 4–52: *Śrāvakanaya* (*pratītyasamutpāda*)

vv. 4–14: A lifecycle interpretation of the chain of the *pratītyasamutpāda*

vv. 15–31: On the correct and reverse sequences of the chain of the *pratītyasamutpāda* with an account of the chain of events (in the form of the butterfly effect)**(vv. 4–31: see Appendix I)**

vv. 32–52: The Noble Ones' Four Truths

vv. 53–64: *bodhisattvanaya*

vv. 65–87: *mantranaya* **(vv. 65–87: see Appendix I)**

vv. 65–66: Homage to Heruka

v. 67: The Vajrayāna is *buddhavacana*

vv. 68–69: Etymologies of *mantra*

v. 70: On *mantra* practitioners (including non-Buddhists, *śrāvaka*s, and *bodhisattva*s)

vv. 71–78: On the generation of deities by means of *mantra*s

vv. 79–87: A *mantra*'s effect of altering the value of things

v. 88: Closing verses

The *Nayatrayabheda*, unlike the *Nayatrayapradīpa*, does not focus on ranking the three *nayas*, but rather on presenting a straightforward overview of the core teachings of each *naya*. This character can be seen in the first two verses, listing the main teachings of the three *naya*s, i.e. dependent origination, the Noble Ones' Four Truths, the selflessness of *dharma*s, and mantras:

sattvāśayavaśāc citrāṃ yā sūte phalasampadam |
sā kalpalatikevoccair jainī jayati bhāratī || 1 ||
pratītyotpādasatyārthadharmanairātmyamantravit |
kuśalaśrīḥ samācaṣṭe sarvathā nayasaṅgraham || 2 ||
dvāda$_{(1r2)}$*śāṅgaṃ pravacanaṃ draṣṭuṃ śakto jano na yaḥ* |
tasyāyam udyamo 'nena kriyate 'nujighṛkṣayā || 3 ||

(Transl.) The Victor's speech (*jainī bhāratī*), which gives rise to the various perfections of fruits in accordance with beings' dispositions, rules resoundingly (*uccair*) (i.e. is supreme, *jayati*), like *kalpa*-creepers.[①]

---

① I understand the word *ucchaiḥ* as an adverb used here with a double meaning (*śleṣa*), i.e. "loudly" and "highly, intensely," relating to speech and creepers' growth, respectively.

Kuśalaśrī, knowing the meaning of dependent arising, the [Four] Truths [of the *śrāvakanaya*], the selflessness of phenomena [of the *pāramitānaya*], and mantras, [will now] thoroughly explain [them in] a compendium of the [Three] Methods.

This effort has been undertaken by him out of a wish to benefit (*anujighṛkṣayā*) those persons who cannot see [the meaning of] the twelvefold scripture.

Moreover, the concluding verse of the *Nayatrayabheda* (i.e. v. 88), written in the Rathoddhatā metre, mentions the Tantric path (*vajrasattvapadavī*) and holds up the attainment of the state of *vajrasattva* as the supreme goal:

jainaguhyamatasārasaṅgrahaṃ
kurvato 'sya kuśalaṃ yad asti tat |
vajrasattva(4r5) *padavīm upeyuṣāṃ*①
*sarvam astu jagatāṃ tamopaham*② ||

(Transl.) The virtue that the present author has [acquired by] making [this] compendium of the essence of the Victorious One's (i.e. the Buddha's) secret thoughts (= *Nayatrayabheda*)—may all this [virtue] dispel the darkness of beings who have approached the path to/of Vajrasattva!

The *mantranaya* section of the *Nayatrayabheda* teaches that a harmful thing such as poison can be transformed into a useful thing such as medicine by means of a mantra's efficacy (vv. 79–84). In the same way, when phenomena are not correctly observed, they will confuse minds; but when they are correctly observed, they will become causes that put a stop to mundane activities and the mind's suffering (v. 86). Worldly phenomena lead the ignorant to transmigratory existences, while at the same time providing the wise with supreme bliss (v. 87).

8. The *Nayatrayahṛdaya*

The *Nayatrayahṛdaya* is another unknown work. The work probably consists of 18 verses. Due to damage to the manuscript, verses 13–18 and the colophon of the work, which contains the title

① upeyuṣāṃ] em., upeyuṣaṃ Ms.
② -paham] em., -pahām Ms.

and author's name, are unfortunately in large part illegible. However, the title survives on the folio of the palm-leaf manuscript containing a table of contents. The same title, *Nayatrayahṛdaya*, is found in a birchbark manuscript containing a collection of Tantric ritual manuals preserved at the Tibetan Museum in Lhasa.① The following is an outline of the legible parts:

Śrāvakanaya (vv. 1–7) **(See Appendix II)**

vv. 1–2: *Ātman* does not exist apart from *skandhadhātvāyatana*.

Objections from a non-Buddhist opponent:

v. 3: (1) *Skandhadhātvāyatana* is different from *ātman*, inasmuch as the former is impermanent, while the latter is permanent.

v. 4ab: (2) If *ātman* were impermanent, karmic fruit would disappear.

v. 4cd: (3) If *ātman* were impermanent, the relation between the agent of an action and receiver of its karmic fruit would be inconsistent.

Reply to the three objections:

v. 5: (1) If *ātman* were permanent, we would experience bliss or suffering alone forever.

v. 6: (2) Due to impermanence, karmic imprints can bring forth their fruits without interruption.

v. 7: (3) No one can receive someone else's karmic fruit as long as their mind streams are different from each other.②

Pāramitānaya (vv. 8–11)

v. 8: *Skandhadhātvāyatana* do not exist externally, because they are beyond oneness and multiplicity, in the same way as a dream does not exist in reality but can be perceived.③

v. 9: (Objection:) If so, *ātman* should always exist, for one can always recognize it by perceiving it in one's memory (*smṛti*).④

vv. 10–11: (Reply:) The memory of *ātman* is nothing but a conceptualization, and is to

---

① See Kawasaki 2004 and Kano and Szántó 2020: 33 "A versified short work with the same title *Nayatrayahṛdaya* is found in a collection of miscellaneous tantric works preserved in Potala [*sic* for Norbulingka]." Although the folios which contain this work in the Xizang Museum manuscript are still unavailable, the title was recovered from a folio in the manuscript containing a table of contents (in which the title is written *Nayanatrayahṛdaya*, which we emended to *Nayatrayahṛdaya*).

② Concerning (1) (2) and (3), cf. e.g. *Buddhacarita* 16.78–87.

③ *ekānekatvavirahād ye proktāḥ skandhadhātavaḥ | bāhyaṃ piṇḍaṃ tu cātrāste svapnavac cānubhūtitaḥ ||* (*Pāda* c is partially illegible and may need improvement.)

④ *yady evaṃ tarhi nityaḥ syād ātmā smṛtyanubhūtitaḥ | kāryakāraṇabhāvāc ca tayor jñeyāpy anityatā ||*.

be abandoned by training (*abhyāsa*).①

Mantranaya (v. 12–17)

v. 12: (Objection:) If so, the acquisition of the Buddha's state, which is characterized by the conceptualization of deities through the stages of *mantra* visualization, should also be abandoned by training.②

(vv. 13–18 are illegible in the manuscript due to multiple damage.)

As far as the legible parts of the manuscript are concerned, the work aims to refute the opponent's view on *ātman*. From the *pudgalanairātmya* stance of the *śrāvakanaya*, the author refutes the opponent's view of *ātman* by focusing on its permanence (vv. 1–7), and from the *dharmanairātmya* or emptiness stance of the *pāramitānaya*, he refutes the real existence of the entire world of external objects (which exist only in an illusionary form, like a dream) solely on the basis of one's perception (v. 8). He then refutes the existence of *ātman*, which is assumed on the basis of mistaken conceptualization (*kalpanā*) (vv. 9–11). The opponent then criticizes the practice of visualizing deities in the *mantranaya* for being based on a form of conceptualization similar to that leading to the assumption of *ātman* (v. 12). Unfortunately, the verses that contain the author's reply to this objection are badly damaged in the manuscript.

9. Conclusion

In this paper we have provided a rough overview of the contents of the three *nayatraya* works. In sum, the *Nayatrayapradīpa* focuses on the superiority of Tantric Mahāyāna to non-Tantric Mahāyāna and non-Mahāyāna teachings, the *Nayatrayabheda* concisely represents essential doctrinal topics of the three *naya*s for the sake of beginners, and the *Nayatrayahṛdaya* refutes opponents' objections from the viewpoint of each *naya*.

Although the three works regard the *mantranaya* in common as the highest among the three *nayas*, the Tantric traditions (or personal devotions) to which each author adheres do not seem to be the same: the *Nayatrayapradīpa* deals with the Guhyasamāja tradition, while the author of the *Nayatrayabheda* expresses his homage to Heruka.

---

① Many parts of verses 10–11 are illegible in the manuscript.

② *candravajrakrameṇaiva devatākalpanātmikā* | *buddhatvādiphalāvāptir abhyāsāt kiṃ na hīyate* ||.

Their expositions of the *mantranaya*'s superiority are also different from each other. The *Nayatrayapradīpa* focuses on four points, i.e. the *mantra* teaching (*mantraśāstra*) (1) is free of confusion (*asammoha*), (2) offers many methods (*bahūpāya*), (3) presents no difficulties (*aduṣkara*), (4) and is for practitioners with sharp faculties (*tīkṣṇendriyādhikāra*), while the *Nayatrayabheda* stresses its efficacy in transforming harmful things into useful ones. The *mantranaya* section of the *Nayatrayahṛdaya* for its part is largely illegible due to damage to the manuscript and needs more study.

Turning back to the larger context of the history of Indian Buddhism: As a result of the wide diffusion of the Tantric tradition in Indian Buddhism, the tradition was adopted by Buddhist scholastic communities both inside and outside monasteries. However, because the Tantric tradition contains certain deviations in doctrine and practice from the non-Tantric Buddhist traditions, they had to reconcile it with these latter traditions and represent it to people as internally consistent and superior to them. The three works dealt with in this paper reveal some approaches used by Indian Buddhists when trying to integrate the Tantric tradition into the scholastic tradition. We see in these works the challenges facing them to justify Tantric teachings. Clarifying the relationship between the scholastic tradition and the non-scholastic traditions of Indian Tantric Buddhism (or even anti-scholastic ones, such as that of the Siddhas[①]) is another task, one that is still ongoing.

Appendix I: *Nayatrayabheda* verses 4–31 and 65–87

Appendix 1 presents *Nayatrayabheda* verses 4–31 and 65–87. The diplomatic transcription of the text was prepared by Dr. Li Xuezhu and the present author, and the critical edition was prepared by the latter. A critical edition of the entire work (88 verses in total) is currently under preparation in collaboration with Dr. Li. For opening verses 1–3 and verse 88, see above in this paper. Verses 4–31 deal with *pratītyasamutpāda* of the *śrāvakanaya*, in which verses 4–14 discuss the lifecycle interpretation of the twelve members of the *pratītyasamutpāda* (cf. *Abhidharmakośa* 3.21–24), while verses 15–31 teach the correct and reverse sequences of the chain of causality among the twelve members of the *pratītyasamutpāda* by telling a story that demonstrates the causality. Verses 65–87 are the *mantranaya* section. Verses not included in this paper will be published in collaboration with Dr. Li on another occation. In the following text, sandhi and orthography are standardized, verse numbers are added, and the twelve members of the *pratītyasamutpāda* are bold-faced.

---

① Cf. Szántó 2019.

Verses 4–31 (fol. 1r2–2r2) —*śrāvakanaya* section—

tyaktvā deham upādatte sūkṣmaṃ karmādhivāsitam |

āntarābhāvikaṃ tattadgatisaṃcārakāraṇam || 4 ||

svakarmārjitam āhāraṃ bhuñjānaṃ sthitaye param[1]$_{\text{(1r3)}}$ |

kliṣṭaṃ riraṃsayā yāntaṃ punarjanmamahāṭavīm || 5 ||

***avidy**ācchāditaṃ cittaṃ rūḍhaṃ **saṃskāra**bījataḥ* |

*nītaṃ vāsanayā garbhaṃ **vijñānam** iti saṃjñitam* || 6 ||

sthānāt sthānāntaraṃ gacchan pradīpo 'rthakriyākṣamaḥ |

kṣaṇikatve 'pi vijñā$_{\text{(1r4)}}$*nam evaṃ dehāntaraṃ śrayet* || 7 ||

tat kramākramavaj jñeyaṃ nijām arthakriyāṃ dadhat |

svopādeyasya jananād dīpavad bahukāryakṛt || 8 ||

*gṛhītakalalaṃ tac ca **nāmarūpā**khyayoditam* |

*pūrṇam **indriyaṣaṭkena** yadā cārbudanā*$_{\text{(1r5)}}$*ma tat* || 9 ||

viṣayendriyavijñānasaṃsargād yad udeti tat |

***sparśā**khyaṃ sukhaduḥkhādivedakaṃ **vedano**cyate* || 10 ||

*tajjaṃ **tṛṣṇ**eti vikhyātaṃ snehapāśavaśīkṛtam* |

majjanonmajjanaṃ kurvac chakunta iva palvale || 11 ||

bhogārthaṃ $_{\text{(1r6)}}$*dhāvatas tasya kṛpaṇasyābhilāṣiṇaḥ* |

*nām**opādānam** ity uktaṃ tajjaṃ karma **bhavā**bhidham* || 12 ||

*skandhānāṃ pratisandhānaṃ punar **jātir** iti smṛtā* |

***jarāmaraṇam** ity uktaṃ punaraṅgacatuṣṭayam* || 13 ||

iti saṃsaraṇaṃ jantoḥ kīṭāder brahmaṇo 'pi vā |

cakra$_{\text{(1v1)}}$*vad bhramam āpnoti samyagjñānāvadhiṃ vinā* || 14 ||

yathābhūtadṛśaḥ samyagyuktimārgānusāriṇaḥ |

avismaraṇaśīlasya samyagjñānasamudbhavaḥ || 15 ||

andhadaṇḍābhighātena phenālayavighaṭṭanāt |

daṣṭas taiḥ kukkuras tena yācako 'pi tathā$_{\text{(1v2)}}$*rditaḥ* || 16 ||

kṣiptas tena tam uddiśya daṇḍaḥ sa patitaḥ punaḥ |

kulālabhāṇḍanicaye tatkṣobho 'bhūd ayantritaḥ || 17 ||

taṃ dṛṣṭvā markaṭo bhītaḥ cchitvā rajjuṃ viniryayau |

sarvāśākṣobhaṇavyagraḥ kuceṣṭābhyastacāpalaḥ || 18 ||

---

① param] em., para Ms.

tam u$_{(1v3)}$*ddiśyātha batubhiḥ praharadbhir ito 'mutaḥ* |
rājasūnuḥ kṣatas tena cukṣubhe nagaraṃ bhṛśam || 19 ||
babhūva ghorasaṃgrāmo bahulokakṣayāvahaḥ |
bībhatsarasasaṃsaktajantupatrarathākulaḥ || 20 ||
tataḥ śauryanidhiḥ śrīman pūrṇo$_{(1v4)}$*ttaptapradeśibhiḥ* |
lakṣaṇaiḥ sūcito 'śeṣajagadvinayakauśalaḥ || 21 ||
*rājā vinayavān*① *dhīmāñ chrutavān apramādavān* |
nirjagāma śanais tasya vivektuṃ prabhavaṃ kaleḥ || 22 ||
pūrvapūrvavicāreṇa kāraṇānveṣaṇodya$_{(1v5)}$*taḥ* |
vimṛśya tucchaṃ taddhetum anayac chāntatāṃ raṇam || 23 ||
dviṣaṭkāṅganaye yojyaṃ nidarśanam idaṃ sphuṭam |
neśvarādes tato jātaṃ viśvaṃ nāpy apahetukam || 24 ||
andho ***'vidyā****tra vijñeyā* ***saṃskārā*** *daṇḍasaṃjñayā* |
phenālayābhidhānena prokta$_{(1v6)}$*m* ***aṅgacatuṣṭayam*** || 25 ||
kukkuro ***vedanā*** *jñeyā* ***tṛṣṇā*** *yācaka ity api* |
kulālabhāṇḍanicaya ***upādānam*** *iti smṛtam* || 26 ||
markaṭo ***bhava*** *ākhyāto* ***jātī*** *rājasuto mataḥ* |
nagarakṣobhasaṅgrāmo ***jarāmaraṇa****saṃjñitam* || 27 ||
yo 'sau rājā $_{(2r1)}$ *sa sambuddho 'laṃkṛto lakṣaṇādibhiḥ* |
ajñānadhvāntavidhvansadakṣaḥ ko 'nyas tato 'paraḥ || 28 ||
vilomakramam āśritya vicāryāṅgāni sarvaśaḥ |
avidyāprabhavaṃ viśvaṃ tuccham ity upadiṣṭavān || 29 ||
padāny anyāni yāny atra tair da(t)tā saṅgatiḥ ki$_{(2r2)}$*la* |
kathāyā iti mantavyo dṛṣṭānto 'rthavivakṣayā || 30 ||
anulomavilomābhyāṃ bhavāṅgānāṃ vivecanāt |
catuḥsatyaparijñānaprativedho na durlabhaḥ || 31 ||
iti pratītyasamutpādaḥ ||

Verses 66–87 (fols. 3r6–4r4) —*mantranaya* section—
durdāntadarpadamanikapaṭur vineṣyan
mohebhakṛttikarayugmadhṛtātapatraḥ

① The akṣara *vi* is not clear in the manuscript.

rāgīva bhāti karuṇād[①] *api bhāvagūḍho*
bhūyāt sa herukajino (3v1) *jagataḥ śivāya* || 65 ||[②]

cakāsti yo vineyānāṃ rāgiṇāṃ praṇidhānataḥ |
nīrāgo 'pi mahārāgas taṃ vande 'dbhutaceṣṭitam || 66 ||
avatāraṃ vineyānāṃ sandhāyoktaṃ tathāgataiḥ |
vajrayānam itīttham no gurubhir darśito nayaḥ || 67 ||
mananaṃ paratattvasya trāṇaṃ (3v2) *lokasya sarvataḥ* |
yataḥ pravartate jñānāt tan mantra iti buddhyatām || 68 ||
tadudbhūto 'pi varṇātmā vācako devatākṛteḥ |
ādhivyādhipraśamanān mantra ity abhidhīyate || 69 ||
tapaḥprabhāvasatyādiyuktānāṃ karuṇātmanām |
samīhitārtha(3v3) *siddhyarthaṃ vacanam mantra ucyate* || 70 ||
bodhipakṣyaguṇaugho 'sau yoginīvīravigrahaḥ |
avatīrṇaḥ karuṇayā māṇḍaleyavapur dadhat || 71 ||
adabhrabhramanirmuktasaṃvinmaṇḍalaraśmayaḥ
śakrāyudhavad ābhānti nīrūpā api rū(3v4)*piṇaḥ* || 72 ||
adhimucyettham ātmāto devatākārarūpadhṛt |
bahiḥspharaṇayogena pūjyaḥ sattvārthasiddhaye || 73 ||
bhāti yad yasya tat tasmād abhinnaṃ sukhaduḥkhavat |
ittham advayarūpatvaṃ bhāvyabhāvakayor dvayoḥ || 74 ||
vikalpo devatā(3v5)*kāro viruddhaḥ prakṛtasya yaḥ* |
tasmin sati kathaṃ tasya sambhavas tadvirodhinaḥ || 75 ||
tataḥ prakṛtarūpatvād vikalpo 'bandha eva saḥ |
devatātmā sa evāyaṃ mokṣaḥ sumahimā yataḥ || 76 ||
snehamadvibhramottīrṇaḥ prakṛtyaiva prabhāsvaraḥ |
ma(3v6)*ntriṇaḥ svasvabhāvo 'sāv avilupto*[③] *dṛḍhaṃ smṛteḥ* || 77 ||
anavadyaṃ samāsādya rūpādikam ananyadhīḥ |
mahākāruṇikaṃ tatra pūjayet karuṇāśayaḥ || 78 ||

---

① Here the masculine form *karuṇa* (which, according to Monier-Williams, normally means "causing pity or compassion" as one of the *rasa*s or sentiments of a poem) is used instead of the common feminine form *karuṇā*.

② Metre: Vasantatilakā.

③ avilupto] em., avilupta Ms.

ya[①] *eva bhāvāḥ prāg āsan*[②] *kevalā duḥkhahetavaḥ* |
sāmagryantaram āśritya ta eva sukhakāraṇam || 79 ||
yathā bā$_{(4r1)}$*dhitasāmarthyaṃ mantraiḥ prāg bādhakaṃ viṣam* |
bhūtvā hanti nṛṇāṃ mṛtyuṃ sāmagrīśaktibhedataḥ || 80 ||
tattatsāmagryabhedena bhāvā yānti bhidām amī |
śatapadyā viṣaṃ dṛṣṭaṃ mūrtam āyur nṛṇāṃ ghṛtam || 81 ||
nāgavallī sakramukā kṣāracūrṇavimiśritā |
rāgaṃ sṛja$_{(4r2)}$*ty araktāpi sāmagrīśaktibhedataḥ* || 82 ||
rūpādikaṃ tathaivedaṃ bālajantuvimohakam |
prajñopāyāśrayāt puṃsāṃ viduṣāṃ kleśaghātakam || 83 ||
yo 'sāv abhedaḥ prāg uktaḥ prajñākaruṇayor dvayoḥ |
sa samādhiviśeṣo 'tra prajño$_{(4r3)}$*pāyāśrayaḥ*[③] *smṛtaḥ* || 84 ||
evaṃ pramāṇasiddhe 'pi yasyāsti vimatir mate |
nairātmyādikathā tasya dūre saugatamāninaḥ || 85 ||
avicāritacārutvāc cittavibhramamātrakam |
bhāvā vicāram āpannāś cittanirvṛttihetavaḥ || 86 ||

ye vāsa$_{(4r4)}$*jantum avivekinam asvatantraṃ*
  bhāvā amī bhavarathaṃ bhayadaṃ nayanti |
bhūtā ta eva paramārthadṛśā pratītā
  hlādaṃ paraṃ dadhati kasya na yuktibhājaḥ || 87 ||[④]

Appendix II: *Nayatrayahṛdaya* verses 1–7b

Appendix 2 presents *Nayatrayahṛdaya* verses 1–7b and a translation of them. A full edition of the entire work is currently under preparation in collaboration with Dr. Li. Verses 1–2 teach that there is no such thing as *ātman*, only *skandha*s etc. Verses 2–4 deal with a non-Buddhist opponent's objection that *ātman* exists separately from the *skandha*s, etc. Verses 5–7b present the Buddhist's reply to the objection from the stance of the *śrāvakanaya*.

---

① ya] em., yam Ms.
② āsan] em., āsān Ms.
③ -āśrayaḥ] em., āśraya Ms.
④ |Metre: Vasantatilakā.

pañca skandhān samāsena dvādaśāyatanāni ca |
bhikṣubhyaḥ tattvavit prāha dhātūn aṣṭau tathā daśa || 1 ||
ebhyo 'nyo na padārtho 'sti nityatvādiguṇānvitaḥ |
ya ātmajīvajantvādisaṃjñābhiḥ parikalpitaḥ || 2 ||
athocyate ta evātmā tad ayuktaṃ yatas tu te |
anityā bahurūpāś ca nitya ātmā parair mataḥ || 3 ||
anityāḥ sarvadharmāś cet karmaṇāṃ nāsty ataḥ phalam |
anyena ca kṛtāt puṇyāt phalaṃ bhuṅkte 'nya eva hi || 4 ||
anitye phalasaṃpattiḥ karmaṇāṃ na tu śāśvate |
nityasya caikarūpatvāt sukhito duḥkhabhāk katham || 5 ||
anitye vāsanājātaṃ karmaṇāṃ syāt phalaṃ sphuṭam |
yo 'ṅgo bīje hi vinyastaḥ sa phale dṛśyate yathā || 6 ||
kartur bhuṅkte phalaṃ nānyaḥ tasyāsau bhinnasantatiḥ | 7ab

(Transl.) The one who knows reality (i.e. the Buddha) concisely taught the five *skandha*s, the twelve *āyatana*s, and the eighteen *dhātu*s to monks. (v. 1)

There is no [other] category apart from these, ones which—conceptualized under names such as *ātman, jīva*, or *jantu*—are accompanied by such characteristics as permanence. (v. 2)

(Objection:) If [Buddhists] say that *ātman* is nothing but them (i.e. *skandha*s etc.), this is not appropriate, [1] since others hold that these latter (i.e. *skandha*s etc.) are impermanent and have sundry characteristics (*bahurūpa*), whereas *ātman* is permanent [and always has one unchanging characteristic]; (v. 3)

[2] since if all phenomena were impermanent, there would be no fruit of karmic acts; [3] since one would receive the fruit [resulting] from virtuous activity (*puṇya*) committed by someone else. (v. 4)

(Reply:) [1] Since [*skandha*s, etc.] are impermanent, there is completion of the fruit of karma. But if they were permanent, there would be no [such completion]. As something which is permanent [like *ātman* should always] have one [unchanging] characteristic, how can it, when it is [always] blissful, undergo suffering? (v. 5)

[2] It is obvious that when they (i.e. *skandha*s etc.) are impermanent, karmic fruit is produced from the [invisible] imprints (*vāsanā*) [of previous karma], just as an [invisible] element deposited in a seed will appear [later] in [the form of] its fruit. (v. 6)

[3] Someone whose [mental] continuum is different from [that of the agent of a karmic act] (*bhinnasantati*) does not receive the fruit of the karma of the agent.①

Appendix III: Śrāvakas' Paying Homage to Bodhisattvas

In some texts, *bodhisattva*s are said to be objects of worship and included in the Jewel of the Buddha (*buddharatna*), while in others those monks who do not worship *bodhisattva*s are said to be Hīnayāna Buddhists (i.e. *śrāvaka*). For example, in the *Nanhai jigui neifazhuan* 南海寄歸内法傳, Yijing 義净 (635–713) states that one who worships *bodhisattva*s is called a Mahāyāna Buddhist, and one who does not, a Hīnayāna Buddhist, i.e. a *śrāvaka*:

考其致也，則律撿不殊，齊制五篇通修四諦。若禮菩薩，讀大乘經，名之爲大。不行斯事，號之爲小。②

(Transl.) Concerning the mode [of monastic discipline within the Hīnayāna and Mahāyāna], there is no difference between their Vinaya codes. [Both] commonly establish the five kinds of transgression [taught in the Vinayas] and similarly practice the Noble Ones' Four Truths. When **one pays homage to *bodhisattvas*** and recites Mahāyāna sūtras, one is called a Mahā[yāna Buddhist], whereas when one does not do these, one is called a Hīna[yāna Buddhist].

From its Mahāyāna standpoint, the *Subhāhuparipṛcchā*, for instance, criticizes Buddhists (i.e. *śrāvaka*s) who do not worship *bodhisattva*s:

gang zhig theg pa mchog la sdang ba dang || bdud kyis bshad pa yin zhes zer ba dang || rmongs pa nga la gnod sbyin zhes smra dang || byang chub sems dpa' la ni mi 'dud pa'i || dge slong dge slong ma dang dge bsnyen dang || dge bsnyen ma dang 'jig rten pa rnams kyis || nga yi rigs kyi gsang sngags bzlas brjod na || de dag rnams kyi lus ni myur du 'jig ||

(Transl.) If those who are hostile towards the supreme vehicle (i.e. the Mahāyāna), those who say "It's a demon's theory," fools who call me a *yakṣa*, and the monks, nuns, lay men, lay women, and worldly people **who do not pay homage to *bodhisattva***s chant my *vidyāmantra*s,

① The following translation is also possible: "Some second person who is different from the agent (*kartṛ*) does not partake of the fruit; the latter has a mental continuum different from the former."

② Taishō 54, 205c10–13. For more on the coexistence between *bodhisattva* monks and *śrāvaka* monks with reference to this account by Yijing, see, for instance, Nishimoto 1956: 187.

their bodies will be quickly destroyed.[①]

Candrakīrti's *Triśaraṇasaptati* v. 51 conveys the stance taken by the Pūrvaśailas that Arhats, i.e. a *śrāvaka* or *pratyekabuddha* who has completed the soteriological paths, worship *bodhisattva*s.

pūrvaśailāgame 'rhadbhir bodhisattvās tu vanditāḥ |
ratnatrayān na te bāhyā buddhe 'ntarbhāvato matāḥ ||

(Transl.) In a scripture of the Pūrvaśaila [tradition], on the other hand, it is maintained that ***bodhisattvas* are [to be] praised** by Arhats and that they are not outside of the Three Jewels, for they are included in the [Jewel of] the Buddha.[②]

Avalokitavrata states that the Pūrvaśailas possessed Mahāyāna scriptures in the Prakrit language: "Further, the Pūrvaśailas and the Aparaśailas of the same Mahāsāṃghika school possess the *Prajñāpāramitā* and other Mahāyāna sūtras in the Prakrit language." [③] Therefore, the "scripture" (*āgama*) mentioned in the verse is very probably a Mahāyāna one. Indeed, the passage from the Pūrvaśaila scripture is quoted in Bhāviveka's *Tarkajvālā*,[④] part of which was later extracted in Abhayākaragupta's *Munimatālaṃkāra* (Skt. Ms. fols. 8v4–9r1), composed much later in A.D.1108 or 1109:

bhagavān āha—ye bodhisattā savvadhammasamatāvipañcitassa samādhissa lābhino savve te caturasītisu sattacaritasahassesu yathāpucchārahan dhamma desenti. atha kho tthero subhūtī bhagavantam etad avocat—ṇa tathe sāvakapattekabuddhāṇaṃ visayo iddhī ca, yathe bodhisattāṇaṃ. vandāmi bhagavan bodhisattāṇam iti pūrvaśailanivāsināṃ bodhisattvapiṭake.[⑤]

---

① *Subāhuparipṛcchā*, D805, 137a2–4. See Ōtsuka 2013: 925.

② See Kano and Li 2014: 7.

③ The translation is from Skilling 2009: 202. For the original Tibetan text, see *ibid.* 205: *dge 'dun phal chen sde nyid kyi shar gyi ri bo'i sde dang nub kyi ri bo'i sde dag las kyang 'phral skad du* | *shes rab kyi pha rol tu phyin pa la sogs pa theg pa chen po'i mdo dag 'byung ba'i phyir ro* ||

④ *Tarkajvālā*, D3856, 176a2–7. I owe this valuable reference to Dr. Vincent Tournier (in a personal communication in November 2020). The passage was translated by Nozawa 1973 and Eckel 2008: 167–168. Skilling (1997: 612) pointed out the link between the passage and the *Triśaraṇasaptati*.

⑤ A diplomatic transcription of the manuscript is as follows: *bhagavān āha* | *ye bodhisatvā sarvvadharmmasamatāvipañcitassa samādhi*$_{(9r1)}$*ssa lābhino sarvve te caturaśītisu sattacaritasahassesu yathāpucchārahan dharmma deśenti* | *atha kho ttharo subhūtī bhagavantam etad avocat* | *ṇa tathe sāvakapattekabuddhāṇaṃ visayo iddhī ca yathe bodhisattāṇaṃ vandāmi bhagavan bodhisattāṇam iti pūrvvaśailanivāsināṃ bodhisatvapiṭake* |. I am grateful to Dr. Tournier for his valuable suggestions on the readings of the above-quoted passage from the *Munimatālaṃkāra*.

(Transl.) The Bhagavat said: "All the *bodhisattva*s who attain the *samādhi* called 'equality regarding all phenomena' teach dharma in accordance with the 84,000 kinds of [mental] activities of sentient beings." Then the elder Subhūti said to the Bhagavat: "The *viṣaya* and *ṛddhi* of *śrāvaka*s and *pratyekabuddha*s are not like those of *bodhisattva*s. [Therefore], O Bhagavat, I bow down to *bodhisattva*s." [This much was taught] in the *bodhisattvapiṭaka* of the Pūrvaśailanivāsins.

This passage from "the *bodhisattvapiṭaka* of the Pūrvaśailanivāsins" is a Prakrit version of the *Brahmaviśeṣacintiparipṛcchā*.① Bhāviveka also quotes passages from scriptures of various other schools that teach the worship of *bodhisattva*s by *śrāvaka*s (they were again extracted by Abhayākaragupta).②

Turning back to the *Triśaraṇasaptati* verse above (which very probably presupposes the *Tarkajvālā*): Who are the "*bodhisattva*s to be worshipped," and who are the "*bodhisattva*s included in the Jewel of the Buddha?" In this regard, the following passage from the *Tarkajvālā* is again noteworthy:

de lta bas na yon tan dang ldan pa'i khyim pa rnams ni yon tan gyis dbul bar gyur pa'i rab tu byung ba dag gis phyag bya ba kho na yin te.

(Transl.) This is why renunciants who are poor in virtue should definitely pay homage to virtuous householders.③

Since this passage is followed by the above-cited Pūrvaśailanivāsins' *āgama* passage, Bhāviveka has in mind that the "*bodhisattva*" here is a householder. Moreover, in the same context, the *Munimatālaṃkāra* states:

*atra ca dvividho buddhaḥ, pāramārthikas trikāyasaṃgṛhītaḥ, sāṃketikaś ca dhātustūpapratimācaityabodhisattvarūpaḥ, eteṣu pūjiteṣu buddhā bhagavantaḥ pūjitā iti vacanāt.*④

---

① The passage corresponds to *Brahmaviśeṣacintiparipṛcchā*, D160, 73b2–3; Taishō vol. 15, 20a20–b1; *ibid.* 50c21–51a1; *ibid.* 83b22–c9. For the seven *piṭaka*s of the Pūrvaśailanivāsins, see *Triśaraṇasaptati* vv. 57–58 and Baba 2022: 50. For the inscriptions that mention Pūrvaśailanivāsins, see Tsukamoto 2001: 72.

② *Tarkajvālā*, D3856, 175a7–179b1 (cf. Nozawa 1973: 212–213, Skilling 1997, Eckel 2008: 166–173); *Munimatālaṃkāra*, Skt. Ms. fols. 8v2–9r4.

③ Tibetan text: D3856, 175a7 = Eckel 2008: 348. Translation by Eckel 2008: 166.

④ *Munimatālaṃkāra*, Skt. Ms. fol. 8r3–4.

(Transl.) And in this context, [the Jewel of] the Buddha is of two kinds: the ultimate one, which is included in the three bodies [of the Buddha], and the conventional one, which has the nature/shape (*rūpa*) of a relic, stūpa, image, caitya, or *bodhisattva*, for it is stated that when these are worshipped, illustrious buddhas are worshipped.

Here, Abhayākaragupta lists such objects of worship as stūpas included in the Jewel of the Buddha, and at the end of the list one finds "*bodhisattva*". In this regard, Bhāviveka says, "One should pay homage to a Bodhisattva in the same way that one pays homage to a Buddha, because they belong to the same continuum, just as one pays homage to the sapling of a fig tree and the son of a Cakravartin, as if both were fully grown".① Echoing this statement, Abhayākaragupta says that *bodhisattva*s are "sprouts" of a buddha, and so are conventionally buddhas since they belong to the same continuum leading from a cause to its result, like the continuum running from a sprout to the fully grown fig tree.② Although Bhāviveka does not specify who the householder *bodhisattva*s to be paid homage to by monks are, he may have been hinting at powerful mundane patrons, such as local kings or royal families. There may be other possible interpretations,③ but the one being proposed can certainly not be discarded. This is just a partial description of the relationship between *bodhisattva*s and *śrāvaka*s, further details of which I will leave to another article.

References

Baba, Norihisa 馬場紀寿. 2022. 仏教の正統と異端—パーリ・コスモポリスの成立 [Buddhist Orthodoxy and Heresy: The Birth of the Pāli Cosmopolis]. Tokyo: Tokyo daigaku shuppankai.

Deokar, Lata Mahesh. 2021. "Unknown Buddhist Narratives as Cited in the Kavikāmadhenu." In: Lata Mahesh Deokar (ed.), *Saṃkathā: Proceedings of a Seminar on Buddhist Narrative Literature*. Pune: Department of Pali, Savitribai Phule Pune, 127–136.

Dhīḥ.1997. *Tattvaratnāvaloka*. Rare Buddhist Texts Series 14. Sarnath: Central Institute of Higher Tibetan Studies: 81–103 (Reprint: *Bauddhalaghugranthasamgraha* [*A Collection of Minor Buddhist Texts*]. Sarnath: Central Institute of Higher Tibetan Studies, 2021, 129–149).

---

① This translation is taken from Eckel 2008: 174. See *Tarkajvālā*, D3856, 180a2 (Eckel 2008: 355).

② *Munimatālaṃkāra*, Skt. Ms. fol. 8v1: *te hi buddhāṅkurāḥ sāṃketikā buddhā hetuphalabhāvenaikasantānatvāt*. The Tibetan translation (D3903, 83b1) adds here: *n-ya gro dha'i myu gu dang n-ya gro dha'i ljon shing gi rgyun bzhin no*.

③ For instance, the *bodhisattva* referred to here can may have been a *bodhisattva* statue.

Eckel, Malcolm David. 2008. *Bhāviveka and His Buddhist Opponents: Chapters 4 and 5 of the Verses on the Heart of the Middle Way (Madhyamakahṛdayakārikāḥ) with the Commentary Entitled The Flame of Reason (Tarkajvālā).* Harvard: Harvard University Press.

Hahn, Michael. 1981. "Ajātaśatrvavadāna: A Gopadatta Story from Tibet." In: Jata Shankar Jha (ed.), *K. P. Jayaswal Commemoration Volume*. Patna: K. P. Jayaswal Research Institute, 242–276.

Isaacson, Harunaga. 2001. Ratnākaraśānti's *Hevajrasahajasadyoga* (Studies in Ratnākaraśānti's tantric works I). In: Rafaele Torella (ed.), *Le parole e i marmi: Studi in onore di Raniero Gnoli nel suo 70' compleanno*. Roma, Istituto Italiano per I' Africa e l'Oriente, 457–487.

Isaacson, Harunaga. 2015. Strategies of Supremacy: Claims for the Superiority of the Mantranaya over the Pāramitānaya in Late Indian Tantric Buddhist Texts. Handout, September 20th, 2015. Nihon Indogaku bukkyōgakkai, Kōyasan.

Isaacson, Harunaga and Sferra, Francesco. 2014. *The Sekanirdeśa of Maitreyanātha (Advayavajra) with the Sekanirdeśapañjikā of Rāmapāla: Critical Edition of the Sanskrit and Tibetan Texts with English Translation and Reproductions of the MSS*. Napoli: Universita degli Studi di Napoli "L'Orientale."

Isoda, Hirofumi 磯田熙文. 1979.『Nayatrayapradīpa』について [On the *Nayatrayapradīpa*]. 印度学仏教学研究 *Indogaku bukkyōgaku kenkyū* 28–1: 408–411.

Kano, Kazuo 加納和雄. 2014.『普賢成就法』の新出梵文資料について [Newly Available Sanskrit Materials of Jñānapāda's *Samantabhadrasādhana*]. 密教学研究 *Mikkyōgaku kenkyū* 46: 61–73.

Kano, Kazuo 加納和雄. 2019. アドヴァヤヴァジュラ編とされる新出の梵文詞華集 [Newly Surfaced Tantric Anthology Ascribed to Advayavajra from a Sanskrit Manuscript Collection Preserved at Norbulingka]. 密教学研究 *Mikkyōgaku kenkyū* 52: 23–38.

Kano, Kazuo 加納和雄. 2021. *Nayatrayapradīpa, Nayatrayabheda, Nayatrayahṛdaya*— 顕密の体系を概述する三点の梵文作品 [*Nayatrayapradīpa, Nayatrayabheda, Nayatrayahṛdaya*: Three Works that Summarize Tantric and Non-tantric Systems]. 印度学仏教学研究 *Indogaku bukkyōgaku kenkyū* 69–1: 129–136.

Kano, Kazuo and Li Xuezhu 加納和雄, 李學竹. 2014. "Sanskrit Verses from Candrakīrti's *Triśaraṇasaptati* Cited in the *Munimatālaṃkāra*." *China Tibetology* 22: 4–11.

Kano, Kazuo and Li Xuezhu 加納和雄, 李學竹. 2019. *Nayatrayapradīpa*—新出梵本の予備的報告 [Preliminary Survey of the Sanskrit Manuscript of Trivikrama's *Nayatrayapradīpa*]. *Journal of World Buddhist Cultures* 2: 125–140.

Kano, Kazuo and Li Xuezhu 加納和雄, 李學竹. 2020. 声聞による大乗の真実観批判—

Nayatrayapradīpa 梵文校訂と訳注（1）[The Śrāvakas' Criticism of Mahāyāna's Position on Tattva and its Refutation: Sanskrit Text and Translation of the *Nayatrayapradīpa* [1]]. 駒澤大学仏教学部論集 *Komazawa daigaku bukkyōgakubu ronshū* 51: 77–102.

Kano, Kazuo and Li Xuezhu 加納和雄, 李學竹. 2021. 声聞の離欲と菩薩の大悲—*Nayatrayapradīpa* 梵文校訂と訳注（2）[Śrāvakas' Detachment and Bodhisattvas' Compassion: Sanskrit Text and Translation of the *Nayatrayapradīpa* (2)]. 駒澤大学仏教学部論集 *Komazawa daigaku bukkyōgakubu ronshū* 52: 95–131.

Kano, Kazuo and Szántó, Péter-Dániel. 2020. "New Pages from the Tibet Museum Birch-bark Manuscript (1): Fragments Related to Jñānapāda." 川崎大師教学研究所紀要 *Kawasakidaishi kyōgakukenkyūjo kiyō* 5: 27–51.

Kawasaki, Kazuhiro 川崎一洋. 2004. "On a Birch-bark Sanskrit Manuscript Preserved in the Tibet Museum." *Journal of Indian and Buddhist Studies* 52/2: 50–52.

van der Kuijp, Leonard W.J. 2020. "Indo-Tibetan Tantric Buddhist Scholasticism: Bhavyakīrti and His Summary of Sāṃkhya Philosophy (part I)." *Journal of Tibetan and Himalayan Studies* 5: 1–40.

Kuranishi, Kennichi 倉西憲一. 2014. "Dauḍīpāda and the *Guhyāvalī*." *Indogaku bukkyōgaku kenkyū* 62/3: 1267–1271.

Kyuma, Taiken 久間泰賢. 2009. "Superiority of Vajrayāna, Part I: Some Remarks on the **Vajrayānāntadvayanirākaraṇa* (*rDo rje theg pa'i mtha' gñis sel ba*) Ascribed to Jñānaśrī." In: Shingo Einoo (ed.), *Genesis and Development of Tantrism*. Tokyo: Sankibō: 469–486.

Matsuda, Kazunobu 松田和信. 2021. 不浄観を説く中阿含 139 経—三啓集から回収された梵文テキストと和訳 [Sanskrit Text and Japanese Translation of the *Madhyamāgama* 139 (**Śivapathikāsūtra*) Based on the Tridaṇḍamālā Manuscript]. 佛教大学仏教学会紀要 *Bukkyōdaigaku bukkyōgakkai kiyō* 26: 63–81.

Namai, Chishō 生井智紹. 1996. 真言門より行を行ずる菩薩—大乗仏教における密教の形成過程という観点から [On Bodhisattvas Who Practise according to the Mantra Method]. 高野山大学論文集 *Kōyasan daigaku ronbunshū*: 163–180.

Namai, Chishō 生井智紹 . 1998. 真言理趣による行の確立—大乗仏教における密教の形成についての一視座 [Establishing the Mantranaya Practice: On the Formation of the Esoteric Buddhism in Mahāyana Buddhism]. In: Yukei Matsunaga (ed.), インド密教の形成と展開 *Indo mikkyō no keisei to tenkai*. Kyoto: Hōzōkan, 103–138.

Nishimoto, Ryūzan 西本龍山. 1956. 讃稱せらるべき大乘戒観 [Perspectives on the Mahāyana Disciplines That Are to Be Praised]. 印度学仏教学研究 *Indogaku bukkyōgaku kenkyū* 4–1:

184–187.

Nozawa, Jōshō 野澤静證. 1973. 清弁の声聞批判一インドにおける大乗仏説論 [Annotated Japanese Translation of Bhāviveka's *Madhyamakahṛdayavṛtti Tarkajvālā* Chapter 4, Śrāvakatattvanirṇayāvatāra]. 函館大谷女子短期大学紀要 *Hakodate ōtani joshi tankidaigaku kiyō* 5: 203–221.

Onians, Isabelle. 2002. *Tantric Buddhist Apologetics, or Antinomianism as a Norm*, D.Phil. dissertation, Oxford, Trinity Term.

Ōtsuka, Nobuo 大塚伸夫. 2013. インド初期密教成立過程の研究 [A Study on the Development of the Early Esoteric Buddhism in India]. Tokyo: Shunjūsha.

Ōtake, Susumu 大竹晋. 2020. セルフ受戒で仏教徒一五戒・八戒・菩薩戒、インド直伝実践マニュアル [On Being a Buddhist by Self-ordination]. Tokyo: Kokushokankōkai.

Schopen, Gregory. 2005. *Figments and Fragments of Mahāyāna Buddhism in India: More Collected Papers*. Honolulu: University of Hawai'i Press.

Skilling, Peter. 1997. "Citations from the Scriptures of the 'Eighteen Schools' in the Tarkajvālā." In: Petra Kiffer-Pülz and Jens-Uwe Hartmann (eds.), *Bauddhavidyāsudhākarah: Studies in Honour of his 65th Birthday*. Indica et Tibetica 30. Swisttal-Odendorf: Indica et Tibetica Verlag, 605–614.

Skilling, Peter. 2009. "Prakrit *Prajñāpāramitās*: Northwest, South, and Center: Gleanings from Avalokitavrata and Haribhadra." *Bulletin of the Asia Institute*, New Series 23: 199–208.

Sobisch, Jan-Ulrich. 2002. *Three-Vow Theories in Tibetan Buddhism*. Wiesbaden: Reichert Verlag.

Sugiki, Tsunehiko. 1999. Kṛṣṇācārya の四次第 [Kṛṣṇācārya's Four Stage Meditational Process]. 印度学仏教学研究 *Indogaku bukkyōgaku kenkyū* 47–2: 142–145.

Szántó, Péter-Dániel. 2015. "Tantric Prakaraṇas." In: *Brill's Encyclopedia of Buddhism*, vol. 1. Leiden/Boston: Brill, 756–761.

Szántó, Péter-Dániel. 2019. "Siddhas." In: *Brill's Encyclopedia of Buddhism*, vol. 2. Leiden/Boston: Brill, 443–451.

Szántó, Péter-Dániel. 2020. "The Road Not to Be Taken: An Introduction to Two Ninth-Century Works Against Buddhist Antinomian Practice." In: Cristina Pecchia and Vincent Eltschinger (eds.), *Mārga: Paths to Liberation in South Asian Buddhist Traditions. Papers from an International Symposium Held at the Austrian Academy of Sciences, Vienna 17–18 December, 2015*. Wien: VÖAW.

Takada, Ninkaku 高田仁覚. 1965. インド密教から見た仏教の輪郭 [A Few Hasty Outlines of Indian Buddhism Seen from the Viewpoint of Mantrayāna]. 密教文化 *Mikkyō bunka* 71/72: 66–72.

Tanemura, Ryūgen 種村隆元. 2008. 密教はなぜ顕教より優れているのか？ ―ジュニャーナシュリー作『金剛乗に関する二つの極端の排除』について [Why Is Tantric Buddhism Superior to non-Tantric Buddhism? Jñānaśrī's **Vajrayānāntadvayanirākaraṇa*]. 現代密教 *Gendai mikkyō* 19: 145–155.

Tsukamoto, Keishō 塚本啓祥. 2001. インド仏教の虚像と実像 [Hollow Images and True Images of Indian Buddhism]. Tokyo: Sankibō.

Yoritomi, Motohiro 頼富本宏. 1990. 密教仏の研究 [Research on Esoteric Buddhism]. Kyoto: Hōzōkan.

Post script: After submission of the manuscript of the present paper, the following relevant papers have been published:

Kano Kazuo, Li Xuezhu 加納和雄, 李學竹. 2023a. "The Dependent-origination teaching in the *Nayatrayabheda* of Kuśalaśrī —Sanskrit text and Japanese translation of verses 1–31." *Mikkyo Bunka* 249/250: 7–26.

Kano Kazuo, Li Xuezhu 加納和雄, 李學竹. 2024a. "The Four Truths of Noble Ones and Bodhisattva's Path in the *Nayatrayabheda* of Kuśalaśrī—Sanskrit text and Japanese translation of verses 32–64." *Mikkyo Bunka* 251/252.

Kano Kazuo, Li Xuezhu 加納和雄, 李學竹. 2025a. "The Mantra path in the *Nayatrayabheda* of Kuśalaśrī—Sanskrit text and Japanese translation of verses 65–88." *Mikkyo Bunka* 253/254.

Kano Kazuo, Li Xuezhu 加納和雄, 李學竹. 2022. "Superiority of the Mahāyāna: Sanskrit Text and Translation of the *Nayatrayapradīpa* (3)." *Komazawadaigaku bukkyōgakubu ronshū* 53: 71–98.

Kano Kazuo, Li Xuezhu 加納和雄, 李學竹. 2023. "Superiority of the Mantranaya: Sanskrit Text and Translation of the *Nayatrayapradīpa* (4)." *Komazawadaigaku bukkyōgakubu ronshū* 54: 67–82.

Kano Kazuo, Li Xuezhu 加納和雄, 李學竹. 2024. "Variety of Means of Practice in the Mantranaya: Sanskrit Text and Translation of the *Nayatrayapradīpa* (5)." *Komazawadaigaku bukkyōgakubu ronshū* 55.

Kano Kazuo, Li Xuezhu 加納和雄, 李學竹. 2025. "Preliminary remarks on a collection of miscellaneous texts of Saṃmitīya — Studies of Bhaikṣukī manuscripts from Potala Palace (1) —." *Journal of the Faculty of Buddhism of the Komazawa University* 83: 33–64.

Buddhist Narrative and Non-Narrative Sources on the Salvation of the Patricidal King Ajātaśatru*

Wu Juan 吴　娟
Depatment of Chinese Language and Literature, School of Humanities, Tsinghua University

1. Introduction: Diverse Attitudes to the Salvation of Ajātaśatru in Indian Buddhism

Buddhist stories from various sources tell us that soon after the death of his father, Ajātaśatru remorsefully confesses his crime of patricide to the Buddha and becomes one of the Buddha's chief lay disciples. Since patricide is one of the five most heinous crimes according to Indian Buddhist ethics, questions such as what spiritual status a committer of this crime could reach and whether or how he could ultimately attain liberation have significant implications for Buddhist ethics and soteriology. Although ancient Indian Buddhist authors generally agreed that after having visited the Buddha (or encountered a deputy of the Buddha) Ajātaśatru was psychologically relieved of the anguish of guilt and the fear of hell, they nonetheless differed greatly in determining the spiritual and karmic benefits gained by him. The benefits mainly cover three aspects: his immediate spiritual attainment during the visit (or encounter), the mitigation or elimination of his infernal punishment in the next life, and his eventual spiritual attainment in the future. For instance, the Pāli *Sāmaññaphalasutta* says that while listening to the Buddha's sermon, Ajātasattu fails to attain

---

* This article has previously been published in the *Annual Report of the International Research Institute for Advanced Buddhology at Soka University*, Vol. XXVI, 2023, pp.167–188. The research was sponsored by the National Social Science Foundation of China under Grant No. 2018VJX071, Tsinghua University Initiative Scientific Research Program (No. 2021THZWWH03), and Tsinghua University Essential Humanities Development Program (清華大學基礎文科發展項目).

the Dhamma-eye (*dhammacakkhu*), the basic insight into the Buddhist Truths, precisely due to his patricide.① Contrastingly, the **Ajātaśatru-kau*kṛtya*vinodana* (AjKV), the oldest extant Mahāyāna text dealing with his salvation, tells us that having heard the bodhisattva Mañjuśrī's exposition of emptiness (*śūnyatā*), Ajātaśatru attains the "conforming acceptance of states of existence" (**ānulomika[dharma]kṣānti/ānulomikī [dharma]kṣānti*).② The AjKV predicts that he will be reborn in hell but will feel no pain there, after which he will rise from hell and eventually attain buddhahood. On the other hand, both the 5th-century Pāli commentator Buddhaghosa and the 11th-century Sanskrit poet Kṣemendra agreed that Ajātaśatru will attain pratyekabuddhahood in the future.

An examination of how and why Buddhist authors③ disagreed on the benefits Ajātaśatru gained through contact with the Buddha (or with a deputy of the Buddha, such as Mañjuśrī) may open windows not only into their attitudes toward saving this archetypal criminal in particular, but also into their understandings of karmic responsibility and spiritual liberation in general. Further, since whatever benefits assigned to Ajātaśatru can only make full sense against certain narrative or doctrinal backgrounds, an examination of this kind may also help us appreciate the multiple ways in which the salvation of Ajātaśatru is placed in different contexts and the specific meanings it embodies. The AjKV mentioned above provides a telling example in this regard, where the thorough salvation of Ajātaśatru by Mañjuśrī, as Harrison and Hartmann rightly put it, demonstrates "the capacity of the perfection of wisdom (*prajñāpāramitā*) and insight into emptiness (*śūnyatā*) to radically transform suffering consciousness into awakening." ④

To be sure, the salvation of one guilty of an *ānantarya* crime is not something novel in Indian Buddhist soteriology. Jonathan A. Silk notes, "Crimes such as the sins of immediate retribution are serious ... but the tradition appears to be (nearly) unanimous in considering that they do not result

---

① DN I 86,2–5.

② See T. 627 (xv) 422b8 (*juan xia*): 柔順法忍；D 216, *mdo sde*, Tsha 252a4; S 223, *mdo sde*, Za 325a2: *stong pa nyid kyi rjes su 'thun pa'i bzod pa* (**śūnyatānulomikā/°kī kṣānti*). However, the earliest Chinese version of the AjKV speaks of Ajātaśatru's attainment of "joyful and faithful acceptance (of states of existence)" (T. 626 [xv] 401b13 [*juan xia*]: 所喜信忍；404b14–15: 歡喜信忍). The conforming intellectual receptivity to states of existence (*ānulomika[dharma]kṣānti/ānulomikī [dharma]kṣānti*)–or as Lamotte (1944–1980: IV.1789; V. 2380) renders it, "conviction préparatoire"–is a feature realized by a bodhisattva at the sixth *bhūmi* ("stage") toward buddhahood according to the *Daśabhūmikasūtra* (Rahder 1926: 47.19–23 [text]; Honda 1968: 187 [tr.]; Kondō 1936: 96.12–13; Strauch 2010: 38), or at the seventh *bhūmi* according to the *Śūraṃgamasamādhisūtra* (Lamotte 1965: 162 n. 119 = 1998: 145).

③ Kṣemendra was a Vaiṣṇava by faith but deeply influenced by Buddhism (see Mejor 1992: 2 n. 2). His *Bodhisattvāvadānakalpalatā* is a collection of poetic retellings of Buddhist stories largely—but not entirely—taken from the Mūlasarvāstivāda *Vinaya* (see Panglung 1981: 209–210).

④ Harrison and Hartmann 2000: 168.

in one's permanent estrangement from ultimate awakening, bodhi or nirvāṇa." [①] In other words, most Indian Buddhist authors accepted the possibility of one guilty of an *ānantarya* crime attaining ultimate liberation. This is the case for all those who commit one or more of the five *ānantarya* crimes. What is interesting about Ajātaśatru is that he is not only a committer of an *ānantarya* crime, but also an eminent lay disciple of the Buddha. He is acclaimed as a model of rootless faith in a number of Buddhist texts.[②] According to Buddhaghosa, there is no ordinary worldly man as faithful as Ajātasattu.[③] The transformation from an archetypal villain into a great devotee of the Buddha is the most fascinating trait of Ajātaśatru in Indian Buddhism. Thus his personality is a unique combination of two almost contradictory identities—the identities as a paradigmatic sinner and as an exemplary Buddhist *upāsaka*.[④]

To thoroughly save Ajātaśatru–which is to say, to deliver him from the cycle of rebirths–is not just to save a patricide, but to save one who transforms from a patricide into a model *upāsaka* in the

---

① Silk 2007: 273.

② For an overview of Indian Buddhist sources on Ajātaśatru's rootless faith, see Wu 2016: 105–111.

③ See Sv 610,23–24: *sakko āha bhante puthujjano nāma ajātasattunā samo saddho n'atthi na so mama vacanaṃ karissati* ("Sakka said, 'Sir, there is no ordinary man as faithful as Ajātasattu. He will not follow my word"). The reason why Sakka says this is that those holding wrong views (*micchādiṭṭhikā*) ask Sakka to contrive a strategy to take away the share of the Buddha's relics obtained by Ajātasattu. See also Sv 238,10–11: *pothujjanikāya saddhāya samannāgato nāma iminā raññā sadiso nāma nāhosi* ("Indeed, no one endowed with the faith of ordinary people was equal to this king [Ajātasattu]"). The term *puthujjana* ("ordinary, worldly man") refers to one who has not entered the noble path to liberation, a follower of the Buddha who has not attained *sotāpatti* or stream-entry (see Cone 2020: 500–501, s.v.). The *Puggalapaññatti* ("Designation of Persons") says (pp.12, 30–32): *katamo ca puggalo puthujjano. yassa puggalassa tīṇi saññojanāni appahīnāni na ca tesaṃ dhammānaṃ pahānāya paṭipanno. ayaṃ vuccati puggalo puthujjano* ("What kind of person is 'ordinary man'? The man whose three fetters [i.e., *sakkāyadiṭṭhi* 'belief in self,' *vicikicchā* 'doubt,' and *sīlabbataparāmāsa* 'clinging to rules and rituals'] have not been eliminated and who is not practising to eliminate these things. Such a man is called 'ordinary man'"); also tr. in Law 1979 (1924): 19. The *Puggalapaññatti* commentary explains (pp-a 183, 26–29): *tesaṃ ca dhammānan ti tesaṃ saṃyojanadhammānaṃ. maggakkhaṇasmiṃ hi tesaṃ pahānāya paṭipanno nāma hoti ayaṃ pana maggakkhaṇe pi na hoti* ("'These things' refer to the fetters. Because at the moment of [entering] the path one is practising to eliminate them, this man [i.e., a *puthujjana*] has not yet reached the moment of [entering] the path").

④ There are also two other notorious sinners (both monks) guilty of *ānantarya* crimes featured in Indian Buddhist literature: Devadatta, who is said to have committed three *ānantarya* crimes including creating a schism in the *Saṃgha*, wounding the Buddha, and killing the *arhatī* Utpalavarṇā (Lamotte 1944–1980: II. 868–876; Mukherjee 1966: 45–94, 125–126; Bareau 1991: 97–100, 120, 122), and Mahādeva, the putative instigator of the schism between the Mahāsāṃghikas and the Sthāviras, who is also said to have committed three *ānantarya* crimes including patricide, matricide, and killing an *arhat* (Silk 2009: 17–20, 38–57). In Sinhalese Buddhism, the *Cūlavaṃsa* (Geiger 1925: XXXVIII 80–XXXIX 59 [text]; 1929: 38–50 [tr.]) speaks about King Kassapa I, who is said to have committed patricide and later repented (DPPN, s.v. 12. Kassapa; Obeyesekere 1989: 246–251; 1990: 174–180). But there is no mention of his change into a Buddhist *upāsaka*.

same lifetime. Given this transformation, the salvation of Ajātaśatru offers a convenient platform for Buddhist authors to express their ideas on how to balance the workings of *karma* and other factors (for instance, the salvific power of the Buddha, the efficacy of the Buddhist Dharma, the merit of Buddhist faith, the role of repentance, etc.), thereby to illustrate their different soteriological emphases. For instance, in his commentary on the *Sāmaññaphala-sutta*, Buddhaghosa shows that because of hearing the Buddha's sermon, Ajātasattu, after staying in hell for a while, will be released and finally attain liberation as a *paccekabuddha*.① Ajātaśatru's release from hell and his pratyekabuddhahood are also predicted in the Chinese translation of the *Ekottarikāgama* (EĀc 38.11) and in the *Āshěshìwáng wèn wǔnì jīng* 阿闍世王問五逆經 ("Scripture on King Ajātaśatru's Inquiry into the Five Most Heinous Crimes", T. 508).② In both texts his future rising from hell and eventual awakening are explained as the long-term karmic rewards for his Buddhist faith established in this life, not as the results of hearing a particular sermon preached by the Buddha. This subtle difference of emphasis is understandable. Buddhaghosa relates Ajātasattu's future rebirths in his commentary on the *Sāmaññaphalasutta* primarily for an exegetical purpose. He wants to use Ajātaśatru's final liberation to demonstrate the salvific efficacy of the Buddha's sermon on the fruits of the ascetic life. In EĀc 38.11 and T. 508, however, the story of Ajātaśatru's salvation is not told for an exegetical purpose, but serves to illustrate the incredible karmic effects of establishing Buddhist faith, and ultimately to demonstrate the Buddha's capability of arousing faith even in the worst criminal and consequently leading him to awakening.

In studying Indian Buddhist attitudes toward the salvation of Ajātaśatru, there is one more point we cannot neglect, namely that the story of Ajātaśatru's transformation and his salvation forms part of the polemics against the archetypal schismatic Devadatta. While the story of Ajātaśatru's or Kūṇika's causing the death of his own father was told both by Buddhists and by Jainas, only the Buddhists adapted it into a polemic device to condemn a schismatic monk—Devadatta, the notorious cousin and adversary of the Buddha. A number of Buddhist texts show that in his early days Ajātaśatru assists Devadatta in several attempts on the Buddha's life. Desirous of supplanting the Buddha to become head of the monastic community, Devadatta incites Ajātaśatru to kill his own father, King Bimbisāra, a chief patron of the Buddha, and to usurp the throne of Magadha. With the schismatic legend of Devadatta as a backdrop, Ajātaśatru's confession of his patricide to the Buddha and his transformation into a Buddhist *upāsaka* can be seen as marking the downfall of

---

① See Sv 237,23–238,13.

② See T. 125 (ii) 726a5–16 (*juan* 32); T. 508 (xiv) 776a4–26.

Devadatta and the victory of the Buddha, since they show that even the chief patron of Devadatta goes over to the Buddha's party. This implication is most clearly suggested by the fact that the *Śrāmaṇyaphalasūtra*, which describes Ajātaśatru's visit to the Buddha after his patricide, is incorporated in full into the *Saṃghabhedavastu* of the Mūlasarvāstivāda *Vinaya*, where Ajātaśatru's change into a disciple of the Buddha and his withdrawal of support for Devadatta constitute an immediate cause leading to Devadatta's committing of a third *ānantarya* crime (i.e., his killing of the *arhatī* Utpalavarṇā). Moreover, since it is Devadatta who persuades Ajātaśatru to commit the patricide and thereby leads him to suffer the karmic retribution of being reborn in hell in the next life, and since it is through the Buddha that Ajātaśatru becomes relieved of his anguish of guilt and starts accumulating good *karma*, stories of his transformation and salvation also serve to demonstrate the "good friend" (*kalyāṇamitra*) image of the Buddha in contrast with the "evil friend" (*pāpamitra*) image of Devadatta. This contrast is made explicit, for instance, in the *paccupannavatthu* or "story of the present" of the Pāli *Saṃkicchajātaka*, where we are told: "He [Ajātasattu], after having, because of Devadatta and following his counsel, killed his own father, ..., became fearful and gained no hearty enjoyment from his royal splendour," and "now, having approached the Tathāgata, through contact with a good friend, his fear has gone away and he enjoys the happiness of rulership." ①

There can be little doubt that Indian Buddhist authors did not share the same opinion on whether to have Ajātaśatru saved from *saṃsāra*, or how to have him saved, even though they may have agreed on the possibility of his ultimate liberation. There is a remarkable diversity both in Buddhist interpretations of the personality of Ajātaśatru, and in Buddhist treatments to his sinful condition. A relatively early story tradition represented by the Pāli *Sāmaññaphalasutta* focuses on the karmic obstacle caused by his patricide to his spiritual cultivation. Attempts to bring him to ultimate liberation (either as a *pratyekabuddha* or as a *buddha*) likely represent later developments. In order to attain a more complete picture of the diverse ways in which Indian Buddhist authors dealt with the theme of the salvation of Ajātaśatru, we need to take an overview of related Buddhist narrative and non-narrative sources. In what follows, I will first introduce all major narrative sources concerning the salvation of Ajātaśatru, and then proceed to look at non-narrative (expository or argumentative) sources related to this theme.

---

① Ja V 261,33–262,34: *so hi devadattaṃ nissāya tassa vacanena pitaraṃ ghātāpetvā ... bhīto rajjasiriyā cittassādaṃ alabhi* (B[e]: *na labhi*) *... so dāni tathāgataṃ āgamma kalyāṇamittaṃsaggena vigatabhayo issariyasukhaṃ anubhotī*. Translated also in Cowell 1895–1907: V. 134–135.

2. An Overview of Narrative Sources on the Salvation of Ajātaśatru

While only a small number of Jaina texts give accounts of Kūṇika's remorse and his subsequent death,① there is a very rich body of Buddhist literature dealing, at various levels of detail, with Ajātaśatru's repentance, his transformation into a Buddhist *upāsaka*, his future rebirths, and/or eventual awakening. The Indian Buddhist narrative cycle of the salvation of Ajātaśatru basically comprises five subcycles: (1) stories of his repentance for the patricide and conversion by the Buddha (i.e., the frame story of the *Śrāmaṇyaphalasūtra* and its adaptations); (2) stories of his repentance for the patricide and conversion by someone other than the Buddha; (3) stories of his conversion unrelated to his repentance for the patricide; (4) prophecies of his future rebirths and pratyekabuddhahood; (5) prophecies of his future rebirths and buddhahood. The chart below offers an outline of the five subcycles and their corresponding textual sources:

Table 1: The Narrative Cycle of the Salvation of Ajātaśatru in Indian Buddhism

Subcycle I	Ajātaśatru's Repentance and His Conversion by the Buddha: Five Versions (1–5) and Three Adaptations (6–8) of the Frame Story of the *Śrāmaṇyaphalasūtra*
1	*Sāmaññaphalasutta* in the Pāli *Dīghanikāya* (DN 2 at DN I 85,6–86,5)
2	Part of the *Saṃghabhedavastu* of the Mūlasarvāstivāda *Vinaya* in Sanskrit and Tibetan versions②
3	*Shāménguǒ jīng* 沙門果經 ("Scripture on the Fruits of Śramaṇa-hood") in the Chinese version of the *Dīrghāgama* (DĀc 27)③
4	*Jìzhìguǒ jīng* 寂志果經 ("Scripture on the Fruits of Being a *Samaṇa/ Śamaṇa," T. 22)④

(Continued)

① For an overview of Jaina sources on Kūṇika's remorse over the death of his father Śreṇika and/or his subsequent death, see Wu 2019: 93–103.

② For the Sanskrit text, see SBhV II 251.19–254.4 (tr. MacQueen 1988: 100–103); for the Tibetan counterpart, see D 1, *'dul ba*, Ṅa 284b2–286a6; S 1, *'dul ba,* Ṅa 392a5–394b7. Yìjìng 義净 's translation of the *Saṃghabheda-vastu* ends abruptly before the Buddha preaches a sermon to Ajātaśatru (T. 1450 [xxiv] 206a4 [*juan* 20]). It is unclear how the Indic original used by Yìjìng described Ajātaśatru's reaction to the Buddha's sermon.

③ See T. 1 (i) 109b12–109c21 (*juan* 17); tr. Meisig 1987: 360–376; MacQueen 1988: 47–50.

④ See T. 22 (i) 275c28–276b6; tr. Meisig 1987: 361–379; MacQueen 1988: 68–71. The Chinese *jìzhì* 寂志 ("one whose mind is tranquilized") was most likely translated from a Prākrit form, either *samaṇa* or *śamaṇa* (Karashima 2016: 108–110).

5	Untitled *sūtra* in the Chinese version of the *Ekottarikāgama* (EĀc 43.7)①
6	*Paccuppannavatthu* of the *Sañjīvajātaka* (Ja I 508,9–510,11)
7	*Paccuppannavatthu* of the *Saṃkiccajātaka* (Ja V 261,32–263,2)
8	Part of the *Fànxíng pǐn* 梵行品 ("Chapter on Pure Practice") ② of the *Mahāparinirvāṇa-mahāsūtra* (Chinese versions [T. 374, T. 375], Tibetan version [D 119/P 787/S 333] translated from T. 374)③
Subcycle II	Ajātaśatru's Repentance and His Conversion by Someone Other Than the Buddha
1	By an anonymous Buddhist monk: **Ajātaśatrvavadāna* ascribed to Gopadatta (ca. 400–800)④

(Continued)

① See T. 125 (ii) 764a13–b11 (*juan* 39); tr. Meisig 1987: 358–371; MacQueen 1988: 87–89. There is no mention of Ajātaśatru in the Sanskrit fragments of the EĀ from Gilgit, which consist entirely of sections of the *nipāta*s on ones and twos (Ōkubo 1982; Tripāṭhī 1995: 120–218). No mention is made of him in the published fragments of the EĀ from the Berlin Turfan collection either (besides the references given in Allon [2001: 10–11] and Tripāṭhī [1995: 19], see also SHT VI 1326, Bl.178 [cf. IX p.439]; SHT VIII 1829, 1957; SHT IX 2071; SHT X 3459; SHT XI 4542).

② While the Sanskrit equivalent to *fànxíng* 梵行 could be either **brahmacarya* or *°caryā*, the former is more common (cf. SWTF, vol. 19, p.265, s.v. brahma-carya; Lamotte 1944–1980: I. 467; Olivelle 1993: 80 n. 22).

③ See T. 374 (xii) 474a26–485b11 (*juan* 19&20) = T. 375 (xii) 717a14–728c3 (*juan* 17&18). The story told in T. 374 is translated into Japanese and discussed in Sadakata 1986: 13–100, 185–227; for previous studies, see Hirakawa 1971: 2–5; Mochizuki 1988: 137–154; Radich 2011: 34–39; Granoff 2012: 203–210. For an English translation from T. 375 (or rather, from a modern Japanese translation of T. 375), see Yamamoto 1973–1975: II. 451–495. On the complex textual history of the *Mahāparinirvāṇa-mahāsūtra* (MPM), see Shimoda 1997: 155–235; Habata 2007: xxxiv–xlii (§§13–18); Radich 2015: 20–21. The southern Chinese recension T. 375 is a revision of the northern recension T. 374; the Tibetan translation (D 119, S 333) was also based on T. 374. Thus neither T. 375 nor this Tibetan translation can be taken as an independent witness. There is yet another Chinese translation (T. 376) and another Tibetan translation of the MPM (D 120, S 179), both independently made from Indic originals. Hirakawa (1971: 2, 11 n.5) notes that neither T. 376 nor the independent Tibetan translation (D 120, S 179) contains much detail on Ajātaśatru's salvation. He further notes that these two versions share a common episode with T. 374 and T. 375 (ibid.: 4). According to that episode, after his patricide Ajātaśatru comes to blame the Buddha for having ordained Devadatta while knowing Devadatta's evil nature. In response, the Buddha admonishes Ajātaśatru not to look for others' fault, but to reflect on his own crime and to seek remedies. This episode is arguably of an Indian origin. It implies that Ajātaśatru's crime can be mitigated through some remedial measures.

④ According to Hahn (1992: 17), the **Ajātaśatravadāna* "was accessible only in the form of Rāhula Sāṅkṛtyāyana's transcript of a fragmentary Sanskrit manuscript found in Xizang. The manuscript consists of five leaves, but since the final part of the story is missing neither the author nor the title of the legend is given". Hahn (1981: 257–276) offers a revised edition of the **Ajātaśatravadāna* based on Sāṃkṛtyāyana's transcript and other relevant sources. On the authorship of this work, its title reconstruction, as well as its structural and poetical features, see Hahn 1981: 242–256. On the date of Gopadatta, see Hahn 1992: 28. The **Ajātaśatrvavadāna* is listed both in Rāhula Sāṅkṛtyāyana's and Frank Bandurski's inventories of Sanskrit manuscripts in Xizang (see Harrison 2014: 281).

2	By a Buddhist layman: *Xiángxiàng pǐn* 降象品 ("Chapter on Subjugating an Elephant") of the *Fó běnxíng jīng* 佛本行經 ("Scripture on the Buddha's Former Deeds," T. 193)①
3	By the elder Maudgalyāyana: *Tiáodá rù dìyù pǐn* 調達入地獄品 ("Chapter on Devadatta's Entering into Hell") of the *Fó běnxíng jīng* (T. 193)②
4	By an anonymous Buddhist monk: *Kalpadrumāvadānamālā* no. 20 *Śrīmatyavadāna* (Story of Śrīmati)③
5	By the bodhisattva Lokeśvara: *Kalpadrumāvadānamālā* no. 28 *Ajātaśatruparidāpitāvadāna* ("Story of the Converted Ajātaśatru") or *Ajātaśatruparibodhitāvadāna* ("Story of the Exhorted Ajātaśatru")④
Subcycle III	Ajātaśatru's Conversion Unrelated to His Repentance for the Patricide
1	Related to Indra's worship of the Buddha: *Avadānaśataka* no.16 *Pañcavārṣikāvadāna* ("Story of the Quinquennial Festival")⑤
2	Related to Indra's worship of the Buddha: *Kalpadrumāvadānamālā* no. 24 *Dharmabuddhinṛpāvadāna* ("Story of King Dharmabuddhi"), parallel to the *Pañcavārṣikāvadāna*⑥

(Continued)

① See T. 193 (iv) 93a9–95c13 (*juan* 5). The traditional attribution of T. 193 in seven fascicles to the Chinese translator Bǎoyún 寶雲 (376–449) is problematic. The *Chū sānzàng jìjí* 出三藏記集 compiled by Sēngyòu 僧祐 in 515 CE, which is usually deemed credible, mentions a *Fó běnxíng jīng* in five fascicles among anonymous scriptures (T. 2145 [lv] 21c12 [*juan* 4]). Higata Ryūshō (1966: 341) suggests that T. 193 may have been translated after Zhī Qiān 支謙 (fl. ca. 223–253) but before Kumārajīva (ca. 350–409); see also Willemen 2009: xv. Higata (1966: 341–344) further notes that while T. 193 shares with Aśvaghoṣa's *Buddhacarita* many stanzas, its content clearly differs from that of the *Buddhacarita*.

② T. 193 (iv) 98b29–103a7 (*juan* 6).

③ This story is summarized in Mitra 1882: 300.

④ This story is summarized in Mitra 1882: 303. According to Feer (1879: 304; 1979 [1891]: xxvi) and Filliozat (1941: 14, nos. 26–27), the manuscript of the *Kalpadrumāvadānamālā* in the Bibliothèque Nationale de France gives the title *Ajātaśatruparidāpitāvadāna*. This title reappears in Matsunami (1965: 231). However, the manuscript of the *Kalpadrumāvadānamālā* in the Cambridge University Library (MS Add.1590; Bendall 1883: 131) gives the title *Ajātaśatruparibodhitāvadāna* (see folio 269a7–8 at http://cudl.lib.cam.ac.uk/view/MS-ADD-01590/541 [accessed 29 May 2022]).

⑤ See Avś I 88–92; translated into French in Feer 1979 (1891): 72–76. For the Tibetan counterpart, see D 343, *mdo sde*, Am 46b2–49a4; S 252, *mdo sde*, Sha 70b4–73b7. In the Chinese version of the *Avadānaśataka* (T. 200 [iv] 210a22–c8 [*juan* 2]) the story appears as the 15th (rather than the 16th) chapter. Its content largely agrees with, but still differs from, that of the Sanskrit version.

⑥ The story is summarized in Feer 1979 (1891): 75–76; Mitra 1882: 301. Feer (1879: 304; 1979 [1891]: xxvi) gives the title *Dharmabuddhinṛpa*; Filliozat (1941: 14) gives the title *Dharmabuddhanṛpa*. According to the Cambridge MS Add.1590 (folio 235b1 at http://cudl.lib.cam.ac.uk/view/MS-ADD-01590/470 [accessed 14 October 2016]), the title reads *Dharmabuddhinṛpāvadāna*. The story mentions a king (one of the Buddha's past existences) named Dharmabuddhi. On the correspondence between this story and the *Pañcavārṣikāvadāna* of the *Avadānaśataka*, see Feer 1879: 304; Speyer 1902–1909: II. XXII.

3	Related to the Buddha's subjugation of a drunken elephant: *Shǒucái zuìxiàng tiáofú pǐn* 守財醉象調伏品 ("Chapter on Subjugating the Drunken Elephant Dhanapāla") of the *Fó suǒxíng zàn* 佛所行讃 (Chinese translation of the *Buddhacarita*, T. 192), and its counterpart in the Tibetan translation (D 4156/P 5656)①
4	Related to the Buddha's subjugation of 500 drunken elephants: *Fènnù pǐn* 忿怒品 ("Chapter on Anger") of the *Fǎjù pìyù jīng* 法句譬喻經 (T. 211), partly parallel to the story above in T. 192②
5	Related to the Buddha's curing of a plague in Magadha: Part of the *Bhaiṣajyavastu* ("Section on Medicine") of the Mūlasarvāstivāda *Vinaya* in Chinese and Tibetan versions③
Subcycle IV	Prophecies of Ajātaśatru's Future Rebirths and Eventual Pratyekabuddha-hood
1	Part of Buddhaghosa's commentary on the *Sāmaññaphalasutta* (Sv 237,23–238,13)
2	Part of an untitled *sūtra* in the Chinese *Ekottarikāgama* (EĀc 38.11)④
3	*Āshèshìwáng wèn wǔnì jīng* 阿闍世王問五逆經 ("Scripture on King Ajātaśatru's Inquiry into the Five Most Heinous Crimes," T. 508), containing a prophecy parallel to that found in EĀc 38.11⑤

(Continued)

① See T. 192 (iv) 40c19–41b3 (*juan* 4); tr. Willemen 2009: 153–155. The Chinese version agrees closely with the Tibetan (D 4156, *skyes rabs*, Ge 76a7–78a1; P 5656, *mdo 'grel*, Ṅe 92a8–94a5; tr. Johnston 1984 [1936]: III. 60–63, vv. 37–65), which was translated independently from Sanskrit. According to Sēngyòu 僧祐 (T. 2145 [lx] 12a25 [*juan* 2]), the translator of the *Fó suǒxíng zàn* 佛所行讃 in five fascicles (T. 192) is Bǎoyún 寶雲, not Tán Wúchèn 曇無讖 (*Dharmakṣema). Ōminami (2002: 139–145) supports Sēngyòu's attribution of T. 192 to Bǎoyún.

② See T. 211 (iv) 596a5–b2 (*juan* 3); paraphrased in Beal 1878: 121–123; Lamotte 1944–80: IV. 1773; see also Japanese translations in Tanabe 2000: 142–145; Kamitsuka et al. 2001: II. 43–47. According to Sēngyòu 僧祐 (T. 2145 [lv] 10a1–3 [*juan* 2]), T. 211 was translated by Fǎjù 法炬 and Fǎlì 法立 in 290–311 CE. Brough (1962: 38) notes that T. 211 is a selection of verses taken from T. 210 (an earlier Chinese translation of the *Dharmapada*), "together with explanatory stories, and is thus similar to a somewhat condensed Dhammapada Aṭṭhakathā." Mizuno (1981: 341–355) convincingly argues that T. 211 is not a pure translation of an Indic text but contains episodes added or changed by the translators in China; see also Enomoto Fumio's remarks in Kamitsuka et al. 2001: II. 275–282. As for the present story of Ajātaśatru, Mizuno (1981: 351) suggests that it is difficult to determine whether it was translated from an Indic original or composed in China. The story has no parallel in the Pāli *Dhammapadaṭṭhakathā*.

③ See the Chinese version at T. 1448 (xxiv) 19c2–20c20 (*juan* 5); the Tibetan version at D 1, *'dul ba*, Kha 13a6–17a6; S 1, *'dul ba*, Ka 454a4–*kha* 7a2 (summarized in Panglung 1981: 20–21; see a Japanese translation by Yao 2013: 81–86). No Sanskrit version of this part of the *Bhaiṣajyavastu* has been identified.

④ T. 125 (ii) 726a6–16 ≈ 726a29–b8 (*juan* 32); tr. Wu 2014: 157.

⑤ The prophecy appears at T. 508 (xiv) 776a4–c17. In EĀc 38.11 and T. 508, prophecies of Ajātaśatru are placed within the Vaiśālī plague legend. Yet another Chinese text titled *Púsà běnxíng jīng* 菩薩本行經 ("Scripture on the Bodhisattva's Former Deeds," T. 155) also predicts Ajātaśatru's future lives and places the prediction within the Vaiśālī plague legend, but without mentioning his pratyekabuddhahood (T. 155 [iii] 116a9–117b20 [*juan zhong*]).

4	Pallava 45 *Ajātaśatrupitṛdrohāvadāna* ("Story of Ajātaśatru's Malice toward His Father") of Kṣemendra's *Bodhisattvāvadānakalpalatā*①
Subcycle V	Prophecies of Ajātaśatru's Future Rebirths and Eventual Buddhahood
1	Chapter 11 of the *Ajātaśatrukaukṛtyavinodana* preserved in two Chinese translations (T. 626, T. 627), one Tibetan translation (D 216/P 882/S 223), and one fragmentary Sanskrit version (Harrison and Hartmann 2000a)②
2	*Āshěshìwáng shòujué jīng* 阿闍世王授決經 ("Scripture on the Prediction of King Ajātaśatru's [Future Buddhahood]," T. 509)③
3	*Āshěshìwáng shòujì pǐn* 阿闍世王受記品 ("Chapter on King Ajātaśatru's Receiving of a Prophecy [of His Future Buddhahood]") of the *Shǒuhù guójièzhǔ tuóluóní jīng* 守護國界主陀羅尼經 ("Scripture on the Dhāraṇīs for Safeguarding Rulers of States," T. 997)④

In addition, it might be worth mentioning that the *Rgya gar chos 'byung* ("History of Buddhism in India") completed by the Tibetan scholar Tāranātha in 1608 CE speaks of Ajātaśatru's future attainment of stream-entry. Tāranātha's account runs as follows:⑤

In this way Ānanda guarded teachings for forty years. In the next year King Ajātaśatru also passed away. Having been reborn in hell for a short while, after dying from there, he was reborn in heaven. [There] hearing the Dharma from the noble Śāṇavāsika, he attained the status of a stream-enterer (*rgyun du zhugs pa*, **srotāpanna*). Thus it was said.

As far as I am aware, this is the only account of Ajātaśatru's future rebirths that relates him to Śāṇavāsika (also called Śāṇavāsa or Śāṇakavāsin), the Buddhist patriarch who is said to have

① See Das and Vidyābhūṣaṇa (1888–1918: I. 1070–1087), based on a bilingual blockprint containing both the Sanskrit text (in Tibetan script) and the Tibetan translation. The Sanskrit text was reproduced in Vaidya (1959: 280–284). See also textcritical remarks by de Jong (1979: 27–35), based on the Das-Vidyābhūṣaṇa edition, two Cambridge manuscripts (Add. 1306, Add. 913), and the Tibetan translation in Peking Tanjur.

② For the Chinese versions, see T. 626 (xv) 404a14–c10 (*juan xia*) [tr. Sadakata 1989: 158–164]; T. 627 (xv) 425b28–426a24 (*juan xia*). For the Sanskrit version (in fragmentary form) and a translation of the Tibetan counterpart (D 216, Tsha 260b5–262b4; S 223, Za 338b1–341b3; P 882, Tsu 272b3–274b6), see Harrison and Hartmann 2000: 204–212. The chapter divisions are taken from Dharmarakṣa's Chinese version (T. 627), and not found in any other version of the text.

③ For translations of T. 509, see Sadakata 1986: 151–155.

④ T. 997 (xix) 571c16–574c24 (*juan* 10).

⑤ I translate from the Tibetan text edited by Schiefner (1868: 7.6–9 = TBRC W12434, 12.17–13.2): *de ltar na kun dga' bos lo bzhi bcur bstan pa bskyangs | de'i phyi lo rgyal po ma skyes dgra yang 'das te | yud tsam dmyal bar skyes nas | de las shi 'phos nas lhar skyes te | 'phags pa sha na'i gos can la chos nyan pas rgyun du zhugs pa thob par grags so |* Translated also in Schiefner 1869: 9–10; Chimpa and Chattopadhyaya 1990 (1970): 25. The closing expression *grags so* indicates the hearsay nature of this account.

received the mastery of the Dharma from Ānanda and then passed it on to Upagupta.① Tāranātha's account is likely based on an earlier source (or sources). But since he does not indicate what source was used here, it is unclear whether this account has an Indian origin.

3. An Overview of Non-Narrative Sources on the Salvation of Ajātaśatru

A number of Buddhist texts present Ajātaśatru's future destiny (or more precisely, his descent into hell and subsequent release from it) not as part of a story, but as part of doctrinal or scholastic argumentation. For instance, the **Abhidharma-mahāvibhāṣā* translated by Xuánzàng 玄奘 (602–664) gives five explanations of Ajātaśatru's rootless faith immediately after an exposition of the notion of "serenity based on a realization [of the Buddhist Truths]" (Chin. *zhèngjìng* 證净, Skt. **avetyaprasāda*).② The fifth explanation reads:③

Furthermore, the faith attained by King Ajātaśatru does not exempt him from falling into the evil destiny [i.e., hell], and is therefore called "rootless." After his death he temporarily fell into hell and, after undergoing a little bit of suffering there, he will be reborn in heaven.

Here the last sentence on Ajātaśatru's mild suffering in hell, his release from hell, and his ensuing rebirth in heaven has no parallel in Buddhavarman's translation of the **Abhidharma-vibhāṣā*.④ Regarding this sentence, there are two possibilities: First, it could have originally belonged to the Indic text of the **Abhidharma-mahāvibhāṣā* from which Xuánzàng translated. Second, it

---

① On Śāṇavāsika/Śāṇakavāsin as one of the five "masters of the Dharma" (*dharmācārya*s, including Mahākāśyapa, Ānanda, Madhyāntika, Śāṇakavāsin and Upagupta) who are said to have successively preserved and transmitted Śākyamuni Buddha's teachings, see Strong 1992: 66–67. Interestingly, a fragment of an old Uigur text called *ötüg* ("annals") narrates the happenings after the Buddha's *nirvāṇa* as follows: when Ānanda sustained the Buddha's teachings within the *Saṃgha*, Ajātaśatru supported the Buddha's teachings outside the *Saṃgha*; after Ānanda entered *nirvāṇa*, Ajātaśatru was reborn in heaven; during the reign of Ajātaśatru's son Udāyin, while Śāṇavāsa sustained the Buddha's teachings within the *Saṃgha*, Udāyin supported the Buddha's teachings outside the *Saṃgha* (see Zhang and Zieme 2013: 405–406; Zieme 2014: 402–404). This Uigur text highlights the parallelism between the *Saṃgha* and the state in terms of their roles in preserving the Buddha's Dharma. Since it associates Ajātaśatru with Ānanda, and Ajātaśatru's son Udāyin with Śāṇavāsa, it still differs from Tāranātha's account.

② T. 1545 (xxvii) 536b9–25 (*juan* 103), translated and discussed in Wu 2016: 121–130.

③ T. 1545 (xxvii) 536b23–25 (*juan* 103): 復次，未生怨王所成就信未免惡趣，故名無根。彼後命終暫墮地獄，受少苦已，方生天故。

④ Buddhavarman's translation only says that "although [Ajātaśatru] has such faith, he is not exempted from the evil destiny, and therefore [his] faith is called 'rootless'" (T. 1546 [xxviii] 387b19 [*juan* 54]).

could have been added as an explanatory gloss by Xuánzàng (or by someone else) based on a certain Buddhist source about Ajātaśatru known to him. In either case it is likely that this sentence ultimately derives from an Indic origin, since a similar (though much more elaborated) prophecy is found in the Sanskrit, Tibetan and Chinese versions of the **Ajātaśatru-kau*kṛtya*vinodana*, which describes Ajātaśatru's brief stay in hell, his feeling of no pain while staying there, and his ascent to heaven after emerging from hell.①

Another Buddhist text that speaks of Ajātaśatru's rebirth in hell as part of doctrinal exegesis is the anonymous *Sàpóduō píní pípóshā* 薩婆多毘尼毘婆沙 (**Sarvāstivādavinaya-vibhāṣā*, T. 1440) translated perhaps in the Qin 秦 period (351–431).② This text is a detailed commentary on the *Shísòng lǜ* 十誦律 (T. 1435), the Chinese version of the Sarvāstivāda *Vinaya*. In the **Sarvāstivādavinayavibhāṣā* we find the following passage explaining the salvific power of the Three Jewels (the Buddha, the Dharma, and the *Saṃgha*):③

Question: If one commits an enormous crime, even the Buddha cannot save him. If one commits no crime, he would not need the Buddha to save him. Why is it said that the Three Jewels are capable of salvation and protection?

Answer: Although Devadatta took refuge in the Three Jewels, his heart was insincere. He was dissatisfied with the three refuges, always hankering for worldly profit and fame. He claimed himself to be an omniscient one, competing against the Buddha. For these reasons, even though the Three Jewels have great power, they cannot save him. As for King Ajātaśatru, although he had committed an *ānantarya* crime and was supposed to enter the Avīci hell,④ due to his sincere mind toward the

---

① See Harrison and Hartmann 2000: 204–206.

② On the date of the translation of T. 1440, see Hirakawa 1960: 259–260; Funayama 1998: 280; 2006: 44.

③ T. 1440 (xiii) 505b9–16 (*juan* 1): 問曰：若有大罪，佛不能救。若無罪者，不須佛救。云何三寶能有救護？答曰：提婆達多雖歸三寶，心不眞實。三歸不滿，常求利養名聞。自號一切智人，與佛共競。以是因緣，三寶雖有大力，不能救也。如阿闍世王，雖有逆罪應入阿鼻獄，以誠心向佛故，滅阿鼻罪，入黑繩地獄。如人中七日，重罪即盡。是謂三寶救護力也。This passage is reproduced verbatim in the *Dàfāngbiàn fó bàoēn jīng* 大方便佛報恩經 ("Scripture on the Great Skilful Means of the Buddha's Compassionate Recompense"), cf. T. 156 (iii) 156b19–27 (*juan* 6). As already noted by Naitō (1955), T. 156 is not a translation of any Indic text, but a compilation made through recycling existing Chinese Buddhist scriptures. Recently Funayama (2016) convincingly argues that T. 156 was most likely compiled in China during the 5th century CE, and that it consists of excerpts taken from more than ten Chinese Buddhist texts (including, *inter alia*, T. 1440). On T. 156, see also Funayama 2002: 15; 2014: 138–139; Schaik and Galambos 2011: 113–115.

④ Not all Buddhist traditions agree that Ajātaśatru's patricide leads him to the Avīci hell. For instance, Buddhaghosa (Sv 237,32–238,4) shows that Ajātasattu will be reborn in the hell of copper pot (*lohakumbhī*). Silk (2007: 254 n. 2) observes that according to the AKBh and the **Abhidharma-Mahāvibhāṣā* (T. 1545), "sins other than the creation of a schism in the monastic community do not necessarily result in rebirth in the worst of the hells, Avīci, ..., although they might."

Buddha, his crime leading to Avīci was eliminated, and he entered the Black-String (Kālasūtra) hell. [There] his weighty crime became extinguished within a period as long as seven days in the human world. This is called the salvific and protective power of the Three Jewels.

This passage contrasts the savable Ajātaśatru with the unsavable Devadatta. It highlights the extent to which the karmic consequence of Ajātaśatru's patricide can be mitigated through cultivating a sincere mind toward the Buddha. The punishment in the Kālasūtra or "Black-String" hell is certainly less severe than the punishment in Avīci. In Buddhist traditions, Kālasūtra is either listed among the eight great hot hells (*mahānarakas*, including Saṃjīva, Kālasūtra, Saṃghāta, Raurava, Mahāraurava, Tapana, Pratāpana and Mahāvīcī),① or belongs to a group of five hells (Saṃjīva, Kālasūtra, Saṃghāta, Raurava and Avīci).② The *Mahāvastu* contains a detailed depiction of torments in the Kālasūtra hell,③ and explains that the hell is so named because hell-beings there are cut to pieces with black strings.④ Some scholars have pointed out that those who lack respect for their parents tend to fall into the Kālasūtra hell.⑤ According to a careful study by Funayama Tōru, T. 1440 is not a pure translation, but "a mixture of a translation of an Indic text, which constitutes the greater part, and a certain amount of exegetical elements" that were interpolated by the translator in order to help a Chinese audience understand the text.⑥ So far I have not found any Sanskrit, Pāli or Tibetan parallel to the statement above concerning Ajātaśatru's rebirth in the Kālasūtra hell and the exhaustion of his evil karma within seven days. Given the Sino-Indian hybrid nature of T. 1440,

① See AKBh ad III.58 (tr. Yamaguchi and Funahashi 1955: 382; see also La Vallée Poussin 1923–1931: II.149); Feer 1892: 191–196; Kirfel 1920: 201–206; Sadakata 1997 (1973): 48.

② Mvu I 42.16–17, 53.13–14, 337.5; Tournier 2017: 434 (text), 486 (tr.).

③ Mvu I 12.15–13.10 (tr. Leumann and Shiraishi 1988 [1952]: 30–31), I 17.8–20.11 (tr. Leumann and Shiraishi 1988 [1952]: 35–39).

④ Mvu I 20.11–12: *kenedaṃ kālasūtraṃ | tatra nairayikān nirayapālā ārdravṛkṣe vā varjetvā kālasūtravaśena takṣanti tenaiṣa kālasūtranirayo yathākartavyo ||* My translation: "Why is it [called] 'Black-String'? There hell-guards, having impaled hell-beings on verdant trees (cf. BHSD, 471, s.v. *varjayati*; or, having hewed them like verdant trees [cf. Leumann and Shiraishi 1988 (1952): 39]), cut them by means of black strings. For this reason, it is named 'Black-String Hell', just as it should be described." Moreover, Mus (1939: 79) explains the torture instrument *kālasūtra* as "un cordeau de charpentier, noirci avec du charbon, du goudron, etc."

⑤ For instance, Feer (1892: 192) says: "Il dit que ce lieu est réservé à ceux qui ont manqué de respect à leurs père et mère, au Buddha et à la confrérie"; see also Kirfel (1920: 202): "Diese Hölle ist bestimmt für Lügner, schlechte Söhne, schlechte Frauen usw." For occurrences of the Kālasūtra hell in Brahmanical literature, see Kirfel 1920: 149–171. According to the *Bhāgavata Purāṇa* (5.26.14), a killer of a brahmin falls into Kālasūtra (see Jacobsen 2009: 391). The *Mānava Dharmaśāstra* mentions Kālasūtra twice: at 3.248 it says that if one, after eating an ancestral offering, gives his leftovers to a Śudra, that one falls into Kālasūtra (Olivelle 2005: 121 [tr.], 494.10 [text]); at 4.88 Kālasūtra is listed as one of the hells to which a person goes, who accepts a gift from a greedy king deviating from the Law (Olivelle 2005: 128 [tr.], 521.8 [text]).

⑥ See Funayama 2006: 45. On T. 1440, see also Funayama 1998: 280–285; 2002: 20–21; 2006: 44–46.

unless we find an Indic parallel to this statement, it would be difficult to determine whether it reflects a genuine Indic conception of Ajātaśatru's experience in hell.

Further, the *Karmavibhaṅga* ("Classification of Acts") uses Ajātaśatru's present life and his next birth to illustrate a type of act that results in an immediate release from hell. The Sanskrit version of the text reads:①

> Among these [i.e., the acts enumerated earlier in the text], what is the act, being affected by which a person passes away immediately upon being reborn in hells?② It is replied:
>
> Someone here [i.e., in this world] has done a deed leading to hell, and has accumulated such a deed. Having done it, he feels distressed, ashamed, repentant,③ and disgusted [by his own deed]. He declares it, confesses it, [and] makes it public. He attains restraint in the future.④

---

① Lévi 1932: 49.14–50.2, §29; Kudō 2004: 84–87 (MS[A]25v3–26r4, MS[B]14v6–15r4): *tatra*[1] *katamat karma yena samanvāgataḥ pudgalo narakeṣūpapannamātra eva cyavati. ucyate.*[2] *ihaikatyena*[3] *nārakīyaṃ karma kṛtam bhavaty upacitaṃ ca.*[4] *sa tat kṛtvāstīryati.*[5] *jihrīyati.*[6] *vigarhati.*[7] *vijugupsati. ācaṣṭe. deśayati. vyaktīkaroti.*[8] *āyatyāṃ saṃvaram āpadyate. na punaḥ kurute.*[9] *sacen*[10] *narakeṣūpapadyate upapannamātra eva*[11] *cyavati. yathā*[12] *rājājātaśatruḥ. tena devadattasahāyenānantaryakarma kṛtam. pitṛvadhaḥ saṃghabhedaḥ dhanapālamokṣaṇam śilāyantramokṣaṇam devadattasyādeśena tasmād avīcinarakagamanaṃ*[13] *śrutvā tena saṃvignena bhagavati cittam prasāditam. śrāmaṇyaphalasūtre 'tyayadeśanaṃ*[14] *kṛtam.*[15] *pratisaṃdadhāti*[16] *kuśalamūlāni. tena maraṇakāle cittam*[17] *prasāditam. asthibhir api*[18] *buddham*[19] *bhagavantaṃ śaraṇaṃ gacchāmi. sa upapannamātra eva cyavati. idaṃ karma yena samanvāgataḥ pudgalo narakeṣūpapannamātra eva*[20] *cyavati.*
1) MS[A] omits *tatra* 2) MS[B] omits *ucyate* 3) MS[A]: *ihaikatyaina* 4) MS[B] omits *ca* 5) MS[A]: *kṛtvā ārttīyati*; MS[B]: *sa taṃ kṛtvā ārttīyati* (on *āstīryati*, see Karashima, Fukita and Kudō 1999: 99–101) 6) MS[A]: *jihrīyate*; MS[B]: *jehrīyati* (ibid.: 101–103) 7) MS[A] omits *vigarhati*; MS[B]: *vitarati* (Lévi 1932: 49 n.4) or *vibharati* (Kudō 2004: 85) 8) MS[B]: *vyantīkaroti* 9) MS[B]: *kurate* (scribal error) 10) MS[A]: *sa*; MS[B]: *sacet* 11) MS[A] omits *eva* 12) MS[A] adds *sa* 13) MS[A]: *devadattasyāvījigamanaṃ* instead of *devadattasyādeśena tasmād avīcinarakagamanaṃ* 14) MS[A]: °*deśanā* 15) MS[A] omits *kṛtam* 16) MS[A]: *pratisandadhāni* (scribal error) 17) MS[A]: *citta* 18) MS[A]: *aṣṭhibhir iti* instead of *asthibhir api* 19) MS[B] omits *buddham* 20) MS[A] omits *eva*
For previous studies, see Lévi 1932: 122–123, §XXIX (French tr.); Namikawa 1984: 60–62; Kudō 2004: 250, Note 22 (annotation); 2009: 141 (Japanese paraphrase). For a parallel in the Tocharian *Karmavibhaṅga*, see Lévi 1933: 86–87 (ed.), 100 (tr.); Sieg 1938: 11–12 (remarks on Lévi's ed.); Pinault 2007: 209–212 (revised ed.).

② I follow Lévi (1932: 122) who translated *samanvāgata* (literally "furnished, endowed") as "affecté".

③ I translate *vitarati* as "he feels repentant." Of the two Sanskrit manuscripts (A&B) on which Lévi's edition is based, MS[B] reads *vitarati* (Lévi 1932: 49 n. 4) or *vibharati* (Kudō 2004: 85), whereas MS[A] omits the word. Based on the Tibetan translation *smod pa* ("to blame"), Lévi (1932: 47 n. 8) gives the reading *vigarhati*. However, according to de Jong (1960: 66), it is unnecessary to change *vitarati* into *vigarhati*, and the Tibetan *smod pa* in fact represents *vijugupsati* (or *jugupsate*). De Jong further points out that the Tibetan translation of the phrase in question, *ngo tsha bar 'dzin la 'gyod cing smod pa* (D 338, *mdo sde*, Sa 282b4 = Lévi 1932: 191.23), indicates **jihrīyati vitarati vijugupsati* (or *jugupsate*), with *'gyod pa* ("to repent") suggesting *vitarati*.

④ Here *saṃvara* ("restraint") may refer to the threefold restraint: *kāyasaṃvara* ("restraint of body"), *vāksaṃvara* ("restraint of speech"), and *manaḥsaṃvara* ("restraint of mind"). On the threefold restraint, see AKBh ad IV.18a (Pradhan 1967: 208.21–22); tr. Funahashi 1987: 137; see also La Vallée Poussin 1923–31: iii. 52 [based on Saeki 1887: 592].

He never commits it again. If he is reborn in hells, immediately upon being reborn, he passes away.

It is just like King Ajātaśatru. In the company of Devadatta, he committed an *ānantarya* crime.① Under the advice of Devadatta, he killed his own father, splitting the monastic community, releasing [the elephant] Dhanapāla [to attack the Buddha], and releasing a rock-device [to kill the Buddha].② Having heard the [fate of] going into the Avīci hell as a result of this [i.e., patricide],③ being terrified, he cultivated a serene and faithful mind (*cittaṃ prasāditaṃ*) toward the Blessed One.④ In the Scripture on the Fruits of the Ascetic Life, he confessed his transgression. He made connection again to the wholesome roots. At the moment of death, he cultivated a serene and faithful mind, thinking, "Even with my bones I go to the Buddha, the Blessed One, for refuge!" Immediately upon being reborn [in hell], he passed away.

Such is the act, being affected by which a person passes away immediately upon being reborn in hells.⑤

The *Karmavibhaṅga* claims that Ajātaśatru not only commits patricide, but also splits the monastic community and casts down a rock to kill the Buddha, whereas a more common Buddhist

---

① Lévi's translation "En compagnie de Devadatta, il avait commis ces péchés capitaux" (1932: 122) appears to be problematic. The text reads *devadattasahāyenānantaryakarma kṛtam*, clearly referring to only one *ānantarya* crime.

② On this entire sentence, see discussion below.

③ According to Kudō (2004: 86–87), MS[B] reads *tasmād avīcinarakagamanaṃ śrutvā*, while MS[A] reads *devadattasyāvījigamaṇaṃ śrutvā* ("having heard Devadatta's going into Avīci"). The Tibetan version (D 338, *mdo sde, sa* 282b6 = Lévi 1932: 191.28) reads: *las des mnar med pa'i sems can dmyal bar 'gro bar thos nas* ("having heard the going into the Avīci hell because of this deed"), which agrees with MS[B].

④ The word *prasādita* is the past passive participle of the causative of *pra-√sad*. The nominalized causative of *pra-√sad* is *prasāda*. Gethin (1992: 112) notes that *pasāda* (Pāli equivalent to Skt. *prasāda*) "conveys at the same time notions of a state of mental composure, serenity, clarity or purity, and trust; it is almost impossible to translate effectively" (cited in Rotman 2009: 66). In Hindu religious contexts, *prasāda* has an entirely different meaning, since it "commonly refers to materials that have been 'tasted' by the gods and returned to devotees for consumption" (Pinkney 2014: 103).

⑤ There is another short account about Ajātaśatru in the Sanskrit *Karmavibhaṅga*, according to which he suffers intense headache due to the lingering effects of the remnant of his bad *karma*. It reads (Lévi 1932: 56.9–10, §XXXII; Kudō 2004: 108–109): *yathā rājājātaśatrur aparipūrṇa* (MS[A], [B]: °*pūrṇṇa*) *eva nairayikāyuḥpramāṇe* (MS[B]: °*yika-m-āyuṣpramāṇe tataś*) *cyutaḥ* | *abandhyatvāt* (MS[A]: °*tvāc ca*) *karmaṇāṃ kadācid atīva śirorujā bhavati* | "It is just like King Ajātaśatru, who died even when his lifespan in hell was not completed. Because his acts were not barren [i.e., still yielding karmic effects], sometimes he felt intense headache"; also tr. in Lévi 1932: 128; Kudō 2009: 141. See the Tibetan counterpart at D 338, Sa 285b5–6; P 1005, Shu 296a8–b1. No parallel is found in Chinese.

story tradition holds that Devadatta alone takes responsibility for the latter two crimes.① This text shows that despite his patricide and his involvement in the attempts on the Buddha's life, Ajātaśatru is almost totally exempted from infernal punishment, insofar as, although he still goes to Avīci, he immediately passes away upon being reborn there. The act (or rather, series of acts) leading to his immediate release from the hell includes his confession of misdeeds, his reconnection to wholesome roots, and his continual cultivation of a pious and serene mind toward the Buddha up to the moment of his death. Thus this text lays emphasis on the efficacy of confession, moral restraint and pious mental status in mitigating the consequences of bad *karma*. Granoff has amply shown that the importance of the moment of death and the deathbed thought in determining one's next birth is widely stressed by Buddhists, Jainas and Hindus alike.② All three Indian religions see the moment of death as "the deciding moment in the salvational history of the individual," ③ and all agree that proper mental states at death are essential in securing a good rebirth. Despite such shared beliefs, Buddhists and Jainas hold different views on whether a positive mindset at the moment of death can substantially reduce the effects of bad *karma*. The present case of Ajātaśatru shows that a positive deathbed mental status can lead to an extreme reduction of one's lifespan in hell, whereas in Jaina tradition such reduction would be impossible.④

The counterpart in the *Las rnam par 'byed pa* (D 338/P 1005), the Tibetan translation of the *Karmavibhaṅga*, curiously incorporates a verse between Ajātaśatru's pre-death statement and the

---

① In examining what kind of individual is qualified to motivate a schism, Silk (2007: 259–260) observes that according to Buddhist legal and scholastic literature, the instigation of a schism "must be brought about by a legitimate, and indeed respected and honorable, member of the community in question", not by a layman, a nun, or any other. Thus, legally speaking, it is impossible for Ajātaśatru to play any direct role in splitting the Buddhist monastic community. The episode that Devadatta hurled down a piece of rock at the Buddha was widely known among Indian Buddhist storytellers (see Mukherjee 1966: 67–70). Apart from the *Karmavibhaṅga*, there seems to be no other Buddhist text claiming Ajātaśatru's role in this episode.

② See Granoff 2007. According to Edgerton (1926–1927), the belief that the moment of death has a decisive importance for the post-mortem fate of the dying person is found not only in Indian religions, but also in Christianity and Judaism. He argues that this belief was originally separated from the doctrine of *karma* (ibid.: 21).

③ Granoff 2007: 73.

④ According to Jaina *karma* theory, the *nāraka-āyus sthiti* (duration of one's lifespan in hell) can never be shorter than ten thousand years, that is, the minimum duration in the first hell (see Umāsvāti's *Tattvārthādhigamasūtra* 3.6 and 4.44 [tr. Jacobi 1906: 311, 324]; Wiley 2003: 351).

concluding sentence. The Tibetan translation reads:[1]

> (...) He accumulated wholesome roots, and at the moment of death, he proclaimed, "Even when I become bones, I go to the Buddha for refuge!" As it is said,
>
> "When one commits extremely terrible crimes,
>
> although they (the crimes) can be diminished through self-reproach, thorough confession and undertaking restraint,
>
> it cannot be said that they totally vanish."
>
> Such is the act, being possessed of which a person passes away immediately upon being reborn in hell.

The verse in question, while admitting the salvific value of self-reproach, confession and moral restraint, stresses that even these positive actions cannot eradicate one's crimes. In the present context, this verse may serve to explain why Ajātaśatru has to fall into hell anyway, even though his lifespan in hell is reduced almost to a blink. I have not identified the textual source of this verse. In any event, we can be sure that the Tibetan version was translated from an Indic recension of the *Karmavibhaṅga* different from the Sanskrit version quoted above (or more precisely, the Sanskrit manuscripts edited by Sylvain Lévi and Noriyuki Kudō).

In two Chinese versions of the *Karmavibhaṅga*, namely, the *Fó wèi shǒujiā zhǎngzhě shuō bàoyè chābié jīng* 佛爲首迦長者説業報差别經 ("Scripture on the Buddha's Explanation of the Differences of Karmic Retributions to the Householder Śuka", T. 80) translated in the Suí 隋 dynasty (581–618), and the *Fēnbié shàn'è bàoyìng jīng* 分别善惡報應經 ("Scripture on Distinguishing the [Karmic] Retributions for Good and Evil", T. 81) translated in the late 10th century, we find the following two passages corresponding to the account quoted above from the Sanskrit *Karmavibhaṅga*:[2]

---

① D 338, *mdo sde*, Sa 282b6–283a1; P 1005, *mdo sna tshogs*, Shu 293a6–8 (see also Lévi 1932: 191.31–37 [cited from Narthang Kanjur 323]): (...) *dge ba'i rtsa ba bsags pa dang tshe 'pho kar rus pa yan cad kyang sangs rgyas la skyabs su mchi'o zhes gsol ba lta bu ste* | *de skad du* | *shin tu* (P: *du*) *mi bzad* (P: *zad*) *las rnams byas pa ni* || *bdag la smod dang rab tu bshags pa dang* || *sdom par byed pas de dag srabs 'gyur gyis* || *shin tu* (P: *du*) *rtsa nas phyin ces mi smra'o* || *zhes gsungs pa lta bu ste* | *las de lta bu dang ldan na gang zag sems can dmyal bar skyes ma thag tu tshe 'pho bar 'gyur ba'o* | Translated into Japanese in Namikawa 1984: 60. The Tibetan version of the **Karmavibhaṅga-nāma-dharmagrantha* only mentions Ajātaśatru's name, without giving details on his actions (D 339, *mdo sde*, Sa 304a6–b2; P 1006, *mdo sna tshogs*, Shu 316a5–7; tr. Feer 1883: 265–266).

② There is no mention of Ajātaśatru in the other four Chinese versions of the *Karmavibhaṅga* (T. 26 [170], T. 78, T. 79, T. 755). On the extant Chinese versions of the *Karmavibhaṅga*, see Lévi 1932: 2–3, 14–19; Kudō 2004: xx.

Passage 1 (from T. 80):[①]

Furthermore, there is an act which can make living beings who fall into hell temporarily enter and immediately get out. Suppose that some living being has committed an action leading to hell. Having done it, he becomes fearful. He gives rise to an ever-increasing faith, and generates a mental state of embarrassment and shame. He loathes and abandons [his misdeed], deeply repenting, and never commits it again. For example, King Ajātaśatru, [due to] his patricide and other crimes, temporarily fell into hell, and was immediately released [from there]. Thereupon the World-Honoured One spoke a verse:

"If a person commits a weighty crime,
having done it, he deeply reproaches himself.
He repents and never commits it again.
This suffices to extirpate his root transgression." [②]

Passage 2 (from T. 81):[③]

Furthermore, what is the act, [being affected by which] a *pudgala* ("person"), upon being reborn in hell, immediately dies? Here [in this world] a *pudgala*, having committed his misdeed [leading to hell], feels repentant, disgusted, and perturbed. He confesses, invalidates, eliminates, and keeps away from [his misdeed], saying, "Mental afflictions are sharp [and thus hurting] like spikes, in which one cannot take pleasure. I shall never commit it again." For example, King Ajātaśatru, having committed the crime of patricide, repented and confessed, "I have done an evil deed. I myself

---

① T. 80 (i) 893c6–13: 復有業能令衆生墮於地獄暫入即出。若有衆生造地獄業，作已怖畏。起增上信，生慙愧心。厭惡棄捨，慇重懺悔，更不重造。如阿闍世王，殺父等罪，暫入地獄，即得解脱。於是，世尊即説偈言："若人造重罪，作已深自責。懺悔更不造，能拔根本業。"

② Here the Chinese 根本业 is most possibly a translation of **mūlāpatti* ("fundamental transgression, cardinal sin"). The *Ākāśagarbhasūtra* ("Scripture on the Womb of Space") cited in Śāntideva's 8th-century *Śikṣasamuccaya* lists five *mūlāpatti*s of a consecrated *kṣatriya* (Bendall 1897–1902: 59.10–60.8; tr. Bendall and Rouse 1922: 61–62). Of the five, the fourth concerns the committing of one of the five *ānantarya* crimes (Bendall 1897–1902: 60.3–6). For a discussion on this Sanskrit passage from the *Ākāśagarbhasūtra*, as well as its Chinese and Tibetan parallels, see Silk 2007: 257–259.

③ T. 81 (i) 898a20–27 (*juan shang*): 復云何業，有補特伽羅地獄中生即便命終？此一補特伽羅作彼業已，悔、嫌、躁擾。説言、撥無、解除、遠離："煩惱鋒利，不可愛樂。我更不作。"如阿闍世王，作殺父罪已，悔過發露："我作惡業，應當自受。"對佛懺悔，解説前非。佛愍彼王，令觀罪性：從緣幻有，了不可得。故此補特伽羅處地獄中，即便命終。The Chinese word 闍 is a misprint of 闍 in the Taishō edition. I thank the late Professor Seishi Karashima for his valuable comments that enabled me to better understand this passage (email 14 November 2016).

should bear the consequences." He expressed remorse before the Buddha, and explained his prior offences. The Buddha took pity upon this king, making him examine the nature of his crimes as follows: they exist as illusions caused by certain conditions, completely beyond mental conception.① Thus this *pudgala* [Ajātaśatru], upon being reborn in hell, immediately dies.

These two Chinese passages focus primarily on the salvific efficacy of repentance and confession. Strikingly, the verse spoken by the Buddha in the Chinese version T. 80 claims that self-reproach, repentance and moral restraint have the power of eradicating one's crimes, thus conveying an idea exactly opposite to what the Tibetan verse discussed above conveys.② It is hard to say to what extent T. 80 and the Tibetan version accurately reflect the contents of their Indic originals, but one thing is clear: their Indic originals were different from the Sanskrit version, which incorporates no verse at all while speaking about Ajātaśatru.

Yet another text that presents Ajātaśatru's immediate release from hell in a non-narrative (or expository) context is the *Tarkajvālā* ("Blaze of Reasoning") written by the 6th-century Indian scholar Bhāviveka (or Bhavya), a prose auto-commentary on his *Madhyamakahṛdaya-kārikā* ("Verses on the Heart of the Middle Way"). In the fourth chapter of the *Tarkajvālā* preserved in the Tibetan translation *Dbu ma'i snying po'i 'grel pa rtog ge 'bar ba* (D 3856/P 5256), Bhāviveka uses Ajātaśatru's experience in hell to argue that even the gravest of crimes can be uprooted without denying the law of *karma*. The text reads:③

---

① Chin. 從緣幻有，了不可得. The expression 不可得 may be a translation of **nopalabhyate* or **anupalabhyamāna* (or its variant), which means "not being perceived [as true and real]" and implies, in the present context, that Ajātaśatru's crimes do not really exist. Steinkellner (1992) notes that in early Buddhist canonical literature the term *anupalabdhi* ("non-perception") does not directly mean non-existence, but only implies non-existence. This Chinese phrase is reminiscent of the story told in the AjKV, which, as Harrison (1993: 153–154) aptly summarizes it, "Mañjuśrī manages to convince Ajātaśatru that since all *dharma*s are empty, wrong actions and the retribution they incur are also empty, and have no power to affect the mind that sees them for what they are." In the present text the Buddha, instead of Mañjuśrī, makes Ajātaśatru realize the empty, illusionary nature of his crimes.

② The Tibetan verse reads (D 338, *mdo sde*, Sa 282b7; P 1005, *mdo sna tshogs*, Shu 293a7 (see also Lévi 1932: 191.32–35): *shin tu* (P: *du*) *mi bzad* (P: *zad*) *las rnams byas pa ni* || *bdag la smod dang rab tu bshags pa dang* || *sdom par byed pas de dag srabs 'gyur gyis* || *shin tu* (P: *du*) *rtsa nas phyin ces mi smra'o* ||.

③ D 3856, *dbu ma*, Dza 185b1–6; P 5256, *dbu ma*, Dza 202a3–b1 (cited in Eckel 2008: 363): *gal te sdig pa shin tu zad par 'gyur ba yin na* |[1] *ci'i phyir sngon gyi las kyi rnam par smin pa*[2] *ni ma gtogs so zhes bstan ce na* | *dmus long dang* |[3] *mig gcig pa dang* | *zha bo dang* | *theng*[4] *po dang* |[5] *lkugs*[6] *pa dang* | *'on pa la sogs pa'i ngo bo nyid du gyur pa'i rgyud 'bras*[7] *bu nye bar longs spyod pa las dgongs nas bstan pa yin te* | *gang gi phyir rnam par smin pa'i gnas skabs kyi ngo bor gyur pa'i las rnams kyi 'bras bu ni yongs su zad par nus pa yod pa ma yin no* || *rgyur gyur pa'i sems pas mngon par 'dus byas pa ni sems pa'i khyad par gzhan thob pa na*[8] *yongs su zad par 'gyur ba yin te* | *ji ltar sor mo'i phreng ba dang* | *ma skyes dgra dang* | *sva ka dang* | *pha*[9] *gsod pa dang* | *mya ngan med pa la sogs pa dag la brten pa bzhin no* || *gal te ma skyes dgra dang* | *ma gsod pa dag la dge ba'i sems pa gzhan skyes pa yod bzhin du ci'i phyir las zad par ma gyur nas mnar med pa dag tu skyes* （转下页）

[Objection:] If evil can be completely eliminated, why is it taught, "not including the ripening of previous action" ?①

[Reply:] This statement refers to the experience of results in the personality-continuum (*rgyud*, **santāna*) of people who are by nature blind, one-eyed, lame, maimed, dumb, deaf and so on, because the results of actions that have the nature of being in the state of ripening cannot be totally eliminated. When an action has been performed with an intention serving as its cause,② if [subsequently] another distinctive intention is attained, [then the aforesaid action] can be totally eliminated, as in the cases of Aṅgulimāla, Ajātaśatru, who killed his own father,③ Aśoka, etc.

[Objection:] If Ajātaśatru and a matricide generated other wholesome intentions, why were they reborn in Avīci, with their [evil] actions not being eliminated?④

[Reply:] It is taught that they were reborn in Avīci and so forth, in order to generate confidence (*yid ches pa*, **sampratyaya*) in action and result (i.e., in the law of *karma*), but it is not the case that their actions were not eliminated without remainder. Just as a silk ball is beaten down⑤ and then bounces up, similarly they were reborn there [in Avīci] and then released. They were not even touched by the row of flames of hell and etc. In this way, while evil becomes uprooted, it is not karmically fruitless.

（接上页）*she na |*[10] *de'i las dang*[11] *'bras bu yid ches pa bskyed pa'i phyir mnar med pa la sogs par skye ba bstan pa yin gyi | las rnams lhag ma ma lus par ma zad pa ni ma yin te | dar gyi pho long brdabs pa las 'phar ba bzhin du der skyes shing thar pa yin la | dmyal ba'i me'i phreng ba la sogs pas kyang reg pa ma yin te | de ltar sdig pa shin tu rtsa ba nas 'byin par yang grub la | las la 'bras bu med pa yang ma yin no ||*

1) P omits *shad* 2) P: par 3) P omits *shad* 4) P: 'theng 5) P omits *shad* 6) P: klug 7) P: 'dras 8) P: ni 9) DP: phag 10) P omits *shad* 11) P adds *shad*

See also a translation in Eckel (2008: 184–185) and a discussion in Jenkins (2011: 320–322). I thank Professor Helmut Tauscher for his valuable comments on my draft translation of this passage (personal communication).

① According to Skilling (1992: 148–149 [cited in Eckel 2008: 184 n. 320]), the Sanskrit original of this quote was probably the stock phrase *varjayitvā paurāṇaṃ karmavipākam*.

② Eckel (2008: 185) translates *rgyur gyur pa'i sems pas* as "by thought that is still in its causal state." However, it seems to me that the text refers to "action after having intended," i.e., bodily or verbal action resulting from intention (*cetanā*). See AKBh ad IV.1c (Pradhan 1967: 192.9): *sūtra uktaṃ dve karmaṇī cetanā karma cetayitvā ce ti | yat tac cetayitvā cetanākṛtaṃ ca tat |* "It is said in the Scripture, 'There are two types of action: intention, and the action after having intended. The action after having intended is that which is produced by intention"; see also La Vallée Poussin 1923–1931: III.1–2; Funahashi 1987: 2.

③ I follow Eckel (2008: 185 n. 322) to emend *phag gsod pa* ("pig-killer") into *pha gsod pa* ("father-killer").

④ Eckel (2008: 185 n. 323) renders *ma gsod pa* as "one who was determined to kill his mother" and suggests that Aṅgulimāla is referred to here. But as far as I am aware, Aṅgulimāla's rebirth in the Avīci hell is not stated anywhere in Buddhist literature. A number of Buddhist sources tell us that he attained arhatship in this life.

⑤ Tib. *brdabs pa*, past tense form of *rdeb pa* ("to strike, to beat"); cf. TSD, vol.6, 2766, s.v. *brdabs pa*.

According to Bhāviveka, the great evils done by Ajātaśatru, the serial-killer Aṅgulimāla, and the cruel king Aśoka, were completely eliminated as a result of their subsequently forming wholesome intentions. As Eckel has pointed out, here Bhāviveka describes the mechanism of conversion, showing that a positive intention (i.e., "another distinctive intention" [*sems pa'i khyad par gzhan*] stated in the passage above) arises and replaces the preceding negative intention.[①] In the case of Ajātaśatru, although he was reborn in Avīci, he was not touched by the flames of hell and thus underwent minimal suffering. Bhāviveka compares Ajātaśatru's descent into and ascent from hell to a silk ball's falling down and bouncing up. This comparison indicates that his stay in hell was extremely brief.[②] The use of the metaphor of a bouncing ball to characterize Ajātaśatru's next birth in hell is also seen in some other Tibetan or Chinese Buddhist texts. For instance, the 6th-century Indian Yogācāra scholar Sthiramati's sub-commentary (**Sūtrālaṃkāravṛttibhāṣya*) on the *Mahāyānāsūtrālaṃkāra* 3.8 speaks of a similar metaphor as follows:[③]

> Furthermore, because of the power of his lineage [i.e., bodhisattva-gotra], even [a bodhisattva] who has committed the five *ānantarya* crimes experiences the suffering of a hell-being only as little [with regard to length] as it takes for a silk ball to bounce back, just like King Ajātaśatru.

In the *Āshěshìwáng wèn wǔnì jīng* 阿闍世王問五逆經 or "Scripture on King Ajātaśatru's Inquiry into the Five Most Heinous Crimes," the Buddha predicts that Ajātaśatru, after finishing this life, "will fall into hell in a way similar to the bounce of a ball." [④] In the *Shǒuhù guójièzhǔ tuóluóní jīng* 守護國界主陀羅尼經 or "Scripture on the Dhāraṇīs for Safeguarding Rulers of States" the

① Eckel 2008: 185 n. 321.

② In some Buddhist texts (for instance, T. 100 [ii] 423c21–23 [*juan* 7], T. 203 [iv] 449a4–7 [*juan* 1]) the metaphor of a bouncing ball, when used to describe one's rebirth in hell or in heaven, serves to indicate the inevitable and immediate nature of such rebirth.

③ D 4034, *sems tsam*, Mi 46b1; P 5531, *sems tsam*, Mi 50b3–4: *de yang dper na rgyal po ma skyes dgra lta bu mtshams med pa lnga byas kyang rigs kyi mthus sems can dmyal ba'i sdug bsngal dar gyi pho long bsdabs* (D: *bsdams*) *pa tsam zhig myong ba lta bu'o* | Quoted also in Eckel (2008: 185 n. 324). Both *bsdams* in the Derge edition and *bsdabs* in the Peking edition seem to be scribal errors, and may be emended to *brdabs*, in light of the reading *dar gyi pho long brdabs pa* in the *Tarkajvālā* (D 3856, Dza 185b5; P 5256, Dza 202a8). The **Sūtrālaṃkāra-vṛttibhāṣya* is a commentary on the *Sūtrālaṃkāravyākhyā*, which, in turn, is a commentary on the *Mahāyāna-sūtrālaṃkāra*. I thank Professor Jowita Kramer for her illuminating comment on this Tibetan sentence (email 22 January 2017).

④ T. 508 (xiv) 776a6: 當墮地獄如拍毱 .

Buddha says to Ajātaśatru:①

> You have created evil *karma*, and are supposed to enter the great Avīci hell to undergo suffering for one *kalpa*. Because you wisely confess [your crime] and repent, you will temporarily enter [the hell] and immediately get out. It is just as a strong man or woman hits a ball with his or her hand, and [the ball] temporarily touches the ground and immediately bounces up. When you finish your life there [i.e., in the Avīci hell], you will be reborn in the Tuṣita Heaven, where you will meet the Compassionate Honourable One [Maitreya] and will receive from him a prophecy [of buddhahood].

This passage gives a vivid picture of the bounce of a ball, and makes it clear that Ajātaśatru's rebirth in hell is a very quick process. Given that both Bhāviveka's *Tarkajvālā* and Sthiramati's **Sūtrālaṃkāravṛttibhāṣya* use the metaphor of a bouncing ball to depict Ajātaśatru's infernal experience, there can be little doubt that such a metaphor is of Indic origin. In the passage cited above from the *Tarkajvālā* Bhāviveka argues that the Buddha, for the sake of generating people's confidence in the law of *karma*, taught that Ajātaśatru was reborn in hell, but that in fact Ajātaśatru's evil *karma* had been totally eliminated. Interestingly, later in the *Tarkajvālā* Bhāviveka makes a similar point when discussing negative karmic results (such as physical injuries and ailments) suffered by the Buddha. There he explains as follows:②

> All these [negative results] are displayed [by the Buddha] with skill-in-means (*thabs la mkhas pa*, **upāyakauśalya*) in order to discipline sentient beings. The Blessed One does not have even the slightest bit of [bad] *karma* ... However, most sentient beings waste③ karmic maturation, and the Tathāgata teaches [that he experiences] karmic maturation in order to teach

① T. 997 (xix) 574c17–20 (*juan* 10): 汝造惡業，合入阿鼻大地獄中一劫受苦。由汝有智發露懺悔，暫入便出。如壯男女以手拍毬，暫時著地，即便騰起。從此命終，生兜率天，見慈氏尊，便得授記。

② D 3856, *dbu ma*, Dza 186b2–3, 6; P 5256, *dbu ma*, Dza 203a7–8, 203b3–5 (quoted in Eckel 2008: 364–65): *'di dag thams cad ni thabs la mkhas pas sems can gdul bar mdzad pa'i phyir bstan pa yin gyi* | *bcom ldan 'das la ni 'phrin* (D: *phrin*) *las kyi cha shin tu phra ba yang mi mnga' ste* | ... | *'on kyang sems can phal cher las kyi rnam par smin pa chud gson* (P: *son*) *pa dang* | *las kyi rnam par smin pa la yid mi ches pa de rnams la las kyi rnam par smin pa bstan par bya ba'i phyir de bzhin gshegs pas phrin las kyi rnam par smin pa bstan te* | See also a translation in Eckel 2008: 187. For karmic explanations of the Buddha's ailments and afflictions in his final life, see Lamotte 1976: 294–298; Strong 2012.

③ Tib. *chud gson pa* literally means "to waste" (Zhang 1985: 815, s.v. *chud gson pa*; Jäschke 1881: 159, s.v. *chud*). Here it may well have the connotation of "to neglect, to be unaware of."

karmic maturation to those who have no confidence in karmic maturation.

Thus in Bhāviveka's view, just as the Buddha's display of his foot being pierced by a thorn should not be taken as an indication that he still has bad *karma*, in a similar way, the Buddha's teaching of Ajātaśatru's rebirth in Avīci should not be taken to mean that Ajātaśatru's bad *karma* has not been eradicated. Rather, both the Buddha's display of physical injuries and his teaching in question are only skill-in-means to convince sentient beings of the law of *karma*.

4. Conclusion

The present paper provides an overview of both narrative and non-narrative sources related to the salvation of the patricidal king Ajātaśatru in Indian Buddhist traditions. In terms of narrative sources, of the five subcycles of stories of the salvation of Ajātaśatru outlined above in Table 1, Subcycles I, IV and V are the most important. In Subcycle I, most versions and adaptations of the *Śrāmaṇyaphalasūtra* (except T. 22 and the story of Ajātaśatru in the "Chapter on Pure Practice" of the Mahāyāna *Mahāparinirvāṇasūtra*) present an overall balanced picture: on the one hand, Ajātaśatru's confession and taking refuge demonstrate the Buddha's personal charisma and the great impact of his teaching; on the other hand, Ajātaśatru's failure to make substantial spiritual progress during his visit to the Buddha as a result of his patricide indicates the inescapability of karmic effects. The situation is rather different in Subcycles IV and V, which respectively comprise prophecies of his pratyekabuddhahood and prophecies of his buddhahood. Through granting ultimate awakening and liberation to this archetypal sinner, Buddhist authors of these prophecies illustrated the temporary nature of karmic obstacles to spiritual growth, the salvific power of the Buddha (or the bodhisattva Mañjuśrī in the case of the AjKV), the efficacy of the Buddhist Dharma, and the overwhelmingly positive nature of Buddhist soteriology. In terms of non-narrative (namely scholastic, expository or argumentative) sources, we have seen that the **Abhidharma-mahāvibhāṣā* (T. 1545), the **Sarvāstivāda-vinaya-vibhāṣā* (T. 1440), the *Karmavibhaṅga*,[①] and two Mahāyāna treatises (the *Tarkajvālā* and **Sūtrālaṃkāravṛttibhāṣya*) all speak, for one reason or another, about the mitigation or elimination of Ajātaśatru's punishment in hell. The fact that the theme of the

① Regarding the sectarian affiliation of the *Karmavibhaṅga*, according to Kudō (2004: ix), the most dominant hypothesis has been that it belongs to the Vātsīputrīyas or, more likely, to the Saṃmitīyas.

salvation of Ajātaśatru recurs in both narrative and non-narrative sources suggests that this theme is arguably important not only for our understanding of Buddhist narrative traditions of this particular character, but also for a better appreciation of the ways in which Indian Buddhist philosophers exploited narrative material for the purpose of scholastic argumentation.

Abbreviations

All references to Pāli texts are to the Pali Text Society editions, using the standard abbreviation system set up in Helmer Smith's "Epilegomena" of CPD, vol. I, 5*–15*.

AjKV **Ajātaśatrukau*kṛtya*vinodana*

AKBh P. Pradhan (ed.), *Abhidharmakośabhāṣya of Vasubandhu*. Patna: K. P. Jayaswal Research Institute, 1967.

Avś J. S. Speyer (ed.), *Avadānaçataka: A Century of Edifying Tales, Belonging to the Hināyāna*. Bibliotheca Buddhica III. St.-Pétersbourg: Commissionnaires de l'Académie Impériale des Sciences, 1902–1909.

B^e Burmese Chaṭṭha Saṅgāyana edition of Pāli texts

BHSD Franklin Edgerton, *Buddhist Hybrid Sanskrit Grammar and Dictionary*, Vol. II: Dictionary. New Haven: Yale University Press, 1953.

CPD V. Trenckner et al. (eds), *A Critical Pāli Dictionary*. Copenhagen: Royal Danish Academy; Bristol: The Pali Text Society, 1924–2011.

D *Bka' 'gyur* (*sde dge par phud*). 103 vols. Buddhist Digital Resource Center, TBRC W22084. Delhi: karmapae chodhey gyalwae sungrab partun khang, 1976–1979.

DĀc Chinese translation of the *Dīrghāgama*

DPPN G. P. Malalasekera (ed.), *Dictionary of Pāli Proper Names*, 2 vols. London: The Pali Text Society, 1937–1938.

EĀc Chinese translation of the *Ekottarikāgama*

MPM *Mahāparinirvāṇa-mahāsūtra*

Mvu Émile Senart (ed.), *Le Mahāvastu*. Societe Asiatique, Collection d'Ouvrages Orientaux, Seconde Série. 3 vols. Paris: L'Imprimerie Nationale, 1882–1897.

P *The Tibetan Tripitaka: Peking Edition–Kept in the Library of the Otani University, Kyoto–Reprinted under the Supervision of the Otani University, Kyoto*. 168 vols. Tokyo–Kyoto: Tibetan Tripitaka Research Institute, 1955–1961.

S *Bka' 'gyur* (*stog pho brang bris ma*). 109 vols. Buddhist Digital Research Center, TBRC W22083. Leh: Smanrtsis shesrig dpemzod, 1975–1980.

SBhV Raniero Gnoli (ed.), *The Gilgit Manuscript of the Saṅghabhedavastu, Being the 17th and Last Section of the Vinaya of the Mūlasarvāstivādins*. 2 Parts. Roma: Is. M. E. O., 1977–1978.

SHT Ernst Waldschmidt et al. (eds.), *Sanskrithandschriften aus den Turfanfunden*, Teil 1–12. Wiesbaden/Stuttgart: Steiner Verlag, 1965–2017.

Skt. Sanskrit

SWTF *Sanskrit-Wörterbuch der buddhistischen Texte aus den Turfan-Funden und der kanonischen Literatur der Sarvāstivāda-Schule*, begonnen von E. Waldschmidt, hg. von H. Bechert, K. Röhrborn, J.-U. Hartmann, Bd. I ff., Göttingen 1973 ff.

T. *Taishō Shinshū Daizōkyō* 大正新脩大蔵経

Tib. Tibetan

tr. translated; translation

TSD J. S. Negi (ed.), Tibetan-Sanskrit Dictionary, 16 vols. Sarnath, Varanasi: Central Institute of Higher Tibetan Studies, 1993–2005.

References

Allon, Mark. 2001. *Three Gāndhārī Ekottarikāgama-Type Sūtras: British Library Kharoṣṭhī Fragments 12 and 14*. Seattle: University of Washington Press.

Bareau, Andre. 1991. "Les agissements de Devadatta selon les chapitres relatifs au schisme dans les divers Vinayapiṭaka." *Bulletin de l'École Française d'Extrême-Orient* 78: 87–132.

Beal, Samuel. 1878. *Texts from the Buddhist canon, commonly known as Dhammapada, with accompanying narratives*. London: Trübner & Co.

Bendall, Cecil. 1897–1902. *Çikshāsamuccaya: A Compendium of Buddhist Teaching Compiled by Çāntideva, Chiefly from Earlier Mahāyāna-sūtras*. St. Petersburg: Imperial Academy of Sciences.

Bendall, Cecil and W. H. D. Rouse (trs.). 1922. *Śikshā-Samuccaya: A Compendium of Buddhist Doctrine*. London: John Murray, Albemarle Street, W.

Brough, John. 1962. *The Gāndhārī Dharmapada*. London: Oxford University Press.

Chimpa, Lama, and Alaka Chattopadhyaya. 1970. *Tāranātha's History of Buddhism in India*. First pubnished in Simla. Reprint: Delhi: Motilal Banarsidass, 1990.

Cone, Margaret. 2020. *A Dictionary of Pāli*, Part III: p–bh. Bristol: Pali Text Society.

Cowell, Edward Byles,et al. 1895–1907. *The Jātaka: Stories of the Buddha's Former Births*. 6 vols. Cambridge: Cambridge University Press.

Das, Sarat Chandra, and Hari Mohan Vidyābhūṣaṇa (and Satis Chandra Vidyābhūṣaṇa). 1888–

1918. *Bodhisattvāvadānakalpalatā*. 2 vols. Calcutta: Baptist Mission Press.

Eckel, Malcolm David. 2008. *Bhāviveka and His Buddhist Opponents*. Cambridge, Massachusetts and London, England: Harvard University Press.

Edgerton, Franklin. 1926–1927. "The Hour of Death: Its Importance for Man's Future Fate in Hindu and Western Religions." *Annals of the Bhandarkar Oriental Research Institute* 8 (3): 219–249.

Feer, Léon. 1879. "Études bouddhiques: le livre des cent légends (*Avadâna-çataka*)." *Journal Asiatique* 14, 273–307.

Feer, Léon. 1883. *Fragments Extraits du Kandjour*. Annales du Musée Guimet 5. Paris: Ernest Leroux.

Feer, Léon (tr.). 1891. *Avadâna-çataka: Cent légendes bouddhiques*. First published in Paris. Reprint: Amsterdam: Oriental Press, 1979.

Feer, Léon. 1892. "L'enfer indien." *Journal Asiatique* 8 (20): 185–232.

Filliozat, Jean. 1941. *Catalogue du fonds sanscrit. Fascicule I–Nos 1 à 165*. Paris: Librairie d'Amérique et d'Orient.

Funahashi Issai 舟橋一哉. 1987. *Kusharon no genten kaimei: gōbon* 倶舎論の原典解明：業品 [A Textual Study of the *Abhidharmakośa*: The Chapter on Karma]. Kyoto: Hōzōkan.

Funayama Tōru 船山徹. 1998. "Mokuren mon kairitsu chū gohyaku kyōjūji no genkei to hensen"『目連問戒律中五百軽重事』の原形と變遷 [The *Mulian wen jielü zhong wubai qingzhongshi*: Its Urtext and the Transformations]. *Tōhō Gakuhō* 东方學報 70: 203–290.

Funayama Tōru 船山徹. 2002. " 'Kanyaku' to 'Chugoku senjutsu' no aida: Kanbun butten ni tokuyū na keitai o megutte."「漢訳」と「中国撰述」の間–漢文仏典に特有な形態をめぐって [Mediating 'Chinese Translations' and 'Chinese Compositions': Regarding Some Figures Special to Chinese Buddhist Literature]. *Bukkyō Shigaku Kenkyū* 仏教史学研究 45 (1): 1–28.

Funayama, Tōru. 船山徹. 2006. "Masquerading as Translation: Examples of Chinese Lectures by Indian Scholar-Monks in the Six Dynasties Period." *Asia Major* 19, no.1–2: 39–55.

Funayama Tōru 船山徹. 2014. *Butten wa dō kan'yakusaretanoka: Sūtora ga kyōten ni naru toki* 仏典はどう漢訳されたのか——スートラが経典になるとき [How Buddhist Scriptures Were Translated into Chinese: Making Sūtras into Classics]. Tokyo: Iwanami Shoten 岩波書店.

Funayama Tōru 船山徹. 2016. '*Da fangbian fo bao'en jing* bianzuan suoyinyong di hanyi jingdian'《大方便佛報恩經》編纂所引用的漢譯經典 [Translated Chinese Scriptures Cited in the Composition of the *Da fangbian fo bao'en jing*]. Translated by Wang Zhaoguo 王招國. *Fojiao wenxian yanjiu* 佛教文獻研究 2: 175–202.

Geiger, Wilhelm (ed.). 1925. *Cūlavaṃsa, Being the More Recent Part of the Mahāvaṃsa*, Vol. I. London: The Pali Text Society.

Geiger, Wilhelm (tr.). 1929. *Cūlavaṃsa, Being the More Recent Part of the Mahāvaṃsa*, Part I. London: The Pali Text Society.

Gethin, Rupert. 1992. *The Buddhist Path to Awakening: A Study of the Bodhi-Pakkhiyā Dhammā*. Leiden: Brill.

Granoff, Phyllis. 2007. "Fasting or Fighting: Dying the Noble Death in Some Indian Religious Texts." In: Phyllis Granoff and Koichi Shinohara (eds.), *Heroes and Saints: The Moment of Death in Cross-cultural Perspectives*. Newcastle, UK: Cambridge Scholars Publishing, 73–100.

Granoff, Phyllis. 2012. "After Sinning: Some Thoughts on Remorse, Responsibility, and the Remedies for Sin in Indian Religious Traditions." In: Phyllis Granoff and Koichi Shinohara (eds.), *Sins and Sinners: Perspectives from Asian Religions*. Leiden: Brill, 175–215.

Habata, Hiromi. 2007. *Die zentralasiatischen Sanskrit-Fragmente des Mahāparinirvāṇa-Mahāsūtra: kritische Ausgabe des Sanskrittextes und seiner tibetischen Übertragung im Vergleich mit den chinesischen Übersetzungen*. Indica et Tibetica 51. Marburg: Indica et Tibetica Verlag.

Hahn, Michael. 1981. "Ajātaśatrvavadāna–A Gopadatta Story from Tibet." In: J. S. Jha (ed.), *K. P. Jayaswal Commemoration Volume*. Patna: K. P. Jayaswal Research Institute, 242–276.

Hahn, Michael. 1992. *Haribhaṭṭa and Gopadatta: Two Authors in the Succession of Āryasūra. On the Rediscovery of Parts of Their Jātakamālās*. Second edition. Tokyo: The International Institute for Buddhist Studies.

Harrison, Paul. 1993. "The Earliest Chinese Translations of Mahāyāna Buddhist Sūtras: Some Notes on the Works of Lokakṣema." *Buddhist Studies Review* 10 (2): 135–177.

Harrison, Paul. 2014. "Earlier Inventories of Sanskrit Manuscripts in Tibet: A Synoptic List of Titles." In: Paul Harrison and Jens-Uwe Hartmann (eds.), *From Birch Bark to Digital Data: Recent Advances in Buddhist Manuscript Research*. Wien: VÖAW, 279–290.

Harrison, Paul, and Jens-Uwe Hartmann. 2000. "Ajātaśatrukaukṛtyavinodanāsūtra." In: Jens Braarvig et al. (eds.), *Manuscripts in the Schøyen Collection: Buddhist Manuscripts, Volume I*. Oslo: Hermes Publishing, 167–216.

Higata Ryūshō 干潟龍祥. 1966. "Memyō no Busshogyō san to sono yoei" 馬鳴の仏所行讃とその余影 [Aśvaghoṣa's Buddhacarita and Its Influence]. In: Kanakura Hakushi Koki Kinen Ronbunshū Kankōkai 金倉博士古稀紀念論文集刊行会 (ed.), *Kanakura hakushi koki kinen: Indogaku Bukkyōgaku ronshū* 金倉博士古稀紀念：印度学仏教学論集. Kyoto: Heirakuji Shoten, 337–357.

Hirakawa Akira 平川彰. 1960. *Ritsuzō no kenkyū* 律蔵の研究 [A Study of the *Vinaya-Piṭaka*]. Tokyo: Sankibō Busshorin.

Hirakawa Akira 平川彰. 1971. "Daijō kyōten ni hattatsu no ajaseō setsuwa" 大乗経典の発達と阿闍世王説話 [The Origins of Mahāyāna Scriptures and the Story of King Ajātaśatru]. *Indogaku Bukkyōgaku Kenkyū* 印度學佛教學研究 [*Journal of Indian and Buddhist Studies*] 20 (1): 1–12.

Honda Megumu. 1968. "Annotated Translation of the Daśabhūmika Sūtra." In: Denis Sinor (ed.), *Studies in South, East and Central Asia: Presented as a Memorial Volume to the Late Professor Raghu Vira*. New Delhi: International Academy of Indian Culture, 115–276.

Jacobi, Hermann. 1906. "Eine Jaina-Dogmatik: Umāsvati's *Tattvārthādhigama Sūtra*." *Zeitschrift der Deutschen Morgenländischen Gesellschaft* 60: 287–325.

Jacobsen, Knut A. 2009. *The Functions of Hell in the Hindu Tradition*. Numen 56 (2/3): 385–400.

Jäschke, H. A. 1881. *A Tibetan-English Dictionary, With Special Reference to the Prevailing Dialects*. Reprint: Delhi: Motilal Bandarsidass Publishers.

Jenkins, Stephen. 2011. "On the auspiciousness of compassionate violence." *Journal of the International Association of Buddhist Studies* 33 (1–2): 299–331.

Johnston, E. H. (ed. and tr.). 1936. *Aśvaghoṣa's Buddhacarita or Acts of the Buddha*. 3 Parts. First published in Lahore. Reprint: Delhi: Motilal Banarsidass, 1984.

de Jong, Jan Willem. 1960. "Vitarati." *Indo-Iranian Journal* 4 (1): 65–67.

de Jong, Jan Willem. 1979. *Textcritical Remarks on the Bodhisattvāvadānakalpalatā (Pallavas 42–108)*. Tokyo: The Reiyukai Library.

Kamitsuka Yoshiko 神塚淑子 et al. (trs.). 2001. *Shinri no uta to monogatari: Hokku hiyukyō gendaigoyaku* 真理の偈と物語：『法句譬喻経』現代語訳 [Stories of Truth and Verses: A Modern Japanese Translation of the *Faju piyu jing*]. 2 vols. Tokyo: Daizō shuppan.

Karashima, Seishi. 2016. "Indian Folk Etymologies and Their Reflections in Chinese Translations–*brāhmaṇa, śramaṇa* and *Vaiśramaṇa*." *Annual Report of the International Research Institute for Advanced Buddhology at Soka University* 19: 101–123.

Karashima Seishi 辛嶋静志, Fukita Takamichi 吹田隆道 and Kudō Noriyuki 工藤順之. 1999. "Mahākarmavibhaṅga to Karmavibhaṅgopadeśa (1): Nepāru kokuritsu komonjo-kan shozō no shahon"「Mahākarmavibhaṅga と Karmavibhaṅgopadeśa (1): ネパール国立古文書館所蔵の写本 [Mahākarmavibhaṅga and Karmavibhaṅopadeśa (1): Two Original Manuscripts preserved in National Archives of Nepal]. *Annual Report of the International Research Institute for Advanced Buddhology at Soka University* 2: 93–128.

Kirfel, Willibald. 1920. *Die Kosmographie der Inder: nach den Quellen dargestellt*. Bonn & Leipzig: Kurt Schroeder.

Kondō Ryūkō 近藤隆晃 (ed.). 1936. *Bonbun daihō kōbutsu kegonkyō jūjibon* 梵文大方廣佛華嚴經十地品: *Daśabhūmīśvaro nāma mahāyānasūtraṃ*. Tokyo: The Daijyō Bukkyō Kenkyū-Kai.

Kudō, Noriyuki. 2004. *The Karmavibhaṅga: Transliterations and Annotations of the Original Sanskrit Manuscripts from Nepal*. Tokyo: The International Research Institute for Advanced Buddhology, Soka University.

Kudō Noriyuki 工藤順之. 2009. "(Mahā-)Karmavibhaṅga shoin kyōtenrui kenkyū nōto (3): Zan'yo no bunken" (Mahā-)Karmavibhaṅga 所引経典類研究ノート (3): 残余の文献 [Philological Notes on the Quotations in the (Mahā-)Karmavibhaṅga (3): Miscellaneous texts]. *Annual Report of the International Research Institute for Advanced Buddhology at Soka University* 12: 123–152.

Lamotte, Étienne. 1944–1980. *Le Traité de la grande Vertu de Sagesse de Nāgārjuna (Mahāprajñāpāramitāśāstra)*. 5 vols. Reprint: Louvain: Université de Louvain, 1970–1981.

Lamotte, Étienne. 1976. *The Teaching of Vimalakīrti*. Translated by Sara Boin. London: The Pali Text Society.

Lamotte, Étienne. 1998. *Śūraṃgamasamādhisūtra: The Concentration of Heroic Progress. An Early Mahayana Buddhist Scripture*. Translated from the French edition of 1965 by Sara Webb-Boin. London: Curzon Press.

La Vallée Poussin, Louis de. 1923–1931. *L'Abhidharmakośa de Vasubandhu*. Paris: Paul Geuthner.

Law, Bimala Charan. 1924. *Designation of Human Types* (*Puggala-Paññatti*). Reprint: London: The Pali Text Society, 1979.

Leumann, Ernst, and Shiraishi Shindō 白石真道. 1952. "Mahāvastu, ein buddhitischer Sanskrittext, übersetzt von Prof. Dr. Ernst Leumann, Albert-Ludwigs-Universitat Freiburg in Baden, in Verbindung mit Sindō Siraishi (Shindō Fujita), Heft I," *Yamanashi Daigaku Geigakubu Kiyō* 山梨大学藝学部紀要 /*Proceedings of the Faculty of Liberal Arts and Education, Yamanashi University* 1: 1–78. Reprinted in: Shiraishi Hisako 白石寿子 (ed.), *Shiraishi Shindō Bukkyōgaku Ronbunshū* 白石真道・仏教学論文集 [The Collected Papers of Shiraishi Shindō]. Sagamihara-shi, Japan: Kyōbi Shuppansha, 1988, 15–78.

Lévi, Sylvain. 1932. *Mahākarmavibhaṅga (La Grande Classification des Actes) et Karmavibhaṅgopadeśa (Discussion sur le Mahākarmavibhaṅga)*. Paris: Ernest Leroux.

Lévi, Sylvain. 1933. *Fragments de textes koutchéens (Udānavarga, Udānastotra, Udānālaṁkāra et Karmavibhaṅga)*. Cahiers de la Société Asiatique 2. Paris: Imprimerie Nationale.

MacQueen, Graeme. 1988. *A Study of the Śrāmaṇyaphala-sūtra*. Wiesbaden: Otto Harrassowitz.

Meisig, Konrad. 1987. *Das Śrāmaṇyaphala-sūtra: Synoptische Übersetzung und Glossar der chinesichen Fassungen verglichen mit dem Sanskrit und Pāli*. Wiesbaden: Otto Harrassowitz.

Mejor, Marek. 1992. *Kṣemendra's Bodhisattvāvadānakalpalatā: Studies and Materials. Studia Philologica Buddhica*. Tokyo: The International Institute for Buddhist Studies.

Mitra, Rājendralāla. 1882. *The Sanskrit Buddhist Literature of Nepal*. Calcutta: Asiatic Society of Bengal.

Mizuno Kōgen 水野弘元. 1981. *Hokkugyō no kenkyū* 法句経の研究 (A Study of the *Dharmapada*). Tokyo: Shunjūsha.

Mochizuki, Ryōkō 望月良晃. 1988. *Daijō Nehangyō no Kenkyū* 大乗涅槃経の研究 [A Study of the Mahāyāna *Mahāparinirvāṇa-sūtra*]. Tokyo: Shunjūsha.

Mukherjee, Biswadeb. 1966. *Die Überlieferung von Devadatta, dem Widersacher des Buddha in den Kanonischen Schriften*. München: J. Kitzinger.

Mus, Paul. 1939. *La Lumière sur les Six Voies: Tableau de la transmigration bouddhique d'après des sources sanskrites, pāli, tibétaines et chinoises en majeure partie inédités*. Paris: Institut d'ethnologie.

Naitō Tatsuo 内藤龍雄. 1955. "Daihōbenbutsu hōongyō nitsuite." 大方便仏報恩経について [On the *Da-fangbian-fo-baoen-jing*]. *Indogaku Bukkyōgaku Kenkyū* 3 (2): 313–315.

Namikawa Takayoshi 並川孝儀. 1984. "Mahākarmavibhaṅga shoin no kyō ritsu ni tsuite" Mahākarmavibhaṅga 所引の経・律について [On the Sūtras and Vinayas Quoted in the Mahākarmavibhaṅga]. *Bukkyō daigaku kenkyū kiyō* 佛教大学研究紀要 68: 53–76.

Obeyesekere, Gananath. 1989. "The Conscience of the Parricide: A Study in Buddhist History." Henry Myers Lecture 1988. *Man* 24 (2): 236–254.

Obeyesekere, Gananath. 1990. *The Work of Culture: Symbolic Transformations in Psychoanalysis and Anthropology*. Chicago: The University of Chicago Press.

Ōkubo, Yusen. 1982. "The Ekottara-āgama Fragments of the Gilgit Manuscript—Romanized Text—." *Bukkyōgaku Seminā* 仏教学セミナー 35: 120 (1)–91(30).

Olivelle, Patrick. 1993. *The Āśrama System: The History and Hermeneutics of a Religious Institution*. New York: Oxford University Press.

Olivelle, Patrick. 2005. *Manu's Code of Law: A Critical Edition and Translation of the Mānava-Dharmaśāstra*. New York: Oxford University Press.

Ōminami Ryūshō 大南龍昇. *Busshogyōsan* 仏所行讃. In *Shin kokuyaku Daizōkyō* 新國訳大蔵経, series 2, *Hon'enbu* 本縁部, vol.1, 125–426. Tokyo: Daizō Shuppan.

Panglung, Jampa Losang. 1981. *Die Erzählstoffe des Mūlasarvāstivāda-vinaya analysiert auf Grund der tibetischen Übersetzung*. Tokyo: The Reiyukai Library.

Pinault, Georges-Jean. 2007. "Concordance des manuscrits tokhariens du fonds Pelliot." In: Melanie Malzahn (ed.), *Instrumenta Tocharica*. Heidelberg: Winter, 163–219.

Pinkney, Andrea Marion. 2007. "*Prasāda*, the Gracious Gift, in Contemporary and Classical South Asia." *Journal of the American Academy of Religion* 81(3): 734–756.

Radich, Michael. 2011. *How Ajātaśatru Was Reformed: The Domestication of "Ajase" and Stories in Buddhist History*. Tokyo: The International Institute for Buddhist Studies.

Radich, Michael. 2015. *The Mahāparinirvāṇa-mahāsūtra and the Emergence of Tathāgatagarbha Doctrine*. Hamburg: Hamburg University Press.

Rahder, Johannes (ed.). 1926. *Daśabhūmikasūtra et Bodhisattvabhūmi: Chapitres Vihāra et Bhūmi*. Paris: Paul Geuthner ; Louvain: J.-B. Istas.

Rotman, Andy. 2009. *Thus Have I Seen: Visualizing Faith in Early Indian Buddhism*. New York: Oxford University Press.

Sadakata Akira 定方晟. 1986. *Ajase no Sukui* 阿闍世のすくい [The Salvation of Ajātaśatru]. Kyoto: Jinbun shoin.

Sadakata Akira. 1989. *Ajase no Satori* 阿闍世のさとり [The Awakening of Ajātaśatru]. Kyoto: Jinbun shoin.

Sadakata, Akira. 1997. *Buddhist Cosmology: Philosophy and Origins*. Translated from the Japanese edition 須弥山と極楽：仏教の宇宙観 [*Mt. Sumeru and Paradise*: Buddhist Cosmology] by Gaynor Sekimori. Tokyo: Kōsei Publishing Co.

Saeki Kyokuga 佐伯旭雅. 1887. *Kandō abidatsumakusharon* 冠導阿毘達摩俱舎論. 3 vols. continuous pagination. Reprint: Kyoto: Hōzōkan, 1978.

Schaik, Sam van, and Imre Galambos. 2011. *Manuscripts and Travellers: The Sino-Tibetan Documents of a Tenth-Century Buddhist Pilgrim*. Berlin & Boston: Walter de Gruyter.

Schiefner, Antonius. 1868. *Târanâthae de doctrinae Buddhicae in India propagatione narratio. Contextum tibeticum e codicibus petropolitanis*. Petropoli: Academiae scientiarum Petropolitanae.

Shimoda Masahiro 下田正弘. 1997. *Nehangyō no kenkyū: daijō kyōten no kenkyū hōhō shiron* 涅槃経の研究：大乗経典の研究方法試論 [A Study of the *Mahāparinirvāṇa-sūtra*, with a Focus on the Methodology of the Study of Mahāyāna Scriptures]. Tokyo: Shunjūsha.

Sieg, Emil. 1938. "Die Kutschischen Karmavibhaṅga-Texte der Bibliothèque Nationale in Paris (zu Prof. Sylvain Lévi's Ausgabe und Übersetzung)." *Zeitschrift für Vergleichende Sprachforschung* 65: 1–54.

Silk, Jonathan A. 2007. “Good and Evil in Indian Buddhism: The Five Sins of Immediate Retribution.” *Journal of Indian Philosophy* 35 (3): 253–286.

Silk, Jonathan A. 2009. *Riven by Lust: Incest and Schism in Indian Buddhist Legend and Historiography*. Honolulu: University of Hawai‘i Press.

Skilling, Peter. 1992. “The Rakṣā Literature of the Śrāvakayāna.” *Journal of the Pali Text Society* 16: 110–182.

Steinkellner, Ernst. 1992. “Lamotte and the concept of anupalabdhi.” *Asiatischen Studien/ Études asiatiques* 46: 398–410.

Strauch, Ingo. 2010. “More Missing Pieces of Early Pure Land Buddhism: New Evidence for Akṣobhya and Abhirati in an Early Mahayana Sutra from Gandhāra.” *The Eastern Buddhist* 41(1): 24–66.

Strong, John S. 1992. *The Legend and Cult of Upagupta: Sanskrit Buddhism in North India and Southeast Asia*. Princeton, NJ: Princeton University Press.

Strong, John S. 2012. “Explicating the Buddha’s Final Illness in the Context of his Other Ailments: the Making and Unmaking of some *Jātaka* Tales.” *Buddhist Studies Review* 29 (1): 17–33.

Tanabe Kazuko 田辺和子 (tr.). 2000. *Hokku hiyukyō* 法句譬喩経. Shin kokuyaku daizōkyō, Indo-senjutsu, Hon’en-bu 5 新国訳大蔵経・インド撰述部・本縁部 5. Tokyo: Daizō shuppan.

Tournier, Vincent. 2017. *La formation du Mahāvastu et la mise en place des conceptions relatives à la carrière du bodhisattva*. Paris: École française d’Extrême-Orient.

Tripāṭhī, Chandrabhal. 1995. *Ekottarāgama-Fragmente der Gilgit-Handschrift*. Reibek: Dr. Inge Wezler Verlag für Orientalistische Fachpublikationen.

Vaidya, P. L. 1959. *Avadāna-Kalpalatā of Kṣemendra*. 2 vols. Darbhanga: The Mithila Institute.

Wiley, Kristi L. 2003. “The Story of King Śreṇika: Binding and Modifications of *Āyu Karma*.” In: Olle Qvarnström (ed.), *Jainism and Early Buddhism: Essays in Honor of Padmanabh S. Jaini*. Fremont: Asian Humanities Press, 337–358.

Willemen, Charles (tr.). 2009. *Buddhacarita: In Praise of Buddha’s Acts*. Berkeley, California: Numata Center for Buddhist Translation and Research.

Wu, Juan. 2014. “Violence, Virtue and Spiritual Liberation: A Preliminary Survey of Buddhist and Jaina Stories of Future Rebirths of Śreṇika Bimbisāra and Kūṇika Ajātaśatru.” *Religions of South Asia* 8(2): 149–179.

Wu, Juan. 2016. “The Rootless Faith of Ajātaśatru and Its Explanations in the **Abhidharma-mahāvibhāṣā*.” *Indo-Iranian Journal* 59/2, 101–38.

Wu, Juan. 2019. "The Buddhist salvation of Ajātaśatru and the Jaina non-salvation of Kūṇika." *Bulletin of the School of Oriental and African Studies* 82 (1): 85–110.

Yamaguchi Susumu 山口益, and Funahashi Issai 舟橋一哉. 1955. *Kusharon no genten kaimei: Sekenbon* 倶舎論の原典解明：世間品 [A Textual Study of the *Abhidharmakośa*: The Chapter on Cosmology]. Kyoto: Hōzōkan.

Yamamoto Kōshō(tr.). 1973–1975. *The Mahāyāna Mahāparinirvāṇa-Sūtra*: A Complete Translation from the Classical Chinese in 3 Volumes, Annotated and with Full Glossary, Index and Concordance. Ube: Karinbunko.

Yao, Fumi 八尾史. 2013. *Konponsetsuissaiuburitsu yakuji* 根本説一切有部律薬事 [The *Bhaiṣajyavastu* of the Mūlasarvāstivāda *Vinaya* (annotated Japanese translation)]. Tokyo: Rengō shuppan.

Zhang Yisun 張怡蓀 et al. (eds.). 1985. *Bod Rgya tshig mdzod chen mo/Zanghan da cidian* 藏漢大辭典 (The Great Tibetan-Chinese Dictionary). Beijing: Minzu chubanshe.

Zhang, Tieshan, and Peter Zieme. 2013. "A Further Fragment of Old Uigur Annals." *Acta Orientalia Academiae Scientiarum Hungaricae* 66 (4): 397–410.

Zieme, Peter. 2014. "Collecting of the Buddhist Scriptures: Notes on Old Uigur 'annals'." *Annual Report of the International Research Institute for Advanced Buddhology at Soka University* 17: 401–422.

Retrieving the *Oral-Tradition Gems*

Iain Sinclair
The University of Queensland

Thirty-seven verses quoted by *paṇḍita* Vanaratna (1384–1468) in the course of his teaching tours in Xizang have been transmitted as an anthology with the abbreviated title *Chain of Essential Oral-Tradition Gems* (*Zhal lung rin po che'i snying po'i phreng ba, Mukhāgamaratnasārāvalī*). This anthology was compiled by Vanaratna's translator, Bsod nams rgya mtsho (1424–1482), on the *paṇḍita*'s third and last visit to Xizang, which ended in the year 1454. The *Gems* have since been propagated as a Sanskrit–Tibetan bitext in printings of the Tibetan *Bstan 'gyur*. There has been no study of this anthology as yet, apart from passing references to it in accounts and studies of Vanaratna's life. The aim of this paper is to retrieve, for the first time, a coherent Sanskrit text from the *dbu can* transliterations in the *Gems*. The quotations' sources are traced here, where possible, and the process of their transmission, translation and arrangement in an anthology is exposed in some detail. Thirty verses have been located in the known Sanskrit corpus. The most prominent voices are the luminaries of Vajrayoginī praxis going back to Śabarapāda and Advayavajra. Non-tantric Buddhist scriptures and authors are also quoted. On the whole, the *Gems* display strong connections with the Buddhist world of the 15th-century Kathmandu Valley, where Vanaratna spent most of his later life.

1. The *paṇḍita*, the anthology and its compiler

Vanaratna, the last Buddhist *paṇḍita* to travel from the Indo-Gangetic plain to the Himalayas, needs little introduction. Thanks to Vanaratna's fruitful encounters with his Tibetan coreligionists, his life is one of the best documented of any Buddhist born on the subcontinent in the early second millennium. A full chapter of the *Deb ther sngon po* of Gzhon nu dpal (1392–1481), completed in 1476, is devoted to Vanaratna, and became widely read in the West via *The Blue Annals*, the 1949 translation published by George Nikolas de Roerich (1902–1960). While Tibetan hagiographic writing on Vanaratna has enjoyed sustained attention (Ehrhard 2002; Parajuli 2014; Damron 2021), the *paṇḍita*'s own works — which form a vital part of the picture of late South Asian Buddhism — have barely been noticed. The pressing need to learn more about the state of Buddhism at this point in history provides one incentive for retrieving the "oral-tradition gems" in the form that they were known to Vanaratna.

The anthology of quotations conveyed by Vanaratna is given the full title *Grub pa'i dbang phyug paṇḍi ta chen po shrī ba na ratna'i zhal lung rin po che'i snying po'i phreng ba* (*Siddheśvaramahāpaṇḍitaśrīvanaratnamukhāgamaratnasārāvalī*) in Tibetan catalogues. It is provisionally translated here as *Chain of Essential Oral-Tradition Gems of the Glorious Vanaratna, the Great Pundit and Lord of Adepts*.[①] The title harks back to the anthology's closing remarks, which liken Vanaratna to a *rin po che* and describe him as the foremost scholar of Jambūdvīpa. A Sanskrit-Tibetan bitext of the anthology has been transmitted in various printings of the *Bstan 'gyur*: Pe cin (Q), Snar thang (N) and Dpe bsdur ma (A), among others, but not the Sde dge (D) printing. The bilingual format of the text is shared with a number of other texts in the *Bstan 'gyur*. Remarks on various works transmitted in this format were offered by Michael Hahn (1987: 51–52), but there is as yet no complete inventory of such bitexts. More continue to be discovered in manuscript; the *Amṛtasiddhi* (Schaeffer 2005) and *Āmnāyamañjarī* (Tanaka 2017) bilingual codices are two important recent finds. Besides the bitext of the *Oral-Tradition Gems*, there is another recension that contains just the Tibetan translation, and which is noticed only in passing here. The various witnesses are discussed further in this paper's textual criticism section.

One of the remarkable features of the *Gems* is the fact that its circumstances of compilation are known in some detail, unlike so much of what was written in the Sanskritic Buddhist world. A biography of the compiler, Bsod nams rgya mtsho, records that he often heard Vanaratna recite

---

① In this study, *sāra* is construed as an adjective qualifying *ratna* with the meaning "vital," "essential". At one point, however, before the *āvalī* element had been added, *sāra* meant "essence" in the sense of a selective anthology; an earlier title is reported to have been *Zhal lung rin po che'i snying po dam pa'i cho*[*s*] (cf. Damron 2021: 116)–which is also awkward to Sanskritise. The artificial title *Xīdì zìzàizhě dà bāndǐdá jíxiáng Línbǎo shī kǒuchuán xīnsuǐ bǎo mán* 悉地自在者大班抵達吉祥林寶師口傳心髓寶鬘 is given in the Chinese appendix (Hànwén shǔ mùlù 漢文屬目録) to the Pe cin *Bstan 'gyur*, Q, according to Otani 1965: 1024. This title transposes the elements *rin po che* (寶) and *snying po* (心髓): *Chain of Gems of Quintessence of Oral Tradition*.

certain verses to other cognoscenti on tour in Xizang, or when the *mahāpaṇḍita* was resting. These verses are said to have been translated by Bsod nams rgya mtsho on the spot, and were later compiled into the present anthology after Vanaratna left Xizang for the last time. So we are told in a passage of the *Thams cad mkhyen pa lo tsā ba chen po'i rnam par thar pa Ngo mtshar rgya mtsho* located and translated by Ryan Damron (2021: xxxii). The verses of the *Gems* do represent an oral tradition, but not an exclusively oral one; the present study will show that most of the verses are transmitted in other texts, and that some of them appear to have been conveyed to the compiler in writing.

2. The contents of the *Oral-Tradition Gems*

The *Oral-Tradition Gems* bring together quotations from a variety of authorities who are prominent in the post-Indian, Himalayan Buddhist faithspace. Common topics of interest in this milieu are covered: the nature of existence; the self and the mind; causality; emptiness; the virtues of the guru who liberates from rebirth. These quotations are sourced from tracts on tantric yoga, treatises of Mādhyamika and Yogācāra orientation, and anthologies of Mahāyānasūtras. The sources are not always correctly identified in the *Gems*, and some of these misidentifications may reflect an oral mode of transmission, as I argue in the philological commentary on verses 18, 24 and 30, among others. In the words of the compiler, the anthology offers "the essence of sūtra and mantra teaching" (*mdo sngags kyi bstan pa'i snying po*).

The anthology does not include a word from the conservative scriptural tradition that Vanaratna is understood to have encountered during his six years of study in Sri Lanka, which concluded in 1412. While it may be that Vanaratna's Tibetan associates in general sought to downplay his schooling in Thera institutions (Damron 2021: 19, 41), Sanskritic Buddhism — which Vanaratna had adopted before reaching the Himalayas — has no room for the competing and incompatible authority claims of the Pāli *āgama*s. The discourse captured in the *Oral-Tradition Gems* is, as its very title indicates, a testament of a living, immediate spirituality, one that holds out the promise of rapid liberation — an antithesis of "early" Buddhism, so called. Although Vanaratna has been characterised as belonging to "the esoteric-ritualistic, or Tantric, strand of" Buddhism, in the words of Martin Delhey (2021: 379), this anthology makes clear that Vanaratna was concerned with the entirety of Buddhist discourse as it then existed in the religion's heartland, even if only a tiny fraction of this discourse is conveyed in the *Oral-Tradition Gems*.

The largest share of the *Gems* belongs to the Vajrayoginī praxis tradition descended from Advayavajra. This *paṇḍitāvadhūta* is quoted most often (vv. 10, 11, 16, 30). Two verses are ascribed to Advayavajra's guru Śabarapāda (vv. 19, 36), and two to Saraha (w. 2, 12). The *Marmakalikā* commentary on the *Tattvajñānasaṃsiddhi* (a work on Vajrayoginī composed by Advayavajra's Nepalese student Śūnyasamādhivajrapāda) supplies two verses (vv. 21, 23). Other luminaries quoted in the *Gems* represent a potpourri of tantric religiosity. There are verses from pseudo-Āryadeva (vv. 13, 24), Daüḍīpā (v. 29), Kāṇeripā (v. 31), and Raviśrī's Kālacakra-oriented *Amṛtakaṇikā* commentary (v. 18). A stanza by Saraha (v. 12) and the well-known vajra song of the *Hevajratantra* (vv. 25–28′) are conveyed in the original Apabhraṃśa. These quotations are presented without stating their affiliation to particular praxis traditions or objects of worship, apart from the vajra song, which is credited by name to the *Hevajratantra*.

A smaller portion of the anthology is sourced from non-tantric Buddhism. One half-verse is taken from the *Niraupamyastava* of Nāgārjuna (v. 15cd), and one full verse from Candrakīrti's *Madhyamakāvatāra* (v. 18). Two verses of Mahāyāna scripture are quoted via Candrakīrti (v. 32) and Nāgārjuna the anthologist (v. 15). Kambalapāda's *Ālokamālā*, from which two verses are quoted (vv. 6, 17), is a work of the Yogācāra, albeit one that had strong appeal to tantric Buddhists. Three quotations in the *Gems* are the work of the poet Bhartṛhari, who is often identified as a non-Buddhist, yet in these verses Bhartṛhari expresses a feeling of resignation or dispassion (*vairāgya*) that is closely aligned with Buddhist sentiments. Certain verses ascribed to Nāgabodhi (v. 14), Nāgārjuna (v. 20), Virūpākṣa (v. 32) and others (vv. 5, 8, 33) have not yet been located in other sources. The first verse in the anthology is said to have been composed in honour of Vanaratna by his Indian acquaintance Āditya (v. 1). This verse cannot, however, be located in Āditya's extant *saptaka* eulogy dedicated to Vanaratna. Additional details on the various sources of the *Oral-Tradition Gems* are given in a concordance accompanying the text edition, and the attributions of quotations taken from them are discussed further in the philological commentary section.

3. Reflections of the *Gems* in Nepalese manuscripts

Most of the quotations compiled in the *Oral-Tradition Gems* are preserved in the Nepalese Sanskrit corpus. Some of the source texts have, moreover, been preserved only in Nepal, such as Daüḍīpā's *Guhyāvalī* (v. 29) and Kāṇeripā's *Śucikaraṇa* (v. 31). These works were not translated into Tibetan. Vanaratna also had access to texts besides those circulating in the Kathmandu Valley.

At least two identifiable works quoted in the *Gems* are not available in the Nepalese corpus: the *Sūtrasamuccaya* attributed to Nāgārjuna (v. 15) and Candrakīrti's *Madhyamakāvatāra* (v. 9). Sanskrit witnesses of both works have now been found in the present-day Xizang Autonomous Region of China. The *Gems*' quotation from the *Madhyamakāvatāra* could have been sourced from a Sanskrit manuscript currently stored at the Potala Palace in Lhasa; the text of this quotation hardly varies from that of the manuscript studied by Li Xuezhu (李學竹). It has also been found that Vanaratna had to draw on local Sanskrit manuscript libraries while teaching in Xizang, China.① There is the additional possibility that the *Gems* include verses from texts that Vanaratna had acquired in India, as he is known to have had manuscripts copied there (Damron 2021: 62–64).

The strands of teaching gathered in the *Oral-Tradition Gems* are then grounded for the most part, though not entirely, in the 15th-century manuscript corpus of Nepal. The Nepalese corpus offers prospects for establishing the textual traditions of the *Gems*' verses and for diagnosing problems in their transmission. One possible case of a misreading of a manuscript kept in Nepal is discussed in the philological commentary on verse 2. But in seeking to identify possible lines of descent into the *Gems*' exemplars, it should also be acknowledged that textual transmission also flowed in the other direction, namely, from Vanaratna into Nepal. Nepalese manuscripts associated with Vanaratna and his circle have been attracting more scholarly attention. Chief among them is the "Vanaratna codex" (Royal Asiatic Society MS Hodgson 35, Cowell & Eggeling 1876: 26–27) formerly kept in Nepal, which was scribed by the *mahāpaṇḍita* himself (Damron 2021: 189–90; Delhey 2021: 385 n. 26). The first text in the codex is the *Amṛtakaṇikā*, the commentary that supplies two verses of the *Gems* (vv. 18, 19) and was copied by Vanaratna's Nepalese students.② This codex further includes texts translated by Vanaratna from spoken and written Tibetan into Sanskrit — probably in Xizang

① Of the twenty-odd texts taught by Vanaratna at rTses thang in Xizang, according to the list compiled by Damron (2021: 176), only the *Ḍākinīvajrapañjara*, the *Sekoddeśa* commentary by *Bodhivajra, and the *Mañjuśrīnāmasaṃgīti* commentary by *Amoghadeva (Don yod lha) have not yet been located in the Nepalese manuscript corpus. This list also contains confirmed or probable sources of the Gems: the *Amṛtakaṇikā* (vv. 18, 19), the *Prasannapadā* (v. 7?), a *dohā* collection (v. 12?) and Advayavajra's *amanasikāra* works (vv. 10, 11, 16ab, 30).

② A manuscript of the *Amṛtakaṇikā*, MS NGMPP B 24/23, was copied by two of Vanaratna's Newar disciples, Rūparāja and Ravicandra. It is described by Damron (2021: 124 n. 106), with reference to Lal (1994: 110 MS *ka*), as undated. It is in fact dated to year 600 (of the Nepal era), corresponding to 1480 CE — about twelve years after Vanaratna's passing: *abde vyomaviyat ṣaḍānanayute kṛṣṇe sacaitre phālguṇe*. This statement of the date of copying was, moreover, rephrased by the anonymous 20th-century copyist of its apograph, MS NGMPP B 103/14, as follows: *naipālīyasamvat 600 mite likhitān prācīnatāḍapatrapustakāl likhitam*. Ravicandra is mentioned elsewhere in the Nepalese corpus as having participated in the copying of MS NGMPP A 936/11 (cf. Damron *ibid.*), which has been noticed by Pandey (1989: 7–28) under the artificial title **Sādhanavidhāna Bauddhagranthasaṃgraha*. Its contents include a rare copy of Śabarapāda's *Vajrayoginīsādhana*, the opening part of the *Guhyāvalī* and other esoterica reflected in the *Gems*.

itself, according to Damron (2021: 212–213). Of greater interest here are the overlooked Nepalese anthologies that show commonalities with the sources and themes of the *Gems*.

3.1 A codex containing the Tattvajñānasaṃsiddhi, 1454 CE

A hitherto unstudied manuscript that is contemporaneous with Vanaratna and gives special attention to a verse included in the *Gems* is a codex of Vajrayoginī-related texts, MS University of Tokyo 149 (Matsunami 1965: 63). The first part of this codex was copied soon after Vanaratna had returned to Nepal, in late 1454 (*samvat 575 poṣamāse*). The codex begins with an exposition of the opening verse of the *Marmakalikā*, verse 23 of the *Gems*. Each word in the verse is glossed with terse Sanskrit expressions. (A transcript is given in the philological commentary.) The commentator uses very simple constructions, as though trying to reach a typical Newar audience that knows little if any Sanskrit. Expositions of this type are rarely seen in Nepalese manuscripts. This unusual, unpolished short text appears to record an oral commentary, and the Sanskrit-speaking expert on the Vajrayoginī system best known in Nepal at the time was Vanaratna.

After the exposition of *Marmakalikā* 1.1, the codex goes on to give the full text of the *Tattvajñānasaṃsiddhi*, followed by a series of unattributed and decontextualised verses from tantric texts including the *Hevajra*, Advayavajra's *Mahāyānaviṃśikā* (and probably also his *Pañcatathāgatamudrāvivaraṇa*), and a couple of Kālacakra verses.① These texts overlap with the small set of sources for the *Oral-Tradition Gems*. These verses continue right after the *Tattvajñānasaṃsiddhi* as part of the same scribal campaign and were presumably meant to facilitate the study of that text. Following this is the *Marmakalikā* commentary on the *Tattvajñānasaṃsiddhi*. The whole codex is a manifest product of a literate Newar Vajrayoginī praxis tradition of the mid-15th century. Its selection of material is in many cases similar to that of the *Gems*; it can be suspected to have been written down by someone close to Vanaratna.

3.2 The Tantraślokasaṃgraha of Jīvaharṣa, c. 1474 CE

Another Nepalese text that resonates with Vanaratna's oeuvre and the *Gems* is a unique anthology of quotations, the *Tantraślokasaṃgraha* compiled by Jīvaharṣa. This anthology is witnessed

① The correspondences are as follows: MS University of Tokyo 149 ff. 8r6–9r1 ≡ *Samvarodayatantra* vv. 33.16–23 and 33.5–7ab; f. 9r1–4: unidentified (presumably also from the *Samvarodayatantra*); f. 9r4–7 ≡ *Hevajratantra* vv. II.2.40–42; f. 9r7–8: unidentified; f. 9r8–9 ≡ *Hevajratantra* v. II 2.51; f. 9v1 ≡ *Pañcatathāgatamudrāvivaraṇa* 4+ (ex *Vajraśekhara*, cf. ed. Mathes 2015: 374), also quoted in other works; f. 9v2 ≡ Advayavajra's *Mahāyānaviṃśikā* v. 7; f. 9v2–3: *Hevajratantra* I.1.12; f. 9v3–5 ≡ *Sekoddeśa* 157–158, most likely via Raviśrījñāna's *Guṇabharaṇī* (cf. ed. Sferra 2000: 114).

in MS Royal Asiatic Society Hodgson 52 (Cowell & Eggeling 1876: 40), which is undated but written in a hand typical of the 15th or 16th century. Its compiler was active in Kathmandu around the year 1474, judging from a reference to a person of the same name occurring in that year.① He was then old enough to have known Vanaratna or at least the Nepalese students of his who were still alive then. The *Tantraślokasaṃgraha* displays similarities not only in the selection of sources, but also in the choice of literary form. Like the *Gems*, it is an unusual collection of quotations of tantric and non-tantric Buddhist *āgama* and *śāstra*, in which each quotation is followed by an attribution.

The *Tantraślokasaṃgraha* draws its 154 numbered verses from a variety of works. Some are quoted by name, others are quoted anonymously. The anthology shares some sources with the *Oral-Tradition Gems*: the *Hevajratantra*, the *Svādhiṣṭhānaprabheda* of pseudo-Āryadeva (*Gems* v. 54 ≡ *Tantraślokasaṃgraha* v. 117) and the *Niraupamyastava* (*Gems* v. 18 ≡ *Tantraślokasaṃgraha* v. 120). Some of its quotations are taken from other works of authors quoted in the *Gems* — for instance, from Advayavajra (his *Pañcākāra* 2 ≡ *Tantraślokasaṃgraha* v. 89) and from Śabarapāda (an unattributed verse of his *Vajrayoginīsādhana*② ≡ *Tantraślokasaṃgraha* v. 63). Jīvaharṣa draws on the *Amṛtasiddhi*③ of Virūpākṣa, another author who is quoted by name in the *Gems* (v. 32). The compiler often quotes the *Hevajratantra* and some of its commentaries as well as Kālacakra texts (vv. 32, 36, 37, 135 etc.). The works that interest the compiler are again more closely aligned with Vanaratna's teaching than with the mainstream of medieval Newar Buddhism.

While a few verses of the *Tantraślokasaṃgraha* are shared with the *Gems*, there is little other overlap between the two anthologies, which is remarkable given that so much source material is shared between them. Another striking coincidence is that both anthologies quote Bhartṛhari, who is a virtual unknown in Newar Buddhist circles (although his work was being copied in 15th-century

---

① The compilation concludes as follows: *iti tantraślokasaṃgraha samāpta || kṛtir iyaṃ vajragurujivaharkhena saṃgraha iti* (*sic*, MS Royal Asiatic Society Hodgson collection 52 f. 13v6). Cowell & Eggeling *ibid.* read *-jinaharkhena*, although the MS reads -जिव- (*sic*). The title *vajraguru* is unusual and is not necessarily equivalent to *vajrācārya*. A person of the same name is mentioned in MS India Office Library 7820 (Sarvajñamitra's *Sragdharāstotra*), copied "for the monk" (*śākyabhikṣu*) "śrī Jīvaharshapāla, son of the wife Kusumalakshmīmayī of the monk Harsharājapāla" on "Wednesday, the twelfth day of the dark fortnight of the month Caitra, under the *Uttara-Bhadra nakshatra*, in Nepal *saṃvat* 594 or 597" (Keith & Thomas 1935: 1427). Only the former year resolves to a date on a Wednesday, that is, April 13, 1474.

② The verse *aguhye jāyate vighnaṃ siddhihānis tathaiva ca | nānārogavyādhiś caiva · jāyate †ṇarkaḥ† raurave ||* (*sic*, MS Royal Asiatic Society 62 ff. 6v7–7v1) corresponds to verse 9cd–10ab of the currently unpublished *Vajrayoginīsādhana* of Śabarapāda.

③ *Amṛtasiddhi* ed. Satapathy 2018: 37, 83, vv. 87, 201 ≡ *Tantraślokasaṃgraha* vv. 23, 107. Both quotations are attributed to the *Amṛtasiddhiyoga*, the same title as Satapathy's MS.

Nepal; see e.g. MSS NGMPP A 1027/11, C 4/5). His name is given in the *Tantraślokasaṃgraha* with a misspelling similar to that of the *Gems*.[1] The many unusual commonalities shared by Jīvaharṣa's anthology and Bsod rnams rgya mtsho's anthology point to Jīvaharṣa having been acquainted with Vanaratna's teaching tradition in some way. It is possible that he had access to the *Oral-Tradition Gems* in some form, although no copies have surfaced in Kathmandu Valley to date.

3.3 The tantric Buddhist Subhāṣitasaṃgraha, c. 1400s

The undated, anonymously compiled *Subhāṣitasaṃgraha* anthology of tantric and Mādhyamika-Yogācāra teaching first edited by Cecil Bendall has several sources in common with the *Oral-Tradition Gems*. Among them are Kambalapāda's *Alokamālā*, Daüḍīpāda's *Guhyāvalī* and the *Hevajratantra*. Both anthologies draw on the sixth chapter of Candrakīrti's *Madhyamakāvatāra*, which was hardly noticed by other late tantric commentators whose works are preserved in Sanskrit (cf. Li 2015: 1–2). Both anthologies include several verses in Apabhraṃśa. There are other unusual commonalities: Saraha, who is inaccurately credited in the *Gems* as the speaker of v. 2, is likewise inaccurately credited as the speaker of at least two verses in the *Subhāṣitasaṃgraha* (cf. ed. Bendall 1905: 21 n. 2). The arbitrary assignment of otherwise unattributed verses to Saraha was not a widespread convention and leaves the impression that the two anthologies were conceived under similar circumstances, if not by the same person. The witness of the *Subhāṣitasaṃgraha* copied for Bendall was "written on palm-leaf in an archaic form of Bengali writing, probably about the XVth century" (Bendall *ibid.*). This would be an apt description of Vanaratna's handwriting, although the copyist of this palmleaf MS is named as an otherwise unidentified Vidyāpatidatta at Vaḍa-grāma. The circumstances of the *Subhāṣitasaṃgraha*'s compilation and its connections with Vanaratna's *oeuvre* warrant further investigation.

4. The reception and transmission of the *Gems*

The Tibetan translations of individual verses in the *Oral-Tradition Gems* are almost all new. The originality of these translations lends support to the anthology's self-presentation as a record

---

① *Tantraślokasaṃgraha* v. 104, corresponding loosely to one of Bhartṛhari's epigrams (ed. Kosambi 1948: 204 v. 838), is attributed to *bharathalī satake*. *Gems* v. 34 (Bhartṛhari's *Vairāgyaśataka* 2) is ascribed to *bhartha ha ri*.

of "oral tradition" that was rendered into Tibetan as soon as it was heard. Most of the Tibetan translations in the *Gems* differ substantially from other translations of the same verses transmitted in the *Bstan 'gyur*. Only in the case of one sūtra quotation transmitted in Candrakīrti's *Prasannapadā* (v. 7) does Bsod rnams rgya mtsho give a translation that follows the canonical translations word for word. Here he might have remembered or recognised the verse from a previous encounter with it in a Tibetan monastic curriculum.①

4.1 Indications of written transmission at the source

It is also evident that many of the quotations in the *Gems* were transmitted through the mediation of writing at or near the point of origin, and as such are not "oral-tradition gems" proper. The fact that the compiler worked with source material in an Indic writing system is clear from the many errors in the *dbu med* transliterations caused by misreadings of an exemplar written in an Eastern Indian or Nepalese script. There are several cases of glyphs marked with *virāma* being incorrectly copied as glyphs with subscribed *r*. For example, in v. 3a, the word *sragvī* was miscopied as *sra gra bī* (witnesses A and N), misreading *g-virāma* as *gra* (i.e. ག྄ as གྲ). In v. 23a, the *Gems*' exemplar must have had *viracayan̦* (ན྄) *līnaḥ for viracayaṃl līnaḥ*, i.e. with *n-virāma* before the word break (cf. MS Matsunami 149 f. 1v4), as the former word was conveyed as *bi ra tsa ya nra* (ནྲ) in blockprint Q. In v. 13c the word *yat* has been correctly transcribed with *t-virāma* (*t*, ཏ྄ using Tib. *halant*) in Q, but incorrectly as *tra* (ཏྲ , using Tib. *r-btags*) in A. Other examples of this confusion occur in vv. 5a and 8b. We also find confusions of *la* with *na* (v. 9a) and *lya* ལྱ with *lpa* ལྤ (vv. 2c, 16d, 18c). Errors of this kind would not have originated in misheard speech; they are miscopyings. Cases of stylised small-*m* word final (ཾ) being read as *visarga* (◌ཿ) and vice versa are numerous (vv. 9d, 16d, 32d, 33d, 37b). All such errors come out of transmission in the medium of an Indic writing system.

Another artefact of written transmission is the rare *upadhmānīya*-prefixed ligature *ḫpha* (ཧྥ) standing for *ṣpha* in vv. 4c (N and Q) and 34b. This glyph results from hypercorrection by a scribe or a blockprint carver, not a misrepresentation of a spoken syllable. It was hypercorrected again to *nypha* (ཉྥ) in printing A. Furthermore, in *Gems* vv. 5a, 7d and 19b there are instances of Tib. *paluta* (྅), which corresponds to *avagraha*. While *avagraha* marks can of course be used in transcribing speech into writing, *avagraha*s are not used consistently in the Sanskrit portions of the *Gems*. Their

① The verse that is ascribed to the otherwise unavailable *Anavataptahradāpasaṃkramaṇasūtra* in Candrakīrti's *Prasannapadā* (*Gems* v.7) also occurs in Kamalaśīla's *Madhyamakāloka* (D 3887), the *Madhyamakāvatārabhāṣya* (D 3862) and the *Catuḥśatakaṭīkā* (D 3865), among others.

few occurrences appear to result from arbitrary scribal intervention or from the scribe drawing on different textual sources.

The quality of translation varies throughout the anthology. A few examples will be highlighted here; more discussion takes place in the philological commentary section. In *Gems* v. 2a, drawn from Munidatta's *Caryāgītikośa* commentary, the Tibetan translation reads **vicitrayati* (*rnam par bkra bar*) instead of *viracayati*. In v. 2d, the term *savinayam*, which qualifies the act of prostration, is understood by the translator literally as an act of discipline (*dul bar byas pa'i*), whereas the parallel translation of this verse in D 2293 grasps the appropriate sense: "well-behaved" (*gus par*). The phrase *ca indriyabalāni* in *Gems* v. 18b, taken from the *Amṛtakaṇikā*, was read as **uccendriyabalāni* (Tib. *mtho dbang po'i stobs*) in the Tib. *Gems*. Then in v. 18d the phrase *aharahaḥ* is translated *a la la* (**aho aho*), whereas the parallel in the Tibetan translation of the *Amṛtakaṇikā* (D 1395) reads *nyin bzhin 'bab 'gyur*, corresponding to *ahar-ahar*. In *Gems* v. 19a, the translation of *tadubhayī nāpy anubhayī* as *de dag skye 'jig pa'ang ma yin pa* seems to have instead understood *tadudayī nāpi*. The shakiness of the *Gems*' translation in such cases leads to doubt about whether Vanaratna was always consulted on the translation, and adds to the indications that Bsod rnams rgya mtsho worked on some of the verses alone, using written exemplars.

5. Editorial policy and procedure

The present edition aims to restore the text to the state in which it was known to its compiler. This effort to recover the "compiler's text" does not, however, necessarily entail the removal of all obvious problems, given that the compiler cannot be ruled out as a source of some of these problems. The Tibetan translation in some cases rests on flawed understandings of a Sanskrit text which itself contains flaws. The bitextual mode of transmission makes the cause of many of these flaws unusually clear, as can be seen from the examples given in the previous section. Editorial policy therefore focuses on rectifying accidental errors, such as the transposition of two syllables, as well as errors of *sandhi* and metre, while readings that are supported by the translation are accepted wherever they can be. This approach is balanced with the need to instil coherence and to preserve as much of the received textual tradition as possible.

One type of error that pervades the transcriptions in the blockprints — the loss of vowel-lengthening marks (Tib. *chung*) due to insufficient separation between lines — is recorded in the apparatus only if there are other problems with the lemma. The reader is alerted to discussions in the philological commentary by the use of asterisks, and wavy underlines draw attention to doubtful passages.

5.1 Witnesses for the Gems

The Qianlong printing of the *Oral-Tradition Gems* (Otani 1965: 1024 No. 5096, siglum Q) forms the base text of the Sanskrit edition. The Sanskrit readings of the Snar thang printing (vol. 89, fols. 399–412, No. 3885, siglum N), which are often better than those of the Qianlong printing, are also collated. The Dpe bsdur ma printing (Vol. 48 *rgyud* No. 2852, pp.696–708, siglum A) provides the base text for the Tibetan verses and its Sanskrit readings are collated. The Gser bris ma printing is partly illegible and was not collated. All of these printings were consulted between August 2021 and May 2022 in the form of digital scans, of varying quality, distributed online by the Buddhist Digital Resource Center (library.bdrc.io). Tibetan textual parallels cited throughout this study have been sourced from digital e-texts originating with the Asian Classics Input Project (asianclassics.org) unless stated otherwise. References to folio numbers of Tibetan blockprints are not accompanied by line references, which are now largely redundant for locating canonical passages in this era of widespread digitization.

The textual criticism of the *Mukhāgamaratnasārāvalī* presented below includes a work-in-progress edition of the Sanskrit verses, followed by philological commentary, a list of Tibetan words and their Sanskrit or Apabhramśa referents, and an English translation of the verses. There should be no expectation of a definitive treatment at this time, given that a number of the quotations remain unidentified. It should be noted that the Tibetan part of the bitext, and the prose introductions in particular, have not been as rigorously edited as the Sanskrit text. Variants in the stand-alone Tibetan translation of the *Gems* (*Zhal lung rin po che'i phreng ba*, Q 5099, N 3888, A *rgyud* 2853), which lacks the Sanskrit verse transcriptions, have been collated only opportunistically.

5.2 On the English translation

The English translation gives priority to the edited Sanskrit text over the associated Tibetan translations. However, the authorial attributions of verses added to the Tibetan text are carried over into the English translation, even where these attributions are doubtful, in order to show how the verses were presented to their Tibetan audience. It is not easy to translate a collection of verses assembled from such a miscellany of sources in a consistent and fluid way, but translation ought to be attempted in any serious labour of textual criticism.

The Tibetan translations of the verses often differ substantially from the Sanskrit. The lexical data appended to the edition lays out these differences systematically. The Tibetan sentences composed by the compiler to introduce each verse provide insights into how the anthology was organised, but they have little philological value and are not translated here. An English translation of the complete Tibetan text represents a project in its own right. The door is then left open for the Tibetan *Oral-Tradition Gems* to be translated in full in further work on the anthology and its place in the Tibetosphere.

I thank Dr Sabine Klein-Schwind (S. K-S. in the notes) and Dr D. Templeman for helpful remarks on my earlier draft editions and translations of selected verses of the *Gems*, while I take responsibility for all errors. I also thank the symposium organisers for the opportunity to put this work in progress before learned colleagues at Tsinghua University. Their feedback has been incorporated into the present version of the paper. I dedicate this chapter to the memory of Tschen Yin-Koh (陳寅恪), the subject of the symposium at which these findings were presented, and who, like Vanaratna, travelled to distant places in search of learning at a time when he had no opportunity to study Sanskrit in his homeland.

6. Textual criticism

Abbreviations

A	Dpe bsdur ma printing of the Tibetan Tripiṭaka
D	Derge (Sde dge) printing of the Tibetan Tripiṭaka
Gems	*Mukhāgamaratnasārāvalī*
MS	manuscript
N	Narthang (Snar thang) printing of the Tibetan Tripiṭaka
NGMPP	Nepal-German Manuscript Preservation Project
Q	Qianlong (Pe cin) printing of the Tibetan Tripiṭaka
Skt.	Sanskrit
T	Taishō (SAT 大蔵経 2015) edition of the Chinese Tripiṭaka
Tib.	Tibetan
*	discussion in the notes or introduction
	virāma mark
conj.	conjecture
corr.	correction

ed. edition

em. emendation

om. omits

6.1 Concordance of identified authors and works

	AUTHOR (Tib. *Gems*)		IDENTIFIED AUTHOR	IDENTIFIED WORK
1)	mi'i nyi ma	*Maṇuṣyasūrya	Āditya	**untraced**
2)	klu sgrub zhabs la sha ba ra dbang phyug	*Nāgārjunapāda–Śabareśvara	Sarahapāda	via Munidatta's *Caryāgītikośavṛtti* on Lūyīpādagīta 1
3)	paṇḍita bhartṛ ha ri	Bhartṛhari	Bhartṛhari (attr.)	Bhartṛhari's epigrams
4)	'phrog byed don 'dzin	*Bhartṛhari	Bhartṛhari	*Vairāgyaśataka* 39
5)	kho dpon la springs pa zhal		**untraced**	
6)	la ba pa'i *snang ba'i phreng ba*	Kambala's *Ālokamālā*	Kambalapāda	*Ālokamālā* 274
7)	zhes pa mdo las	**iti sūtre*	via Candrakīrti	via *Prasannapadā* 212
8)	la ba'i na bza' can	*Kambalāmbara	**untraced**	
9)	dpal ldan zla ba	*Śrīcandra	Candrakīrti	*Madhyamakāvatāra* 6.107
10)	a dwa ya badzra	Advayavajra	Advayavajra	*Yuganaddhaprakāśa* 7
11)	me tri'i zhabs	Maitrīpāda	Advayavajra	*Pañcatathāgatamudrāvivaraṇa* 1
12)	sa ra ha'i zhabs	Sarahapāda	Sarahapāda	*Dohā* (Sarahapādīya) II.9
13)	klu sgrub kyi zhal snga nas	*Nāgārjuna	pseudo-Āryadeva	*Svādhiṣṭhānaprabheda* 59
14)	nāga bo dhi	Nāgabodhi	*āgama*	via Munidatta's **Caryāgītikośavṛtti* on Bhusukupādagīta 2
15)	ārya klu'i zhabs	*Āryanāgārjuna	via Nāgārjuna (Samuccayakāra)	via *Sūtrasamuccaya* 8 (ex *Vīradattaparipṛcchā*)
16)	klu grub kyi zhal snga nas	*Nāgārjuna	Advayavajra & Nāgārjuna	*Mahāyānaviṃśikā* 8ab + *Niraupamyastava* 15cd

(Continued)

	AUTHOR (Tib. *Gems*)		IDENTIFIED AUTHOR	IDENTIFIED WORK
17)	la ba pa'i zhabs	*Kambalapāda	Kambalapāda	*Ālokamālā* 128
18)	dauḍi pra bandha	Daüḍi	*ukta*	via *Amṛtakaṇikā* on *Nāmasaṃgīti* 9.6
19)	ri khrod zhabs	*Śabarapāda	*gurūpadeśakrama*	via *Amṛtakaṇikā* on *Nāmasaṃgīti* 4.1
20)	'phags pa klu'i zhabs	*Āryanāgārjuna	**untraced**	
21)	brtson 'grus dpal bshes gnyen	Vīryaśrīmitra	Vīryaśrīmitra	*Marmakalikā* on *Tattvajñānasaṃsiddhi* 2.1
22)	dzā landha ri pa	Jālandharipā	via Jālandharipāda	via *Vajrapradīpā* 22
23)	birya shrī mi tra	Vīryaśrīmitra	Vīryaśrīmitra	*Marmakalikā* 1
24)	ārya de ba	Āryadeva	pseudo-Āryadeva	*Svādhiṣṭhānaprabheda* 40abc+45d
25)	*rdo rje'i rgyud kyi rgyal po*	**Hevajratantrarāja*		*Hevajratantra* II 4.6
26)	"	"		" 4.7ab
27)	"	"		" 4.7cd
28)	"	"		" 4.8ab
28′)	"	"		" 4.8cd
29)	ḍau di pra bandha	Daüḍī-prabandha	Daüḍīpāda	*Guhyāvalī* 7
30)	*zung 'jug gsal ba*	**Yuganaddhaprakāśa*	Advayavajra	*Tattvaprakāśa* 6–7ab
31)	zhal byung ngo	**mukhodgata*	Kāṇeripā	*Śucikaraṇa* 31
32)	bi ru pākṣa	Virūpākṣa	**untraced**	
33)	zhal byung nyid do	**mukhodgata*	**untraced**	
34)	bhartha ha ri	Bhartṛhari	Bhartṛhari	*Vairāgyaśataka* 2
35)	*mdza' mo'i bu'i rtogs pa brjod pa*	*Avadāna of Mdza' mo'i bu*	**untraced** (35abc), *Pañcatantraka* Aparīkṣitakāraka 22 (35d)	
36)	sha ba rā sya	Śabara	via Śāntarakṣita	via *Tattvasiddhi et al.*
37)	slob dpon chen po dpa' bo	*Mahācārya-Śūra	**Dharmadāsa**	*Vidagdhamukhamaṇḍana* 1

6.2 Sanskrit metres

Anuṣṭubh (*śloka*) vv. 8, 10, 14, 16, 20, 22, 24, 30, 31, 32, 35, 36

Ārdrā v. 9

Indravajrā vv. 6, 11, 13, 15

Upajāti vv. 7(?), 21

Ṛddhi v. 33

Vaṃśastha v. 5

Vasantatilakā vv. 2, 37

Śārdūlavikrīḍita vv. 4, 18, 23, 29, 34

Śikhariṇī v. 3, 17, 19

undetermined metre v. 1

6.3 Edition of the Mukhāgamaratnasārāvalī bitext

Siddheśvaramahāpaṇḍitaśrīvanaratnamukhāgamaratnasārāvalī

(*Grub pa'i dbang phyug paṇḍi ta chen po shrī Ba na ratna'i zhal lung rin po che'i snying po'i phreng ba*)

§ /rgya gar shar phyogs Sadna ga ra'i mkhas pa chen po/ mchog grub pa'i dbang phyug shrī Ba na ratna'i zhal gyi lung/ ched du gdams pa kha 'thor[1] ba dang bcas pa gnas skabs gang yang rung ba rnams su thos pa la/

1). pratyakṣavītarāgaṃ[2] prakṣālitaṃ bhavajakalmāṣakalaṅkam[3] |
bhajata janā bhavaśāntyai[4] bhaktyā Vanaratnamahāsthaviram[5] ||

/srid par skye ba'i nyon mongs rnyog pa rnams/
/rab tu bkrus las mngon sum chags bral ba/
/gnas brtan chen po Nags kyi rin chen la/

① 'thor Q mthor A*rgyud*2853

② vītarāgaṃ em. bī ta ra gaṃ ANQ

③ prakṣālitaṃ bhavajakalmāṣakalaṅkam em. pra kṣha ni ta bha wa dza ka lma kha ka lāṃ kaṃ ANQ -prakṣālitabhavajaṃ kleśakalaṅkaṃ ed. Damron 2021: 54 n.31

④ bhavaśāntyai corr. bhavaśantyai ed. Damron 2021: 54 n.31 bha wa sha ntyai ANQ

⑤ bhaktyā vanaratnamahāsthaviram corr. (cf. parallel, Hahn 1996: 36) bha ktya ba na ra tna ma ho stha bi raḥ NQ bha ktya ba na ra tna ho stha bi raḥ A

/srid pa zhi byed skye bos gus bsten kye/

/paṇḍi ta chen po Mi'i nyi mas ched du brjod pa'o// 1 //

je dang por thun mong ma yin pa'i bshes gnyen bsten tshul la gdams pa/

2). yā sā saṃsāracakraṃ viracayati manaḥsaṃniyogārthahetoḥ①*

sā dhīr yasya② prasādād viśati③ nijabhuvaṃ svāmino niṣprapañcam④ |

tac ca pratyātmavedyaṃ⑤ samudayati sukhaṃ kalpanājālamuktaṃ⑥

kuryāt* tasyāṅghripadmaṃ⑦ śirasi savinayaṃ sadguroḥ⑧sarvakālam⑨||

/yid ni don la mngon par zhen pa'i rgyu las 'khor ba'i

'khor lo rnam par bkra bar byed pa'i blo/

/gang yin de ni rje bo gang gi drin las

spros pa med pa'i rang gi sa la rab tu 'jug/

/de yang rtog⑩ pa'i dra ba las grol yang dag

bde bar 'char ba⑪ so so rang gis rig bya ba/

/bla ma dam pa de yi zhabs kyi padmar dul bar

byas pa'i mgo bos rtag tu phyag bgyi'o/

Klu sgrub zhabs la Sha ba ra dbang phyug gis so// 2 //

de nas mi rtag pa nyid kyis nges par 'byung ba'i gnas la gdams pa'i phyir/

---

① manaḥsaṃniyogārthahetoḥ em. (Tib. yid ni don la mngon par zhen pa'i rgyu las) manaḥ-sanniyoga-ātma-hetoḥ (parallel, Kværne 1977: 71) ma naḥ sa nni pe shā rṣha he toḥ ANQ

② sā dhī rya sya NQ sī dhā rya sya A sā dhīr yasyāḥ (parallel Kværne 1977: 71) dhīryasya (parallel, Sen 1977: 5)

③ viśati em. (parallel Kværne 1977: 71; Tib. rab tu 'jug) dhi sha ti Q ddhi sha ti AN diśati (parallel, Sen 1977: 5)

④ niṣprapañcaṃ corr. ni nypra pa nytsaṃ AN ni kpra pa nytsāṃ Q

⑤ tac ca pratyātmavedyaṃ corr. ta tsa pra tyā tma be dyaṃ AQ ta tsa pra tyā po dya N

⑥ kalpanajālamuktaṃ corr. (parallel, Kværne 1977: 71) ka lya na dzā la mu ktaṃ AQ ka lya na dzā lya na dzā la mu ktaṃ N kalpanāmalamuktaṃ (parallel Sen 1977: 5)

⑦ ta syā ngghri pa dmaṃ QN (Tib. de yi zhabs kyi padmar) tasya aṃhri-yugmaṃ (parallels, Kværne 1977: 71; Sen 1977: 5)

⑧ sa dgu roḥ NA sa dgu reḥ Q

⑨ sarvakālam em. (S. K-S.) sa rbba kā laḥ QNA

⑩ rtog QN tshog A

⑪ ba QN ta ba A

3). yathā sragvī tūryair① janaparivṛto* vadhyapuruṣaṃ②
prayad vadhyasthānaṃ③* nipatati viṣāde④ pratipadam |
evaṃ* he⑤ bhogasthā divasadivasair mṛtyunikaṭaṃ⑥
vrajanto⑦ mā yūyaṃ bhavata vibhavair⑧ dṛptamanasaḥ⑨ ||

/gsad bya'i skyes bu me tog thod can rol mo
dang ldan skye bo mang pos yongs bskor ba/
/gsod pa'i gnas su 'gro bzhin pa ni
gom pa re res nyam ngar ltung ba ji lta bar/
/longs spyod gnas bcas rnams kye 'di ltar
nyin re nyin res 'chi ba la ni nges btsun te/
/mngon par chas pa khyed rnams longs spyod dag
gis yid la khengs pa 'byung bar 'gyur ba ci/
/paṇḍi ta Bhartṛhari'i gzhung las so// 3 //

ma brtags pa'i bsod nyams kyi chags pa dag las khyad par du yid 'byung bar bya ba la gdams pa/

4). āyur varṣaśataṃ nṛṇāṃ⑩ parimitaṃ rātrau tadardhaṃ⑪ gataṃ
tasyārdhasya parasya cārdham⑫ aparaṃ bālatvavṛddhatvayoḥ |
śeṣaṃ vyādhiviyogaduḥkhasahitaṃ⑬ sevādibhir nīyate⑭*

---

① sragvī tūryair em. (parallel, Kosambi 1948: 182) sra gra bī tū rye AN sra gra gi tu rye Q
② janaparivṛto vadhyapuruṣaṃ em. (Tib. gsad bya'i skyes bu; parallel, Kosambi 1948: 182) ba hu dza na pa ri vṛ to ba ddhya pu ru ṣhaṃ NQ ba ddha pu ru ṣhaṃ A
③ prayad vadhyasthānaṃ em. mra yā nwā ddhya sthā naṃ N mra yā nrā ddhya sthā naṃ Q mra yā nwā sthā A
④ bi ṣhā de AN bi ṣhā di Q
⑤ evaṃ he ANQ (Tib. kye 'di ltar) tathā he (parallel, Kosambi 1948: 182)
⑥ -divasair mṛtyunikaṭaṃ corr. di ba sai rmṛ rtu ni kā ṭaṃ N di ba sau rmṛ rtu ni kā ṭaṃ Q sa di ba sor ma rdu ni kā ṭaṃ A
⑦ vrajanto corr. prajanto ANQ
⑧ vibhavair em. (parallel, Kosambi 1948: 182) bi bha bhai r- N bha bai r- AQ
⑨ dṛpta- em. (parallel, Kosambi 1948: 182; Tib. yid la khengs pa) tṛpta- ANQ
⑩ varṣaśataṃ nṛṇāṃ corr. ba ṣha śsha t nnṛ ṇāṃ N ba rṣha śa t-i nnra ṇāṃ AQ
⑪ tadardhaṃ corr. ta ta rdhaṃ NQ ta rdhaṃ A
⑫ parasya cārdham em. (parallel, Kosambi 1948: 80) dha dā rdha ma rdha m- Q rddha sya dha da rddha m- N dā rdha ma rdha m- A
⑬ vyādhiviyoga- corr. (parallel, Kosambi 1948: 80) byā dzhi bi yo ga N byā dzhi bi yo ga yo ga AQ
⑭ sevādibhir nīyate em. (parallel, Kosambi 1948: 80) se bā ni ḫpha lā NQ se bā ni nyphe lā A

jīve vāritaraṅgacañcalatare saukhyaṃ kutaḥ prāṇinām[1] ||

/mi rnams tshe tshad lo brgya nyid na'ang

mtshan mo rnams kyis de'i phyed song/

/de yi[2] phyed ni byis pa nyid de

gzhan phyed rgan po nyid kyis 'das/

/lhag ma phrad dang 'bral ba'i sdug bsngal

nad bcas re* ba 'bras bu med/

/srog ni chu yi rlabs[3] ltar g.yo ba[4]

mi rnams ci phyir shin tu bde/

/'phrog byed don 'dzin gyi gzhung[5] las so// 4 //

de ltar shes pa las bde bar gshegs pa'i brtan pa bdud rtsi lta bu la brten par gdams pa/

5). yathā ghṛtārthe[6] puruṣo 'bhimanthanād

jalaṃ[7] samāpnoti ghṛtaṃ na kaś canam[8] |

asau gataṃ* mārgam apīha[9] sevayan

naras tathā naiva vimuktibhāg bhavet[10] ||

/ji ltar su yang rung ba'i skyes bu mar don gnyer ba yis/

/chu ni mngon par bsrubs kyang mar rnyed 'gyur ba ma yin pa/

/de bzhin bde bar gshegs pa'i lam 'di la yang mi bsten[11] pa'i/

/mi yis rnam par grol ba rnyed par 'gyur ba ma yin nyid/

kho dpon la springs pa zhal las so// 5 //

---

① prāṇinām corr. (parallel, Kosambi 1948: 80) prā ṇi nāḥ ANQ
② de yi QN de'i *Argyud*2853
③ rlabs QN brlabs *Argyud*2853
④ ba QN na *Argyud*2853
⑤ gzhung A gzhud Q
⑥ ghṛtārthe corr. ghṛ tā rthi ANQ
⑦ 'bhimanthanād jalaṃ em. `bhi ma na tha yra na dza la d- NQ `bhi mra na tha ya nra dza lad- A
⑧ kaś canam conj. ka shtsa na ANQ
⑨ apīha corr. a pi ha ANQ
⑩ bhavet corr. bha beḥ NQ -hra beḥ A
⑪ bsten pa'i em. (cf. Skt. sevayat) brten pa'i ANQ

thun mong ma yin pa'i phyi nang gi khyad par bstan pa las rnam par grol ba'i bstan pa'i snying po la gdams pa/

6). sarvaḥ samānaḥ pravibhajyamānaḥ①*
sūkṣmekṣikākṣāmadhiyā kṛtāntaḥ② |
bauddhasya bāhyasya vibhāgakartā③
na syād ihaikā yadi śūnyatoktiḥ④ ||

/sangs rgyas pa dang mu stegs kun nas mtshungs snyam⑤ du/
/rnam dbye byed po med las gal te 'dir dbye ba/
/chen po'i blo dang ldan pas zhib mor mthong ba gang/
/mthar thug pa ni stong nyid gcig pur gsungs pa'o/
/La ba pa'i *Snang ba'i phreng ba* las so// 6 //

de lta bas na/

7). yaḥ pratyayair⑥ jāyati sa hy⑦ ajāto
na tasya utpāda⑧ svabhāvato 'sti |
yaḥ pratyayādhīna⑨ sa śūnya ukto⑩
yaḥ śūnyatāṃ jānati so 'pramattaḥ ||

/gang zhig rkyen las skyes pa de ma skyes/

---

① sarvaḥ samānaḥ pravibhajyamānaḥ em. (parallel, Śāśanī 2017: 187)　sa rbba sa mā na pra bi bha dzṛ ma naḥ NQ　sa rbba sa mda na pra bh-i dzra ma naḥ A

② sūkṣmekṣikākṣāmadhiyā kṛtāntaḥ em. (parallel, Lindtner 1985: 214)　sū kṣhmi kṣhi kā kṣhya ma dhi yaṃ kṛ ta nta AN　sū kṣhmi kī kā kṣhya m dhi yaṃ kṛ ta nta Q　sūkṣmekṣikākṣāmadhiyāṃ kṛtāntaḥ (Śāśanī 2017: 187)

③ bauddhasya bāhyasya vibhāgakartā em. (parallel, Lindtner 1985: 214)　bau ddha sya bi bha ga rttā N　bau ddha sya ba hmā sya bi bha ga ka rttī Q　bau ddha sya bi hmā sya bi bha ga ka rtti A　bauddhasya bāhyasya vibhāgakartrī (parallel, Śāśanī 2017: 187)

④ śūnyatoktiḥ (parallel, Lindtner 1985: 214)　shū nya to kti ANQ

⑤ snyam Q　nyams A*rgyud*2853

⑥ pratyayair em. (parallel, la Valleé Poussin 1913: 239)　pra tyai r- ANQ

⑦ sa hy NQ　sa dy- A

⑧ u tpā da N　u tpā ta A　u tpā Q　utpādu (parallel, la Valleé Poussin 1913: 239)

⑨ pratyayādhīna corr.　pra tya yā dzhī na ANQ

⑩ śūnya ukto corr. (parallel, la Valleé Poussin 1913: 239)　sū nya taṃ u kte ANQ

/de la[1] skye ba rang bzhin yod ma yin/
/rkyen la rag las gang de'ang stong par bshad/
/gang zhig stong nyid shes de bag yod pa'o/
/zhes pa mdo las so// 7 //

stong pa nyid de yang nam mkha'i me tog dang mo sham gyi bu lta bu gtan med nyid can gyi dgag pa ni ma yin no zhes gdams pa/

8). notpādo[2] bhāvarūpeṇa nānutpādaḥ khapuṣpavat[3] |
anutpādasvabhāvena utpādaḥ śūnyatā[4] matā ||

/ngo bo nyid kyis dngos skye med/
/mkha'i me tog bzhin pa skyes min/
/skye ba med pa'i rang bzhin gyis/
/skye ba stong par bzhed pa yin/
La ba'i na bza' can gyis so// 8 //

de'i phyir/

9). na tattvataś[5] cet khalu[6] santi bhāvās
teṣām asattvaṃ[7] vyavahārato 'pi |
syād eva vandhyātanayasya yadvat
svabhāvataḥ sattvam ato 'sti teṣām[8] ||
/dngos po rnams kyi de kho na nyid kyang/
/nges par med na mo sham bu ji bzhin/
/tha snyad du yang med pa nyid 'gyur te/

---

① de la NQ de yi A*rgyud*2853
② notpādo corr. no tya do ANQ
③ khapuṣpavat corr. kha pu ṣhya bra tra Q kha bu nya ba ta A
④ u tpā daḥ shū nya tā Q u tpā daḥ shū nya ta N ut pā da shū nya tā A
⑤ ta twa ta sh- AN ta twa sh- Q
⑥ khalu corr. kha nu ANQ
⑦ -a sa twaṃ AN -a sa twa Q
⑧ teṣām (parallels, Li 2015: 17) te ṣhāḥ A te ṣhaḥ NQ

/rang bzhin nyid yod ’di las de rnams yod/
/dpal ldan Zla ba’i’o// 9 //

yod pa de yang med pa’i zlas drangs par ni ma yin no zhes rten cing ’brel par ’byang ba’i rang bzhin gyi tshul la gdams pa/

10). naiḥsvabhāvyād① ajātatāṃ② pratyayād aniruddhatā |
bhavābhāvāv③ ato na ’sto yuganaddhaṃ tu jāyate④ ||

/skye med nyid phyir rang bzhin med/
/’gag pa med las rten ’byung ba/
/yod dang med pa⑤ nyams ’di las/
/zung ’jug nyid du skye bar ’gyur/
/A dwa⑥ ya badzra gyi’o// 10 //

mtshan nyid de dag dang ldan pa’i mtshan gzhi ni sems kyi rang bzhin gyi tshul las gzhan ma yin no zhes gdams pa/

11). pratītyajātāḥ parikalpaśūnyāḥ⑦
śūnyāḥ svabhāvena na vastusantaḥ⑧ |
nocchedinaś citravidekarūpā⑨*
rūpādayaḥ pañcajinā jayante⑩* ||

/skye ba kun rtog gi stong rten ’byung ba/
/stong pa’i rang bzhin gyis na dngos por med/

---

① naiḥsvabhāvyād corr. nai swa bhā byā d- A nai swa bha bya d- N ni swa bha byā d- Q
② a dza ta tāṃ AN a dza ta tā Q ajātatvaṃ (parallel, Mathes 2015: 449)
③ bhavābhāvāv (parallel, Mathes 2015: 449) bha bā bhā bau b- A bha bā bha bo b- NQ
④ jāyate corr. dza ya te ANQ bhāṣate (parallel, Mathes 2015: 449)
⑤ pa AN ba Q
⑥ a dwa corr. a dra ANQ
⑦ pari- corr. pa ti- ANQ
⑧ vastusantaḥ corr. ba stu sa nta ANQ
⑨ citravidekarūpā corr. tsi tra bi te ka rū pa ANQ citracidekarūpā (parallel, Mathes 2015: 371)
⑩ jayante em. jayanti (parallel, Mathes 2015: 371) ≍ dza ya nti ANQ

/chad min bkra ba sems kyi ngo bor gcig/
/gzugs sogs rgyal ba lnga rnams rgyal gyur cig/
Me tri'i zhabs kyi'o// 11 //

de nyid ni lhan cig skyes pa bde ba chen po brjod pa dang bral ba'i kho na nyid mthar thug pa te/

12). ṇa ttaṃ bāï guru kahaï ˌ ṇa ttaṃ bujjaï sīsa① |
sahaja amiasuha sa alajaï ˌ kāsu② kahijjaï③ kīsa* ||

/bla mas brjod pa de yang ma yin zhing/
/de ni slob mas go ba'am thob pa med/
/lhan cig skyes pa'i bde ba bdud rtsi ste/
/su la su zhig gis ni brjod par byed/
/Sa ra ha'i zhabs kyi glu'o// 12 //

'di nyid brtan g.yo'i khyab bdag rgyu'i rdo rje 'dzin pa'o zhes khyad par gyi gnas la gdams pa/

13). ye④ parvatā aṣṭamahāsamudrā
dvīpāś ca⑤ sarve narakādibhedāḥ⑥ |
yat⑦ sthāvaraṃ jaṅgamam eva⑧ sarvaṃ⑨*
tat tat svayaṃ Vajrabhṛd⑩* eva nānyat⑪ ||

/gang zhig ri dang rgya mtsho chen po brgyad/
/gling dang dmyal sogs dbye ba thams cad dang/

---

① taṃ bujjaï sīsa em. (parallel, Lal 1994: 179) taṃ bujjhaï śīṣa parallel (Pandey 1988: 36) tta mwā ba r-i i si sa N tta mwā bu r-i i si sa A tta mrā bu r-i i si sa Q
② kāsu corr. kā sū ANQ
③ -jjaï corr. dzdza ANQ
④ ye ANQ yaṃ (parallel, Pandey 1997: 45)
⑤ dvīpāś ca corr. (parallel, Pandey 1997: 45) dwa pi shtsa ANQ
⑥ narakādibhedāḥ corr. (parallel, Pandey 1997: 45) na ra kā di bhe da ANQ
⑦ ya t Q ya tra A ya ta N
⑧ jaṅgamam eva em. (parallel, Pandey 1997: 45) dza ga la me ba A dzaṃ ga la me ba NQ
⑨ sa rbbaṃ ANQ (Tib. thams cad) dṛṣṭaṃ (parallel, Pandey 1997: 45)
⑩ ba dzra bhṛ d- ANQ sarvavid (parallel, Pandey 1997: 45)
⑪ nānyat corr. (parallel, Pandey 1997: 45) na nyaḥ A na nnyaḥ NQ

/brtan pa dang ni g.yo ba thams cad gang/
/de de gzhan min rdo rje 'dzin rang nyid/
/Klu sgrub kyi zhal snga nas so// 13 //

'o na don gzhan du snang ba ci zhe na/ gsungs pa/

14). śūnyataiva① bhaved bhāvo vāsanāvāsitā satī |
vātāvartair② dṛḍhībhūtā āpa③ eva ghanopalāḥ ||

/stong nyid* bag chags kyis bsgos na/
/stong pa nyid ni dngos por 'gyur/
/rlung gis dkrugs las brtan por ni/
/gyur pas chu nyid chab phrom mo/
/Nāga bo dhi'i'o// 14 //

de lta mod kyi rang bzhin gzhan ru gyur ba ni ma yin no zhes bya ba'i tshul gyis lam gyi shes pa ye shes kyi phyogs nyid la dpes gdams pa/

15). aṅgāram④ ādāya yathā hi bālo gharṣed ayaṃ⑤ yāsyati śuklabhāvam |*
yāti kṣayaṃ naiva tu śuklabhāvaṃ bālasya buddhir vitathābhimānā⑥ ||

/ji ltar byis pas 'di la dkar po nyid/
/'ong snyam sol ba blangs nas bdar ba yis/
/zad par song mod dkar por mi 'gyur ba/
/byes blo brdzun pa'i mngon rlom de bzhin no/
/Ārya Klu'i zhabs kyi'o// 15 //

de'i phyir rang bzhin kha na la lam gyi snying por bya ba ste/

---

① śūnyataiva corr.　shū nya tā shū nya tai ba ANQ
② vātāvarttair em.　bā tā ba rta r- N　sa ti bā tā ba rta r- AQ
③ dṛḍhībhūtā āpa corr.　dzṛ ḍi/bhū tāḥ a pa N　dṛ ḍī bhū tāḥ a pa AQ
④ aṅgāram corr.　aṃ sha ra m- ANQ
⑤ gharṣed ayaṃ em.　ga rṣha de yaṃ ANQ　ghṛṣyed ayaṃ (parallel, Bendall 1902: 231)
⑥ bi ta thā bhi mā nā N　ba ti thā bhi mā nā AQ

16). na kleśā bodhito bhinnā[①] na bodhau kleśasaṃbhavaḥ[②] |
kleśaprakṛtitaś[③] caiva tvayāmṛtam upārjitam[④] ||

/byang chub nyon mongs las gzhan min/
/byang chub nyon mongs las ma byung/
/nyon mongs rang bzhin nyid las ni/
/khyod kyis bdud rtsi brnyes pa lags/
/Klu grub kyi zhal snga nas so// 16 //

rang bzhin las gzhan du nam 'gyur ni med bzhin du sdang ba brdzun pa kho na ste/

17). aho citraṃ citraṃ[⑤] samaviṣamanimnonnatagatau
dhiyaṃ[⑥] dhatte bhrāntiṃ[⑦] viditam api bhūtārthavidhinā |
anādau saṃsāre hṛdayagaganābhogalikhitair[⑧]*
alīkaiḥ saṃkalpais tribhuvanam idaṃ saṃgraham iva ||

/e ma'o bden pa'i don ni cho gas rtogs
kyang 'khrul pa'i blo dag la/
/mnyam dang mi mnyam mtho dma'i 'gro ba
sna tshogs bkra ba rnam bkod pa/
/srid pa gsum gyis bsdus pa 'di ni
kun tu rtog pa brdzun pa yis/
/thog ma med pa'i 'khor bar snying gi
nam mkha'i khongs su bris pa bzhin/
/La ba pa'i zhabs kyis so // 17 //

---

① na kleśā bodhito bhinnā corr. (parallel, Mathes 2015: 467) na kle sha bo dhi to bhi nna NQ na kle sha bo dhi to bhi nni A

② kleśasaṃbhavaḥ corr. (parallel, Mathes 2015: 467) kle sha saṃ bha ba AQ kle sha saṃ bbha ba N

③ kleśaprakṛtitaś corr. kle sha pra kṛ ti ta AN kle sha pra k-i ti ta Q

④ upārjitam corr. (parallel, Tucci 1932: 318) -u pā rdzi taḥ Q -u pa rdzi taḥ AN

⑤ tsi traṃ tsi traṃ NQ tsa tsi traṃ tsi traṃ A

⑥ dhi yaṃ ANQ dhiyā (parallel, Lindtner 1985: 164)

⑦ dhatte bhrāntiṃ em. (parallel, Lindtner 1985: 164) da tte bha ntiṃ NQ da tte bhi ntiṃ A

⑧ hṛdayagaganābhogalikhitair corr. (S. K-S.) hṛ da ya ga ga nā bho ga li khi tai r- AQ hṛ da ya ga ga nā bho ga N hṛdayagagane bhāgalikhitair parallel (Lindtner 1985: 164)

de nyid kyis na rang bzhin bde ba chen po so so rang gis rig pa'i ngo bo nyid du mngon du bya ba'i rnam par mi rtog pa'i sgo thun mong ma yin pa la gdams pa/

18). ete te viṣayās ta eva manasaḥ pañca pravṛttikṣaṇāḥ[①]*
tair evotsukavanti[②] cendriyabalāny utkleśabījāni naḥ[③] |
vandyaḥ[④] sadgurupādapaṅkajarajaḥsparśaḥ[⑤] svayaṃ yad vaśād
etan[⑥] māmakasāram ity aharahaḥ syandati[⑦]* tattvāmṛtam[⑧] ||

/bdag po nyon mongs sa bon gyis mtho dbang po'i
stọbs dang de rnams nyid kyis rtsol ldan par/
/yid ni rab tu 'jug pa lnga po rnams kyi
skad cig yul 'di rnams te de nyid ni/
/phyag 'os bla ma dam pa'i zhabs kyi chu skyes
rdul la rang nyid reg pa'i dbang gang las/
/bdag gi snying po zhes bya de kho na nyid
bdud rtsir son par gyur pa a la la/
Dau ḍi pra bandha las so// 18 //

de las ji ltar de kho na nyid kyi bdud rtsi'i gnas la son pa gsal bar 'doms pa/

19). na satyā nāsatyā na ca tadubhayī* nāpy anubhayī
nirullekhā sarvākṛtivaramayī[⑨] madhyamakadhīḥ[⑩] |

---

① pañca pravṛttikṣaṇāḥ (parallel, Lal 1994: 80) pa nya pra bhṛ tti kṣhā ṇā N pa nya pra bṛ tti kā ṇā Q pa nya pra bhṛ tti kṣha ṇā A

② tai r e bo ttshu kha ba nti N ati re o ttshu kha ba nti Q ti re bo tchu kha ba nti A tāny evotsukavanti (parallel, Lal 1994: 80)

③ u tkle sha bī dzā ni naḥ Q (Tib. nyon mongs sa bon gyis ... nyid kyis) -u t kle sha bi dzā ni naḥ N -u tkle sha bi dzā ni na naḥ A utkleśabījānilaḥ (parallel, Lal 1994: 80)

④ vandyaḥ em. (parallel, Lal 1994: 80) ba ndya ANQ

⑤ -sparśaḥ corr. sparśaḥ (parallel, Lal 1994: 80) sya rsha ANQ

⑥ yad vaśād etan corr. (parallel, Lal 1994: 80) ya dwa shā ta na ANQ

⑦ aharahaḥ syandati em. (S. K-S.; Tib. ...'bab 'gyur) -a ha ra ha sya nda nti AQ -a ha ra ha sya nta nti N aharahaḥ spandanti (parallel, Lal 1994: 80)

⑧ tattvāmṛtam (parallel, Lal 1994: 80) ta twā mṛ taḥ ANQ

⑨ sarvākṛtivaramayī corr. sa rbbā kṛ ti ba ta ma yī ANQ

⑩ madhyamakadhīḥ corr. (parallel, Lal 1994: 13) ma dhya na ka dhi Q ma dhya na ka dhī AN

jinaḥ śāstā saiva sthiracalajagattattvam iti① sā
svasaṃvittir② devī jayati sukhavajrapraṇayinī ||

/bden dang kun du brdzun min de dag
skye dang 'jig pa'ang ma yin pa/
/rang bzhin spros med dbu ma'i
blo ni kun du thams cad byed po mchog/
/brtan g.yo'i 'gro ba'i de kho na zhes
rgyal ba ston pa nyid kyis te/
/de ni bde ba'i rdo rjer gyur ma
so so rang rig lha mo rgyal//
Ri khrod zhabs kyis so// 19 //

bde ba de rang gis rig na rang la bya byed srid par thal ches pa nyid du dogs pa la gsungs pa/

20). kena jñāyate③ saukhyam iti vedyavedakaṃ④ manaḥ |
vedyavedakabhāvo vidoṣo⑤ no* niḥsvabhāvataḥ ||

/bde de gang gis shes snyam na/
/yid kyis rig par byed mod kyang/
/rang bzhin med⑥ phyir rig bya dang/
/rig byed gyur pa'i skyon med do/
/'phags pa Klu'i zhabs kyi'o// 20 //

so so rang gis rig bya'i lha mo'i nges pa gsungs pa/

---

① iti ANQ api (parallel, Lal 1994: 13)
② svasaṃvittir corr. swa saṃ bi tti r N swa saṃ bi tti rra Q sve se vi tti rri A
③ kena jñāyate em. (Tib. de gang gis) ke na ta tra dznye ya te NQ ke na: ta ta dzhe ya te A
④ vedya- corr. (Tib. rig par byed) be da ANQ
⑤ vedyavedakabhāvo vidoṣo em. be dya be da ka bhrā bo bi do ṣho Q be dya be da ka bhrā bo bi do ṣho N be da be da ka bhā bo pi do ṣho A
⑥ med AQ; N om.

21). nirātmakatvāt khalu dharmadhātor viśuddhitaḥ suptaśavo vimānaḥ |
tatrotthite 'yaṃ① suviśuddhadharma · dhātusvarūpo② jagadekarūpaḥ③||

/bdag med nyid phyir nges par chos kyi dbyings/
/rnam par dag pas ro dag nyal ba'i gnas/
/shin tu rnam dag chos dbyings rang bzhin gyis/
/der ni bzhengs 'di 'gro ba gcig pa'i sku/
/Brtson 'grus dpal bshes gnyen gyi'o// 21 //

de nyid kyis na rang byin gyis brlab pa'i gnas la gdams pa/

22). abhrāntatattvalābhāya④ saṃbhogakam⑤* iti smṛtam |
hūm phaṭkāravinirmuktaṃ sattvabiṃbaśivaṃ⑥* param⑦ ||

/ma 'phrul ba yi de nyid thob/
/longs spyod rdzogs pa'i sku zhes dran/
/huṃ phaṭ yi ge las grol ba/
/sems dpa'i gzugs brnyan zhi ba mchog/
Dzā landha ri pa'i'o// 22 //

de'i nges pa la kho nar rgyu 'brus kyi Tsaṇḍalī dang lhan cig skyes pa gnyes kyi nges pa la gdams pa/

---

① tatrotthite 'yaṃ conj. (S. K-S.; Tib. der ni bzhengs 'di)　tatrotthiteyaṃ (parallel, Pandey 2000: 35 n.2; Tib. der ni bzhengs 'di)　ta tro tsthi ti yaṃ NQ　ta tro hsī te yaṃ A

② -dhā tu swa rū po A　-dhā tu sra rū po Q　-dhā tu sra rū paḥ N　-dhātusvarūpā　(parallel, Pandey 2000: 36)

③ dza ga te ka rū paḥ AQ　jagad ekarūpā (parallel, Pandey 2000: 36); N om.

④ abhrāntatattvalābhāya corr.　a bha nta ta twa la bhā ya AQ　a bha nta ta twa la N

⑤ saṃbhogakam em.　saṃ bho gaṃ ga m- ANQ　saṃbhogam (parallel, Gerloff 2017: 240)

⑥ sattvabiṃbaśivaṃ corr. (Tib. sems dpa'i gzugs brnyan zhi ba)　sa twa biṃ bi shi baṃ NQ　sa twa biṃ bi shi ba A　sattvabiṃbasamaṃ (parallel, Gerloff 2017: 240)

⑦ param em.　pa raḥ ANQ

23). Caṇḍālīkaralīlayā① nijapadād ullālito② 'pi svabhūr③
viṣvagbhūri④ mahāsukhaṃ viracayaṃl⑤ līnaḥ svabodhodaye |
ambhojāgragato 'pi⑥ nirvṛtipadaṃ prāpto 'pi dhatte yayā
drāgadrāv* udayadvayaṃ ca sahajānandāya vandāmahe ||

/Gtum mo'i 'od kyi rol pas rang gi gnas las
g.yo ba'ang rang 'byung bde ba cher/
/thim las rgya cher khyab cing gsal bzhin pa la
rang nyid rtogs pa shar ba gang/
/chu skyes rtse mor son pa'ang 'phel ba
gang gis myang 'das go 'phang thob pa yang/
/re gnyis dag la shar ba'i lhan cig skyes dga'i
skad cig ma ste bdag 'dud do/
/Bīrya shrī mi tra'i 'o// 23 //

de'i phyir mdzon par gsal ba'i rgyus 'bras bu la ji ltar mtshams sbyor ba'i nges pa gsungs pa/

24). ekamudrāsamāyuktaś caturmudrāyuto 'tha vā |
antaḥpuragato* vāpi māyādeham* anusmaret ||

/kun tu phyag rgya gcig sbyor dang/
/phyag rgya bzhi la sbyor ba 'am/
/btsun mo'i grong du 'jug pa'ang rung/
/sgyu ma'i lus ni rjes dran bya/
/Ārya de ba'i'o// 24 //

de ji ltar rjes su dran par bya ba'i btsan thabs kyi sbyor ba la gdams pa/

---

① caṇḍālī- corr. (parallel, Pandey 2000: 1) tsa ṇḍā lo ANQ
② -u llā li to ANQ ullāsito (parallel, Pandey 2000: 1)
③ 'pi swa bhū r ANQ (cf. Tib. rang 'byung) viśvabhūr (parallel, Pandey 2000: 1)
④ bi ṣhwa gbhū ri NQ bi ṣhwa bbhū ri A viśvagbhūri (parallel, Pandey 2000: 1)
⑤ viracayaṃl corr. (parallel, Pandey 2000: 1) bi ra tsa ya nra AQ bi ra tsa ya na N
⑥ pi AQ; N omits

25). Kollaïre ṭṭhia bolā ˌMummuṇire kakkolā[1] |
ghaṇe[2] kipiṭa ho vājjaï[3] ˌkaruṇe kiaï[4] ṇa rolā ||

26). tahiṃ bala khājaï ˌgāḍhem[5] maaṇā pijjaï |
hale Kāliṃjara paṇiaï ˌdunduru tahiṃ vājjiaï ||

27). caüsama katthuri ˌsihlā[6] kāppura lāïaï* |
mālaïindhaṇaśālia[7] ˌtahiṃ bharu khāïaï ||

28). peṃkhaṇa kheṭa karante[8] ˌsuddhāsuddha ṇa maṇiaï[9] |
niraṃśu aṅge caḍābiaï ˌtahiṃ ja sarāva paṇiaï ||
[28′).] malaaje[10] kunduru vāṭaï[11] ˌḍiṇḍima tahiṃ ṇa vājjiaï ||

/shes rab kyi ni ka kko llar/
/thabs kyi bo lla rab bzhag nas/
/yang yang bsrubs gyur sgra sgrogs par/
/der ni snying rje cis mi skye// 25 //

/skabs der sha ni bza' bya zhin /
/rgyan du chang yang btung bar bya/
/kye skal ldan phyi rol mi btang bar/
/de chu skal med spang bar bya// 26 //

/bzhi mnyam gla rtsi si hla/

---

① kakkolā (parallel, Gerloff 2017: 113) ka kko llā ANQ
② ghaṇeṃ conj. ghaṇe (parallel, Gerloff 2017: 113) gha ṇa ï ANQ *gha 佉 (lacunose) T 892
③ vājjaï em. (cf. Gerloff 2017: 113; 末惹伊 T 892) ba dzdza i ANQ
④ karuṇe kiaï corr. (parallels, Gerloff 2017: 113; 葛嚕尼 吉阿伊 T 892) ka ru ṇe ki a N ki ru ṇe ka a i AQ
⑤ gāḍheṃ corr. (parallels, Gerloff 2017: 113; 誐引遲 T 892) gā ḍeṃ NQ khā ṭeṃ A
⑥ sihlā corr. (parallels, Gerloff 2017: 113; Tib. si ngla; 悉羅 T 892) si hla N sa hli Q si hphi A
⑦ -śālia corr. (parallels, Gerloff 2017: 113) sā li a i NQ *śā li 娑隸 T 892
⑧ karante corr. (parallels, Gerloff 2017: 113; 葛陵諦 T 892) ka ra nta ANQ
⑨ ma ṇi a i ANQ (Tib. yid) muṇiaï (parallel, Gerloff 2017: 113) *ja ṇi a i 惹抳阿伊 T 892
⑩ mala aje corr. (parallel, Gerloff 2017: 113) ma la a dza ANQ *ma la ya je 末隸野囒 T 892
⑪ vāṭaï corr. (parallels, Gerloff 2017: 113; 末吒伊 T 892) bā da i AQ bā pa i N

/e ma'o ka ppur dang li shi/
/ma la ya skyes bud shing gis/
/sā li ji tsam 'dod der bza'// 27 //

/yongs brtags dum bu gcig nyid bya/
/dag dang ma dag yid mi bya/
/mi rus phyag rgya lus la gdags/
/der skyes mnga' ni phyi rol btang// 28 //

/ma la ya skyes 'khrig sbyor bas/
/'jug bya rigs ngan der mi spang// [28′] //
/rdo rje glu'i sbyor ba/ *Kye'i rdo rje'i rgyud kyi rgyal po*r ro//

/de nyid kyi rtsa ba'i nges pa mthar thug pa la gdams pa/

29). rāgānte[1] viramapraveśasamaye candre svabhāvasthite
yā vṛttir[2] manasaḥ pravṛttir aparā vāyor niruddhā gatiḥ[3] |
tatkāle yad ananyasaṃbhavasukhaṃ[4] sākṣāt paraṃ tat padaṃ[5]
tatra[6] svānubhavo hi[7] yasya sa punaḥ[8] siddho mahāmudrayā ||

/chags pa'i mtha' ni chags bral dang po
'jug pa'i dus su 'jug pa yi ni yid gang zhig/
/zla ba'i rang bzhin gnas pa na ni gzhan la
rab tu 'jug ste rlung gi rgyu ba 'gag/
/de yi dus su bde ba gang zhig 'byung ba

---

① rāgānte corr. rā shā nte ANQ
② yā vṛttir corr. (S. K-S.) ya vṛ tti r- ANQ yā vittir (parallel, n.a. 2008a: 119; Tib. yid gang zhig) ya vitir parallel (Sen 1977: 39) yo cittir (parallel, Kværne 1977: 125)
③ gatiḥ corr. (Sen 1977: 39) gati ANQ srutiḥ (parallel, n.a. 2008a: 119)
④ ananya- (parallels, Sen 1977: 39, n.a. 2008a: 119) a na nnya- ANQ (Tib. gzhan min) anya- (parallel, Kværne 1977: 119)
⑤ sākṣātparaṃ tatpadaṃ (parallels, Kværne 1977: 119; Sen 1977: 39; n.a. 2008a: 119) sa kṣha tpa daṃ ta tpa raṃ N sa kṣha d pa da ta raṃ Q sa kṣha da taṃ dpa raṃ A
⑥ tatra parallels ni tya- ANQ
⑦ hi em. (Tib. de ni; parallels, Kværne 1977: 119; Sen 1977: 39; n.a. 2008a: 119) sti NQ staṃ A
⑧ punaḥ corr. pu na ANQ

gzhan min mngon sum pa yi go ’phang mchog/
/de ni gang gis rtag par yang yang nyams su
myong las phyag rgya chen po’i dngos grub ’gyur/
/Ḍau di① pra bandha las so// 29 //

phyag rgya chen po’i dngos grub kyi rang bzhin gsungs pa/

30). evaṃ prabhāsvarāc cittāt sattvārthas tu pravartate |
bhoganirmāṇakāyābhyāṃ pratītyapraṇidhānataḥ |
tau ca tasmān na bhinnau② ca tayos tu tatsvabhāvataḥ ||
/’di ltar ’od gsal ba’i sems las/
/sems can don du rdzogs longs spyod/
/sprul pa’i sku dag smon lam dang/
/rten cing ’brel ’byung las ’jug pa/
/de rnams kyi ni de dag gi/
/rang bzhin las gzhan ma yin no/
/Zung ’jug gsal ba las so// 30 //

de’i phyir sems can sgol ba’i khur khyer ba’i lhag pa’i bsam pa can bdag legs su ’dod pa dag gis gnas ’di kho na la yid gcig tu bya bar gdams pa/

31). yatra caikaṃ③ manaḥ kṛtvā dhyāyate④ paramaṃ padam |
tatraiva labhate siddhir ālambaṇena⑤* kiṃ phalaḥ ||

/gang du ’ang mchog gi go ’phang la/
/yid gcig pa yis bsam byas na/
/de las dngos grub rnyed ’gyur te/
/byang⑥ mang rtsom la ’bras bu ci/

---

① ḍau di corr. ḍo dri ANQ
② tau ca tasmān na bhinnau em. (parallel) to tsai ta sma nna dzhi nnau NQ to tsi ta sma nni dzhi nnau nna A
③ ya tra tsai kaṃ N ya twa tse kaṃ Q ya twa tsai kaṃ A
④ kṛtvā dhyāyate corr. kṛ twa dhya ya te ANQ kuryād *jāyate parallel
⑤ siddhir ālambaṇena conj. si ddhi ra na dza le na ANQ siddhiḥ *rājajālena parallel
⑥ byang N bya Q

/zhal byung ngo // 31 //

de lta bas na 'chi ba med pa nyid kyi gan sa la yang ngo zhes gdams pa'i phyir/

32). cittaṃ ca śūnyatā proktā mahāmudrātmikā① parā |
taṃ ca bhāvayitvā② nityaṃ mṛtyur āyate vañcanam③ ||

/sems kyang stong pa nyid du gsungs/
/phyag rgya chen po'i bdag nyid gsungs*/
/de yang rtag tu sgom pa las/
/'chi ba bslu bar 'gyur ba nyid/
/Bi ru pākṣha'i 'o// 32 //

de ltar shes pa nas sgrub pa kho na snying por bya ba'i phyir nags su gnas pa'i skabs kyi phan yon la gdams pa/

33). na dṛśyate④ krūramukhaṃ⑤* narāṇāṃ
nīcasya garvo⑥ 'pi na dṛśyate vā⑦ |
na dṛśyate bandhujanasya⑧ śokaḥ
sthitir vane sādhutarā narāṇām⑨ ||

/mi rnams kha nas gya gyur smra ba mi thos shing/
/dman pa rnams kyi khengs pa mthong ba min pa dang/
/gnyen gyi skye bo'i mya ngan mthong ba ma yin pas/
/nags su gnas na mi rnams shin tu legs pa nyid/
/zhal byung nyid do// 33 //

---

① mahāmudrātmikā corr. ma hā mu drā tmi ka AQ ma hā mu drā tmi N
② bhāvayitvā em. (kha nas gya gyur Tib.) bhā ba ya twā ANQ
③ āyate vañcanam corr. -ā ya te ba nytsa naḥ ANQ āyāti vañcanam (parallel, Schneider 2010: 117)
④ dṛśyate conj. (Tib. thos) dṛ shṛ te ANQ
⑤ krūramukhaṃ conj. (Tib. kha nas gya gyur lan smra ba) tsa kra su khaṃ ANQ
⑥ garvo em. (Tib. khengs pa) ga rbho ANQ
⑦ vā em. tsa ANQ
⑧ bandhujanasya corr. ba ntsu dza na sya N ba nytsu dza na sya Q na ba nytsa na sya A
⑨ narāṇam corr. na rā ṇaḥ ANQ

chags sdang gi rkyen spangs pa la sogs pas chags bral gyi nges pa la gnas pa nyid kyang chags pa chen po'i nges pa la mi ston na slar zhing sred pa brtas pa'i rgya'o zhes bya ba'i tshul gyis sred pa las nges par 'byang ba la khyad par du gdams pa/

34). bhrāntvā① deśam anekadurgaviṣamaṃ kiñcin na prāptaṃ mayā②*
tyaktvā śīlakulābhimānam③ ucitaṃ sevā kṛtā niṣphalā④ |
bhuktaṃ⑤ mānavivarjitaṃ paragṛheṣv āśaṅkayā kākavat⑥
Tṛṣṇe vairiṇi⑦ pāpakarmanirate⑧ nādyāpi santuṣyasi ||

/bgrod dka'i yul ni mang por 'khyams nas
bdag gis cung zad kyang ni ma rnyed par/
/tshul khrims rigs kyi nga rgyal dor nas
phyug po* bsten par byas kyang 'bras bu med/
/gus pa spangs pa'i gzhan gyi khyim du
bya rog lta bur dogs dang bcas shing zos/
/da dung tshim par ma gyur sdig pa'i las la
dga' ba'i dgra bo Sred pa skye/
/Bhartha ha ri'i'o// 34 //

khyad par gyi sred pa las nges par 'byang ba la 'dir zhes da migs kyi sgo na sa bla lhag tu gdams pa/

---

① bhrāntvā (parallel, Kosambi 1948: 58)　bha ntya NQ　bha ndya A
② ki nytsi nna pra pta mma yā ANQ　prāptaṃ na kiñcit phalaṃ parallels
③ shī la ku lā bhi mā na m- ANQ　jātikulābhimānam (parallel, Kosambi 1948: 58)
④ sevā kṛtā niṣphalā (parallel, Kosambi 1948: 58)　se tsa kṛ tā ni ḥpha lā Q　se tsa kṛ tā ni ḥpha la N　se tsa kṛ tā ni bpha la A
⑤ bhuktaṃ parallel (Kosambi 1948: 58)　bhu nydza m- ANQ
⑥ paragṛheṣv āśaṅkayā kākavat em. (parallel, Kosambi 1948: 58)　pa ra gṛ he sā sha ngka yā kā ka ba NQ　pa ra gṛ he sā sha ngka yā kā ka pa A
⑦ tṛṣṇe vairiṇi em. (parallel, Kosambi 1948: 58 var. MS H)　tṛ ṣhṇi bai re ṇi N　tṛ ṣhṭi be re ṇi Q　tṛ ṣhṇa bai re ṇi A
⑧ pā pa ka rmma ni ra te AQ　pā pa ka rmma ni ra te A　pāpakarmapiśune (parallel Kosambi 1948: 58)

35). ekadṛṣṭād dṛṣṭaśataṃ① dṛṣṭapañcaśatādhikam②*|
atitṛṣṇapuruṣasya③ cakraṃ bhramati mastake ||

/gcig mthong ba nas brgya mthong zhing/
/brgya phrag lnga dbang mthong nas ni/
/shin tu sred pa'i skyes bu yi/
/mgo④ po la ni 'khor lo 'khor/
/*Mdza' mo'i bu'i rtogs pa brjod pa* las so// 35 //

de lta bu'i bsgrod pa gcig pa'i lam gyi gtso bo'i snod kyi khyud par la gdams pa/

36). bhikṣubhāve sthitā⑤ ye ca ye ca tarkaratā narāḥ |
vṛddhabhāve⑥ sthitā ye ca teṣāṃ tattvaṃ na deśayet ||

/gang yang dge slong dngos gnas dang/
/mi gang rtog ge la dga' dang/
/gang zhig rgan po'i dngos gnas pa/
/de la de nyid bstan mi bya/
/Sha ba rā sya yaṃ// 36 //

de ltar theg pa thams cad kyi nges par 'byung ba mthar thug pa'i sting po rnyed nas rgyal ba'i bstan pa'i snying po la rton pa nyid kyis yon tan shes pas de kho na'i ched du rang dang gzhan gyi phun sum tshogs pa thams cad sbyar ba gcig pa'i lhag pa'i bsam pa bla na med pa la gdams par bzhed pas de yun du gnas pa las brtsams pa'i mchog tu shis pa brdzod pa/

37). siddhauṣadhāni bhavaduḥkhamahāgatānāṃ
puṇyātmanaṃ⑦* paramakarṇarasāyanāni |

---

① ekadṛṣṭād dṛṣṭaśataṃ em. (gcig mthong ba nas Tib.) e kaṃ dṛ ṣhṭa sha taṃ dṛ ṣhṭa AN e kaṃ dṛ ṣhṭa dṛ ṣhṭa sha taṃ Q
② dṛṣṭapañcaśatādhikam conj. dṛ ṣhṭa pa nytsa sha tā ni shtsa ANQ
③ atitṛṣṇapuruṣasya corr. a ti tṛ ṣhṭa sya pu ru ye ṣha sya ANQ
④ mgo Q mgon A
⑤ bhikṣubhāve sthitā em. (cf. v. 36c; parallel, Sakurai 1996: 419) bhi kṣhu bhā ba sthi tā ANQ
⑥ vṛddhabhāve corr. bṛ dwa bhā be ANQ
⑦ puṇyātmanaṃ em. (Tib. bsod nams kyi ni bdag nyid rnams la) pu ṇyā tma naṃ ANQ

prakṣālanaikasalilāni① manomalānāṃ②
Śauddhodaneḥ③ pravacanāni ciraṃ jayante④ ||

/srug bsngal nad chen ldan pa'i srid pa rnams kyi grub pa'i sman/
/bsod nams kyi ni bdag nyid rnams la rna ba'i bcud len mchog/
/kun tu yid kyi dri ma 'khrud par byed pa'i chu gcig pu/
/Zas gtsang sras po'i gsung rab rnams ni yun du rgyal gyur cig/
slob dpon chen po Dpa' bo'i'o// 37 //

'Dzam bu'i gling gi mkhas pa mtha' dag gi thig le mtshan brjod par dka' ba'i grub pa'i dbang phyug shrī Ba na ratna'i zhal snga nas/ mdo sngags kyi bstan pa'i snying po la⑤ do gal du yi dam du bya ba'i gnas che⑥ long la gdams pa'i gzhung zhal las 'byang ba'i shas 'ga' zhig zin pa rnams/ paṇḍi ta chen po de nyid kyi bka' drin gyis 'tsho ba'i dge slong rnal 'byor spyod pa rgya mtsho'i sde zhes bya bas bskyad par phangs pa kho na'i lhag pa'i bsam pas⑦ bzhed pa ji lta bar bsgyur zhing/

rin po che'i snying po dam pa'i phreng ba lta bu ba sgrigs te yi ger spel ba re shig go//

6.4 Philological commentary

1): The opening lines of the *Oral-Tradition Gems* attributed to Mi'i nyi ma, "Sun of men," present a number of problems. Its forty syllables do not form metrical verse (– – ⏑ – ⏑ – – – – ⏑ – ⏑ ⏑ ⏑ – – ⏑ ⏑ – – / ⏑ ⏑ ⏑ ⏑ – ⏑ ⏑ – – – – ⏑ ⏑ – ⏑ ⏑ – ⏑ ⏑ –). Nor is it found in its ostensive source, the *Ratnastotrasaptaka* of Āditya, also called *Vanaratnastotra*. This short work is extant in Sanskrit and two Tibetan translations (ed. Hahn 1996: 36; D 1177/Q 5044, Q 5101), all attributed to Āditya (*nyi ma*). From its various witnesses it is clear that this *Ratnastotrasaptaka* is not the source for *Gems* v. 1.

Ryan Damron (2021: 54 n.30) studied this verse of the *Gems* and noticed that it is incorporated in Gzhon nu dpal's *Deb ther sngon po* (trans. Roerich 1949: 798). The diction in the *Deb ther sngon po* verse (quoted below from Sakya Research Centre text R909) is nonetheless quite different from that of the *Gems*:

---

① prakṣālanaikasalilāni em. parallel   pra kṣha la nai ka sha la lā ni N   pra kṣha la nai ka li lā ni AQ
② manomalānāṃ corr.   ma no ma lā nā ANQ
③ śauddhodaneḥ em. (zas gtsang sras po'i Tib.)   shau ddho da niḥ ANQ
④ ciraṃ jayante corr. (yun du rgyal gyur cig Tib.)   tsi ṃ dza ya nti Q   tsi ri dza ya nti N   tsa ra dza ya nti A
⑤ la AQ   las N
⑥ gnas che AQ   gnad che N
⑦ bsams pas N   bsam pa Q

/gnas brtan chen po nags kyi rin chen ni/
/srid skyes nyon mongs rnyog pa rab bkrus nas/
/chags bral mngon du mdzad do skyes bo dag/
/srid pa zhi phyir gus pas bsten par gyis/

Gzhon nu dpal's version of the verse appears to have been translated into Tibetan afresh. His translation remains consistent with the Sanskrit text and follows it better in *pāda* d, for instance: *srid pa zhi phyir* (*bhavaśāntyai*) *gus pas* (*bhaktyā*) *bsten par gyis* (*bhajata*). There then appears have been a common source for the two different Tibetan translations, Gzhon nu dpal's and Bsod rnams rgya mtsho's. This leads to the conclusion that a different Sanskrit verse or poem in praise of Vanaratna, also attributed to Āditya, was in circulation.

The unmetricality of this 40-syllable verse raises doubts about whether it could be the work of the Āditya who penned the well-formed Toṭaka stanzas of the *Ratnastotrasaptaka*. Little is known about Āditya apart from this one work and Tibetan accounts of his meeting with Vanaratna, which Damron (2021: 53) locates in present-day Andhra Pradesh. There is an unnoticed disparity between Āditya's role as "the leader of a community of renunciants (Tib. *dge sbyor*; Skt. *śramaṇa*)" in this region (Damron *ibid.*) and his self-identification as a *Magadhadeśīyaparamopāsaka in the colophons of the Tibetan translations of the *Ratnastotrasaptaka* (*ma ga dha'i yul du byung ba'i dge bsnyen*, Q 5101; *yul ma ga dhā nas byung ba'i dge bsnyen dam pa*, D 1177). The terms *śramaṇa* or *upāsaka* could, however, indicate a non-Buddhist religious affiliation such as Jainism. Damron (2021: viii) also states that the name *Narāditya "mistranslates" the Tibetan name Mi'i nyi ma (as used in the *Gems*) and that the correct form, as used by Gzhon nu dpal in Sanskrit transliteration, is Manuṣasūrya, but the possibility that Gzhon nu dpal is using an artificial back-translation here has certainly not been excluded. The name Āditya is witnessed in the colophon of the Sanskrit manuscript of the *Ratnastotrasaptaka* kept at Ngor monastery (cf. Bandurski 1994: 81 No. 42, MS Xc 14/43–45; ed. Hahn *ibid.*). Here I refer to the Göttingen photographs of this manuscript, scans of which were kindly shared with me by Kazuo Kano.

2): This homage to the guru, the second verse of the *Gems*, is taken from Munidatta's commentary on the opening song (attributed to Lūyīpā) of the *Caryāgītikośa*. In this part of the commentary (cf. ed. Kværne 1977: 71), Munidatta quotes Nāgārjuna's *vajrajāpa* (section of the *Pañcakrama*, i.e., v. 1.67; cf. ed. Mimaki and Tomabechi 1994: 12, D 1340), and then gives the verse in question from the "musical composition" of Saraha (*sarahapādair apy uktaṃ prabandhe*; D

2293: *sa ra ha'i zhabs kyis bshad sbyar las kyang gsungs te*). In the *Gems*, by contrast, the verse is presented as Śabareśvara's personal reply to Nāgārjuna (*klu sgrub zhabs la sha ba ra dbang phyug gis*), as though the verse is part of a dialogue between the two. It is doubtful that Śabareśvara has been confused with Saraha accidentally, in view of Vanaratna's fervent and literate devotion to the former (Mathes 2008). The Great Śabara and Saraha are, then, two appellations for the same person, according to this anthology.

In *Gems pāda* 2a, the reading *manaḥsaṃniyogārthahetoḥ* is accepted as germane to this textual tradition, with the support of *don la* for *-artha-*, over the much more preferable reading *-ātmahetoḥ* (cf ed. Kværne *ibid.*). The received reading of the *Gems, sa nni pe shā rṣa he toḥ*, may derive from a graphic confusion. In the facsimile edition of Munidatta's *Caryāgītikośa* commentary published by Sen (1977: 5), his manuscript, MS NGMPP A 39/18, which is copied in an Eastern Indian hand, can be seen to break mid-compound to accommodate a string hole, such that *yo* যো could be taken for *pe* followed by a space filler character পে¦. Here *ga* গ is also confusable with *śa* শ . Another witness for Munidatta's commentary formerly kept in a Nepalese collection, MS Cambridge Or.715.3, has not been identified as such in manuscript catalogues and remains unstudied (it does not contain the text of the verse in question; it comprises a single folio covering Guṇḍarīpāda's song and its commentary, ed. Kværne 1977: 87, 89).

Apart from its inclusion in the *Gems*, this verse has so far been located only in Munidatta's commentary. More generally, its wording echoes another verse of guru devotion that begins *yasya prasādakiraṇaiḥ spharitātmatattvaḥ* and is often encountered in the Hevajra tantric system and in various late Buddhist works authored in Nepal (cf. Sinclair 2016: 335, 346). The verse moreover calls to mind Hindu guru devotion verses such as those found in the *Vākyavṛtti* of Śaṅkara (*yasya prasādād aham eva viṣṇuḥ ... tasyāṅghripadmaṃ praṇato 'smi nityam*; cf. Jagadananda 1979: 2), in the *Yatidharmaprakāśa* of Vāsudevāśrama (cf. ed. Olivelle 1976: 65) — a possible contemporary of Munidatta — and so on.

3): The anthology's third verse is one of the epigrams attributed to Bhartṛhari. The edition referred to here is that of Kosambi (1948: 182 v. 665). The textual condition of this verse in the *Gems* is unusually poor, probably reflecting poor (Nepalese?) source material. In *pāda* 3a, *bahu-* in *bahujanaparivṛto* is hypermetrical (assuming Śikhariṇī metre) and most likely an inserted gloss. For *pāda* 3b, witness N has the transliterated reading *mra yā nwā ddhya sthā naṃ*; Kosambi accepts the reading *prayātavyasthānaṃ* here, while the reading of his MS M4 has *prayād vadhyasthānaṃ*. A reading such as *prayat* conceivably underlies the *Gems*' translation *gsod pa'i gnas su* (*vadhyasthāna*) *'gro bzhin pa ni* (*pra*- $\sqrt{}$ *yā*). The adoption of this reading then requires, for metrical compliance, the emendation of the beginning of the third *pāda* from *evaṃ* (*'di ltar*) to the reading of Kosambi's edition, *tathā*; however, the latter reading is foreign to the *Gems*' textual tradition and has not been adopted here. The compound *mṛtyunikaṭaṃ* "closeness to death" in 3c is translated as *'chi ba la ni nges* "determining the moment of death," **mṛtyuniścayam*. In *pāda* 3d the reading *vibhogair* is unmetrical — it is possibly caused by contamination from 3d — and Kosambi's edition again guides the emendation to *vibhavair*.

4): Bhartṛhari's *Vairāgyaśataka* (cf. ed. Kosambi 1948: 80, v. 200) is the source of this verse. In *pāda* 4b, the transcription *se bā ni ḫpha lā* (*sevā niṣphalā*) is translated *re ba 'bras bu med*, which would correspond to a reading such as **niṣphalaṃ kāṃkṣate*, unless *re ba* is a miscopying of *se ba*. In any case, the received texts of the *Gems* lack the desired verb *nīyate*, which is accepted in Kosambi's edition and most of his witnesses.

5): The source of this verse, *kho dpon la springs pa zhal las*, has not been determined. The conjecture *abhimanthanād jalam* in the first *pāda* (Tib. *chu ni jalam mngon par bsrubs kyang*) is a conjecture based on two presumed errors in the transcription *yra na*: graphic confusion of *d-virāma* as *yra*, and metathesis of *nā* and *d-virāma*. The translator understood the sequence *a sau ga taṃ* in 5c to mean *asaugatam*, an unattested word apparently taken to mean "un-Buddhist" : *bde bar gshegs pa'i lam* (*sau ga taṃ mā rga m-*) *'di la yang* (*a pi* [*i*] *ha*) *mi* (*a-*) *bsten pa'i* (*se va ya n-*). It is conjectured that the verse here read *asau gataṃ mārgam*, referring in its original context to some non-conducive path, and that its referent has been lost in the anthologising process. As it stands in the *Gems*, it could refer to the miserable life lamented by Bhartṛhari in v. 4.

6): Whereas this is an authoritative verse for some tantric authors, especially Advayavajra (*Pañcatathāgatamudrāvivaraṇa* v. 19), it is attributed here to its classical locus, the *Ālokamālā* of Kambalapāda. The Sanskrit text of this verse published by Lindtner (1985: 214 v. 274) is lacunose in its first *pāda*, but this lacuna can be restored from Lindtner's own MS, Matsunami 1965: 26 No. 59 f. 25r2–3, read with the aid of the University of Tokyo's "Database for Sanskrit manuscripts in the UT Library — Preliminary edition for Palm leaves" (Tōkyō Daigaku Sōgō Toshokan shozō Sansukritto shahon Dētabēsu 東京大学総合図書館所蔵サンスクリット写本データベース 貝葉写本先行公開版): *sa* [*rrva*] *sa mā* [*naḥ*] *pra ci bha jya mā naḥ*. Advayavajra's students Sahajavajra and Rāmapāla also quote this verse. It is attributed to Kambalāmbarapāda in Rāmapāla's

Sekanirdeśapañjikā, which is available in Sanskrit (ed. Śāśanī 2017: 187). The Tibetan translation of this verse in the *Sekanirdeśapañjikā* (D 2253) is much the same as that of the Tibetan translation of Sahajavajra's **Tattvadaśakaṭīkā* (D 2254); see Nagashima 2002: 46–47. The translation in the *Gems* is different from these and, again, appears to be original. In *pāda* 6b, the compound *sūkṣmekṣikākṣāmadhiyā* is translated as *chen po'i* (*-a-kṣāma-*?) *blo dang ldan pas* (*-dhiyā*) *zhib mor* (*sūkṣma-*) *mthong ba* (*-īkṣikā-*) *gang*. In the Tibetan **Tattvadaśakaṭīkā et al.* part of the compound is left untranslated: *phra rab* (*sūkṣma-*) *lta bas* (*-īkṣikā-*) *blo yis* (*-dhiyā*).

7): The *Gems* attributes this verse to "a *sūtra*". Different second-hand attributions for this verse are given in the Sanskrit corpus. In Candrakīrti's *Prasannapadā* the verse is attributed to an otherwise unavailable *Anavataptahradāpasaṃkramaṇasūtra*, perhaps through an incorporated marginalium (the title of this text is omitted in the Tibetan translation, D 3860: *ji skad du mdo las*). In *Pañcatathāgatamudrāvivaraṇa* 15 (D 2242) the verse is said to come from the *Candrapradīpa*, i.e., the *Samādhirāja*. In view of the fact that Advayavajra is cited so often in the *Gems*, his *Pañcatathāgatamudrāvivaraṇa* may have been Vanaratna's direct source here.

8): This verse has not yet been located in Kambalapāda's known works.

9): The sixth chapter of Candrakīrti's *Madhyamakāvatāra*, from which this verse of the *Gems* has been extracted (*Madhyamakāvatāra* 6.107), has been published in Sanskrit by Li (2015: 17).

10): The edition of Advayavajra's *Yuganaddhaprakāśa* v. 7 referred to here is Mathes 2015: 176.

11): The most significant variant for this verse attested in the *Gems* occurs in v. 3c: *citravidekarūpāḥ*. The edition of the *Pañcatathāgatamudrāvivaraṇa* of Mathes (2015: 371) reads *citracidekarūpāḥ* here. The *Gems*' translation *bkra ba sems kyi ngo bor gcig* understands *citravidekarūpāḥ*, as does the canonical Tibetan translation, D 2242: *sna tshogs gcig pa'i sems*. The variant *-vid-* is also attested in the *Kalparājatantra*, a 19th-century Nepalese anthology (cf. e.g. Bibliothèque nationale de France MS Sanscrit 47, ark:/12148/btv1b10082301d, f. 36v5–6).

12): This verse is included in the Tibetan translation of Saraha's *Dohākośa* (D 2224, cf. trans. Schaeffer 2005: 312):

/bla mas bstan pa brjod min na/ /slob mas go ba ma yin te/
/lhan cig skyes pa bdud rtsi'i ro/ /gang gis ji ltar bsten par bya/

A similarly worded translation is given in a commentary on the Sarahapādīya *Dohākośa*, namely, the **Nijatattvaprakāśa* attributed to Advayavajra (D 2257). This verse is not part of the 105-verse recension of Saraha's *Dohākośa* (Shahidullah 1928: 145 n. 30), but it is included in other *dohā* collections ascribed to Saraha; see e.g. Bagchi (1935: 7 v. 9, 28 vol. I). Bagchi notes that "it is quoted in the *Kriyāsamuccaya* as a citation from Sarahapāda (*Sarahapādair api-uktam*) in corrupt form"; it has also been transcribed from one witness of the *Kriyāsamuccaya* by Pandey (1988: 35). More to the point, the verse by Saraha occurs in a work that Vanaratna is known to have used. Vibhūticandra quotes it, without attribution, to elucidate the word *avācya*, "unspeakable" "inexpressible", in his *Nibandha* subcommentary (on Raviśrījñāna's *Amṛtakaṇikā* commentary) on *Nāmasaṃgīti* 8.27. The following *chāyā* conveys the present editorial understanding of this verse:

ṇa ttaṃ bāï guru kahaï ˌ ṇa ttaṃ bujjaï sīsa |
sahaja amiasuha sa alajaï ˌ kāsu kahijjaï kīsa ||

*na tad vācayā guruḥ kathayati na tad budhyati śiṣyaḥ |
*sahajāmṛtasukhaḥ sakalajagate kasya kathyate kīdṛśaḥ ||

This *chāyā* draws on vocabulary compiled by Shahidullah (1928: 202–228). At points it differs from that of Bhayani (1996: 26 v. 73), who worked with a textual tradition of the verse having the variant *rasu* (**rasa*, Tib. *ro*, as in D 2224) in place of *suha* (**sukha*) in the third *pāda*. The word *kīsa* is translated as *bsten par bya* in some Tibetan translations (D 2224, 2257), which would indicate an underlying word related to √ *sev*, but here ought to correspond to some conjugation of √ *kṛ* such as *kriyase*. There is no direct translation of the word *bāï*, v. 12a, in the Tibetan *Gems*; it is translated as *brjod* in D 2224.

13): Pandey (1997: 45) has *sarvavid eva* for 13c, whereas the Tibetan translation of the *Gems* understands *vajrabhṛd eva* (*rdo rje 'dzin rang nyid*). The canonical translation of the *Svādhiṣṭhānaprabheda*, D 1805, likewise reads *rdo rje 'dzin*. In *Gems* v. 13c, further, the received reading *sarvvaṃ* (*thams cad*) seems to be contamination from 13b, as it is paralleled by *dṛṣṭaṃ* in the *Svādhiṣṭhānaprabheda* (cf. D 1805: *blta*).

14): This verse has not been located in a work by Nāgabodhi/Nāgabuddhi, although its cosmogenetic subject matter is also treated in Nāgabuddhi's *Samājasādhanavyavastholi* and *Karmāntavibhāga*. The *Gems'* direct source for this verse was most likely Munidatta's *Caryāgītikośavṛtti* (ed. Kværne 1977: 237). In the *Gems*' Tibetan translation of *pāda* 14b, the term *stong yid* is superfluous; compare the parallel translation of the *Caryāgītikośavṛtti*, D 2293 (*stong nyid de nyid gyur pa yis/dngos po'i bag chags kyis bsgos 'gyur*). Some equivalent of *avāsitā* (e.g. *blangs med*) would be expected in order to accord with the Sanskrit text here.

15): This verse originates in the *Vīradattaparipṛcchā*, a Mahāyānasūtra, which is quoted by name in the *Sūtrasamuccaya* attributed to Nāgārjuna. There are a number of quotations from the *Vīradattaparipṛcchā* in topic 8 of the *Sūtrasamuccaya*, as witnessed in the Tibetan translation of the *Sūtrasamuccaya*. It is not yet known whether this verse is included in the fragments of the palmleaf *Sūtrasamuccaya* manuscript recently identified in China by Zhang Meifang 張美芳, on which see Wang *et al.* (2020: 59–60). The verse is also quoted with attribution to the *Vīradattaparipṛcchā* in *pariccheda* 13 of Śāntideva's *Śikṣāsamuccaya*, a related anthology (ed. Bendall 1902: 231). As such, there is abundant if indirect testimony for this verse from the Tibetan and Chinese translations of the *Vīradattaparipṛcchā, Sūtrasamuccaya*, and *Śikṣāsamuccaya*, although it has not been located in the patchy Chinese translation of the *Sūtrasamuccaya* (T 1635). One of the canonical Chinese translations of the *Vīradattaparipṛcchā,* the *Wúwèishòu suǒ wèn dàchéng jīng* 無畏授所問大乘經 (T 331 $68a_4$), follows the Sanskrit text well: 譬如 (*yathā hi*) 愚者 (*bālam*) 取 (*ādāya*) 于炭 (*aṅgāram*) 勤力摩 (*gharṣet*) 治欲 (*yāsyati*) 令白 (*śuklabhāvam*). The phrase *yāsyati śuklabhāvam* in 15b is apparently understood as **yāsyeti śuklabhāvam* in the Tibetan translation of the *Sūtrasamuccaya*, D 3934: *dkar por bya zhes*.

16): The first half of this stanza is taken from Advayavajra's *Mahāyānaviṃśikā* v. 8ab (ed. Mathes 2015: 467). The whole of verse 8 is also quoted in Munidatta's *Caryāgītikośavṛtti* (ed. Kværne 1977: 260) in his comments on a song by Bhusukupā, where it is attributed simply to *āgama*. The second half of the stanza corresponds to the second half of Nāgārjuna's *Niraupamyastava* v. 15 (ed. Tucci 1932: 318). The variants of these half-verses in the *Gems*' textual tradition are trivial.

17): The *Ālokamālā* edition of Lindtner (1985: 164) gives for *pāda* 17c of this verse (v. 128) the reading *bhāgalikhitaiḥ*, whereas the Gems has the transcription *bho ga li khi tai r-* (blockprint Q) and the translation *khongs su bris pa*. The canonical Tibetan translation, D 3895, *khyab par/ bris pa'i*, supports *-ābhogalikhitaiḥ* (as suggested by S. K-S.).

18): The attribution of this verse to Daüdipā has no known basis. It may be due to an error in the transmission of the *Gems*, perhaps again occurring at the source as a misremembered attribution. The same subject matter is treated in the *Guhyāvalī* and the first *pāda, ete te viṣayās ta eva manasaḥ pañca pravṛttikṣaṇāḥ*, has a little similarity with a verse of the same metre beginning *ete pañca nayanti* in Daüdipā's *Guhyāvalī* (v. 17). In fact, the present verse of the Gems occurs as an anonymous quotation (*uktaṃ ca*) in Raviśrījñāna's *Amṛtakaṇikā* (ed. Lal 1994: 80) commentary on the epithet *aśeṣabhāvārtharatiḥ* in *Nāmasaṃgīti* 9.6. The term *pravṛttikṣaṇa*, occurring in the first *pāda*, is attested Abhidharma and Yogācāra jargon and so is preferable to **prabhṛtikṣaṇa* (blockprint N).

19): The transcription of this verse in the *Gems* agrees largely with the text of the *Amṛtakaṇikā* edited by Lal (1994: 13), apart from the usual haphazard losses of *a chung* marks in the *Gems*' Sanskrit transcriptions. The *Amṛtakaṇikā* attributes the present verse to a *gurūpadeśakrama* (D 1395: *bla ma'i man ngag gi rim pa*). The *Gems*' identification of this guru as Śabarapāda has not found support in other sources.

20): No trace of this verse has been found in the works of Nāgārjuna, nor elsewhere. The expression *vedyavedakabhāva* occurs in *pramāṇa* texts such as Mokṣākaragupta's *Tarkabhāṣā*. The transcriptions of the fourth *pāda* transmit the reading *no niḥsvabhāvataḥ* (N & Q blockprints), in which the word *nas* has no obvious referent in the Tibetan translation. The Tibetan *Gems* reads this verse as an internal response to a question: *yid kyis rig par byed mod*(?) *kyang*. It can be conjectured that the text read *yo* or *ko niḥsvabhāvataḥ*, although neither of these conjectures would be prone to confusion with *no*.

21): This verse conflates the opening and closing half-verses from two stanzas introduced with the words *tathā ca* in the *Marmakalikā* commentary on Śūnyasamādhivajrapāda's *Tattvajñānasaṃsiddhi* 2.1 (ed. Pandey 2000: 35–36). The *Gems* translates *vimānaḥ*, in *pāda* a, as *gnas*, whereas the canonical translation of the *Marmakalikā* (D 1585) here translates in the better known sense of *gzhal med khang*.

22): The source of this verse is an unattributed quotation in the *Vajrapradīpā* of Jālandharipā (ed. Gerloff 2017: 240). As Gerloff notes (*ibid.*, 379), this verse is not found in the Tibetan translation of the *Vajrapradīpā* (D 1237). The second *pāda* of Gerloff's edition of this verse, *saṃbhogam iti smṛtam*, is not marked in that edition as being hypometrical. In the Tibetan *Gems*, 22b, *longs spyod rdzogs pa'i sku* clearly understands **saṃbhogakāyam* or an element standing for *-kāyam*. The metrically compliant emendation *saṃbhogakam* has been adopted here. The Sanskrit transcripts of the *Gems* blockprints convey the variant *-śivam* in the fourth *pāda*, 22d: *sattvabiṃbaśivaṃ param* (witness N, Tib. *sems dpa'i gzugs brnyan zhi ba*). The highly doubtful reading *śivaṃ* may have originated as a shift from *sattvabiṃba-samam* (ed. Gerloff *ibid.*) to *sattvabiṃba-śamam* (*śamam* also corresponds to *zhi ba*), which was later hypercorrected to *-śivam*. From the context of Jālandharipā's discussion, and from its sources in turn, it is clear that *sattvabiṃba* should be taken in the sense of *bodhisattvabiṃba* or *buddhabiṃba*.

23): This is the opening verse of Vīryaśrīmitra's *Marmakalikā pañjikā* on the *Tattvajñānasaṃsiddhi*. It has been edited in Sanskrit by Pandey (2000: 1). The terse Sanskrit commentary (*vyākhyā*) on this verse uniquely documented in MS University of Tokyo General Library No. 149 (Matsunami 1965: 63), f. 1r1–1v1, has been mentioned earlier. The commentary on the whole verse is given here (in tentative form, unedited apart from a few silent corrections), in view of its potential relevance to the Vanaratna teaching tradition and the textual tradition of the *Gems*:

> ৺ Caṇḍālītyādiślokasya vyākhyānam āha || **vandāmahe** | namas kurmahe | ke ca yaṃ | kaṃ | **rāgadrāv udayadvayaṃ** | viśvabhūvaṃ | rāgāḍ | drāk | īṣaṭ | udayaḥ | prakāśaḥ | dvayāt | paramaviramākhyātvāt | yasya | saḥ | rāgathā | kathaṃ ca | asti | ko yaḥ | **viśvabhūḥ** parameśvaraḥ | **sahajānandaḥ** | viśvaṃ | jagata | bhavati | prabhavati | yasmāt | suviśvabhūḥ | kiṃ viśiṣṭaḥ | **līno** vilīnaḥ | kasmin | **svabodhodaye** | svasaṃvedyajñānādaya | kiṃ kurvan | **viracayan** | anubhavan | kiṃ **viśvagbhūri mahāsukhaṃ** | viṣvag dharmodayā | tatra bhūri pracuraṃ | mahat sukhaṃ , sahajasukham iti | kiṃ viśiṣṭa san | **ullālitaḥ** | utkṣipaḥ | kasmāt | **nijapadāt** | svakīyasthānāt | kayā | **Caṇḍālīkaralīlayā** | Caṇḍālī | Madhyamā | kundurupravṛttavāyusaṃharṣāt | vidyurūpā | kaṃ syāḥ | karakiraṇaḥ | tasya | līlā , rilā | tayā | **dhatte** | vibhartti | kiṃ , **nirvṛttipadaṃ** | mokṣapadaṃ | kiṃ viśiṣṭaḥ | **prāptaḥ** | samanugataḥ | †samāl iti tāyā vata† | kayā | **yayā** | Caṇḍālyā | kiṃ viśiṣṭa san | **aṃbhojāgragataḥ** | aṃbhasi

jāyate iti | aṃbhojaṃ , kamalaṃ | tasyāgrā śikharaṃ | tatra gata iti | īṣat kṣaraṇordhvagatatvāt | katham api punaḥ ||

The glyph sequence in 23cd, *ya yā drā ga dra b-* (according to Q), is parsed as *yayā đ rāgadrāv*, the latter term being glossed as *drāk* in harmony with the Tibetan *Gems* (*skad cig ma ste*). In the Tibetan translation of the *Marmakalikā* (D 1585), we have *myur zhing myur bar*, which seems to understand *drāk-ādrau*.

24): This verse concatenates three quarter-verses (v. 40abc) and a quarter-verse (v. 45d) from pseudo-Āryadeva's *Svādhiṣṭhānaprabheda* (ed. Pandey 1997: 44). Its subject has thereby been changed from *svādhiṣṭhāna* to *māyadeha*. It is hard to discern the rationale for this substitution, as the different *mudrā* configurations clearly do not define the illusory body in *Svādhiṣṭhānaprabheda* 45. Is this a deliberate reworking, or a misremembering, of the original verse?

25–28′): The text of this famous *vajragīti* from the *Hevajratantra* was first published long ago by Bagchi (1935: 36 IX). For nearly as long its semantics have been glossed over in modern studies. There is a philologically valid but semantically devolved exegesis that substitutes the codewords of the song with the corresponding euphemisms supplied in *Hevajratantra* II.3, which has been the usual approach in Anglophone as well as Tibetan scholarship, continuing up to Gerloff (2017: 145). One attempt to convey the *vajragīti* in language closer to its literal sense is made in a recent English translation of the song as it occurs in *Saṃpuṭodbhava* Ⅵ .1.3–7 (Dharmachakra 2020). The present English translation of the song moves further in the direction of literalism as a step towards exposing more of its metaphorical framework. An in-depth discussion of its metaphors would require a separate article, but it can mentioned in passing that the metaphorical source domain encompasses spices and aromatics that have rich potential for *double entendre*, as I have pointed out elsewhere (Sinclair 2019).

The Apabhraṃśa text of the *vajragīti* has been translated here with substantial guidance from glosses in the Sanskrit Haivajrika literature (Pandey 1988: 30), but also by referring to the *Gems*' Tibetan translation. The published Sanskrit exegetical material on the *Hevajra* is scant at the time of writing, if growing slowly, and the present edition and translation of the *vajragīti* likewise remains a work in progress. Alternative testimony for the text of the song is available outside the Sanskrit manuscript tradition in dozens of canonical Tibetan translations of texts of the Hevajra tantric system, in which Apabhraṃśa words are often preserved in Tibetan phonetic transcription. The only external testimony for the song collated here is sourced from the Chinese translation (*Fóshuō Dàbēi kōngzhì jīngāng dàjiàowáng yíguǐ jīng* 佛説大悲空智金剛大教王儀軌經 , T 892 597b_{25}–c_{5}; cf. Willemen 1983: 95), because it represents an early textual tradition entirely independent (as far as is known) of the Tibetan translations. Although the *Gems* conveys few interesting variants or interpretations, the Tibetan translation of v. 27ab is noteworthy:

caüsama katthuri sihlā kāppura lāïaï |
/bzhi mnyam gla rtsi si hla/ /e ma'o ka ppur dang li shi/

There is no word corresponding to *li shi*, "cloves," in the Apabhraṃśa text. With this change, there are four items associated with the *caüsama*, such that *lāïaï* (Skt. **labhyate*) was somehow read as a Prakritic word for cloves such as *laṅ* (cf. Turner 1966: 637 No. 10977, Skt. **lavāṅga*).

In the present edition the half-verse beginning *malaaje kunduru vāṭaï* is numbered with a prime, v. 28′, as it is orphaned without numbering in the blockprints of the *Gems*. However, this half-verse is usually counted as part of the *vajragīti*. Note also that the present edition pays no attention to the metre of this block of verses.

29): The source of this verse, the *Guhyāvalī*, has been edited in Sanskrit (n.a. 2008a: 119 v. 7). There is no complete Tibetan translation of the *Guhyāvalī*, although the *Guhyāvalī* was cited in other texts and some of these citations were translated into Tibetan. Kuranishi (2014: 204) notes, in his concordance of the *Guhyāvalī* citations, that this verse is also cited in Munidatta's *Caryāgītikośa* commentary. It is attributed to Daṛatipāda in Kværne's Sanskrit edition (1977: 125), but to Uḍi zhabs in the Tibetan translation (D 2293, ed. Kværne 1977: 126); neither of these names looks right. As Kuranishi anticipates, and as the manuscript confirms (Sen 1977: 37 f.19a3), the name here is *da u ḍī*, which Sen *ibid.* reads as *daḍatī*.

30): These three half-verses are found in neither the *Yuganaddhaprakāśa* of Advayavajra nor in *Rāhulaśrīmitra's **Yuganaddhaprakāśa nāma Sekaprakriyā* (D 1818). Their source is Advayavajra's *Tattvaprakāśa* vv. 6–7ab. As the *Tattvaprakāśa* is another short work by Advayavajra that ends in the word *prakāśa*, this misattribution may be due to faulty memory — Vanaratna's?

In the *Tattvaprakāśa*, the first *pāda* of this block reads *evam anāśravād dharmāt* (ed. Mathes 2015: 438–439), whereas the *Gems* reads *evaṃ prabhāsvarāc cittāt*. This is a significant difference, as the former reading refers to the *dharmakāya* — at least in the understanding of

Mathes (2015: 164) — in the context of a discussion of the bodies of a Buddha. In the context of the *Gems*, this verse's tacit reference to the *dharmakāya* has been lost. The *Gems*' translation is slightly awkward — splitting the compounds *bhoganirmāṇakāyābhyāṃ* and *pratītyapraṇidhānataḥ* across different quarter-verses — compared to the cleaner Tibetan translation of the *Tattvaprakāśa* (D 2241): /longs spyod sprul pa'i sku dag gis/ /rten 'brel smon lam dag gis ni/

31): Kāṇeripā's *Śucikaraṇa* v. 81 is the source of this verse. The reading of the fourth *pāda* is marked as uncertain in the edition published in *Dhīḥ* (n.a. 2008b: 139): *siddhiḥ *rājajālena*. The *Gems* blockprints all read *si ddhi ra na dza le na*. The second word is translated as *byang mang rtsom la*, probably understanding **ārambhaṇena*, "by getting started," in the *Gems*. But as Kāṇeripā is drawing a contrast with mental processes, as opposed to non-mental ones, the reading here is conjectured to be *ālambaṇena*, "with a physical support/meditation object."

32): This verse imputed to Virūpākṣa remains untraced. It has not been located in Satapathy's 2018 *editio princeps* of the *Amṛtasiddhi* attributed to Virūpākṣa. What is clear at present is the affinity of this verse with Vāgīśvarakīrti's *Mṛtyuvañcanopadeśa* 4.75 (ed. Schneider 2010: 117):

> tattvaṃ ca śūnyatā proktā sarvākāravarātmikā |
> tām evābhyasyato nityaṃ mṛtyur āyāti vañcanām ||

The Tibetan *Gems* translates *parā* in 32b as *gsungs*, probably due to contamination from 32a; *gzhan* would be expected (cf. 4b).

33): No written source for this verse "from the mouth" (*zhal byung nyid*) has been located. Its four-part structure is typical of *nīti* maxims. In the absence of parallels, the Sanskrit transcription has been heavily emended to follow the Tibetan translation. For instance, the word transcribed as *tsa kra su khaṃ* in 33a is conjectured to have come about, through metathesis and graphic confusion at the Tibetan end, from **krūramukhaṃ* on the basis of Tib. *kha nas gya gyur lan smra ba*, which, however figuratively understands *-mukham* (as speech, *thos*) and **krūra-* (as *gya gyur*, "twisted").

34): The incoherent parts of the transcript of this verse of the *Gems* have had to be emended here with extensive reliance on Kosambi's edition (1948: 58 v. 148) of the *Vairāgyaśataka*. It is noteworthy that much of the variation transmitted in the *Gems* is reflected in Kosambi's "Northern Recension," version H (*ibid.*: 27). In 34a, the reading *kiñcin na prāptam mayā* is accepted here as the reading of the textual tradition of the *Gems* even though *na* is hypometrical; Kosambi's edition here instead reads *prāptaṃ na kiṃcit phalaṃ*. The translation of *ucitam* in v. 34b as *phyug po* is hard to explain except as a free translation; it may be a misreading of *phal pa*.

35): The received text of this verse is unmetrical and incoherent: *e kaṃ dṛ ṣhṭa sha taṃ dṛ ṣhṭa dṛ ṣhṭa pa nytsa sha tā ni shtsa | a ti tṛ ṣhṭa sya pu ru ye ṣha sya tsa kra bhra ma ti ma sta ke* (witness N). It has been emended here with a low degree of confidence. In the second *pāda*, there is no correlate for Tib. *dbang* in the received Sanskrit text. In the context it seems to mean "more than" (**adhikam*). The second half of the verse has a striking parallel in a *śloka* of the *Pañcatantra* of Visṇuśarman, Aparīkṣitakāraka v. 22cd (ed. Parab & Wâsudev 1925: 214):

atilobhābhibhūtasya cakraṃ bhramati mastake ||

In the context of the *Pañcatantra*, this verse refers to a Brahmin who was cursed for his greed by a wheel grinding down his head. The stated source of the verse in the *Gems* is an **avadāna* or *jātaka* (*rtogs pa brjod pa*) of Mdza' mo'i bu. This title could represent various underlying Sanskrit names and has not yet been identified in the *avadāna* corpus.

36): The ascription of this well-known verse to Śabara is peculiar to the *Gems*. It is a verse that occurs without clear attribution throughout the tantric Buddhist scholastic corpus, from pseudo-Āryadeva's *Caryāmelāpakapradīpa* (D 1803) up to Darpaṇa's *Kriyāsamuccaya* (D 3305). Previous studies — above all that of Szántó (2010: 293), which puts this verse at the centre of an article-length discussion — have not located its point of origin. A relatively early citation is found in Śāntarakṣita's *Tattvasiddhi*, where it is attributed to the Bhagavat (D 3708: *de yang bcom ldan 'das kyis*). Śāntarakṣita here finds the "state of a monk" (*bhikṣubhāva*) — the "monastic life" — to be synonymous with lack of means-and-insight (*prajñopāyarahita*) and to therefore be inappropriate for sustained tantric praxis. This verse is said by Śāntarakṣita to have a scriptural origin, an origin that would be expected to be akin to the other *mahāyoga*-genre tantras cited in the *Tattvasiddhi*. A slightly different form of the verse appears in the *Vajrahṛdayālaṃkāratantra* (D 451), which could be classified as *mahāyoga*—at any rate, this tantra knows of the *rnal 'byor chen po* category. The translators, Kamalagupta and Mnga' bdag lha Ye shes rgyal mtshan, read:

> /de bas dge slong dngos gnas dang/ /de bzhin rtog ge rgan po dang/
> /rang gi bu dang rgyal po la/ /de nyid yang dag bshad mi bya/

The underlying text can be conjectured as follows (the alternative conjecture **svaputrā rājāno ye ca* would also fit *pāda* c):

> *bhikṣubhāvā vṛddhā ye ca ye ca tarkaratā tathā |
> *rājānaḥ svaputrā ye ca teṣāṃ tattvaṃ na deśayet ||

The third *pāda*, which states that kings or one's sons should not be taught "reality," did not propagate further, although others seem to have been aware of this variant of the verse. It is clearly echoed in a paraphrase that opens Vāgīśvārakīrti's *Saṃkṣiptābhiṣekavidhi*, v. 4c: *na rājñe 'pi na putrāya* ...; D 1887: *rgyal po la min by la min* (cf. eds. Sakurai 1996: 410, 427). This verse on the qualities of an initiand conveyed an important idea for Vāgīśvārakīrti; his opening paraphrase gives it in full, albeit with a minor variant in *pāda* a (*bhikṣubhāve ratā ye ca*, cf. ed. Sakurai 1996: 419, which displays contamination from *pāda* b). The sentiment expressed in this verse would have been far more appropriate for Vanaratna's Newar audience than for Tibetan monastics.

Given that this verse is tied to the exegesis of the *Guhyasamājatantra* from an early stage, its association with the Vajrayoginī tradition in the *Gems* is an oddity that most likely originates with Vanaratna. The lone ascription to *sha ba ra* does not occur elsewhere in the anthology, so it is unlikely to have become attached to this verse accidentally. It is, however, found in a number of Yoginītantric works in the Nepalese Sanskrit corpus including the *Kriyāsamuccaya* (D 3305) and Ratnarakṣita's *Padminī* (D 1420) commentary on the *Saṃvarodaya*.

37): This is the opening verse of Dharmadāsa's *Vidagdhamukhamaṇḍana*. The author crafts a consonance here between the words *siddhauṣadhāni* and *śauddhodaneḥ*. In *pāda* b, an emendation to *puṇyātmanāṃ* from the received reading *puṇyātmanaṃ* was required to comply with the Vasantatilakā metre. This is a fitting verse for wrapping up the anthology.

6.5 Tibetan–Sanskrit/Apabhramśa lexica

TIB. (VERSE)	SKT./APB.
a la la **18d**	*aho aho
e ma'o **17a**	aho
ka kko llar **25a**	kakkolā
ka ppur **27b**	kāppura
kyang **17a**	api
kyang **9a**	cet khalu
kye **26c**	hale
kye **3c**	he
kun tu yid kyi dri ma **37c**	manomalānām
kun tu rtog pa **17c**	samkalpaiḥ
kun du thams cad byed po mchog **19b**	sarvākṛtivaramayī
kun nas **6a**	sarvaḥ
kha nas gya gyur smra ba **33a**	*krūramukham
khyed rnams **3d**	yūyam
khyod kyis **16d**	tvayā
khengs pa **33b**	garvaḥ
gang **13c**	yat
gang **36b**	ye
gang **7c**	yaḥ
gang gi **2b**	yasya
gang gis **23c**	yayā
gang gis **29d**	yasya
gang du **31a**	'ang
gang zhig **13a**	ye
gang zhig **36c**	ye ca
gang zhig **7a, 7d**	yaḥ
gang yang **36a**	ye ca
gang yin **2b**	yā
gcig **6d**	ekā
gcig pa yis **31b**	ekam
gcig pa'i sku **21d**	ekarūpaḥ
gcig mthong ba nas **35a**	ekadṛṣṭāt
gnyen gyi skye bo'i **33c**	bandhujanasya
gtum mo'i 'od kyi rol pas **23a**	caṇḍālīkaralīlayā
gdags **28c**	caḍābiaï
gnas **21b**	vimānaḥ
gnas na **33d**	sthitiḥ
gnas brtan chen po nags kyi rin chen **1d**	vanaratnama-hāsthaviram
gzhan **4b**	parasya
gzhan gyi khyim du **34c**	paragṛheṣu
gzhan ma yin no **30f**	na bhinnau
gzhan min **13d**	nānyat
gzhan la **29b**	aparāḥ
g.yo ba'ang **23a**	ullālitaḥ
grub pa'i sman **37a**	siddhauṣadhāni
gal te **6b**	yadi
gla rtsi **27a**	katthuri
gling **13b**	dvīpāḥ
gsad bya'i skyes bu **3a**	vadhyapuruṣaḥ
gsal ba **30**	prakāśa
gsung rab rnams ni **37d**	pravacanāni
gsungs **32a**	proktā
gsod pa'i gnas su **3b**	vadhyasthānam
gus **1c**	bhaktyā
gus pa spangs pa'i **34c**	mānavivarjitam

go ba'am thob pa **12b**	bujjhaï
go 'phang **29c**	tatpadam
go 'phang la **31a**	padam
gom pa re res **3b**	pratipadam
nges par **21a**	khalu
nges par med na **9b**	syād eva
ngo bo nyid kyis dngos **8a**	bhāvarūpeṇa
ci **31d**	kim
ci **3d**	mā
cis mi skye **25d**	kiaï ṇa
cung zad kyang ni **34a**	kiñcit
chags pa'i mtha' ni **29a**	rāgānte
chags bral dang po 'jug pa'i dus su **29a**	viramapraveś-asamaye
chab phrom mo **14d**	ghanopalāḥ
chu **14d**	āpaḥ
chu ni **5b**	jalam
chu yi rlabs ltar g.yo ba **4d**	vāritaraṅgacañ-calatare
chu skyes rtse mor son pa'ang 'phel ba **23c**	ambhojāgragataḥ
chu skal med **26d**	dunduru
chen po'i blo dang ldan pas zhib mor mthong ba gang **6c**	sūkṣmekṣikākṣā-madhiyā
chos kyi dbyings **21a**	dharmadhātoḥ
ji bzhin **9b**	yadvat
ji tsam 'dod **27d**	bharu (*sic*)
ji lta bar **3b**	yathā
ji ltar **15a**	yathā hi
ji ltar **5a**	yathā
nyam ngar **3b**	viṣāde
nyams **10c**	na 'staḥ
nyid **9c**	api
nyid kyis **18a**	naḥ
nyid du **10d**	tu
nyid na'ang **4a**	parimitam
nyid yod **9d**	sattvam
nyin re nyin res **3c**	divasadivasaiḥ
nyon mongs **16a**	kleśāḥ
nyon mongs rang bzhin nyid las ni **16c**	kleśaprakṛtitaḥ
nyon mongs las ma byung **16b**	na kleśasambhavaḥ
tha snyad du **9c**	vyavahārataḥ
thabs kyi **25b**	kollaïre
thams cad **13c**	sarvam
thams cad **13b**	sarve
thim las **23b**	līnaḥ
thog ma med pa'i **17d**	anādau
thob pa **23c**	prāptaḥ
da dung tshim par ma gyur **34d**	nādyāpi santuṣyasi
dkar po nyid **15a**	śuklabhāvam
dkar por **15c**	śuklabhāvam
dag dang ma dag **28b**	suddhāsuddha
dgra bo **34d**	vairiṇi
dge slong dngos gnas dang **36a**	bhikṣubhāve sthitāḥ
dang **13b**, **19a**, **36b**	ca
dang de rnams **18a**	tāni
dang ni g.yo ba **13c**	jaṅgamam

dngos grub **31c**	siddhiḥ
dngos po rnams kyi **9a**	bhāvāḥ
dngos por **14b**	bhāvaḥ
dbang gang las **18c**	yad vaśāt
dbye ba **6b**	vibhāgakartā
dbu ma'i blo ni **19b**	madhyamakadhīḥ
dman pa rnams kyi **33b**	nīcasya
dmyal sogs dbye ba **13b**	narakādibhedāḥ
drin las **2b**	prasādāt
dul bar byas pa'i **2d**	savinayam
de **26d**	tahim
de **7a**, **7d**	sa
de kho na nyid **9a**	tattvataḥ
de kho na nyid bdud rtsir **18d**	tattvāmṛtaḥ
de gang gis **20a**	kena
de nyid **36d**	tattvam
de nyid ni **18b**	ta eva
de dag gi **30e**	tayoḥ
de dag skye 'jig pa'ang **19a**	*tadudayī
de de **13d**	tat tat
de ni **12b**	ttam
de ni **2b**, **19d**	sā
de ni **29d**	hi
de bzhin **5c**	tathā
de yang **12a**	ttam
de yang **2c**	tac ca
de yang **32c**	taṃ ca
de yi **2d**	tasya
de yi dus su **29c**	tatkāle
de yi phyed ni **4b**	tasyārdhasya
de rnams **9d**	teṣām

de rnams kyi ni **30e**	tasmāt
de la **36d**	teṣām
de la **7b**	tasya
de las **31c**	tatraiva
de'i phyed **4a**	tadardham
der **27d, 28′b**	tahim
der ni **21d**	tatra
der skyes **28d**	tahim ja
dogs dang **34c**	āśaṅkayā
dor nas **34b**	tyaktvā
nags su **33d**	vane
pur gsungs pa **6d**	uktiḥ
phyag bgyi'o **2d**	kuryāt
phyag 'os **18c**	vandyaḥ
phyag rgya gcig sbyor **24a**	ekamudrāsamā-yuktaḥ
phyag rgya chen po'i dngos grub **29d**	siddho mahāmu-drayā
phyag rgya chen po'i bdag nyid **32b**	mahāmudrātmikā
phyag rgya bzhi la sbyor ba **24b**	caturmudrāyutaḥ
phyi rol btang **28d**	paṇiaï
phyi rol mi btang bar **26c**	paṇiaï
phyir rang bzhin med **10a**	naiḥsvabhāvyāt
phyug po **34b**	ucitam
phyed **4b**	ardham
bag chags kyis bsgos **14a**	vāsanāvāsitā
bag yod pa **7d**	apramattaḥ
bgrod dka'i yul ni mang por **34a**	deśam anekadurgaviṣamam
bcas shing **34c**	kṛtā
btung bar bya **26b**	pijjaï

bdag gi snying po **18d**	māmakasāram
bdag gis **34a**	mayā
bdag po nyon mongs sa bon gyis **18a**	utkleśabījāni
bdag med nyid phyir **21a**	nirātmakatvāt
bdag 'dud **23d**	vandāmahe
bdar ba yis **15b**	gharṣet
bdud rtsi **16d**	amṛtam
bde **20a**	saukhyam
bde **4d**	saukhyam
bde ba gang zhig 'byung ba gzhan min **29c**	ananyasambhava-sukham
bde ba cher **23a**	mahāsukham
bde ba'i rdo rjer gyur ma **19d**	sukhavajrapraṇayinī
bde bar **2c**	sukham
bde bar gshegs pa'i ... mi **5c**	asaugatam (*sic*)
bden **19a**	satyā
bden pa'i don ni cho gas **17a**	bhūtārthavidhinā
btsun mo'i grong du 'jug pa'ang **24c**	antaḥpuragataḥ
bzhag nas **25b**	ṭṭhia
bzhi mnyam **27a**	caüsama
bzhin **17d**	iva
bzhengs 'di **21d**	utthite 'yaṃ
bzhed pa yin **8d**	matā
bza' **27d**	khāïaï
bza' bya zhin **26a**	khājaï
bya rog lta bur **34c**	kākavat
byang chub **16b**	bodhau
byang chub **16a**	bodhitaḥ

byang mang rtsom la **31d**	*ālambaṇena
byas na **31b**	kṛtvā
byis pa nyid de **4b**	bālatva
byis pas **15a**	bālaḥ
byis blo **15d**	bālasya buddhiḥ
byed **12d**	kīsa
brgya phrag lnga dbang mthong nas ni **35b**	*dṛṣṭapañcaśatā-dhikam
brgya mthong zhing **35a**	dṛṣṭaśatam
brjod pa **12a**	kahaï
brjod par byed **12d**	kahijjaï
brnyes pa **16d**	upārjitam
brtan g.yo'i 'gro ba'i de kho na **19c**	sthiracalajagat-tattvam
brtan pa **13c**	sthāvaram
brtan por ni gyur pas **14c**	dṛḍhībhūtāḥ
brdzun pa yis **17c**	alīkaiḥ
brdzun pa'i mngon rlom **15d**	vitathābhimānā
brdzun min **19a**	nāsatyā
bla ma dam pa **2d**	sadguroḥ
bla ma dam pa'i zhabs kyi chu skyes rdul la **18c**	sadgurupādapa-ṅkajarajas
bla mas **12a**	guru
blangs nas **15b**	ādāya
blo dag la **17a**	dhiyam
bstan mi bya **36d**	na deśayet
bsten kye **1c**	bhajata
bsten pa'i **5c**	sevayan
bsten par byas **34b**	sevā
bsdus pa **17c**	samgraham

bsam **31b**	dhyāyate
bslu bar **32d**	vañcanam
bsod nams kyi ni bdag nyid rnams la **37b**	*puṇyātmanaḥ
bo lla rab **25b**	bolā
ma ’phrul ba yi de nyid thob **22a**	abhrāntatattval-ābhāya
ma yin nyid **5d**	naiva
ma yin pa **19a**	nāpi
ma yin pa **5b**	na
ma yin zhing **12a**	ṇa
ma rnyed par **34a**	na prāptam
ma la ya skyes bud shing gis sā li **27cd**	mālaïindhaṇaśālia
ma la ya skyes **28′a**	mala aje
ma skyes **7a**	ajātaḥ
mkha’i me tog bzhin pa **8b**	khapuṣpavat
mgo po la ni **35d**	mastake
mgo bos **2d**	śirasi
mnga’ **28d**	sarāba
mngon par chas pa **3d**	vrajantaḥ
mngon par bsrubs kyang **5b**	abhimanthanāt
mngon sum chags bral ba **1a**	pratyakṣavītarāgam
mngon sum pa yi **29c**	sākṣāt
mchog **22d**, **29c**	param
mchog gi **31a**	paramam
mnyam dang mi mnyam mtho dma’i ’gro ba **17b**	samaviṣamanim-nonnatagatau
mthar thug pa ni **6d**	kṛtāntaḥ
mtho dbang po’i stobs **18a**	indriyabalāni

mthong ba ma yin pas **33c**	na dṛśyate
mthong ba min pa dang **33b**	api na dṛśyate vā
mtshan mo rnams kyis **4a**	rātrau
mtshungs **6a**	samānaḥ
mya ngan **33c**	śokaḥ
myang ’das go ’phang **23c**	nirvṛtipadam
mar **5b**	ghṛtam
mar don gnyer ba yis **5a**	ghṛtārthe
mi **36b**	narāḥ
mi thos shing **33a**	na dṛśyate
mi ’gyur ba **15c**	naiva
mi yis **5d**	naraḥ
mi rnams **33a**, **33d**	narāṇām
mi rnams **4d**	prāṇinām
mi rnams **4a**	nṛṇām
mi rus phyag rgya **28c**	niramśu
mi spang **28′b**	ṇa vājjiaï
mu stegs **6a**	bāhyasya
me tog thod can **3a**	sragvī
med **12b**	ṇa
med na **9b**	na... syāt
med pa nyid **9c**	asattvam
med las na **6b**	syāt
mo sham bu **9b**	vandhyātanayasya
mod **15c**	tu
tsi phyir shin tu **4d**	kutaḥ
tshul khrims rigs kyi nga rgyal **34b**	śīlakulābhimānam
tshe tshad **4a**	āyuḥ
zhabs kyi padmar **2d**	aṅghripadmam

zhes **19c**	iti
zhes dran **22b**	iti smṛtam
zhes bya **18d**	iti
zad par **15c**	kṣayam
zla ba’i rang bzhin gnas pa na ni **29b**	candre svabhāvasthite
zas gtsang sras po’i **37d**	*śauddhodaneḥ
zung ’jug **10d**, **30**	yuganaddha
zos **34c**	bhuktam
’khyams nas **34a**	bhrāntvā
’khrig 28′a	kunduru
’khrud par byed pa’i chu gcig pu **37c**	prakṣālanaikaśajalāni
’khrul pa’i **17a**	bhrāntim
’khor **35d**	bhramati
’khor ba’i ’khor lo **2a**	saṃsāracakra
’khor bar **17d**	samsāre
’khor lo **35d**	cakram
’gag **29b**	niruddhā gatiḥ
’gag pa med las **10b**	aniruddhatā
’gyur **14b**	bhavet
’gyur **29d**	asti
’gyur te **9c**	santi
’gyur ba **5d**	bhavet
’gyur ba nyid **32d**	āyate
’gro ba **21d**	jagad
’gro bzhin pa ni **3b**	*prayat
’chi ba **32d**	mṛtyuḥ
’chi ba la ni nges btsun **3c**	*mṛtyunikaṭam
’das **4b**	gatam
’di ni **17c**	idam
’di la **15a**	ayam
’di la yang **5c**	apīha
’di ltar **3c**, **30a**	evaṃ
’di las **9d**, **10c**	atas
’dir **6b**	iha
’byung bar ’gyur ba **3d**	bhavata
’bral ba’i snyug bsngal nad bcas **4c**	vyādhiviyogaduḥkhasahitam
’bras bu **31d**	phalaḥ
’bras bu med **4c**, **34b**	niṣphalā
’am **24b**	atha vā
’ong snyam **15b**	yāsyati
’od gsal ba’i sems las **30a**	prabhāsvarāc cittāt
yang **23c**	api
yang **26b**	gāḍhem
yang **9c**	api
yang dag... ’char ba **2c**	samudayati
yang med pa **9c**	asattvam
yang yang **29d**	punaḥ
yang yang bsrubs gyur **25c**	ghaṇem kipiṭa ho
yid **31b**	manaḥ
yid kyis **20b**	manaḥ
yid gang zhig **29a**	yā vittiḥ
yid ni **18b**	manasaḥ
yid ni don la mngon par zhen pa’i rgyu las **2a**	manaḥsanniyogārthahetoḥ
yid mi bya **28b**	ṇa maṇiaï
yid la khengs pa **3d**	dṛptamanasaḥ
yun du **37d**	ciram
yul ’di rnams te **18b**	ete te viṣayāḥ

yongs brtags dum bu gcig nyid bya **28a**	pemkhaṇa kheṭa karante
yod **9d**	asti
yod dang med pa **10c**	bhavābhāvau
yod ma yin **7b**	na... asti
rkyen la rag las **7c**	pratyayādhīna
rkyen las **7a**	pratyayaiḥ
rgan po nyid kyis **4b**	vṛddhatvayoḥ
rgan po'i dngos gnas pa **36c**	vṛddhabhāve sthitāḥ
rgya cher khyab cing **23b**	viṣvagbhūri
rgya mtsho chen po brgyad **13a**	aṣṭamahāsamudrāḥ
rgyan du chang **26b**	ma aṇā
rgyal **19d**	jayati
rgyal gyur cig **37d**	jayante
rgyal ba **19c**	jinaḥ
rgyu ba **29b**	pravṛttir
rang gi gnas las **23a**	nijapadāt
rang gi sa la **2b**	nijabhuvam
rang nyid **13d**	eva
rang nyid **18c**	svayam
rang nyid rtogs pa shar ba gang **23b**	svabodhodaye
rang bzhin **9d**	svabhāvataḥ
rang bzhin med phyir **20c**	niḥsvabhāvataḥ
rang bzhin las **30f**	svabhāvataḥ
rang 'byung **23a**	svabhūr
rje bo **2b**	svāminaḥ
rjes dran bya **24d**	anusmaret
rnyed 'gyur ba **5b**	samāpnoti
rnyed 'gyur **31c**	labhate
rtag tu **2d**	sarvakālaḥ
rtag tu **32c**	nityam
rtag par **29d**	nitya
rten 'byung ba **10b**	pratyayāt
rtog ge la dga' **36b**	tarkaratāḥ
rtog pa'i dra ba las grol **2c**	kalpanājālamuktam
rtogs **17a**	viditam
rdo rje 'dzin **13d**	vajrabhṛt
rna ba'i bcud len mchog **37b**	paramakarṇarasā-yanāni
rnam dbye byed po **6b**	vibhāgakartā
rnam par grol ba rnyed par **5d**	vimuktibhāk
rnam par dag pas **21b**	viśuddhitaḥ
rnam par bkra bar **2a**	*vicitrayati
rab tu bkrus las **1a**	prakṣālitam
rab tu 'jug **2b**	viśati
rab tu 'jug pa lnga po rnams kyi skad cig **18b**	pañca pravṛttikṣaṇāḥ
rtsol ldan par **18a**	utsukavanti
rdzogs longs **30b**	pravartate
rlung gi **29b**	vāyor
rlung gis dkrugs las **14c**	vātāvartte
ri **13a**	parvatāḥ
rig par byed **20b**	vedyavedakam
rig bya **20c**	*vedyam
rig byed gyur pa'i **20d**	vedya ... bhāvaḥ
rigs ngan **28′b**	ḍiṇḍima
rung **24c**	vāpi
re gnyis dag la shar ba'i **23d**	udayadvayam

re ba (?) **4c**	sevā
reg pa'i **18c**	sparśaḥ
ro dag nyal ba'i **21b**	suptaśavaḥ
rol mo dang ldan **3a**	tūryaiḥ
lags **16d**	caiva
ltung ba **3b**	nipatati
lam **5c**	mārgam
las gzhan min **16a**	na ... bhinnā
lha mo **19d**	devī
lhag ma **4c**	śeṣam
lhan cig skyes dga'i **23d**	sahajānandāya
lhan cig skyes pa'i bde ba bdud rtsi **12c**	sahaja amiasuha
li shi **27b**	lāïaï (*sic*)
lus la **28c**	aṅge
lo brgya **4a**	varṣaśatam
longs spyod gnas bcas rnams **3c**	bhogasthāḥ
longs spyod dag gis **3d**	*vibhogaiḥ
longs spyod rdzogs pa'i sku **22b**	sambhogakam
sha ni **26a**	bala
shin tu rnam dag chos dbyings rang bzhin gyis **21c**	suviśuddhadhar-madhātusvarūpaḥ
shin tu legs pa nyid **33d**	sādhutarā
shin tu sred pa'i skyes bu yi **35c**	atitṛṣṇapuruṣasya
shes **20a**	jñāyate
shes **7d**	jānati
shes rab kyi ni **25a**	mummuṇire
skad cig ma ste **23d**	drāgadrau
skabs der **26a**	tahim

skye ba **8d**	utpādaḥ
skye ba med pa'i rang bzhin gyis **8c**	anutpādasva-bhāvena
skye ba rang bzhin **7b**	utpāda svabhāvato
skye bar 'gyur **10d**	jāyate
skye bo mang pos yongs bskor ba **3a**	*bahujanaparivṛtaḥ
skye bos **1c**	janāḥ
skye med **8a**	notpādaḥ
skye med nyid **10a**	ajātatām
skyes pa **7a**	jāyati
skyes bu **5a**	puruṣaḥ
skyes min **8b**	nānutpādaḥ
skyon med **20d**	vidoṣaḥ
skal ldan **26c**	kālimjara
sgyu ma'i lus ni **24d**	māyādeham
sgra sgrogs par **25c**	vājjaï
sgom pa las **32c**	bhāvayitvā
sangs rgyas pa **6a**	bauddhasya
snyam du **6a**	pravibhajyamānaḥ
snyam na **20a**	iti
snying gi nam mkha'i khongs su bris pa **17d**	hṛdayagaganāb-hogalikhitaiḥ
snying rje **25d**	karuṇe
stong nyid **6d**, **7d**, **14a**	śūnyatā
stong pa nyid du **32a**	śūnyatā
stong pa nyid ni **14b**	śūnyataiva
stong par **8d**	śūnyatā
stong par bshad **7c**	śūnya uktaḥ
ston pa nyid kyis **19c**	śāstā
sdig pa'i las la dga' ba'i **34d**	pāpakarmanirate

sdug bsngal nad chen ldan pa'i srid pa rnams kyi **37a**	bhavaduḥkhamahāgatānām
sna tshogs bkra ba **17b**	citram citram
spang bar bya **26d**	vājjiaï
spyod sprul pa'i sku dag **30bc**	bhoganirmāṇakāyābhyām
spros pa med pa'i **2b**	niṣprapañcam
spros med **19b**	nirullekhā
sbyor bas **28′a**	vāṭaï
smon lam dang rten cing 'brel 'byung las **30cd**	pratītyapraṇidhānataḥ
srid pa gsum gyis **17c**	tribhuvanam
srid pa zhi byed **1c**	bhavaśāntyai
srid par skye ba'i nyon mongs rnyog pa rnams **1b**	bhavajakalmāṣakalaṅkam
sred pa **34d**	tṛṣṇe
srog ni **4d**	jīve
slob mas **12b**	sīsa
si hla **27a**	sihlā
su zhig gis ni **12d**	kahi
su yang rung ba'i **5a**	kaś cana
su la **12d**	kāsu
sems kyang **32a**	cittam ca
sems can don du **30b**	sattvārthāḥ
sems dpa'i gzugs brnyan zhi ba **22d**	*sattvabimbaśivam
so so rang gis rig bya ba **2c**	pratyātmavedyam
so so rang rig **19b**	svasaṃvittiḥ
song **15c**	yāti
song **4a**	gatam
son par gyur pa **18d**	syandati
sol ba **15b**	aṅgāram
hum phaṭ yi ge las grol ba **22c**	hūmphaṭkāravinirmuktam

6.6 Translations of the verses, with emic attributions

Chain of Essential Oral-Tradition Gems of the Glorious Vanaratna, the Great Pundit and Lord of Adepts

To ease rebirth, folks, please revere
in faith Vanaratna *mahāsthavira*,
Who washed off the dregs and stains of lives,
whose dispassion appears before the eyes. (1)
—the commendation of the great pundit Sun Of Men.

One should modestly do [bowing][①] with the head

① *kuryāt*: in the sense of *namaskuryāt*, cf. Tib. *Gems*: *phyag bgyi'o*; D 2293: *'dud.*

at all times to the lotus feet of him, the true guru,
By whose grace that thought
which constructs the round of rebirth
Due to the cause of the goal[①]-directed mind
enters nonproliferation at the master's own level,
And the bliss of freedom from the web of aspersion
emerges, knowable by each individual. (2)
—spoken by Śabareśvara[②] to Nāgārjunapāda.

Just as a condemned man — headbanded, surrounded by people and music
—falters in dread with each step on the way to the place of execution,
Hey, hedonists, in this way death looms with each passing day.
Aren't you all pushed by the influences[③] of a narcissist mind? (3)
—from a book of pundit Bhartṛhari.

Human life lasts a hundred years at most. Half of it goes in the night,
And another half of the other half in childhood and old age.
The rest, tied up with illness, partings and woe, is led in servitude and such.
Where is the happiness for beings in a life as uneven as waves on water? (4)
—from a book of Bhartṛhari.

Just as a person seeking butter from churning
water gets no butter anywhere,
A man, if[④] he resorts to a non-Buddhist path here,
would likewise have no part in liberation at all. (5)
—from the mouth of Kho dpon la springs pa.[⑤]

The whole system of tenets,[⑥] on being analysed

① *-ārtha-* ≍ Tib. *Gems*: *don la*; parallels: *-ātma-* "soul".
② Originally (in Munidatta's *Caryāgītikośa* commentary) Saraha.
③ *vibhavair* (em.); *Gems* blockprints: *vibhogair.*
④ *api*: read *yady api*.
⑤ Unidentified.
⑥ *kṛtāntaḥ*: "tenet system", "dogma" (D 2242: *grub pa'i mtha'*); Tib. *Gems*: *mthar thug pa ni.*

by one of lean wits and an eye for detail, is samey,
If it were not for the single teaching of emptiness here
differentiating between the Buddhist and the outsider. (6)
—from Kambalapāda's *Garland of Light*.

That which arises through conditions is simply unarisen;
its production is not due to inherent nature.
That which depends on conditions is called empty;
he who knows emptiness is clear-headed. (7)
—from a *sūtra*.[①]

[There is] no arising as real existence,
Nor non-arising like a sky-flower [eye disorder].
Arising with the inherent nature of non-arising
is understood to be emptiness. (8)
—by Kambalāmbara.

"If existences do not exist in reality,
they have no being conventionally either.
They would be just like a barren woman's son.
Hence, there is being, intrinsically." (9)
—[an objection presented] by Śrīcandra(kīrti).

[Existences have] beginninglessness due to lacking self-existence,
ceaselessness due to conditions.
Hence, neither existent nor nonexistent exist;
[existences are] born coupled together. (10)
—Advayavajra.

The Five Victors prevail as form and so on,
in individual form as a variegated perception, not isolated,

---

① Attributed to an *Anavataptahradāpasaṃkramaṇasūtra* in the *Prasannapadā*.

Empty, empty of determinations, arising from causes
not substantially extant in their intrinsic nature. (11)
—Maitrīpāda.

The guru doesn't explain it in words,
the student doesn't fathom it.
Who in the whole world can explain to whom①
the bliss of the ambrosial innate? (12)
—From the song of Sarahapāda.

Any mountains, eightfold great oceans,
islands, all levels of hell and so on —
Whatever is inanimate, let alone alive, everything —
that itself is none other than the Vajra-bearer proper. (13)
—From the mouth of Nāgārjuna.②

Emptiness alone, imbued with latent imprints,
could become existence.
With whirlings of wind, water alone
becomes condensed into thick clouds. (14)
—Nāgabodhi.

How a child, taking [a lump of] coal, might polish it:
"this becomes bright."
But it just crumbles without becoming bright,
the child's intellect having a false conceit.③ (15)
—(via) Nāgārjuna.

---

① *kāsu kahijjaï kīsa*: Skt. **kasya kathyate kīdṛśaḥ* (see the philological commentary). *Kīsa* is translated as "who" after Tib. *Gems' su zhig gis*, but we should understand "how", as the guru might still explain (albeit in an unfathomable way) *sahaja amiasuha*.

② Pseudo-Āryadeva, in his *Svādhiṣṭhānaprabheda*.

③ The *Gems* omits the succeeding verse in the source *sūtra*, the *Vīradattaparipṛcchā* (as quoted in Nāgārjuna's *Sūtrasamuccaya*), which begins *evaṃ hi yaś caukṣamatir manuṣyaḥ* ..., "So too a man who is fixated on cleanliness ...".

Defilements are not separate from the awakened,
nor is [there] arising of defilements in awakening.
And from the primal nature of defilement itself
immortality is procured by you. (16)
—from the mouth of Nāgārjuna.[①]

Ah, one directs wandering thought in diverse ways,
Along high, low, flat and rugged courses — even [when] observing with a fact-oriented approach.
In the unbegun round of rebirth, this triple world is like [their] totality,
Inscribed in the expanse of the heart's sky by noxious concepts. (17)
—Kambalapāda.

These very sense objects, precisely these,
have the five emergent moments of the mind.
Through them indeed, our sense faculties and powers
and seeds of disorder get agitated.
Venerable is the touch of the dust of the true guru's lotus feet,
that by the power of which — of its own accord —
This ambrosia of reality, the "essence of mine,"
flows day by day. (18)
—from Daüḍi's *prabandha*.

Neither true nor untrue,
nor both of these, nor neither,
She is indescribable, made of all the best parts,
the thought of the centre.
As the Victor, the teacher, is himself the
reality of the animate and inanimate world,
She, the goddess of self-aware cognition, vanquishes

① The first half of the verse is from Advayavajra's *Mahāyānaviṃśikā*, the second from Nāgārjuna's *Niraupamyastava*.

aiming for the thunderbolt of bliss. (19)
—Śabarapāda.

With what is blissfulness to be experienced?
[With] the mind that is the knower and the knowable,
Which,[①] arising as [both] knower and knowable,
is flawless due to lack of inherent nature. (20)
—[attributed to] Ārya Nāgārjuna.

Because of the very lack of selfhood, due to the Dharmadhātu's
purity, a numb corpse is a flying castle.
When it gets up, it has the inherent nature of the well-purified
Dharmadhātu that is uniform with the world. (21)
—Vīryaśrīmitra.

In order to grasp reality unmistaken
the enjoyment body is taught,
Unimpaired by the syllables *hūm* or *phaṭ*,
calm as an [awakening] being, supreme. (22)
—[via] Jālandharīpā.

The self-arisen, while shaken up from its state
by the play of Caṇḍālī's light,
Is dissolved in the arousal of the self-aware
experiencing great bliss abundantly and pervasively.
Going to the tip of the lotus, as well,
the nirvanic state is also had, by which
The innate joy I salute obtains
the quick and the running, the two emergents. (23)
—Vīryaśrīmitra.

① *yaḥ* (conj.); *Gems* blockprints: *naḥ*.

One should think of the illusory body as conjoined with one *mudrā*
Or escorted by four *mudrā*s, or even as being among a harem.① (24)
—[Pseudo-]Āryadeva.

Myrrh② sits at Mount Kolla, pepper at Mummuni.
The woods boom deeply, ahoy! Love happens, not noise. (25)

Then he eats the power,③ squeezes the ornament tight.
Hello! The Kāliñjaran is to lead; the deniers④ have to keep out. (26)

He gets the foursame: musk, Shallaki resin, camphor, [cloves⑤].
He eats lots of jasmine wood-fired rice product there. (27)

We do swinging and snot, not minding clean or unclean,
Putting drab⑥ on the body. The platter is put in there. (28)

Olibanum abounds in the sandal grove.
Bongos⑦ are not to be kept out of there. (28′)
—the vajra song from the *Hevajratantrarāja.*

At the end of *rāga*, at the time of entering *virama*,
when the moon is in its natural state,

---

① *antaḥpuragataḥ*: the "apartments of seclusion"; Tib. *Gems*: *btsun mo'i grong du 'jug pa'ang* (D 1805: *btsun mo'i 'khor na bzhugs pas*). The word *pura* can also refer to maṇḍala superstructure.

② *bolā... kakkolā*: these are words for aromatics plants. Here, *bola* is regarded as synonymous with *ela* (cardamom), among other possible referents (see e.g. Turner 1966: 704 No. 12154). Pepper (cubeb) is one meaning of *kakkola* (Turner 1966: 127 No. 2586). These identifications have been proposed and discussed elsewhere (Sinclair 2019). *Gems* Tib.: *shes rab kyi ni ka kko llar/thabs kyi bo lla* "the *kakkola* of insight, the *bola* of means," cf. *Hevajra* II.4.50ab: *bolasaukhyaṃ mahāmudrā vajrāyatanam upāyakam* (ed. Tripathi & Negi 2001: 183).

③ *bala*: *Gems* Tib.: *sha* "meat."

④ *durduru*: apparently synonymous with *durdurūṭa* "atheist," "an abusive word," or *durdhūr* "difficult to be restrained," as glossed by Monier Williams 1872: 422. Tib. *Gems*: *skal med* "unfortunate one," cf. *Hevajra* II.3.57c: *abhavyaṃ dunduraṃ khyātam* (ed. Tripathi & Negi 2001: 169).

⑤ *li shi* (*Gems* Tib. only). See also the philological commentary on this verse.

⑥ *niraṃśu*; *Gems* Tib.: *mi rus* "human bone."

⑦ *ḍiṇḍima*; Tib. *Gems*: *rigs ngan* "outcaste" (**cāṇḍāla*).

The mode which the mind has, different to [its] activity,
is the arrested motion of the winds.
At that time, the bliss that has no other origin
is manifestly the supreme state.
For he who has personal experience in this is,
moreover, a *siddha* by way of the Great Seal. (29)
—from Daüḍi's *prabandha*.

The needs of living beings are furthered
in this way due to radiant mind
By the Enjoyment and Emanation bodies,
as a result of causation and solicitation.
Because that [mind] is their own nature,
the two are not, therefore, separate. (30)
—from the *Prakāśa*.

When the mind, having been made one,
meditates on the highest state,
Siddhi is to be had right then.
What result [is had] from [meditating on] an object? (31)
—From the mouth (of Kāṇeripā).

Mind is called emptiness, the transcendence consisting of the Great Seal.
And having meditated on that, death shall always be cheated. (32)
—Virūpākṣa.

See not the cruel face① of men; neither see the hubris of a lowlife.
See not the grief of kith and kin. Better that men stayed in the forest. (33)
—oral tradition.

---

① *krūramukhaṃ* conj.; *tsa kra mu khaṃ* blockprints, cf. Tib. *Gems*: *kha nas gya gyur smra ba* "swirling speech from the mouth."

Roaming a treachery-skewed land, I gained nothing in return.
Putting aside just pride in clan and mores, I did fruitless service.
In others' houses, I ate heedlessly out of worry, like a crow.
O Desire, you crone bent on bad karma, are you not satisfied even now? (34)
—Bhartṛhari.

From one view, a hundred views [arise], increasing to five hundred views.
For a person of acute desires, a wheel always spins in the head. (35)
—from the *Story of Mdza' mo'i bu*.

Those who abide in the state of a monk, who are sophistry-loving men,
And who abide in an elderly state are not to be taught reality. (36)
—Śabara.

May the potent medicines for the ills of rebirth's pangs,
The ultimate feasts for the ears for worthy souls,
The singularly cleansing waters for tainted minds —
The Buddha's teachings — endure through the ages. (37)
—the great *ācārya* Vīra.

References

Canonical Tibetan texts

D 451 Bcom ldan 'das de bzhin gshegs pa (Kamalagupta & Lha ye shes rgyal mtshan, trans.). *Dpal rdo rje snying po rgyan gyi rgyud* (*Vajrahṛdayālaṃkāratantra*).

D 1177 Nyi ma pa (Gzhon du dpal, trans.). *Dpal ldan bla ma nags kyi rin chen gyi bstod pa bdun pa* (*Ratnastotrasaptaka* of Āditya). Skt.: Hahn 1997: 36–37.

D 1237 Dzā landha ri zhabs (Mañjuśrī & Nyi ma rgyal mtshan, trans.). *Kye rdo rje'i sgrub thabs kyi mdor bshad pa dag pa rdo rje sgron ma zhes bya ba* (*Vajrapradīpā nāma ṭippaṇīviśuddhi* of Jālandharipā). Skt.: Gerloff 2017: 163–267.

D 1395 Nyi ma'i dpal ye shes (Nor bu dpal ye shes, Nyi ma'i dbang po'i 'od zer & Chos rje dpal, trans.). *'Phags pa mtshan yang dag par brjod pa bdud rtsi'i thig pa zhes bya ba* (*Amṛtakaṇikā nāma Śrīnāmasaṅgītiṭippaṇī* of Raviśrī). Skt.: Lal 1994.

D 1420 Ratnarakṣita (Thams cad mkhyen pa'i dpal & Blo brtan, trans.). *Dpal sdom pa 'byung ba'i rgyud kyi rgyal po chen po'i dka' 'grel padma can* (*Śrīsamvarodayamahātantrarājasya Padminī nāma pañjikā* of Ratnarakṣita).

D 1585 Brtson 'grus dpal bshes gnyen (Mañjuśrī, Jetakarṇa & Nyi ma rgyal mtshan, trans.). *De kho na nyid ye shes yang dag par grub pa'i rgya cher 'grel pa de kho na nyid bshad pa* (*Marmakalikā nāma Tattvajñānasaṃsiddhipañjikā* of Vīryaśrīmitra). Skt.: Pandey 2000.

D 1802 Klu sgrub (Śraddhākaravarman & Rin chen bzang po, trans.). *Rim pa lnga pa* (*Pañcakrama* of Nāgārjuna). Skt.: Mimaki and Tomabechi 1994.

D 1803 Āryadeva (Śraddhākaravarman & Rin chen bzang po, trans.). *Spyod pa bsdus pa'i sgron ma* (*Caryāmelāpakapradīpa* of pseudo-Āryadeva).

D 1805 'Phags pa lha (Śraddhākaravarman & Rin chen bzang po, trans.) *Bdag byin gyis brlab pa'i rim pa rnam par dbye ba* (*Svādhiṣṭhānaprabheda* of pseudo-Āryadeva). Skt.: Pandey 1997: 40–45.

D 1818 Sgra gcan 'dzing dpal bshes gnyen (Śākyaśrībhadra & Kun dga' rgyal mtshan trans.). *Zung du 'jug pa gsal ba zhes bya ba'i dbang gi bya ba* (**Yuganaddhaprakāśa nāma Sekaprakriyā* of *Rāhulaśrīmitra).

D 1887 Nag gi dbang phyug grags pa (Sumatikīrti, Klog skya gzhon nu 'bar & Mar pa chos kyi dbang phyug, trans.). *'Dus pa'i dbang bskur ba'i cho ga mdor bsdus pa* (*Saṃkṣiptābhiṣekavidhi* of Vāgīśvārakīrti). Skt.: Sakurai 1996: 409–421.

D 2224 Saraha (n.a. trans.). *Do ha mdzod kyi glu* (*Dohākośa* of Saraha). Skt.: Shahidullah 1928: 123–165.

D 2241 Gnyis med rdo rje (n.a. trans.). *De kho na nyid rab tu bstan pa* (*Tattvaprakāśa* of Advayavajra). Skt.: Mathes 2015: 437–441.

D 2242 Gnyis med rdo rje (Phyag na rdo rje & Rma ban chos 'bar, trans.). *De bzhin gshegs pa lnga'i phyag rgya rnam par bshad pa* (*Pañcatathāgatamudrāvivaraṇa* of Advayavajra). Skt.: Mathes 2015: 371–384.

D 2253 Dga' ba skyong (Samantabhadra & Nag tsho, trans.). *Dbang bskur ba nges par bstan pa'i dka' 'grel* (*Sekanirdeśapañjikā* of Rāmapāla). Skt.: Śāśanī 2017.

D 2254 Lhan cig skyes pa'i rdo rje (Vajrapāṇi, Kalyāṇavarma & Jñānakara, trans.). *De kho na nyid bcu pa'i rgya cher 'grel pa* (**Tattvadaśakaṭīkā* of *Sahajavajra).

D 2257 Gnyis su med pa'i rdo rje (Prajñāśrījñānakīrti, trans.). *Mi zad pa'i gter mdzod yongs su gang ba'i glu zhes bya ba gnyug ma'i de nyid rab tu ston pa'i rgya cher bshad pa* (**Nijatattvaprakāśa* of Advayavajra).

D 2293 Thub pas byin (Kīrticandra & Grags pa rgyal mtshan, trans.). *Spyod pa'i glu'i mdzod* *kyi 'grel pa* (**Caryāgītikośavṛtti* by Munidatta). Skt.: Kværne 1977.

D 3305 'Gro ba'i me long (Mañjuśrī & Blo gros rgyal mtshan, trans.; rev. Vajraśrī). *Rdo rje slob dpon gyi bya ba kun las btus pa* (*Kriyāsamuccaya* of Darpaṇa).

D 3708 Zhi ba 'tsho (Dīpaṃkaraśrījñāna & Rin chen bzang po, trans.; rev. Kumārakalaśa & Shākya 'od). *De kho na nyid grub pa zhes bya ba'i rab tu byed pa* (Tattvasiddhi of Śāntarakṣita).

D 3860 Zla ba grags pa (Mahāsumati & Pa tshab Nyi ma grags, trans.). *Dbu ma rtsa ba'i 'grel pa tshig gsal ba zhes bya ba* (*Prasannapadā* of Candrakīrti). Skt.: la Valleé Poussin 1913.

D 3862 Zla ba grags pa (Kanakavarman & Pa tshab ni ma grags, trans.). *Dbu ma la 'jug pa'i bshad pa* (*Madhyamakāvatārabhāṣya* of Candrakīrti).

D 3865 Zla ba grags pa (Dīpaṃkaraśrījñāna & Tshul khrims rgyal ba, trans.). *Byang chub sems dpa'i rnal 'byor spyod pa bzhi brgya pa'i rgya cher 'grel pa* (*Catuḥśatakaṭīkā* of Candrakīrti).

D 3887 Kamalaśīla (Śīlendrabodhi & Dpal brtsegs rakṣita, trans.). *Dbu ma snang ba* (*Madhyamakāloka* of Kamalaśīla).

D 3895 Kambala (Shākya 'od, trans.). *Snang ba'i phreng ba zhes bya ba'i rab tu byed pa* (*Ālokamālā* of Kambala). Skt.: Lindtner 1985.

D 3934 Āryanāgārjuna (Jinamitra, Śīlendrabodhi & Ye shes de, trans.). *Mdo kun las btus pa* (*Sūtrasamuccaya* compiled by Nāgārjuna).

Q 5044: see D 1177.

Q 5096 Śrīvanaratna. *'Grub pa'i dbang phyug paṇḍi ta chen po shrī ba na ratna'i zhal lung rin po che'i snying po'i phreng ba* (*Siddheśvaramahāpaṇḍitaśrīvanaratnamukhāgamaratnasārāvalī* compiled by Sāgarasena).

Q 5099 Śrīvanaratna. *Zhal lung rin po che'i phreng ba* (*Mukhāgamaratnāvalī*).

Q 5101 Nyi ma (Rgya mtsho sde, trans.). *Bstod pa rin po che bdun pa* (*Ratnastotrasaptaka* of Āditya). See also D 1177.

Secondary studies

Bendall, Cecil (ed). 1902. *Çikshāsamuccaya: a compendium of Buddhistic teaching.* Bibliotheca Buddhica, 1. St. Pétersbourg: Imperial Academy of Sciences.

Bendall, Cecil (ed). 1905. *Subhāṣita-saṃgraha.* Extrait du «Muséon» Nouvelle série, IV–V. Louvain: J.-B. Istas; London: Luzac; Paris: Leroux; Leipsic, Harrassowitz.

Bandurski, Frank. 1994. "Übersicht über die Göttinger Sammlungen der von RĀHULA SĀṄKṚTYĀYANA in Tibet aufgefundenen buddhistischen Sanskrit-Texte (Funde buddhistischer Sanskrit-Handschriften, III)." In: Frank Bandurski, Bhikkhu Pāsādika, Michael Schmidt and

Bangwei Wang (eds.), *Untersuchungen zur buddhistischen Literatur*. Göttingen: Vandenhoeck & Ruprecht, 12–126. urn:nbn:de:bvb:12-bsb00040415–7.

Bhayani, H C. 1997 (ed. and trans.) *Dohā-gīti-kośa of Saraha-pāda (A Treasury of Songs in the Dohā Māde nyid kyis na rang bzhin bde ba chen po so so rang gis rig pa'i ngo bo nyid du mngon du bya ba'i rnam par mi rtog pa'i sgo thun mong ma yin pa la gdams patre) and Caryā-gīti-kośa (A Treasury of the Caryā Songs of various Siddhas)*. Ahmedabad: Prakrit Text Society.

Cowell, E. B. & Eggeling, J. 1876. "Catalogue of the Buddhist Sanskrit Manuscripts in the possession of the Royal Asiatic Society (Hodgson Collection)." *Journal of the Royal Asiatic Society (New Series)* 8(1): 1–52.

Damron, Ryan C. 2021. "Deyadharma–A Gift of the Dharma: The Life and Works of Vanaratna (1384–1468)." PhD diss., University of California, Berkeley.

Delhey, Martin. 2021. "The 'Vanaratna Codex': A Rare Document of Buddhist Text Transmission (London, Royal Asiatic Society, Hodgson MS 35)." In: Stefanie Brinkmann, Giovanni Ciotti, Stefano Valente and Eva Maria Wilden (eds.), *Education Materialised: Reconstructing Teaching and Learning Contexts through Manuscripts*. Berlin, Boston: De Gruyter, 379–397. doi:10.1515/9783110741124–018.

Dharmachakra Translation Committee. 2020. *The Foundation of All Tantras, the Great Sovereign Compendium "Emergence from Sampuṭa". Saṃpuṭodbhavasarvatantranidānamahākalpa rājaḥ*. 84000: Translating the Words of the Buddha. (Version 1.11.15, 2022.) https://read.84000.co/translation/UT22084-079-008.html.

Ehrhard, Franz-Karl (ed.) 2002. *A Buddhist correspondence: the letters of Lo-chen Bsod-nams-rgya-mtsho. Facsimile edition of a 15th century Tibetan manuscript*. Lumbini: Lumbini International Research Institute.

Gerloff, Torsten. 2017. "Saroruhavajra's Hevajra-Lineage: A Close Study of the Surviving Sanskrit Works." PhD diss., Universität Hamburg.

Hahn, M. 1987. "Sanskrittexte aus dem tibetischen Tanjur (I). Das Nāgārjuna zugeschriebene Daṇḍakavṛttastotra." *Berliner Indologische Studien* 3: 51–102.

Hahn, M. 1996. "Das *Vanaratnastotra* des Āditya." In: Jens-Uwe Hartmann, Roland Steiner and Helmut Eimer (eds.), *Suhṛllekhāḥ. Festgabe für Helmut Eimer*. Swisttal-Odendorf: Indica et Tibetica Verlag, 29–42.

Jagadananda, Swami (ed.) 1979. *Vakyavritti and Atmajnanopadeshavidhi of Sri Sankaracharya*. Mylapore, Madras: Sri Ramakrishna Math.

Keith, Arthur Berriedale and Frederick William Thomas (eds.) 1935. *Catalogue of the Sanskrit and Prākrit Manuscripts in the Library of the India Office. Vol. II part II: Nos. 6628–8220*. Oxford University Press.

Kosambi, D. D. (ed.) 1948. *The Epigrams Attributed to Bhartrhari, including the Three Centuries*. Bombay: Singhi Jain Śastra Sikshapitha, Bharatiya Vidya Bhavan.

Kuranishi, Ken'ichi. 2014. "Dauḍīpāda and the *Guhyāvalī*." *Journal of Indian and Buddhist Studies* 62(3): 1267–1271. doi:10.4259/ibk.62.3_1267.

Kværne, Per. 1977. *An Anthology of Buddhist Tantric Songs. A Study of the Caryāgīti*. Oslo/Bergen/Tromsø: Universitetsforlaget.

Lal, Banarsi. 1994. *Āryamañjuśrīnāmasaṁgīti with Amṛtakaṇikā-ṭippaṇī by Bhikṣu Raviśrījñāna and Amṛtakaṇikodyota-nibandha of Vibhūticandra*. Sarnath: Central Institute of Higher Tibetan Studies.

Li, Xuezhu 李學竹. 2015. "*Madhyamakāvatāra-kārikā* Chapter 6." *Journal of Indian Philosophy* 43: 1–30. doi:10.1007/s10781–014–9227–6.

Lindtner, Chr. 1985. "A Treatise on Buddhist Idealism. Kambala's *Ālokamālā*." In: Chr. Lindtner, Miscellanea Buddhica, Indiske Studier V. Copenhagen: Akademisk Forlag, 109–219.

Mathes, Klaus-Dieter. 2008. "The *Śrī-Śabarapādastotraratna* of Vanaratna." In: Dragomir Dimitrov, Michael Hahn and Roland Steiner (eds.), *Bauddhasāhityastabakāvalī: Essays and Studies on Buddhist Sanskrit Literature dedicated to Claus Vogel by Colleagues, Students, and Friends*. Marburg: Indica et Tibetica Verlag, 245–268.

Mathes, Klaus-Dieter. 2015. *A Fine Blend of Mahāmudrā and Madhyamaka. Maitrīpa's collection of Texts on Non-conceptual Realization (Amanasikāra)*. Wien: Österreichische Akademie der Wissenschaften.

Matsunami, Seiren 松濤誠廉. 1965. *A Catalogue of the Sanskrit Manuscripts in the Tokyo University Library*. Tokyo: Suzuki Research Foundation.

Mimaki, Katsumi and Tomabechi, Tooru. 1994. *Pañcakrama: Sanskrit and Tibetan Texts Critically Edited with Verse Index and Facsimile Edition of the Sanskrit Manuscripts*. Tokyo: The Centre for East Asian Cultural Studies for Unesco, the Toyo Bunko.

Monier Williams, M. 1872. *A Sanskṛit-English dictionary*. Oxford: Clarendon Press.

N.a. 2008a. "Guhyāvalī of Siddhācārya Dauḍīpāda with Vivṛti by Paṇḍitasthavira Śrīghanadeva." *Dhīḥ* 46: 111–130.

N.a. 2008b. "Śucikaraṇam of Kāṇeripā." *Dhīḥ* 46: 131–141.

Olivelle, Patrick (ed.) 1976–1977. *Vāsudevāśrama Yatidharmaprakāśa*. 4 vols. Vienna: Indologisches Institut der Universität Wien.

Otani University Library. 1965. *A Comparative Analytical Catalogue of Tanjur Division of the Tibetan Tripitaka* 大谷大学図書館蔵 西蔵大蔵経 丹殊爾勘同目録. Tokyo: Tibetan Tripitaka Research Institute.

Pandey, Janardan Shastri. 1988. "Apabhraṃśa vacana saṃgraha." *Dhīḥ* 5: 29–36.

Pandey, Janardan Shastri. 1989. 'Introduction of Rare Texts.' *Dhīḥ* 8: 6–34.

Pandey, Janardan Shastri. (ed.) 1997. *Durlabha Bauddha Grantha Parichaya (Part-II)*. Sarnath: Rare Buddhist Texts Research Project, Central Institute of Higher Tibetan Studies.

Pandey, Janardan Shastri. 2000. *Tattvajñānasaṃsiddhiḥ of Śūnyasamādhīpāda with Marmakalikāpañjikā of Vīryaśrīmitra*. Sarnath: Rare Buddhist Texts Research Unit.

Parajuli, Punya Prasad. 2014. "Vanaratna and His Activities in Fifteenth-Century Nepal." In: Andrew Quintman and Benjamin Bogin (eds.), *Himalayan Passages: Tibetan and Newari Studies in Honor of Hubert Decleer*. Boston: Wisdom, 289–300.

Roerich, George N. 1949. *The Blue Annals*. Calcutta: Royal Asiatic Society of Bengal. (2nd ed.: Delhi, 1976.)

Sakurai, Munenobu 桜井宗信. 1996. *Indo mikkyō girei kenkyū: kōki Indo mikkyō no kanjō shidai (インド密教儀礼研究—後期インド密教の灌頂次第)*. Kyoto: Hōzōkan.

Sakya Research Centre. https://sakyaresearch.org [Accessed 14 February 2022].

Sāṅkṛtyāyana, Rāhula. 1937. "Second Search of Sanskrit Palm-leaf Mss. in Tibet." *Journal of the Bihar and Orissa Research Society* XXIII (I): 1–57.

Śāśanī, Ṭhinalerāma (ed.) 2017. "Sekanirdeśapañjikā." *Dhīḥ: Journal of Rare Buddhist Texts Research* LVII: 169–206.

Satapathy, Bandita (ed.) and Niradbaran Mandal (trans.) 2018. *Amṛtasiddhiyogaḥ*. Pune: Kaivalyadhama.

Schaeffer, Kurtis R. 2002. "The Attainment of Immortality: From Nāthas in India to Buddhists in Tibet." *Journal of Indian Philosophy* 30 (6): 515–533. doi:10.1023/A:1023527703312.

Schaeffer, Kurtis R. 2005. *Dreaming the Great Brahmin: Tibetan Traditions of the Buddhist Poet-Saint Saraha*. New York: Oxford University Press.

Schneider, Johannes. 2010. *Vāgīśvarakīrtis Mṛtyuvañcanopadeśa, eine buddhistische Lehrschrift zur Abwehr des Todes*. Wien: Österreichische Akademie der Wissenschaften.

Sen, Nilaratan (ed.) 1977. *Caryāgītikoṣa*. Simla: Indian Institute of Advanced Study.

Sferra, Francesco. 2000. *The* Ṣaḍaṅgayoga *by Anupamarakṣita with Raviśrījñāna's* Guṇabharaṇīnāmaṣadaṅgayogaṭippaṇī. *Text and annotated translation*. Roma: Istituto Italiano per l'Africa e l'Oriente.

Shahidullah, M. 1928. *Les chants mystiques de Kāṇha et de Saraha: Les Dohā-koṣa (en apabhraṃśa, avec les versions tibétaines) et les Caryā (en vieux-bengali)*. Paris: Adrien-Maisonneuve.

Sinclair, Iain. 2016. "The appearance of tantric monasticism in Nepal: A history of the public image and fasting ritual of Newar Buddhism, 980–1380." PhD diss., Monash University. doi:10.4225/03/58ab8cadcf152.

Sinclair, Iain. 2020. "Spice as soteriology: The transcendent signification of *bola* and *kakkola*." Paper presentation, Käte Hamburger Kolleg, Centre for Religious Studies, Ruhr-Universität Bochum.

Szántó, Péter-Dániel. 2012. "The case of the *vajra*-wielding monk." *Acta Orientalia Academiae Scientiarum Hungaricae* 63 (3): 289–299. doi:10.1556/Aorient.63.2010.3.5.

Tanaka, Kimiaki 田中公明. 2017. "New Material on the Āmnāyamañjarī." *The memoirs of Institute for Advanced Studies on Asia* 172: 37–48. doi:10.15083/00074379.

Tripathi, Ram Shankar and Thakur Sain Negi. 2001. *Hevajratantram With Muktāvalī Pañjikā of Mahāpaṇḍitācārya Ratnākaraśānti*. Sarnath: Central Institute of Higher Tibetan Studies.

Tucci, Giuseppe. 1932. "Two Hymns of the Catuḥ-stava of Nāgārjuna." *Journal of the Royal Asiatic Society* 64 (2), 309–325. doi:10.1017/S0035869X00112079.

Turner, Ralph L. 1966. *A Comparative Dictionary of the Indo-Aryan Languages*. London: Oxford University Press.

Ui, Hakuju 宇井伯寿, Suzuki, Munetada 鈴木宗忠, Yenshô, Kanakura 宗忠金倉, Tada Tôkan 多田等観. 1934. *A complete catalogue of the Tibetan Buddhist Canons (Bkaḥ-ḥgyur and Bstan-ḥgyur)* (西藏大藏經總目錄 東北帝国大学藏版). Sendai: Tōhoku Imperial University.

La Valleé Poussin, Louis de. 1913. *Madhyamakavṛttiḥ: Mūlamadhyamakakārikās (Mādhyamikasūtras) de Nāgārjuna avec la Prasannapadā Commentaire de Candrakīrti*. St-Pétersbourg: l'Académie impériale des sciences.

Wang Junqi, Zhang Meifang, Lü Xiaofang, Xin Song, Kawa Sherab Sangpo, Dazhen. 2020. "A Preliminary Study on a Newly Discovered Sanskrit Manuscript of Nāgārjuna's *Sūtrasamuccaya*." *Journal of Buddhist Studies* 17: 59–88.

Willemen, Ch. 1983. *The Chinese Hevajratantra. The scriptural text of the ritual of the great king of the teaching, the adamantine one with great compassion and knowledge of the void*. Leuven: Uitgeverij Peeters.

敦煌宗教与世俗文献

藏译疑伪经《北斗七星经》再探

才　让

西北民族大学铸牢中华民族共同体意识研究院

中国佛教界一般将造于本土的佛经称为“疑伪经”。部分中土疑伪经曾被译成藏文，或收入《甘珠尔》中，或收入《陀罗尼集》中，得以在藏地流传，对藏传佛教产生了一定的影响。疑伪经《北斗七星经》（སྨེ་བདུན་ཞེས་བྱ་བ་སྐར་མའི་མདོ༎）有回鹘文、蒙古文、藏文等文字的译本，在多民族间传播而影响较广。由此该经颇受海内外学者重视，傅海波（H. Franke）[①]等诸多著名学者发表有相关的研究成果。其中，邦隆（L. Panglung Jampa）研究了其藏译本并将之译成德文[②]，约翰・艾维尔斯科（Johan Elverskog）[③]、松川节[④]、苏鲁格[⑤]等人的研究成果中亦或多或少涉及藏译本。本文在已有的研究基础上，对藏译《北斗七星经》之版本、译跋、藏译文之特色及流传等问题进行再探讨。

---

① H. Franke, “The Taoist Elements in the Buddist Great Bear Sūtra (Pei-tou ching),” *Asia Major,* Vol. 3, No.1, 1990, pp.75-111.

② L. Panglung Jampa, “Die tibetische Version des Siebengestirn-Sūtras,” in E. Steinkellner ed., *Tibetan History and Language. Studies dedicated to Uray Géza on his 70th Birthday, Vienna*:University of Vienna, 1991, pp.399-416.

③ Johan Elverskog, “The Mongolian Big Dipper Sūtra,” *Journal of the International Association of Buddhist Studies,* Vol. 29, No. 1, 2008, pp.87-123.

④ 松川节著，杨富学、秦才郎加译:《蒙古语译〈佛说北斗七星延命经〉中残存的回鹘语因素》,《甘肃民族研究》2007年第2期，第75—80页。原文被收入森安孝夫编:《中央アジア出土文物論叢》，朋友书店2004年版，第85—92页。

⑤ 苏鲁格:《汉、回鹘、蒙古三种文字〈北斗七星经〉之考释》,《蒙古学信息》2004年第4期，第69—75页。

一、藏译本之版本

1.《甘珠尔》版本

松川节已指出最早收入《北斗七星经》的藏文《甘珠尔》是永乐版，但对永乐版所依据的底本曾有不同的说法。东噶先生认为明朝的使臣在纳塘寺获得该寺所编的《甘珠尔》，以此为母本刻印了永乐版[①]。最早的纳塘本目录，目前能看到的有两种，一是卷丹柔贝热止（བཅོམ་ལྡན་རིག་པའི་རལ་གྲི）所编《佛教广弘庄严日光》（བསྟན་པ་རྒྱས་པ་རྒྱན་གྱི་ཉི་འོད）。《东噶藏学大辞典》中称此目录为“甘珠尔和丹珠尔目录佛教广弘”，编者当时不知道该目录的存世情况，后来发现于哲蚌寺乃久（十明）殿。该目录遵照了吐蕃时期的目录编纂法，将经论汇编在一起，未分《甘珠尔》和《丹珠尔》。另，《东噶藏学大辞典》中还认为卷丹柔贝热止著有《甘珠尔目录·日光》（简目），但整理出版的《卷丹柔贝热止文集》（二卷本）中未见该目录。纳塘版之第二种目录即纳塘寺卫巴·洛赛造贝僧格（དབུས་པ་བློ་གསལ་རྩོད་པའི་སེང་གེ）所著《论典目录》（བསྟན་བཅོས་དཀར་ཆག），这应是最早的《丹珠尔》目录。《佛教广弘庄严日光》的编排法与永乐版《甘珠尔》相比，差别很大，可以断定永乐版不是以纳塘版为底本的。

现在学界一般认为永乐版的底本是完成于蔡巴·贡噶多杰（1309—1364）时期的《蔡巴〈甘珠尔〉》[②]。在蔡贡塘寺，首先由贡噶多杰的父亲莫兰多杰于1310—1328年间准备编纂《甘珠尔》，“第五饶迥水猪年（1323年）到第六饶迥土鼠年（1348年）期间，蔡巴·贡噶多杰掌政（指贡噶多杰担任蔡巴万户的万户长——译者注），修就了用金银汁混合书写的一套完整的《甘珠尔》，迎请遍知的布顿大师进行校订，这部甘珠尔的目录是蔡巴·贡噶多吉自己编制的，目录的题为《新造佛说甘珠尔之目录——白册》，……通常称为‘《蔡巴〈甘珠尔〉》’”[③]。该写本《甘珠尔》有260函。编纂于蔡贡塘寺的《蔡巴〈甘珠尔〉》中，收入同期翻译的《北斗七星经》是非常有可能的，也能说明何以在永乐版中出现了此经。该经在永乐版的经部ཨ༨函。新出《甘珠尔（对勘本）》经部《北斗七星经》之对勘记中云：“此经德格版、理塘版、纳塘版、卓尼版、库伦版、拉萨版不收，以永乐版为底本，与北京版进行

---

① 东嘎·洛桑赤列著，陈庆英、敖红译：《藏文文献目录学》（上），《西藏研究》1987年第4期，第124页。

② 参见嘉措等：《拉萨现藏的两部永乐版〈甘珠尔〉》，《文物》1985年第9期，第85—88页；王尧：《藏文大藏经 丽江一里塘版甘珠尔经述略》，《中央民族学院学报》1986年第3期，第71—77页；辛岛静志：《论〈甘珠尔〉的系统及其对藏译佛经文献学研究的重要性》，《中国藏学》2014年第3期，第31—37页。

③ 东嘎·洛桑赤列著，陈庆英、敖红译：《藏文文献目录学》（上），第124页。《蔡巴〈甘珠尔〉》曾请布顿大师校订，在永乐版目录《如来大宝佛语目录·佛法增盛之日光》中有说明，言永乐版《甘珠尔》随顺布顿大师所抉择之目录，参见中国藏学研究中心《大藏经》对勘局编：《甘珠尔（对勘本）》（藏文），中国藏学出版社2008年版，第105卷，第375—482页。

了对勘。”[①]

以永乐版为母本的《甘珠尔》刻印本中收有《北斗七星经》，如之后的万历版《甘珠尔》以永乐版为底本在北京重新刊刻，只是该版本大都亡佚无存。[②]景泰年间用金粉抄写了一套《甘珠尔》，其底本可能是永乐版或抄自西藏的永乐版母本。对此抄本，后来在清康熙年间孝庄太皇太后命人对景泰抄本重新抄写，称为《龙藏经》，大部分藏台北故宫博物馆。[③]《龙藏经》中是否有《北斗七星经》待查。

清康熙年间（1662—1722）以永乐版为底本刊刻了《甘珠尔》，被称为北京版《甘珠尔》，乾隆年间此版曾数次增补修订。[④]北京版同样收有《北斗七星经》，也为学界所熟知。邦隆以拉萨版《陀罗尼集》所收《北斗七星经》为底本，与北京版《甘珠尔》，以及其他写本（藏于德国柏林国家图书馆的《甘珠尔》）校勘，校勘记有 161 条，但未能使用永乐版。《甘珠尔（对勘本）》中，对勘永乐版与北京版，校勘记有 8 条，并统计出二者字数均是 2 806 字，可见永乐版和北京版差别不大。但所作对勘有所遗漏，如永乐版和北京版的最大区别主要在第一位藏译者的名称写法不同，永乐版作མ་ཧུ་པ་ལ།，而北京版作མ་ཧཱ་པ་ལ།[⑤]。此点，对勘本未能校出。

2.《陀罗尼集》中所收

藏文大藏经《甘珠尔》将短小的经咒汇编在一起，名为གཟུངས་བསྡུས（陀罗尼集）。[⑥]这种做法可能源于印度，敦煌藏文文献中亦有短小咒语的汇编。《甘珠尔》之《陀罗尼集》所收经文有三类：第一是短小的密宗陀罗尼经，如《圣度母陀罗尼》；第二是祈愿文类，如《催破大千经所说祈愿文》；第三是吉祥颂类等，如《吉祥偈》。《陀罗尼集》所收经文的特点是现实功用极为突出，对于解决群体或个人遭遇的困难很有针对性。《陀罗尼集》在民间受到欢迎，成为举行禳灾仪式的常用法本。由此，出现了单独印行的《陀罗尼集》，而且内容不断增加，将可疑的伪经、伏藏文献、本土大师的作品等收入其中，与《甘珠尔》中的《陀罗尼集》间差别较大。松巴堪布在批驳《陀罗尼集》中的疑伪经时，提出了两种《陀罗尼集》版本。一是觉囊派多罗那他时期出现的，即达丹版；二是清代北京印刷的《陀罗尼集》，言其

---

① 中国藏学研究中心《大藏经》对勘局编：《甘珠尔（对勘本）》（藏文），第 76 卷，第 806 页。

② 波兰的克拉科夫亚盖隆大学图书馆藏有部分万里版《甘珠尔》，参见龙达瑞：《波兰亚盖隆大学藏万历版〈甘珠尔〉》，《西南民族大学学报》（人文社会科学版）2017 年第 1 期，第 88—93 页。也有研究者认为万里版是永乐版的重印，而非重刻，参见巴多、张智瑜：《清代官版藏文〈大藏经〉之刊刻考》，《西南民族大学学报》（人文 社会科学版）2022 年第 2 期，第 30—45 页。

③ 辛岛静志：《论〈甘珠尔〉的系统及其对藏译佛经文献学研究的重要性》，第 33 页。

④ 巴多、张智瑜：《清代官版藏文〈大藏经〉之刊刻考》，第 30—45 页。

⑤ 此点在松川节的论文中已经提及。北京版《甘珠尔》经部第 93 函，第 286 叶 b—290 叶 a，参见佛教数字资源中心（BDRC）W1PD96684。

⑥ 汉文《大藏经》中有《陀罗尼集经》十二卷，唐代天竺三藏阿地瞿多译，亦汇集了佛菩萨等的咒语、手印法等，但与藏文《陀罗尼集》不同。

所收文献又有所增加，如收进了《白伞盖赞》《度母赞》等。松巴堪布所列伪经中有《北斗七星经》，疑所举两种《陀罗尼集》中收有该经。

最晚编纂的《陀罗尼集》名为《经咒经典海中众多心要、名号、陀罗尼汇编》（མདོ་སྔགས་གསུང་རབ་རྒྱ་མཚོ་སྙིང་པོ་མཚན་གཟུངས་མང་བསྡུས），是由定日哇·曲吉坚赞（དིང་རི་བ་ཆོས་ཀྱི་རྒྱལ་མཚན།）出资刻印的（1949 年刻印，BDRC 标为 1947 年）[①]，共上下两卷。后印版存于拉萨，故此《陀罗尼集》又称为拉萨版。该《陀罗尼集》问世最迟，所收经文的数量又超过了以往的版本，尤其收入格鲁派大师的一些作品，如六世班禅的《香跋拉祈愿文》。松巴堪布所指出的疑伪经，拉萨版中亦大多收有。《北斗七星经》（སྨེ་བདུན་ཞེས་པ་སྐར་མའི་མདོ།），在拉萨版下卷第 228 叶 a—233 叶 b 间，首题汉、蒙古、藏三语对照经名，经文后面有译跋和翻译题记。相比于永乐版、北京版，拉萨版《陀罗尼集》所收《北斗七星经》经过了后人的订正，文字错误较少。

此外，此经还有单行本，民间有收藏。又收入一些文献汇编中，如《重要古籍抄本汇编》（དཔེ་རྙིང་རྩ་ཆེན་བྲིས་མའི་སྐོར་ཕྱོགས་བསྡུས།）[②]、《经集》（མདོ་མང་།）[③]、《日常诵念经典汇编·善道明灯》（ཆོས་སྤྱོད་ཕྱོགས་བསྒྲིགས་ལམ་བཟང་གསལ་བའི་སྒྲོན་མེ།）[④] 等。

二、藏译本现存译跋之翻译及第二位译者身份之补证

松川节等主张该经首先被翻译成了回鹘文，之后从回鹘文译成蒙古文本，蒙古文本又译成藏文本，藏文本又回译成蒙古文本。蒙古文本之初译者是必兰纳识理，但不清楚其译本是否存世。松川节认为蒙古文本可分为五类，但又言受到藏译本之影响。约翰·艾维尔斯科、苏鲁格等人认为蒙古文本译自汉文本，之后被翻译成了藏译本。但苏鲁格本人翻译成汉文的蒙古文本，实则源自藏文本，因其上署有藏译本译者题名。

藏译本的正文后面附有译跋，其中第一部分是偈颂体，第二部分是散文体，说明了此经翻译成回鹘、霍尔（蒙古）文、藏文以及刻印流通的情况。学界对源自藏文本的蒙古文译本之译跋已有汉文翻译，但所译与笔者之理解多有不同，现依据永乐版，将跋文再翻译如下：

---

① BDRC. W1KG12113。

②《重要古籍抄本汇编》（དཔེ་རྙིང་རྩ་ཆེན་བྲིས་མའི་སྐོར་ཕྱོགས་བསྡུས།）第 36 卷，第 1031—1044 页，但所收《北斗七星经》是刻本，第一位藏译者名作མ་ཧཱ་པ་ལ།与永乐版同（参见 BDRC.WZPD19899）。

③《经集》（མདོ་མང་།）第 2 卷，梵夹装印本，第 713—730 页，wA rA Na si，1971 年（参见 BDRC. W1KG12536）。该本中第一位译者同样作མ་ཧཱ་པ་ལ།。

④《日常诵念经典汇编·善道明灯》，西藏人民出版社 1999 年版，第 560—573 页。

“导师正觉所讲说（སྟོན་པ་རྫོགས་པའི་སངས་རྒྱས་ཀྱིས་གསུངས་པ།།），

于此北斗七星经（ཙི〔སྡི〕[1]་བདུན་ཞེས་པའི་སྐར་མའི་མདོ་སྡེ་འདི།།），

能依心忆并供养（བརྟེན་པའི་སེམས་ཀྱིས་དྲན་ཞིང་གང་མཆོད་པ།།），

彼得利益因深知（དེ་ལ་ཕན་པ་འབྱུང་ཞེས་རབ་ཤེས་ནས།།）。

乌汝波噶名苏古且（ཨུ་རུག་པོ་གའི་མིང་ཅན་ཟུ་གུར་ཆེ།།[2]），

幼时时常于此法（ཆུང་ངུའི་དུས་ནས་རྟག་པར་ཆོས་འདི་ལ།།），

具足信念常诵供（ཡིད་ཆེས་ལྡན་པས་རྒྱུན་དུ་གློག་ཅིང་མཆོད།།），

为求高位而祈愿（རང་གི་གོ་འཕང་ཆོལ་ཞིང་གསོལ་འདེབས་པས།།），

相应得佑具福分（འཐུན〔མཐུན〕[3]་པར་སྐྱོབ་པའི་བདག་པོའི་བསོད་ནམས་ཅན།།）。

令行解脱导师佛化身（གྲོལ་མཛད་སྟོན་པ་སངས་རྒྱས་སྤྲུལ་པ་གང་།།），

图贴睦尔王子为长寿（ཐོག་ཐེ་མུར་རྒྱལ་བུ་ཡུན་དུ་ཚེ་རིང་ཞིང་།།），

并愿成为慈悲大皇帝（ཐུགས་ཅན་རྒྱལ་པོ་ཆེན་པོར་འགྱུར་བར་འདོད།།），

具足智慧菩萨此主宰（བློ་ལྡན་བྱང་ཆུབ་སེམས་དཔའ་བདག་པོ་དེ།།），

修习而登薛禅汗宝座（སློབ་ནས་སེ་ཆེན་རྒྱལ་པོའི་གདན་སར་བཞུགས།།）。

‘因吾心愿得满足（བདག་གི་ཡིད་ལ་འདོད་པའི་ཚིམ་གྱུར་པས།།），

于此无惑生定解（ཐེ་ཚོམ་མེད་པར་ཆོས་འདིར་ངེས་ཤེས་ཅས།།），

回鹘文之此经典（ཡུ་གུར་ཡི་གེར་ཆོས་ཀྱི་མདོ་སྡེ་འདི།།），

以前他人若未译（སྔོན་ཆད་གཞན་གྱིས་བསྒྱུར་བ་མེད་པས་ན།།），

令诸蒙古信供奉（མང་པོའི་ཧོར་རྣམས་དད་པས་མཆོད་གྱུར་ཅེས།།）。’

由吾译成蒙古文（བདག་གིས་ཧོར་གྱི་སྐད་དུ་བསྒྱུར་བ་ཡིན།།）。

‘若吾所愿能实现（ང་ཡིས་ཇི་ལྟར་བསམས་པ་འགྲུབ་འགྱུར་ན།།），

万千有情所有愿（སེམས་ཅན་ཁྲི་ཕྲག་སྟོང་ཕྲག་འདོད་པ་ཀུན།།），

如我一般满足云（བདག་ཉིད་ཇི་བཞིན་ཚིམ་པར་གྱུར་ཅིག་ཅེས།།）。’

印刷千册施诸人（སྟོང་ཕྲག་པར་དུ་བཏབ་ནས་ཀུན་ལ་བཀྱེ།།），

以此福德果报力（འདི་ཡི་བསོད་ནམས་དྲིན་གྱི་འབྲས་བུའི་མཐུས།།），

皇帝皇后及后嗣（བདག་པོ་རྒྱལ་པོ་དཔོན་མོ་བརྒྱུད་པར་བཅས།།），

寿命恒长增福德（ཡུན་དུ་སྐུ་ཚེ་རིང་ཞིང་བསོད་ནམས་འཕེལ།།），

究竟获得佛之位（མཐར་ཐུག་སངས་རྒྱས་གོ་འཕང་རྙེད་གྱུར་ཅིག།）。

国境仇敌纷争消（རྒྱལ་ཁམས་དགྲ་དང་འཁྲུག་པ་ཞི་བ་དང་།།），

无有魔障及瘟疫（གདོན་དང་བར་ཆད་རིམས་མེད་བདེ་གྱུར་ཅིག།），

---

① ཙི：永乐版、北京版均如此，尾题经名中亦作ཙི་，应是སྡི之误。拉萨版《陀罗尼集》本中均作སྡི。

② ཟུ་གུར་ཆེ：或作ཟུ་གུར་ཆེ།，其义不明，或刻印有误。

③ འཐུན：拉萨版《陀罗尼集》本作མཐུན，应是。

风调雨顺无饥荒（ཆར་རླུང་དུས་འབབ་མུ་གེ་མེད་འགྱུར་ཞིང་།།）。

愿吾心愿令实现（བདག་གིས་སྨྲས་དང་བསམ་དོན་འགྲུབ་གྱུར་ཅིག།），

我及父母儿子等（བདག་དང་ཕ་མ་བུ་སོགས་གཉེན་རྣམས་དང་།།），

兄弟及众有情等（འཚོ་བའི་དཔུན ① ་དང་སེམས་ཅན་མང་པོར་བཅས།།），

于此世间法愿满（འཇིག་རྟེན་འདིར་ཡང་ཆོས་ཀྱི་འདོད་པ་ཚིམ།།），

极乐刹土常到达（བདེ་བ་ཅན་ཞིང་རྟག་པར་ཕྱིན་གྱུར་ཅིག།）。

天历元年（1328 年——译注）即龙年十月初一进行了印刷。（ཐེན་ལི་དང་པོའི་ལོ་འབྲུག་གི་ལོ་ཟླ་བ་བཅུ་པའི་ཚེས་གཅིག་ལ་སྤར་དུ་བཏབ་པ་ཡིན།།）

此经由一位印度班智达和唐三藏从印度携带至汉地并翻译，在汉地广为流传。在大皇帝之大臣，出生于菩萨种，具足信仰、智慧、禅定的金紫光禄大夫御史大夫乌汝波噶的鼓励下，回鹘教法之主必兰纳识里将其译成蒙古语文，印刷两千册。阿邻铁木尔大司徒将它翻译成回鹘文，在蒙古和回鹘广为流传。大夫（指乌汝波噶——译注）以前持蒙古之教法，因此法之加持转而信仰佛教并出家，体悟此法之诸功德。后于阴火牛年由译师玛哈巴拉和释阿难达巴陀罗在贡塘寺译成藏文并于校订。（མདོ་འདི་རྒྱ་གར་གྱི་ཡུལ་ནས་རྒྱ་གར་གྱི་པཎ་ཌི་ཏ་གཅིག་དང་། ཐང་ཟམ་ཚང་གིས་ཁྱེར་ཏེ་རྒྱའི་ཡུལ་དུ་བསྒྱུར་རོ།། རྒྱ་ཆེན་པོའི་ཡུལ་དུ་རྒྱས་པར་གྱུར་ཅིང་གནས་པ་ལས། རྒྱལ་པོ་ཆེན་པོའི་བློན་པོ་བྱང་ཆུབ་སེམས་དཔའི་རིགས་སུ་བྱུང་བ་དད་པ་དང་ཤེས་རབ་དང་། ཏིང་ངེ་འཛིན་དང་ལྡན་པའི་གིམ་ཙེ་གོང་ལུ་ཏའི་ཏུའི་གཡུའི་ཤྲཱི་ཐའི་ཏུ་ཨུ་རུག་པོ ② ་གས་བསྐུལ་ཏེ། ཡུ་གུར་གྱི་བསྟན་པའི་བདག་པོ་པྲཛྙཱ་ཤྲཱིས་ཧོར་གྱི་སྐད་དང་ཡི་གེར་བསྒྱུར་ནས་སྟོང་ཕྲག་གཉིས་སྤར་དུ་བཏབ། ཨ་ལིན་ཏེ་མུར་ཏའི་སི་དུས་ཡུ་གུར་གྱི་སྐད་དུ་བསྒྱུར་ཏེ། སྟོང་ཕྲག་གཅིག་སྤར་དུ་བཏབ་ནས་ཆོས་ཀྱི་སྦྱིན་པ་བྱས་ཏེ། ཧོར་དང་ཡུ་གུར་ལ་རྒྱས་པར་བྱས་ཤིང་། ཏའི་ཏུ་ཉིད་ཀྱང་སྔོན་ཆད་སོག་པོའི་ཆོས་ལུགས་འཛིན་པ་ལ། ཆོས་འདིའི་བྱིན་བརླབས་ཀྱིས་སངས་རྒྱས་ཀྱི་ཆོས་ལ་ཞུགས་ཤིང་རབ་ཏུ་བྱུང་ཏེ། འདིའི་ཡོན་ཏན་རྣམས་ཉམས་སུ་མྱོང་བར་གྱུར་པའོ།། སླད་ཀྱིས་མེ་མོ་གླང་གི་ལོ་ལ་ལོ་ཙྪ་བ་མ་ཧཱ་པ་ལ་དང་། ཤཱཀྱ་ཨཱ་ནནྡ་བྷ་དྲས་གུང་ཐང་གི་གཙུག་ལག་ཁང་དུ། བོད་ཀྱི་སྐད་དང་ཡི་གེར་བསྒྱུར་ཞིང་ཞུས་ཏེ་གཏན་ལ་ཕབ་པའོ།། ||）

该跋文偈颂体部分中，“导师正觉所讲说”至“相应得佑具福分”，是在说明元朝大臣乌汝波噶对该经的推崇，下文亦言蒙文本的翻译是在他的鼓励下完成的。“令行解脱导师佛化身”至“修习而登薛禅汗宝座”，是言图贴睦尔即元文宗（1304—1332）在登基之前就重视《北斗七星经》，并将其登基的原因归功于此经。之后的“因吾心愿得满足”至“令诸蒙古信供奉”应是元文宗之旨令，让译者将《北斗七星经》从回鹘文本译成蒙古文。之后加了单引号的三句话亦应是元文宗之语。蒙古文本的翻译年代是 1328 年，正是元文宗登基之年。这段跋文的记载也得到了史书的证明。研究者指出，《元史》载元文宗时期（1328—1332）曾两次“祭星消灾”，这说明元文宗登基后同样重视《北斗七星经》，并举行相关仪式。之后“以此福德果报力”以下诸句，是译者必兰纳识里的祈愿文。从偈颂文看，回鹘文译本早于蒙古文本。

---

① དཔུན：北京版作དབུན，དཔུན、དབུན均误。拉萨版《陀罗尼集》所收文本中作སྤུན（232 叶 a），应是。

② པོ：前文作བོ。北京版前文作པོ，下文作བོ。

跋文之散文体部分，介绍了该经的来历，及蒙古文本之翻译者、印刷的册数、回鹘文之译本等。从语气看，散文体译跋似是藏译者所加，与最后一句藏译本译者题记是完整的一段。因此笔者以为现存的《北斗七星经》译跋说明回鹘本早于蒙古文本[①]，蒙古文本是在回鹘本基础上翻译的，但也不排除译者通数种文字，翻译时对汉译本有所参考。

藏译本翻译的时间是阴火牛年，即元顺帝至元三年（1337 年）。贡塘寺又称蔡贡塘寺，属于蔡巴噶举派。元代时蔡巴噶举成为地方势力，乃十三万户之一，万户长一职由噶氏家族世袭。第一位译者之梵语名，按《北京版》所载为མ་ཏི་ཕ་ལ，邦隆还原为藏文是 Blo-gros-stobs（བློ་གྲོས་སྟོབས，意译“智慧力”）或 Blo-gros-skyoṅ（བློ་གྲོས་སྐྱོང，意译“智慧护”）。但是早于北京版之永乐版中作མ་ཏྣ་ཕ་ལ，故有可能མ་ཏི 是མ་ཏྣ之误。此人作为藏译本之主译者，应是一位精通藏蒙两种文字的译师，但笔者尚未发现与其生平等信息相关的线索。

第二位译者署名同样用梵语，作ཤྲཱི་ཨཱ་ནནྡ་བཛྲ（Śri-Ānandavajra），邦隆还原为ཀུན་དགའ་རྡོ་རྗེ（应是དཔལ་ཀུན་དགའ་རྡོ་རྗེ），并指向蔡巴・贡噶多杰。但邦隆又言此人不能确定即为蔡巴・贡噶多杰，理由之一是丽江版（即理塘版）中没有收入《北斗七星经》，而丽江版的底本是《蔡巴〈甘珠尔〉》，故推测《蔡巴〈甘珠尔〉》中亦无《北斗七星经》。笔者以为无论《蔡巴〈甘珠尔〉》是否收有《北斗七星经》，此处的译者可以确定就是蔡巴・贡噶多杰，别无他人。

也有学者推断元文宗下令西藏僧侣崇拜星星，即向西藏推广《北斗七星经》，《北斗七星经》可能由此传到西藏。但藏文译经题记并未说明奉旨译经事，应是贡噶多杰等人了解到此经在皇室及汉、回鹘、蒙古多民族传播之情形而将其翻译成了藏文。蔡巴・贡噶多杰（1309—1364）所著的《莫兰多杰传》对蔡巴万户与元朝皇室之间的频繁往来和密切关系多有反映，又涉及贡噶多杰本人的部分历史。如言金猴年（1320 年）时，元英宗命蔡巴万户长莫兰多杰赴大都觐见，其因故派子贡噶多杰代为前往，贡噶多杰时年十二岁，随萨迦本钦俄色僧格赴内地。[②] 贡噶多杰至大都，拜见元英宗并受到其礼遇，获得各种赏赐、诏书，亦得到帝师贡噶罗追坚赞等上层之关照。阴水猪年元月（1322 年），贡噶多杰返回蔡巴。[③] 虽

---

① 吐鲁番出土的回鹘文《北斗七星经》刊本之跋文中，提到此回鹘文本在癸丑年（1313 年）印刻了 1 000 部（参见上揭松川节文）。

② 俄色僧格是第十三任本钦，《西藏通史》言《红史》等未提及此人入朝事，《莫兰多杰传》对其入朝之记载，可补史书之阙。

③《东噶・藏学大辞典》中言贡噶多杰在十五岁时，即在水猪年（1323 年）被任命为万户长，木牛年（1325 年）即其十七岁时（《西藏通史》言十六岁）赴大都觐见元泰定帝也孙铁木耳（1323—1328 年在位），获得银印等封赏。恰白・次旦平措等人编的《西藏通史・松石宝串》亦言贡噶多杰十七岁时赴大都觐见泰定帝。《莫兰多杰传》中言莫兰多杰卸任万户长是在年四十岁的水猪年（1323 年），将万户长之职交给贡噶多杰。莫兰多杰于阳土龙年（1328 年，时年四十五岁）出家为僧。贡噶多杰之相关史事之记述，《莫兰多杰传》所载更为可信。参见东噶・洛桑赤列：《东噶藏学大辞典：藏文》，中国藏学出版社 2002 年版，第 1698 页；恰白・次旦平措等编，陈庆英等译：《西藏通史——松石宝串》，西藏古籍出版社 1996 年版，第 539 页；蔡巴・贡噶多杰：《莫兰多杰传》，民族文化宫图书馆抄本，第 27 页 a。

书中未言贡噶多杰在赴京期间曾学习过蒙古文，但其在内地居住近一年，自然有机会接触和学习蒙古文。从《莫兰多杰传》看，贡塘寺与元朝皇室间关系非凡，寺中建有忽必烈影堂，元庭重视蔡巴和贡塘寺，皇帝及部分皇室成员对贡塘寺之赏赐、供养源源不断，来自朝廷的金字使者络绎不绝。贡噶多杰作为蔡巴之首领，又有内地之行的经历，耳闻目睹，必能了解朝廷推崇《北斗七星经》之风尚。

蔡巴・贡噶多杰的著作喜欢用梵语署名，如他撰写的《莫兰多杰传》中，其名作ཨ་ནནྡ་བཛྲ；而且，其撰写《红史》中的蒙古早期世系（忽必烈及以前）时，言从典籍ཐོབ་ཆེན中将重要的部分摘录而成，ཐོབ་ཆེན（Thob chen）即《脱卜赤颜》。[①] 又用蒙古语将《红史》称为ཧུ་ལན་དེབ་གཏེར，[②] 说明贡噶多杰很可能掌握了蒙古文，才能参与翻译之事。因此，这个译经题记对研究蔡巴・贡噶多杰而言，非常有价值。上文亦言永乐版中收入有《北斗七星经》，而永乐版的底本是《蔡巴〈甘珠尔〉》，后者正是在贡噶多杰时期完成的。所以蔡巴・贡噶多杰将自己的译作收入他所编的《甘珠尔》，似乎也是顺理成章之事。问题是，如邦隆所指出的，以《蔡巴〈甘珠尔〉》为底本的丽江版中因何无《北斗七星经》，这一问题尚难以被圆满地回答。《蔡巴〈甘珠尔〉》完成于 1347 年，而丽江版全部完成于 1623 年，间隔近三百年的时间。丽江版目录由六世红帽活佛之弟子孜夏寺喇嘛安噶（ཇེ་ཤག་ལྷ་མ་མཛོན་དགའ་མིང་ཅན།）完成，[③] 经典的编排方式与《永乐版》有很大的差异。目录前言中言该版本经宣尼扎巴坚赞、噶玛派历代黑红帽活佛等之校订、注释、辨析，在雪域之地已无可匹敌。[④] 故可知，丽江版所依据的《蔡巴〈甘珠尔〉》已历经了多次重修，亦有可能《北斗七星经》因非正宗佛典而被剔除。

三、藏译本与汉文本之比较

国内编的历代《大藏经》均未收《北斗七星经》，主要保存在日本，据松川节的研究，该经收录在日本编的《大正藏》《享和仪轨》《大日本缩刷大藏经》《卍续藏经》等中。后来，

① 蔡巴・贡噶多杰著，东嘎・洛桑赤列校注：《红史》（藏文），民族出版社 1981 年版，第 30 页。

② 蔡巴・贡噶多杰著，东嘎・洛桑赤列校注：《红史》（藏文），第 149 页。

③《甘珠尔（对勘本）》第 106 卷所收理塘版目录《如来佛语藏译一切原本刻印目录・能仁欢喜》，署名为第六世红帽・噶尔旺曲吉旺楚，但最新的研究表明作者是第六世红帽之弟子名安噶者，参见巴多、张智瑜：《滇藏等地多民族文化交流之实证研究——理塘版〈甘珠尔〉刻经的若干史实及版本源流考证》，《中国藏学》2021 年第 4 期，第 98—107 页。另，该目录有 1982 年日本东京国际佛学研究影印版。

④ 中国藏学研究中心《大藏经》对勘局编：《如来佛语藏译一切原本刻印目录・能仁欢喜》，《甘珠尔（对勘本）》（藏文），第 106 卷，第 4 页。该目录跋文中言丽江版完成于金鸡年（1621 年）。

在中国山西曲沃县广福院发现了雕版印刷于雍熙三年（986 年）的《北斗七星经》残片，[①] 证明了此经 10 世纪时在国内有流传。而在元代，此经转而被翻译成多民族语言，也证明当时不仅存在汉文母本，而且流通广泛、影响广大。藏文本不是直接译自汉文，而是转译自蒙古文，这种间接的翻译方式会使文本发生什么样的变化，与原本有多大的差异，这些问题在该经藏译本的研究中值得关注。笔者依据《大正藏》本和宋代刻本残片，与藏译文进行了对勘，得出如下看法：

第一，藏译本与“大正本”“曲沃本”相比，既有阙失的部分，又有多出的部分，有可能元代回鹘文本、蒙古文本所依据的汉文本与存世汉文本有差异。“大正本”经文前，首先绘有图像（见下图），第一列是七星神像，皆手持笏板，站立状。其中第二像旁边有一头戴官帽、双手作揖状小像，代表武曲星旁边的小星。每位神像右首分别标日文“チ”“ト”“ヘ”“ニ”“ホ”“ハ”“ロ”“イ”。第二列是星图，用圆形表示，相互间用横线连接，如北斗七星状，每星上或下标星名。第三列是代表七星的星符。现存藏文本阙失七星图和星符，而后者是实现本经功能的主要依靠，是制作护身符和经幡的关键因素，这一缺失致使仅凭藏译本无法实施相关仪轨。星符阙失的原因不明，或其所依据的蒙古文本本就无星符，或藏文刻本因星符繁杂，刻印有难度而放弃。藏译文中提到星符时，只言“其之星符是此”，因无具体图形，使人不知所指。可见星符的阙失，是藏译本丢失的最为重要的信息。后人在编写相关供养祭祀仪轨时（见下文），对星符不着一字，权当星符不存在或无关紧要。

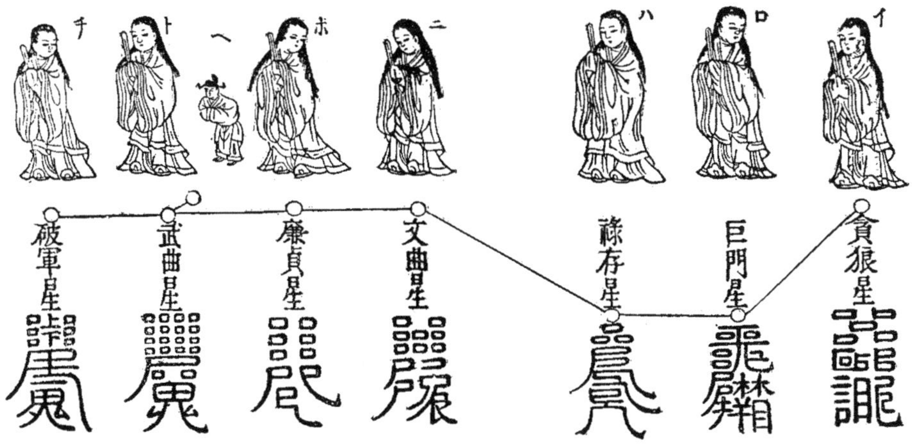

第二，藏文本部分词汇的翻译不够准确，或者与原汉文本之间有较大的差别，二者很难对等。以“禄食”为例：

---

① 赵冬生：《山西曲沃县广福院发现宋金（齐）佛经》，《文物》1994 年第 7 期，第 44—51 页。

“大正本”：“子生人，向此星下生，禄食黍。有厄，宜供养此经及带本星符，大吉。”

藏译本：སྨི་བདུན་ཞེས་བའི་སྐར་མ་ནི་ཐོག་མར་ཐམ་ལང་ཞེས་པའི་སྐར་མའོ།།བསྲུང་བའི་འཁོར་ལོ་ནི་འདི་ཡིན་ནོ།།བྱི་བ་ལོ་པའི་མི་དག་སྐར་མ་འདིའི་རིས་སུ་སྐྱེས་པའོ།།མཆོད་པའི་ཟས་ནི་གྲུས་མ་སྦོམ་པོའོ།།གདོན་དང་བར་དུ་གཅོག་པ་བྱུང་ན་ཆོས་འདི་མཆོད་ནས་བསྲུང་བ་འདི་གདགས་པར་བྱའོ།།བར་ཆད་ཐམས་ཅད་ཞི་ནས་དགའ་བར་རྒྱ་ཆེན་པོ་འཐོབ་པར་འགྱུར་རོ།།

藏文还译：“北斗七星之首是贪狼星，其之星符是此。鼠年生人等属于此星之种类，供养的食物是脱壳粗大（谷物）。若有魔障，则供养此经而戴此星符，会消除一切障碍，获得大欢喜。”

从汉文本之内容看，经文似是紧随星符之下，故省去了星名。“向此星下生”，藏译本理解为属于此星之种类。“禄食”是指不同年份出生的人所能享用的俸禄用粮食来代表，寓意其命运。而藏文将其译为མཆོད་པའི་ཟས།（供养的食物），即供养星神的用品（苏鲁格译文中译为“供祭的食物”）。“星符”译为བསྲུང་བའི་འཁོར་ལོ，直译为“护轮”，一般指护身符，与星符相类似。

藏译本中有关“禄食”之翻译与汉文原文比对如下：

黍——གྲུས་མ་ སྦོམ་ པོ། 粟——གྲུས་མ་ཕྲ་མ། 粳米——འབྲས 小豆（麦）——གྲོ། 麻子——བཙོ་མའི་འབྲས་བུ། 大豆——སྲན་མ་ནག་པོ། 小豆——སྲན་ཆུང་།

黍去皮后叫黄米，比小米稍大，藏文译为གྲུས་མ་ སྦོམ་ པོ།，意为“脱壳粗大”，不够准确。苏鲁格译为“糜子”。第二种禄食粟译为གྲུས་མ་ཕྲ་མ།，意为“脱壳细小”，苏鲁格译为“谷子”。《汉藏对照词典》中，“黍”对应的藏文词是ཁྲ，但《藏汉大辞典》中将此字又释为“糜子”“小米”。糜子又名穄子，与黍相近，但无黏性，不是黍。粟，即谷子，也叫小米。《汉藏对照词典》中将“糜子”“粟”“小米”对应词均作ཁྲེ。第四种禄食汉文本中的“小豆”应是小麦之误。第六种禄食大豆，藏文译为སྲན་མ་ནག་པོ།，藏文意为“黑豆”，一般指豌豆。汉语中的大豆即黄豆，《汉藏对照词典》作སྲན་ཆེན།或སྲན་སེར。第七种禄食小豆藏文译སྲན་ཆུང་།，藏文意为“小豆”。苏鲁格译为“绿豆”。小豆即红豆，《汉藏对照词典》作སྲན་དམར།。

可知，藏文本身对“黍”“粟”等谷物没有对应的词汇，再加转译自蒙古文，译者要准确把握和表达这些谷物的名称，是一件十分困难的事。

第三，七佛与七星之关系。汉文本中将七星直接视为某某佛，而藏文本将七星理解为某某佛之化身。比对如下：

“大正本”：“南无贪狼星，是东方最胜世界运意通证如来佛。”

藏译本：ཕྱག་འཚལ་དེ་ནི་བདག་ཅག་ཏམ་ལང་ཞེས་བ་ཡི།།སྐར་མའི་གོ་འཕང་ལའོ་ཚོད་ནི་ཤར་ཕྱོགས།།ཀུན་ནས་འཕགས་པའི་འཇིག་

ཧེན་དག་ཏུ་རྒྱལ་བ་ནི།།བློ་གྲོས་དབང་གིས་ཡོན་ཏན་རྫོགས་པའི་སྤྲུལ་པའོ།།དེའི་གཟུངས་ནི་འདི་ཡིན་ནོ།།ན་མཿས་མན་ཏ་བུདྡྷ་ནན།ཨོཾ་ཨ་མི་རྟ་ཡ་ཡ་སྭཱ་ཧཱ།།

藏文还译:“敬礼彼者即吾等称为贪狼星位者，汝是东方最胜世界等处之胜者，即智慧自在功德圆满之化身。彼之陀罗尼是此：南无萨满大布达南，嗡阿弥达雅亚娑哈!”

七星均有各自的咒语，而“大正本”缺。另，回鹘文本、藏文本均有对七星之赞颂文和献酥油灯之日期，“大正本”本亦缺。①

第四，关于制作本命经幡。

曲沃本:“若善男子善女人，造本命幡子，书此神符，须用净物，即得福。生金命人白幡子，木命人青幡子，水命人黑幡子，火命人赤幡子，土命人黄幡子。”② 这一段“大正本”缺，但回鹘文译本、藏译本中均有。藏译本译为:

吉祥金人身白色（དཔལ་ལྡན་གསེར་གྱི་མི་ནི་གཟུགས་དཀར་པོ།།），
吉祥木人身青色（དཔལ་ལྡན་ཤིང་གྱི་མི་ནི་གཟུགས་སྔོན་པོ།།），
吉祥水人身黑色（དཔལ་ལྡན་ཆུའི་མི་ནི་གཟུགས་ནག་པོ།།），
吉祥火人身赤色（དཔལ་ལྡན་མེའི་མི་ནི་གཟུགས་དམར་པོ།།），
吉祥土人身黄色（དཔལ་ལྡན་སའི་མི་ནི་གཟུགས་སེར་པོ།།）。

གཟུགས有多种含义，如身体、颜色等，松传节将其译为“容颜”。藏文本与汉文原文差别较大，藏文本未翻译“命”“幡子”这两个重要的词汇（回鹘文本中有“幡子”），经文原文是指根据每个人的五行属性来制作幡子，幡子颜色与五行相符，即金——白色，木——青色，水——黑色，火——赤色，土——黄色。藏文的翻译使人觉得五行属性不同，则人的身体或容貌的颜色不同。不过，在藏地挂代表个人命运的经幡时，往往根据五行的属性来选择经幡的颜色，与本经的宗旨相同，可能源自五行占算法。

通过以上的比对，可以看到间接翻译过来的藏文本与汉文原本之间有较大的差异，某些部分只能说主旨、大意存焉。一种文本转换为另一种文本时，自然会出现增减，或有意，或无意，这是译作中常见现象，更不用说这种多种语言间的辗转翻译。翻译本身就以对跨文化文本的理解为前提，这一过程中出现的某些“走样”，可能是与本土文化对接发生的创造性

① 孔庆典、江晓原认为:“在后世流传下来的回鹘、蒙、藏三个版本的《佛说北斗七星延命经》中，讲述每月何日烧香拜经的内容很可能是由回鹘人在14世纪初首先传入；而对这些日期的选择体现了具有佛教密宗和印度色彩的二十七宿纪日法。”见孔庆典、江晓原:《11～14世纪回鹘人的二十八宿纪日》，《西域研究》2009年3期，第9—21，136页。

② 赵冬生:《山西曲沃县广福院发现宋金（齐）佛经》，第46页，图一。

阐释。如藏文本中对部分粮食种类的翻译，是在无法找到准确的藏语对应词时的一种变通。对无法阅读汉文原本者而言，藏译本是唯一的，其所讲的一切只能视为理应如此、原本如此。就此而言，《北斗七星经》藏译本与原本间存在的明显差异造就了一种新的文本。

二、《北斗七星经》在藏传佛教界的流传

邦隆认为《北斗七星经》在藏地影响不大，约翰·艾尔沃斯科格认可了这种说法。但该经收入《陀罗尼集》等众多文献集中，说明此经在翻译成藏文后一直在流通，尤其受到民间的重视。不仅有藏传佛教界的两位学者对该经进行评述，而且有相关仪轨文献问世。

16 世纪泽塘寺学者班盖桑波（པད་དཀར་བཟང་པོ།）受扎巴迥乃坚赞[①]之命所著的《经部提要》（མདོ་སྡེ་སྤྱིའི་རྣམ་བཞག）中，对《北斗七星经》有概要介绍，指出此经中的讲法者是导师（即释迦牟尼），求法者是文殊菩萨，并言："此经之意义，即占算所谓七星，具有对利益和损害能快速判断的特殊法。此经义之概要：所谓七星者，对众生所造之利益和损害，开示对此等损害能守护之方法、供养的七食、彼等主宰之七年（实际是十二属相——译注）、修习之七陀罗尼、所变化之七佛、占算七善果等。"[②]这算是藏传佛教界学者对《北斗七星经》的最早认知，作者未怀疑此经之来源，认为它是可靠的佛经，并将此经归于大集部（འདུས་པ་ཆེན་པོའི་མདོ）。但作者对经义的概括也不精准，因此经的作用是"有大威神，有大威力，能救一切众生重罪，能灭一切业障"，而不是说利益和损害是北斗七星造成的，北斗七星是七佛之化身，岂能造损害业。

至 18 世纪时，格鲁派著名学者松巴堪布在八十岁高龄时，撰写了一部名为《纯净佛典·净化水垢摩尼澄水珠》（གསུང་རབ་རྣམ་དག་ཆུའི་དྲི་མ་སེལ་བྱེད་ནོར་བུ་ཀེ་ཏ་ཀ།）的著作，除了重复《如意宝树史》中对宁玛派密续和伏藏文献的看法外，集中讨论了《陀罗尼集》中的疑伪经问题，提出了尖锐的批评。根据笔者的统计，松巴堪布提出的疑伪经约 52 种[③]，包含三部译自汉文

---

① 此人似是第九任帕竹第斯阿旺扎西扎巴之子，约于 1524 年担任丹萨替寺之京俄（《西藏通史·松石宝串》汉译本第 440 页）。

② ཆོས་འདིའི་དགོས་པའི་དོན་ནི། སྐར་བདུན་ཞེས་པའི་སྐར་མ་རྩིས་པས་ཕན་པ་དང་གནོད་པའི་འབྱུགས་དཔྱོད་ཁྱད་པར་ཅན་དུ་འགྱུར་བའོ།འདིའི་བསྡུས་པའི་དོན་ནི། སྐར་བདུན་ཞེས་བྱ་བའི་སྐར་མ་བདུན་གྱིས་འགྲོ་བ་ལ་ཕན་པ་དང་། གནོད་པ་བྱེད་པས་དེ་དག་གི་གནོད་པ་བསྲུང་བའི་བསྲུང་བ་དང་། མཆོད་པའི་ཟས་བདུན་དང་། དེ་དག་གིས་བདག་བྱེད་པའི་ལོ་བདུན་དང་། སྒྲུབ་པའི་གཟུངས་བདུན་དང་། སྤྲུལ་བྱེད་ཀྱི་སངས་རྒྱས་བདུན་དང་། དགེ་བ་རྩིས་འབྲས་བདུན་ལ་སོགས་པ་བསྟན་པའོ། 见班盖桑波著，木雅·贡布整理：《经部提要》（བསྟན་པ་སྤྱིའི་རྒྱས་བྱེད་ལས་མདོ་སྡེ་སྤྱིའི་རྣམ་བཞག་བསྟན་བསྡུ་བཞི་བྱ་བའི་བསྟན་བཅོས་བཞུགས་སོ），民族出版社 2006 年版，第 547 页。该著原是手抄本，共收 327 部佛经，成书于第 9 饶迥的木牛年（1565 年）。

③ 才让：《〈陀罗尼集〉中的疑伪经——松巴堪布的质疑与批判》，《西北民族研究》2019 年第 1 期，第 119—130 页。

的疑伪经，其中一部就是《北斗七星经》。他认为此经译自汉、蒙古文，七星的名称类似汉语或回鹘语（Yu gur）；经中所言七星是七佛的化身，有违佛理；此经经名用三种语言，即汉语、蒙古语和藏语，足以说明其渊源。松巴堪布虽未深入探讨，但其所言可谓一针见血，寥寥数语便表达了他对此经面貌的看法。松巴堪布的观点遭到了第三世土观之反驳，师徒二人由此交恶。但是当时的藏传佛教其他人物对松巴和土观之争保持了沉默，藏传佛教界中并未因此掀起辨伪存真之风潮，同样没有对《北斗七星经》等疑伪经的传播产生任何影响。但对《北斗七星经》类经典持怀疑态度的仍大有人在，如格鲁派隆务寺高僧赤干·绛央图丹嘉措（1866—1928）的闻法录中亦言卓尼版《甘珠尔》中无《北斗》《星经》两部经，后者属于疑伪类，不需要教敕传承云云。

《北斗七星经》在流传过程中，出现了藏传佛教式的祭祀仪轨，如《北斗七星供养法·如意宝王》（མིས་བདུན་སྐར་མ་ལ་མཆོད་པ་འབུལ་ཚུལ་བསམ་འཕེལ་ཡིད་བཞིན་དབང་གི་རྒྱལ་པོ།），[①] 使《北斗七星经》完全融入到藏传佛教文化体系中。据该文后记，作者署名布斯固什玛底萨热哇悉地（ཧྲུ་ཤུ་གུ་ཤུ་མ་ཏི་ཨནྡྲ་སིདྡྷི），是受到胡尔察贝利克塔脱颜洛桑喜饶（ཧུར་ཚེ་པེ་ལིག་ཁ་ཐོ་ཡོན་བློ་བཟང་ཤེས་རབ།）之请而撰写，文字的书写者亦是请求者。从署名看，作者应是蒙古族僧人，请求者洛桑喜饶似是其弟子，二人俱通藏文。后记未言其成书年代。该仪轨分为如下内容：

第一，对《北斗七星经》之大致介绍。作者首先概括了《北斗七星经》之利益，言鼠年等十二属相之人属于七星之种类（རིགས།），对自己所属之星辰按各自之供品加以供养，则可获得消除魔障、福德增长等诸多益处。

第二，供养。又分对七星的分别供养和整体供养。针对前者，作者引述了《北斗七星经》中关于七星之供品等内容。言准备之供物除每一星辰之禄食外，还要准备五种供品为一组的共七组供品。首先，行皈依发心、四无量、观想等，继以《北斗七星经》中所述供养七星益处相关经文作祈愿。之后，分别介绍了七星的迎请、献供、赞颂等，其中还包含对七星的坐骑、手持的物品、调伏的对象及其他星宿眷属的描述。此部分内容不见于《北斗七星经》，可能是作者参照密宗仪轨及五行占算等添加的。

以第一位贪狼星之供养仪轨为例，书中言其“身体白色光灿然，手持邬东波罗花，骑乘白色狮子上，调伏天神此星星，是为善逝佛化身”[②]，并称此星主宰昴宿、觜宿、参宿、氐宿（原文作ནམ་སོ།，似是ནམ་འོག）、鬼宿、柳宿等七宿。仪轨包括：诵念咒语，加持供物；献供物，提及供品之名；赞颂祈愿，引述有“吉祥金人是白色身”等经文内容。之后，分列其他六星献供仪轨，与贪狼星之献供仪轨类似。

其他六星的坐骑和眷属如下：

---

① 该文献是手抄本，似藏于蒙古国图书馆，参见 BDRC. WA1NLM3588。落桑东知博士提供了相关信息及电子版，在此向他致谢。

②《北斗七星供养法·如意宝王》第 6 叶 b。

巨门星“身体白色光灿然，手持白螺与宝剑，骑乘白色骏马上，调伏人类此星星，是为善逝佛化身”①，同样被视为东方之星座，连同昴宿等一起邀请；

禄存星“身体黑绿怖畏相，手中持有蛇之绳，骑乘凶狠青蛙上，调伏龙类此星星，是为善逝佛化身”②，是南方星宿之主，眷属有星宿、张宿、翼宿、轸宿、角宿、亢宿等；

文曲星“身体蓝绿光灿然，手持光灿之珠宝，骑乘具威疯虎上，调伏夜叉此星星，是为善逝佛化身”③，亦被视为南方之星系；

廉贞星“身体白色光灿然，手持黄金之宝剑，各种光芒射四方，骑乘如云青龙上，调伏天干（དབང་ཐང་།）此星星，是为善逝佛化身”④，被视为西方星宿之主，眷属有房宿、心宿、尾宿、箕宿、斗宿、女宿和牛宿；

武曲星“身体金色光灿然，手持燃烧之云朵，骑乘美丽之孔雀，住于日月之宝座，调伏地神此星星，是为善逝佛化身”⑤，属于西方之星系；

破军星“身体黑色颈灿然，手持燃烧之天仗，骑乘于共鸣鸟，调伏诸鬼此星星，是为善逝佛化身”⑥，为北方星系之主，眷属有室宿、壁宿、危宿、虚宿、奎宿、娄宿、胃宿。

接下来是煨桑（བསངས་གཏོང་བ།）、招福运（གཡང་འགུགས།）等仪式，以念诵相关颂词为主。

以上将北斗七星信仰与二十八宿相结合的做法，作者可能有所凭依，但二十八星宿之方位划分，与中国传统的东方青龙七宿（角、亢、氐、房、心、尾、箕）、北方玄武七宿（斗、牛、女、虚、危、室、壁）、西方白虎七宿（奎、娄、胃、昴、毕、觜、参）、南方朱雀七宿（井、鬼、柳、星、张、翼、轸）的划分法不同。该仪轨视贪狼星、巨门星为东方七宿之主，禄存星、文曲星为南方七宿之主，廉贞星、武曲星为西方七宿之主，破军星单独为北方七宿之主。中国古代亦有以四宿分别配七斗者，如保存在日本的天宫图上，最上一层绘制北斗七星，均是佛的形象，图中右上角有星名，左下方和右下方是四星宿名⑦。另外，该仪轨将北斗七星的形象密教化，标明了其肤色、手持的法物和坐骑，以及调服教化之对象，类似密教的护法神。

该仪轨的问世说明藏传佛教界中尤其是蒙古族地区仍有《北斗七星经》之信奉、实践

① 《北斗七星供养法·如意宝王》，第 8 叶 b。
② 《北斗七星供养法·如意宝王》，第 9 叶 b。
③ 《北斗七星供养法·如意宝王》，第 10 叶 b。
④ 《北斗七星供养法·如意宝王》，第 11 叶 b。
⑤ 《北斗七星供养法·如意宝王》，第 12 叶 b。
⑥ 《北斗七星供养法·如意宝王》，第 13 叶 a。
⑦ 汪悦进（Eugene Wang）著，杨钧译，李清泉校：《没有修持者的宗教仪式？瑞光寺塔里的 11 世纪初陀罗尼印本》，《美术大观》2022 年第 2 期，第 30—39 页。

者。该仪轨完全遵循了藏传佛教同类仪轨的撰写模式，推进了《北斗七星经》的藏传佛教化。而且这一仪轨的制定，是以阙失星符的藏译本为基础的，可视为是对藏译本的一种诠释，解决或明确了实现本经功能的途径或方法。又在密教的语境下，进一步强化、延伸或扩展了经典的功能。值得注意的是，作者将སྨེ་བདུན写成了མེས་བདུན།，意为“七祖先”，或是有意为之，或是抄写之误。

附录：藏文《北斗七星经》之译文

汉语：北斗七星经。蒙古语：do’u lon e bug an ner thu ho don nu su dur/ 藏语：sme bdun zhes bya ba skar ma’i mdo。

向七如来敬礼！天中天薄伽梵向菩萨妙吉祥童子授教云：“北斗七星之首是贪狼星，其之星符是此。鼠年生人等属于此星之种类，供养之食物是脱壳粗大（谷物）。若有魔障，则供养此经而佩戴此星符，将消除一切障碍，会得大欢喜。第二名是巨门星，其之星符是此。牛年和猪年生人等属于此星之种类，供养之食物是脱壳细小（谷物）。若有魔障，则供养此经而佩戴此星符，将消除一切障碍，会得大欢喜。第三名是禄存星，其之星符是此。虎年和狗年生人等属于此星之种类，供养之食物是米。若有魔障，则供养此经而佩戴此星符，将消除一切障碍，会得大欢喜。第四名文曲星，其之星符是此。兔年和鸡年生人等属于此星之种类，供养之食物是麦子。若有魔障，则供养此经而佩戴此星符，将消除一切障碍，会得大欢喜。第五名廉贞星，其之星符是此。龙年和猴年生人等属于此星之种类，供养之食物是麻子。若有魔障，则供养此经而佩戴此星符，将消除一切障碍，会得大欢喜。第六名武曲星，其之星符是此。羊年和蛇年生人等属于此星之种类，供养之食物是黑豆。若有魔障，则供养此经而于身上佩戴此星符，将消除一切障碍，会得大欢喜。第七名破军星，其之星符是此。马年生人等属于此星之种类，供养之食物是黑豆。若有魔障，则供养此经而佩戴此星符，将消除一切障碍，会得大欢喜。

敬礼彼者即吾等称为贪狼星位者，汝是东方最胜世界等处之胜者，即智慧自在功德圆满之化身。彼之陀罗尼是此：南无萨满大布达南，嗡阿弥达雅亚娑哈！敬礼彼者即吾等称为巨门星位者，汝是东方殊胜大宝世界等处之胜者，即光音自在（佛）之化身。彼之陀罗尼是此：南无萨满大布达南，嗡阿次达尼娑哈！吾等敬礼称为禄存星位者，汝是东方如同满月刹土之金色等觉的化身。彼之陀罗尼是此：南无萨满大布达南，嗡尼玛日尼阿噶达那巴热玛如提斯娑哈！吾等敬礼称为文曲星位者，汝是东方世界之悔恨及众多忧苦中的胜者，即最神圣福德位（佛）的化身。彼之陀罗尼是此：南无萨满大布达南，嗡卫哈娑哈！吾等敬礼称为廉贞星位者，汝是东方世界纯净刹土中，智慧无碍广大[①]佛化身。彼之陀罗尼是此：南

① 藏译文原文为བློ་དང་ཤེས་རབ་ནི།།མཁྱེན་པ་ཐོགས་མེད་རྒྱས་པ，བློ、ཤེས་རབ།、མཁྱེན་པ།同义，意为“智慧”。

无萨满大布达南，嗡帕热提杂热玛热那娑哈！吾等敬礼称为武曲星位者，汝是东方世界信奉佛法法海欢喜之能仁如来佛的化身。彼之陀罗尼是此：南无萨满大布达南，嗡萨跋达热萨玛叶娑哈！吾等敬礼称为破军星位者，汝是东方世界大宝琉璃所成刹土之药师琉璃光佛的化身。彼之陀罗尼是此：南无萨满大布达南，嗡萨跋达巴热密尼杂娑哈！凡何人于本年之行走（རང་གི་ལོའི་འགྲོས།）[1]中若遭遇障碍，则其人对此法宝敬礼七次，就能消除一切障碍。”

尔时，天中天佛告妙吉祥菩萨：“文殊！吾所说此经，具足法之殊胜光明，有大威力，能成一切有情从错乱罪业中获得救护的所依处。能清净并消除一切罪业和障蔽，及一切魔之冤孽。若比丘或比丘尼，或男女施主，或男女家主，或具足声望成为圣者之男士或妇女，值得尊敬或不值得尊敬，或大小何种，皆于北斗七星之类属下出生。若有人闻此经，并学习、记忆，以身供养，逐次劝朋友、亲戚等受持，则以此福德之恩德（དྲིན）和果报（འབྲས་བུ）于此世能获得。若善男子善女人，为利益堕生地狱而感受各种粗重痛苦之人，则对此经以虔诚心尊敬、供养，之后，彼等之识从地狱之苦中获得解脱并减轻，往生极乐世界无量光佛刹土。若善男子善女人，或被魔鬼、大种魔等压服，或厉魔迫害，或梦不详，或见恶兆，或心中恐怖，则听闻此经而持之，并记忆、行供养，从此等魔障获得解脱并减轻，其心得安，令其之一切担忧和恐惧消失。若有善男子善女人，或希冀出行之时，与自己之长官结伴，得其欢喜并爱护，或被派遣时，此人遇此经，以随喜心恭敬而供养，则此后彼长官对此人和颜并爱护，使此人之名望大增，获得大欢喜。若善男子善女人患重病而受苦，若从病患中欲求解脱，于净处焚香而供养此经，并诵念，则能从所患一切疾病中得解脱。若有善男子善女人，如田地庄稼和果树未得（丰收），并牲畜患病，[2]则于干净之地，焚香后供养此宝经，使所有庄稼丰收、牲畜繁衍，亦无魔障。复有善女子，若怀胎，而出现障碍之月份，则以虔心对此经尊敬而供养，彼等障碍中无病解脱，所生之子或女等，亦具足福德、吉祥和长寿。复次，善男子善女人，凡所生之一切人，北斗七星皆了知并主宰。所生存之一生中，凡出现的灾厄、无意义之争吵，及如此上百恶兆等一切，皆受北斗七星之主宰。若知此而对此经尊敬并虔诚心供养，则任何魔鬼和灾厄所不能损害。”

尔时，妙吉祥童子等集会之四众弟子，对此法语恭而尊敬，并领会，行五体礼而返。南无热达那孜然杂底摩诃底杂孜然啊哇扎阿格娑哈。天中天佛所说北斗七星延命法经品。

吉祥金人身白色，[3]吉祥木人身青色，吉祥水人身黑色，吉祥火人身红色，吉祥土人身黄色。

---

① 汉文本中作“行年”。

② 汉文本中作“或养蚕虚耗、六畜不安”，藏译本中未反映出“养蚕”“六畜”等词义。

③ 曲沃本在此句前尚有：“尔时，文殊师利菩萨言：‘若有善男子善女人，不能添寿益命，唯造五逆不祥，冲秽日月星辰，造作种种恶业；若遇行年窒塞，所事不成；或被太岁、太阴、将军、黄幡、豹尾、大煞、小煞、五鬼、诸神、星宿所临。即于净室，烧香供养此经，即得人神尧满，具足延年。若善男子善女人，造本命幡子，书此神符，须用净物，即得福。’”

对北斗七星的祈愿赞文是如此：住于地藏上方高八万由旬须弥山之顶端，于此四大洲世间具足权势之汝，乃吾之神；向四生和五业之一切有情行救护者是汝；汝似串联的珠子般成天神王帝释之顶饰，以日月、七曜、行星和三十万亿星（向汝）供养；吾之神，汝令此世所愿诸事成就，即所愿诸事如同心愿般令我满足；使成百魔障和灾厄消除者是汝，吾之神；汝令吾之寿命长久，善语皆成就。

述说给北斗七星献酥油灯（之日期）：孟春月初七日，仲春月初四日，季春月初二日；孟夏月二十七日，仲夏月初五日，季夏月初三日；孟秋月二十日，仲秋月初七日，季秋月二十日；孟冬月初十一日，仲冬月初十五日，季冬月初八日，于以上时间献酥油灯。[①] 北斗七星经完毕。

导师正觉所讲说，
于此北斗七星经，
能依心忆并供养，
彼得利益因深知。
乌汝波噶名苏古且
幼时时常于此法，
具足信念常诵供，
为求高位而祈愿，
相应得佑具福分。
令行解脱导师佛化身，
图贴睦尔王子为长寿，
并愿成为慈悲大皇帝，
具足智慧菩萨此主宰，
修习而登薛禅汗宝座。
“因吾心愿得满足，
于此无惑生定解，
回鹘文之此经典，
以前他人若未译，
令诸蒙古信供奉。”
由吾译成蒙古文。
“如吾所愿能实现，
万千有情之心愿，

① 以上祈愿文和献灯日之相关内容，不见于“大正本”和“曲沃本”。

如我一般满足云。”
印刷千册施诸人，
以此福德果报力，
皇帝皇后及后嗣，
寿命恒长增福德，
究竟获得佛之位。
国境仇敌纷争消，
无有魔障及瘟疫，
风调雨顺无饥荒。
吾语愿望令实现，
我与父母亲人等，
助友及众有情等，
于此世间满法愿，
极乐刹土常到达。
天历元年（1328年——译注）即龙年十月初一进行了印刷。

此经由一位印度班智达和唐三藏从印度携带至汉地并翻译，在汉地广为流传。在大皇帝之大臣，出生于菩萨种，具足信仰、智慧、禅定的金紫光禄大夫御史台乌汝波噶的鼓励下，回鹘教法之主必兰纳识里将其译成蒙古语文，印刷两千册；阿邻铁木尔大司徒翻译成回鹘文，在蒙古和回鹘广为流传。大夫（指乌汝波噶——译注）以前持蒙古之教法，因此法之加持转而信仰佛教并出家，体悟此法之诸功德。后于阴火牛年由译师玛哈巴拉和释阿难达跋陀罗在贡塘寺译成藏文并校订。

从《吐蕃大事纪年》看吐蕃巡守制度*

黄维忠
中国人民大学国学院

在敦煌藏文文献中，涉及吐蕃大事纪年的卷号共五件，分别为P.T.1288、IOL Tib J 750、Or. 8212.187、IOL Tib J 1368、Dx 12851。学界常合称前三件文书为《吐蕃大事纪年》。[①] 国内外对《吐蕃大事纪年》的研究已经非常深入，巴考（Jacques Bacot）、托马斯（Frederick W. Thomas）、杜散（Charles G. Toussaint）、[②] 张琨[③]、王尧、陈践[④]、黄布凡、马德[⑤]、杜晓峰（Brandon Dotson）[⑥]、

* 本文为中国人民大学重点课题“《古藏文辞典》编纂”（项目号21XNL005）、中国藏学研究中心重点课题“西藏文化史”（项目号2020ZD001）的阶段性成果。本文曾以简要报告形式在清华大学中文系、清华大学人文与社会科学高等研究所于2021年10月15日举办的“纪念陈寅恪先生——西域和佛教语文学国际研讨会”上发表。与会学者提出的问题对本文的完善提供了有益的借鉴；另外，在本文撰写过程中，笔者经常就语法问题与中国社会科学院的尹蔚彬研究员、中央民族大学格日杰布老师进行讨论，受惠甚多，特此一并致谢！原载于《中国藏学》2021年第4期，第59—70页，略有修订。

① 它们又和P.T.1286《小邦邦伯家臣及赞普世系》、P.T.1287《吐蕃赞普传记》合称为学界熟知的《敦煌本吐蕃历史文书》。

② Jacques Bacot（巴考）, Frederick W. Thomas（托马斯）, Charles G. Toussaint（杜散）, *Documents de Touen-houang relatifs a l'histoire du Tibet*（敦煌吐蕃历史文书）, Paris: Libraire Orientaliste Paul Geuthner, 1940.

③ Kun Chang（张琨）, “An Analysis of the Tun-Huang Tibetan Annals（敦煌本吐蕃纪年之分析）,” *Journals of Oriental Studies* (Hong Kong), Vol.5, No.1−2, 1959/1960, pp.123−173.

④ 王尧、陈践译注:《敦煌本吐蕃历史文书（增订本）》，民族出版社1992年版。后收于氏著:《敦煌古藏文文献探索集》，上海古籍出版社2008年版。又收于《王尧藏学文集》（卷一），中国藏学出版社2012年版。

⑤ 黄布凡、马德:《敦煌藏文吐蕃史文献译注》，甘肃教育出版社2000年版。

⑥ Brandon Dotson（杜晓峰）, *The Old Tibetan Annals: An Annotated Translation of Tibet's First History. With an Annotated Cartographical Documentation by Guntram Hazod*（吐蕃大事纪年译注并附图说）, Wien: Verlag der Österreichischen Akademie der Wissenschaften, 2009. 任小波对该书有一详细书评，可参见任小波:《评多特生、哈佐德〈吐蕃纪年译注并附图说〉》，载姚大力、刘迎胜主编《清华元史》（第三辑），商务印书馆2015年版，第466—474页。

止贡噶举澈赞法王（H. H. the Drikung Kyabgon Chetsang）[①] 等学者的论著受到学界的广泛关注，研究吐蕃史的学者更是离不开《吐蕃大事纪年》这一重要文献。学界对相关成果已经进行过总结和评述，此不赘述。[②] 总体而言，学界均未关注到吐蕃时期的巡守制度问题。文章尝试以《吐蕃大事纪年》为主要材料，讨论吐蕃的巡守制度。

巡守之原意是指古代的帝王到各地巡视。[③]《孟子 · 梁惠王下》曰："天子适诸侯曰巡狩，巡狩者，巡所守也。"《文选 · 东都赋》注引"逸礼"曰："巡狩者何？巡者，循也；狩，牧也。谓天子巡行守牧也。"从"巡狩"的"狩"到"守"，这一个字的变化，是巡狩内涵的延展和演绎，是由以军事为主向以政治为主的时代性的变化。

根据学者的研究，中国古代巡守制度的产生"应在夏代以前的尧舜时期"。[④]《左传》即载，哀公七年"禹合诸侯于涂山，执玉帛者万国"。"联盟首领同参盟各邦发生政治联系的渠道最初只能有两条，即要求各盟邦的统治者前来朝拜和自身离开首邦到外地去巡视。借朝拜和巡视之机，还可集全部或一方'诸侯'进行大会。"[⑤]"迄至先秦，又演变为帝王对部落、方国以及诸侯封国巡察、征伐的政治军事活动，并成为控扼天下、巩固王权的重要举措。春秋战国至秦汉，巡狩逐渐由军事为主转为政治为主；在儒学文化思想的构建与演绎下，'天子非展义不巡守'。巡狩逐渐制度化、系统化、理论化和礼仪化，其历史文化涵蕴和意义亦日渐广博、深远。"[⑥] 秦汉以后，巡狩作为封建王朝的统治运作模式，不仅是传统礼俗社会以礼教万民的治国要道，更是其"内圣外王"理想政治的社会实践。

学界对中国古代历朝巡守制度的讨论十分热烈，但对吐蕃巡守制度却几未着墨。而要讨论吐蕃巡守制度，关键在于对《吐蕃大事纪年》中གཤེགས一词的理解。以下我们将在分析གཤེགས一词的基础上，展开对吐蕃巡守制度的讨论。

在讨论之前，我们先对本文引用的《吐蕃大事纪年》行数和十二生肖纪年作一说明。先举一例：

---

① H. H. the Drikung Kyabgon Chetsang, *Tun hong bod kyi yig rnying las byung ba/ bod btsan po'i rgyal rabs*, Dehra Dun, India: Songtsen Library, 2010. 该书英文译本参见 Meghan Howard with Tsultrim Nakchu trans., *A History of the Tibetan Empire: Drawn from the Dunhuang Manuscript*, Dehra Dun, India: Songtsen Library, 2011。

② 有关《吐蕃大事纪年》的研究，西文研究方面的综述可参见前揭书所附参考文献目录。藏文研究方面的综述，可参见桑吉东知：《敦煌藏文文献研究综述——以藏文论文为中心（1982—2014）》，《中国藏学》2016 年第 3 期，第 66—74 页。新近的综述可参见朱丽双、黄维忠：《〈古藏文编年史〉研究综述》，《敦煌学辑刊》2018 年第 3 期，第 101—125 页；李锋、杨铭：《近年来敦煌本吐蕃历史文书研究成果评析——从民族史的角度》，《西南民族大学学报》（人文社会科学版）2021 年第 9 期，第 38—44 页。

③ 赵世超：《巡守制度试探》，《历史研究》1995 年第 3 期，第 4 页。

④ 赵世超：《巡守制度试探》，第 5 页。

⑤ 赵世超：《巡守制度试探》，第 6 页。

⑥ 何平立：《中国古代帝王巡狩与封建政治文化》，《社会科学》2006 年第 3 期，第 155 页。

285/233 ༄༅།།སྦྲུལ་གྱི་ལོ་ལ། བཙན་པོ་དབྱརད: ཆབ་སྲིད་ལ་གཤེགསྟེ། 286/234……དགུན་ཆབ་སྲིད་ལས: སླར་བྲག་མར་དུ་གཤེགསྟེ།[①]

及至蛇年。夏（741 年），赞普以政事巡狩。……冬（741—742），〔赞普〕结束政事活动后巡狩扎玛。[②]

以上为本文引用《吐蕃大事纪年》原文和译文的格式。

说明一：285/233 系《吐蕃大事纪年》行数，前一个数字是 P.T.1288 加上 IOL Tib J 750 的总行数，后一个数字是 IOL Tib J 750 的行数。[③] 两者相差的 52 行，系 P.T.1288 的行数（以下引文中如仅出现一个数字，系 P.T.1288 的行数）。学界对 P.T.1288 行数的认定有两种说法，一种为 51 行，[④] 一种为 52 行。两者的差别由第三行而起。第三行因残缺不全，现存的文书上并没有显示有文字存在（参见下图 P.T.1288 前 18 行）。这样，有学者认为该行应该没有文字，有的则认为应该有文字，杜晓峰甚至推测有 9 个字左右。[⑤] 本文采用后一种说法。

图 1　P.T.1288《吐蕃大事纪年》局部

① 本文所引《吐蕃大事纪年》原文主要依据国际敦煌学网站的高清图版所录，同时参照《王尧藏学文集》（卷一）、《敦煌藏文吐蕃史文献译注》《吐蕃大事纪年译注并附图说》（此书录文为藏文拉丁字母转写）等书的录文。此后不再一一出注。

② 本文汉译文系在参照《王尧藏学文集》（卷一）、《敦煌藏文吐蕃史文献译注》等书译文的基础上翻译而成。因对གཤེགས一词的理解与前贤有所不同，故译文亦有差异。如本引文的汉译，《王尧藏学文集》（卷一）第 207 页的译文为“夏，赞普以政务出巡临边。……冬，赞普牙帐自边地还至札玛”，《敦煌藏文吐蕃史文献译注》第 53 页的译文为“夏，赞普以政务出巡。……冬，（赞普）从视政地返扎玛尔”。为节省版面，差异之处不一一出注。

③ 这种行数的标注方法首先由杜晓峰采用，参见 Brandon Dotson, *The Old Tibetan Annals: An Annotated Translation of Tibet's First History. With an Annotated Cartographical Documentation by Guntram Hazod, part* II.《吐蕃大事纪年译注并附图说》第二部分。Brandon Dotson，前揭书。

④ 国内常见的为 51 行的说法。如《王尧藏学文集》（卷一）、《敦煌藏文吐蕃史文献译注》等。

⑤ Brandon Dotson, *The Old Tibetan Annals:An Annotated Translation of Tibet's First History. With an Annotated Cartographical Documentation by Guntram Hazod*, p.81.

说明二：吐蕃十二生肖纪年中的冬季、春季都是跨年度的（参见表 1[①]），因此在无法确定冬季、春季的确切月份时，需要标注两个年度，如上引文中蛇年的冬季应为 741—742 年。在以下的汉译中，如文书确切记载为夏、秋季的，则仅标注一个年份，记载为冬、春季的，则标注两个年份。

表 1：吐蕃纪年与公历月份对照表

吐蕃纪年	公历	吐蕃纪年	公历	吐蕃纪年	公历	吐蕃纪年	公历
春三月	四月	夏三月	七月	秋三月	十月	冬三月	第二年一月
夏一月	五月	秋一月	八月	冬一月	十一月	春一月	第二年二月
夏二月	六月	秋二月	九月	冬二月	十二月	春二月	第二年三月

一、对གཤེགས一词的分析

学界已经关注到《吐蕃大事纪年》的规范用字遣词问题。林冠群指出，“吾人观《吐蕃大事纪年》的载记，对于王室成员的行止、各种活动，以及政府官员所作各种措施等，每件相同的活动、措施，都使用相同的词汇，例如赞普居处所在用‘བཞུགས།’，跸所移至他处用‘གཤེགས།’，赞普去世用‘དགུང་དུ་གཤེགས།’，臣下去世则使用‘གུམ།’，为区别君臣，二者明显使用不同词汇，于此可见有所规范”[②]。龚煌城认为藏语敬语词普遍有个腭化音作中缀，当这种音与边音结合时会变成ཞ。[③]格日杰布也认为古藏语清浊交替，这种规则是成立的，如གཤེགས、བཞེད、བཞུགས、བཞེས、བཞེངས、ཞལ等词语是吐蕃赞普的专用词汇。[④]通过对གཤེགས一词的分析，我们认为གཤེགས确系赞普专用词。具体来说，གཤེགས在《吐蕃大事纪年》中有多重含义，以下我们分别讨论。

1. 行走、来、去

表示“行走、来、去”的གཤེགས在《吐蕃大事纪年》中出现了两次，系གཤེགས的本义。

---

① 此表引自 Brandon Dotson, *The Old Tibetan Annals:An Annotated Translation of Tibet's First History. With an Annotated Cartographical Documentation by Guntram Hazod*, p.13。

② 林冠群:《从〈吐蕃大事纪年〉论唐代吐蕃的史学》,《中国藏学》2013 年第 1 期，第 15 页。

③ Gong Hwang-cherng, “Ancient Tibetan y and related questions,” *Bulletin of the Institute of History and Philology* 48.2, 1977, pp.205–228.

④ 这是上《吐蕃大事纪年》课程时，格日杰布提出的观点。

248/196 ༄།:།འབྲུགི : ལོ་ལ།བཙན་པོ : དབྱརད : མཚོ་བགོ : ཕོལ : གངས : ན་བཞུགས : པ་ལས།སླར : བོད་ཡུལ : དུ་གཤེགསྟེ།

及至龙年。夏（728 年），赞普驻于措高之包冈，后，还至蕃地。

282/230 །བཙན་པོ : ཡབ : དགུན་བོད་ཡུལ : དུ་སླར་གཤེགས།

冬（739—740），赞普父王还至蕃地。

2. 宾天[①] དགུང་དུ་གཤེགས

དགུང་དུ་གཤེགས 表示“宾天”，这一意思在《吐蕃大事纪年》中出现了 3 次。

15 ॥ དེ་ནས : ལོ་དྲུག་ནའ། བཙན་པོ : ཁྲི་སྲོང་རྩན་དགུང་དུ་གཤེགསོ།

（649—650）六年后，赞普赤松赞宾天。

66/14 ༄།:།བྱི : བའི་ལོ་ལ : བབ་སྟེ་དབྱརད : བཙན་པོ : སྤྲགས : གྱི་ཤ་ར་ན་བཞུགས་ཤིང། དགུན་ཚང་བང་སྣ་ནས།ཁྲི་ 67/15 མང : སློན་དགུང་དུ་གཤེགས།

及至鼠年。夏（676 年），赞普驻于札之鹿苑，冬，赞普赤芒伦于仓邦那宾天。

148/96 | དགུན་བཙན་པོ : ཆབ་སྲིད་ལ : མྱུ་ལ་གཤེགས : པ་ལས། དགུང་དུ་གཤེགས།

〔及至龙年。〕冬（704—705），赞普以政事巡狩蛮地，宾天。

དགུང་དུ་གཤེགས། 可译为逝往天界、逝归天界、宾天、升遐。这在 P.T.1287、P.T.1286 中也有相关例子：

P.T.1287/83 ॥བཙན་པོ་ཡབ་ཁྲི་སློན་བཙན॥ 84 དགུང་དུ་གཤེགས། །

赞普父王赤伦赞宾天。

P.T.1287/164 རྒྱལ་སྟག་བུ་དགུང་དུ་གཤེགསོ།

达布王宾天。

P.T.1286/47 ॥འདི་ཡན་ཆད་འདྲའ་སྟེ་། སྲས་ཆིབས་ཀ་ཐུབ་ན་། ཡབ་དགུང་དུ་གཤེགས་སོ་॥

以上〔诸王〕大致相同，王子能骑马时父王即逝归天界。

“宾天”“逝往天界”“逝归天界”应为དགུང་དུ་གཤེགས的引申之意，其原意则是去天上、回归天界，用的是གཤེགས“行走、来、去”的本意。P.T.1287、P.T.1286 中同样有相应的例子。

P.T.1287/6 །མངོན་ 7. བར་དགུང་དུ་གཤེགས་པ་ལ་སྩོགས་པ་འཕྲུལ་དང་བྱིན་ཆེད་པོ་མངའ་བས། ངོད་དང་དྲེགས་མ་ཐུབ་སྟེ॥

却具当众升天等巨大神通与幻化之力，故不能克制其狂躁与骄慢。

---

① 宾天：委婉语，谓帝王之死，亦泛指尊者之死。

P.T.1286/43.ཁྲི་འི་བདུན་ཚིགས་ཀྱི་སྲས། ལྡེ་ཉག་ཁྲི་བཙན་པོ། ས་དོག་ལ་ཡུལ་ཡབ་ཀྱི་རྗེ་དོག་ཡབ་ཀྱི་ཆར་དུ་གཤེགས་ནས། །ལྷ་སྲས་མི་
44. ཡུལ་གྱི་རྒྱལ་མཛད་ཅིང་བཞུགས་པ་ལས། མངོན་དུ་ཐལ་བྱུང་དགུང་དུ་གཤེགས་པ། །

赤顿祉之子即岱·聂赤赞普来作雅砻大地之主，降临父辈之地，天神之子做人间之王，后又为人们目睹直接回归天界。

值得注意的是，在《吐蕃大事纪年》中，表示去世，吐蕃赞普、王室成员和大臣采用的是不同的词。吐蕃赞普用དགུང་དུ་གཤེགས，王室成员用ནོངས，大臣则用གུམ。①

ནོངས一词在《吐蕃大事纪年》中出现 8 次，表示王室成员的去世。比如：

281/229 །སྲས་ལྷས : པོན : ཇོན་ན་བཞུགས། བཞུགས་ 282/230 པ་ལས : ནོངས། བཙན་པོ : ཡབ : དགུན་བོད་ཡུལ : དུ་སླར་གཤེགས། བཙན་མོ : ཀིམ་ཤེང : ཁོང་ཅོ་ནོངས་པར : ལོ་ཆིག།

〔及至兔年。(739—740)〕王子拉本驻于准，其间薨逝。赞普父王于冬季返回吐蕃本部。金城公主薨逝。是为一年。

本例句中，王子、金城公主均为王室成员，用ནོངས理所当然。不过，下面的这个例子就饶有趣味了。

Or. 8212.187/49 ༎ དགུན་སྨད་རྒྱ་རྗེ : ནོངས་ནས༎ རྒྱ་ 50 རྗེ་གསར་དུ་བཙུག : པ༎

冬末，唐王薨逝，新王登基。

这里的唐王指肃宗（756—762），新王指代宗（762—779），肃宗去世用ནོངས，是把唐帝当成吐蕃王室成员看待？还是因唐蕃甥舅关系？或者说把唐帝仅仅看成是四周的一个王？这是一个值得细究的问题。②

གུམ一词在《吐蕃大事纪年》中出现 13 次，其中 1 次为人名，其余 12 次均表大臣去世之意。

48 ༄༅།།ཡོས་བུའི་ལོ་ལ། བཙན་པོ : འོར་མང་དུ་གཤེགས་སྟེ། བློན་ཆེ་སྟོང་རྩན་རིས་ཕུར་གུམ་པར : ལོ : གཅིག།

及至兔年（667—668），赞普巡狩倭儿芒，大论东赞薨于日布。是为一年。

---

① 有学者已经注意到描述不同人群去世使用不同的词。上文提及，林冠群已指出吐蕃赞普、大臣采用的是不同的词，但他并未提及王室成员。参见林冠群：《从〈吐蕃大事纪年〉论唐代吐蕃的史学》，第 15 页。另外，刘凤强在《敦煌吐蕃历史文书的“春秋笔法”》中对这三种情况有详细的讨论，详见刘凤强：《敦煌吐蕃历史文书的“春秋笔法”》，《中国藏学》2014 年第 1 期，第 103—108 页。

② 拟与其他词汇一起专门论述，在此不展开讨论。

以上两种意思在《藏汉大辞典》中均有标注，一是行走、来、去，二是死、逝。[①]表明这一词汇一直沿用至今，但已作为一般词汇使用，而非赞普专用词汇了。

3. 巡狩

གཤེགས一词在《吐蕃大事纪年》中出现36次，除以上几例外，均为巡狩之意。试举一二例：

232/180 ༄༅༎ བྱི་བའི་ལོ་ལ། བཙན་པོ་ : དབྱར་ད་སྤེལ་ན་བཞུགས་ཤིང། བྱང་རོལ་དུ་གཤེགས་སྟེ། ཁོ་ཉེ་དུ་རུར། གཡག་རྒོད་ལ་ : རོལ་མོ་ : མཛད། 233/181 གཡག་རྒོད་སྒྲོག་དུ་བཀུག།

及至鼠年夏（724年），赞普驻于“拜”，巡狩北方，于“科聂都若”捕猎野牦牛，以索缚野牦牛。

175/123 ༄༅༎ ཁྱི་ལོ་ : ལ་བབ་སྟེ། བཙན་པོ་ : བལ་པོ་ན་ : བཞུགས། ཕྱི་དྲོན་ན་བཞུགས། མཁྲིས་པ་ཐང་དུ་ : འདུན་མ་ : འདུས་སྟེ : 176/124 བཙན་མོ་ : ཁོང་ཅོ་གཤེགས་ : པའི་ཡོ་ : བྱད་བཀྲལ། ཞང་བཙན་ཏོ་རེ་ལྷས་ : བྱིན་ལས་ : སྐྱོགས་པས། གཉེ་པོ་བགྱི་ 177 /125 སྟེ། བཙན་མོ་ : ཀིམ་ : ཤང་ཁོང་ཅོ་ : ར་སའི་ཤ་ཚལ་དུ་གཤེགས། དགུན་བཙན་པོ་ : སྤྲངས་དབྱལ་ : བྲག་མར་ན་བཞུགས་ : །

及至狗年（710—711），赞普驻于跋布川，祖母驻于准；于墀帕塘召集会盟，准备与赞蒙公主联姻之物具，以尚·赞咄热拉金等人为迎婚使，将赞蒙金城公主迎娶至逻些之鹿苑。冬，赞普伉俪驻于札玛。

需要指出的是，此句中出现了两个གཤེགས。第一个གཤེགས : པའི་ཡོ : བྱད，གཤེགས后加པ，把动词转成了名词，此处的པ为名物化标记，གཤེགས名物化后再限定中心语ཡོ་བྱད，因此结合上下文，གཤེགས : པའི་ཡོ : བྱད可理解为联姻的物具。第二个གཤེགས，作为动词，也可作“联姻”解释，在行文中可翻译成“迎娶”。作“联姻”的གཤེགས字在《吐蕃大事纪年》中共出现了6次，在第二部分我们会展开讨论。

通过以上的分析可知，གཤེགས有三种意思：一为行走、来、去之意；二为宾天；三为巡狩。且专用于赞普。前两种相对较少，第三种最多，均与赞普巡狩有关。

以下我们就གཤེགས的第三种含义所体现的相关制度再进行具体分析。

二、吐蕃巡守制度分析

巡守制度是“一种承载文化思想和维护统治秩序的礼仪制度”[②]。中国古代五礼（吉礼、

① 张怡荪主编：《藏汉大辞典》（下册），民族出版社1993年（2004年重印）版，第2876页。

② 郭旭东：《卜辞与殷礼研究》，陕西师范大学哲学系2010年博士学位论文，第79页。

嘉礼、宾礼、凶礼、军礼）中，不少内容都涉及巡狩。有学者指出："巡狩既是祭祀天、地、君、亲、师、社稷、鬼神的吉礼和亲万民和合人际关系的吉庆嘉礼，又是包含有亲邦国、朝觐、交聘、通好、交际之宾礼和哀邦国、悼亡、救患、问疾、恤灾之凶礼，亦是同邦国、耀武、征服不驯的征伐之军礼等等。"[①] 显然，巡狩活动是一个包含多种礼仪的综合活动。

（一）吐蕃赞普巡狩频率分析

根据《吐蕃大事纪年》，吐蕃几任赞普在任期间外出巡狩共计 29 次。其中有 3 任赞普的数据具有统计意义。在 664—676 年、686—704 年、724—746 年间（共 55 年）巡狩 27 次，平均两年一次，其中也有一年两次的。具体而言，3 任赞普情况有所差别。（参见表 2）

表 2：吐蕃赞普巡狩一览表

赞普时期	时　间	地　点	目　的	巡狩频率
松赞干布（630—649 年在位）	641—642	吐蕃	政事（联姻）	
芒伦芒赞（649—676 年在位）	鼠年（664—665）	北方	猎	13 年间，8 次巡狩，平均约 1.6 年一次
	兔年（667—668）	倭儿芒	避寒	
	羊年冬（671—672）	多鱼之园	避寒	
	羊年冬（671—672）		政事（联姻）	
	猴年冬（672—673）	南几林	避寒	
	鸡年冬（673—674）	襄之让噶园	避寒	
	狗年冬（674—675）	仓邦那	避寒	
	猪年春（675—676）	谐辛	避寒	
赤都松（686—704 年在位）	鼠年（688—689）	达域	政事（联姻）	在位 19 年，12 次巡狩，平均约 1.6 年一次
	牛年（689—690）	吐谷浑	政事（联姻）	
	兔年夏（691 年）	色乌秀	政事（集会）	
	羊年夏（695 年）	登木	政事	
	羊年冬（695—696）	扎玛	政事	
	狗年夏（698 年）	北方	政事（托言猎）	

① 何平立：《巡狩与封禅——封建政治的文化轨迹》，齐鲁书社 2003 年版，绪论第 3 页。

续　表

赞普时期	时　间	地　点	目　的	巡狩频率
赤都松（686—704 年在位）	狗年冬（698—699）	帕尔	政事	
	猪年夏（699 年）	跋布川哲乌塘	政事	
	鼠年夏（700 年）	下枯零之孙可	政事	
	鼠年秋（700 年）		政事（军事）	
	兔年冬（703—704）	南诏	政事（军事）	
	龙年冬（704—705）	蛮地	政事	
赤玛蕾（705—712 年执政）	狗年（710—711）	逻些之鹿苑	政事（联姻）	
赤德祖赞（712—754 年在位）	鼠年夏（724 年）	北方	猎	23 年间，7 次巡狩，平均约 3.3 年一次
	兔年夏（727 年）	吐谷浑	政事	
	兔年夏（739 年）	毕	政事	
	蛇年夏（741 年）		政事（军事）	
	蛇年冬（741—742）	扎玛	政事	
	猴年夏（744 年）	北方	猎	
	狗年夏（746 年）	塞孔	猎?	

芒伦芒赞（643—676）于 649—676 年在位 27 年，8 次巡狩，平均 3 年多一次。实际上，芒伦芒赞继赞普位后，直到 664 年才外出巡狩。此前一则因为赞普年幼，二则忙于安排对外扩张事宜，尤其是吞并吐谷浑是吐蕃自松赞干布以来的既定目标，为此吐蕃花费了长达 30 年的时间。663 年，吐蕃最终灭吐谷浑。从 664 至 676 年 13 年间，芒伦芒赞 8 次巡狩，平均约 1.6 年一次，巡狩内容涉及狩猎、政事巡狩、避寒等，尤其以避寒次数最多。

赤都松（676—704）于 686—704 年在位 19 年，12 次巡狩，平均约 1.6 年一次。巡狩内容涉及狩猎、政事巡狩等，其中 698 年的巡狩，是借狩猎之名进行铲除噶尔家族的活动，实际上也属于政事巡狩。因此可以说赤都松在位期间的 12 次巡狩均为政事巡狩，而且 4 种政事巡狩的情况均有出现，显示出赤都松赞普忙于各种政务活动，且大多围绕铲除噶尔家族、对外扩张活动而展开。704 年冬，赤都松年仅 29 岁宾天，恰是其巡狩蛮地之时。

值得注意的是，P.T.1287《吐蕃赞普传记》有一段关于赤都松的记载，正与狩猎有关。

སྟགི་རྣ་བ་ལ་བཟུང་བ་ལ་སྩོགས་པའ།།

赞普赤都松，年虽幼冲，曾劈野猪，绊野牛，捉虎耳，诸如此类等。

这一记载表明，吐蕃赞普在未成年时，有狩猎的训练，狩猎的对象包括野猪、野牛、老虎等。有研究者指出，狩猎的功效在于，吐蕃赞普的“控制能力在狩猎这一领域中的清晰展示，自然地暗示了他在其他方面的能力，例如税收或镇压暴乱”，因此，“狩猎有效地重申了统治者参与和管理大型机构的能力，即统治”。① 对赤都松这一活动的特别记载，显示出赤都松相对于其他赞普而言，其狩猎能力突出，这才有 691 年夏于“色乌秀”召集会议后，年仅 15 岁的赤都松亲自巡狩，698 年更是实施了借狩猎之名铲除噶尔家族活动的妙计。

赤德祖赞（704—754）于 712—754 年在位 43 年，7 次巡狩。但因《吐蕃大事纪年》缺失 7 年记事（748—754），所以有记录可查的仅 36 年，可推测其巡狩频率平均 5 年多一次。赤德祖赞在 712 年继赞普位后，因其年幼、忙于对外扩张事务，直到 724 年才外出巡狩。724—746 年，23 年间赤德祖赞 7 次巡狩，平均约 3.3 年一次。巡狩内容涉及狩猎、政事巡狩等，不过仍以政事巡狩为主。

（二）吐蕃赞普巡狩内容分析

《吐蕃大事纪年》所载的 29 次巡狩，根据内容可分为 3 种情况，即狩猎、政事巡狩和避寒。

1. 狩猎（བྱང་རོལ་དུ་གཤེགས）

狩猎是吐蕃赞普巡狩活动的重要组成部分，在《吐蕃大事纪年》中记载有 4 次。

（1）44 ༄ཿ།བྱི་བའི་ལོ་ལ། བཙན་པ : བྱང་རོལ་དུ་གཤེགས་ཤིང།

及至鼠年（664—665），赞普巡狩北方。

（2）232/180 ༄ཿ།བྱི་བའི་ལོ་ལ། བཙན་པོ : དབྱརད་སྤེལ་ན་བཞུགས་ཤིང། བྱང་རོལ་དུ་གཤེགསྟེ། ཁོ་ཉེ་དུ་ཙུར། གཡག་རྗོད་ལ : རོལ་མོ : མཛད། 233/181 གཡག་རྗོད་སྒྲོག་དུ་བཅུག།

及至鼠年夏（724 年），赞普驻于“拜”，巡狩北方，于“科聂都若”捕猎野牦牛，以索缚野牦牛。

（3）296/244 ༄ཿ།སྤྲེའུ : ལོ : ལ།བཙན་པོ : དབྱརད་བྱང་རོལ་དུ་གཤེགས : པ་ལས : སྣར : འཁོརདེ།

① 大卫·托马斯·普利兹克：《丝绸之路上的文化交流——吐蕃时期的艺术珍品》，载王旭东、汤姆·普利兹克主编《丝绸之路上的文化交流——吐蕃时期艺术珍品》，中国藏学出版社 2020 年版，第 21 页。

及至猴年。夏（744 年），赞普巡狩北方而还。

这一活动，在 Or. 8212.187 中也有记载，但并未标明是在夏天。

སྤྲེའི་ལོ་ལ : བབ་སྟེ། བཙན་ཕོ་ཕོ་བྲང། མཚར : དུ་བདབ་སྟེ། བྱང་རོལདུ་གཤེགས།

及至猴年（744—745）。赞普牙帐驻于册尔，巡狩北方。

（4）Or. 8212.187/6 །ཁྱི་ལོ་ལ་བབ་སྟེ། དབྱར་ 7 བཙན་པོ་ན་མར་ན་བཞུགསྟེ། གསེར་ཁོང་དུ་རོལ་དུ་གཤེགས།

及至狗年。夏（746 年），赞普驻于那玛尔，至塞孔巡狩。

以上 4 次狩猎活动，明确标明བྱང་རོལདུ་གཤེགས巡狩北方的有 3 次。狩猎的时间一般在夏季，因此狗年夏（746 年）的记载尽管没有明确说明狩猎，我们还是把它归入了狩猎活动。

狩猎的对象以牦牛为主。敦煌藏文文献中关于狩猎对象的记载很少，前文提及的 P.T.1287《吐蕃赞普传记》中提到赤都松狩猎的对象包括野猪、野牛、老虎等。此外，吐蕃墓棺板画保留的狩猎图像中，其主要狩猎对象是牦牛、鹿，以牦牛居多。郭里木吐蕃墓棺板画第 1 号载："骑射图像集中分布在棺板左半部分，内容分为上下两组。上组为向右驰骋的前一后三夹击两头受惊狂奔的牦牛的四名骑士。其中，在牦牛前面骑士扭身回射，后面三骑上部二人满弦瞄准牦牛，下面一骑因画面受损不见骑者，但结合整体画面，可以肯定原也为一名射牦牛的猎手。另外，牦牛前侧并排还有一只飞奔的猎犬回首朝向牦牛。"[①]

图 2：青海郭里木吐蕃墓葬 1 号棺板画（线描图）上、A 板（局部）（线描图由仝涛绘）[②]

---

① 马冬：《考古发现所见吐蕃射猎运动——以郭里木吐蕃棺板画为对象》，《西安体育学院学报》2008 年第 6 期，第 64—65 页。

② 线描图采自王旭东、汤姆·普利兹克主编：《丝绸之路上的文化交流——吐蕃时期艺术珍品》，第 19 页。

2. 政事巡狩

政事巡狩的情况相对复杂，又可细分为 4 种：一为以打猎为名，铲除噶尔家族的活动；二为标明为ཆབ་སྲིད进行巡狩的；三为联姻；四为军事活动。

一是以打猎为名进行政治活动。从《吐蕃大事纪年》来看，为铲除噶尔家族，吐蕃赞普赤都松至少有 5 次名为打猎的巡狩活动。

> 127/75 ༄༅།ཁྱི་ལོ་ལ་བབ་སྟེ།བཙན་པོ་: དབྱར་བྱང་རོལ་དུ་གཤེགས།དགུན་བློན་ཆེན་པོ་: ཁྲི་འབྲིང་གྱིས།ཙོང་ཀ་ཆེ་ཆུང་དུ་དྲང་སྟེ། 128/76 རྒྱའི་དམག་དཔོན་ཆེན་པོ་: ཏུག : ཧུ་ཤི་བཟུང། དེའི་: དགུན་མགར་ལ་: བཀོན་པབ་སྟེ་: བཙན་པོ་: ཕར་དུ་གཤེགས་པར་ [ལོ་] ཅིག།
>
> 及至狗年。夏（698 年），赞普巡狩北方。冬（698—699），大论钦陵发兵大小宗喀开战，并俘获唐大将军都护使。冬，噶尔〔家族〕获罪。赞普巡狩帕尔。是为一年。

关于此事，《资治通鉴》卷二〇六圣历二年载：

> 〔二月〕初，吐蕃赞普器弩悉弄尚幼，论钦陵兄弟用事，皆有勇略，诸胡畏之。钦陵居中秉政，诸弟握兵分据方面，赞婆常居东边，为中国患者三十余年。器弩悉弄浸长，阴与大臣论岩谋诛之。会钦陵出外，赞普诈云出畋，集兵执钦陵亲党二千余人，杀之，遣使召钦陵兄弟，钦陵等举兵不受命。赞普将兵讨之，钦陵兵溃，自杀。夏四月，赞婆帅所部千余人来降。太后命左武卫铠曹参军郭元振与河源军大使夫蒙令卿将骑迎之。以赞婆为特进、归德王。钦陵子弓仁，以所统吐谷浑七千帐来降，拜左玉钤卫将军、酒泉郡公。[①]

“赞普诈云出畋”，在《新唐书·吐蕃传》记为“赞普托言猎”，说明《吐蕃大事纪年》中赤都松“赞普巡狩北方”并非一次纯粹的狩猎活动，而是其以狩猎为名，提前部署，铲除噶尔家族的政事活动。

结合汉藏文文献，事件的经过如下：698 年夏天，赤都松赞普托言猎，提前布置。699 年 2 月，赤都松与钦陵开战。钦陵在其亲信两千余人倒戈之后，誓死不屈，在战场上自杀。噶尔家族获罪。699 年夏 4 月，钦陵之弟和千余亲随以及钦陵的儿子弓仁、七千帐吐谷浑人投唐，唐加以安抚。封赞婆为特进、归德王，弓仁拜左玉钤卫将军、酒泉郡公。

实际上，从《吐蕃大事纪年》来看，吐蕃王室铲除噶尔家族的活动，从 685 年就已经开始了。此后，“694 年论岩在赞普的安排下主持集会议盟；695 年赞普亲自主持集会议盟，宣

---

① 苏晋仁编：《通鉴吐蕃史料》，西藏人民出版社 1982 年版，第 43 页。

布赞辗恭顿（勃伦）背叛；696 年又由论岩主持集会议盟；698 年冬，趁钦陵引兵赴大宗喀之机，向噶尔家族发难，即这里所记的‘噶尔家族获罪’之事；次年（699 年）又清查获罪家族财产”①。这些内容均可以在《吐蕃大事纪年》中找到蛛丝马迹。其中,羊年夏（695 年）赤都松巡狩登木、羊年冬（695—696）赤都松巡狩扎玛，与诛杀噶尔·赞辗恭顿（禄东赞之子）有关；猪年夏（699 年）赤都松自帕尔前往跋布川哲乌塘巡狩，同样与铲除噶尔家族的活动有关。吐蕃赞普赤都松的这些巡狩活动均可归入政事巡狩范畴。

二为政事（ཆབ་སྲིད）巡狩②。此类巡狩最多，其中 5 次明确标明为政事（ཆབ་སྲིད）巡狩。

（1）132/80 ༄༅། བྱི་བའི་ལོ་ལ་བབ་སྟེ། བཙན་པོ : དབྱརད་མོང་ཀར་ནས : ཆབ་སྲིད་ལ : ཤ་གུ : ཉིང་སུམ : ཕོལ་དུ་གཤེགས་ཤིང་།

及至鼠年。夏（700 年），赞普以政事从蒙噶尔前往下枯零之孙可巡狩。

（2）148/96 དགུན་བཙན་པོ : ཆབ་སྲིད་ལ : མྱྭ་ལ་གཤེགས : པ་ལས། དགུང་དུ་གཤེགས།

〔及至龙年〕，冬（704—705），赞普以政事巡狩蛮地，宾天。

总体来看，冬天一般而言是吐蕃赞普避寒之时，但在 704 年底或 705 年初，吐蕃赞普赤都松领兵出征南诏，表明此时吐蕃正是扩张之际。可惜的是，赤都松年仅 29 岁逝于蛮地。

（3）243/191 ༄༅། ཡོས : བུའི་ལོ་ལ། བཙན་པོ : དབྱར་ཆབ་སྲིད་ལ : འ་ཞ་ཡུལ་དུ་གཤེགསྟེ།

及至兔年。夏（727 年），赞普以政事巡狩吐谷浑。

（4）281/229 ༄༅། ཡོས : བུའི : ལོ་ལ། བཙན་པོ : དབྱརད་ཆབ་སྲིད་ལ : བེག་དུ་གཤེགསྟེ།

及至兔年。夏（739 年），赞普以政事巡狩“毕”地。

（5）286/234……དགུན་ཆབ་སྲིད་ལས : སྐར་བྲག་མར་དུ་གཤེགསྟེ།

冬（741—742），〔赞普〕结束政事活动后巡狩扎玛。

还有一次巡狩活动发生在 691 年。

108/56 ༄༅། ཡོས་བུའི་ལོ་ལ་བབ་སྟེ། བཙན་པོ……། དབྱར་འདུན : སེའུ་གཞུག་དུ : འདུས : པ་ལས། 109/57 ལྷ་གཤེགས་ནས། ཁྲ་སྣར་འདོངསྟེ།

及至兔年。赞普……夏（691 年），于“色乌秀”召集会议，巡查，迁至“查那”。

ལྷ་གཤེགས，学界有多种理解。杜晓峰认为是一个地名，并专门对该词做了一个注释：“这种

① 王尧：《王尧藏学文集》（卷一），第 259 页。

② P.T.1047 第 63 行也记载：“国王为政事巡狩，大功告成。”

结构说明 Lha-gshegs 和查那都属于广义上的色乌秀。Lha gshegs 字面意是‘神离开（the god departed）’，所以这里流传的神话可能影响了该地区的名字。”① 王尧、陈践翻译成“赞普驾临”，黄布凡、马德翻译成“因王赴会”。②

实际上，我们认为可以将其理解成赞普巡狩，以ལྷ指代赞普。P.T.1287 便有ལྷ་གཤེགས这样的例子：

491 ཅོག་རོ་ཟམ་མཆིད་གླངས་པ་འི་ཆོག་ལ། །ཀྱེ་འདམ་གྱི་ནི་ཐང་ཀར་རུ། ལྷ་གཤེགས་ནི། 492 ཞལ་མ་འཚོལ། །ལྷ་གཤེགས་ནི་ཞལ་འཚོལ་ན། དུད་དེ་ནི་ཕྱག་ཀྱང་འཚལ།།ཕྱག་མདའ་ནི་སྤྲིན་ཀྱིས་འཛིན།།

属庐萨应对而歌：“噫！在达木平坝上，赞普巡狩而未见尊颜，赞普巡狩若见尊颜，俯身恭致敬，信息传来即收下。”

在古代，帝王巡狩的一个重要目的就是稳定地方秩序。691 年夏，赤都松赞普在“色乌秀”召集会议后巡查地方，本身就是一种对地方的震慑。

三为联姻。在《吐蕃大事纪年》中，由赞普主持的联姻活动共有 5 次。发生在 641—711 年之间，时间跨度 50 年。

（1）11[བ]: ཙན་མོ : མུན་ཆང : ཀོང་ཅོ། མགར : སྟོང་རྩན་ཡུལ་ཟུང་གྱིས : སྤྱན་དྲངསྟེ : བོད་ཡུལ་ 12 དུ : གཤེགསོ།

〔641—642 年，〕赞蒙文成公主由噶尔·东赞域宋护送，迎娶至吐蕃。

（2）52 ༄༅།།ལུག་གི་ལོ་ལ་བབ : སྟེ : བཙན་པོ : དབྱརད : ལྡམ : གྱི་ར་སྔོན་ན་བཞུགསྟེ།དགུན་ན་ཉ་མངས་ཚལ་དུ་གཤེགས་ 53 ཤིང།བཙན་མོ : ཉ་མོ : སྟེངས : ཉ་ཤུར : སྤུངས : ཏེ་རྒྱུག་ལ : བག་མར : གཤེགས : པར : ལོ་གཅིག།

及至羊年。夏（671 年），赞普驻于登木之绿苑；冬（671—672），巡狩多鱼之园，将赞蒙聂媚登公主嫁与聂秀绷野究为妻。是为一年。

（3）100/48 ༄༅། བྱི་བའི་ལོ ལ་བབ་སྟེ། བཙན་པོ་ཉེན་ཀར་ན་བཞུགས་ཤིང། དབྱར : འདུན : ཟུ་སྤུག་དུ : འདུས། དགུན : དབོན་ད་རྒྱལ་ 101/49 ཁྲི་ཟུང་གྱིས། ཤོགས : གྱི་ཚུར་ལུང་དུ་བསྡུས། བཙན་མོ : ཁྲི་མོ་སྟེངས : དགས : ཡུལ་དུ་ཆབ : སྲིད་ལ་གཤེགས་སྟེ་ལོ་ཆིག།

及至鼠年（688—689）。赞普驻于年噶，夏（688 年），于苏浦（ཟུ་སྤུག）召集会盟；冬（688—689），派坌达延墀松于晓之粗垅召集〔盟会〕，赞蒙墀顿去达域联姻。是为一年。

（4）102/50 ༄༅། གླང་གྱི་ལོ་ལ་བབ་སྟེ།བཙན་པོ་ཉེན་ཀར་གྱི་ཐང་བུ་ར་ན་བཞུགས་ཤིང།བཙན་མོ : ཁྲི་བངས།འ་ཞ་རྗེ་ལ : བག་མར : 103/51 གཤེགས།

及至牛年（689—690）。赞普驻于年噶之塘卜园，将墀邦公主嫁与吐谷浑王为妻。

① Brandon Dotson, *The Old Tibetan Annals: An Annotated Translation of Tibet's First History. With an Annotated Cartographical Documentation by Guntram Hazod*, p.97, n.192.

② 王尧：《王尧藏学文集》（卷一），第 197 页；黄布凡、马德：《敦煌藏文吐蕃史文献译注》，第 44 页。

（5）175/123 ༄༅།། ཁྱི་ལོ་ : ལ་བབ་སྟེ། བཙན་པོ་ : བལ་པོ་ན : བཞུགས། ཕྱི་དོན་ན་བཞུགས། མཁྲིས་པ་ཏང་དུ : འདུན་མ : འདུས྄ྟེ :176/124 བཙན་མོ : ཁོང་ཅོ་གཤེགས : པའི་ཡོ : བྱད་བཀྱལ། ཞང་བཙན་ཏོ་རེ་ལྷས : བྱིན་ལས : སྙོགས་པས། གཉེ་པོ་བཀྱི 177 /125 སྟེ། བཙན་མོ : ཀིམ : ཤང་ཁོང་ཅོ : ར་སའི་ཤ་ཙལ་དུ་གཤེགས། དགུན་བཙན་པོ : སྤངས་དབྱལ : བྲག་མར་ན་བཞུགས : །

及至狗年（710—711）。赞普驻于跋布川，祖母驻于准；于墀帕塘召集会盟，准备与公主联姻之物具，以尚·赞咄热拉金等人为迎婚使，将金城公主迎娶至逻些之鹿苑。冬，赞普伉俪驻于札玛。

以上5例中，动作行为的发出者均为赞普。第3例的情况相对复杂，我们详细分析一下：赞普驻于年噶，其后有一连词ཤིང，表明其后动作行为的发出者仍然是赞普；夏季会盟的召集所用动词是འདུས（自动词），表明召集者是赞普；冬季会盟的召集所用动词是བསྡུས（使动词），表明会盟的召集者并非坌达延墀松，而是赞普（发出者）；同样的，后一句用赞普专用词汇གཤེགས，表明动作行为真正的发出者仍是赞普，而非赞蒙墀顿。

值得注意的是，《吐蕃大事纪年》中还有两个联姻的例子，但并未用གཤེགས一词。

268/216 ༄༅།། ཁྱིའི : ལོ་ལ།བཙན་པོ : ཕོ་བྲང་དབྱརད : དོན་ན་བཞུགས།……ཇེ་བ : འདྲོན་མ : ལོད་དུར 269/217 གྱིས : ཁ་གན་ལ : བག་མར་བཏང།

及至狗年。夏(734年)，赞普牙帐驻于准。……公主卓玛蕾嫁与突骑施可汗。

283/231 ༄༅།། འབྲུག་གི་ལོ་ལ། བཙན་པོ : ཕོ་བྲང། དབྱརད་མཆར་བུ : སྣའི་ངང་མོ : གླིང་ན་བཞུགས་སྟེ། ཇེ་བ : ཁྲི་མ་ལོད་བྲུ་ཞ་རྗེ་ལ : བག 284/232 མར་བཏང།

及至龙年。夏（740年），赞普牙帐驻于册布那之昂木林。墀玛类公主嫁与小勃律王为妻。

有学者推测，未用གཤེགས一词的原因有两个。其一，是ཇེ་བ（公主）的身份。已经有研究者指出，“je-ba也可能是表示赞普王后或小王妃的姐姐，因为她们不具有实际意义上的王室血统”。① 其二，这一联姻的提议可能并非来自吐蕃赞普，而是联姻的另一方。“这可能是732年来访的突骑施使臣一手策划的。”②

四为军事巡狩。《吐蕃大事纪年》记载有3次与军事巡狩有关的活动。前两次发生在赤都松时期，后一次则在赤德祖赞时期。

---

① Brandon Dotson, *The Old Tibetan Annals: An Annotated Translation of Tibet's First History. With an Annotated Cartographical Documentation by Guntram Hazod*, p.119, n.294.

② Brandon Dotson, *The Old Tibetan Annals: An Annotated Translation of Tibet's First History. With an Annotated Cartographical Documentation by Guntram Hazod*, p.119, n.294.

（1）133/81 སྟོན་བཙན་པོ་གཤེགས་སྟེ : ག་ཆུར་དྲངས།
秋（700 年），赞普巡狩，发兵河州。
（2）145/93 དགུན་བཙན་པོ : འཇང་ཡུལ་དུ་གཤེགས་སྟེ་།འཇང་ཕབ་ཁར : ལོ་གཅིག།
〔及至兔年〕冬（703—704 年），赞普巡狩南诏，攻陷南诏。
（3）285/233 ༄༅།།སྦྲུལ་གྱི་ལོ་ལ། བཙན་པོ : དབྱརད་ཆབ : སྲིད་ལ་གཤེགས་སྟེ།རྒྱའི་མཁར་དར : ཁྭ : ཧྭན་ཕབ།
及至蛇年。夏（741 年），赞普以政事巡狩，攻陷汉城达化县。

3. 避寒

避寒同样是巡狩的重要活动之一。唐朝的皇帝们便喜欢到两京周围的行宫中避暑寒。据吴宏岐统计，隋唐两京有避暑宫 19 所，“长安周围有 15 所，洛阳周围有 4 所”；温泉宫“以华清宫、凤泉宫和汝州温泉宫最为有名”。① 吐蕃因地处高原，无须避暑，吐蕃赞普的巡狩主要为避寒，时间以冬、春为多，《吐蕃大事纪年》记有 6 次避寒活动。

（1）48 ༄༅། ཡོས་བུའི་ལོ་ལ། བཙན་པོ : འོར་མང་དུ་གཤེགས་སྟེ།
及至兔年（667—668）。赞普巡狩倭儿芒。
（2）52 ༄༅། ལུག་ལོ་ལ་བབ : སྟེ : བཙན་པོ……། དགུན་ཉ་མངས་ཚལ : དུ་གཤེགས།
及至羊年。冬（671—672），赞普……巡狩多鱼之园。
（3）54/2 ༄༅། སྤྲེའུ་ལོ་ལ་བབ་སྟེ། བཙན་པོ :……།དགུན : ནམ་ཅེ : སླིང་དུ : 55/3 གཤེགས་སྟེ།
及至猴年。赞普……冬（672—673），巡狩南几林。
（4）56/4 ༄༅། བྱ་གགི་ལོ་ལའ : བཙན་པོ :……58/6 དགུན་པོ་བྲང : ཤངས : གྱི་རབ་ཀ : ཚལ་དུ་གཤེགས་ཤིང་།
及至鸡年。冬（673—674），赞普巡狩“襄”之“让噶园”。
（5）60/8 ༄༅། ཁྱི་ལོ : ལ་བབ་སྟེ།བཙན་པོ :……དགུན་ཚང་བང་སྣར། གཤེ 61/9 གས་སྟེ།
及至狗年。赞普……冬（674—675），巡狩仓邦那。
（6）62/10 ༄༅། ཕགི་ལོ་ལ : བབ་སྟེ། བཙན་པོ : དཔྱིད : ཞེ་ཤིང་དུ་གཤེགས་སྟེ།
及至猪年。春（675—676），赞普巡狩“谐辛”。

三、初步结论

གཤེགས一词在《吐蕃大事纪年》中出现了 36 次，作为吐蕃赞普的专用词汇，除少数几例

① 吴宏岐：《隋唐帝王行宫的地域分布》，《中国历史地理论丛》1994 年第 2 期，第 73—74 页。

外，均为巡狩之意。吐蕃赞普的巡狩活动至少包含了狩猎、政事巡狩、避寒等内容。通过狩猎，吐蕃赞普可以证明其有能力调度人力，在政治舞台上同样可以发号施令。内容丰富的政事巡狩，包括联姻、巡查地方，更是吐蕃赞普统治能力的展示，尤其是以狩猎为名剪除禄东赞家族所进行的一系列活动，更是将狩猎的政治意涵发挥得淋漓尽致，凸显了吐蕃赞普借巡狩这一形式强化统治、稳定秩序。

由于史料的缺乏，我们对吐蕃赞普的巡狩规模、巡狩前的祭祀活动等信息一无所知。但通过对《吐蕃大事纪年》相关内容的分析，可以在很大程度上确认吐蕃时期存在巡守制度。正如前文所提及的，巡守制度是"一种承载文化思想和维护统治秩序的礼仪制度"[①]。作为吐蕃王朝中央政权强有力的标志，赞普的巡狩既是和合人际关系的嘉礼，又是蕴含联姻、交聘、通好的宾礼，亦是耀武、征伐的军礼，在在显示出吐蕃巡守制度的丰富内涵。

吐蕃巡守制度是探究吐蕃礼仪制度的重要门径之一，值得学界持续关注。期待学界同好发表高论，以推进我们对吐蕃时期巡守制度的认识。

---

① 郭旭东:《卜辞与殷礼研究》，第 79 页。

曹议金东征甘州回鹘史事证补

——浙敦114号《肃州府主致沙州令公书状》译释*

任小波

复旦大学历史地理研究中心

一、引　　言

2000年，浙江教育出版社影印出版《浙藏敦煌文献》，刊布了一批以佛典残叶为主的藏文写本。其中，一件墨书秀丽、钤有朱印的世俗文书颇为引人注目，此即浙敦114号（浙博89号）藏文写本。此本首尾、右部俱残，粘于浙敦113号（浙博88号）汉文写本纸背，原系著名学者张宗祥（1882—1965）旧藏。就其款式和内容判断，此本应是吐蕃统治结束以后的一件河西官府文书的正本残叶，笔者拟题《肃州府主致沙州令公书状》。《浙藏敦煌文献》将其断为“五代写本”，拟题则作“河西历史故事”①。2004年，武内绍人先生发表《吐蕃统治结束直至西夏时期（9—12世纪）藏文在西域行用的社会语言学影响》，简要提及此本年代当在10世纪末叶（980年代），推定其系曹氏归义军压服了肃州的反抗以后，肃州汉人向归义军节度使“令公”的效忠誓辞（a pledge of allegiance）②,然而他并未对此进行文本译释和深入研究。

---

* 本文原载沈卫荣主编：《西域历史语言研究集刊》第10辑，科学出版社2018年版，第433—441页。发表以后，承蒙冯培红先生赐教（2019年6月17日），得以纠正疏失，于此特致谢忱！此次重刊，又有部分修订。

① 毛昭晰等主编：《浙藏敦煌文献》，浙江教育出版社2000年版，图版第207页，叙录第21页。

② Tsuguhito Takeuchi, “Sociolinguistic Implications of the Use of Tibetan in East Turkestan from the End of Tibetan Domination through the Tangut Period (9th-12th c.),” in D. Durkin-Meisterest, S.-C. Raschmann et al. eds., *Turfan Revisited: The First Century of Research into the Arts and Cultures of the Silk Road*, Berlin: Dietrich Reimer Verlag, 2004, pp.341–343.

浙敦 114 号卷首、卷末骑缝之处，分别钤有署作“肃□之□”“□州□印”的同一枚阳文朱印。浙敦 113 号骑缝之处的朱印，亦与浙敦 114 号从同。经过缀合识别，均系“肃州之印”。官府文书上的骑缝朱印，功能在于接续纸张、防止造伪。浙敦 113 号写有“同光年”三字，且与印文叠合，似乎表明作为公文用纸，此纸应接裱于同光年间（923—926）。同卷题跋“此为后唐时人书”，即是出自张宗祥手笔。浙敦 114 号、113 号所存印文吻合，表明此本首尾部分虽被揭取，但仍保有原始装裱状态。值得注意的是，PT 1190.v 号书状末尾年款上的“肃州之印”，PT 1189.r 号书状正面下部末尾、背面骑缝之处的“肃州之印”①，亦与浙敦 114 号、113 号相同。PT 1190.v 号汉文书状，尾题“乾符□年正月贰拾壹日”，可知年代当在乾符某年（874—879）；PT 1189.r 号藏文书状，据考年代当在乾德五年（967 年）前后。② 准此判断，张氏以及曹氏归义军时期，无论对肃州的实际控制程度和统属关系如何，肃州官府沿用着同一枚唐代所颁的“肃州之印”。

二、浙敦 114 号藏文录文及汉文译文

根据《浙藏敦煌文献》所收浙敦 114 号藏文写本彩色、黑白两种图版，兹将此本的拉丁转写和笔者的汉文译文移录如下：

[---] {1} dgongs te gdan gshegs // kam cur pho nya brdzangs // go[-] [te] {2} gin dang / blon po dang / ru ru'i to dog las stsogs pa / zhu ba g[s]o[l] [---] {3} 'tshal zhing / sdums la mchis / tha tshigs gsar du brnan [---] {4} bde ba la bkod nas / yar gshegs // yar gshegs pa'i gti [bas] [bsam] {5} pa ngan pa ma bor nas // sug cur shod ma yang byas / dbang po la [---] {6} glo ba 'phreng nas // leng kong du ma zhus / gros ma bstun ste [---] {7} g.yabs pa dang // pho nya bzungs nas // leng kong gyi thugs [rg]y[al] [---] {8} yang ma legs te nos // rje leng [kong] yang / btsan mag mang po [---] {9} byon // sgo mnan nas / so sor gum chad du gyur nas // [---] {10} 'bangs kyang / sems grangs te / glo ba chung / 'jigs pa '[-] [---]

{11} $ // slad kyis // rje leng kong yang / byang cub gyi sems rgya b[skyed] [---] {12}

---

① 森安孝夫:「河西帰義軍節度使の朱印とその編年」,『内陸アジア言語の研究』第 15 號，2000 年，第 118 頁。

② 赤木崇敏:「帰義軍時代チベット文手紙文書 P.T.1189 訳註稿」，收入荒川正晴編『東トルキスタン出土「胡漢文書」の総合調査』，平成 15—17 年度科学研究費補助金研究成果報告書，2006 年，第 83—84 頁。

'bangs kyi tshis su / tha tshigs gsar du gso bar gnang // tha [tshigs] [---] {13} du gsos tshun cad // sug cu dbang po dang / 'bangs byin dang / lung 'bangs kyang // he[-] [---] {14} las stsogs pas / kyang // rje leng kong la / snying log par bsam [---] {15} btsal re // 'bangs chang kyu / rje khud par myi bgyi re // yar te [---] {16} te / lha klu gnyen po // mched sum brgya' drug cu // byang phyo[gs bdag] {17} po byi sha ra ma ne // sha cu'i kyim an shan shin las stsogs pa [---] {18} gzur gsol cig // gos na smos pa las mna' [---] {19} bya dgur myi legs / bsam dgur ma grub // lo phyugs ma [b]ye[d] [---] {20} sar mtshon sna dgu lus la phog // langs na / mdung dang ral [gri] [---] {21} shog // yul shor nas // ma bzhi g.yas / bu bzhi g.yon du [---]

释词：{3} tha tshigs > tha tshig. {7} bzungs > bzung. {8} btsan mag > btsan dmag. {10} grangs > grang. {13} byin > byings. {15} chang kyu > chang khyu; yar > g.yar. {17} kyim > khyim. {18} gos > bsgos. {21} shor > gshor.

……，思虑……，并且前往。〔肃州〕遣使甘州，祈请……狄银及其臣僚、茹茹都督等，达成和断，新立咒誓，入于安乐。此后，前往上部。前往上部者称："〔彼等〕未弃恶念，亦未知会肃州。对于府主，……顾虑；对于令公，未作通报。商议不谐，调集〔军兵〕，扣留使者。"于是，令公发愤，又获恶〔讯〕。人主令公，遣去众多劲旅，制服门戍，各各处死。〔官〕民痛心失意，……苦难。

因此，人主令公，发菩提心，为求利益百姓，新增咒誓。新增咒誓有云："尔后，肃州府主、一切百姓、龙家等，对于人主令公，决不心生邪念。百姓民众，决不自立为王。"趋前……，祈请神龙眷属、三百六十兄弟、北方之主毗沙门、沙州家安善神等，以作证盟，规诫晓谕。〔若违〕誓辞，诸事不佳，众愿难遂，农牧无功。所居之处，各色兵器，击刺其身。一经起身，……戟剑。划定辖境之后，母族在右，子嗣在左……

三、曹议金东征甘州回鹘以及遣使后唐

浙敦 114 号所记史事，当与曹议金任归义军节度使期间（914—935）东征甘州回鹘之役有关。根据相关敦煌文书，归义军与甘州回鹘之间，相隔不过一年两次交兵。李军先生考证，这两次战事分别为甘州（张掖）之战、肃州（酒泉）之战。① 第一次是由于甘州回鹘阻塞归义军通贡中原之路，归义军主动征讨，双方战于甘州。根据 P 3270 号《儿郎伟》，甘州

① 李军：《晚唐五代肃州相关史实考述》，《敦煌学辑刊》2005 年第 3 期，第 96—97 页。

回鹘“数年闭塞东路”，“今遇明王利化，再开河陇道衢。太保神威发愤，遂便点缉兵衣。略点精兵十万，各各尽擐铁衣”。此处“明王利化”，系指同光二年（924年）五月后唐庄宗授予曹议金归义军节度使之事。第二次是由于甘州回鹘兵侵肃州龙家，侵逼归义军东境，归义军出兵自卫，双方战于玉门、肃州。然而，对于战事的进程和细节，相关论著之中仍有不少歧义。

P 4011号《儿郎伟》颇能贯通战事全貌，参照原卷图版以及诸家录文，[1] 兹将此本全文厘定如下：

驱傩之法，送故迎新。且要扫除旧事，建立芳春。便获青阳之节，八方启（稽）颡来臻。

自从太保利化，千门喜贺殷勤。甘州数年作贼，直拟欺负侵凌。去载阿郎发愤，点集兵钾（甲）军人。亲领精兵十万，围绕张掖狼烟。未及张弓拔剑，他自放火烧然（燃）。一齐披发归伏，献纳金银城川。遂便安邦定国，永世钦伏于前。

不经一岁未尽，他急逆乱无边。准拟再觅寸境，便共龙家相煎。又动太保心竟（境），跛（叵）耐欺负仁贤。缉练精兵十万，如同铁石心肝。党（当）便充（冲）山进路，活捉猃狁狼烟。未至酒泉小郡，他自魂胆不残。便献飞龙白马，兼及绫锦数般。王子再拐无数，散发纳境相传。

因兹太保息怒，善神护我川原。河西一道清泰，天子尉（慰）曲西边。六蕃总来归首，一似舜日尧年。大都渴仰三宝，恶贼不打归降。万性（姓）齐唱快活，家家富乐安眠。比至三月初首，天使只（旨）降宣传。便拜三台使相，世代共贼无缘。万性（姓）感贺太保，直得千年万年。

荣新江先生指出，归义军趁甘州回鹘内乱、汗位交替之际发动战争，战事当发生于同光二年末、同光三年初，且在同光三年六月以前。[2] 同光二年十一月，甘州回鹘可汗仁美之弟狄银（Tegin）居功夺权、嗣立为汗，给予曹议金东征可乘之机。尤其根据S 5139.v号《凉州节院使押衙刘少晏状》所谓“回鹘三五年来自乱”，“曹太保阿郎政直（整治），开以河西老道”，以及尾署“乙酉年六月□日”，战事在同光三年六月以前可成定谳。

同光二年末或该年十一月，狄银继任甘州回鹘可汗以后，[3] 曹议金亲征甘州。同光三年

---

① 周绍良：《敦煌文学“儿郎伟”并跋》，《出土文献研究》第1辑，1985年，第179页。荣新江：《归义军史研究：唐宋时代敦煌历史考索》，上海古籍出版社2015年版，第321—322页。

② 荣新江：《曹议金征甘州回鹘史事表微》，《敦煌研究》1991年第2期，第8—10页。《归义军史研究：唐宋时代敦煌历史考索》，第312—313、324—325页。

③ 冯培红：《敦煌的归义军时代》，甘肃教育出版社2013年版，第327页。

初，亦即该年六月以前，归义军与甘州回鹘鏖战于玉门，进而挺进肃州。根据 P 2058.v 号《儿郎伟》，甘州回鹘“三五年间作贼，令公亲自权兵”，亦与浙敦 114 号吻合。曹议金东征之役胜利前后，甘州回鹘可汗狄银亡故，阿咄欲（Adruq）嗣立。根据《新五代史·回鹘传》，“阿咄欲，不知其为狄银亲疏，亦不知其立卒”[①]。然据 P 4011 号“王子再抈无数，散发纳境相传”，这位“王子”或指狄银之子阿咄欲。此后，曹议金又将其与甘州回鹘公主李氏所生之女嫁予阿咄欲，改变了此前“可汗是父，天子是子”的甘、沙关系格局。归义军两度击败甘州回鹘，打通经由张掖绿洲入贡中原的河西通道，然而终究未能长期控制甘、肃二州。

基于敦煌文书中的纪年史料，荣新江先生揭出曹议金同光二年前后称司空，同光三年始称太保，天成三年（928 年）至长兴二年（931 年）称令公，长兴二年始称大王。[②] P 4011 号记述曹议金东征之役，通篇将其称作“太保”，适与如上论断吻合。钢和泰（Alexander von Staël-Holstein）藏卷《于阗使臣上沙州太保书状》（出自敦煌，925—927），则以藏文 The po 或 The bo 对译曹议金的汉文衔称“太保”[③]。长兴二年正月，后唐以曹议金兼中书令。然于此前，曹议金已在境内冒称令公、自封使相。根据 P 2675.bis.v 号《曹议金状》，曹议金称“太保兼令公”。此件文书，或即后唐以曹议金兼中书令以后，曹议金上呈某位“相公”的答谢书状底稿。P 4011 号通篇称曹议金为太保，然其结尾又称“比至三月初首，天使只（旨）降宣传”，“便拜三台使相”，或系此后传抄添缀之辞。浙敦 114 号五次出现“令公”（Leng kong）衔称，显然是指曹议金。尤其第 7—8 行所谓“令公发愤”（leng kong gyi thugs [rg]y[al]），“众多劲旅”（btsan mag mang po）等句，正与 P 4011 号所谓“去载阿郎发愤”“亲领精兵十万”，以及“又动太保心竟（境）”“缉练精兵十万”相符，均指曹议金东征之役。准此研判，浙敦 114 号约书写于天成三年至长兴二年之间。

同光年间，归义军先后两次遣使后唐：第一次于同光二年四月抵达洛阳，五月获授归义军节度使；第二次于同光四年（926 年）正月、二月分作两批抵达洛阳。此后天成年间，归义军是否遣使于史无征。荣新江先生推断，P 4011 号应系天成二年末曹议金太保、令公衔称并用，或其将从太保改称令公时的产物。[④] 曹议金称令公的有纪年的最早书证，见于 P 2814 号《都头知悬泉镇遏使安进通状》，题作天成三年二月。曹议金冒称令公以后，或曾还有遣使之举。浙敦 113 号上的“州般”二字，当“沙州入朝般次”之义。同卷内题九字：

中书门下平章事崔□。

---

① 欧阳修撰：《四夷附录·回鹘传》，《新五代史》，中华书局 1974 年版，卷 74，第 916 页。

② 荣新江：《归义军史研究：唐宋时代敦煌历史考索》，第 103、107 页。

③ G. Uray, “L’emploi du tibétain dans les chancelleries des états du Kan-sou et de Khotan postérieurs à la domination tibétaine,” *Journal Asiatique*, Vol. 269, No. 1-2, 1981, pp.81-82.

④ 荣新江：《曹议金征甘州回鹘史事表微》，第 7 页；《归义军史研究：唐宋时代敦煌历史考索》，第 322 页。

根据《新五代史·唐明宗本纪》，天成二年（927年）正月“太常卿崔协为中书侍郎、同中书门下平章事”，卒于四年（929年）二月。[①] 又据洛阳所出《崔协墓志》，天成二年正月“制授中书侍郎、平章事”，三年三月“又进门下侍郎、平章事”，卒于四年二月。[②] 所谓“崔□”，极有可能是崔协。天成三年五月，后唐为“沙州节度使曹义（议）金加爵邑”[③]。如上题字写于沙州，时间当在天成三年前后，似与后唐加赐“爵邑”相关。

浙敦113号写本内有思妇词、宫词、《定西番》、愿文、王播《题木兰院二首之一》、杂写等项。[④]《定西番》所谓“夜久更兰（阑）欲暮深，圣泽远闻天下静”，应与归义军政治、军事相关。愿文则作：

> 次（此）则我皇帝之德业也。沙州，最陲西苗裔也。四邻，并是戎狄也……次则伏惟我当座都僧统和尚：才明（名）绝代，动必应机。五百挺生，千贤间生。故富通……

虽为残抄，然亦可知其系天成三年以后沙州富通和尚所撰。如上“都僧统和尚”，联系浙敦114号“令公”以及浙敦113号“崔协”的年代背景，或指河西都僧统阴海晏（926—933年在位），其时正值曹议金任归义军节度使的后半期。

四、多部族、多语言环境下的政治生态

浙敦114号涉及曹议金东征甘州回鹘之役，以及此后肃州官民向曹议金所立的誓辞。兹将相关信息汇释如下：（1）第1—2行 [Te]gin，应指甘州回鹘可汗“狄银”。此词源自突厥文 Tägin，原指突厥可汗子弟，汉文史籍通常记作“特勤”[⑤]。这一称谓，后为回鹘等族袭用。（2）第2行 Ru ru'i to dog，或可译作“茹茹都督”。其中 Ru ru 似为柔然，汉文史籍通常记作“茹茹”“蠕蠕”。至于 To dog，当系汉文“都督”之音译。根据行文，此词表明茹茹依属甘州回鹘。（3）第6、7、8、11、14行 Leng kong，当系汉文“令公”之音译，均指归义军节度

---

① 欧阳修撰：《唐明宗本纪》，《新五代史》，卷6，第57、60页。

② 仇鹿鸣：《新见五代崔协夫妇墓志小考》，《唐史论丛》（第14辑），陕西师范大学出版总社有限公司2012年版，第234页。

③ 薛居正等撰：《唐书·明宗纪》，《旧五代史》，中华书局1976年版，卷39，第538页。

④ 黄征、张崇依：《浙藏敦煌文献校录整理》下册，上海古籍出版社2012年版，第485—487页。并参上册《前言》，第4页。

⑤ 沙畹（Éd. Chavannes）、伯希和（P. Pelliot）：《摩尼教流行中国考》（*Un traité manichéen retrouvé en Chine*），收入冯承钧编译《西域南海史地考证译丛》第8编，中华书局1958年版，第81页。

使曹议金。（4）第13行Sug cu dbang po，译为“肃州府主”。此处的dbang po正是唐宋之际河西汉文官府文书中“府主”之对称。[①]（5）第13行Lung 'bangs，译为“龙家”。根据行文，此词表明龙家活跃于肃州一带。（6）第17行Sha cu'i kyim An shan shin，实为沙州遣往肃州的主盟官员。其中Sha cu'i kyim（< Sha cu'i khyim），译言“沙州家”；至于An Shan shin，可以译作“安善神”。根据敦煌汉藏写本中的“五姓”资料，An正是汉文“安”姓之对音，[②]此人或许具有粟特背景。

浙敦114号第4行yar（译言“上部”，多指西部），当即PT 1189.r号《肃州府主致河西节度书状》（964年）第12—15行所引达怛（Da tar）、仲云（Ju ngul）、回鹘（Hor，甘州回鹘右翼）等部誓辞中的yar sha cab phyogs（上部Sha cab方面）、sha cu phyogs（沙州方面），均指归义军辖境。此处Sha cab，当系Sha cu（沙州）的一种变体或异写。准此可知，甘、肃二州常以yar这一地缘名词指称西部的归义军政权。浙敦114号第13行Lung 'bangs，系指活跃于归义军东境的肃州龙家。唐宋之际河西龙家部族，出自西晋以来焉耆龙氏王国。PT 1287号《吐蕃赞普传记》第381行Lung gi rgyal po，即是出征河陇的吐蕃军将对于“龙氏国王”的称谓。PT 1089号《吐蕃职官表状》（821年）第40行凉州军镇（mKhar tsan khrom）下的Lung dor，曾有学者推论Lung与吐蕃辖下的龙氏部族有关，然而对于Dor的所指尚未形成确信的结论。[③]840年以后回鹘西迁，庞特勤率部占据焉耆，或许正值此背景，龙氏王族率部流落河西。[④]龙家之名突现于公元9世纪下半叶的敦煌汉文、胡语文书，适与上述历史过程相符。PT 1263（P 2762）号《藏汉对照词汇》第8行，即以Lung rje对译龙家首领“龙王”。根据S 367号《沙州伊州地志》（885年），“龙部落本焉耆人，今甘、肃、伊州各有首领，其人轻锐，健斗战”，亦与浙敦114号所述甘州、肃州地望吻合。

大中三年（849年），归义军收复吐蕃占领下的肃州。中和四年（884年），甘州龙家等部迫于回鹘的军事压力，并入归义军辖下的肃州。根据S 389号《肃州防戍都状》（884年），“甘州共回鹘和断”“龙家共回鹘和定”。此系归义军节度使张淮深（867—890年在位）时期，肃州防戍都基于肃州周边形势所上的书状。此后，归义军由于防戍力量有限，逐渐丧失了对肃州的控制，汉人、龙家等部建立肃州政权。张氏后期以及曹氏时期，归义军仅保有肃州西境。曹氏后期，肃州日益投附于甘州回鹘，最终成为甘州回鹘属郡。根据《新五代史·回鹘

---

① G. Uray, “The Title dBaṅ-po in Early Tibetan Records,” in P. Daffinà ed., *Indo-Sino-Tibetan: Studi in Onore di Luciano Petech*, Rome: Bardi Editore, 1990, pp.419–433.

② 高田時雄：「五姓を説く敦煌資料」,『国立民族学博物館研究報告』別冊14號『漢族と隣接諸族』, 1991年，第261頁。

③ 岩尾一史：「ドルポ考—チベット帝国支配下の非チベット人集団—」,『内陸アジア言語の研究』第31號，2016年，第11—13頁。

④ 荣新江：《龙家考》，收入中国中亚文化研究协会编《中亚学刊》（第四辑），北京大学出版社1995年版，第148—150、155—156页。

传》，甘州回鹘“又有别族号龙家”[①]，反映了如上历史过程的结果。张广达先生指出，唐宋之际河西“各部首领和各地首脑，需要时时通过‘和定’（又称‘和断’）来调整彼此的利害关系和结束冲突”[②]。浙敦 114 号第 3 行 sdums，译为“调解”“议和”，正可对称“和断”等词。

东征之役胜利以后，曹议金除了遣使后唐、获取封赐之外，另一举措便是巩固肃州防戍、确保东境安定。浙敦 114 号所记肃州官民向曹议金宣誓效忠，双方达成和断，即为上述举措的重要内容。肃州对于甘、沙交涉的特殊地位，亦于此役期间再次得以凸显。暂时掌控肃州局势以后，曹议金进而谋求与甘州回鹘关系的长久稳定。根据 P 2992.v 号长兴二年《曹议金致甘州顺化可汗书状》：

> 自去年兄大王当便亲到甘州，所有社稷久远之事，共弟天子面对商仪（议）。平稳已讫，兄大王当便发遣一伴般次入京。

长兴元年（930 年）夏秋曹议金亲赴甘州，会晤甘州回鹘可汗仁裕（又作“仁喻”），[③]商议“所有社稷久远之事”，此后双方遣使后唐。次年，后唐“以沙州节度使曹义（议）金兼中书令”[④]。准此可知，此时沙、甘关系已是兄弟之国，双方希望同保河西安定、贡道畅通。归义军与肃州之间的盟誓，应在曹议金东行以前。

浙敦 114 号第 13 行 Byi sha ra ma ne（< Vaiśramaṇa），当指北方天王“毗沙门”（rNam thos sras）。对于此词，PT 960 号《于阗教法史》第 16、31 行又作 Be sha ra ma ne、Bɨ sha ra ma nɨ。毗沙门天王即多闻天王，系佛教所谓护持世间的四大天王之一，因居北方故称“北方之主”（Byang phyogs bdag po）。约于公元 6 世纪初叶，于阗多闻天王信仰传入敦煌，受到河西官民的敬奉。中唐以后及至归义军时期，多闻天王信仰在敦煌臻于鼎盛。曹氏归义军时期，多闻天王信仰与转轮圣王观念相表里，形成鲜明的政治文化意涵。根据 PT 1189.r 号，曹元忠（944—974 年在位）任归义军节度使时期，由于西州回鹘离乱、逃人越境东奔，河西地区劫盗频发，达怛、仲云、回鹘等部，于肃州大云寺（De'i yun zi）内“共以多闻天王证盟”（gnam mtho mtha' tshigs bgos, > rnam thos tha tshig bsgos）[⑤]。PT 1189.r 号第 12 行 mtha'

---

① 欧阳修撰：《四夷附录·回鹘传》，《新五代史》，卷 74，第 916 页。

② 张广达：《唐末五代宋初西北地区的般次和使次》。原载李铮、蒋忠新主编：《季羡林教授八十华诞纪念论文集》下册，江西人民出版社 1991 年版。此处引自张广达：《张广达文集：文书、典籍与西域史地》，广西师范大学出版社 2008 年版，第 188—190 页。

③ 哈密顿（J.R. Hamilton），耿昇、穆根来译：《五代回鹘史料》（*Les Ouïghours à l'épouque des Cinq Dynasties d'après les documents chinois*），新疆人民出版社 1986 年版，第 122 页，注释 1—2。荣新江：《归义军史研究》，第 328—329 页。

④ 薛居正等撰：《唐书·明宗纪》，《旧五代史》，卷 42，第 575 页。

⑤ 任小波：《唐宋之际河西地区的部族关系与护国信仰——敦煌 PT 1189.r 号〈肃州府主致河西节度书状〉译释》，原载《西域历史语言研究集刊》第 7 辑，2014 年。此处引自余欣主编：《瞻奥集：中古中国共同研究班十周年纪念论丛》，上海古籍出版社 2021 年版，第 43—44 页。

tshigs，亦即浙敦 114 号第 3、12 行 tha tshigs（咒誓）之变体。正是基于这种护国祐方的政治文化愿望，河西官民不仅广为崇奉多闻天王，甚至以其作为重大盟誓的知鉴。P 4011 号所谓“善神护我川原”，此处“善神”（*lha dge ba）或即多闻天王。

五、结　语

浙敦 114 号所记史事，兹可结合上文所论概述如下：甘州回鹘及其属部茹茹等族兵侵肃州龙家，肃州府主为此遣使甘州[①]，祈请甘州回鹘可汗狄银新立咒誓，节制回鹘臣僚、茹茹都督等部。然而，甘州回鹘图谋西进、不愿休兵，并未知会肃州，亦未通报沙州。由于商议不谐，甘州回鹘不仅继续调集军兵，而且扣留肃州使者。于是，肃州府主派员前往沙州求助，将此军情通报归义军节度使曹议金。鉴于东境安全遭受威胁，曹议金愤而出兵玉门、肃州，讨击甘州回鹘。经过激烈战斗，甘州回鹘溃败，肃州亦遭浩劫。东征之役胜利以后，曹议金为保东境安定，遂与肃州府主新增咒誓。肃州官民、龙家部族，皆向曹议金承诺永远效忠、决不叛离。沙州官员安善神受命主盟，并以护国祐方之神多闻天王证盟。肃州既系甘、沙间的缓冲区域，又是龙家部族盘踞之地，战略地位极其重要。根据 P 4011 号，甘州回鹘“准拟再觅寸境，便共龙家相煎”，恰与如上背景和史事吻合。又据 P 2970 号《阴善雄邈真赞》（931 年以后），阴善雄曾以归义军常乐县令身份参与东征之役，“达怛犯塞，拔拒交锋。统领军兵，临机变策”，表明除了茹茹都督之外，甘州回鹘亦曾纠合北境的达怛等部为其外援。

综合上文考证，浙敦 114 号的书写年代，当在天成三年左右曹议金冒称令公以后，长兴元年夏秋曹议金亲赴甘州以前，亦即 928—930 年之间。武内绍人先生将其断为 10 世纪 80 年代，显然失之过晚。肃州官民向曹议金宣誓效忠，并非所谓肃州的某次反抗被归义军压服的结果，而是居于甘、沙两强夹缝下的肃州审度时势所作出的选择。参与盟誓的肃州官民，亦非仅是汉人，还有龙家等部。根据浙敦 114 号，曹议金东征之役的目标，不仅在于打通与凉、灵二州以及中原的政治联系，更是在于有效安抚或统合临边各部，持续享有丝绸之路上的中转贸易权益。归义军与周边的回鹘、达怛、茹茹、龙家等部族或政权的交往，造就了唐宋之际河西一带交融共生的多部族、多语言环境。如若这种交往涉及三个以上操不同语言的部族，藏语作为官方通用语言的功能便会凸显出来。此即吐蕃统治结束以后，藏语得以长期而持续地行用于河西地区的社会语言学机制。这一机制生成的基石，正是盛极一时的吐蕃帝国对于河西乃至西域诸族的军事征服、政治统合和文化影响。

---

① 补注：关于“肃州遣使甘州”一事，由于浙敦 114 号多有残缺，本文初稿将其拟作“沙州遣使甘州”。承蒙冯培红先生赐教，指出当系“肃州遣使甘州”。再次考量藏文原文和前后语境，笔者认为此说合乎情理，可以采信，故而重新改写了译文和正文。

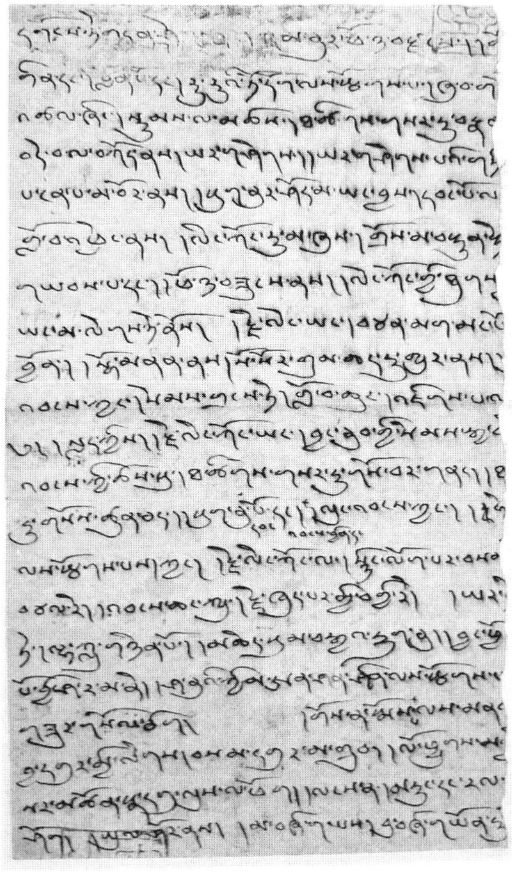

图 1 浙敦 114 号

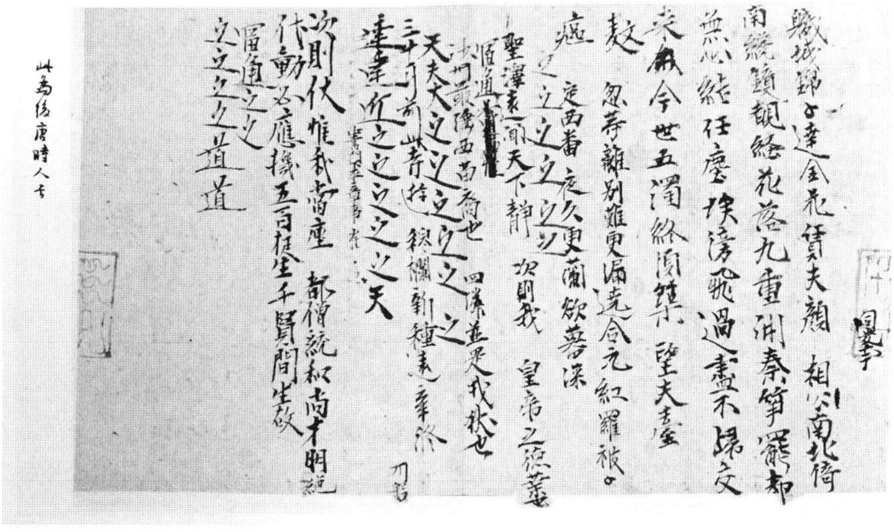

图 2 浙敦 113 号

国之神祇

——一篇来自敦煌的 9 世纪 *Tridaṇḍaka* 祈祷文（*rGyud chags gsum*）*

Lewis Doney　著

波恩大学（University of Bonn）

扎　西　译**

中国人民大学

一、引　言

近期发现了一篇很重要的藏文祈祷文书，年代为公元 9 世纪中晚期，本文将对该文书的若干细节进行探讨。该文本（IOL Tib J466/3）发现于著名的莫高窟藏经洞，11 世纪初被封存，然而这一 *Tridaṇḍaka* 祈祷文（*rGyud chags gsum*）的核心部分，或于吐蕃帝国时期（约 600—842）被书写 / 翻译 / 编辑。IOL Tib J466/3（以及同出自藏经洞的 Pelliot tibétain 177）中的某些段落与吐蕃赞普赤松德赞（742—约 800）时期铸造的桑耶寺钟的铭文相一致。从内容上看，该文献介于末代吐蕃时期的宗教祈祷文与 12 世纪所传之吐蕃宫廷诗篇之间，这些诗篇现载于那些关于佛法如何传入西藏的神话性的历史材料中。因此该文书对于研究早期吐蕃佛教赞颂文献（praise literature），其与印度佛教及汉地佛教的更广泛的关联，以及后世西藏历史编纂的材料来源均有重要意义。本文将对 IOL Tib J 466/3 号文本与更早的王室祈祷文——如桑耶寺钟铭文等做比较研究，以资古藏文祈祷文献研究之借鉴。本文特别关注的是，与统

---

* 本文为笔者在参与“超越边界：宗教、区域、语言与国家（Beyond Boundaries: Religion, Region, Language and the State）”项目时，由欧洲研究委员会（European Research Council）资助完成（ERC Synergy Project 609823 ASIA）。

** 本文译自 Lewis Doney, “Imperial Gods: A Ninth-Century Tridaṇḍaka Prayer (rGyud chags gsum) from Dunhuang,” *Central Asiatic Journal*, 2018, Vol. 61, No. 1, Old Tibet and its Neighbours (2018), pp.71−101。

治权意象相关的“四方”是如何逐渐被佛教宇宙观中的“十方”（通常与“三宝”相关联）所替代的，以及印度神祇是如何融入到这篇藏文 *Tridaṇḍaka* 所展示的藏族人的宇宙观中的。

二、（吐蕃）帝国佛教

在许多关于佛教进入西藏的早期历史记载中，桑耶寺的建成和开光（8 世纪）伴随着许多不可思议的神迹和盛大的庆祝仪式。[①] 靠着桑耶寺东面墙，在大门的南面有一条红色石柱，毫无疑问，对于许多造访此地的人而言，这条石柱是十分显眼的。而凿刻在石柱上的巨大的文字，则是我们能够找到的少数关于桑耶寺建造的吐蕃时期的记号之一。[②] 这些文字包含的是一份书面的誓言（见 Scherrer-Schaub 2012），宣告了永久性地给予佛教以官方的资助。同桑耶寺的建筑和壁画一样，这样的铭文或许将佛教世界的秩序加在了公共空间之上。因此在阅读以下文献时应十分仔细，应注意其中所承载的吐蕃赞普对自身在王权和宗教方面的形象刻画（见 Doney 2013b）。

该铭文写道：“为了违反此誓之事不会被犯或被引起，[③] 祈请世出世间众神与精灵（非人）作为见证”，立誓维护三宝（*triratna*；*dkon mc[h]og gsum*）之供奉，从而维持佛教在卫藏之修习。[④] 正如克里斯蒂娜·舍勒-肖布所言（Cristina Scherrer-Schaub 2014），无论是该文的语气还是所祈请的神祇，均没有体现明显的佛教特征，从而避免激怒王廷那些非佛教势力：

> 此诏令命令维持佛教的建立，以未来世代赞普的名义进行宣誓，赞普及其执政大

---

① 相关研究见 Doney 2013a。*dBa' bzhed* 中并没有描绘这一场景（见 Pasang Wangdu and Diemberger 2000），但在 *sBa bzhed* G（57），*sBa bzhed* S（48）和 *sBa bzhed* P——也就是 KGT（354—355）中有类似的描述，在 Mes dbon gsum gyi rnam thar（117a—b）中也有特写。而 Chos 'byung me tog snying po sbrang rtsi'I bcud（MTNd 302.20—03.12）则提供了一个大体一致而略有不同的版本。参见 Sørensen 1994, p.398。

② 该文转写和翻译见 Tucci 1950, pp.43, 94–95；亦见于 Richardson 1949，pp.57–58; 1985, pp.26–29；亦见于 Li and Coblin 1987, pp.186–192。转写见于 Iwao ed.2009, pp.11–12；最新翻译见 Willis 2013, p.152 以及 Schaeffer, Kapstein and Tuttle 2013, p.65。关于该文中吐蕃帝国和赞普赤松德赞形象的自我呈现的相关讨论，见 Doney 2013b, pp.69–71。Helga Uebach（2010）基于古文书学，对 Richardson 1985 (p.27) 等文将该铭文归于 8 世纪提出了质疑。亦见 Scherrer-Schaub 2014, p.146。

③ Hugh Edward Richardson（1985, p.29）将 *myi bsgyur bar* 翻译为“为了……它（誓言）不会被改变”；但此处笔者沿袭 Li and Coblin 以及 Tucci 的译法，将该短语与 *mna' kha dbud pa dag* 而不仅仅是 *mna' kha* 连在一起，因为文中有个 *gyang*。

④ 本文所使用的古藏文转写系统对部分读者而言可能有些陌生，但笔者遵循的是“线上古藏文文献”（Old Tibetan Documents Online: http://otdo.aaken.jp/site/editorialPolicy）规定的转写规则。“桑耶寺铭文”第 14—18 行是这样写的：myi bgyI myi bsgyur bar/ 'jIg（15）rten las/ 'da's pa' dang/（16）'jIg rten gyi lha dang/ myI ma yin（17）ba'/ thams cad gyang dphang du/（18）gsol te/

臣亦起誓，以世出世间之神祇作为见证而确保誓言生效。然而无论是赤松德赞，或是其执政大臣均未列名为佛教僧团的施主（*yon bdag*）。赤松德赞是一位富有政治手段的君主。①

在这份宣誓的一个更长的版本中——很有可能亦发自公元 8 世纪吐蕃赞普——对祈请的神祇有一个更为详细的列举，并且显然更贴合佛教语境。② 该文写道：

> 祈请十方一切佛，一切正法，一切菩萨众 / 一切菩萨僧，③ 一切圆觉及声闻，依天地秩序之一切神，藏地的本命神（*sku lha*），一切九尊，一切龙、夜叉、非人作为此誓之见证，令知此诏令不可更改。

这份宣誓中的神祇所扮演的角色与上文桑耶寺铭文十分一致，即被祈请作为誓言的见证者以确保誓言的永恒性。因此，从现存最早的支持佛教的宣言中可以看出，这些神祇——无论是世间的，还是出世的——都与佛教在藏地的命运绑在一起。④

上文所述桑耶寺铭文，结合其较长版本的内容，显示出赤松德赞将自身置于维护与弘传佛教的中心位置。在桑耶寺发现的另一吐蕃时期的铭文中，亦祈愿此赞普能够获得证悟（*byang chub*）。在桑耶寺一口铜钟的宗教铭文中，⑤ 赤松德赞的一位王妃祈愿其获得证悟：

---

① Cristina Scherrer-Schaub 2014, p.151.

② 见 Tucci 1950, pp.44–47, 95–97；Richardson 1998[1980]，pp.91–93, 95–96 对 dPa' bo gTsug lag phreng ba（1504—1566）之 KGT 第 370—376 页的转写和翻译，该部分显然为对这一 8 世纪文本的照实誊抄。Richardson 1985, p.27 将这一文本归于与“桑耶寺铭文”相同的年代，即 779 年到 782 年之间。他还写道：“〔在〕PT（即 KGT）109a 这一更为具体的诏令中，祷文显示出更多的佛教面目。”（同文第 31 页，注 2）

③ 这是笔者自己提供的另一种译法。Richardson 亦将 *byang chub sems dpa'i dge 'dun* 中的属格视为实有属格：木头碎片（*shing gi tshal ba*）仅仅是某木制品的一部分，因此众——*dge 'dun* 仅仅是 *byang chub sems dpa'* 能形成的某种形态。很难确定该文本中 *dge 'dun* 想要表达的是众（正如 Richardson 所认为的）还是个体的和尚与尼姑（僧），更重要的是，*byang chub sems dpa'* 所指到底是“已经证悟”还是“正在证悟路上”。关于早期藏文史料中将 *byang chub sems dpa'* 一词用于描述吐蕃赞普的相关研究，见 Doney 2013b, pp.75–76 以及 Doney 2015。

④ 翻译遵照 Richardson 1998[1980], p.92，并做少许校改。KGT 371.19–72.1 是这样写的：#[无 mgo yig]/ 'di ltar yi dam bcas pa / phyogs bcu'i sangs rgyas thams cad dang / [无垂符] dam pa'i chos thams cad dang / byang chub sems dpa'i dge 'dun thams cad dang / rang sangs rgyas dang nyan thos thams cad dang / gnam sa'i rim pa lha'o [lha'o] cog dang / bod yul gyi sku lha dang / lha dgu thams cad dang / klu dang / gnod sbyin [gnods byin] dang mi ma yin pa thams cad（第 372 页）dbang du gsol te [ste] / gtsigs 'di [di] las mi 'gyur bar mkhyen par bgyis so//（方括号中标示出的是 Richardson 1998[1980], p.96 文中主要的错误）

⑤ 转写和翻译见 Richardson 1985, p.32–35，以及 Li and Cobin 1987, p.332–339，亦可参考 Iwao ed. 2009, p.70。Walter and Beckwith 2010, p.304 将这座钟的年代归于吐蕃帝国时期。关于该钟铭文中对赤松德赞形象刻画的讨论见 Doney 2013b, p.71–72，以及 Scherrer-Schaub 2014, p.146。笔者即将发表的文章中将对所有吐蕃帝国时期的寺钟做艺术—历史和物质—文化方面的研究。

王妃 rGyal mo brtsan 母子铸此钟以供奉十方之三宝，祈愿借此福德之力，令天赞普（*lHa bTsan po*）[①] 赤松德赞父子、夫妇俱得六十妙音、获无上证悟。[②]

正如较长版的诏令，这一祈愿文提及“十方”非如《吐蕃大事纪年》（*Old Tibetan Annals* Or. 8212/187，第 16—19 行）[③] 中所载的“四方”。笔者在其他文章中业已指出，这一佛教的惯用修辞（*topos*），对于吐蕃赞普的形象转换而言十分重要。它标志着卫藏地区宇宙方位观念发生了转变，由宽泛的欧亚大陆的四方观念转向了以“菩萨赞普”为中心、周围环绕着开悟的人格化形象的印度佛教景观（Doney 2015，第 38—39 页）。另外，在此处王妃用了一个奇怪的词组——“十方之三宝”，这几乎不见于任何其他藏文佛教文献。[④] 因此，我对上文较长版本的诏令做了翻译上的调整，以反映一种可能性，即十方不仅作为佛而且亦作为法、僧（或者其他神祇，至少是佛教神祇）的居所。

令人惊讶的是，我在另外一个文本中也找到了“十方之三宝”这一奇怪的词组。该文本即发现于敦煌莫高窟藏经洞，现存于不列颠图书馆的 IOL Tib J 466 号写本。[⑤] 构成该写本第三部分的祈祷文——IOL Tib J 466/3——以这一有趣的意象开篇，并在赞颂之余提供了近乎史学的叙事，因此不同于桑耶钟铭的内容，更像是祈愿式的祷文（aspirational prayer）。铭文的大部分内容都寓意着一个理想的未来（以 *smond to* 结尾），而这更常见于捐赠者题词以及后来的祈愿文（*smon lam*）中。桑耶钟铭将赤松德赞刻画为行进在证悟之路上的形象，而我下面要讨论的祈祷文则将他的证悟视为历史事实，或者至少是作为一种笃定的信念来叙述。

---

① 参见 Doney 2013b, p.76 及注 61 对穷结（’Phyongs rgyas）碑铭中的“（’phrul gyi）lha btsan po”这一头衔 / 修饰词的研究。似乎其既具有世俗层面的含义，又具有超越世俗的含义。

② 桑耶寺钟上的铭文是这样写的：jo mo rgyal mo brtsan yum（第 2 行）sras kyIs phyogs bcu’I（3）dkon mchog gsum la（4）mchod pa’I slad du cong（5）’di bgyis te// de’i bso-（6）-d nams kyI stobs kyis（7）lha btsan po khrI srong lde b-（8）-rtsan yab sras stangs dbya-（9）-l gsung dbyangs drug（10）cu sgra dbyangs dang ldan te（11）bla na myed pa’I byang chub（12）du grub par smond to//

③ 本文中标为“Or.”或“IOl Tib J”，以及标为“Pelliot tibétain”的文本，均来自中国敦煌莫高窟。前两者现藏于不列颠图书馆（British Library），后者则藏于法国国家图书馆（Bibliothèque nationale de France）。大多数文本的影像均可在“国际敦煌项目”（International Dunhuang Project http://idp.bl.uk）和“艺术图像数据库”（Artstor http：//www.artstor.org/index.shtm）上找到。

④ 最近（2017 年 6 月 25 日与 Michelle Wang 私下交流时），笔者发现，赞颂“十方三宝”在唐代（618—907）汉文文献中亦出现过。在三十卷本的《佛说佛名经》中，指示祈愿者礼敬十方的佛、法、僧（*Buddhanāma sūtra* T14.441，300c19—20：“今者归命十方佛、归命十方法、归命十方僧”）。这一文本与忏仪有关，而从敦煌地区文书来看，该经显然曾十分流行（见 Kuo 1994）。这一词组在《华严经》（*Avataṃsaka sūtra*）的序言或注释中亦有（Xuanhua 1982, p.120），该经包含《入法界品》（*Gaṇḍavyūha sūtra*）和《普贤行愿品》（*Bhadracarīpraṇidhāna* 见下文）。但在《华严经》正文中，或是在该经藏译本中，均未能找到这一表述。这一有趣的发现，尚待更进一步的探索。

⑤ 见 Dalton and van Schaik 2006，pp.209–212。亦见 van Schaik and Doney 2007, pp.195–196；Dalton 2011, pp.62–66；Doney 2015, pp.40–41。Doney 2013, p.78 页以及 Doney 2017, pp.314–315 中亦有简要介绍。

三、涉及吐蕃赞普的早期祈祷文

IOL Tib J 466/3 号文本被发现于莫高窟第十七号，该洞窟于 11 世纪早期被封存，但其书写的年代可能更接近于吐蕃帝国时期，并且可能书写于帝国中心区域。一些证据表明，如果说该祈祷文本是后吐蕃时期的产物的话，那么它也是在吐蕃灭亡不久之后写成。该祈祷文与许多写于公元 9 世纪 40 年代——即吐蕃占领敦煌的末期或稍晚于这一时期——的《大乘无量寿宗要经》（*Aparimitāyurnāma[mahāyāna] sutra; Tshe dpag tu myed pa zhes bya ba theg pa chen po's mdo*）的抄本一样，都是用相同的纸张和手写体书写（见 Dotson 和 Doney 即将发表的文章）。IOL Tib J 466 上标记的位置索引是 Ch.79.XIII.4，很可能是斯坦因（Aurel Stein）在最初接触到这些写本时标记的，与其编号相同的还有另一卷中的 IOL Tib J 310.4 号文本（卷数 88:002，位置索引 Ch.79.XIII.1）。[①] IOL Tib J 310 被用以标识敦煌发现的所有《大乘无量寿宗要经》的藏文抄本。IOL Tib J 310.4 为众多抄本之一，共有三页，附有标明抄写者和编辑者的题记。抄写者拥有一个汉文名字，转写成藏文作 lu dze shing（第 3 页，第 38 行：*lu dze shing bris//*），编辑团队则至少包含两名僧人——Shes rab 和 dPal mchog（第 3 页，第 39 行用红色墨水写着：*$/: /shes rab zhus / jI^i na yang zhus / dpa+l mchog sum zhus*）。这两个文本（译者按：IOL Tib J 466 与 IOL Tib J 310）均写在纸片（panels）上，并且有同样的位置索引，表明斯坦因是在同一地方发现它们的；亦有可能它们被放置在洞窟中的同一处（或许与同一位置索引的汉文文书放在一起？），并且在历史上有某种关联。

这一古藏文 *Tridaṇḍaka* 祈祷文同时具备宗教性、历史性、宇宙观和本土性。其中间部分由韵文写成，以顶礼构想中的佛陀（及其弟子）时代的印度众神作为开头。结尾处则向护卫藏土道场（如拉萨大昭寺）的本土神祇献供，并向吐蕃的大师致敬，还提到了赞普赤松德赞本人（仿效伟大的印度法王）。除了引用印度文献和陀罗尼，这一文本还包含了一些古藏文概念，如“大王”（*rgyal po chen po*）以及难以确定意涵的“*phyva*”一词。IOL Tib J 466/3 号文本还提到赤松德赞手握天神众（*gnam gyI lde*）之剑，这可能与赞普先祖源自天上神祇的早期传说有关。因此，应当就赞普和神祇的形象刻画，将 IOL Tib J 466/3 与（上文）桑耶钟铭以及下文将讨论的文本做比较，以供更广泛的古藏文祈祷文献研究参考。

黄维忠（2007a）专门撰文介绍了与吐蕃帝国时期有关的敦煌祈祷文，并参考了与这些

---

① Ch.79.XIII 下的其他文本均为汉文文本，而需要说明的是，目前在 IDP 网站上编号为 IOL Tib J 310.4 号的文本影像与该文本并不相符。

祈祷文相关的二级文献。[①] 爱德华 · 理查生（Hugh Edward Richardson 1992）对其中一些文本，包括涉及赤松德赞的文本做了讨论。他认为：

> 敦煌发现的《吐蕃大事纪年》和《吐蕃赞普传记》中包含有关西藏早期历史的重要史料，与之相比，其他敦煌写本……很少有披露赞普事迹者，除非是在庄重的宗教语境中……在印度事务部图书馆（India office library）第 370（5）号文件——“从天上降下的正法之卷（A volume of the Dharma that came down from Heaven）”[②] 中，提到了赤松德赞的名字。推测而言，他亦可能是 Pell. T. 1091 号文本中所提到的统治者，我认为这一残破文本与大约公元 797 年沙洲（sha—cu）的一次反抗吐蕃统治的起义有关。（Richardson 1992, 5）

① 在该作品的开头（Huang 2007a，29），作者列举了载有这些祈愿文的文本，对文本的类型做了简单提示并标明了文本的行数（感谢 Emanuela Garatti 在汉文方面对笔者的帮助）：
—Pelliot tibétain 1（《赞普愿文》和《奉请十方佛发愿文》）；分别为 16 行和 18 行
—Pelliot tibétain 2（《迎请诸佛愿文》和《奉请酥油灯愿文》）；分别为 43 行和 32 行
—Pelliot tibétain 16（《赞普愿文》）；106 行
—Pelliot tibétain 17（《为亡者而作的忏愿文》）；82 行
—Pelliot tibétain 18（《为死亡和转世的危险而作的忏愿文》）；29 行
—Pelliot tibétain 45（《酥油灯愿文》）；53 行
—Pelliot tibétain 130（《赞普愿文》）；20 行
—Pelliot tibétain 131（《赞普愿文》）；34 行
—Pelliot tibétain 132（《赞普愿文》）；38 行
—Pelliot tibétain 134（《赞普愿文》）；50 行
—Pelliot tibétain 154（《忏愿文》）；19 行
—Pelliot tibétain 175（《吐蕃法事发愿文本》）；30 行
—Pelliot tibétain 230（反面载有一《赞普愿文》）；（25+）11 行
—Pelliot tibétain 1123（《赞普愿文》）；33 行
—IOL Tib J 76/2（《酥油灯愿文》）；22 行
—IOL Tib J 452/2（《忏愿文》）；40 行
—IOL Tib J 751/1（《赞普愿文》）；54 行
—IOL Tib J 1107（反面载有一《赞普愿文》）；（11+）2 行
—IOL Tib J 1371（《赞普愿文》）；15 行
—IOL Tib J 1772/5（《奉请十方佛发愿文》）；9 行
—甘博 10565（《赞普愿文》）；15 行
作者没有对所有这些祈愿文都进行深入研究，此外，不知为何他还漏掉了 IOL Tib J 783 号文本（见 Thomas 1951, pp.112–113）。他可能亦不知晓 IOL Tib J 374 号文本，当然这是可以理解的。Chen 2014, p.249 和 p.254 注 44 引用了黄维忠于同一年发表的另一藏文祈愿文研究作品（Huang 2007b），然而目前为止笔者未能见到这一作品。

② 这一材料（Richardson 1977 中有详细的讨论）现在被称为“一卷从天上落下的正法”（Single Volume of the Dharma that Fell from Heaven），并且还被辨认出与敦煌文书中的 IOL Tib J 370/6 号文本（IOL Tib J 370 号文本的第 6 部分，而非第 5 部分）一致。（关于该文本的）更多讨论参见 Dalton and van Schaik 2006, p.105；van Schaik and Doney 2007, pp.196–197。

在理查生写作此文时，他还不知道 IOL Tib J 466/3 号文本，但他详述了其他与吐蕃赞普，特别是与赤祖德赞（815—841 年在位）[①] 相关的敦煌写本。通常认为这位赞普为反佛赞普朗达玛（乌东赞 841—842 年在位）[②] 所害，但是理查生注意到了一个向这位据说是离经叛道的赞普祈祷的文本（Pelliot tibétain 134；同上 Richardson 文，第 6 页）。他还翻译了两篇祈祷文（Pelliot tibétain 131 和 230），内容则是致力于确保继承人沃松（'Od srung，约 846—约 893）安康，如此，他便可以继续保护正法（同上 Richardson 文，第 7—10 页）。[③] 因此，敦煌文献见证了佛教对于吐蕃赞普的描述（至少在修辞学上），在雅砻王朝（Yar klung）的崩溃之后，作为一脉相承的王统世系，一直持续到了"分裂期"（*sil bu'i dus*）。

山口瑞凤（Yamaguchi Zuihō 1996）和克里斯蒂娜·舍勒-肖伯（Cristina Scherrer-Schaub 1999—2000）均将 Pelliot tibétain 134 中所载的祈祷文归于乌东赞名下，[④] 并分别提供了该文本下半部分和整个文本的翻译。[⑤] 以下是由萨姆腾·卡尔迈（Samten Karmay）提供的摘要：

> 该文开头以赞普的名义礼敬佛教三宝，接下来是一套供养和忏罪的惯用语词。以赞普的名义做忏悔，因其在保护佛教或处理帝国事务时，对敌人施以极刑。然后是恳请诸佛继续传法，同时这些受统治者供养的人乞求赞普确保其臣民能自由地供养〔僧人〕，便于他们获得解脱，并有能力为其他有情众生带来利益和福德。该文结尾处则写道："我

---

① Richardson 没有提到涉及这位赞普的祈祷文还有一篇，即 Thomas 1951，第 112—113 页中的 IOL Tib J 1371 号文本。Thomas 在该文中声称这一祈祷文"很显然是 IOL Tib J 751 号文本的又一抄本，或者是该文本的另一版本"。

② Brandon Dotson（2009，第 143 页）遵从了山口瑞凤（Yamaguchi 1996）对年代的划分，其他学者如 Michael L. Walter（2009，第 233 页；2013，第 417 页）则有不同看法，他给出的在位时间为 815—836 年，但并没有做出解释。

③ Macdonald and Imaeda 1978—1979 翻印了 Pelliot tibétain 131 和 230 号写本，分别为 153、166—167 页插图。Scherrer-Schaub（1999—2000，第 219 页注 7，以及同书第 235 页注 62）基于 Richardson 的介绍对这两个有关沃松的祈祷文做了讨论。同上书第 239 页注 73 中，Scherrer-Schaub 提到：Richardson 1988 年的文章中将 Pelliot tibétain 134 与 Pelliot tibétain 132（与赤祖德赞相关）相提并论，认为两者均为针对两位继任者的祈祷文；但事实上，Richardson 将 Pelliot tibétain 134 号文本与 Pelliot tibétain 131 号文本相混淆了，因为后者与 Pelliot tibétain 132 号文本有更多的相似性，而 Pelliot tibétain 134 号文本与另两者均非如此相似，亦可见本文下面对这些写本的物理特征的描述。在 Huang 2007a，第 38 页有一个 Pelliot tibétain 230 号文本的简单条目，另外，这三个写本在该著作中多次被提及。

④ Scherrer-Schaub（1999—2000，第 233—234 页）强调，Pelliot tibétain 134 号文本与另一篇祈祷文——Pelliot tibétain 175 号文本——在描述该赞普时，有一些相似的类型化的表述。在该书第 219—220 页，对 Pelliot tibétain 175 号文本有所讨论，Scherrer-Schaub 将该文描述为一篇"忏愿文以及天赞普与其王廷的誓愿"（Prière de repentance et vœu du divin empereur du Tibet et de sa cour）；同文第 221 页注 16 亦有讨论，此处该内容被描述为"一篇对治王朝动荡、敌人、恶咒师以及其他灾难的祈祷文"（une prière adressée pour contrer les instabilités du royaume, les ennemis du Tibet, les mauvais magiciens et autres calamités）。

⑤ 这篇祈祷文在 van Schaik and Doney 2007 中亦有提及。此外，Huang 2007a，第 37—38 页亦可参考。亦可参见 Scherrer-Schaub 2014，第 136 页。

们祈愿赞普不会见到任何噩兆，祈愿他免受恶灵之害，免受一切怨敌之害，永生不死；我们祈愿梵天（Brahma）、因陀罗（Indra）、四大天王（the four Lokapala）〔世界的守护者们〕，以及十方守护者赐予他力量和荣耀；我们祈愿他免受一切恶灵之害，受到保护。”（Karmay 2003, 58—59）

与此祈祷文相同的是，IOL Tib J 466/3 号文本亦包含对三宝的赞颂、对一位既是统治者又是佛教徒的吐蕃赞普的赞诗，同时两者享有一个共同的宇宙观——包括本土神祇和印度神祇。舍勒 - 肖伯（Scherrer-Schaub 1999—2000，第 218 页）认为《普贤菩萨行愿赞》——她将其称为“卓越的大乘祈愿文”（la prière mahayanique par excellence）——对此类藏文祈愿文（*praṇidhāna*；*smon lam*）或曰公开礼赞文产生了深远影响，为后者提供了一种源自印度佛教的范式。此外她指出这类文献也受到《三聚经》（**triskandhaka*；*pung po gsum pa*；译者按：此处的“pung”应为“phung”之笔误）的影响，这在敦煌文书中能够找到证据（上揭文第 220 页）。《普贤行愿》这类祈祷文，如赞颂其美德的《入法界品》，对早期西藏佛教的修法和文献具有很重要的影响，而其“七支”（*yan lag bdun*）的结构在下文将要讨论的许多祈祷文中均能找到。[①] 正如雅各 · 道尔顿（Jacob P. Dalton 2011，第 62—66 页）所指出的，IOL Tib J 466 号文本亦遵循了七支的结构。

一个同样重要的文献，亦是在藏学研究中具有更悠久历史的文献，即所谓的“De ga g.yu tshal 寺祈祷文”，该文献的内容是庆祝在赤祖德赞时期 De ga g.yu tshal 地区的“法令寺”（temple of the treaty-edict；*gtsigs kyi gtsug lag khang*，见 Kapstein 2009，第 65 页，注 47）的建成。[②] 迈克尔 · 沃尔特（Michael L. Walter 2013）则在最近发表的研究这一文献的文章中

---

① 参见 Scherrer-Schaub 1999—2000，第 220 页；van Schaik and Doney 2007，第 185—186 页；Sernesi 2014，第 144 页。Osto 2010 对梵文本做了翻译和讨论，并研究了其与《入法界品》之间的关系。Richard K. Payne 和 Charles D. Orzech（2011，第 135—136 页）提供了“七支无上供”（*Saptavidhā-anuttarapūjā*）的大纲，即以这篇祈祷文为代表的“七支无上供养”:“七支无上供”的七要素为顶礼（*vandanā*），供养（*pūjanā*），忏悔（*deśanā*），随喜（*modanā*），请转法轮（*adhyeṣaṇā*），祈请不入涅槃（*yācanā*），回向（*nāmanā*）。然而，他们随后又补充道，并非所有祈祷文均严格遵照七支的结构（同文第 136 页），随后在 Yönten 1996 中即找到了例证。

② 该文被写在一个 20 页的贝叶（*pothī*）写本上，目前被分为了两部分，即 Pelliot tibétain 16（第 22—34 页）和 IOL Tib J 751（第 35—41 页），该抄本正反面均有四行文字。该文本最早由 F.W. Thomas 进行了转写、翻译和广泛的讨论（1951，第 92—109 页；1955，第 4—5 页、第 42—46 页）。OTDO（http://otdo.aaken.jp/text/93［2017-6-4］）上则可获取该文本完整的转写，以及直到千禧年左右的与该文本相关的二级文献。最近的一条是 Kapstein 2004，该文翻译了这一祈祷文中描述寺院的那一部分（Pelliot tibétain 16, 26b1-28b3；Kapstein 2004，第 111—114 页）。Kapstein 还发表过一篇更深度的研究，并探讨了该文本中的历史和地理参照（Kapstein 2009，文中有一个校订过但更短的翻译，见该文第 45—47 页）。此外，还有一篇简短的关于该寺位置再探讨的文章（Kapstein 即将发表），该文认为最有可能是位于甘南的大夏，即战略性地定位在唐帝国和吐蕃帝国之间，作为最有可能的候选地。在 2009 年那篇文章中，Kapstein 展示了这一祈祷文的结构，即由一系列祈祷构成，而其中七个留存了（转下页）

指出，根据古文字学分析，这一文献应为后世的仿作，而非公元 9 世纪早期的作品，其根据是对该文献所做的古文字学分析，而这一研究结果与其早先的结论（Walter 2009，第 233 页）相悖。本章之后会附上这一文献的译文及注解。至关重要的是，沃尔特（Walter 2013，第 425 页）提示了法令寺祈祷文与 Pelliot tibétain 1 号文本[①]（二者或许出自同一抄手）以及 Or.15000/379 号文本在语言上的相似性，而武内绍人也注意到了这一点。[②] 法令寺祈祷文标题为忏悔和祈愿（*'Gyod tshangs dang smon lam*），敦煌遗书中亦发现有同一标题的文本，尽管其内容并不相同。[③] 举例而言，Pelliot tibétain 177 号文本即以这样的句子作为开头："一切修善者〔应〕于十方至宝前坦白〔他们的过失〕并忏悔"（Pelliot tibétain 177，1r1：*dge ba cI bgyIs pa de dag thams cad phyogs bcu'I dkon mchog thams cad kyI spyan sngar 'thol zhIng bshagso//*），这可与本文开头所讨论的桑耶钟铭的相关表述做比较。[④] 一系列错综复杂的佛教术语似乎正在逐渐兴起，笔者倾向于称其为"帝国时期的藏文"（imperial-period Tibetan）。

然而，沃尔特（2013，第 425 页）接着又做了十分重要的区分："总体而言，这些文献的语言是相似的，并且看起来并不十分古老，可以肯定并非吐蕃时期的。在某些方面，PT016 号文本（Pelliot tibétain 16 和 IOL Tib J 751 号文本的合称）的语言与这些忏悔类文本不同，尽管它们有着相似的主题。这是因为该文本的某些段落更为古朴，具有一些文体上的特点，其适用范围则更窄，即指向了某些特定的重要人物。"最后他在文章结尾处写道：

（接上页）下来（其中五个的来源是可以辨认的，Kapstein 2009，第 33 页）。此外，还可参考 Scherrer-Schaub 1999—2000 中的注释（尤其是该书第 219 页，注 6），以及 Huang 2007a，第 32—37 页。此外还有 Hill 2013，第 174—175 页；2015，第 54 页分别对 Pelliot tibétain 16 中与神权统治相关的古藏文术语以及 sku bla 仪式的讨论。

① Walter 2013，第 419 页等处；Huang 2007a，第 32 页也对 Pelliot tibétain 1 有著录，作者于此处提到了 IOL Tib J 1772/5 号文本（该文本乃是一份用藏文转写的向十方诸佛祈祷的汉文祈祷文），并将之与 Pelliot tibétain 1/3（即 Pelliot tibétain 1 号文本的第三部分）关联起来。作者还引述了 Simon 1957，而 Simon 的这篇文章即将这两者联系了起来。目前笔者手上没有这篇文章，但既然"十方"在此处扮演了重要角色，那么这种联系就值得深究。

② 见武内绍人（Takeuchi）1998，第 1 卷、第 159、491 页。F.W. Thomas（1951，第 112—113 页，注 21）描述了 IOL Tib J 783 号文本中的另一祈祷文，认为也与 De ga g.yu tshal 文本相似。他写道："这一段很明显是上文提到的 No.19 号长文本（即 IOL Tib J 751）的又一抄本或另一版本的一部分。尽管其大多数部分都过于残破，以致很难连贯，但总体而言这种联系是很显然的。文中祈愿：'凭借彼王子（prince; *lha sras*）赤祖德赞的功业，僧众、尼众、及一切有情得享幸福和永生'；祈愿：'王子本人，无病无痛，治土大盛，摒除一切敌人等等，愿其于今生得证佛果'；祈愿：'其治下之人长寿、无疾病'；并祈愿：'遍蕃域内的无数有情众生均幸福圆满，人畜无病，常年丰收。'"（Thomas 1951，第 113 页）

③ 武内绍人（1998，第 1 卷，第 159 页）声称："*'Gyod tshangs dang smon lam* 这一标题在第 1 页正面（r1）和第 2 页反面（v2），但是文本内容与以下具有相同或类似标题的敦煌写本并不一致：VP[de la Vallée Poussin 1962]208.209—10，247，452.2；P[elliot tibétain]17，18，24，175—177。"

④ 此外，该文还是一篇没有提到吐蕃的标准祈祷文（尽管其中载有与 IOL Tib J 466/3 号文本相似的段落和标点符号，并且提到了"善知识" f. 3r2–3）。文本的背面是《金刚经》（*Vajracchedikā*）的汉译本。祈祷文的后面有写手的练笔，内容显然来自该祈祷文。

一个次要的结论是，PT016号文本以及PT001文本的编辑是为了给后帝国时代的僧伽提供范本，以在宫廷或其他重要场合中举行忏罪仪轨。通过使用帝国时代流传下来的本子，并将它们缀合成连贯的文本，敦煌地区的僧伽为自己提供仪轨，而这些仪轨则依托于强大且受人尊敬的佛教君主的身份之上。由于参考点是热巴坚（Ral-pa-can）统治时期，这些文本似乎是针对于866年左右甚至更晚时期仍对新疆和北部安多（Amdo）地区有部分控制权的那些藏族统治者的——如青唐（Chingthang）。（Walter 2013，432）

沃尔特反对将De ga g.yu tshal祈愿文归于赤祖德赞统治时期，他的这一观点颇具争议，但并非是本文关注的重点。反而是其关于将新旧不同层次的文本融合于同一祈祷文的提示，对我们下文讨论IOL Tib J 466/3号文本有所影响。

对于评估吐蕃时期和后吐蕃时代早期的汉藏关系而言，另一个重要的祈祷文本即是“燃灯祈祷文”（燃灯文，藏文为*mar mye kha*），该文保存于Pelliot tibétain 1123号文本中。① 该文是献给赤祖德赞的（Richardson 1992，6），文中赞扬了他的军事成就，并传达了如今看来更为传统的佛教（以及儒家?）价值观。②

最后需要提到的是，三折页IOL Tib J 374号文本中所载的一份不完整的“为藏地的祈祷文”，该文或许展示了一个更为印度化的语境（Dalton and van Schaik 2006，第108—109页）。③ 非常有趣的是，每一处提到藏地——Bod Khams——的文字，均被“部分地”涂掉了，这一改动的时间则应在11世纪初封闭藏经洞之前（见上文第108页）。该祈祷文祈求诸佛、菩提萨埵、阿罗汉、色界与欲界诸神、四大天王以及十个护方神，清除藏地的障碍，并向他们献上无上的赞美/供养（*bla myed mchod pa 'di phul bas/*）。每一群体均被献予一

---

① Pelliot tibétain 1123号文本被复制为MacDonald and Imaeda 1978—1979，第452页插图，在国际敦煌项目（IDP）网站上亦有。该文本为卷轴样式，尺寸为30 × 48 cm。

② 见Chen 2014，第249—252页，作者陈怀宇（Chen Huaiyu）错误地将赤祖德赞在位年代归在了赤德松赞名下。MacDonald and Imaeda 1978—1979，第452页复印件第10、14、16、20、23、27和32行均明确提到的是赤祖德赞；例如，第32—33行这样写道：“*btsan po khri gtsug lde brstan gyi sku la gnod byed kyi/ bgegs thams cad kyi myi tsugs/ par srung zhing bskyabs par bskul lo ...*”

③ 这一写本的“为吐蕃的祈祷文”这一部分的转写和翻译见Sam van Schaik的博客：https://earlytibet.com/2009/05/22/a-prayer-for-tibet/（发表于2009年5月22日；笔者检视时间为2017年6月4日）。Sam van Schaik还更新了Dalton and van Schaik 2006，第108—109页中对该写本的著录，两位作者发现此文本的最后一页的背面是由另一个密教祈祷文构成的。情况很复杂，因为历史上某位曾接触到该文本的读者（缺失了第1页之前的那部分祈祷文，该部分结尾为…*dgong shIg/*，写于1a1？）在最后一页的背面而不是正面标上了藏文页码3（*gsum*）。笔者认为，这一写本应该被分成IOL Tib J 374/1和IOL Tib J 374/2。IOL Tib J 374/1号文本结尾写着“摄供品”（*//$//mchod pa bsdus pa'I le'u rdzogs+ho/*）；Sam van Schaik在其博客中翻译为“摄集供养的章节”（The chapter summarizing the offerings），并且将“供养品”归于比丘吉祥积名下（*dge slong dpal brtsegs gyi mchod pa'I le'u <g>lags s+ho//://*），所指或许是也或许不是8世纪著名译师尕娃吉祥积（sKa ba dPal brtsegs）（Dalton and van Schaik 2006，第108页）。

个 8 至 11 句的诗节，其中一部分则遵从七音律，并且它们是以各个群体中某个具名的个体或子群体作为编号。这种模式包括这些神祇（尽管顺序不一致）亦出现在 IOL Tib J 466/3 号文本中，接下来我们将对其内容做进一步讨论。这将使我们看到这一 *Tridaṇḍaka* 祈祷文与更广泛的祈祷文献之间的其他关联，而这种关联或能更深入地反映这一时期的祷告实践传统。

四、IOL Tib J 466/3 号文本的内容

对于 IOL Tib J 466/1 号和 2 号文本，笔者未能在多尔顿和舍克（Dalton and van Schaik 2006，第 209—210 页）所提供的有用信息上做任何补充。然而有证据表明第一页，即写有 IOL Tib J 466/1 号文本（一篇未被确认的祈祷文）和 466/2 号文本（《尊胜佛母陀罗尼》*Uṣṇīṣavijaya-dhāraṇī*）的那一页，与该写本之后的几页并不构成一个整体，而这使得从第二页开头的 *Tridaṇḍaka* 祈祷文变得更为重要。IOL Tib J 466/3 号文本写在轻薄的淡棕色纸上，用的是略显方正（square-ish）的乌金体小字（*dbu can*）。IOL Tib J 466/4 号及其后的文本出自同一人之手，中间几无间隔。比较而言，IOL Tib J 466/1 号和 466/2 号文本则出自另一人之手，或者至少是写于另一时间。第一页上书写了两列文字，而第二列文字则由 24 行组成，在这一点上与后面的几页是一致的。① 然而，第一页的笔迹相较于后几页在垂符（*shad*）的弯曲以及 *ka*、*kha*、*ga*、*nga* 的笔序上有显著差异。特别是，笔者注意到从第二页开始，*na ro* 这一符号的右面那一勾有水平角；而细直的 *'greng bu* 则回笔至自身而非将笔提离纸面。与这些差异相印证的是：第一页纸的质量更为粗糙，没有划线，没有圆形装饰垂符或者红色记号，以及诸如此类的标记（*merkmals*）。② IOL Tib J 466/3 文本从新的一页的首行开始。然而，明显可以看出第一页和第二页纸曾被粘在一起（在某一时刻），因为在第一页的正面第

---

① 据 de la Vallée Poussin（1962，第 466），每一开页（每一列）有“24 和 25 行”。第一开页有两列，分别为 16 和 24 行，第一列最初由多少行组成则已不得而知。在文本被封存在洞窟里之前，就已对纸片做了保护措施，现在看起来比原稿纸暗一些的纸是在纸片被用来写字（或重新写上字）之前，粘在原纸张背面以进行修补的。在第 11 行，暗一些的纸上写着 *[rgyal m]tsan*，在第十二行写着 *[su]gsol//*，抑或还有其他的字。不幸的是，在印度事务部（India Office）或不列颠图书馆对该纸片做文物保护工作时，其被贴在了档案纸上，因此原来背面的内容已看不到了。这种暗纸补丁在第 2 列第 23 行亦很明显。

② 在这一纸片上没有明显的准线、边框或书脊线，然而所写文字大概在一个未成型的，不规整的边框内。在第 2 列有 0.6—1.6 cm 的左边距，0.8—1.3 cm 的右边距，上边距未知（这一纸片的最上面一部分丢失了），0.5—1.8 cm 的下边距，以及 1—1.2 cm 的行距。在这一列有一些写在行间的字，很小（第 15 行 *'i*，第 17 行 *-d*），并且用叉标记。这种标记形式在后面几页中也有，但这种用叉标记的情形在藏文文本中也不算十分罕见。

二列和第二页反面第三列处均发现了粘合的痕迹。

关于第一页的这项结论令我们的 IOL Tib J 466/3 号文本变得更为重要。因为如果我们抛开 IOL Tib J 466/1 号和 466/2 号文本，那么就可以将 IOL Tib J 466/3 号文本作为这一写本的第一部分（“*rgyud chags dang po*”），而不仅仅是埋藏于一系列文本中的一个部分。这些发现亦将使 IOL Tib J 466/4 号、466/5 号、466/6 号文本成为其从属的部分，它们或为 IOL Tib J 466/3 的接续，或为其附录。与之相反，IOL Tib J 466/1 号和 466/2 号文本最初则与 IOL Tib J 466/3 号文本并不相关。然而写着这两部分的这一页，与写着以 IOL Tib J 466/3 起首的其他文本的那几页又被缀合在了一起。其中原因，或许即是笔者下文将要阐述的，《尊胜佛母陀罗尼》和跟随其后的 *rGyud chags gsum* 祈祷文之间存在仪轨和文字上的关联。

第二页，也就是 IOL Tib J 466/3 号文本开始的那一页的开头是这样写的：“这是第一个 *rgyud chags*，无曲调地念诵。”（第 3 列，第 1 行：*$/*：*/rgyud chags dang po ste/ dbyangs tang myI sbyor bar klags/*）这样就将 IOL Tib J 466/3 号文本的第一部分（第 3 列，第 1—19 行）与其中间部分（*rgyud chags bar ma*；第 3 列，第 19 行—第 11 列，第 15 行）和结尾部分（*rgyud chags tha ma*；第 11 列，第 15—21 行）区分开来了。同样的指示也出现在第三部分的开头，说明了第一部分和第三部分应当无曲调地念诵。然而中间部分（也是最长的部分）则如其开头的指示（第 3 列，第 20 行：*dbyangs dang sbyar ba/*：*/*），应当结合曲调念诵。

rGyud chags gsum（*pa*）或者说 *Tridaṇḍaka* 在佛教经典文献中有所提及，但目前为止尚未能找到其印度范例。[①] 作为一个结合音律的作品，这一文本是唯二的违反佛教对寺庙作乐的一般性禁止的作品之一（至少在文本意义上是如此）。另一个则是《佛功德赞》（*Śāstṛguṇasaṃkīrtta*，这或许不是一个真实存在的文本），而这一文本是用来赞颂佛祖的。格雷戈里·肖本（Gregory Schopen 2010，第 118 页，注 35）告知我们，这些祈祷文都应该伴随着标准的语调来念诵，然而佛律（*Vinaya*）又暗示这一规则并不总是需要遵从。从 IOL Tib J 466/3 号文本来看，也并不是整个 *rGyud chags gsum* 都要伴随音乐——仅仅是中间的赞颂部分而已。

后来的西藏传统中保留了“三常念（*rgyun chags gsum pa*）”，比如噶举派的“大愿”（*sMon lam chen mo*，第一卷，第 1—6 页）。《藏汉大辞典》（张怡荪等编，2003[1985]，上卷第 576 页）定义 *rgyud gsum* 为 *rgyun chags gsum*，但也解释为萨迦道果法（*Lam 'bras*）的一部分。而在 IOL Tib J 466 中，*rGyud chags gsum* 和 *rGyud gsum pa* 看起来既不相同却又有联

---

① 见 Schopen 1997，第 231—233 页，注 62 关于佛教《根本说一切有部律》（*Mūlasarvāstivāda-vinaya*）中的《衣事》（*Cīvara-Vastu*）和《毗奈耶杂事》（*Vinayakṣudraka-vastu*）的讨论。在耆那教中似乎也没有这样的文本。Peter Flügel（2010，第 455 页，注 176）认为 Schopen 所描述的寺院举行葬仪所含的最主要的五个仪轨元素（包括 *Tridaṇḍaka*，被列为第二个仪式），“在耆那教中有相应的仪轨，并且指示了古代共通的寺院葬仪文化”。然而，Flügel（在 2017 年 3 月 8 日的私人交流中）也指出，*Tridaṇḍaka* 与其说是一种文本特载的耆那教寺院仪轨，不如说更普遍地体现在耆那教修行者留给在家信众的葬仪的某些部分当中。

系，IOL Tib J 466/3 号文本由前者组成，而 IOL Tib J 466/4 号文本又是后者。关于这一点请看下文（以及 Dalton 2011，第 62—66 页和 Dolton 2016）。

rGyud chags dang po

从第一行我们就可以看出，（该文本的）书写者始终倾向于将 dang 写成 tang，将 sdug 写成 stug，等等。[①] 此外偶尔也会出现别的语法上或正字法上的错误，这使得对 IOL Tib J 466/3 号这一长篇幅、内容独特的祈祷文做全文翻译在目前而言是不可行的。因此，为了达到我们的研究目的，笔者将概括该文本中最重要的一部分。这一部分又由三个部分组成：第一部分为分别向三宝（*dkon mchog gsum*），即佛、法、僧祈祷；第二部分将三者作为一个整体；最后一部分则是念诵遍满十方佛土的《供养云陀罗尼》(《云供咒》*Pūjāmegha dhāraṇī*)，对象是作为三宝之首的佛（但或许从提喻法上来讲对象是三者全部）。[②] 这一部分所用的陀罗尼除了一处细小差别外，与 IOL Tib J 369 号文本（2r3—5）是一致的。[③] 第 16—17 行将《供养云陀罗尼》描述为“使十方一切佛土生起供养之云的陀罗尼”（*phyogs bcu'I sangs rgyas kyI zhIng thams cad du// mchod pa'I sprIn byung ba'I gzungs*）。这种对十方的强调，与 IOL Tib J 369/2 号文本中所载的《供养云陀罗尼》是一致的。这为我们更广泛的讨论提供了论据，即随着佛教的传入，在藏地，“四方”这一意象逐渐被“十方”宇宙观所代替。需要注意的是，在赤松德赞那篇较长版的诏令中（前文“帝国佛教”部分已有翻译），十方亦是宇宙观念上的诸佛居所，或者说是所有三宝的处所（佛作为三宝的一个部分）。

rGyud chags bar ma

在 *rGyud chags dang po* 中被赞颂和祈求的三宝，在 *rGyud chags bar ma* 的开头被称作“十方三宝”，其亦为这一部分第一节的供奉对象（*/: /'phyogs bcu'i dkon mchog gsum la mchod pa /:/*）。公元 8 世纪的桑耶钟铭中也包含这一短语，此外亦有其他一些在 *rGyud chags*

---

① 就这一点而言，这一文本不算特别，更非极端例子。例如，对于 Pelliot tibétain 1030 号文本的开头部分，Lalou 1950，第 40 页是这样描述的：“d 始终写为 t 的片段（Fragment où les *d* sont toujours écrits comme des *t*.）开头（Débute）：*bcom ltan 'tas la 'ti skat cig gsol to// bcom ltan 'tas 'dzam bu ling gi sems can 'ti 'tag na// gcig gis gcig bskyet te// thog ma...*”

② 该文本为七音节诗歌，偶尔会有出入。此处，笔者用 *rkang pa*（字面意思为“脚”）来区分诗的行数和构成散文的更常规的行数（lines）。唯一明显的分节符号，是在分别向“三宝”祈祷的祈祷文的结尾（第 11 行），有一个圆圈。以及从此处数 15 诗行（*rkang pa*），在向“三宝”整体祈祷之后（第 16 行），有两个标红的竖直排列圆圈。

③ 这一反复的陀罗尼，几乎与 IOL Tib J 369 2r3—5 一字不差（除了拼写上的变体 / 错误和一些垂符的使用地方不同外）。此外，在 IOL Tib J466 第 17 行写着：*ma h'a bo di/ man ṭo/ pa sang gra ma na {bad}*（写法为 b+d）*dzre/*；而 ITJ 369 2r5 写的是：*ma h'a bo d+hi man to pa sang kra ma na*（没有 bad rdze）/。在经折本上发现的陀罗尼，即 IOL Tib J 140 反面 1r2 与 IOL Tib J 466 号文本相同（与 369 号文本不同）写的是“*pa sang gra ma na ba dzre/...*”。

bar ma 开头（第 4 列，第 1 行）能够找到的词或短语，如 *dbyangs* 和 *bla myed*。[①]

或有一种耐人寻味的可能性即桑耶寺钟铭文参考了这篇罕见的唱诵祈祷文，而这篇祈祷文可能自吐蕃帝国毗邻的任一或多个佛教传播的区域传入。这样的推测是十分恰当的，因为该铭文被刻在能够产生声音的钟上面，并且由六十个音节组成，而这六十个音节映射的正是铭文中所提到的佛之六十妙音（Richardson 1985，第 35 页，注 3）。[②] 其后的昌珠（Khra 'brug）钟（亦以音乐为主题）铭文中声称，其乃由一位汉僧应业已受戒的王后的请求浇铸而成（同上文第 82—83 页），这一事实加强了寺庙之间的关联。此外，叶巴（Yer pa）钟铭则载有另一广泛流通的祈祷文——《普贤行愿赞》（引言部分有提及）的一部分，同时还用某种印度字体转录了著名的《缘起法颂》（*ye dharmā* ）字符（Richardson 1985，第 144—147 页）。或者是，IOL Tib J 466/3 号文本要么参考了桑耶钟铭，要么作为吐蕃和后吐蕃时代早期的一种普遍类型的佛教祈祷文，与后者享用同一个语库。我们可以看到，桑耶钟铭的赞颂对象——赤松德赞，亦作为一个亡故的赞普出现在了下文要介绍的 *rGyud chags bar ma* 里。这一提法增强了文本与吐蕃帝国的联系，也表明文本中这一层垒至少可以追溯到赤松德赞亡故（8 世纪末）之后。

rGyud chags bar ma 的其他部分由赞颂诗节组成，对象是佛教神祇、佛教历史叙事中的神话英雄以及藏地的重要人物和精灵。这些诗节先描述其赞颂的对象，举出其中的一两名代表或子群（subgroups），然后以重复的赞颂惯用语结尾。在这一点上，其与上文讨论过的 IOL Tib J 374 号文本（"为藏地的祈祷文"），以及 Pelliot tibétain 1345 号文本中的"守护者们最后的告诫"（Scherrer-Schaub 1999—2000，第 227 页，第 48 行）是相类似的。然而，目前而言，除了语言之外，没有任何证据表明这一祈祷文为藏地原创（同样，亦不能证明其出自汉地）。

rGyud chags bar ma 的赞颂诗节自毗卢遮那佛开始，将之放在了释迦佛前面，尽管或许他们在各自的佛土中有同等的地位（第 4 列，第 1—2 行：*bcom ldan rnaM par snang mdzad tang// 'dren pa shag kya thub ba lastsogs//*）。一些密续则直接将释迦牟尼指为"遍照佛"（Vairocana；见 Snellgrove 1987，第 120、152 页），例如《净治一切恶趣》（*Sarvadurgatipariśodhana*）。[③] 将

---

① 请注意以下桑耶钟铭中笔者以斜体标出的部分：jo mo rgyal mo brtsan yum(2)sras kyIs *phyogs bcu'I*（3）*dkon mchog gsum la*（4）*mchod pa*'I slad du cong（5）'di bgyis te// de'i bso-（6）-d nams kyI stobs kyis（7）lha btsan po khrI srong lde b-（8）-rtsan yab sras stangs dbya-（9）-l gsung *dbyangs* drug（10）cu sgra *dbyangs* dang ldan te（11）*bla na myed pa*'I byang chub（12）du grub par smond to//。

② De ga g.yu tshal 祈祷文中声称佛陀拥有 62 梵（Brahmā）音（Pelliot tibétain 16，30r2–3: *gsung tshangs pa'I dbyangs (30r3) drug cu rtsa gnyIs dong ldan bas*）

③《净治一切恶趣密续》（*Sarvadurgatipariśodhana tantra*; *Ngan song thams cad rnam par sbyong ba'i rgyud*;Q.116）旨在遮阻投生下三道，并且其与《顶髻尊胜总持经》（*Uṣṇīṣavijaya dhāraṇī sutra*; *gTsug tor rnam par rgyal ba'i gzungs*;Q.197 和 Q.198）密切相关，而后者本身即被抄写在 IOL Tib J 466/2 中。这一密续也是被严格保密的仪轨之一，因其被视作能够保障吐蕃王室的权力，故而其翻译和流通似乎都受到了严格的控制（Dalton 2011，第 57 页）。然而，lHan kar ma 目录中则记录了一部赤松德赞时期由佛护（Buddhagupta）撰写的释论（Kapstein 2000，第 63 页）。

毗卢遮那佛置于首位或许反映了与密续的联系，与吐蕃佛教，尤其是在赤松德赞及其继任者治下佛教的联系，亦或者是反映了其后密教发展的趋向。① 紧随其后的是诸声闻（*śrāvaka*）、佛（*jina*）等等，有时赞颂指向的对象是令人费解的。但除了语言以外，就目前这一部分而言，没有任何迹象表明这篇祈祷文编撰的藏地背景，抑或汉地背景，更有可能的是，这篇祈祷文的大部分都是来自于印度的 *Tridaṇḍaka* 祈祷文。

rGyud chags bar ma 中与藏地有关的内容

在这之后（第 10 列，第 12 行结尾），该祈祷文从四句一偈的形式转变为更短的偈颂形式，直到几乎不能构成诗节。在这一部分内容中，与藏地有关的人物终于"登上了舞台"：

敬颂往昔之亲教师（*upādhyāya*）、圣者（*āryan*）：论典（*śāstra*）众河之源头，心智广深似大海，身具辞章（*kāvya*）之海潮，外道（*tīrthika*）狂风浑不动。Nāgārjuna（龙树，约 1—2 世纪）、Āryadeva（提婆，约 2—3 世纪）、Ashva ka（Aśvaghoṣa——马鸣?）②、Ma tri tse ta（Mātṛceṭa；约 2—3 世纪?）、Klu mtsho（Klu 'tsho，Nāgarakṣita——龙护?）③、Ārya Asang（Asaṅga——无著；约 4—5 世纪）、dByig gi gnyen（po）（Vasubandhu——世亲；约 4—5 世纪）、phyogs kyI glang po（Dignāga——陈那；约 480—540 年）、Shu ra（Āryaśūra——圣勇猛；约 4 世纪?）以及 Shan ta ra kshI ta（Śāntarakṣita——寂护；约 8 世

① 关于将赤松德赞等同于毗卢遮那的可能性，特别是对桑耶寺布局的研究，见 Kapstein 2000，第 60—65 页。他将《净治一切恶趣密续》视为"西藏最早与毗卢遮那有关的文本之一"（同上书，第 63 页）。同时，毗卢遮那佛亦为位于 De ga g.yu tshal 寺中心的佛像（Pelliot tibétain 16，27a4）；该文本的翻译和相关讨论分别见于 Kapstein 2009，第 46 页和第 48 页。Dalton and van Schaik（2006，第 280—281 页）亦认为 IOL Tib J 579 号文本可能能够为"桑耶坛城（bSam yas *maṇḍala*）"提供文本来源。他们是这样描述这一份写成贝叶格式（*pothī*）的文本："一份完整的灌顶仪轨（dbang chog）的实操手册，并与《净治一切恶趣密续》（Q.116）有关……主要是利用了这一密续的第二品，其第一部分描述了一个由 43 个神祇构成的坛城……这或许是一个重要的描述，因为此中 42 神祇或许能解释桑耶寺顶层的布局——据说这一层有一尊普明毗卢遮那佛（与《净治一切恶趣密续》有关），并且由 42 个神祇伴随。"（Dalton and van Schaik 2006，第 280 页）这为之后的研究提供了有启发性的线索。然而，在讨论早期西藏佛教中毗卢遮那的重要性时，亦不应忘记《一切如来真实摄》（*Sarvatathāgatatattvasaṃgraha*）和《文殊根本续》（*Mañjuśrīmūlakalpa*）中所包含的印度背景，以及在《大毗卢遮那成佛神变加持经》（*Mahāvairocana tantra*）中，正是由"毗卢遮那"释迦牟尼讲法（Snellgrove 1987，第 152 页）。

② 马鸣（Aśvaghoṣa，约 80—150 年）在 17 世纪时被称为 *Aśvaka*（Kilty trans. 2010，第 143 页），从现在的角度来看这是非常晚的事情了。上书还给出马鸣的另外两个名字（Mātṛceṭa 和 Matrcitra 译者按：此处应为 Maticitra 的误写），显然是同一名字的不同写法，而这一名字正是我们的列表中的下一位。

③ 笔者未能找到任何与 Nāgasaras（Klu mtsho 龙湖）相关的信息，而 Klu 'tsho 在古藏文文献中是西藏人的名字（或名字的一部分 Thomas 1951，131，M.I. xxviii，2），所以如果有一个印度的佛教徒叫作 Nāgarakṣita，那么在 ITJ 466/3 号文本中很有可能就会写作 Klu 'tsho。这就意味着抄写员在此处将一个常见的名字误写成了"Klu mtsho"，而这是不大可能的。我们很有可能是在寻找一个传统上被认为生活于公元 3—4 世纪的人。

纪）等等业已涅槃的大师，他们令愚痴〔而导致〕生盲之人睁眼，乃是存续〔三〕宝（或宝〔佛〕）之人。向他们顶礼并献上供养。

IOL Tib J 466 第 10 列，第 12 行—第 11 列，第 1 行；sngon gyi mkhan po 'phags pa rnams la mchod pa / / bstan bcos chu klung mang po'i gnas / / blo dkyel mtsho chen gting yangs shIng / / snyan dngags rIg pa'I mtsho rlabs can / / mu stegs rlung gIs myI bskyod pa / / {'phags}（写作：g+s）pa na ga rdzu na {(插入 <)d(> 插入)ng}（读作：dang）/ / ^a rya de ba ^ashva ka / / ma trI tse ta klu mtsho dang / / ^a rya ^a sang dbIig gI gnyen / / phyogs kyI glang po shu ra dang / / shan ta ra {kshI}（写作：k+sh）ta lastogs / / ston pa mya ngan 'das {phyI na}（读作：phyIn）/ / ma rIg dmus long dmyIg 'byed cing / / dkon mchog gdung 'dzIn thams cad la / / phyag 'tshal bsnyen bkur mchod pa dbul /。

关于早期西藏佛教徒对印度佛教历史的了解，这是最早的材料之一。从该文可以看出，吐蕃帝国时期或后帝国时代早期，不仅有人知道这些论主，而且能够按照时间予以排序（除了 Āryaśūra）。此外，这些南亚的佛教高僧似乎被分为了两个谱系，从龙树至提婆以降代表印度哲学传统，而 Mātṛceṭa 追随马鸣之后的诗学传统——Nāgasaras（Klu mtsho）/ Nāgarakṣita（Klu 'tsho）亦属于这一传承？复次，还有一点也与 *rGyud chags bar ma* 作为吟唱祈祷文的特性相符。正如我们即将看到的，接下来的“法王”们也是按照年代来排序的，并且他们也同样在教授人们佛法之后“入于涅槃”。

寂护位于这一传承的末尾，并且他是（这其中）唯一一位踏足过藏地的大师（8 世纪晚期）。① 对于这样一个短短的列表而言，强调其有所遗漏或许是不智的，但是还是要指出，该文本没有提到月称（Candrakīrti）和法称（Dharmakīrti），而两者与寂护（包括在赤松德赞时期亦到过藏地的 Kamalaśila——莲花戒）是有关联的。同样，汉传佛教的大师亦不在其列，说明这一文本并非由一位懂藏文并愿意展示汉地佛教历史知识的汉人编纂。

该祈祷文接着赞颂了佛教传统中的世俗政权人物：

赞颂我们藏地的善知识（*kalyāṇamitra*）——以大王赤松德赞为首的伟大的法王（*dharmarāja*）们。掌握了 *phyva* 之王法，并以天神的武器〔统治〕王国的 *'phrul rje*（王）赤松德赞，以及阿育王（Dharmāśoka）、迦腻色伽王（Kaniṣkā）、戒日王（Śīlāditya/Harṣa）等等，他们是业已涅槃的大师，是弘扬教法者，向他们顶礼并献上供养。

IOL Tib J 466，第 11 列，第 1—4 行：bdag cag bod khams kyI dge ba'I bshes nyen //

① 见 IOL Tib J 689/2 号文本，在此处其被视为桑耶寺和大昭寺的首位善知识（*kalyāṇamitra*；*dge ba'i bshes gnyen*）（见 Karmay 1988，第 76—80 页；Uebach 1990，第 407—413 页）。Van Schaik and Doney 2007；Doney 2015、2017 中提供了关于这一人物在后世西藏史料中的更多信息。

rgyal po chen po khri srong lde brtsan lastsogs pa / / chos kyI rgyal po chen po rnams la mchod pa / / phyva'I rgyal thabs mnga' brnyes shing / / chab srId gnam gyI lde mtshon can / / 'phrul rje khrI srong lde brtsan dang / / dar ma sho ka / ka ni sk'a / shI la ^a tI da tya lastsogs / / ston pa mya ngan 'das {phyI na}（读作：phyIn) / / bstan pa rgyas mdzad thams cad la / / phyag 'tshal bsnyen bkur mchod pa dbul / /。

此处，又将一个公元 8 世纪的人物列入到了印度佛教徒中，但与寂护不同的是，这是一个藏人——吐蕃赞普赤松德赞。这里仅列出他，或许提示我们可以将这一作品，或者这一部分内容写成的时间追溯到公元 8 世纪。因为如果该作品是在公元 8 世纪后某位（或某几位）赞普的统治之后完成的，那么可以假定，作者会将这位（几位）君主的名字与赤松德赞的名字放在一起。除非这一祈祷文的创作时间在 10 世纪末期，而编纂者认为仅有赤松德赞是值得一提的佛教君主的典范。然而，手稿学、古文字学和语言学方面的特征并不支持后一种推测。

正如 IOL Tib J 466 中所呈现的，*rGyud chags gsum* 祈祷文将赤松德赞视为如寂护一样的善知识，同时又将该赞普尊奉为一位证悟了的导师。上文桑耶钟铭中所记载的祈祷文暗示其将会获得证悟，而这篇祈祷文则声称赤松德赞如之前的印度君主一般业已涅槃。同时，还给予了赤松德赞 *'phrul rje* 的头衔，这一头衔或与其他吐蕃时期铭文中的 *'phrul gyi lha bTsan po*（见 Stein 1985）类似。最后，在描述这位赞普时，用到了 *phyva*（王室祖先神?）和 *gnam gyI lde*（天神众）等特殊的术语。[①] 因此，这一文本既将赤松德赞视为吐蕃的统治者，同时也将其视为本土神祇的统治者。该文本还将赞普描述为一位“善知识”（*kalyāṇamitra*）。[②] 或

① 以往关于这一诗节的研究见本文注 17。

② 将赤松德赞或者其他统治者描述为“我们”藏土的一位“善知识”，可以说是很奇怪的。鉴于我们对于“善知识”和吐蕃赞普之间的关系的了解（见 van Schaik and Doney 2007，第 192—193 页；Doney 2017，第 311—314 页），这种奇怪之处驱使我们去寻找笔误的迹象。这一诗行缺少了一个音节，因此我们或许可以在 *dge ba'i bshes gnyen* 后面加一个作格，这样这一句代表的则是由“善知识”发出的动作，而不是将其作为动作的对象。然而，这样一来则与其他诗节中的结构不一致了，因为其他诗节均在开头陈述赞颂的对象。这些诗节中从未说明赞颂的发出者是谁；笔者推测其指的就是负责念诵这一“*rGyud chags gsum*”的僧人——而不是尊贵的（以及特指的）被称为“善知识”的那些寺院头领（因为他们中的一人也是这些诗节的赞颂对象）。事实上，“我们的”藏土是与他们的自我指涉联系最紧密的一个词，这也是我们在翻译这一诗节时需要十分谨慎的一个原因。

或者，这里缺失的不仅仅是一个音节，而是这一诗节的一大部分？或许在赞颂印度大师之后的诗节中，赞颂的对象应该是其他的善知识，比如寂护，而不是这些国王。这就意味着，有可能在抄写时产生了错误，使得除了开头一句保留了下来，这一诗节的大部分内容均遗失了。这是有可能的，但同时，关于国王的那一诗节的第一句也遗失了，这是十分巧合的（当然这也解释了这一错误缘何未被注意到）。另一种可能性是，尽管在吐蕃帝国时期，统治者们不被视为“善知识”，但在稍后的时期，他们已被塑造为导师。比如，Pelliot tibétain 149 号文本中，赤松德赞可以依止寂护，在这里，后者是赞普的导师。但 Pelliot tibétain 149 号文本中也记载有赞普说 dBa' dPal dbyangs（桑耶寺和大昭寺的另一个“善知识”）“是我的一个弟子（*slob ma*）沙门”（Pelliot tibétain 149 正面，第 8 行：*bdag gi slob ma dge sbyong zhig lags so zhes gsol ba dang/*）。也就是说，正如我们这篇祈祷文一样，该文本暗示赤松德赞是一名导师，甚至是一名“善知识”。

许最好还是不要宣称在一篇吐蕃时期的祈祷文中，赤松德赞被描述为一位“善知识”。然而，如果这一行（*rkang ba*）是被插入进去的，那么插入此句的人无疑是想要将赤松德赞刻画为“我们藏土”的一位“善知识”。

接下来一节是赞颂藏土（*bod yul*）的神祇（*lha rnams*），或者说是西藏（*bod*）的地方神（*yul gyi lha rnams*）：

> 向藏土的神祇，如乾达婆之王〔和〕“具五顶髻者”父子；向所有令人敬畏的地方神（*yul bdag gnyan po*），如于环绕〔西藏〕的铁山、银山、金山、水晶山和雪山中产出人之珍宝与珍宝之珍宝，并且行善法与天道的，威力巨大的诸神（*lha dang sman*）。我以虔敬的方式，献上纯净的吉祥之物，如香氛、香（或者好闻的香，*dri spos*）和花朵。
>
> 第 11 列，第 4—8 行：/ drI za’I rgyal po gtsug pud lnga pa {yab}（写作：y+b) sras lastsogs pa /:/ bod yul gyI lha rnams la mchod pa / / lcags rI dngul rI gser gyI ri / / shel rI gangs rI khyad kor na / / myI dang nor gyi dbyig ’byung zhIng / / chos bzang gnam lugs spyod pa yI / / mthu chen lha dang sman lastogs / / yul bdag gnyan po thams cad la / / rje sa rI mo’i tshul bzung ste / drI spos men tog bzang lastogs / / bkra shis gtsang ma’I rdzas rnams ’bul /。

这一节所赞颂的三种类型的神祇，即 *yul bdag*，*sman* 和 *yul lha*，也载于“木简牍”之上，而这是我们所能掌握的最早的关于西藏非佛教仪轨的资料之一。舍克（Sam van Schaik 2013，第 246 页）认为：“其中一条（IOL Tib N 255）记载了一种直接面向本地神祇——被称作 *yul lha yul bdag*——的仪轨，这种短语结构亦出现在 Pelliot tibétain 1042 号文本中。这种仪轨还提到了 *sman* 这种神灵。”① 在文本的这一节中，*sman* 看起来应为 *yul bdag* 的一个子类，而非另一种类型的神祇。特意指出的神应该是非凡的，而“具五顶髻者”通常即指乾达婆王。在后世的作品中，该名字的拥有者被认为是西藏本地神——gNyan chen thang lha（念青唐古拉）。② 然而，在此文本中，似乎用父子（*yab sras*）将二者区分开了；此外，“具五顶

---

① 这一木简的照片见 van Schaik 2013，第 246 页，其转写见同文注 39：“IOL Tib N 255（M.I.iv.121）：$// yul lha yul bdag dang/ sman gsol ba’i zhal ta pa/ sku gshen las myi[ng] b[sgrom] pa/ gy-d[-] zhal ta pa/ gsas chung lha bon po/ blo co[com] [rno]/ -m pos sug zungs/ la tong sprul sug gzungs/.” 亦可参见 Thomas 1951，第 395 页（然而 Thomas 误把 *sman* 翻译成了医生）。van Schaik 2013，第 247 页及同文注 42 还转写了与此类似的另一木简：“IOL Tib N 873（M.I.xxvii.15）：$:/./yul lha yul bdag dang sman gsol ba’i zhal ta pa/ dang sku gshen dpon yog//：/blon/ man gzigs blon mdo bzang.” 同样，亦可参见 Thomas 1951，第 395 页。

② 在娘·日光（Nyang Nyi ma ’od zer，1124—1192）所著的《赤铜洲》（*Zangs gling ma*）中，莲花生（Padmasambhava）将念青唐拉（gNyan chen thang lha）称为“五髻食香王（Dri za’i rgyal po Zur phud lnga pa）”。见 *ZL*h 28a3–4 和 *ZL*i 23b5，见 Doney 2014，第 128 页和第 248 页。然而，在这部文献中，这只是他的众多名字之一，并且可能引用了关于乾达婆国王的早期叙事。

髻者”（古典藏文作 *zur phud lnga pa*）亦是文殊师利的异名。这些神祇中还包括威力巨大的、有能力的（*mthu chen*）这一子类，*mthu chen* 这一表达在 *rGyud chags bar ma* 的结尾（见下文）再次出现，而在 Pelliot tibétain 134 号等祈祷文本中，*mthu* 常常与 *byin* 结合，用来描述赞普。舍勒-肖伯（Scherrer-Schaub 1999—2000，第 238 页等）将这些术语翻译为“（君主的）力量与威严”（la force et la magnificence du souverain）。此外，完满清净之力也用来描述法性（*dharmatā*，见上书第 227 页，第 44 行：*chos nyid rnam par dag pa'i mthus*）。这一节还提到诸神行善法（*chos bzang*）和天道（*gnam lugs*），既可能是说佛教，也可能是说吐蕃帝国的神权信仰（见 Stein 1985）。

在最后一节，该祈祷文又坚定地转回了佛教领域。首先，总共用了七句，“赞颂被菩提心摄受的众凡夫”（第 11 列，第 8 行：*byang chub kyI sems kyIs zin pa'I so so'i skye bo rnams la mchod pa//...*）。然后，“赞颂具有加持力的仪轨物品 / 供养物”（第 10 行：*lha rdzas byin can la mchod pa*）。*lha rdzas* 这种表达在十二行的 De ga gyu tshal 祈祷文中出现得相当频繁。

rGyud chags bar ma 以一个祈求作为结尾：“愿所有统治 / 控制整个世界的具威严力的（/ 者）〔和？〕修行者，令至上的安乐和教法遍布整个世界。”（第 14—15 行：*'jIg rten kun la 'ang mnga' mdzad pa'I// mthu chen drang srong thams cad kyIs// 'jIg rten mtha' bdag mchog tu skyid pa dang/ bstan pa rgyas par mdzad du gsol/*）除了此处的祈求外，*rGyud chags bar ma* 的所有内容均为赞颂，这或许与该部分作为唯一需要唱诵的部分有关。再次强调，除此以外被僧侣团体允许伴乐唱诵的“文本”，仅有赞颂佛陀的《佛功德赞》。

rGyud chags tha ma

在得出最终结论之前，我们需要对 *Tridaṇḍaka* 的结尾部分进行讨论。*rGyud chags tha ma* 特别强调其不应用来唱诵（第 11 列，第 15—16 行），正如 *rGyud chags dang po* 一样（第 3 列，第 1 行，见上文）。其以十方佛为开端（而非十方三宝），祈愿他们的愿望得到满足（第 16—18 行）。在上文提到的较长版本的诏令中，也提到了十方佛，当然这样的表达是比较常见的（如在《普贤行愿赞》中），因此笔者也无意宣称两者有何关联。

rGyud chags tha ma 更像是一份祈愿文（*smon lam*），这作为祈祷文的结尾部分是合适的。除了开头与结尾以外，这一部分的中间并没有用红字来划分区块。或许红字是作为装饰，又或者是用以标示这一部分不应出声诵读，换句话说即正如开头所指示的一般（第 15—16 行）。最后，以“*rGyud chags* 竟”作为结束（第 21 行）。与之后的“第三续”（*rGyud gsum pa*）祈祷文相关的研究，见多尔顿的文章（Dalton 2011，第 62—66 页，以及 Dalton 2016），此处不复赘述。唯一需要注意的是，若这一部分并非后人添加上去的，那么通过将其与 IOL Tib J 466/3 号文本放在同一抄本中，是能够令“第三续”更深地融入吐蕃时代的氛围中的。

五、结　　论

相较于其最终归宿地敦煌而言，IOL Tib J 466/3 号文本的核心部分最初或许是在更接近吐蕃帝国时期并且在更接近吐蕃中心区域的地方被缮写、翻译或编辑的。通过古文字学与手稿学的分析，并将其与其他写本进行比较，可以知晓其仅仅稍微晚于吐蕃帝国时期。使用相同的纸张和页面布局（*mis en page*），以及该写本可能是在十七号洞窟与吐蕃时期的《大乘无量寿宗要经》的抄本一同发现，种种迹象都表明抄写 IOL Tib J466/3 时使用了吐蕃时期原本要用来抄写《无量寿宗要经》的纸，这或许与 Lu Dze Shing 的缮写室有关联。

在对 IOL Tib J 466 第一页和第二页做更进一步的古文书学方面的比较之后，我们对该写本的内容有了新的认识，意识到 IOL Tib J 466/3 的重要性，因为或许这才是原初写本的第一部分。现存 *rGyud chags gsum* 祈祷文的内容，介于吐蕃帝国时期的桑耶钟铭和后世西藏王庭的各类诗歌（载于本文开头引用的历史著作中，见本文注 2）之间。我们可以看到，象征统治权的“四方”，逐渐被佛教宇宙观中的“十方”（尤其与“三宝”结合）所替代，同时还将印度神祇吸收进西藏的宇宙观中。IOL Tib J 466/3 值得与更早的吐蕃帝国时期的祈祷文——如桑耶钟铭以及未来会发现的其他文本——做进一步的比较研究，以作为更广泛的古藏文祈祷文献研究的一部分。

在本文开头我们提到，沃尔特（Michael L. Walter）认为 De ga g.yu tshal 祈祷文是由新旧两层文本混合而成的，因此他将整个文本的编辑时间归属于西藏佛教祈祷文献发展过程中一个较晚的时期。他认为（Michael L. Walter 2013，第 435 页，注 9）在 De ga g.yu tshal 祈祷文中发现的，与赤祖德赞相关文本中相类似的古藏文语词有可能是从铭文里抄录出来的（亦见上文）。与此不同的是，笔者并不认为我们需要担心 IOL Tib J 466/3 号文本有类似的情况，因为该文本中涉及的赞普很明显（在文本形成时）已经去世了。除了指出该文本系伪造，Walter 还注意到“法令寺”祈祷文和法令铭文极度相似（同上书，第 427—428 页），包括在一些非常罕见的短语上。他声称除了《吐蕃大事纪年》以外，这一文本是与吐蕃时代铭文最为接近的文本，但现在他或许可以将 IOL Tib J 466/3 和 Pelliot tibétain 177 号文本的一些短语加入这一列表当中，这些短语与桑耶钟铭（扩展来看或许亦与赤松德赞较长版本的诏令）有对应关系。

将 IOL Tib J 466/3 号文本置于同类型的祈祷文献中来看，其与 Pelliot tibétain 134 的乌东赞祈愿文一样都包括对三宝的赞颂，包括向一位作为君主同时作为佛教徒的吐蕃赞普敬献的颂歌，以及一个既包括本地神祇又包括印度诸神的宇宙观。每一个被赞颂的群体都拥有一个长度为 8—11 行句子的诗节，而有的诗节则遵从七音律，此外这些群体常常都由列名的某一位或某个子群体作为代表。后面这种模式亦见于 Pelliot tibétain 134“为背教者祈祷（prière pour un apostat）”和 IOL Tib J 466/3“为藏地的祈祷文”两篇祈愿文中。

OL Tib J 466/3 号文本的前一部分显示出一种南亚社会语境，而后一部分则透露出西藏化的语境。该文本没有特别指涉汉地或北部中亚地区，尽管赞颂十方三宝这种表达在同时期唐代的汉文文献中也有出现（见上文，注 13）。当然我们亦不能排除这种可能性，即与其说 *rGyud chags gsum* 引用汉文材料，不如说汉文文献吸收了 *Tridaṇḍaka* 祈祷文。许多术语是泛佛教化的；舍勒-肖伯（Cristina Scherrer-Schaub 2014，第 150—151 页）也指出碑铭文献语料库（inscriptional corpus）“表明从桑耶法令开始，在公共档案中逐渐地引入了一套术语，这套术语在后来的几个世纪被普遍运用于佛教世界中”。需要注意的是，不应将影响这一祈祷文形成的因素归于某一单一方面。尽管如此，看起来该藏文祈祷文的大部分来自印度的 *Tridaṇḍaka*，并且加上了一些密教和西藏本土的元素（许多元素是比较隐晦的），其年代属于吐蕃时代晚期或后吐蕃帝国时代的早期。其中的一些西藏本土的元素不具备严格的史料价值，更接近神话传说，或出自某个了解印度佛教的学者、诗人和国王的世系的人之手。此外，这一藏文 *Tridaṇḍaka* 还把吐蕃赞普赤松德赞崇奉为一位已获得证悟的大师，就像其前辈——印度的诸位“法王”一样。

最后，IOL Tib J 466/3 号文本包含了其他非佛教仪轨文本中亦有的三种神祇，即 yul bdag、sman，或许还有 yul lha，而这些神祇都是修习善法的。其关于非佛教的诸神、诸天的描述与 IOL Tib J 1746 号文本是相似的。① 而与后者对非佛教信仰的攻击不同，我们可以看到这一 *rGyud chags gsum* 祈祷文明确地将这些本土信仰与赞普的权力关联在一起。舍克曾提到：

> IOL Tib J 1746 号文本是这类仪轨文本中的另类，其将佛塑造为一种平等对待所有人的慈悲形象……IOL Tib J 1746 号文本是早期材料中极少数以一般性的方式（而非具体的仪轨操作）明确提及藏地的非佛教修习的材料之一；这些非佛教信仰始终被认为是

---

① Sam van Schaik（2013，第 230—233 页）曾讨论过 IOL Tib J 1746 号文本，他基于手稿学、古文书学和语言学的分析，将其归于吐蕃帝国时期。他注意到该文本的两页的布局（尺寸为 28 × 41.5 cm，每一页分作两列），与《无量寿宗要经》（*Aparimitāyurnāma sūtra*）抄本类似，后者产生的年代为赤祖德赞时期，或稍晚于这一时期。而从 IOL Tib J 1746 号文本的书法（Sam van Schaik 所谓“方形风格”）和正字法（比如使用 *da drag*，见下文）来看，其风格更为古早，并且能反映出《吐蕃大事纪年》的书写风格（见上文第 231 页）。尽管用于《无量寿宗要经》抄本的版纸比 IOL Tib J 1746 文本稍大一些，但尺寸变化亦常发生，而且后者只有两页，亦算不上是科学样本（scientific sample）。IOL Tib J 466 号文本由八页组成，尺寸则为 31.5 × 45 cm 左右，换句话说这是吐蕃控制下的敦煌地区所使用的标准尺寸（见 Iwao 2012，第 103 页）。IOL Tib J 1746 号文本的内容是与佛教相关的，具体来说是“论述佛教之于吐蕃本土信仰和仪轨的优越性……（以及）以佛教徒的观点来描述非佛教的信仰——敬奉（*bskurd*）诸神和天”（同上 Sam van Schaik 文，第 231—232 页）。尽管 IOL Tib J 1746 号文本并没有提及统治者的王廷，但其关于非佛教的诸神和天的描述，与 IOL Tib J 466/3 号文本是类似的，而我们的 IOL Tib J 466/3 号文本则明确将这些与赞普的权力联系在一起。

chos（法）的一种：要么被称为“恶法”（*chos ngan pa*），要么被称为“小法”（*chos chu ngu*）。而佛教，作为佛的教法，或称佛法（*chos 'b'u dha*），则是善法（*chos bzang po/chos legs pa*），正法（*chos yang thag pa*）或大法（*chos chen po*）。（van Schaik 2013，第233页）

显然 IOL Tib J 466/3 号文本并没有如此将天、神视为与佛教对立的“恶法”，因为其同时运用两种类型的语言来描述护法赞普赤松德赞，而没有给人任何的矛盾和不协调的感觉。相反，IOL Tib J 1746 号文本将“善”和“恶”两种信仰呈现为相互竞争的语域，这反映了佛教徒与非佛教徒在真理与社会方面的身份地位。

看起来似乎 IOL Tib J 466/3 与为亡者祈祷的仪轨——《净治一切恶趣续》有一定的关联。这种明显的仪轨上的关联，在其他敦煌文本中亦能找到，如后吐蕃帝国时代的《生死轮回故事》（*sKye shi'i lo rgyus*）这一与皈依佛教有关的叙事文本，该文正是模仿《净治一切恶趣续》以及本文引言中提到的《入法界品》而写的。[①] 该文讲述了国王沃巴甲（'Od 'bar rgyal，他模仿了该续中某个人物的名字，见 Kapstein 2000，第 206 页，注 20）之死，以及其子仁钦（Rin chen）在佛教诸神的帮助下寻找对治死亡和（重）生的方便（正如《入法界品》中一样）。在故事的结尾（Pelliot tibétain 218 ng—na 页背面，第 7 行），释迦牟尼狠批那些信仰颠倒法（*log pa'i chos*）的人，认为他们是永远不能对治死亡的愚人（这与 IOL Tib J 1746 号文本所持立场是相似的，而我们的这份 *Tridaṇḍaka* 祈祷文则并不如此）。释迦牟尼建议仁钦念诵《尊胜佛母陀罗尼》以对治死亡，并且“将其仪轨视为避免堕入恶趣（*durgati*）的唯一可靠的方便”（Imaeda 2007, 第 170 页）。事实上，这一陀罗尼在藏文大藏经中的一个异名即《净治一切恶趣》（**sarvadurgatipariśodhana*；*ngan 'gro thams cad yongs su sbyong ba*；见 Imaeda 2007，第 132 页）。或许这种吐蕃时期和后吐蕃时代早期的仪轨传统的关联，正是导致 IOL Tib J 466 号文本的第一页——包括《尊胜佛母陀罗尼》那一页——看起来很适合添加在文本开头的原因之一。IOL Tib J 466/3 号文本中的赞歌与颂扬死者有关，因为在其更为历史性的部分，赞颂的所有人物都明确地被称为已死亡（并入于涅槃）。这种死后（即“中阴”）的状态在《入法界品》（反而其赞颂的是《普贤行愿》）中也十分重要，而不知何故，对于西藏人来说，在这种语境下赤松德赞又是一个需要提到的十分重要的人物（见 van Schaik 和 Doney 2007 年发表的关于 Pelliot tibétain 149 号文本的研究）。

---

① 今枝由郎相关著作有两篇（Imaeda 1981 和 Imaeda 2007）。今枝由郎发现并拼合的九篇敦煌残卷是（Imaeda 2007，第 114 页）：Pelliot tibétain 218；Pelliot tibétain 219；Pelliot tibétain 220；Pelliot tibétain 366；Pelliot tibétain 367；IOL Tib J 99；IOL Tib J 345；以及斯坦因收藏第 69 卷第 17 页（也就是 IOL Tib J 1302）。今枝由郎强调了《净治一切恶趣密续》和《入法界品》对于这一叙事的重要性，同上文第 119—120 页以及第 132—133 页。

在本文开篇，笔者曾提到后世史料对于桑耶寺建成开光时有美妙音乐演奏的描述。这事实上与 IOL Tib J 466/3 号文本构成一种连续性，因为这些都是后世西藏佛教对吐蕃时期的赞颂文的叙事化描写。然而，显然敦煌藏经洞中留存下来的藏文 *Tridaṇḍaka* 的编辑者们心中有某种更为严肃的想法，因此我们还是应该简要地谈谈“来世”。今枝由郎（Imaeda，2007）非常有洞见地描述了上一段提到的印度作品对吐蕃时期和后吐蕃帝国早期西藏人的死亡、重生和宇宙观念的改变（亦见 Kapstein 2000，第 42—46 页中更为综合性的讨论）。这些印度作品本身所处的文本环境即吸纳婆罗门教（Brahmanism）中的大小神祇，作为使他们和他们的信徒们皈依佛教的一种手段（Snellgrove 1987，第 150 页）。*rGyud chags gsum* 祈祷文中所表述的广阔的宇宙观和历史编纂学展现出早期佛教化西藏的上述两种进程。

最后，笔者认为以一份较晚时期的关于吐蕃帝国时期葬仪的“权威神话”（charter myth）作为结束是比较合适的。在《巴协》（dBa’ bzhed）——关于佛教传入藏地和桑耶寺的修建的历史——中有一份附录，即《施食史》（History of Food Provisioning; *Zas gtad kyi lo rgyus*），这是一份宝贵的早期叙事文本。[①] 正如《净治一切恶趣续》以无垢威光（Vimalatejaḥprabha）之死作为开端，《生死轮回故事》以国王沃巴甲之死作为开端，《施食史》的开端是这样的：“在马年孟春，赞普赤松德赞薨逝。〔他的〕儿子牟尼赞普年幼，[②]〔所以他〕对于修习教法（*chos*）没有什么兴趣……” [③] 苯教徒们抓住了这一机会，试图通过为他的父亲举行葬礼，将他们的教法重新凌驾于佛教之上。然而，他（牟尼赞普）又详细叙述了一个梦境，在梦里他看见赤松德赞与毗卢遮那（Śrī Vairocana）、金刚手（Vajrapāṇi）以及文殊（Mañjuśrī Kumārabhūta）一起坐在阿孥迦婆底天（Aḍakavatī），教授经论中的教法。牟尼赞普说：“如果将这一预言性的梦境与我父亲神子（*devaputra*）的葬礼联系起来，那么其按照苯教的方式来完成是不合适的，因为必须按照〔佛教〕白法（*dkar chos*）的方式来完成。” [④] 他命令召开会议来决定这件事，而巴阁 · 毗卢遮那（Pa gor Vairocana）最终为佛教徒赢得了胜利（见 Dotson 2013，第 70—75 页）。正如《生死轮回故事》中释迦牟尼建议仁钦念诵《尊胜佛母陀罗尼》以对治死亡，《施食史》结尾是这样写的：

---

① *dBa’ bzhed* 26a2—31b6；见 Pasang Wangdu and Diemberger 2000，第 92—105 页。Zeff Bjerken（2005）亦指出了这一文本、《生死轮回故事》以及《净治一切恶趣密续》之间的关联。

② 或许此处将牟尼赞普与牟如赞普（Mu rug，800—约 802 年在位，804 年薨）相混淆了。牟尼赞普（797—798 年在位）似乎于 798 年先其父薨逝；见 Dotson 2009，第 143 页。

③ 翻译遵从 Pasang Wangdu and Diemberger 2000，第 95 页。*dBa’ bzhed* 26a2—3：// rta’i lo’i dpyid zla ra ba’i ngo la btsan po khri srong lde btsan ’das/ sras mu ne btsan po ni sku chungs/ chos spyod pa la dga’ ba’ang nyung ste/

④ *dBa’ bzhed* 26a8：mtshan ltas ’di dang sbyar na lha sras yab kyi ’dad ni bon du byar mi rung gi/ dkar chosu bya dgos pas...

此后，葬仪均依照《净治恶趣密续》，依照普明佛（Vairocana）和九顶髻〔佛〕的坛城来执行。从那以后，所有的葬仪都依照佛法仪轨来执行……此外，愚蠢的苯教修习者们埋藏了很多〔死者〕的财物，佛教传承（*lugs*）的大师们知道这样做有百害而无一利，有鉴于此，他们制定了〔向死者〕施食（*zas gtad*）的仪轨。《施食史》竟。①

根据《施食史》这一附录的叙述，佛教系统的葬仪是依照《净治恶趣密续》，其实践则基于普明（*sarvavid*）毗卢遮那佛坛城。此外，这些葬仪是优于非佛教（在这里指“苯教”）葬仪的，特别是在赤松德赞葬仪的执行上。因此，看起来后来对于赞普的佛教化历史叙事中对于亡者祈祷文的描述来自祈祷文本身。就此而言，它们可以说是对敦煌 *rGyud chags gsum* 祈祷文所呈现的这种祈祷文历史编纂学（devotional historiography）的一种继承。

参考文献

藏文材料：

dBa’ bzhed: 2000. “dba’ bzhed.” In: Pasang Wangdu, and Hildegard Diemberger (eds.), *Dba’ bzhed: The Royal Narrative Concerning the Bringing of the Buddha’s Doctrine to Tibet*. Wien: Verlag der Österreichischen Akademie der Wissenschaften, 123–156.

sBa bzhed G: mGon po rgyal mtshan (ed.) 1980/1982. *sBa bzhed: sba bzhed ces bya ba las sba gsal snang gi bzhed pa bzhugs*. Beijing: Mi rigs dpe skrun khang.

sBa bzhed P: verbatim quotes contained in dPa’ bo gTsug lag phreng ba. 2002. *Chos ’byung mkhas pa’i dga’ ston*. Varanasi: Vajra Vidya.

sBa bzhed S: 1961. “btsan po khri srong lde btsan dang mkhan po slob dpon padma’i dus mdo sngags so sor mdzad pa’i sba bzhed zhabs btags ma.” In: R. A. Stein (ed.), *Une Chronique ancienne de bSam-yas: sBa-bźed*. Paris: Adrien-Maisonneuve, 1–92.

KGT: dPa’ bo gTsug lag phreng ba. 2002. *Chos ’byung mkhas pa’i dga’ ston*. Varanasi: Vajra Vidya.

Mes dbon gsum gyi rnam par thar pa: “mi rje lhas mdzad byang chub sems dpa’ sems dpa’ chen po chos rgyal mes dbon rnam gsum gyi rnam par thar pa rin po che’i phreng ba.” In: *Rin chen gter mdzod chen po’i rgyab chos collected by Dingo Chentse Rinpoche*, 1980. Paro: Ugyan Tempai

① dBa’ bzhed 31b2—6：de nas phyis ngan song sbyong rgyud la brten nas kun rig dang gtsug tor dgu’i dkyil ’khor la brten nas shid rnaMs byas so// grir shi ba la khro bo nyi ma’i dkyil ’khor la brten nas shid byas/ de’i gtad yar dang ! gri ’dul laswo pa rnaMs mdo sde’i khungs dang sbyar nas mdzad/ dus de nas shid thaMd chos lugs su byed pa byung ste/ de yang bon lugs glen pa dag nor longs spyod mang po gter du sbed pa yod skad/ de ni god che la phan chung bar dgongs nas chos lugs mkhas pa dag gis zas gtad kyi phyag bzhes ’di mdzad skad do// zas gtad kyi lo rgyus rdzogs+ho//

Gyaltsen, vol. 7.

sMon lam chen mo: Bokar Rinpoché (ed.) 2004. *Zhal 'don gces btus / dbu lags so / / 'gro mgon bka' brgyud pa'i dge 'dun smon lam /*. Dharamsala: Dhorphen.

MTNd: *Chos 'byung me tog snying po sbrang rtsi'i bcud*. Lhasa: Bod ljongs mi dmangs dpe skrun khang.

其他文字材料：

Bjerken, Zeff. 2005. "Of Mandalas, Monarchs, and Mortuary Magic: Siting the Sarvadurgatipariśodhana Tantra in Tibet." *Journal of the American Academy of Religion* 73 (3): 813–841.

Chen, Huaiyu. 2014. "Multiple Traditions of One Ritual: A Reading of the Lantern-Lighting Prayers in Dunhuang Manuscripts." In: Tansen Sen (ed.), *Buddhism Across Asia: Networks of Material, Intellectual and Cultural Exchange*. Singapore: Institute for Southeast Asian Studies, 233–257.

Dalton, Jacob P. 2011. *The Taming of the Demons: Violence and Liberation in Tibetan Buddhism*. London: Yale University Press.

Dalton, Jacob P. 2016. "How Dhāranīs WERE Proto-Tantric: Liturgies, Ritual Manuals, and the Origins of the Tantras." In: David B. Gray, and Ryan Richard Overby (eds.), *Tantric Traditions in Transmission and Translation*. Oxford: Oxford University Press, 199–229.

Dalton, Jacob, and Sam van Schaik. 2006. *Tibetan Tantric Manuscripts from Dunhuang: A Descriptive Catalogue of the Stein Collection at the British Library*. Leiden: Brill.

Doney, Lewis. 2013a. "Nyang ral Nyi ma 'od zer and the Testimony of Ba." *Bulletin of Tibetology* 49 (1): 7–38.

Doney, Lewis. 2013b. "Emperor, Dharmaraja, Bodhisattva? Inscriptions from the Reign of Khri Srong lde brtsan." *Journal of Research Institute, Kobe City University of Foreign Studies* 51: 63–84.

Doney, Lewis. 2014. *The Zangs gling ma: The First Padmasambhava Biography. Two Exemplars of the Earliest Attested Recension*. Andiast: International Institute for Tibetan and Buddhist Studies.

Doney, Lewis. 2015. "Early Bodhisattva-Kingship in Tibet: The Case of Tri Songdétsen." *Cahiers d'Extême Asie* 24: 29–47.

Doney, Lewis. 2017. "Narrative Transformations: The Spiritual Friends of Khri Srong lde brtsan." In: Eva Allinger et al (eds.), *Interaction in the Himalayas and Central Asia: Processes of Transfer, Translation and Transformation in Art, Archaeology, Religion and Polity*. Vienna: Verlag der Österreichischen Akademie der Wissenschaften (Austrian Academy of Sciences Press), 311–320.

Doney, Lewis. forthcoming. "Temple Bells from the Tibetan Imperial Period: Buddhist Material Culture in Context." In: Elizabeth Cecil, and Lucas den Boer (eds.), *Comparisons Across Time and Space: Papers from the Seventh Leiden Asian Studies Symposium*. Berlin: De Gruyter.

Dotson, Brandon. 2007. "'Emperor' Mu-rug-brtsan and the 'Phang thang ma Catalogue." *Journal of the International Association for Tibetan Studies* 3: 1–25.

Dotson, Brandon. 2009. *The Old Tibetan Annals: An Annotated Translation of Tibet's First History, With an Annotated Cartographical Documentation by Guntram Hazod*. Wien: Verlag der Österreichischen Akademie der Wissenschaften.

Dotson, Brandon. 2013. "The Dead and Their Stories: Preliminary Remarks on the Place of Narrative in Tibetan Religion." In: Christoph Cüppers et al (eds.), *Tibet after Empire: Culture, Society and Religion between 850–1000*. Lumbini: Lumbini International Research Institute, 51–83.

Dotson, Brandon, and Lewis Doney. forthcoming. "A Study of the Tibetan Aparimitāyur-nama mahāyāna-sūtras kept in the British Library in cooperation with Dongzhi Duojie."

Flügel, Peter. 2010. "The Jaina Cult of Relic Stūpas." *Numen* 57 (3): 389–504.

Hill, Nathan. 2013. "'Come as lord of the black-headed'–an Old Tibetan mythic formula." In: Christoph Cüppers et al (eds.), *Tibet after Empire: Culture, Society and Religion between 850–1000*. Lumbini: Lumbini International Research Institute, 169–180.

Hill, Nathan. 2015. "The sku bla Rite in Imperial Tibetan Religion." *Cahiers d'Extême Asie* 24: 29–47.

Huang, Weizhong 黄维忠. 2007a. "Dunhuang zangwen fayuanwen yanjiu zongshu 敦煌藏文发愿文研究综述" [A Summary of Dunhuang Literature.]. *Dunhuangxue jikan* 敦煌学辑刊 [Journal of Dunhuang Studies] 1: 29–39.

Huang, Weizhong 黄维忠. 2007b. *Ba zhi jiu shiji zangwen fayuanwen yanjiu: yi Dunhuang zangwen fayuanwen wei zhongxin* 8—9 世纪藏文发愿文研究：以敦煌藏文发愿文为中心 [A Study on Tibetan Prayers from the Eighth and Ninth Centuries: With Special Attention to the Tibetan Prayers from Dunhuang]. Beijing 北京 : Minzu chubanshe 民族出版社.

Imaeda, Yoshiro. 1981. *Histoire du cycle de la naissance et de la mort. Étude d'un texte tibétain de Touen-houang*. Geneva, Paris: Librairie Droz.

Imaeda, Yoshiro. 2007. "The History of the Cycle of Birth and Death: a Tibetan narrative from Dunhuang." In: Matthew T. Kapstein and Brandon Dotson (eds.), *Contributions to the Cultural History of Early Tibet*. Leiden: Brill, 105–181.

Iwao, Kazushi. 2012. "The Purpose of Sutra Copying in Dunhuang under the Tibetan Rule."

In: Irina Popova, and Liu Yi. St (eds.), *Dunhuang Studies: Prospects and Problems for the Coming Second Century of Research*. Petersburg: Slavia. 102–05.

Iwao, Kazushi et al. (eds.). 2009. *Old Tibetan Inscriptions: Old Tibetan Documents Online Monograph Series*, 2. Tokyo: Research Institute for Languages and Cultures of Asia and Africa.

Iwao, Kazushi et al. (eds.). 2012. *Old Tibetan Texts in the Stein Collection Or.8210*. Tokyo: Toyo Bunko.

Kapstein, Matthew T. 2000. *The Tibetan Assimilation of Buddhism: Conversion, Contestation, and Memory*. Oxford: Oxford University Press.

Kapstein, Matthew T. 2004. "The Treaty Temple of De ga g.Yu tshal: Iconography and Identification." In: Huo Wei 霍巍 (ed.), *Essays on the International Conference on Tibetan Archaeology and Art*. Chengdu 成都 : Sichuan Renmin Chubanshe 四川人民出版社 , 98–127.

Kapstein, Matthew T. 2009. "The Treaty Temple of the Turquoise Grove." In: Matthew T. Kapstein (ed.), *Buddhism Between Tibet and Rgya*. Boston: Wisdom. 21–72.

Kapstein, Matthew T. forthcoming. "The Treaty Temple of De ga g.yu tshal: Reconsiderations." *Journal of Tibetan Studies* (Sichuan University) 10: 32–47.

Karmay, Samten Gyaltsen. 1988. *The Great Perfection (Rdzogs Chen): A Philosophical and Meditative Teaching of Tibetan Buddhism*. Leiden: Brill.

Karmay, Samten Gyaltsen. 2003. "King Lang Darma and his Rule." In: Alex McKay (ed.), *Tibet and Her Neighbours. A History*. London: Edition Hansjörg Mayer, 57–68.

Kilty, Gavin (trans.) 2010. *The Mirror of Beryl: A Historical Introduction to Tibetan Medicine by Desi Sangyé Gyatso*. Somerville MA: Wisdom.

Kuo, Li ying. 1994. *Confession et contrition dans le bouddhisme chinois du Ve au Xe siècle*. Paris: Publications de l'École Française d'Extrême-Orient.

Lalou, Marcelle. 1950. *Inventaire des manuscrits tibétains de Touen-houang conservés à la Bibliothèque Nationale (Fonds Pelliot tibétain) Nos 850–1282*, Volume 2. Paris: Bibliothèque Nationale.

Li, Fang-Kuei, and W. South Coblin. 1987. *A Study of the Old Tibetan Inscriptions*. Taipei: Institute of History and Philology, Academica Sinica.

Macdonald, Ariane, and Imaeda Yoshiro. 1978–1979. *Choix de Documents tibétains conservés à la Bibliothèque nationale complété par quelques manuscrits de l'India Office et du British Museum*. Vols. 1–2. Paris: Bibliothèque nationale.

Osto, Douglas. 2010. "A New Translation of the Sanskrit Bhadracarī with Introduction and Notes." *New Zealand Journal of Asian Studies* 12 (2): 1–21.

Pasang Wangdu, and Hildegard Diemberger. 2000. *Dba' bzhed: The Royal Narrative Concerning the Bringing of the Buddha's Doctrine to Tibet*. Wien: Verlag der Österreichischen Akademie der Wissenschaften.

Payne, Richard K., and Charles D. Orzech. 2011. "Homa." In: Charles D. Orzech et al (eds.), *Esoteric Buddhism and the Tantras in East Asia*. Leiden: Brill, 133–140.

Richardson, Hugh Edward. 1949. "Three Ancient Inscriptions from Tibet." *Journal of the Royal Asiatic Society of Bengal* 15: 45–64.

Richardson, Hugh Edward. 1977. "'The Dharma that Came Down from Heaven': A Tunhuang Fragment." In: Leslie S. Kawamura, and Keith Scott. Emeryville (eds.), *Buddhist Thought and Asian Civilization: Essays in Honor of Herbert V Guenther on his Sixtieth Birthday*. CA: Dharma Publishing, 219–229.

Richardson, Hugh Edward. 1985. *A Corpus of Early Tibetan Inscriptions*. London: Royal Asiatic Society.

Richardson, Hugh Edward. 1988. "The Succession to Glang Darma." In: Gherardo Gnoli, and Lionello Lanciotti (eds.), *Orientalia Iosephi Tucci Memoriae Dicata*. Roma: Serie Orientale, 1221–1229.

Richardson, Hugh Edward. 1992. "Mention of Tibetan Kings in Some Documents From Tunhuang." *Bulletin of Tibetology* new ser. 2: 5–10.

Richardson, Hugh Edward. 1998 [1980]. "The First Tibetan chos-'byung." In: Michael Aris (eds.), *High Peaks Pure Earth*. London: Serindia, 89–99.

Schaeffer, Kurtis R., Matthew T. Kapstein, and Gray Tuttle (eds.). 2013. *Sources of Tibetan Tradition*. New York: Columbia University Press.

Schaik, Sam van. 2013. "The Naming of the Tibetan Religion: Bon and Chos in the Tibetan Imperial Period." *Journal of the International Association for Bon Research* 1: 227–257.

Schaik, Sam van, and Lewis Doney. 2007. "The Prayer, the Priest and the Tsenpo: An Early Buddhist Narrative from Dunhuang." *Journal of the International Association of Buddhist Studies* 30 (1–2): 175–218.

Scherrer-Schaub, Cristina A. 1999–2000. "Prière pour un apostat: Fragments d'histoire tibétaine." *Cahiers d'Extrême-Asie* 11: 217–246.

Scherrer-Schaub, Cristina A. 2002. "Enacting Words: A Diplomatic Analysis of the Imperial Decrees (bkas bcad) and their Application in the sGra sbyor bam po gnyis pa Tradition." *Journal of the International Association of Buddhist Studies* 25 (1–2): 263–340.

Scherrer-Schaub, Cristina A. 2012. "Tibet: An Archæology of the Written." In: Cristina A.

Sherrer Schaub (ed.), *Old Tibetan Studies: Dedicated to the Memory of R. E. Emmerick. Proceedings of the Tenth Seminar of the International Association for Tibetan Studies, 2003*. Leiden: Brill, 217–254.

Scherrer-Schaub, Cristina A. 2014. "A Perusal of Early Tibetan Inscriptions in Light of the Buddhist World of the 7th to 9th Centuries A.D." In: Kurt Tropper (ed.), *Epigraphic Evidence in the Pre-Modern Buddhist World. Proceedings of the Eponymous Conference Held in Vienna, 14–15 Oct. 2011*. Wien: Arbeitskreis für Tibetische und Buddhistische Studien Universität Wien, 117–165.

Schopen, Gregory. 1997. *Bones, Stones, and Buddhist Monks. Collected Papers on Archaeology, Epigraphy, and Texts of Monastic Buddhism in India*. Honolulu: University of Hawaii Press.

Schopen, Gregory. 2010. "On Incompetent Monks and Able Urbane Nuns in a Buddhist Monastic Code." *Journal of Indian Philosophy* 38: 107–131.

Sernesi, Marta. 2014. "A Prayer to the Complete Liberation of Mi la ras pa." In: Stephan Conermann, and Jim Rheingans (eds), *Narrative Pattern and Genre in Hagiographic Life Writing: Comparative Perspectives from Asia to Europe*. Berlin: EB Verlag, 141–185.

Simon, Walter. 1957. "A Chinese Prayer in Tibetan Script." *Sino-Indian Studies* 5 (3–4): 192–199.

Snellgrove, David L. 1987. *Indo-Tibetan Buddhism: Indian Buddhists and their Tibetan Successors*. London: Serindia.

Sørensen, Per K. 1994. *Tibetan Buddhist Historiography: The Mirror Illuminating the Royal Genealogies. An Annotated Translation of the XIVth Century Tibetan Chronicle Rgyal-rabs Gsal-ba'i Me-long*. Wiesbaden: Harrassowitz.

Stein, R. A. 1985. "Tibetica Antiqua III: à propos du mot gcug-lag et de la religion indigène." *Bulletin de l'École Française d'Extrême-Orient* 74: 83–133.

Takeuchi, Tsuguhito. 1998. *Old Tibetan Manuscripts from East Turkestan in The Stein Collection of the British Library*, Vol. 2. London: British Library Press.

Thomas, Frederick William. 1935. *Tibetan Literary Texts and Documents Concerning Chinese Turkestan*, Vol. 1. London: Luzac & Co.

Thomas, Frederick William. 1951. *Tibetan Literary Texts and Documents Concerning Chinese Turkestan*, Vol. 2. London: Luzac & Co.

Tucci, Giuseppe. 1950. *The Tombs of the Tibetan Kings*. Rome: Serie Orientale.

Uebach, Helga. 1990. "On Dharma-Colleges and Their Teachers in the Ninth Century Tibetan Empire." In: Paolo Daffina (ed.), *Studi in Onore di Luciano Petech*. Roma: Bardi Editore, 393–417.

Uebach, Helga. 2010. "Notes on the Palaeography of the Old Tibetan Inscriptions: Zhol and bSam yas." In: Anne Chayet et al (eds.), *Édition, éditions: l'écrit au Tibet, évolution et devenir*. Munich: Indus Verlag, 411–428.

de la Vallée Poussin, Louis. 1962. *Catalogue of the Tibetan Manuscripts from Tun-Huang in the India Office Library (entries 333 to 765)*. Oxford: Oxford University Press.

Walter, Michael L. 2009. *Buddhism and Empire: The Political and Religious Culture of Early Tibet*. Leiden: Brill.

Walter, Michael L. 2013. "Analysis of PT016/IO751: Language and Culture of a Dunhuang Document, Part One." In: Christoph Cüppers et al (eds.), *Tibet after Empire: Culture, Society and Religion between 850–1000*. Lumbini: Lumbini International Research Institute, 417–440.

Willis, Michael. 2013. "From World Religion to World Dominion: Trading, Translation and Institution-building in Tibet." In: Peter Wick, and Volker Rabans (eds.), *"Trading Religions": Religious Formation, Transformation and Cultural Exchange between East and West*. Bochum, Germany: Ruhr-Universität, 141–157.

Xuanhua. 1982. *The Great Means Expansive Buddha Flower Adornment Sutra*, Vol. 40. Talmage, Calif: Dharma Realm Buddhist University & International Institute for the Translation of Buddhist Texts.

Yamaguchi, Zuihō. 1996. "The Fiction of King Dar-Ma's Persecution of Buddhism." In: Jean-Pierre Drège (ed.), *De Dunhuang au Japon–Études chinoises et bouddhiques offertes à Michel Soymié*. Genève: Droz, 231–258.

Yönten, Damchö. 1996. *Ganden Lha Gye: The Guru Yoga of Lama Tsong Khapa*. Bedminster, Bristol: Dharma Therapy Trust.

Zhang, Yisun 张怡荪 et al. 1993 [1985]. *Bod rgya tshig mdzod chen mo/ Zang-Han dacidian* 藏汉大辞典. 3 vols. Beijing 北京: Mi rigs dpe skrun khang.

汉藏佛教文献与艺术

经典、文本、写本

——佛教文献的三个层次*

圣　凯
清华大学人文学院哲学系

经典作为佛陀说法的记录文本，既有佛教“神圣”意义的价值与智慧，又有佛陀乃至高僧说法时对印度、中国社会的批判与开示，更有经典流传区域的历史背景。体现在佛教徒的宗教经验当中，一方面是经典的契入与证悟，即是永恒价值的认同与正觉智慧的体证；另一方面是生活的实践与心性的转化，即是佛教徒在生活中不断思维经典价值与智慧，从而实现心性的不断转化与提升。所以，佛教经典是宗教经验的“圣典”，也是历史的“文化文本”，更是思想的“观念文本”。[①]进而，随着经典的翻译与传播，出现了大量抄写经典的“写本”，但在既有的研究中，往往将写本作为史料应用，并未赋予其宗教学意义上的地位，亦忽视了其社会学意义上的大众传播功能。基于此，本文认为，如何认识经典、文本、写本的内涵与关系，是写本研究、文献学、思想史、宗教史的重要问题。

一、经典与文本

佛教经典作为宗教经典，从印度翻译到中国，既有佛陀精神的传承、印度文明的传播，又有中国译经师的创造性转化，更有中国高僧讲经注释的创新性发展。作为“文化文本”的

---

*　本文为2017年度国家社会科学基金重大项目“汉传佛教僧众社会生活史”（17ZDA233）阶段性成果。

①　基督教释经学的发展也基于圣经的内在张力。圣经是属神的话语，但它却以属人的形式降临到人类面前。神的命令是绝对的，但它却在多变的历史背景中写成，让人难以捉摸它们如何可以成为普遍的基准。见W.W.克莱恩、C.L.布鲁姆伯格、R.L.哈伯德著，尹妙珍等译：《基督教释经学》，上海人民出版社2011年版，第1页。

佛教经典，涉及经典的语言、结集、翻译、保存、印刷等，文献学与历史考证学方法可以适用于对其的研究。此时，文献学、历史考证学作为一种“理性化”的活动，是一种完全排除个人主观情绪与意愿的纯然客观冷静的理智探究，完全不涉及道德的理想或目的。[①]但是作为“圣典”和“观念文本”的佛教经典，关切信仰与思想，包含着基于信仰的内在激情、生命体验与情感，这些方面必须得到重视。

第一，经典所承载的观念世界并不都是“佛陀说”，也记录了后代佛教徒的宗教经验。换言之，经典的“佛说”是群体观念的呈现，而非纯粹的“释迦佛说”。由此，具有永恒价值和意义的“圣典”与寄托着宗教经验的“观念文本”一起构成了“叠加型”的混合观念世界。在此基础上，从观念史的角度探讨“佛说”，是理解与阐释经典的起点。

公元前5、6世纪，佛陀在恒河两岸随缘教化，既无著书立说，其佛弟子亦未记录，故无手稿或刊本流传于世。佛陀的“言教”、制定的生活轨范，通过佛弟子的回忆、结集、口口相传而留了下来。因此，早期佛教公认佛法并不限于佛说。《大智度论》卷二说：“佛法有五种人说：一者，佛自口说；二者，佛弟子说；三者，仙人说；四者，诸天说；五者，化人说。”[②]亦即是说，在家、出家的佛弟子，依佛的教导而修证，证入佛陀自证的境地，本着自己的理解与体验，或用语言、文字表示自己的悟解，或为了化导而自我表达，都是佛法。根源于佛陀而表现于世间的，不只是佛的身、口、意三业德用，也是佛弟子们的清净三业。佛法不是抽象的、疏离于世间的，而是具体的、充实于人之生活的。以佛陀为根本，以僧伽为中心，统摄七众弟子，而展开觉化、净化人间的救世大业，这就是用文句集成圣典的来源。[③]

“如是我闻，一时”体现出“圣典”的历时性特质，是一种佛陀永恒智慧与真理教化、佛弟子体悟的宗教经验不断“叠加”而形成的“观念文本”。对于后代佛弟子而言，听闻释尊法音的同时，也能保有从释尊而来的真正传统的信念，并以此信念作为修道的依据。[④]作为群体经验的共同结晶——“圣典”，圣典的“佛说”意味着经典的神圣性与作为宗教经验的历史性同时存在，即“文化文本”和“观念文本”之间并无任何矛盾，二者不过是“圣典”的不同层面。若按线性的叙述方式，只承认释迦佛所说的教法才是真正的“圣典”，就违背了佛教作为一个历史性的宗教的特性。

若将“圣典”阐释为群体经验，就能解释“大乘是佛说”。下田正弘在研究《涅槃经》

---

① 吴汝钧：《佛学研究方法论》，台湾学生书局1983年版，第103页。

② 龙树菩萨著，鸠摩罗什译：《大智度论》卷二，收入高楠顺次郎、渡边海旭、小野玄妙《大正新修大藏经》第25册，第66页中。

③ 印顺：《原始佛教圣典之集成》，正闻出版社1991年版，第8—9页。

④ 山口益等：《印度圣典的成立及其传播》，收入一平译《佛典研究》（初编），华宇出版社1988年版，第3页。

时，强调部派佛教与大乘佛教的连续性、社会背景研究与思想研究的连接点等。[①] 从经典的成立史来说，佛法思想的发展分化源于理论和实践两大层面，如以修定为修心，引出“心性本净”。《大般若经》卷三十六说：“是心非心，本性净故……于一切法无变异、无分别，是名心非心性。”[②]《般若经》从甚深般若慧的立场，引部派异论的“心性本净”，化为一切法空性的异名，是从修行甚深观慧而来的。[③] 瑜伽行派的唯识思想也是依定境而理解、解释出来的。《解深密经》卷三说：

> 诸毗钵舍那三摩地所行影像，彼与此心当言有异？当言无异？佛告慈氏菩萨曰：善男子！当言无异。何以故？由彼影像唯是识故。善男子！我说识所缘，唯识所现故。世尊！若彼所行影像即与此心无有异者，云何此心还见此心？善男子！此中无有少法能见少法，然即此心如是生时，即有如是影像显现。[④]

瑜伽师通过观行的定境，观察定中影像境界皆为识所缘，从而悟到唯识的道理，并进而发展为认识论意义上的唯识思想。所以“心性本净”的《般若经》、如来藏经典系统，“唯识所现”的瑜伽行派，皆是由修定修心而引出的。[⑤]

可见，要从佛教徒的宗教实践与体验视角，去理解佛教思想体系的变化。同时，大乘经典的历史性并不影响它作为“圣典”的神圣性，二者是缘起的“叠加”。

第二，经典“叠加”着历史与观念。经典作为“文本”，既是一种知识载体，也是一个历时性的传承过程。因此，可以将经典的传播视作一个文化过程，一个文本不断与社会环境、思想氛围等融会的过程。一方面，佛教观念体系具有相对稳定性，标准一致而且数量庞大的藏经汇集并固化了佛教经典传播、注释等有关活动和观念，是佛教徒观念世界最稳定的资源，代代传承；另一方面，在口传、书写、传播、翻译、注释等过程中，经典的价值和意义不断重现，也不断地“叠加”更多的背景与历史信息。因此，文本的稳定性与历史的变动性相结合，大大凸显了佛教经典作为“文化文本”的文化史意义；文本与历史的相互结合，既激活了文本，也刷新了历史。

重视文本的历史性是非常重要的，对于中国佛教来说尤其如此。中国佛教一直依赖佛

---

① 下田正弘：『涅槃経の研究：大乗経典の研究方法試論』，春秋社 2000 年版，第 49 页。

②《大般若波罗蜜多经》卷三十六，收入高楠顺次郎、渡边海旭、小野玄妙《大正新修大藏经》第 5 册，第 202 页上。

③ 印顺：《修定——修心与唯心、秘密乘》，收入氏著《华雨集》第 3 册，正闻出版社 1993 年版，第 159—1160 页。

④《解深密经》卷三，收入高楠顺次郎、渡边海旭、小野玄妙《大正新修大藏经》第 16 册，第 698 页上—中。

⑤ 印顺：《修定——修心与唯心、秘密乘》，收入氏著《华雨集》第 3 册，第 167 页。

教典籍的传入和翻译来理解印度佛教，所以许多印度佛教史著作的叙述方法是基于经典的思想史，抽空了社会环境因素，缺乏印度佛教僧团的现实关切。即便在法显《佛国记》、玄奘《大唐西域记》、义净《南海寄归内法传》中都有对印度佛教现实情况的部分描述，但是大乘佛教只是作为经典传统而存在，传播范围非常有限，教团行持仍然是声闻律传统。如南朝梁陈时期翻译家真谛的出生地为优禅尼国，《历代三宝记》卷十一载："西天竺优禅尼（Ujjayanī、Ujjainī）国三藏法师波罗末陀（Paramārtha），梁言真谛。"①《续高僧传·拘那罗陀传》也载："拘那罗陀，陈言亲依；或云波罗末陀，译云真谛，并梵文之名字也。本西天竺优禅尼国人焉。"②优禅尼国即玄奘《大唐西域记》中提到的"邬阇衍那国"③。真谛所游历的诸国，尤其是以邬阇衍那为中心的西印度，正是正量部的弘化区域。同时，真谛所翻译的典籍中，除了瑜伽行派以外，还出现多部正量部的著作，如《律二十二明了论》《立世阿毗昙论》等正量部论书。所以真谛所属部派应为正量部。④真谛作为世亲《摄大乘论释》的翻译家、摄论学派的创始人，其僧团传统仍然是正量部。

当"圣典"被抽象为文本，只剩下语言、文句乃至思想的探讨，而不重视其背后的历史和社会背景，则会离佛教徒的经验感越来越远。具有讽刺意味的是，翻译家、注释家的出身、立场，尤其是其身份归属、价值立场、思想侧重点等，实际上也会对他们的行动，即对圣典的翻译、解释等产生影响。圣典不能抽离其历史环境，由此可见一斑。

第三，经典的形成不仅源于翻译，本土撰著也不能忽视。如果仅以"翻译标准"确定"经典"，"经典"就会成为客观的历史文献，其思想观念的价值、文明影响力将无法彰显。而如果把"经典"的意义界定拓展到文化价值与影响力，而非将"佛说"局限于"来自印度的翻译"。那么，隋唐以后盛行至今、具有广泛影响力的佛教典籍，如《肇论》《六祖坛经》《宗镜录》《楞严经》《大乘起信论》等大量中国佛教典籍，将不仅具有汉传佛教史上的举足轻重的历史文化意义，而且具有佛教经典的地位。其意义将进一步被发掘，即"经典"作为"圣典"的文本、观念文本意义，在"同情理解""心性体会"的研究价值关怀下，值得佛学研究审视、反思与批判。

与此相关的一个重要问题是经典的"真"与"伪"，涉及经典的身份、内容与翻译等标

① 费长房：《历代三宝记》卷十一，收入高楠顺次郎、渡边海旭、小野玄妙《大正新修大藏经》第49卷，第99页上。

② 道宣：《续高僧传》，收入高楠顺次郎、渡边海旭、小野玄妙《大正新修大藏经》第50卷，第429页下。

③ 玄奘：《大唐西域记》卷十一，收入高楠顺次郎、渡边海旭、小野玄妙《大正新修大藏经》第51卷，第936页下—937页上。

④ 圣凯：《真谛三藏与"正量部"研究》，《华东师范大学学报》（哲学社会科学版）2018年第2期，第46—53页。

准。[1]如智昇《开元释教录》卷十八说：

> 伪经者，邪见所造，以乱真经者也。自大师韬影，向二千年。魔教竞兴，正法衰损。自有顽愚之辈，恶见迷心，伪造诸经，诳惑流俗，邪言乱正，可不哀哉。今恐真伪相参，是非一概。譬夫昆山宝玉与瓦石而同流，赡部真金共铅铁而齐价。今为件别，真伪可分。庶泾渭殊流，无贻后患。[2]

智昇遵循翻译标准，强调印度传入的佛经均属“真经”。因此翻译的佛典是真的，而未经过翻译，中国人自己撰著的典籍，自然够不上经典的资格。这种“真”“伪”观念的背后折射的是智昇对内容和翻译等的评判标准，虽然具有文化和历史意义，但更涉及信仰的正统性等价值与观念。

第四，经典的解释与实践是一体的。根据契理契机的法则，作为佛教神圣与智慧依据的经典文本，必须经过解释与转化，即开示经典的价值与智慧、剖析经典的历史传统、反观生活世界，才能进入时代的观念世界。所以，经典解释是经典进入生活、神圣契入世俗、义理指导实践的重要过程，是印度、中国两种文明的互鉴、融合、汇通的过程，也是中国佛教徒对两种文明的浸润、批判、反思的过程，即文明融合、汇通的过程。

在佛学体系里，从思想到观念，观念到伦理，伦理到社会，存在着一个演进的过程。如北朝佛教的“业”观念，净影慧远《大乘义章》认为“诸业义”共有身等三业、三性业、三受报业、三界系业、三时报业、曲秽浊三业、黑白等四业、五逆业、六业、七不善律仪、八种语、九业、十不善业道、十四垢业、十六恶律仪、饮酒三十五失等十六门[3]，详细论述有关业的教理观念体系。但最重要的还是当时社会大众形成了怎样的“业”观念，所以需要关注具有社会实践意义的造像题记等材料。产生于某一时刻的“术语”进入历史后，经过后代的不断重复而得以延续，并在延续中逐渐产生出指导、促成行动的力量。

文化与社会、经济相关，但并不从属于社会和经济，作为文化的观念具有独立性与能动性。人们的活动总是基于特定的观念、情感与心态进行的，从另一个方向上来看，通过人的行动，得以在实践层面上完成社会内容的建构与意义的重建。这就突破了原先仅仅考察观念演变的研究范式，将观念置入“社会”这一语境之中。而要看到这种文化

---

① 方广锠提出疑伪经的确立，涉及身份标准、内容标准与翻译标准。见方广锠：《从“文化汇流”谈中国佛教史上的疑伪经现象》，收入方广锠主编《佛教文献研究》，广西师范大学出版社2016年版，第一辑，第27—35页。

② 智昇：《开元释教录》卷十八，收入高楠顺次郎、渡边海旭、小野玄妙《大正新修大藏经》第55册，第672页上。

③ 净影慧远：《大乘义章》卷七，收入高楠顺次郎、渡边海旭、小野玄妙《大正新修大藏经》第44册，第597页下—598页上。

的能动性，需要重新思考社会组织的动力与要素，考察在一个社会被组织成为某种特定社会样式的过程中观念所发挥的作用。例如，僧团、社邑乃至今天的佛教居士林等组织，其存在既基于宗教的信仰、传统的传承，也有组织成员的献身精神，更有政治、经济等现实推动力。“观念”与“社会”之间既相互独立，也相互渗透，显示出独立而又相关的叠加感。

所以，经典作为文本，既是具有神圣价值的“圣典”，也是众多观念汇聚的“观念文本”，更是历史的“文化文本”。离开文明的历史、神圣价值，经典作为纯粹的“文本”，将失去其真正的意义。

二、文本与写本

在中国佛教史上，尽管存在单纯强调“文本”作为价值的一面，并导致历史的“消失”，但当进入“写本”时代，经典就重新被灌注了全新的历史意义。通过抄写、雕刻、印刷等形式，“写本”形成了全新的“文本”，但是，写本的“圣典”价值、思想观念等往往成为隐身在“写本”后面的背景，被研究者所忽略。

方广锠在考察汉文大藏经演化的因素时，强调了中国佛教发展、封建王朝的影响、编纂人员、体裁与制作方式、装帧形式等五大因素。[①] 所以“写本”研究不仅涉及写本的历史和社会背景，而且涉及写本的形式。同时，方广锠概括了写本大藏经的基本特点：

> 写本藏经由人工书写修造。这一制作方式，决定了写本藏经的基本特点——唯一性。所谓“唯一性”，是指所写造的任何一部藏经，乃至任何一卷写经，都是唯一的……不同的人抄写的同一部经，乃至同一人先后抄写的同一卷经，相互之间都会有或多或少的差异。从而就某一部经典，乃至就大藏经总体而言，又显示出另一种特性，即形态的不确定性，或称流变性。唯一性与流变性互为表里，成为写本大藏经的基本特点。[②]

唯一性与流变性的产生，实际上是因为经典抄写作为“行动”是不可重复的，这与经典产生的那“一时”具有同等意义。而写本研究的最大冲动，无非是想复原和回到抄写的那

① 方广锠：《中国写本大藏经研究》，上海古籍出版社 2006 年，第 11—13 页。
② 方广锠：《中国写本大藏经研究》，第 25 页。

“一时”，呈现抄经时的观念世界、组织制度、抄经流程乃至纸张、装帧等。唐代道世《法苑珠林》卷十七《敬法篇》阐释了抄经态度与福报之间的关系：

> 纵有抄写，心不至殷，既不护净，又多舛错。共同止宿，或处在门檐，风雨虫宇都无惊惧，致使经无灵验之功，诵无救苦之益。实由造作不殷，亦由我人逾慢也。故《敬福经》云：善男子！经生之法，不得颠倒，一字重点，五百世中堕迷惑道中，不闻正法。[①]

抄经既是宗教性活动，也是一种文化活动；于是，生活世界的现实问题、信仰的宗教归属感等都将通过抄经而最后留在“写本”上。

当然，如果“写本”上明确地留下了抄经那“一时”的相关历史信息，该“写本”的历史价值则明确无疑。但是，敦煌遗书的大量“写本”并没有明确抄写信息，只剩下纸本、书法等非常模糊的时代历史信息。于是，判断“写本”的时间乃至思想属性等，成为敦煌研究、佛教研究等的重要工作。下文以地论宗写本研究为例，说明写本的社会历史信息等如何构成了教理研判的重要依据。

2012年，韩国金刚大学佛教文化研究所汇集中、日、韩学者对藏外地论学派文献进行校录，出版《藏外地论宗文献集成》及《续集》。[②]《藏外地论宗文献集成》收录的文献分为教理集成文献、《华严经》注释书、“五门”文献、“法界图”文献、逸文五个部分；《藏外地论宗文献集成续集》收录的文献分为教理集成文献、《十地经论》注释书、诸经疏、逸文四个部分。这两册书是目前整理得最好的地论学派文献校录本，为深入研究地论学派的文献、历史与思想提供了扎实的基础。

《藏外地论宗文献集成》及《续集》提出的判断地论学派文献的具体标准为：“主要是看是否存在三种判教说（三乘别教、通教、通宗），缘集说（有为缘集、无为缘集、自体缘集）等地论宗固有的教义。”[③]以教义为标准，是一种思想史立场。然而，判断某一敦煌文献是否属于地论学派，必须建立证据效力的强弱标准，才能避免将跨时空的思想或概念传播误解为学派内的历史传承。以敦煌遗书《毗尼心》为例，其末尾提到“小乘教、通教大乘、通宗大乘”三种判教和“有为缘集、无为缘集、自体缘集”三种缘集，于是便被学者列为地论学派

---

① 道世：《法苑珠林》卷十七，收入高楠顺次郎、渡边海旭、小野玄妙《大正新修大藏经》第53册，第415页中—下。

② 青木隆、方广锠、池田将则等：《藏外地论宗文献集成》，大学校文化研究所2012年版；青木隆、荒牧典俊、池田将则等：《藏外地论宗文献集成续集》，大学校文化研究所2013年版。

③ 金天鹤：《藏外地论宗文献集成·序》，载青木隆、方广锠、池田将则等《藏外地论宗文献集成》，第18页。

第二期文献（535—560），[①]归属北朝末年。但是，这三种判教和三种缘集在唐中期的天台、华严文献中皆出现过，永明延寿《宗镜录》卷十八多处引用“自体缘集”[②]，故不能以语词的引用与思想的绵延来判断文献的年代。

不过，从写本研究的信息来看，对《毗尼心》的年代与脉络可以有更稳妥的判断。《毗尼心》的内容出现在莫高窟196窟，根据该窟的题记、空间布局和壁画内容，可以确认该窟为“戒坛窟”，是僧团传授比丘戒等的石窟。进而，将《毗尼心》和196窟的题记与图像进行对照与综合分析，可以窥见敦煌僧团的戒律活动，并由此探讨敦煌律学与南山律学的关系；而从《毗尼心》所引述的各部律论、律宗撰述及其历史文化背景来看，其撰述年代应在道世与义净之间，撰述时间为公元7世纪中期至8世纪初，《毗尼心》的作者则可能是敦煌僧团的“都司”。[③]

因此，探讨某一“写本”的归属，应当优先采信“写本”的历史，其次是写本的语句段落与语法风格，再次是写本中的思想观念，最后是写本中的语词，如此才能建立起研究论证的有效性。

综上可见：一、写本的历史，即其诞生的时间与空间，效力最强。敦煌离长安最近，西魏、北周时期的地论学派文献更容易流传到敦煌，从而保存下来；而在东西魏对立时代，邺城的地论学派文献不容易流传到敦煌。所以，对地论学派文献的判断必须充分考虑各时代各区域的地论学派发展史。二、文本的段落与风格，即作者在撰写文本时使用的语句、段落特点和语言风格，效力较强。如S.4303与S.613V之间，并不是个别语词相同，而是语句、段落相同，无疑可以证明二者的关联性。三、思想观念，即写本所阐述的观念结构，效力较弱。因为思想具有绵延性，一种思想观念可以穿透时空的阻隔，出现在毫不相关的文本里。四、文本的语词，因为语词使用的偶然性与弱相关性，以及时间逻辑的缺乏，效力最弱。随着检索工具的进步，文本之间的语词对应变得愈加容易，也愈加应当谨慎处之。[④]

总之，写本研究重视文本的历史信息，而文本强调语词、段落、风格乃至思想观念。当写本历史信息减弱，变得不可判断，需要通过种种相关性去判断和阐释时，写本就重新回到“文本”的中间地位。

---

① 青木隆：「地论宗の融即论と缘起说」，载荒牧典俊编著『北朝隋唐中国佛教思想史』，法藏馆2000年版，第194—196页。青木隆对敦煌出土的地论宗文献进行分期，将《十地经论》译出的510年至610年分为四期：第一期（510—535），慧光的时代；第二期（535—560），法上、道凭的时代；第三期（560—585），慧远、灵裕的时代；第四期（585—610），最后的时代。

② 延寿：《宗镜录》卷十八，收入高楠顺次郎、渡边海旭、小野玄妙《大正新修大藏经》第48册，第511页上—中。

③ 圣凯：《敦煌遗书〈毗尼心〉与莫高窟196窟比较研究》，《西南民族大学学报》（人文社会科学版）2017年第7期，第41—48页。

④ 圣凯：《南北朝地论学派思想史》，宗教文化出版社2021年版，第17—18页。

三、结语：经典、文本与写本之间的渗透与断裂

写本的唯一性在于时间的不可重复，这是准确无疑的信息；文本毕竟来自作者的观念创作，其中心在于语言，彰显的是作者的主体性；“语境”是连接写本和经典的途径，经典重在神圣价值的永恒性与行动指引的观念动力，其神圣性包含着文本的历史性乃至观念的混杂性。

所以，时间、语言、价值成为写本、文本、经典三者的核心维度。通过这三个维度的转化，经典、文本与写本之间会发生渗透与转化，当然也存在永远不可转化的现象。如从印度翻译过来的经典当中，有相当一部分并没有受到中国佛教僧人和信徒的尊崇；即使编入藏经，也没有获得“圣典”的地位，而只是作为古老的知识文本，借助藏经系统代代相传。与之恰成对比的是，《六祖坛经》作为中国僧人慧能讲经说法的记录，因为禅宗的盛行而受到后代禅门的尊奉与讲授，成为中国汉传佛教最重要的“圣典”。而且，敦煌本《六祖坛经》作为写本，经过整理后，不仅是学术界研究禅宗的知识文本，佛教界亦逐渐接受与应用，也获得了经典的地位。

所以，经典、文本、写本之间是一种缘起的存在，彼此既有相关性，也有独立性，这是研究的始点，也是终点。

从胜迹志文献理解寺庙艺术：以多罗那他的平措林寺为例*

姚 霜

中国人民大学文学院

西藏文化中，圣地（gnas，又作“胜迹”）与朝圣文化（gnas skor）是一个常见且重大的主题。西藏遍地充满了关于圣地的传说，小到洞窟、寺庙，大到神山、湖泊，西藏本土文化对山川地貌的认知都蕴含在对圣地、胜迹的叙事建构中。这些传统文化甚至信仰的创造与延续，渗透在文本叙事中，给予了藏文文献丰富的内涵，而这些记载传说成为我们了解西藏物质与精神文明的素材。

从艺术研究角度来说，藏文文献里有两种与圣地文化息息相关的专门体裁，① 即胜迹志（gnas bshad）与游记（lam yig）。② 长期以来，学界对游记多有关注，这些文本涉及丰富、实用的历史地理信息，因此，对游记中记载的地名、人物、寺庙、艺术遗存等内容的考证成为历史研究的主要对象。然而，当研究者利用文本对上述对象进行历史重构时，往往容易忽略这类文献记载的整体叙述，特别是深受藏传佛教影响的历史叙事。不同的是，西藏的圣地建造文化受到人类学家们持续的关注，正如托尼·休伯（Toni Huber）在其代表作《圣地重生：朝圣与藏土对佛国印度的再造》中所说的，藏传佛教无论是历史的还是当代的发展，都实践

---

* 本文根据 2021 年 10 月“纪念陈寅恪先生西域和佛教语文学国际研讨会”上的报告修订，并在已发表文章《论藏族胜迹文学的叙事策略——以〈甘丹平措林胜迹志〉为例》（载于《民族文学研究》2021 年第 6 期）基础上进行了扩充增补。

① Erberto Lo Bue, “Tibetan Literature on Art,” in J. I. Cabezón and R. R. Jackson eds., *Tibetan Literature: Studies in Genre*, New York: Snow Lion, 1996, pp.470–484.

② 二词的汉译在学界并不统一，如作为胜迹游记（*gnas yid*）的《卫藏道场胜迹志》采用了“胜迹志”的说法，尽管该书应为胜迹志与游记的结合。本论文所讨论的“胜迹志”取藏文本身词汇偏重的含义，直译为“圣地 / 胜迹解说”，以汉文文献中佛教方志或寺志的体裁作为参照，故采用“胜迹志”一词指代 *gnas bshad* 一类文本。参见钦则旺布著、刘立千译注：《卫藏道场胜迹志》，西藏人民出版社 1987 年版。

构建着佛教神圣的空间，以示传法的正统。[①] 除了上述两方面的探索路径，学界鲜有尝试从对艺术文本叙事的分析中去体察圣地传说所蕴含的历史性与宗教性，而这些叙述恰是影响寺庙视觉艺术建造的重要因素。换言之，只有理解了圣地空间构造背后的逻辑，才能探寻到作为圣物被创造出来的艺术作品的内在意义。因此，本文将以藏地的胜迹志为对象，分析具体文本，梳理文本体裁背后的叙事逻辑，理清其分类与叙事结构，试图在文献中探索那些关于胜地历史的、文化的遗珠，透过文本“让所见产生意义”。

一、作为一种文献体裁的“胜迹志”

什么是胜迹志？藏文为“gnas bshad”，原指对圣地的解说。广义上讲，胜迹志往往指对一个神圣场域的建造历程、布局、内部设置的详细描述。有三种胜迹志：一种胜迹志与“历史”（lo rgyud）相结合，除了记录寺庙最珍贵的佛像、佛经藏品等圣物，还将“教法源流”（chos byung）融入其中，形成了我们今天理解的“寺志”，代表有《萨迦圣地解说耳传》（*Sa skya'i gnas bshad snyan brgyud ma*）；另一种是关于胜迹与教法源流融合过程的记载，以“传记”（rnam thar）的形式展现一个寺庙与其相关传承的兴衰过程，代表有《致敬吉祥夏鲁巴教法的善妙士夫传记历史》（*Dpal ldan zhwa lu pa'i bstan pa la bka' drin che ba'i skyes bu dam pa rnams kyi rnam thar lo rgyus ngo mtshar dad pa'i 'jug ngogs*）[②]；此外，我们常见有关胜迹的描述与游记相结合，形成了“圣地游记”（gnas yid）一类文本，代表有《卫藏道场胜迹志》（*Dbus gtsang gi gnas rten rags rim gyi mtshan byang mdor bdus dang po'i so*）[③]、《噶陀司徒卫藏胜迹志》（*Ka thog si tu'i dbus gtsang gnas yid*）[④]。关于圣地建造的详细描述还作为独立的片段被纳入了藏地重要的历史文献之中，比如《拔协》（*Dba bshad*）中有关于桑耶寺建立最早的

---

① Toni Huber, *The Holy Land Reborn: Pilgrimage & the Tibetan Reinvention of Buddhist India*, Chicago and London: The University of Chicago Press, 2008. 关于西方人类学角度的西藏朝圣文化研究综述，参见才贝：《西方“朝圣”视野下藏族“神圣”地理研究及其分析》,《中国藏学》2010 年第 1 期，第 110—117 页。

② 除藏文本外，英译本参见 Puchung Tsering, *The History of Zha Lu Monastery, Ri sbug Hermitage and rGyan gong Temple*, Lhasa: Tibet People's Publishing House, 2017。

③ 除藏文本外，此部经典还有多部汉译、英译著作：Alfonsa Ferrari, *Mk'yen Brtse's Guide to The Holy Places of Central Tibet*, Roma: Istituto Italiano Per il Medio ed Estremo Oriente, 1958; Matthew Akester, *Jamyang Khyentsé Wangpo's Guide to Central Tibet*, London: Serindia Publications, 2016。同时还有依照此游记的西方当代旅行志，见 Keith Dowman, *The Power-Places of Central Tibet: The Pilgrim's Guide*, London: Routledge & Kegan Paul Ltd., 1988。

④ 相关研究参见 Karl-Heinz Everding, “Kah thog Si tu's Account on his Pilgrimage through Central Tibet in Years 1918—1920 *(dBus gtsang gnas bskor lam yig)*,” *Zentral-Asiatische Studien*, 46, 2017, pp.29–35。

叙述，[①]《贤者喜宴》（*Mkhas pa'i dga' ston*）、《安多政教史》（*Deb ther rgya mtsho*）、《后藏志》（*Mnyang Chos 'byung*）等更是包含有诸多寺庙的历史信息。

藏地的游记是长期以来研究西藏以及泛喜马拉雅地区神圣地理（scared geography）的重要文献。游记更多发挥的是一种地图导览的功能，其对某一圣地的解说更多出于朝圣者的观察，可作为重构圣地的佐证，但并不能彻底、全面地，特别是从建造者的角度去了解一处胜迹。例如，在《卫藏道场胜迹志》中，钦则旺波除了记述自己的行程外，还大量征引了其他各地具体的胜迹志来完善自己的游记，如《吉祥大昭寺目录 · 白水晶镜》[②]、《萨迦寺志》（*Sa skya'i gtsug lha khang dang rten gsum gyi dkar chag*）、《觉囊胜迹志》（*Jo nang gi gnas bshad*）等，而在描述各处佛像圣物时，他自述用了"目录"（dkar chag）一类的文本与自己的亲身经验相结合。[③]

区别于游记，狭义的胜迹志作为一种独立的文本，被认为归属于目录体裁。西藏的目录文献是当代藏学家，特别是古藏文文献、历史学家首要关注的领域之一，其包含内容之广度与丰富性超越了其一般仅被认作简单的列表清单的表象。我们常常认为，目录是对文本的一种整理形式，比如《大藏经》的历代目录编纂就体现了不同时代藏传佛教经典发展的语境与诉求。[④]然而，目录作为对圣物的记述，不仅仅只针对佛教经典或注疏。对佛殿（lha khang）或者拥有完整"三所依"的寺庙甚至圣山（属于 gnas chen，即"大胜迹"）的建造的记载与内置的详述也属于此类体裁。有时，对圣物的描述，特别是对佛塔（mchod rten）、灵塔（gser gdung）等重要圣物的建造的描述，甚至可形成长篇巨作，比如第悉 · 桑杰嘉措（Sde srid Sangs rgyas rgya mtsho, 1653—1705）所著的《灵塔》（*Mchod sdong*）就被认为是拥有较为完整的目类文献特点的代表。[⑤]因此，作为文本体裁的"目录"往往可与"胜迹志"互换，我们亦可以通过一部胜迹志窥探到西藏文化的诸多面向——历史、天文、地理、经济、技术、哲学等等。

---

① 桑耶寺文献主要英文研究有 Pasang Wangdu and Hildegard Diemberger, *dBa'bzhed: The Royal Narrative Concerning the Bringing of the Buddha's Doctrine to Tibet*, Wien: Verlag der Österreinchischen Akademie der Wissenschaften, 2000; Per. K. Sørensen, *Tibetan Buddhist Historiography: The Mirror Illuminating the Royal Genealogies*, Wiesbaden: Harrassowitz Verlag, 1994。

② 此书在西方多被称为"拉萨导览"（The Guide to Lhasa），早年曾被译为德文，见 A. Grünwedel, *Die Tempel von Lhasa*, Sitzungsberichte der Heidelberger Akademie der Wissenschaften, Phil.-Hist. Klasse, 1919。

③ Alfonsa Ferrari, *Mk'yen Brtse's Guide to The Holy Places of Central Tibet*, p.21; Karl-Heinz Everding, "Kah thog Si tu's Account on his Pilgrimage through Central Tibet in Years 1918-1920 (*dBus gtsang gnas bskor lam yig*)," p.33.

④ 藏文大藏经编纂历史与各版本的异同可参见 Peter Skilling, "From *bKa' bstan bcos* to *bKa' 'gyur* and *bsTan 'gyur*," in Helmut Eimer ed., *Transmission of the Tibetan Cannon*, Vienna: Verlag derÖsttereichischen Akademie der Wissenschfaften, 1997, pp.99-107.

⑤ 关于目录体裁，详细可参见 Dan Martin, "Table of Contents (*dkar chag*)," in J. I. Cabezón and R. R. Jackson eds., *Tibetan Literature: Studies in Genre*, New York: Snow Lion, 1996, pp.500-514。

这类文本的大量产生又究竟意欲何为呢？丹·马丁（Dan Martin）认为那些描述佛塔圣物的目录文本具有摄受、加持（byin brlabs）的作用。“dkar chag”一词的本义为“白色的佛法如何形成”，或是“如何作功德”，因此，从其制作意图来讲，这些描述都是在颂赞功德，而功德属于建造、资助，乃至参访观礼等所有古往今来与此地、此物相关的人。① 例如，布顿大师（Bu ston Rin chen grub, 1290—1364）完成了近三十年的《丹珠尔》编纂工作之后，造《丹珠尔目录》（*Bstan 'gyur dkar chag*）一部，详细记录了这一编纂过程，其中不仅有关于施主大司徒降曲坚赞、三位担任主要编纂工作的善知识的记载，同时还有上百位不同工种的人员也都被记录在册。② 目录类文本如一部详细的佛教事业计划书，包含了围绕这个事业而展开的所有重要的信息，如建造初衷、设计理念，所涉人力、物力等等。正如藏传佛教哲学史家马修·卡普斯坦（Matthew Kapstein）评论坛城绘画时所言，在藏传佛教，尤其是从印度波罗王朝继承而来的密教传统里，画家、上师、施主、观者等所有“艺术”过程的参与者都属于一个宗教修行的共同体，他们在共同参与建设一个建造世界的工程（a world-constructing enterprise）。③

此外，休伯在对“gnas skor”（朝圣、转经）一词再度分析时提到，“加持”一词很容易被理解为普通的祈福保佑（blessing），而需要强调的是这种行为中的环境空间影响力，即通过围绕圣物、胜迹活动被赋予的力量能够净治罪孽（sdig pa）与遮障（sgrib pa），同时可以帮助生起次第（bskyed rim）的修行，其本身就是在完成一次修行仪轨。④ 如果要将这些笼统的宗教功能进一步具体化的话，那么，神圣空间建造所依据的佛学理论就是后者视觉化的再现，这些有关胜迹的记载正好为后人提供了其所依据的佛学理论的线索。譬如，位于拉萨地区东北的著名的直贡沟是噶举传承的重要圣地，围绕这个区域历史遗迹的朝圣路线被称为“直贡坛城”（Drigung mandala）⑤，而被认为是莲花生大师修行地的“伏藏箧”（gter sgrom）则是其中一处主要胜迹。⑥ 研究者根据游记中的圣地解说、传记等历史文献与田野调查相结合，发现“伏藏箧”中的各处小的供奉点（因此地为山居，并非形成佛殿等的建筑）是对“三根本”（tsa gsum, 上师、本尊、空行）的供奉，如果按照正确的朝圣路线，除了利用他们

① Ibid, pp.505–506.

② Kurtis Schaeffer, “A Letter to the Editors of Buddhist Canon in Fourteenth-Century Tibet: The *Yig mkhan rnams la gdams pa* of Bu ston Rin chen grub,” *Journal of the American Oriental Society*, Vol. 124, No. 2, 2004, p.273.

③ Matthew Kapstein, “Weaving the World: The Ritual Art of the ‘Pata’ in Pala Buddhism and Its Legacy in Tibet,” *History of Religions*, vol. 34, no. 3, 1995, p.244.

④ Toni Huber, “Putting the gnas back into gnas skor: Rethinking Tibetan Buddhist Pilgrimage Practice,” *The Tibet Journal*, Vol. 19, No. 2, 1994, pp.33–50.

⑤ Keith Dowman, *The Power-Places of Central Tibet: The Pilgrim's Guide,*1988, pp.106–122.

⑥ 此处在钦哲旺波原文中写为“*Ti sgrom*”，参见 Alfonsa Ferrari, *Mk'yen Brtse's Guide to The Holy Places of Central Tibet*, p.44, 112。

巨大的加持和威力实现转经所带来的共通利益——净治所遮与烦恼，更深层的是，在这一处修行地按照特定的路线行走观览，即可完成一次实质的修行——不共的密法修行者通过对胜迹里所示的成就法（sgrub thabs, sādhanā）身体力行的观修与现证，实现圆满次第（rdzogs rim）的修行。① 尽管人类学家更多是通过对历史的与当代的朝圣者的经验研究，从而勾勒出胜迹观览的宗教意涵，展现藏传佛教文化发展的活力，而胜迹志或圣物目录的语文学式阅读则会将这一阐释更加具体化，推向接近其建造的原始语境。那些被游记收录、串联的圣地传说，其题材除了经教宣说、佛传故事、授记、大成就者生平，还有民谣、谚语与本土信仰，主要承袭自早期的胜迹文学传统与寺庙传承僧人的传记。这些包罗万象的内容无不是在展现、宣传和强调自己所获圣物、所建胜迹的神圣性与特殊性。②

如果胜迹志只是属于佛教目录类文献中的一种，那么胜迹志是否是西藏特有的一种文献体裁呢？有学者提出胜迹志和圣地游记或与印度 *māhātmya* 赞颂文学有关联。③ 从内容上对比，类似的是，印度的此类文本亦是主要通过对一处地方（山川、河流、湖泊，或人造建筑）外部的描述来定义该地的神圣性，因为这些地方是神所居之处，庙宇建筑与神像是具象的代表。而众所周知的是，西藏寺庙建造起源却是为了镇伏住在山水地域中的罗刹女妖（srin mo），因此对圣物与胜迹的崇拜并非指向所在地本身，而是调伏后的改造。④ 其次，菲利斯·格拉诺夫（Phyllis Granoff）通过对 *māhātmya* 梵文文本的研究，展示了该文学表现中存在着对寺庙里图像崇拜的排斥与妥协。因为正统的婆罗门文化是不允许圣物崇拜的，而在实际世俗需求中又需要使用神像作为仪轨工具，或用美好、神圣的艺术品的庄严感去吸引信众。令格拉诺夫感到惊讶的是，这些所谓的对胜迹的赞颂却往往并未对神像或庙宇本身进行详细的描述，而只是注重于对其外部空间或供奉圣物林伽（*liṅga*）所代表的神山进行描写。⑤ 因此，这与藏地的胜迹志明显不同：除了包含地理环境的描写（一般作为建造的缘起见于

① Andrea Loseries, "Sacred Geography and Individual in Central Tibet: Terdrum Sancturary, a Training Path within the Drikung Mandala," *The Tibet Journal*, Vol. 19, No. 4, 1994, pp.46–58. 关于密续中的圣地作为圆满次第修行中的人身部位的对应研究参见 David Templeman, "Internal and External Geography in Spiritual Biography," *The Tibet Journal*, Vol. 19, No. 3, 1994, pp.66–67.

② Toni Huber, "Guidebook to Lapchi," in Donald S. Lopez ed., *Religions of Tibet in Practice*, Princeton: Princeton University Press, 2007, pp.90–104.

③ Per Sørensen and Guntrum Hazod, *Thundering Falcon: An Inquiry into the History and Cult of Khra-'brug, Tibet's First Buddhist Temple*, Wien: Össterreichische Akademie der Wissenschaften, 2005, p.8.

④ 关于"降伏罗刹女"的叙述研究参见 Janet Gyatso, "Down with the Demoness: Reflections on a Feminine Ground in Tibet," in Jancie B. Willis ed., *Feminine Ground: Essays on Women and Tibet*, New York: Snow Lion, 1989, pp.33–51。有关"伏妖"传说与藏文"胜迹"（*gnas*）一词的关系，以及 *gnas* 本身的文化含义的讨论参见 Toni Huber, "Putting the gnas back into gnas skor: Rethinking Tibetan Buddhist Pilgrimage Practice," p.23–30。

⑤ Phyllis Granoff, "Defining Sacred Place: Contest, Compromise, and Priestly Control in Some Māhātmya Texts," *Annals of the Bhandarkar Oriental Research Institute*, Vol. 79, No. 1/4, 1998, pp.1–27.

开篇），西藏胜迹志主要部分是对佛殿、圣像、佛塔等内外所依（phyi nang gyi rten）进行目录式详述。另一方面，汉地一直有寺庙胜迹描写的传统，从较早的《洛阳伽蓝记》《清凉山志》《吴都法乘》，到历代官修的方志、私家著录，形成了佛学地理志或佛教方志的文献体裁。从内容上对比，汉藏的此类文本均是关于佛教地理环境、传承历史、圣物古迹的记载，包含寺庙、佛塔、圣山等，具有宗教性、历史性、文献性与地域性四个特征。① 然而，就宗教性而言，汉地佛教方志并未受到佛教叙事的强烈影响，虽然其内容可以反映佛教的历史发展，但其人文、世俗普及性远远大于本身的宗教功能，因此它仍属于历史地理的"方志"（gazetteer），而这一点可能影响了当代西藏寺志的编纂。

可以说，西藏胜迹志文本的形成与藏传佛教的发展息息相关，特别是与密教的传播有很深的关联，其体现的佛教宇宙观很大程度上来自印度——即使并非体现在 *māhātmya* 文献中，而在这些叙述建构中所体现的历史性与地理性又是十分丰富且独特的。因此，胜迹志的研究可为理解藏传佛教提供一个整体的、全面的视角，使其能从多个维度——仪轨的、体验的、叙事的、教义的、社会的、物质的——得以展现，从而对建构胜迹的视觉艺术提供内在的逻辑与文化意涵。②

二、胜迹志文本分析：以《甘丹平措林胜迹志》为例

《甘丹平措林胜迹志》（*Dga'ldan phun tshogs gling gi gnas bshad*）是收录于藏地觉囊派 17 世纪祖师多罗那他（Tāranātha，1575—1634）全集的主要胜迹志著作，详述了多罗那他于 17 世纪上半叶历时十三年亲自指导建造的达旦丹曲林寺（Rtag ldan dam chos gling，后改名为"平措林寺"）的缘起、历史、布局、内置等详细内容。始建于 1615 年的平措林寺建造意义重大，它不仅是藏传佛教觉囊派在卫藏地区唯一且最后的大本营，是了解觉囊教义传承发展面貌的重要文物遗址；同时，多罗那他这件庞大的宗教事业（'phrin las）可折射出后藏地区激烈的历史进程。该胜迹志内容大多与《多罗那他自传》（*Tā ra nā tha bdag nyid kyi rnam thar*）等传记文本平行，然而目前所见的两个木刻本（拉达克版、壤塘版）的诸多细节，如

① 汉地佛教方志的定义讨论与文献综述参见曹刚华：《明代佛教方志文献研究概述》，《中国地方志》2007 年第 10 期，第 33—37 页。

② 此处引用了尼尼安·斯马特（Ninian Smart）对于宗教"七个维度"的定义，参见 Ninian Smart, *Dimensions of the Sacred: An Anatomy of the World's beliefs*, Berkley, CA: University of California Press, 1998；关于从南亚到东亚的宗教胜迹形成的多样性与复杂性参见 Phyllis Granoff & Koichi Shinohara, *Pilgrims, Patrons, and Place: Localizing Sanctity in Asian Religions*, Vancouver, Toronto: UBC Press, 2003。

多处含有对多罗那他的尊称，表明该胜迹志为其后人所编写。[①] 这并不影响此胜迹志的内容作为对该寺建造诠释的权威性，因为修建历经数年，这部胜迹文本的生成并非只在一时，稍晚完成的编写被归于多罗那他亦属正常。

从内容结构上看，《甘丹平措林胜迹志》可分为六个部分，分别为：1）顶礼赞颂：展现了觉囊派传承的序列，特别强调对 14 世纪祖师笃布巴（Dol po pa Shes rab rgyal mtshan, 1292—1361）的继承；2）选址的瑞相：描述了觉囊沟口的祥瑞之地；3）授记与建造的缘起：以佛经与古代胜迹历史为源泉建构了寺庙建造的神圣传说；4）中央大殿（gtsug lag khang）三层的内部陈列建造，包括圣物（佛像、佛经）及其装藏与壁画配置；5）周边佛殿的佛像与壁画：依次描述了十五座佛殿的配置，详略不等；6）总结与祈愿；7）后山的建造与配置。其中，前三个部分所含历史信息丰富，对于该寺神圣空间的创建提供了重要文本来源；而周边佛殿、独立佛殿根据设计形制大小篇幅有所不同，多为描述性罗列，为艺术考古图像的重构提供了重要依据。[②]

根据总结部分所说，可以得知这篇早期的胜迹志并非悉数记载了寺庙所有的建筑，然而前四个部分却对寺庙的整体布局与建造初衷做了基调式的解说。值得注意的是，描述各佛殿的段落之间并没有衔接语句，而是类似一本本单独的清单。而根据多罗那他的传记与当代寺志的整理，这些佛殿的叙述次第并非其建造年代的顺序，[③] 从落成方位上看，它们之间也没有关联。这与作为朝圣转经指南的游记具有很大差别，因此挖掘其内在的空间联系还需要更多相关佛学、历史知识的帮助。接下来，本文将就《甘丹平措林胜迹志》的第二、三、四部分进行详细文本分析，展现文本中突出的胜迹制造的元素，揭示在胜迹产生的过程中宗教历史空间观的重要性。

1. 选址

首先，为寺庙修建选择一块上佳的“风水宝地”是胜迹志文本中首要记述的内容之一。《胜迹志》记载：“如此，一切成就处的王主、大山居吉祥觉囊沟胜地的大门，首先就此天然

---

① 目前所见该胜迹志版本有三种，依据时间前后，分别为拉达克木刻本、壤塘木刻本、与基于前两种的校勘本，其内容基本相同。参见闫雪：《西藏甘丹彭措林寺大经堂壁画题记识读与研究》，《中国藏学》2014 年第 3 期，第 164 页。其中，最早的拉达克本指的是如今保存在拉达克斯朵克宫（Stog Palace）的木刻版，出自平措林寺的印经院。然而，“平措林”是该寺改宗格鲁派后的名字，胜迹志记载前后均未有作者题跋信息，因此这些所谓寺志应均为 1658 年以后的作品。后文出现的汉译引文均为笔者译自藏文文献原文，所选翻译底本为《中华大藏经 · 藏文对勘本》，即 Tāranātha, “Dga ldan phun tshogs gling gi gnas bshad bzhugs,” *Dpal brtsegs bod yig dpe rnying zhib 'jug khang nas bsgrigs, Jo nang rje btsun tā ra nā tha'i gsung 'bum dpe bsdur ma*, Pe cin: Krung go'i bod rig pa dpe skrun khang, 2008, vol. 34, pp.160–193。

② 闫雪博士已根据文献就平措林各佛殿建筑佛像配置进行了梳理，参见闫雪：《西藏甘丹彭措林寺建筑格局及其渊源考释》，《民族研究》2016 年第 5 期，第 100—101 页。

③ 平措林寺年代建造一览参见熊文彬、孜强 · 边巴旺堆：《西藏拉孜县平措林寺祖拉康大殿壁画的题材与风格及其流派初探》，《藏学学刊》2016 年第 1 期，第 75—77 页。

成就的瑞相而言，〔它〕稳固威严、高大魁伟、具十亿须弥之吉祥荣光。在被称为‘森林王’的大山脚下，有像守地子面部形状的地貌特色；后山遍布着如意宝般的岩石群，可打败非人与摧毁天众，具有多闻天王的英姿，又有坐立狮子座中的样子。在它面前，宝雨落下，如伏藏瓶般的标识。若从前看，像右旋的螺；〔若从〕后看，像连着台阶佛塔的形状，如与天上的宝尘积混淆。如果说到周围的瑞相，俱全吉祥结等八大吉祥的形状。”① 这一段文字对平措林寺所在的觉囊沟的地貌进行了描绘。位于今天日喀则地区拉孜县的觉囊沟是从 13 世纪伊始藏传佛教觉囊派的驻地，沟内还有早期庙宇建筑、觉囊大塔和山居修行洞窟，多罗那他亦著有对后者的解说，整体所述与此处类似。②

此胜迹志说地貌具有“八吉祥”的形状，是祥瑞的表征，随后即说，“地址的东方与东北方顺势而下，西面与南面逐渐而高，依所有的经，此为所推崇赞颂的建坛城的地址殊胜的性相”③，暗示了密法修行中所代表的内外宇宙的具象化，这些印度密续所建立的宇宙观很大程度影响了藏地对于山水地理的认知。④ 此外，对印度知识体系的积极接收是藏地思想史的一个重要特征，多罗那他正是这样一位代表祖师。⑤ 举例来说，在此段记载“在北方，是被称为‘鲁西达’，吠陀经中所说为‘梵天之子’，盛名的‘一切河流之王’流过，复有河水向右旋转翻涌”⑥ 中，“鲁西达”（lu hi ta），即印度古籍中对布拉马普特拉河的梵文古

---

① Tāranātha, “Dga ldan phun tshogs gling gi gnas bshad bzhugs,” pp.161−162：de ltar na/ sgrub gnas thams cad kyi rgyal po/ ri khrod chen po dpal jo mo nang gi gnas kyi sgo chen por gyur pa ’di nyid la dang por phyi ’byung bas sgrub pa’i dge mtshan gyi dbang du byas na/ brtan cing brjid la mtho zhing lhun chags pa/ lhun po bye ba phrag brgya’i dpal yon can/ nags rgyal zhes bya ri’i dbang po’i ’dabs/ sa bsrung bu yi gdong gi dbyibs can yod/ rgyab ri nor bu’i brag tshogs gtams pa ni/ lha min g.yul ’joms lha tshogs dbugs ’byin mdzad/ rgyal chen rnam mang thos pa ’gying pa’i sku/ seng ge’i khri la bzhugs pa’i rnam pa can/ de yi mdun du rin chen char ’bab cing/ gter gyi bum pa ’dra ba’i rtags mtshan dang/ mdun nas bltas na g.yas su ’khyil ba’i dung/ rgyab bltas bang rim dang bcas mchod rten dbyibs/ rin chen rdul brtsegs mkha’ la rnyog pa ’dra/ de dang nye ba’i ngos la dge mtshan ni/ dpal gyi be’u la sogs bkra shis kyi/ rtags brgyad po rnams yongs su tshang bar yod/

② Tāranātha, “Sgrub gnas skyid phug bde ldan gyi gnas bshad,” *Dpal brtsegs bod yig dpe rnying zhib ’jug khang nas bsgrigs, Jo nang rje btsun tā ra nā tha’i gsung ’bum dpe bsdur ma*, Pe cin: Krung go’i bod rig pa dpe skrun khang, 2008, vol. 34, pp.154−155.

③ Tāranātha, “Dga ldan phun tshogs gling gi gnas bshad bzhugs,” p.162: sa gzhi shar dang dbang ldan phyogs su gzhol/ nub dang lho yi phyogs su pags kyi mtho/ rgyud ste kun las dkyil ’khor bzhengs pa yi/ sa gzhi’i mtshan nyid mchog tu bsngags pa yin/

④ Khendrup Norsang Gyatso, *Ornament of Stainless Light: An Exposition of the Kālacakra Tantra*, Boston: Wisdom Publications, 2004, p.38/44. 时轮修法研究亦可参见 Vesna A. Wallace, *The Inner Kālacakra: A Buddhist Tantric View of the Individual*, New York: Oxford University Press, 2001。

⑤ 关于多罗那他的印度知识参见 David Templeman, “Taranatha the Historian,” *The Tibet Journal*, Vol. 6, No.2, 1981, pp.41−46; “South of the Border: Tāranātha’s Perceptions of India,” *The Tibet Journal*, Vol. 34, No. 3, 2009, pp.231−242。

⑥ Tāranātha, “Dga ldan phun tshogs gling gi gnas bshad bzhugs,” p.162: byang gi phyogs su lu hi tar grags pa/ rig byed gzhung las tshangs pa’i sras su bshad/ chu klung kun gyi rgyal po grags ldan ’bab/ ’bab chu gzhan yang g.yas phyogs khyil bas ’gro/

称“lohitya”，此河在往世书（*Kālika Purāṇa*，即此处所说的“吠陀经”）中被称作梵天之子（*Brahmaputra*），而“一切河流之王”即指雅鲁藏布江。此处将平措林寺门前流经的雅鲁藏布江视为布拉马普特拉河，充分展现了多罗那他对于印藏地理知识的掌握，比起早期研究认为 18 世纪的《松巴佛教史》为最早将悉多河、雅鲁藏布江与布拉马普特拉河联系起来的文献早了一个世纪。①

其次，多罗那他将觉囊沟的地貌特征从东边沿顺时针方向分别比拟为“轮王七宝”（rgyal srid sna bdun, *saptaratna*），即转轮王（*cakravartin*）的七件所属宝物，并提到了“按照汉地的分析算法，东为虎，南为玉龙，西为鸟、北为乌龟”②。多罗那他所说的“算法”（rtsigs）实际指的是藏地的相地术（sa dpyad）③，多罗那他所说的汉地传统应是参照了《玛尼全集》《西藏王统记》等记载的文成公主堪舆建寺的叙事。④通过“轮王七宝”的勾勒，多罗那他将觉囊沟地貌描绘成一尊转轮王的身体，结合下文对前弘期历史的提示，或许这一阐释是在通过追忆吐蕃时期的转轮赞普们塑造此寺庙胜迹的政教权威性，而这一推测在后文中亦可得以证实。⑤

2. 授记与祥瑞

彼得·施维格（Peter Schwieger）在论作为神话的西藏历史之建构时谈到，西藏历史事件与其文化源头的关联不仅仅是以无间断的序列传承的内在性质为纽带，还在于在伟人圆寂之后或发愿者诚心祈祷后，神通、授记、誓言能够持续实现，因此历史是文化起源的直接与相续的纽带。依照这种传承谱系的规律，西藏历史叙事的主要策略是塑造一个先行的（印度的）理想楷模，形成特定的叙事主题去延续这种精神，其中包括对瑞相、神通与授记的描述。⑥多罗那他在胜迹志中详述平措林寺的缘起则是挪用了《大法鼓经》的内容：首先是佛

---

① John A. Ardussi, “The Quest for the Brahmaputra River and its Course According to Tibetan Sources,” *The Tibet Journal*, Vol. 2, No. 1, 1977, pp.35–49.

② Tāranātha, “Dga ldan phun tshogs gling gi gnas bshad bzhugs,” p.162: rgya nag rtsis kyis dpyad nas ’byung ba bzhin/ shar gyi stag dang lho yi g.yu ’brug dang/ nub kyi bya dang byang gi rus spal sogs/

③ 龙珠多杰：《藏族寺院建筑选址文化探微》，《中国藏学》2010 年第 3 期，第 190 页。

④ 对于汉地四大神兽与方位，藏地的传统叙述也有不相同的地方，比如《奈巴教法史》对文成公主建寺的方位就与《西藏王统记》不相同。参见 Per. K. Sørensen, *Tibetan Buddhist Historiography: The Mirror Illuminating the Royal Genealogies*, p.260; Petra Maurer, “When the tiger meets Yul ’khor srung, or how to protect a construction site,” *Études mongoles et sibériennes, centrasiatiques et tibétanines* [Online], Vol. 50, 2019, p.10。

⑤ 藏传佛教寺庙的相地传统多以桑结嘉措的《白琉璃》为主，参见 Gyurme Dorje, *Tibetan Elemental Divination Paintings: Illuminated manuscripts from the White Beryl of Sangs-rgyas rGyas-mtsho with the Moonbeams Treatise of Lo-chen Dharmaśrī*, London: John Eskenazi Ltd., 2001。

⑥ Peter Schwieger, “History as myth: On the Appropriation of the Past in Tibetan Culture, An Essay in Cultural Studies,” in Gray Tuttle & Kurtis R. Schaeffer eds., *The Tibetan History Reader*, New York: Columbia University Press, 2013, p.70, 73.

陀宣说《大法鼓经》，此中的授记指向了笃布巴·喜饶坚赞的出现；其次，凭借笃布巴的预言，多罗那他建立了该寺。

于第一步，如文中所示："对于此大智慧的神变化现，《大鼓品经》所说。无隐藏地现明了说究竟了义的大经，里面以最后的词句作授记，在此瞻部洲南部中，在很晚的时候，童子离车，一切世间见欢喜，比丘持慧便成为名为喜饶坚赞的人。"① 回到《大法鼓经》原文，意思更加明确："如是如来何时〔成为〕该童子？在此娑婆世界，即出现护法名为释迦牟尼的时候，即尔佛。离车童子，取名为一切世间见喜，此后世间界一切护法涅槃后，佛法毁灭时，八十年到时，成为名为持慧的比丘，自寿命与人一样，此经便传出。"② 因此，我们得知，笃布巴是释迦牟尼的直接继承人，在末法时代现出。此经与笃布巴的关系并非多罗那他的独创，而是在笃布巴的生平中不断被提及、圣化的叙述。③ 此外，从教义方面来看，笃布巴彼时在藏地广宣的具有创新的"他空"教法，其经典来源就包含《大法鼓经》，属于其所列的"十部如来藏经"（*snying po'i mdo bcu*）之一，是觉囊派判教依止的"了义经"（*nge don mdo*）。可以说，多罗那他通过延续觉囊的正统——祖师与经教两方面——为自己的寺庙建立找到了第一个吉祥缘起。

其次，授记继续道："不论是过去还是将来的时间里，如此发生，显明我的教法，而即将开示的场所法基，祖拉康之首，正是所谓的'恒常妙法林·了义欢喜园'。实际上，在《大鼓经》中，世尊如来具大悲者亲口授记。遍知法王笃补巴佛陀本人，开显如太阳般的胜教，在八十年间了义教法遍布诸方，而之间未显明开示任何稍微些许了义的教法；复次，法王自己为利益众生持妙善知识的方式，以化身开示了义教法，此授记为：〔《大法鼓经原文》省略〕。在此所说的在南方出现，即是来到瞻部洲南半部希提河的南岸的意思。复次，所说时间的很晚彼将出，是我们的善妙至尊将再宣说了义教法，〔此〕有授记。"④ 这一段对经中授

---

① Tāranātha, "Dga ldan phun tshogs gling gi gnas bshad bzhugs," p.165: de nyid kyi ye shes chen po'i cho 'phrul las sprul pa ni/ rnga po che'i le'u zhes bya ba/ nges don mthar thug ma sbas shing gsar bar bstan pa'i mdo ste chen po de nyid kyi/ tha ma'i tshig gis lung bstan pa/ 'dzam gling lho phyogs kyi rgyud 'dir shin tu phyi mar gyur pa'i dus su yang/ li tsa bī gzhon nu/ 'jig rten kun gyis mthong na dga' ba/ dge slong blo 'chang ste/ shes rab rgyal mtshan ces bya bar gyur pa[de nyid]

② 中国藏学研究中心：《圣大鼓品经·大乘经》，《中华大藏经·甘珠尔》第 63 卷，中国藏学出版社 2007 年版，第 264—265 页：de ltar de bzhin gshegs pa des/gzhon nu de la gang gi tse/'jig rten gyi khams/mi mjed 'dir/ mgon po shākya thub pa zhes bya ba 'byung ba de'i tse/ rgyal po chen po khyod/ litsatsha bī gzhon nu/ 'jig rten thams cad kyis/ mthong na dga' ba zhes bya bar 'gyur te/ de nas 'jig rten gyi khams der/ mgon po yangs su mya ngan las 'das pa'i og tu bstan pa nub pa'i dus kyi tse/ lo brgyad cu lon pa na/ dge slong blo 'chang zhes bya bar gyur nas/ rang gi sog la yang mi lta bar byas te/ mdo 'di 'byin par 'gyur ro/

③ 中国藏学研究中心：《圣大鼓品经·大乘经》，《中华大藏经·甘珠尔》第 63 卷，第 35、196 页。

④ Tāranātha, "Dga ldan phun tshogs gling gi gnas bshad bzhugs," pp.165–166：sngar yang shin tu phyi mar gyur pa'i dus der byung nas/ nga'i bstan pa gsal bar byed do zhes 'byung ba'i gnas gang du bstan pa gsal bar 'gyur ba'i chos gzhi gtsug lag khang gi gtso bo ni/ rtag brtan dam pa'i chos kyi gling nges don dga' ba'i tshal （转下页）

记与笃布巴传法的诠释来自多罗那他的自述。然而，与诸多寺庙历史不同的是，多罗那他将平措林寺的渊源直接与相隔近一百五十年的觉囊祖师进行关联，而非展现历时的代代相传谱系。多罗那他一方面宣称此授记内容正确无误，另一方面却说笃布巴的六支瑜伽修行与如来藏的教法一直保存至他的时代。关于此教派传承的信息十分稀少，直至多罗那他的复兴，期间没有留下任何一部觉囊祖师的著作。[①] 这其中的原因，以多罗那他的说法，亦包含在《大法鼓经》中，根据胜迹志所载，“在彼涅槃灭度后，此后世间化为空，彼说法者圆寂后，如是无现他人，如是僧人难得，次第显现即衰减”[②]。在末法情形下出现救世主无疑是藏传佛教叙事传统中的经典。

之后，如此“顺理成章”的事业之开启迎来的是顺遂的建设过程与神奇瑞相的不断显现。除了天降花雨、地显异象外，胜迹志特意强调了整个工程建造过程毫不费力，仿佛“任运而成”。这些描述着实美化、圣化了实际耗费巨大人力物力、繁复的建造工程，相反，图齐（Giuseppe Tucci）在《西藏画卷》（*Tibetan Painted Scroll*）中谈到这一精美的寺庙称，“〔这些〕工程迫使民众，或短或长时间里都在被强制干活”[③]。除此之外，整篇胜迹志中并未提到赞助人的信息，如此处理更加突出了胜迹志的宗教性。将这些细节与桑耶寺的建造故事进行比对，相似性一目了然。[④] 多罗那他一方面着意于圣域古印度的重构，一方面又潜意识地指向对吐蕃传统的回归，这二者无疑都是围绕佛法初传时对正统性的强调。而这样的叙述建构不仅表现在文本中，还贯穿于整个艺术空间的打造。

3. 圣物选择与装置

当寺庙建筑落成后，接下来最重要的是对佛殿的布置，需要迎请佛像、经书等圣物，举

（接上页）zhes bya ba ’di nyid yin te/ don la bcom ldan ’das de bzhin gshegs pa thugs rje’i bdag nyid can gyi bka’ las lung bstan pa lags/ de yang rnga bo che’i mdo las/ kun mkhyen chos kyi rgyal po dol po sangs rgyas de nyid kyis/ rgyal ba’i bstan pa nyi ma ltar gsal bar mdzad cing/ lo brgyad cu’i bar du nges don gyi bstan pa phyogs thams cad du dar bar gyur la/ de nas bar skabs der cung zad nges pa’i don gyi bstan pa mi gsal bar gyur pa na/ slar yang chos kyi rgyal po de nyid ’gro ba’i don du bshes gnyen dam pa’i tshul bzung ste/ sprul pa’i skus nges pa’i don gyi bstan pa gsal bar mdzad tshul lung bstan pa ni[...] ’dir lho phyogs su ’byung ba zhes bshad pa ni/ ’dzam bu ling gi phyed lho ma chu bo si ti’i lho phyogs su ’byon pa’i don yin la/ de yang shin tu dus kyi tha mar/ de nyid ’byon par gsung pa ni/ bdag cag gi rje btsun dam pa ’dis/ slar yang nges don gyi bstan pa dar bar mdzad pa lung bstan pa yin par gda’/

① Cyrus Stearns, *The Buddha from Dolpo: A Study of the Life and Thought of the Tibetan Master Dolpoba Sherab Gyaltsen*, New York: SUNY Press, 1999, p.60.

② Tāranātha, “Dga ldan phun tshogs gling gi gnas bshad bzhugs,” p.165：de na mya ngan yongs ’das nas/ de ’og ’jig rten stong par ’gyur/ chos smra de ni ’das gyur nas/ de ’dra gzhan ni ’ga’ mi ’byung/ de ’dra’i dge slong rnyed dka’ ste/ rim gyis snang ba nyams par ’gyur/

③ Giuseppe Tucci, *Tibetan Painted Scrolls*, vols. 1, Rome: Libreria dello Stato, 1949, p.200.

④ Pasang Wangdu & Hildegard Diemberger, *dBa’bzhed: The Royal Narrative Concerning the Bringing of the Buddha’s Doctrine to Tibet*, pp.64–69.

行装藏、开光等仪式，还需布局壁画使其内部庄严。藏传佛教将圣物分为“三所依”的佛塔、佛像与佛经，这一分类方式很大程度上成为了胜迹志在详述时的内容架构。[①] 尽管结构划分并不明显，所用笔墨不等，多罗那他仍依照了这一形式分别对“意所依”“身所依”与“语所依”进行了描述。

所谓祖拉康的“身所依”有三种，其详述占有大量篇幅，内容分别为：主尊佛像七勇佛、觉沃佛“胜利十方”、大殿其他塑像与壁画。主尊佛像与圣物均安置于净香殿内。藏学家安德鲁·昆特曼（Andrew Quintman）于 2018 年作文对平措林寺的主尊佛，特别是觉沃佛的塑像，结合纷扰的历史背景进行了深入研究。他指出平措林寺整个寺院造像主题围绕着释迦牟尼佛的单一尊崇，在藏地是罕见的，也体现了多罗那他对印度的致敬；同时，该寺最重要的圣物觉沃佛“胜利十方”是藏巴汗家族的战利品，殊胜的来源使其可与东边拉萨城的两大圣物（大昭寺的觉沃佛与小昭寺的不动金刚）相提并论，暗示了平措林寺享有与拉萨标志性的胜迹相匹敌的地位。[②] 如果结合整个胜迹志的文本阅读与分析，不难肯定昆特曼对圣物论述的合理性。而当对“身所依”的七勇佛塑像、觉沃佛“胜利十方”与其他塑像与壁画作进一步文本分析后，可以看到一些昆特曼在阅读中未关注到的语文学细节，同时对“七勇佛”进行了进一步探讨，在此予以补正：

1）关于觉沃佛的印度来源

据《胜迹志》所说，“就‘觉沃胜利十方’佛而言，佛陀的继承者饮光尊者（迦叶）在狮子座就任后一百年，建了印度金刚座大菩提寺，彼时，工人所造的具幻佛身像出现了很多。神变的觉沃释迦牟尼的伟大传说有很多，但都出自这一时期。吉祥大菩提寺所住的八方，有八座佛坛，在它们每一座里都有佛殿，从八大宏化中，给每一个宏化安放一尊佛像，彼为一切工匠所造佛像之处。此觉沃胜利十方是在其中的调伏守财大象〔的佛像〕”[③]。首先，可以明确的是该佛像是一尊来自印度金刚座（Rdo rje gdan）大菩提寺的塑像。关于金刚座的佛教历史意义于此不予赘述，然而除了表明尊贵的出处，多罗那他在此段叙述中已经隐含着与最知名的二尊觉沃佛做比较的意图。例如此句：“神变的觉沃释迦牟尼的伟大传说有很多，

---

① Dan Martin, “Table of Contents (*dkar chag*),” p.504.

② Andrew Quintman, “Putting the Buddha to Work: Śākyamuni in the service of Tibetan Monastic Identity,” *Journal of the International Association of Buddhist Studies*, vol. 40, 2017, pp.111−156.

③ Tāranātha, “Dga ldan phun tshogs gling gi gnas bshad bzhugs,” p.172：jo bo phyogs las rnam rgyal ’di’i dbang du byas na/ ston pa’i rgyal tshab ’od srung chen po seng ge’i khri la ’khor ’khod pa nas lo brgya tsam na/ rgya gar rdo rje gdan gyi byang chub chen po bzhengs/ dus de tsam na/ lha’i bzo bos bzhengs pa’i sku gzugs ’phrul dang ldan pa mang du byung/ ’phrul snang gi jo bo shAkya mu ni la che ba dbyung ba’i gtam rgyud mi ’dra ba du ma yod kyang/ dus de skabs ka byon par gda’/ dpal byang chub chen po bzhugs pa’i phyogs mtshams brgyad na/ gan doha la brgyad yod/ de dag re re na lha khang re re/ mdzad pa brgyad kyi nang nas mdzad pa re re’i sku brnyan bzhugs/ de thams cad lha’i bzos bos bzhengs pa yin par gda’/ jo bo phyogs las rnam rgyal ’di ni de’i nang nas/ glang po che nor skyong btul ba de yin/

但都出自这一时期。”[①] 根据《玛尼全集》《西藏王统记》等传统史书所载，“神变觉沃”指的是佛陀去世后一位婆罗门夫人命三位儿子建立三座佛教寺院，其中在大菩提寺所建的佛塔式佛殿（gan dho la）中安放的三十岁的佛陀身像[②]；而佛陀出家前所造身像才是藏地历史中著名的“三身”（sku gsum），即佛陀七岁、十二岁与二十五岁的等身相[③]。因此，多罗那他在此区别了觉沃佛的造像类型，并强调了神变觉沃佛的类型之稀有，从而抬高了“胜利十方”的地位。同时，他一方面强调了神变佛像的稀有性，另一方面在八尊中识认了一件重要性相对较低的“调伏疯象”的宏化像[④]，较之于“战胜魔王”“初转法轮”或者“涅槃”的宏化塔而言，这一生动的宏化像仿佛为人们拾起了一段被遗忘在角落中的历史，使其更具有历史真实感。同样的叙事策略亦体现在接下来的叙述中。

2）关于觉沃佛的藏地来源

据《胜迹志》所说，“起初，〔该佛像〕是作为法王松赞干布的本尊像放在宫殿里的；然后，在法王赤松德赞时期，落在桑耶的地方，安放在威檐（bad rngam pa）殿里，后来大洪水灾害出现的时候，在威檐殿和和尚（hwa shang）殿等一带出现水灾，此佛像一时找不到了”[⑤]。此处记载了觉沃佛的塑像从印度直接到了松赞干布的宫殿里，这中间的过程并未说明。然而它来到藏地后仍享有法王“本尊像”的圣物地位[⑥]。其后，它被传承到了桑耶地区。昆特曼将桑耶识认为桑耶寺，认为觉沃佛安住于其中一座名为“bad rngam pa”的佛殿内。[⑦] 然而，仔细考证“bad rngam pa”一词会发现，此应为桑耶僧诤后赤松德赞所新修的一座庙宇之名。“bad rngam pa”，又作“bad rngam po”，字面意为“威檐”，在《巴协》增广本（*Sba bzhed*）中记载：“〔和尚〕然后建了和尚摩诃衍殿，后返回汉地；国王心意已定，在逢集时修

---

① 昆特曼的英文节译并未译出这句话，见 Andrew Quintman, “Putting the Buddha to Work: Śākyamuni in the service of Tibetan Monastic Identity,” p.139。

② Per. K. Sørensen, *Tibetan Buddhist Historiography: The Mirror Illuminating the Royal Genealogies*, pp.66–69.

③ Ibid., p.65.

④ 八塔象征的内容在不同体系中并不一致，在早期佛传艺术中“调伏疯象”很少被单独呈现，多罗那他所理解的“八塔变”图像应是10世纪以后成型的。关于八塔体系在印藏地区流传的讨论参见贾维维：《宋夏河西地区“八塔变”图像的来源与流布》，《文艺研究》2019年第8期，第129—133页；图齐著，魏正中、萨尔吉编译：《梵天佛地》，上海古籍出版社、意大利亚非研究院2009年版，第一卷，第9—11页。

⑤ Tāranātha, “Dga ldan phun tshogs gling gi gnas bshad bzhugs,” p.173：di yang dang por chos kyi rgyal po srong btsan sgam po’i thugs dam gyi rten mdzad cing pho brang du bzhugs pa yin/ de nas chos rgyal khri srong lde btsan gyi ring la/ bsam yas kyi phyogs su phebs/ bad rngam rnam pa’i lha khang du bzhugs pa las/ dus phyis chus gnod pa chen po byung ba’i skabs shig/ bad rngam pa dang hwa shang lha khang sogs mang po zhig la chu skyon byung/ sku ’di re zhig ma rnyed/

⑥ 关于法王的“本尊像”（*thugs dam*）与吐蕃时期寺院建设的关系，以及本尊像是如何从印度来到藏地的历史传说均见于《西藏王统记》等史书，参见 Per. K. Sørensen, *Tibetan Buddhist Historiography: The Mirror Illuminating the Royal Genealogies*, pp.187–193。

⑦ Andrew Quintman, “Putting the Buddha to Work: Śākyamuni in the service of Tibetan Monastic Identity,” p.140.

建威檐殿，后在举办节庆时，全藏人民都聚集而来〔……〕”[①]；同时，据说建于热巴坚时期，藏地著名的前弘期寺院温姜多寺（'U shang rdo'i lha khang）建造时是按先辈的“威檐殿”为蓝图建造了誓愿殿。[②]

因此，虽然此处仍选择将“bad rngam pa”译为“佛殿”，但这座佛殿理当作为一座独立于桑耶寺建筑群之外的庙宇来理解。尽管我们能够于史书中查到这座佛殿，但不同于吐蕃时期流传下来的诸多有名的寺院或者佛殿，[③]此来源实属偏僻小众，多罗那他也未在其他作品中就此有更多的阐释。这尊圣物来自藏巴汗的馈赠，而非多罗那他有意求得，[④]然而他如此强调佛像之印度和吐蕃来源的用意不言而喻，其精心的叙述更让人感佩于作为历史学家的多罗那他本人的博闻强识，而这一思路贯穿于整个平措林寺的艺术建造中。与此同时，多罗那他不仅着意保存继承这些圣物，当那些古老的、经典的造像或者仪轨不再流传时，他则是那一位拥有机缘的、或负有使命的传统接续人。

3）关于“七勇佛”的历史与教法寓意

作为整个平措林寺的主尊佛，“七勇佛”在图像学上的象征意义在先前的研究中并未得到充分的体现。然而，这个与吐蕃佛法初传以及“转轮王”观念息息相关的图像组合，实为整个平措林寺的设计奠定了最重要的基调。“七勇佛”（sangs rgyas dpa' bo bdun），又称“七世佛”（sangs rgyas rabs bdun），《胜迹志》给出了这一组合的出处，即“其作为一切祖拉康最重要的〔部分〕，《别别解脱经》如是云：‘胜观佛、顶髻佛、一切胜佛、灭累佛、金寂佛、饮光佛、释迦牟尼瞿昙天中天，教化驯服人类，〔是〕无上的世间护法，最胜的怙主七佛，具名的别别解脱，此即广大宣说’”[⑤]。随后多罗那他对这一来自律部的传统做了详尽的阐释，其经典来源可见于梵、藏、汉文的《根本说一切有部》《梵网经》《佛说七佛经》等。然

---

① 德吉：《〈巴协〉汇编：藏文》，民族出版社 2009 年版，第 54 页。de nas ha shang ma hA ya na gtsug lag khang bzhengs nas slar rgya nag tu gshegs/ btsun po'i thugs dgongs grub nas/ tshong dus su bad rngam pa'i lha khang bzhengs nas dga' ston mdzad pa'i dus su bod 'bangs thams cad tsogs pa ...

② 德吉：《〈巴协〉汇编：藏文》，第 61 页。关于温姜多寺的研究参见谢继胜、贾维维：《温姜多无例吉祥兴善寺修建史实考述——兼论藏文史书记载的温姜多寺、昌珠寺与于阗工匠入藏的关系》，《故宫博物院院刊》2011 年第 6 期，第 22 页。然而，汉译本《巴协》与该研究中都均未识别“bad rngam pa”一词，故“威檐殿”是否为藏地密檐塔式建筑先例的问题可另作文讨论。

③ 早期吐蕃王室众寺院的研究参见 Per Sørensen and Guntrum Hazod, *Thundering Falcon: An Inquiry into the History and Cult of Khra-'brug, Tibet's First Buddhist Temple*, pp.171–215。

④ 关于之后佛像是如何从乃东寺作为藏巴汗的战利品收入桑珠则（bsam grub tse）宫，随后被彭措南杰（Phun tshogs rnam rgyal, 1550—1620）献给多罗那他的历史渊源参见 Andrew Quintman, “Putting the Buddha to Work: Śākyamuni in the service of Tibetan Monastic Identity,” p.131。

⑤ Tāranātha, “Dga ldan phun tshogs gling gi gnas bshad bzhugs,” p.168：gtsug lag khang thams cad kyi gtso bo 'di nyid kyi dbang du byas na/ so so thar pa'i mdo las/ sangs rgyas rnam gzigs gtsug dor tham cad skyob/ 'khor ba 'jig dang gser thub od srung dang/ shākya thub pa go daṃ lha yi lha/ mi 'dul kha lo bsgyur ba bla na med/ 'jig rten mgon po skyob pa'i mchog sangs rgyas dpa' bo bdun po ste/ grags ldan rnams kyi so so thar/ 'di ni rab tu rgyas par ston/

而，正如昆特曼注意到的那样，七佛的图像组合（iconographic grouping）在藏地十分罕见，不像"三世佛""五方佛"或"药师七佛"等图像组合常见于诸多寺院的塑像和壁画中。如文中所示，是"七勇佛"开启了戒律，根据《大乘法海经》所说，戒律又被称作"七佛之法律"（sangs rgyas rabs bdun gyi chos kyi khrims）。[①] 而多罗那他所引用的《别解脱经》（*Sor mdo, Pratimoksa Sūtra*）[②] 及其释论约在公元 9 世纪初期即被翻译为藏文，而七佛律偈颂在僧团内十分受推崇。石泰安（Rolf A. Stein, 1911—1999）在讨论藏地佛法开端时指出，吐蕃时期留下的历史文书和赞普碑铭题记中出现的"chos khrims"一词揭示了法王（*dharmarāja*）的概念；同时，七佛戒律与十善法的紧密关系，使二者一起成为吐蕃统治的法律基础。[③] 除七佛戒法的广为流传外，与七佛对应的陀罗尼经咒亦很盛行，它们能够护佑人们远离疾苦、消除罪孽。[④] 赤松德赞曾命寂护（Śāntarakṣita）专门撰写了七佛的密教仪轨，供王室信仰之用。[⑤] 这一吐蕃时期的教法传统似乎确实被多罗那他很好地接续了下来，在他所著的仪轨合集《本尊海成就法 · 宝源》（*Yi dam rgya mtsho'i sgrub thabs rin chen 'byung gnas*）中专门收录了七佛的成就法，并提到它们为 13 世纪印度祖师释护（Śakyarakṣita）所传，与藏地其他成就法不同。[⑥]

除了作有七佛仪轨接续了教法传统外，多罗那他对于七佛造像的历史亦有自己的见解，他说道："那么，圣域〔印度〕是佛之正法教授的所在，因此建造七如来身相与祈请等风俗广为流传；然在此方发展，为了设立一个能够流传的范例，最主要的原因还是，身相没有很小、放在一起的七勇佛暂时能够让一切地域诸方欢欣喜乐，长久而言能让见闻觉知解脱，殊

---

① 中国藏学研究中心：《法海》（*Chos rgya mtsho*），《中华大藏经 · 甘珠尔》第 66 卷，第 271 页；此经与汉文《法海经》（T.0034）并不同。

② 中国藏学研究中心：《别解脱经》(*Sor mdo*)，《中华大藏经 · 甘珠尔》第 5 卷，第 22—70 页。胜迹志原文中引用的经文汉译版本为："毗钵尸式弃、毗舍俱留孙、羯诺迦牟尼、迦摄释迦尊、如是天中天、无上调御者、七佛皆雄猛、能救护世间、具足大名称、咸说此戒法。"见义净译：《根本说一切有部戒经》（Taishō 1415），收入高楠顺次郎、渡边海旭、小野玄妙等编《大正新修大藏经》第 25 册，第 507—508 页。

③ Rolf Stein, *Rolf Stein's Tibetica Antiqua: With additional materials,* Arthur P. Mckeown trans., Leiden: Brill, 2010, p.203, n. 17; p.207, n.23; pp.208–209；关于《十善法》与早期吐蕃历史的建构的研究参见沈卫荣、侯浩然：《文本与历史：藏传佛教叙事的形成和汉藏佛学研究的建构》，北京大学出版社 2016 年版，第 65—73 页。

④ 见《佛说七佛经》（*'Phags pa sangs rgyas bdun pa zhes bya ba theg pa chen po'i mdo*，《中华大正藏》，卷八十八，第 112—24 页；英译本见钦哲基金会"八万四千颂"计划：https://read.84000.co/translation/toh852.html）、汉文《虚空藏菩萨问七佛陀罗尼咒经》（Taishō 1333）（转引自 Rolf Stein: *Rolf Stein's Tibetica Antiqua: With additional materials,* p.210）；关于七佛陀罗尼的研究参见 Ronald Davidson, "Studies in Dhāranī Literature III: Seeking the Parameters of Dhāranī-pitaka, the Formation of the Dhāranīsamgrahas, and the Place of the Seven Buddhas," in Richard K. Payne ed., *Scripture: Canon: Text: Context: Essays Honoring Lewis Lancaster*, Berkley: Institute of Buddhist Studies and BKD America, 2014, pp.119–180。

⑤ Matthew T. Kapstein, *The Tibetan Assimilation of Buddhism: Conversion, Contestation, and Memory*, Oxford: Oxford University Press, 2000, p.231; n. 64.

⑥《多罗那他全集》第 30 卷，第 150 页。

胜的种子播种，其〔威力〕比起其他更大，故如是思维。”[①] 多罗那他谈及“七勇佛”的形象在印藏地区的流传，指出自己所造大佛像与印度造像习俗不同，其中中央释迦能仁高二十三卡、其余六佛高二十卡（此七佛像现已无存）。根据印度目前所保存的七佛艺术形象，比如桑齐寺的浮雕，可以发现七佛多为站立像，分隔出现，这也与中国早期克孜尔、云冈、敦煌石窟等造像类似。[②] 而在辽以后，中原寺院出现了装饰大雄宝殿的等身七坐佛造像，其中较具代表性的有辽宁义县辽代奉国寺的七佛像[③]、山西稷山元兴化寺的“七佛说法图”[④]。七佛系列造像虽在藏地鲜有遗存，但据19世纪钦则旺波在多罗那他著作的基础上所著的《成就法集》（*Sgrub thabs kun btus*）中的注解已经提及，“此方亦传授，即前弘期时法王世间自在松赞干布的大昭寺中殿建有七世佛的身像〔……〕”。[⑤]

而为了建造完美的“七勇佛”，多罗那他专门迎请了尼泊尔的工匠，他认定尼泊尔工匠制作出来的佛像最为接近佛法初传时从印度迎请来的佛像。《胜迹志》中记述，请尼泊尔工匠打造佛像的传统亦是吐蕃时期的殊胜做法：“第三次开光时，法王松赞干布建昌珠寺的时候，从索塘首次迎请了佛像，其身粗略天然，〔对此〕尼泊尔工匠作了稍微加工；曼曲卡巴（Sman chu kha pa）将〔此〕无上能仁身像请来，从东边到来，内外来看一切都好，一切善缘巧合。”[⑥] 此处多罗那他首先结合了昌珠寺（Khra ’brug）的建寺传说。昌珠寺位于雅隆河谷，是藏地最早的寺院之一，根据《昌珠寺寺志》记载，松赞干布得到授记在索塘护法山（bzo thang mgon po ri）找到了五方佛的天然石像，并带回请尼泊尔工匠打磨后作为昌珠寺建

---

① Tāranātha, “Dga ldan phun tshogs gling gi gnas bshad bzhugs,” p.169：des na ’phags pa’i yul na sangs rgyas kyi bstan pa rnal ma yod pa’i phyogs su ni/ de bzhin gshegs pa bdun gyi sku gzugs bzhengs pa dang/ gsol ba ’debs pa la sogs pa’i srol ka shin tu dar ba yin/ phyogs ’dir yang de dar bar ’gyur ba’i mig ltas khyad par can bzhag pa’i phyir dang/ don gyi gtso bo sangs rgyas dpa’ bo bdun gyi sku gzugs shin tu chung ba ma yin pa chabs gcig tu bzhugs pa der/ gnas skabs su yul phyogs thams cad bde zhing skyid pa dang/ mthar thug mthong thos dran reg thams cad thar ba mchog gi sa bon thebs par ’gyur pa la gzhan pas kyang lhag par stobs che ba yin bar snang bas de la dgongs pa yin pa ’dug/

② 七佛造像发展历程（特别是河西走廊一带）简要梳理参见董华锋、宁宇：《南、北石窟寺七佛造像空间布局之渊源》，《敦煌学辑刊》2010年第1期，第99—109页。

③ 于博：《辽代七佛造像研究——以辽宁义县奉国寺大雄殿七佛为中心》，首都师范大学美术学2013年硕士学位论文。

④ 孟嗣徽：《兴化寺壁画〈七佛说法图〉》，《紫禁城》1998年第3期，第50—53页。

⑤ *Sgrub Thabs Kun Btus* (block prints), Kangara: Indo-Tibetan Buddhist Literature Publisher, Dzongsar Institute for Advanced Studies, vol. 12, 1902, p.319: phyogs ’dir yang bstan pa snga dar gyi dus su chos kyi rgyal po ’jig rten bdang phyug srong btsan sgam pos ’phrul snang bar khang du sangs rgyas rabs bdun gyi snang brnyan bzhengs par mdzad pa.

⑥ Tāranātha, “Dga ldan phun tshogs gling gi gnas bshad bzhugs,” p.172：chos rgyal srong btsan sgam pos khra ’brug bzhengs dus/ zo thang nas spyan drangs pa’i dang por sku’i rnm pa rags rim byon la / bal po’i bzo bos cung zd tsam sgros gtsang bar byas pa’i thub pa’i sku brnyan bla ma sman chu kha pas spyan drangs te/ shar phyogs nas byon pa sogs phyi nang gi ltas thams cad legs/ rten ’brel thams cad bzang ba’i phyogs su ’grig pa yin par ’dug/

寺的主尊佛像；① 同时，此处所指将佛像带来的人物是曼曲卡巴·洛珠坚赞（Sman chu kha ba Blo gros rgyal mtshan, 1314—1389），早期觉囊派的上师之一，曾追随笃补巴与其主要弟子学习，后于前藏达孜地区曼曲修行处传法。多罗那他不仅将尼泊尔造像的做法与吐蕃传统联系，还关联了早期觉囊派发展的历史，促成了众多“善缘巧合”。

通过对平措林寺圣物装置叙述的详细分析，我们可以看出多罗那他对这一胜迹打造所做的精心策划。他运用自己渊博的历史地理见闻和胜迹文学知识，试图为自己的传承打造一座殊胜的传法圣地。相比于历数伟大传承中的前人功绩，利用教法源流塑造教派身份（monastic identity），这一位觉囊派17世纪极富才华的祖师在寺院建造时直指印度源流，追溯吐蕃历史，无疑都是为了强调佛法的正统。而如此正统的代表并非已经在藏地为人熟知的作品，不论是艺术造像还是仪轨文本，都是同样有着殊胜来源但“被遗忘的”、小众的传承。

4. 开光

任何的佛像或佛塔在建造后都必须要经历装藏（gzungs zhugs）与开光（rab gnas）两个过程，才能圆满其作为宗教圣物的功能。② 主尊“七勇佛”到来后，即举行了装藏与开光仪式，其中“就开光祥时而言，戊午年室宿月十四日至娄宿上旬三日之间，吉祥密集与鲁依巴胜乐，黑阎魔敌，作怖金刚〔大威德〕、无上不动〔忿怒明王〕，忿怒金刚手〔秘主〕，与亥母三十七尊，无我母十五尊，吉祥时轮坛城等，区分后全部一一开光。己未年水月上旬内，佛颅、智慧自在佛母、菩萨释传承的胜乐，在彼三座坛城之上开光三次。此年的箕宿月八日，吉祥黑噜噶胜乐妙金刚的坛城之上，盛大开光一次，简约开光三十次”③。可以看出，大概花了半个月的时间，寺庙为这些新进的尊像一一举行开光仪式，这些数量可观的塑像随后可能被安置在了平措林寺各佛殿中，这也为我们大致了解平措林寺供奉的尊神系统提供了一条重要信息。

当我们进一步在多罗那他的著作中考察这些尊像背后的佛学含义时，会发现这些尊像

---

① Per Sørensen and Guntrum Hazod, *Thundering Falcon: An Inquiry into the History and Cult of Khra-'brug, Tibet's First Buddhist Temple*, pp.60–62, 64.

② 藏传佛教开光仪轨的主要研究参见 Yael Bentor, *Consecration of Images & Stūpas in Indo-Tibetan Tantric Buddhism*, Leiden; New York & Köln: Brill, 1996。

③ Tāranātha, “Dga ldan phun tshogs gling gi gnas bshad bzhugs,” p.171：rab gnas skabs dge mtshan gyi dbang du byas na/ sa pho rta'i lo'i khrums kyi zla ba'i tshes bcu bzhi nas brtsams te/ tha skar gyi yar ngos tshes gsum gyi bar la/ dpal gsang ba 'dus pa dang/ bde mchog lAu hi pa dang/ gshin rje gshed nag po dang/ rdo rje 'jig byed dang/ mi g.yo bla med dang/ phyag na rdo rje gtum po dang/ phag mo lha so bdun ma dang/ bdag med lha mo bco lnga dang/ dpal dus kyi 'khor lo'i dkyil 'khor rnams zhal phye nas rab gnas tshar re re mdzad par gda'/ sa mo lug lo'i chu'i zla ba'i yar ngo'i nang du yang/ sangs rgyas thod pa dang/ ye shes dbang phyug ma dang/ sems 'grel lugs kyi bde mchog ste/ dkyil 'khor de gsum gyi steng nas rab gnas tshar gsum/ lo de nyid kyi chu stod zla ba'i tshes brgyad kyi nyin/ dpal he ru ka 'khor lo bde mchog 'jam pa'i rdo rje'i dkyil 'khor steng nas rab gnas rgyas pa gcig ste mdor na rab gnas tshar bcu gsum dang/

很大程度上是依据多罗那他所传的具有特色的密宗修法传承，是其文本著作的视觉表现。其中，“鲁依巴胜乐”指的是大成就者鲁依巴（Luipa）的胜乐传承[①]，金刚亥母（*vajravārāhī*）主要为胜乐金刚的佛母，无我母（*Nairāymyā*）主要为喜金刚的明妃，其数量之多可以看出多罗那他选择供奉的佛像涵盖了主要的无上密续修法，并非只是一味地突出教派传承的时轮特色。此外，多罗那他特地提到建了三座坛城并为它们开光，即“佛顶盖、智慧自在佛母、菩萨释传承的胜乐”，分别代表的是三部密续修法，即《佛顶盖续》(*Buddhakapāla Tantra*)、《四座释续》(*Catuḥpīthavikhyāta Tantra*）与《三菩萨释》(*Sems 'grel skor gsum*）之一的金刚手菩萨所著的《胜乐经首品释》(*Phyag rdor stod 'grel*)。在《多罗那他全集》中我们均找到了对应的修法仪轨著作。

无论如何，这些佛像的配置似乎都具有理论文本的依据，而这些文本恰恰亦是多罗那他著作的精髓所在。除了这些胜乐、密集、时轮等无上瑜伽修法集合外，多罗那他所著的《宝源》等著作描述了众多本尊形象亦可起到指导造像的作用。将佛法呈现于视觉是藏传佛教艺术的本质，而多罗那他明显是将特定的修法传承有选择性地一一展现，这也适用于《胜迹志》接下来对各佛殿内置佛像、壁画的详述。因此，在佛像名称识认之上，对于研究者而言，重要的是考察其佛像选择的理论依据与排列安置方式背后的逻辑。

三、见即获益：胜迹的意义

如上所述，《胜迹志》中诸多宗教题材的专有名词、故事作为文学母题（motif）均可找到特定传统的出处与渊源。通过精妙编织这一最重要的理解寺庙艺术的文本及其叙事，多罗那他将其整体佛学的成就以寺庙艺术设计的形式得以呈现。这一做法背后的原因又回归到了文章第一部分对于胜迹（gnas）本身的讨论，即这些“三所依”的存在均具有加持的功能。在《胜迹志》中，多罗那他对“胜迹”作了自己的定义：

> 谁在此殊胜之地，〔他的〕贪嗔等烦恼就会减少、善法越来越增长、昏昧显明、所知清净，贪婪心减少、出离心增长，嗔心平息、悲心发展，散乱消除、寂止坚固，邪见不出、胜观自生，如是胜地非有相似。〔那些〕推崇具偏执的赞颂，推崇厉鬼恶魔，凭借谋权与敛财等缘起〔的寺院〕，聚众出现并自许，无明众生如水般流走〔于以上的地

① Jamgön Kongtrul, *Treasury of Knowledge*, Book 8, Part 3, Snow Lion Publications: Ithaca, New York, 2008, p. 28, 44.

方〕，他们幻现此为仙境的存在，〔而这些寺院〕无法与此地相比。比起在他处修习日与月，在此修习仅日与时的功德更大；比起在它处缓慢努力作善事，还不如弃恶行，恭敬佛法与上师，在此处睡觉即亲近无上殊胜菩提。渔夫、旃陀罗、低等的兽类与作无间业等具恶者，不管是自愿还是受他人邀请，在此地转经、看一看祖拉康大殿、沐手、转经、献供，他们的罪行清净后，即〔往〕生天界。何况是其他凡夫，于此胜地，见即获益。①

"见即获益"（mthong ba tsam gyis don dang ldan pa），又称"一见得利""不虚见"，属于藏传佛教"感官解脱"的一种，即"见解脱"（mthong grol），是藏传佛教艺术，特别是密教艺术的普遍（世）宗教内涵。② 多罗那他认为达旦丹曲林是清净无上的，与其他规模较大、财力异常雄厚的寺庙不同，其能让人仅睡一晚即证菩提的胜迹威力正是由他精心布局与安排的艺术工程实现的。对于平措林寺来说，从外象的风水地理，到祖拉康建筑本身，再到里面供奉的主尊佛像、特殊佛像、佛经、其他本尊像与壁画，其"见解脱"的殊胜加持力似乎有内外两个层面：一个层面是属于历史的、文化的，这里所有一切都具有印度的、吐蕃时代的渊源，其古意的力量（archaic power）赋予了此地尊贵的文化地位，使其成为负载着传承的藏土圣地，尽管觉囊沟即使在笃布巴时期也是一处偏远的瑜伽士聚集地；③ 另一个层面则是属于教法的、修行的，从本身具有坛城含义的地貌与祖拉康、七勇佛，再到本尊塑像、图像，均可作为修法仪轨的指示——一切皆可修，所见皆具菩提，其密法的甚深内义为在此地得"见解脱"提供了更加明晰的成道路径。

总的来说，只有将胜迹志置于建造者的知识体系与教法源流之中详细审查，才能读出书

① Tāranātha, "Dga ldan phun tshogs gling gi gnas bshad bzhugs," pp.163–164：gnas mchog dam pa 'dir ni sus 'dug kyang/ chags sdang la sogs nyon mongs shas chung zhing/ dge ba'i chos rnams gong nas gong du 'phel/ gnyid rmugs gsal zhing rig pa dwangs pa'i gnas/ zhen chags chung zhing nges 'byung 'phel ba'i gnas/ gnod sems zhi zhing snying rje rgyas pa'i gnas/ rnam g.yengs sangs shing zhi gnas brtan pa'i gnas/ log lta mi 'byung lhag mthong ngang gis skye/ gnas mchog 'di dang mtshungs pa gzhan yod min/ phyogs 'dzin can gyi bsngags pa brjod pa dang/ the rang 'gong pos grags pa bsrags pa dang/ dbang sdud nor sgrub la sogs rten 'brel gyis/ 'du 'tshog byung zhing grags pa tsam zhig la/ rmongs pa'i 'gro rnams chu ltar rgyug bzhin du/ zhing mchog yin par 'khrul dang 'di mi mnyam/ gzhan du lo dang zla ba bsgoms pa pas/ gnas mchog 'dir ni zhag dang za ma tsam/ bsgoms pa'i phan yon lhag par che ba yin/ gzhan du yun ring dge sbyor 'bad pa bas/ sdig pa'i las spangs chos dang bla ma la/ mos gus byas nas gnas 'dir nyal ba yang/ bla med byang chub mchog la shin tu nye/ nya pa gdol pa ri dwags dman pa dang/ mtshams med byas pa la sogs sdig can yang/ rang nyid dad pa'am gzhan gyis bskul yang rung/ gnas 'di bskor zhing gtsug lag khang la lta/ khrus byas phyag dang bskor ba mchod pa 'bul/ de yi sdig pa dag nas lha yul skye/ skye bo gzhan dag smos kyang ci zhig dgos/ gnas mchog 'di ni mthong ba don ldan yin//

② 相关佛学讨论参见 Holly Gayley, "Soteriology of the Senses in Tibetan Buddhism," *Numen*, Vol. 54, No. 4, Religion through the Senses (2007), pp.459–499; Cynthea J Bogel, *With a Single Glance: Buddhist Icon and Early Mikkyō Vision*, Seattle, WA: University of Washington Press, 2009。

③ 尽管笃布巴在沟内建了觉囊大塔，但目前所见精美的大塔很大程度上是多罗那他时期重修的遗留。参见 Giuseppe Tucci, *Tibetan Painted Scrolls*, p.179。

中记载的祥瑞故事背后的寓意，才能发现如文物清单般罗列的佛殿名、佛像名、壁画内容等等之间的深层关联。如今，虽然同被看作重要的历史文献，但是胜迹志不同于传记、游记、教法源流，其高度的文学叙事构成了其重要的特征，也使得保存了这个叙事传统的胜迹志有别于受到现代史学影响所进行编纂的当代寺志。同时，西藏的胜迹文学是理解寺庙艺术的重要指示，读懂胜迹志不仅需要对其内容中的专有名词进行考证，更需要关注文本中那些看似非历史的、神话的、宗教的叙述，通过语文学式的分析，层层拨开文本中蕴藏的历史文化内涵。

黑水城出土文献与西夏佛教

黑水城的藏传佛教量论之钥：俄藏黑水城文献 912 号研究

马洲洋
奥地利科学院

一、研 究 背 景

在近十年西域佛教研究的诸潮流中，有两个新动向引起了笔者的关注。其中，第一个动向是学界对西夏所流传的藏传佛教的研究的展开。这一展开具有两个新的特征：其一是研究的载体从汉文材料逐渐拓展到西夏文材料；其二是研究的内容从题跋信息等零碎的语文材料拓展到对整篇文本的释读。[①] 第二个新动向与后弘早期的藏传佛教思想史相关。随着《噶当文集》（*Bka' gdams gsung 'bum*）等珍稀藏文文献的出版，学者得以见到一大批此前被认为已经亡佚的文本。这批文本大多与早期噶当派的“经院学”（scholasticism）[②] 相关，涵盖了中观二谛、弥勒五论（Byams chos sde lnga）及量论（tshad ma）等藏传佛教显宗课题。基于对这批文本的研究，学界目前对 11—13 世纪藏传佛教的思想发展的认识有

---

① 这类研究目前成果相当丰硕。其代表性的著作见孙伯君、聂鸿音：《西夏文藏传佛教史料——“大手印”法经典研究》，中国藏学出版社 2018 年版。索罗宁：《大鹏展翅：藏传佛教新旧译密咒在西夏的传播》，上海古籍出版社 2023 年版。

② “经院学”是国际学界假借中世纪基督教经院学概念对藏传佛教中的一部分内容所作出的界定。它的特征大致可概括为：不完全依赖虔信的基础，以理性的方法论证义理的合理性。有关其讨论，见 José Ignacio Cabezón, *Buddhism and Language: A Study of Indo-Tibetan Scholasticism*, Albany: State University of New York Press, 1994。有关本文着重讨论的桑浦经院学，又见 Pascale Hugon, “Mapping Recently Recovered Early Tibetan Epistemological Works,” in Volker Caumanns, Jörg Heimbel, Kazuo Kano and Alexander Schiller eds., *Gateways to Tibetan Studies: A Collection of Essays in Honour of David P. Jackson on the Occasion of his 70th Birthday*, vol. 1, Hamburg: Department of Indian and Tibetan Studies, Universität Hamburg, 2021, pp.415—460。

了极大推进。①

令人激动的是，这两个动向不仅在很大程度上能够相互支持，而且二者的交汇处具有形成一个新研究课题的潜力。这是由于在黑水城所出土的西夏文佛教文献中，除与密教相关的文本外，还有大量记载着藏地后弘早期显教思想的文本。②这一部分文本能与上文所述的新见噶当派藏文文献形成思想史上的联系，从而一方面为我们深入了解西夏所传藏传佛教提供助力，另一方面也能为我们通过西夏材料反向研究当时的藏地传统带来机遇。笔者在过去的研究中，以西夏文量论文本为核心，发现了一批与俄·洛丹喜饶（Rngog Lo tsā ba Blo ldan shes rab，世称“俄译师”，约 1059—1109）所创立的桑浦内邬托寺（Gsang phu ne'u thog，下文简称为“桑浦寺”）经院学传统相关的西夏文藏传佛教义理类文本。③笔者因而提出假设：西夏所流传的藏传佛教义理传统全部来源于桑浦内邬托的学统。④

然而正所谓“大胆假设，小心求证”，我们对任何历史传统的论断必然都要建立在对一个个文本抽丝剥茧的钩沉求索之上。笔者过去对部分文本进行了微观研究，在本文中也将继续这种实践。本文将围绕俄藏黑水城文献第 912 号题名为《正理空幢要门解锁》（𗼃𗣼𗼻𗤶𗥃𘟀𘃣𗖵，以下简称《解锁》）的文本展开。文章先概述文本的内容，再从内容出发，确定其与桑浦传统的关系，最后简要探讨与之相关的其他西夏文本，并在文末附上这一文本的科判与其现量部分的译注。

---

① 其代表性著作见 Kazuo Kano, *Buddha-nature and Emptiness: rNgog Blo-ldan-shes-rab and a Transmission of the "Ratnagotravibhāga" from India to Tibet*, Wien: Arbeitskreis für Tibetische und Buddhistische Studien, 2016; Pascale Hugon and Jonathan Stoltz, *The Roar of a Tibetan Lion: Phya pa Chos kyi seng ge's Theory of Mind in Philosophical Perspective*, Wien: Österreichischen Akademie der Wissenschaften, 2019。

② 最早对这批显教文本进行考述的是索罗宁。详见 Kirill Solonin, "Dīpaṃkara in the Tangut Context: An Inquiry into the Systematic Nature of Tibetan Buddhism in Xixia (part 1)," *Acta Orientalia Academiae Scientiarum Hungaricae* 68, no.4, 2015, pp.425–451; Kirill Solonin, "Dīpaṃkara in the Tangut Context: An Inquiry into the Systematic Nature of Tibetan Buddhism in Xixia: (Part 2)," *Acta Orientalia Academiae Scientiarum Hungaricae* 69, no. 1, 2016, pp.1–25。

③ 参见马洲洋：《西夏文译〈正理除意之暗〉初探》，《中国藏学》2021 年第 3 期，第 138—145 页；Zhouyang Ma, "The *Nyāyabindu* in Tangut Translation," *Journal of Indian Philosophy* 49, no. 5, 2021, pp.779–825; Zhouyang Ma, "Introduction to Speculative Thinking: An Unidentified Work in Tangut Translation of Maja Jangchup Tsöndrü (d. 1185, Tib. rMa bya Byang chub brtson 'grus)," *BuddhistRoad Papers* 1.5, 2022; Zhouyang Ma, "An Inner Asian Buddhist Revolution: The Rise of Tibetan Buddhism in the Tangut Xia State," PhD diss., Harvard University, 2023。

④ 这一假设只涉及传承的内容而并不涉及传承的具体人物和方式。比如，由于许多早期噶当派上师如帕莫竹巴与桑浦寺关系密切，桑浦的经院学传统同样很有可能由噶举派僧众传入西夏，这一点还需进一步考证。此外，这一假设也不排除西夏僧众依据桑浦学统创作本土著作的可能。

二、文本概观

《解锁》的图版被收入了最近出版的《俄藏黑水城文献》第 28 册[①]，使我们能够对全部文本进行研究。据克恰诺夫记载，文本卷装写本，大小为 23 cm × 300 cm，缺开头。[②]图版所见文本同样缺开头，文尾载有文题，不署作者及写作时间。写本中有大量补字、涂改、批注等痕迹，说明使用者曾使用这一文本进行过实际的学习活动。正文中有以“分二”（[illegible]）、“一”（[illegible]）、“二”（[illegible]）等字样组成的科文，符合藏传佛教经院学论议的一般规则。文本以“正理”为题，暗示了它属于藏传佛教量论类文献。[③]文中所出现的量论词汇如“因三相”（[illegible]，*tshul gsum pa'i rtags）、“宗法”（[illegible]，*phyogs chos）、“结果因”（[illegible]，*'bras bu'i gtan tshigs）等与笔者在夏藏量论文本对勘中所见的译语一致，[④]能够说明文本属于藏传佛教量论的大传统。但是，文本中缺乏直接证据表明其译自某一藏文本，因此我们尚需考虑它虽属藏传佛教传统，但为西夏本土创作的可能性。此外，因为现存的全文没有引注任何人名或经典名，所以我们也难以直接确定它所属的传承系统。这必须通过细致的语文学考察才能实现，详见第三节。

该文文题中的“解锁”（[illegible]）二字似乎揭示了这是一部注疏性质的作品，[⑤]文中的体例能够证实这一点。试看如下之一例：

【夏】[illegible]、[illegible][—[illegible]? +[illegible]][illegible]，[illegible]“[illegible]”[illegible]，“[illegible]”[illegible]。“[illegible]”[illegible]，[illegible]。“[illegible]”[illegible]，[illegible]。“[illegible]”[illegible]，[illegible]。[illegible]，“[illegible]”[illegible]。“[illegible]”[illegible]，[illegible]。“[illegible]”[illegible]，“[illegible]”[illegible]。[⑥]

① 《正理空幢要门解锁》（[illegible]，ИНВ. No. 912），收入史金波、魏同贤、克恰诺夫编《俄藏黑水城文献（西夏文佛教部分）》第 28 册，上海古籍出版社 2019 年版，第 5—7 页。以下简称《解锁》。

② Е. И. Кычанов ed., *Каталог Тангутских Буддийских Памятников*, Kyoto: Kyoto University, 1999, p.551.

③ 西夏文的“正理”二字含义非常丰富，至少对应藏文的“rigs pa”和“tshad ma”两个术语。相关讨论见马洲洋：《西夏文译〈正理除意之暗〉初探》，第 143—144 页。

④ 笔者在夏藏《正理滴论》（以下简称《滴论》）的研究中总结了常见夏藏量论词汇的对应关系，详见 Ma, “The *Nyāyabindu* in Tangut Translation,” pp.818–823.

⑤ “解锁”本身不是常见的藏文注疏喻名，难以进行重构。但如果这里是意译的话，则不排除它是对“钥匙”（藏：lde mig；梵：tāla）的翻译。“钥匙”是印藏佛教传统中常见的注疏喻名。

⑥ 《解锁》，第 5 拍第 20 列至第 6 拍第 4 列。本文中所有的西夏文录文除标点外都是原写本的拟真本（diplomatic edition），而非校订本。因此，所有的文字增删等都会被标出。具体体例见附录二。

【译】第二、认识对象[①]的情形[②]即文中从“出世间”到“证得”的部分。所谓“出世”，即生于初地的圣者[③]们。所谓“圣义谛”，即它们被觉察[④]到的法性[⑤]。所谓“显现”，即无思维中的显现和有思维中的显现[⑥]。因为将它们尽皆囊括，所以是“一切法”。所谓“分析”[⑦]，即离于一与多的逻辑原因[⑧]。所谓“存在不成立”，即将“无自性”作为其成立的对象。

这段引文中最引人注目的显然是“即文中从‘出世间’到‘证得’的部分”这句话。这显示《解锁》的作者是在对某一目标文本进行疏释。“文中”（[illegible]）之“文”（[illegible]）字应当指的就是那部文本。这种体例在《解锁》中随处可见。可惜作者在文中各处的引用几乎都只有只言片语，我们难以从中得见根本文之原文。从语境来看，这里的“圣义谛”（[illegible]）、“显现”（[illegible]）、“一切法”（[illegible]）等等都应是根本文中的词汇。作者对每个词作的短小疏释说明了《解锁》应是一部注疏，而《解锁》中另有“后面的讲说依照根本文自然明了”（[illegible]）[⑨]这样的表述，更说明了根本文的存在。从文题来看，我们自然而然会推测《解锁》是对一部名为《正理空幢要门》的文本的注疏。我们将在下文的第四节中详细讨论这一问题。

从整体风格上看，《解锁》的语言非常简明扼要，没有对各种义理问题进行深入讨论，更像是一部平铺直叙的纲要性教科书。这鲜明地体现在它各处的译注中。这种风格似乎正应了“解锁”的含义——它仅作为一部纲要性的著作而存在。从结构上看，《解锁》呼应了法称量论著作尤其是《正理滴论》的基本结构[⑩]。它现存的部分首先讨论现量的定义，再分别叙述四现量。此后，文本再讨论比量的定义，其中又分自利比量与他利比量。接着，文本较为详细地描述了比量中三种真实的逻辑原因以及三种虚假的逻辑原因。最后，文本叙述了认识

① [illegible]，*gzhal bya（梵：prameya），直译“所量”，常与“能量”即认识工具（藏：tshad ma；梵：pramāṇa）配对。见下文就这一问题的讨论。

② [illegible]，*gnas lugs，即某一事物存在的原理，英文常以“mode of existence”翻译。

③ [illegible]，*'phags pa。初地与见道（梵：darśanamārga；藏：mthong lam）相应。大乘菩萨于初地见空性，是为圣者。附录二译注中出现的对瑜伽现量“圣者之智”的陈述亦与此类似。

④ 本文以“觉察”翻译西夏文的 [illegible]，对应藏文的 dmigs pa，梵文的 upalabdhi。

⑤ [illegible]，*chos nyid，即现象的本质。

⑥ 无思维（[illegible]，*rtog [pa] med）的显现即脱离了普遍概念的形象，如心识尚未认识到蓝色时，仅由眼识所觉察的蓝色。有思维（[illegible]，*rtog〔pa〕yod）的显现则相反，它是将认识对象概念化后的形象。前者在时间和空间上都具有唯一性，后者则混合了时间与空间。

⑦ [illegible]，*dpyad pa。

⑧ “离于一与多”（[illegible]，*gcig〔dang〕du〔ma〕dang bral ba；梵：ekānekaviraha），意为某一事物既不是同一的，也不是多重的。印藏以寂护（Śāntarakṣita，8 世纪）为代表的一部分论师以“离于一与多”作为逻辑原因，推导出空性。其公式如下：假如 A 具有“离于一与多”的性质，则 A 自性空。

⑨《解锁》，第 5 拍第 14 列。

⑩ 有关《正理滴论》在西夏量论教学中的重要性，见马洲洋：《西夏文译〈正理除意之暗〉初探》，第 143—144 页；Zhouyang Ma, “The *Nyāyabindu* in Tangut Translation,” pp.788–791。

对象的情形，即以上文之引文开头的部分。

虽然《解锁》正如上文所述缺少开头，但通过文本科判的逻辑，我们能够基本还原出开头的内容。不仅如此，我们还能将全文重组成一个具有多层次的科判。首先，由于文本的最后一目为“第二、认识对象的情形”，我们自然而然会去寻找在它之前的“第一”的内容，但综观所有现存的部分，我们并不能找到一个科目与之相对应。从逻辑上看，既然文本讨论了认识对象，那么就也应讨论认识工具。进一步，由于文本绝大部分都在讨论现、比二量，而现、比二量本身又是法称量论中唯二认可的认识工具，那么显然，文本前面所有的内容都应是“第一、认识工具的情形”。当然，我们不能排除在讨论“认识”这一课题之前《解锁》还讨论了别的科目，但在“认识”这一课题内部，只应有“认识工具”和“认识对象”这两目。

接着，由于文本开始处也不是以“第一”而是以“第二、讲说分别的定义”（[illegible]、[illegible]）开始的，我们还需确定与它同层级的“第一”为何。首先，根据这一目的下级科目，我们得知这里的“分别”显然是就现量和比量而言。其次，既有“分别”，那么似乎就应有“共通”。在量论著述的一般实践中，在分述现、比二量前都要给认识工具下一个一般性的定义，正与这里的结构相符合。因此，与“第二”这一目处同一层级的“第一”就应是“讲说〔认识工具〕共通的定义”。解决了这些问题，我们才能够顺藤摸瓜地将文本前面所有的内容以现代语言重组为附录一科判中1–122.422的内容。

最后剩余的内容是一个处于122.422之后看似独立的“第三、结归”（[illegible]、[illegible]）[1]。这一目的全文如下：

【夏】[illegible]、[illegible]，[illegible]：“[illegible]”[illegible]，“[illegible]”[illegible]。“[illegible]”[illegible]，[illegible]。“[illegible]”[illegible]，[illegible]。“[illegible]”[illegible]，“[illegible]v[illegible]”[illegible]。[2]

【译】第三、结归即文中“此者”到“设置”的部分。所谓“此者”，即之前所说的两种认识工具[3]。“于世间计度”即针对周遍于最上世界的诸多不同众生的作为有法[4]的觉

---

① [illegible]译借为“意系”（主旨的收束？），其意义无法完全确定。从夏、汉藏传密教文本的对勘来看，[illegible]应与汉文“结归”相当。见孙伯君、聂鸿音:《西夏文藏传佛教史料——“大手印”法经典研究》，第231页。比如，密教修法中的“加行”“正体”“结归”分别对应西夏文的[illegible]、[illegible]、[illegible]。如果我们相信这一译语完全译自藏文术语sbyor〔ba〕dngos〔po〕mjug〔pa〕，那么就应译自藏文mjug pa，也就是“总结”之意。“总结”一意亦能与《解锁》中的语境吻合。但[illegible]如何能从字面意义上与mjug pa联系起来则仍不明确。本文权且将所有的[illegible]译为“结归”。

②《解锁》，第5拍第15—19列。

③“……[illegible]……[illegible]”的结构在《滴论》(III.39）中有出现，在本文中亦多有出现。从语境来看，它应当是一个判断句式，能够与汉语中的“……者……之谓”这一结构对应。

④ [illegible]，*chos can（梵：dharmin），或译“性质的载体”。比如，在“声是无常”的论式中，“无常”是“法”（性质），“声”是“有法”（性质的载体）。

察对象的计度。“将认识工具进行设置”即“讲说作为认识工具的现量和比量”。

《解锁》现存的部分并没有任何一目指出它包含了这样的一个“结归”。但从内容来看，这里探讨的应该是设置现、比二量作为认识工具的意义。联想到我们之前已经推导出“第二、讲说〔认识工具〕分别的定义”之前应存在“第一、讲说〔认识工具〕共通的定义”，那么这里的“结归”应当就是对前面这两目的一个总结，而这一目的次序恰好就是“第三”。由此我们可以确定这三目属于同一层级。

综上所述，《解锁》从宏观上看应该是下面这样的结构：

1. 认识工具的情形
    11. 讲说〔认识工具〕共通的定义
    12. 讲说〔认识工具〕分别的定义
    121. 现量
    122. 比量
    13. 结归
2. 认识对象的情形

三、与桑浦量论传统的关系

前文已及，由于《解锁》中没有任何的引注信息，我们无法直接确定它所属的藏传佛教传统。但是，我们仍可根据其内部的线索，经由与藏文文本的比对来确定它与桑浦量论传统的紧密关系。笔者在这里主要利用的藏文文本是杰巴·迅努绛曲（’Jad pa Gzhon nu byang chub，约 1150—1210）所著的《量论真实要集》（*Tshad ma de kho na nyid bsdus pa*，以下简称《量论要集》）①。杰巴是活跃于 12 世纪后期的一名桑浦论师，其量论思想主要承袭于恰

① 杰巴·迅努绛曲（’Jad pa Gzhon nu byang chub，原书误署为龙青饶绛巴〔Klong chen rab ’byams pa〕）：《量论真实要集》（*Tshad ma de kho na nyid bsdus pa*，以下简称《量论要集》），四川民族出版社 2000 年版。这部著作在藏传量论思想史上的重要性早已由范德康（Leonard W. J. van der Kuijp）指出，他同样指出原书所题的作者大概率并不是本书真正的作者。参见 Leonard W. J. van der Kuijp, “A Treatise on Buddhist Epistemology and Logic Attributed to Klong chen rab ’byams pa (1308—1364) and Its Place in Indo-Tibetan Intellectual History,” *Journal of Indian Philosophy* 31, 2003, pp.381–437。但最近，乔纳森·斯托尔茨（Jonathan Stoltz）以翔实的证据指出此书的真正作者是杰巴。详见 Jonathan Stoltz, “On the Authorship of the *Tshad ma'i de kho na nyid bsdus pa,*” *Revue d'Etudes Tibétaines* 56, 2020, pp.48–69。

巴·曲吉僧格（Phya pa Chos kyi seng ge，1109—1169）。[①] 其所著的《量论要集》从体裁上看是一部典型的桑浦“要集”（bsdus pa）[②]，其中的思想基本与恰巴在《量论除意之暗》（*Tshad ma yid kyi mun sel*）中的观点一致，但在思想性和论述语言上相对平实。考虑到《解锁》本身的内容也较为简练而不包含复杂的哲学讨论，《量论要集》应当是一部与之风格上接近而易于比对的文本。

我们首先要考察的是两部文本在结构上的某些相似性。我们发现《量论要集》在现量部分的科判与《解锁》相对应的部分相当一致。下表给出了《解锁》科判中121一目与其所有下级科目以及相对应的《量论要集》科目。为示区别，《量论要集》的科目号用英文字母表示（现量的总标题定为科目A）：

《解锁》科目	原文标题	汉译标题	《量论要集》科目	原文标题	汉译标题
121	[illegible]	讲说现量的定义	A	mngon sum bye brag tu phye ste gtan la dbab pa	特别地划分出现量并将其确立下来
121.1	[illegible]	讲说现量的共通定义	AA	mngon sum gyi thun mong gi mtshan nyid	现量的共通的定义
121.2	[illegible]	〔现量〕分别的定义	AB	mngon sum gyi khyad par gyi mtshan nyid	现量分别的定义
/	/	/	ABA	mtshan nyid kyi rab tu dbye ba	定义的分目
/	/	/	ABB	mtshan nyid dngos	实际的定义
121.21	[illegible]	根识现量的定义	ABB.A	dbang po’i mngon sum gyi mtshan nyid	根识现量的定义
121.22	[illegible]	心识现量的定义	ABB.B	rang rig pa’i mngon sum [gyi mtshan nyid]	自证现量〔的定义〕
121.23	[illegible]	自证现量的定义	ABB.C	yid kyi mngon sum gyi mtshan nyid	心识现量的定义
121.24	[illegible]	瑜伽现量的定义	ABB.D	rnal ’byor gyi mngon sum gyi mtshan nyid	瑜伽现量的定义
121.3	[illegible]	结归	/	/	/

① 有关杰巴的更多分析，参见 Stoltz, “On the Authorship of the *Tshad ma’i de kho na nyid bsdus pa*,” pp.54–59。

② “要集”与“注疏”（’grel pa）相对，指的是不依据某一根本文而系统性地讲述某一领域知识的论著。有关要集见 Hugon and Stoltz, *The Roar of a Tibetan Lion*, p.67。

显然，两部文本在现量部分的科判只有些许表面上的不同：《量论要集》对“现量分别的定义”多出“定义的分目”一目，但这仅是先对现量分类的一个绪论，不影响下面“实际的定义”；《解锁》多出的“结归”则是对现量部分的一个总结，也不影响论述的主体。此外，针对四现量，二者只有论说次序上的不同，而没有实质上的不同。杰巴将自证现量提前其实并没有遵循法称量论传统的一般次序。恰巴在《量论除意之暗》中的次序则与《解锁》保持一致[①]。除这些不同之外，《解锁》与《量论要集》在现量的论述结构上完全一致。

进一步，两部文本在某些具体论述的单元上也极其相似。在叙述根识现量时，《解锁》先指出“仅根识的定义”（[illegible]），再陈述“根识现量的定义”（[illegible]），最后再论述“作为正量[②]的根识现量的定义”（[illegible]）。这样的三重关系恰好可以对应《量论要集》讨论根识现量段落中“定义仅根识的定义”（dbang shes tsam du mtshon pa'i mtshan nyid）、“根识现量的定义”（dbang po'i mngon sum gyi mtshan nyid）和“作为正量的根识现量的定义”（dbang po'i mngon sum tshad ma'i mtshan nyid）三者[③]。

再进一步，两部文本的文字重合度较高。试看下面《解锁》中的一段文字：

【夏】[illegible] v [illegible]，[illegible]，[illegible]，[illegible]。[④]

【译】作为正量的根识现量的定义即依赖于作为主要因缘的根器〔且〕对执持之境不迷乱〔且〕不使之发生欺诈[⑤]。

相呼应的《量论要集》中的文字如下：

【藏】dbang po'i mngon sum tshad ma'i mtshan nyid ni bdag po'i rkyen dbang po gzugs can la rten nas skyes shing gzung don la ma 'khrul ba'i stobs kyis sgro 'dogs gcod byed ces bya ba'o /.[⑥]

【译】作为正量的根识现量的定义即依赖于作为主要因缘的有形的根器而产生，且

---

① 《量论除意之暗》可参见帕斯卡尔·胡贡（Pascale Hugon）所作之科判："Sa bcad of Phya pa Chos kyi seng ge's Tshad ma yid kyi mun sel" [2017-03-04], https://www.oeaw.ac.at/fileadmin/Institute/IKGA/PDF/forschung/tibetologie/Sabcadmunsel.pdf。四现量的四目为 232.2—232.5。

② [illegible]，*tshad ma。在佛教认识论中，“正量”（正确的知识）与“认识工具”为同一主体的不同面向，因此其术语同为 tshad ma（pramāṇa）。这是由于西方哲学将知识定义为一种倾向性状态（dispositional state），但佛教哲学将其定义为获取新信息的认知事件本身。由于与本文相关性不大，此不赘述。

③ 杰巴：《量论要集》，第 165 页。《量论要集》在论述次序上略有不同，它将“定义根识本身的定义”放在最后。

④ 《解锁》，第 1 拍第 14—16 列。

⑤ 本段译文的注释见附录二。

⑥ 杰巴：《量论要集》，第 165 页。

> 依凭对执持之境的不迷乱之力而使增叠[①]断除。

这里，两部文本不仅在意义上相似，在用词和表述上也几乎重合——[illegible]对应 bdag po'i rkyen；[illegible]对 rten；[illegible]对 ma 'khrul；等等。此外，就连虚词和助词也存在相当紧密的对应关系——[illegible]对应 ni；[illegible]对应 la；[illegible]对应 byed；等等。假如我们相信《解锁》是由藏文翻译而来的，则其藏文原本与《量论要集》应有很高的重合度。

综合上面的证据，我们能够确定《解锁》属于桑浦量论传统。事实上，如果我们将《解锁》与恰巴《量论除意之暗》和俄译师《正理滴论复注》[②]等文本进行进一步比对，还能发现更多的证据。此处限于篇幅，不进一步讨论。《解锁》与桑浦量论著作发生语文学关联很可能是源于桑浦传统内部所谓“文本重用”（text re-use）的惯例[③]。帕斯卡尔·胡贡（Pascale Hugon）指出：

> 藏地的量论学者从他们先驱者的著作中利用更早的材料，将它复述为己用而不承认它的外来源流。这种材料的重用在一个或多个层面上展开：内容（content）、结构（structure）以及表述（wording）。
>
> 限于内容的复述揭示出一位作者对他的后继者（们）的影响以及思想家之间连续性印象的结果。在同一“圈子”——这里是桑浦寺——以及同一量论传承中的学者著作中找到这种现象并不奇怪。我因此不再深入探究这一点。
>
> 在这群文本中更为显著的是结构性复述的实践。一种藏文文献中广为流传的实践是以连续性的下属单元将科目进行分层级的组织，它被称作“科判”。两个享有相同科判层级的文本就如同两本具有相同目录的书；尽管单元标题的表述或相同或不同，但书之间享有为课题搭建的相同的组织结构，以相同的次序和相同的门类对其进行探讨。[④]

胡贡接下来又以俄译师和恰巴对法称《定量论》所作的注疏为例展示了具体的表述是如

---

① “断除增叠”（sgro 'dogs gcod byed，另有 sgro 'dogs sel 等表述）是恰巴量论学说中的核心之一。依照恰巴的理论，“增叠”（sgro 'dogs）是覆盖于事物真相上的不真实的部分，凡是正量必须符合增叠被断除的标准。也就是说，恰巴是以排除法对正量进行反向定义的。详见 Hugon and Stoltz, *The Roar of a Tibetan Lion*, pp.68–80。此处的 sgro 'dogs 似不能完全对应西夏文的[illegible]，但这里的区别具有思想史上的意义，详见附录二。

② 有关俄译师《正理滴论复注》的研究，参见 Pascale Hugon, “Tracing the Early Developments of Tibetan Epistemological Categories in Rngog Blo ldan shes rab's (1059—1109) Concise Guide to the *Nyāyabinduṭīkā*”，《藏学学刊》2013 年第 1 期，第 194—234 页。

③ 参见 Pascale Hugon, “Text Re-use in Early Tibetan Epistemological Treatises,” *Journal of Indian Philosophy* 43, no. 4/5, 2014, pp.454–491。

④ Hugon, “Text Re-use in Early Tibetan Epistemological Treatises,” pp.459–460.

何大量跨越两部文本而存在的[①]。在这里，我们在《解锁》和《量论要集》中看到的诸多例证正好呼应了胡贡对桑浦量论传统所建构的语文学上的理论架构。毫无疑问，胡贡提出的三种方面的文本重用——内容、结构、表述，在《解锁》和《量论要集》中都有体现。当然，不同于俄译师和恰巴之间明确的时间先后关系（chronological order），《解锁》和《量论要集》在时间上何者在先，我们尚无法完全确定，但可以肯定的是，它们都来源于桑浦量论的大传统。

四、《正理空幢要门》的系列文本

本文第二节指出《解锁》在体例上是一部注疏，从题名来看，其所注的根本文应该是一部名为《正理空幢要门》的文本。在俄藏黑水城文献中，恰好有一部《正理空幢要门》（Tang. 230），克恰诺夫指出其下有 834、835、890 三个编号的写本[②]。《俄藏黑水城文献》第 28 册刊布了其中的第 835 和 890 号文献，使我们有了研究的机会。然而可惜的是，这两件写本事实上都不是《正理空幢要门》。890 号文献的正确题名为《正理要门记》（[illegible]），这已经由图版的编者更正[③]。而经过笔者的检查，835 号的文本也不是《正理空幢要门》。这一写本缺失篇头，虽然最后有以西夏文楷书所题的“正理空幢要门”几个大字，但正文草书部分的最后实际上写的是“正理要门记竟”（[illegible]）[④]。通过笔者的比对，其草书部分的内容也与 890 号文献一致。这即是说，第 835 和 890 号文献都是一部题为《正理要门记》（以下简称《记》）的文本，克恰诺夫误将这两件写本归入《正理空幢要门》名下。由于 834 号文本尚未刊布，我们难以窥见其面目，只能留待日后继续研究。

但《记》本身也同样应该引起我们的关注。毕竟 835 号文本的最后的确写下了“正理空幢要门”几个字，那么我们就不禁要去思考《记》与《正理空幢要门》的关系。虽然《记》同样没有记载作者等题跋信息，但其文本内部有相当多的语文学线索能为我们所用。首先，我们能确定“记”（[illegible]）在西夏文献中是一种注疏体裁，如作为著名的密教文本《大印究竟要集》（[illegible]）注本的《大印究竟要集记》（[illegible]）。从《记》的内文看也是如此：与《解锁》类似，《记》也存在先引用根本文再疏释的体例。不过最令人惊奇的是，《记》在各处的根本文引文都与《解锁》的引文高度重合。试看下面《记》中的文字：

---

① Hugon, “Text Re-use in Early Tibetan Epistemological Treatises,” pp.460–464.

② Кычанов, *Каталог Тангутских Буддийских Памятников*, Kyoto: Kyoto University, 1999, pp.550–551.

③《正理要门记》（[illegible]，ИНВ. No. 890，以下简称《记》甲本），收入史金波、魏同贤、克恰诺夫编《俄藏黑水城文献（西夏文佛教部分）》第 28 册，第 40—42 页，共 6 拍。

④《正理要门记》（[illegible]，ИНВ. No. 835，以下简称《记》乙本），收入史金波、魏同贤、克恰诺夫编《俄藏黑水城文献（西夏文佛教部分）》第 28 册，第 1—5 页，第 13 拍第 26 列。

【夏】[illegible]、[illegible]：[illegible]“[illegible]”[illegible]。[illegible]：[illegible]，[illegible]，[illegible]。[illegible]？“[illegible]”[illegible]。[1]

【译】第一、讲说分目的名称是一致的。它的文句是“真实的逻辑原因有三种”。它的意义如下：依据三因相，不论是以自身意识而催生决定的真实的逻辑原因，还是以设置三因相的语言作为他人的指授而催生理解的真实的逻辑原因都是三种。若问：那〔真实的逻辑原因〕是什么呢？〔它的文句〕是“即结果、自性、无觉察三者”。

再对比《解锁》中的一段文字：

【夏】[illegible]、[illegible]：[illegible]“[illegible]，[illegible]”[illegible][2]。

【译】第一、讲说分目的名称是一致的。它即文中所说的“真实的逻辑原因有三种，即结果、自性、无觉察”。

可以看出，《记》与《解锁》引用的这段内容（[illegible]）几乎完全一致，其区别仅在于《记》分两次引用，并且尾部多出一“三”（[illegible]）字。此外，二者具有完全相同的科判标题。进一步，《记》于这段文字前出现的“设问”（[illegible]）、“回答”（[illegible]）两目[3]也都能与《解锁》的122.411和122.422两目对应。

上面一例显示的《记》与《解锁》的诸多关系在两部文本中有大量体现。限于篇幅，兹不赘述。这些关系表明，《记》与《解锁》所注释的应当是同一部文本，区别仅在于《记》的注释较详，《解锁》则较略。从文题来看，它们的根本文应当是那部《正理空幢要门》。一旦834号文本得到刊布，我们便有机会确定这一结论。假如《正理空幢要门》和《记》与《解锁》三者间的关系能够得到确定，那么三者就能被归为一类文本群，即以《正理空幢要门》为根本文，以《记》为详注，以《解锁》为略注的系列文本。西夏的量论学习者以这一系列文本来了解法称量论学说中的基本概念。

与《解锁》不同，《记》中存在不少的引注。其中，俄译师的观点被多次引用。试看下例：

【夏】[illegible]，[illegible]：[illegible]、[illegible]；[illegible]、[illegible]

---

① 《记》甲本，第3拍第22—25列。
② 《解锁》，第3拍第15—16列。
③ 见《记》甲本，第3拍第10列，第11列。

[illegible]；[illegible]、[illegible]；[illegible]、[illegible]；[illegible]、[illegible]；[illegible]、[illegible]。[1]

【译】针对此三因相，依照俄师[2]的六个主题来讲说：一、讲说作为定义者的三因相的事例[3]；二、存在于事例中的定义者；三、针对其分目而进行计度的依据；四、存在于其计度依据中的三因相的自体[4]；五、〔表述〕自体的语言的功能；六、决定[5]三因相的认识工具[6]。

《记》的作者对三因相的解释完全因循俄译师所倡导的结构，在解释的过程中还多次直接引用俄译师的话语。由此可见，《记》的解释体系也属于桑浦的教学传统。我们因而可以进一步推测《正理空幢要门》的系列文本应该都是以桑浦教学作为基础的。

五、何谓“空幢”？

“正理空幢要门”中的“空幢”二字无疑是这一文题中最奇怪的地方。如果我们相信这一文题译自藏文，那么“空幢”似乎是从“stong pa'i rgyal mtshan”译来。然而，笔者从未见过任何一部藏文文本的文题中有“stong pa'i rgyal mtshan”这样的词汇。即便我们相信它

---

① 录文据《记》乙本，第 6 拍第 10—12 列。又见《记》甲本，第 1 拍第 3—5 列。但甲本此处有诸多残缺，另有文义不通之处，因而以乙本为佳。

② Ŋwə^{1} dzjịj^{2} [illegible]。Ŋwə^{1} 正对藏文之 rngog。

③ 定义者（mtshan nyid）、被定义者（mtshon bya）、事例（mtshan gzhi）——总称 mtshan mtshon gzhi gsum——是藏传量论中极重要的一环，其理论由俄译师从印度佛教发展而出，由恰巴基本确立下来。简言之，这里由“三因相”（定义者）定义“逻辑原因”（被定义者），而比如“火”就是这样一种定义的具体事例——它是由三因相定义的逻辑原因。有关这种定义理论，详见 Pascale Hugon, “The Origin of the Theory of Definition and Its Place in Phya pa Chos kyi seṅ ge's Philosophical System,” *Journal of the International Association of Buddhist Studies* 32, no. 1/2, 2010, pp.319–368。藏文 mtshan nyid、mtshon bya 和 mtshan gzhi 三者所对应的西夏译语分别是[illegible]、[illegible]和[illegible]，这可由实际的夏藏对勘证明。详见 Zhouyang Ma, “Introduction to Speculative Thinking: An Unidentified Work in Tangut Translation of Maja Jangchup Tsöndrü (d. 1185, Tib. rMa bya Byang chub brtson' grus),” pp.19–23。

④ [illegible]，*ngo bo，或译作“本体”“实体”，此处所指即三种逻辑原因。

⑤ [illegible]，*nges par byed，所谓“决定”，即消除疑问。比如，当用烟推理出火的时候，必须先决定烟的存在而不留疑问。

⑥ 笔者未能在俄译师现存的两部量论著作《正理滴论复注》和《定量论难语释》中找到对应的藏文表述，但俄译师还有一些散佚的著作，如《释量论注》。因此这种六重分类法或许也存在于他的其他著作中。此外，我们也不能排除这种分类法属于一种在桑浦传统中口口相传的教学方法。

是某位作者在文题中加入的特殊的“个人签名”[①]，“stong pa’i rgyal mtshan”也很难说得上是一个有意义的单元。这不禁让我们更加好奇“空幢”的实际意义。

《解锁》和《记》中都没有任何直接解释“空幢”的线索。据笔者所知，在已经发现的全部西夏文献中，除本文研究的《正理空幢要门》系列之外，有且只有一部题名中也含有“空幢”的文本，那就是《四十种空幢要门》（[illegible]，俄藏第871号，以下简称《四十种》）[②]。这部文本的题记中说它是“西天大师地钵迦啰造”（[illegible]）。“地钵迦啰”即阿底峡·燃灯吉祥智（Atiśa Dīpaṃkara Śrījñāna，约982—1054）。《四十种》主要围绕佛教修行人的起信、持戒、善行、恶行等主题展开，一共四十个单元。《四十种》的内容与阿底峡《百法录》（Chos chung brgya rtsa）中的某些“诫语”（gtam）相似，但笔者尚未发现完全一致的藏文本。《四十种》在正文前尚记载有文本创作的缘起和上师传承，明显以第三人称写就，因而我们能够断定《四十种》虽有如是题记，但至少并非全部内容都是阿底峡所作。《四十种》在叙述创作缘起时的最后一句话如下：

【夏】[illegible]，[illegible][+[illegible]][illegible]，[illegible][+[illegible]][illegible]，[illegible]，[illegible]，[illegible]《[illegible]》[illegible]。[③]

【译】然后，在他为西藏人讲说众多秘密法门的时候，他们也不遵从大乘教法而过分放逸。因此，地钵迦啰法师创作了这一从经典和本续等等中集结出的《四十种空幢要门》。

若相信这里的说法，则“空幢”就是阿底峡原题中的内容。然而，阿底峡现存的著作没有任何一部有“空幢”一词在内。由于《解锁》和《记》显然创作在俄译师的时代之后，《正理空幢要门》大概率也是西藏的本土作品，而非阿底峡的著作。因此，“空幢”不应当是阿底峡的“个人签名”。

既然不是“个人签名”，它是否有可能是反映文本内部义理的术语呢？上文已提及，stong pa’i rgyal mtshan（*śūnyadhvaja?）本身不是一个佛教术语，除非在极为特殊的语境中，否则不能成立。从《四十种》的内容来看，它没有任何关于空性的讨论。从《解锁》和《记》的内容来看，除了最后一部分关于认识对象的讨论简单谈到了诸法胜义空的问题，作

① 如炯丹热智·达玛坚赞（Bcom ldan ral gri Dar ma rgyal mtshan，1227—1305）就在自己几乎所有的作品中加入“庄严之花”（rgyan gyi me tog）的个人签名，以示自己的每部作品都是贡献给佛的一束花，其全部作品则构成装饰的花鬘。

② 本文对《四十种空幢要门》的利用得到了喻晓刚博士的帮助，特此致谢！喻博士完成了《四十种空幢要门》的全部译文，尚未发表，但本文出现的与之相关的翻译均出自笔者本人，一切论证和表述上的疏失归本人。

③《四十种空幢要门》（[illegible]，ИНВ. No. 871），收入史金波、魏同贤、克恰诺夫编《俄藏黑水城文献（西夏文佛教部分）》第27册，第335—338页，共12拍。

为全篇主题的量论也和空性没有直接关系，更没有“幢”这个词出现。基于《四十种》和《正理空幢要门》在主题上存在极大的异质性，笔者认为所有将“空幢”作为义理内容的揣测都应排除，否则我们便不能解释阿底峡的诫语和量论有何种空性上的本质联系。

笔者在这里提出的推测如下：西夏文的“空”（[illegible]）字除了能对应藏文的“stong pa”（即空洞、空无之“空”）之外，还能对应藏文的“nam mkha'”（即天空、虚空之“空”）。这已被各种对勘材料证明[①]。假如我们将“空”的藏文定为“nam mkha'”，将“幢”的藏文定为“rgyal mtshan”的话，那么“空幢”就可以构成“nam mkha' rgyal mtshan”，即“南喀坚赞”，常见的藏文法名。那么《四十种》就或许是“四十种南喀坚赞所传之要门”，《正理空幢要门》就或许是“南喀坚赞所传之有关量论的要门”。虽然我们尚无法考证南喀坚赞为何人，但这种解释可以使有关“空幢”的诸多矛盾迎刃而解。考虑到阿底峡的教诫和桑浦的量论都属于噶当派的教法，由同一人传授同样非常合理。这里唯一要考虑的问题就是《四十种》的题记明言为阿底峡创作，但是，上文已经提到，由于文本开头的创作缘起显然不是阿底峡所作，所以至少我们看到的《四十种》是经由他人之手最终整理和呈现的。另一种解释是阿底峡的《四十种》最初是讲授给南喀坚赞的，因此题名为“南喀坚赞要门”。这种情况在印藏传统中非常常见，如摩咥里制吒（Mātṛceta）的《迦腻色伽大王书信》（*Mahārājakaniṣkalekha*，德格 4184 号）——题目中的人名“迦腻色伽大王”事实上是文本内容的接受对象而非作者。

总而言之，笔者认为将“空幢”定为人名“南喀坚赞”而非任何术语或名相是阐释这一词汇的合理方式。随着未来 834 号《正理空幢要门》的刊布以及相关研究的进一步推进，我们将会有更多机会重访这一问题。

六、小　结

俄藏黑水城文献 912 号文献《解锁》为我们深入理解西夏所流传的藏传佛教提供了又一扇窗口。《解锁》以简练的语言勾勒出法称量论学说中的重要概念并加以诠释，为西夏僧众快速高效地趣入这一学说提供了门径。《解锁》与桑浦量论传统的关系能够在语文学研究的基础上得以证实，进一步说明了西夏所传译的藏传佛教经院学与桑浦学统之间千丝万缕的联系。《解锁》作为这一量论传统的导引也并不是单独存在的，而很可能与《记》及《正理

① 见如《滴论》(III. 117, 122, 129, 134)。唯《滴论》中诸处均为“虚空”（[illegible]）而非单字“空”。但据西夏文《同音》，“空”即训为“虚空”（李范文：《简明夏汉字典》，中国社会科学出版社 2012 年版，第 164 页），因此“空”作单字亦可对应 nam mkha' 应无问题。

空幢要门》构成了体系化的教学系统。由于题名中均含有“空幢”,《正理空幢要门》也有可能与《四十种空幢要门》属于同一种传承系统中共同传承的文本。假如我们相信“空幢”事实上是人名“南喀坚赞”的意译，那么虽然其人尚无可考，但能够解释“空幢”同时存在于不同门类文献标题中的原因。黑水城文献中还有许许多多类似《解锁》的文本等待学人去探究。笔者在本文中除了呈现考索本身之外，也希望以这种考索的方式，对未来的研究思路作出某些启发。笔者相信，只要立足于坚实的语文学方法，我们必能听到这些距今近千年的文本对我们的呼唤。

附录一：科判

科　目	西夏文标题	汉译标题	位　置①
*1②	* [illegible]	* 认识工具的情形	—
*11	* [illegible]	* 讲说〔认识工具〕共通的定义	—
12	[illegible]	讲说〔认识工具〕分别的定义	1.1
121	[illegible]	讲说现量的定义	1.1
121.1	[illegible]	讲说现量的共通定义	1.2
121.2	[illegible]	〔现量〕分别的定义	1.11
121.21	[illegible]	根识现量的定义	1.11
121.22	[illegible]	心识现量的定义	1.16
121.23	[illegible]	自证现量的定义	1.22
121.24	[illegible]	瑜伽现量的定义	2.3
121.3	[illegible]	结归	2.7
122	[illegible]	〔讲说〕比量〔的定义〕	2.8
122.1	[illegible]	分目的基础	2.8
122.2	[illegible]	比量名称的意义	2.10
122.3	[illegible]	分目	2.12
122.31	[illegible]③[illegible]	讲说自利比量的定义	2.12
122.32	[illegible]	讲说他利比量的定义	2.22

① 位置的表示方法如下：第一数字为图版拍号，第二数字为列号。如 1.1 表示第 1 拍第 1 列。

② 带 * 号的标题为笔者重构，详见本文第二节。

③ 原文[illegible]作[illegible]，当误。

续 表

科 目	西夏文标题	汉译标题	位 置
122.33	[illegible]	结归	3.7
122.4	[illegible]	讲说共通的逻辑原因	3.10
122.41	[illegible]	讲说具有三因相的真实的逻辑原因	3.11
122.411	[illegible]	设问	3.11
122.412	[illegible]	回答	3.15
122.412.1	[illegible]	讲说分目的名称是一致的①	3.15
122.412.2	[illegible]	讲说各自的定义	3.22
122.412.21	[illegible]	讲说结果因	3.23
122.412.22	[illegible]	讲说自性因	4.9
122.412.23	[illegible]	〔讲说〕无觉察因	4.16
122.412.3	[illegible]	讲说结归	4.23
122.42	[illegible]，[illegible]	为了使人理解它的特殊而讲说虚假的逻辑原因	5.5
122.421	[illegible]	讲说分目的名称相一致	5.6
122.422	[illegible]②	后面的讲说	5.14
13	[illegible]	结归	5.15
2	[illegible]	认识对象的情形	5.20

附录二：现量部分译注③

体例

v 倒字 / □缺字 / [illegible] 较确定的字 /[illegible]？不确定的字 /〔—[illegible]〕原文删字 /〔+[illegible]〕原文增字

---

① 此处说明的是自利比量中的三种真实的逻辑原因与他利比量中的三种在名称上完全一致。

② 虽然 122.42 一目明确指出其下级科目“分二”（[illegible]），但文中只给出了 122.421 的内容。其后紧接着是“后面的讲说依照根本文自然明了”（[illegible]）这样的一句，没有进一步论述。显然这里的“后面的讲说”即当为 122.422 的内容。对比 122.412.1 和 122.412.2 的内容来看，122.422 的内容应该是分别讲说三种虚假原因的具体情况。

③ 这一部分的基本概念与行文脉络均类似法称《正理滴论》，因此，读者可参考王俊淇：《法称〈正理滴论〉与法上〈正理滴论注〉译注与研究》，中国社会科学出版社 2020 年版。本文不再对各种概念进行一一诠释。

【夏】……[illegible]。

【译】……因为没有过失。

【夏】[illegible]、[illegible]：[illegible]、[illegible] [+[illegible]] [illegible]，[illegible]“[illegible]，[illegible]”[illegible]。[illegible]，[illegible]，[illegible]。[illegible]，[illegible]，[illegible]，[illegible]，[illegible]，[illegible]。

【译】第二、讲说分别的定义，分二。其中，第一、讲说现量的定义，分为三种。其中，第一、讲说现量的共通定义。它即文中所说的“脱离了思维而不迷乱[①]即〔它的〕定义”。进一步，应予以脱离的思维是对概念的觉察[②]。虽然〔现量〕与之相脱离，但由于自证[③]是拥有思维的，所以它不是与思维的自体相脱离的。尽管如此，所谓现量，在觉察显明的对象的层面上是与思维的特征相脱离的。[④]

【夏】[illegible]，[illegible]。[illegible]，[—[illegible]？+[illegible]][⑤][illegible]，[illegible]，[illegible] [—[illegible]？+[illegible]][illegible]。[illegible]，[illegible]。[illegible]，[illegible]，[illegible]，[illegible] [illegible]。

【译】所谓迷乱，即对对象的错误觉察。就此而言，对执持之境[⑥]不产生错误是不迷乱[⑦]

---

① “脱离了思维而不迷乱”即法称对现量的著名定义，见于《滴论》I.4 等处。

② 对比杰巴《量论要集》，第 159 页：“因此，思维的定义即被说成是‘对显现为概念之物的认识’。”（de na rtog pa’i mtshan nyid ni spyir snang gi shes pa yin no zhes zer ro / ）

③ [illegible]，*rang rig，即反身认识（reflexive awareness）。

④ 这两句话是说，由于自证是一种反身认识，思维的主体和对象是同一的，所以不能笼统地说是与思维相脱离，否则在否定对象时也否定了主体，以致自证现量无法成立。这里必须要加入限定条件是针对认识对象的思维脱离。对比杰巴《量论要集》，第 160 页，“因此，〔‘与思维相脱离’指的是：〕它不是思维的物质。进一步，‘与思维相脱离’不是针对仅物质所说。如果是那样，则自证现量就会具有思维。那么是怎样的呢？在依赖于自身对境的基础上，它不是思维的物质”。（des na rtog pa’i rdzas ma yin pa’o/ de yang rdzas tsam ma yin pa la ni rtog bral zhes mi brjod do/de lta na rang rig mngon sum kyang rtog bcas su ’gyur bas so/’o na gang yin zhe na rang gi yul la ltos nas rtog pa’i rdzas ma yin pa’o / ）

⑤ 写本中似涂去“[illegible]”字，但它的位置又插入“[illegible]”二字，其意义不完全明确。此处仅作“[illegible]”处理进行翻译。

⑥ 执持之境（gzung yul）、意欲之境（zhen yul）、趣入之境（’jug yul）的对境三分法是桑浦量论的核心之一，经由俄译师对法上相关理论的演绎，由恰巴基本确立。简言之，执持之境是客观显现于心识的对象；意欲之境是心识主动觉察的对象；趣入之境是成为正量的对象。每种对境都对应不同的心识认知情节，详见 Hugon and Stoltz：*The Roar of a Tibetan Lion*, p.5。三种对境的西夏文翻译能由夏藏对勘证明，它们分别是：[illegible]、[illegible]、[illegible]。详见 Zhouyang Ma, “Introduction to Speculative Thinking：A Hitherto Unknown Work of Maja Jangchup Tsöndrü (d. 1185, rMa bya Byang chub brtson’grus) in Tangut Translation,” pp.46—54。

⑦ “不迷乱”（夏：[illegible]；梵：abhrānta；藏：ma ’khrul pa）即感官在认识过程中正常运行而不失灵，与之紧密联系的是正量的定义“不欺诈”（夏：[illegible]；梵：avisaṃvādin；藏：mi slu ba）。详见下文讨论。

的意义，这是因为它不包含显现而不定以及觉察已觉察〔的这两种情况〕[1]。对意欲之境不产生错误并非〔不迷乱的意义〕。进一步，应该知晓：只有在能被“对执持之境不迷乱”定义的情况下，“与思维相脱离”才是对错误认知的遣除。[2]

【夏】[illegible]

【译】第二、〔现量〕各自的定义。它有四种。其中，第一、根识现量的定义即文中所说的“依赖于根器”。仅根识的定义即依赖于作为主要因缘[3]的根器〔且〕能够觉察对境。根识现量的定义即依赖于作为主要因缘的根器〔且〕对执持之境不迷乱。作为正量的根识现量的定义即依赖于作为主要因缘的根器〔且〕对执持之境不迷乱〔且〕不使之发生欺诈。[4]其后的各种应该依照这一种而知晓。[5]

---

① 显现而不定（[illegible]，*snang la ma nges pa）和觉察已觉察（[illegible]，*bcad pa’i yul can）在桑浦量论中被认为是虽属现量（直接知觉）但不属于正量（正确的知识）的两种认知情节。详见 Hugon and Stoltz, *The Roar of a Tibetan Lion*, pp.227—246。对比杰巴《量论要集》，第 160 页：“调伏天（Vinītadeva）师说：所谓‘不迷乱’即不欺诈，因为只要正量的总体定义是不欺诈，那么作为它其中一种的现量就也是。并非如此，因为〔这一定义〕不适用于显现而不定和觉察已觉察的现量。”（slob dpon dul lha na re ma ’khrul ba zhes bya ba ni mi slu ba yin te tshad ma’i spyi’i mtshan nyid mi bslu ba yin tsam na de’i ya gyal mngon sum yang yin pas so/de ni ma yin te mngon sum snang la ma nges pa dang mngon sum bcad pa’i yul can la ma khyab pas so / ）

② 此句是说，单纯的“与思维相脱离”不能排除错误认识，必须附加“不迷乱”的定义。这呼应了法上《正理滴论》注中对“移动的树”（gacchadvṛkṣa）的讨论。详见王俊淇：《法称〈正理滴论〉与法上〈正理滴论注〉译注与研究》，第 72—73 页。又可对比杰巴《量论要集》，第 161 页：“〔反论：〕那么，〔这一定义〕不适用于移动的树的显现等等。〔答语：〕现量的定义不适用于脱离于思维的错误认识——这正是〔我〕所主张的。”（’o na ljon shing ’gror snang la sogs pa la ma khyab bo zhe na/rtog med log shes la mngon sum gyi mtshan nyid kyis ma khyab pa ni ’dod pa nyid do / ）

③ [illegible]，*bdag po’i rkyen（梵：adhipatipratyaya），传统译作增上缘，即对某事来说首要的因缘，如对感官认识来说，感知器官和感知对象就是主要因缘。此缘与下面提到的等无间缘，再加因缘与所缘缘，统称“四缘”，于《阿毗达摩俱舍论》等论著中有详细讨论。

④ 这种三重递进方式明显地将现量本身和作为正量的现量区别开，呼应了上一段对现量定义的限定。桑浦论师普遍接受法上的观点，认为“不迷乱”不等于“不欺诈”，因为“不欺诈”的集合比“不迷乱”的集合要小。所以在这里，“作为正量的现量”必须以“不欺诈”加以限定。此处具有思想史意义的一点是《量论要集》在此处的限定语是“断除增叠”（见本文第三节）。“增叠”（sgro ’dogs）是典型恰巴式的语言，而从对勘经验来看，此处西夏文的[illegible]一般只对 [b]slu ba（欺诈），而没有对 sgro ’dogs 的情况。这一点小的区别或许能帮助我们确定《解锁》在思想史上的下限——它大概率是恰巴思想产生影响之前的作品。

⑤ “其后各种”即其他三种现量。由于只要是现量都要符合“对执持之境不迷乱”的定义，只要是正量都要符合“不欺诈”的定义，所以对后几种现量的具体定义都要遵从这些标准，不再详述。

【夏】[illegible]、[illegible]，[illegible]“[illegible]”[illegible]。[+[illegible]][illegible]，[illegible][+[illegible]]，[illegible]。[illegible]，“[illegible][1][—[illegible]+[illegible]][illegible]，[illegible]”[+[illegible]?]。[illegible]，“[illegible]，[illegible]”[illegible][+[illegible]？—[illegible]？][illegible]。

【译】第二、心识现量[2]的定义即文中所说的“无间”[3]。所谓“无间”，即由根识作为等无间缘所催生，抑或对根识之境不间断的对境的相续的觉察。因此，〔仅心识的定义即〕“依赖于从以根识作为实质诱因[4]的特殊的等无间缘中产生的主要因缘的特殊——心，觉察所觉察的对象的特殊——根识之境不间断的对境的相续”。与之相比，进一步，〔心识现量的定义即〕“依赖于作为主要因缘的心〔且〕对执持之境不迷乱”[5]……是平易的[6]。

【夏】[illegible]、[illegible][+[illegible]][illegible]，[illegible]：“[illegible]”[illegible]。[illegible][+[illegible]？][illegible][+[illegible]]。[illegible]，[illegible]；[illegible]。

【译】第三、自证现量的定义即文中所说的“依凭证悟”，即在对自身……的证悟中不迷乱。进一步，证悟的对象是苦、乐；证悟的主体是意识。

【夏】[illegible]、[illegible]，[illegible]：“[illegible][—[illegible]][illegible]”[+[illegible]。“[illegible]”][illegible]，[illegible]。[illegible]，[illegible]。[illegible]，[illegible]。[+[illegible]，][illegible]□[7] [illegible][+[illegible]][illegible][—[illegible]？][+[illegible]][8][illegible]。

【译】第四、瑜伽现量的定义即文中所说的“产生无漏智”。所谓“漏”即烦恼障。与

---

① “[illegible]”当为“[illegible]”之误。从译语的角度看，“[illegible]”能够完全契合藏文术语 nyer len gyi rgyu’i khyad par；与之相比，“[illegible]”字则无法解释。故译文按“[illegible]”处理。

② 由于各种量论传统对心识现量提出了纷繁复杂的解释，学界迄今难以对其具体含义达成共识。笔者在此仅就字面意义进行翻译，而不深入探讨其义理。总体而言，桑浦传统承袭了法称的基本看法，即由于第一刹那的对境在第二刹那已经消失，根识的认识必须由第三刹那的意识对第二刹那的对境的相续的认识来体现。

③ 所指当是后面紧接着出现的“等无间缘”（[illegible]）。在《滴论》（II.32, 37）中“[illegible]”的用例对应藏文之 thogs pa med pa（“无障碍”）。但根据此处语境，“[illegible]”应翻译的是藏文术语“de ma thag [pa’i rkyen]”（梵：[sam]anantara[pratyaya]）一语，即“〔等〕无间〔缘〕”。

④ [illegible]，*nyer len gyi rgyu（梵：upādānakārana），传统上译作“现取因”，即与结果实质相同的原因，如种子之于新芽。

⑤ 对比杰巴《量论要集》，第167页：“〔心识现量的〕定义即‘依赖于普通人的心而产生，并对执持之境不迷乱’。此为恰巴所言。”（mtshan nyid ni tha mal pa’i yid la brten nas skyes shing gzung don la ma ’khrul ba yin no zhes phya pa zer ro /）

⑥ 此处涂改致使意义不明，推测此处“平易”（[illegible]）应指这一定义在理解上不困难。

⑦ 此字就上下文判断似应为“[illegible]”。

⑧ 此处二字似应倒作“[illegible]”。“[illegible]”能构成完整的语义单元，比较《滴论》（I.11）对瑜伽现量的定义：“[illegible]。”

它相脱离的意识就叫作“无漏智”，是圣者之智。它在初地时产生。因此，〔瑜伽现量的定义即〕凭借对具有真实性对象的修习这一主要因缘之力而产生的对执持之境的不迷乱①。

【夏】𗏁、𗱕𗡶𗵒，𗖵𗰛“𗡞𗢨𗼻𗹦𗖰𗼻”𗢳v𗣼。

【译】第三，结归即文中所说的“容易了知现量是认识工具”。

① 对比杰巴《量论要集》，第168页：“瑜伽现量的定义即依凭对真实性的修习之力而对执持之境不迷乱。”（rnal 'byor gyi mngon sum gyi mtshan nyid ni de kho na nyid goms pa'i stobs kyis gzung don la ma 'khrul ba'o /）注意此处夏藏密合程度很高，尤其西夏文小词“𗹙𗗙”亦严密对应藏文之“stobs kyis”。

噶译师软奴班和大黑天教法在西夏之流传

侯浩然
浙江大学历史学院

噶译师软奴班（Rgwa Lotsāba gZhon nu dpal，约 11—12 世纪）是藏传佛教“新译密续派”（Gsar ma pa）代表性人物之一，曾前往印度求法，回到藏地后为推动密法的传播和发展作出了突出贡献。新近在黑水城出土文献中发现了他从印度带回的大黑天教法，这些教法不仅保存有藏文本，还被翻译成汉文，以至少两种语言在西夏和元代于当地流传。[①] 噶译师软奴班是何许人也？他是如何勾连起印度、西藏和西夏，将大黑天教法传播至黑水城的呢？拂去历史的尘埃，我们带着这些问题走进噶译师软奴班的一生。

一、噶译师出生和藏地求法

本文主要依据噶译师的亲传弟子喇嘛祥·尊珠扎巴（Zhang g.Yu brag pa brtson ’grus grags pa，1123—1193）[②] 所著《噶译师传》（*Dpal chen rgwa lo’i rnam thar*）来重构他的生平事迹。[③]

---

① 目前尚未在黑水城文献中发现西夏文的大黑天文献。有关黑水城出土的大黑天文献，参见 Haoran Hou, “Mahākāla Literature Unearthed From Karakhoto,” in Yukiyo Kasai and Henrik H. Sørensen eds., *Buddhism in Central Asia II: Practice and Rituals, Visual and Material Transfer*, Leiden: Leiden Brill, 2022, pp.400–429。

② 喇嘛祥的生平参见 Per K. Sørensen and Guntram Hazod, *Rulers on the Celestial Plain: Ecclesiastic and Secular Hegemony in Medieval Tibet*, Wien: Verlag der Österreichischen Akademie der Wissenschaften, 2007, pp.30–39。

③ Zhang g.Yu brag pa brtson’ grus grags pa, *Dpal chen rgwa lo’i rnam thar byang chub sems ’byongs ma’* in Lama Zhang Yudrakpa Tsondru Drakpa, *Dpal ldan tshal pa bka’ brgyud kyi bstan pa’i mnga’ bdag zhang g.yu brag pa brtson ’grus grags pa’i gsung ’bum rin po che* [Collected Works of Lord of the Teachings of the Tsalpa Kagyü School, Lama Zhang Yudrakpa Tsondru Drakpa], Kathmandu: Gam po pa Library, 2004, vol. 1, 181–222.

这部写于12世纪晚期的作品是目前已知最早、最详尽的噶译师的传记。① 除此之外，本文还参考了喇嘛祥为噶译师所写的四篇赞颂。② 根据《噶译师传》，他出生在“汉藏交界之地，安多野摩塘之南隅，有属宗喀之域，名曰底乌琼（The'u chung）”③，父亲④ 是一位精通阿毗达摩（*Abhidharma*）的大善知识，母亲为Nyang gza' Tshe sprul。传记中并未交代噶译师的具体出生年，根据前后文推测他或生于11世纪中晚期。⑤ 噶译师少时得名觉色嘉措（Jo sras rGya mtsho），从七岁起，跟随父亲学习佛法，十七岁时，掌握了所有的阿毗达摩教法；二十岁时，在俄译师（rNgog Lotsāwa）的弟子堪布旺敦（*mkhan po* dBang ston）处受比丘戒，从后者处学习了戒律（Vinaya）、中观（Mādhyamaka）和量论（Pramāṇa）。三十岁时，噶译师不顾父母和上师的反对出发前往印度求法，一路以乞食为生；途经卫藏，在内邬宿（sNe'u Zur）向噶当派上师学法，随后前往朗日塘（Glang ri thang），学习“发心”教法（*sems bskyed*）；后辗转到了后藏，在善知识梅格哇（Dge bshes Me dge ba）处学习。他一路筹集前往印度学法的资金，在堆龙（Stod slung）获得大量黄金供养，当到达尼泊尔（Bal yul）时，他一共收集了近六十两黄金（*gser srang*），遂出发前往印度。

喇嘛祥对噶译师在卫藏求法经历，记述颇为简略，未详述其中细节。阿美夏阿旺贡嘎索南（A myes zhabs Ngag dbang Kun dga' bsod nams，1597—1659）在《大黑天教法史》（*Mgon po'i chos 'byung*）中有一些补充：噶译师先在内邬宿向普陀瓦（Po to ba Rin chen gsal，1027—1105）的主要弟子夏惹瓦云丹扎（Sha ra ba Yon tan grags，1070—1141）处求法，后者为他讲授了“无常”（Mi rtag pa）概念；他随后在夏惹瓦的弟子朗日塘巴多杰僧格（Glang ri thang pa rDo rje seng ge，1054—1123）座下学习。根据阿美夏的说法，噶译师最初想在卫藏学法，但无法找到合适的老师。⑥ 这与《噶译师传》中说他从一开始就计划前往印度并不

---

① 维塔利曾依据喇嘛祥写的噶译师传记介绍其生平，参见 Roberto Vitali, “In the Presence of the ‘Diamond Throne’: Tibetans at rDo rje gdan (Last Quarter of the 12th Century to Year 1300),” *The Tibet Journal 34.3/35.2, Special Issue: The Earth Ox Papers* (Autumn 2009–Summer 2010), pp.161–208。

② 四篇赞颂分别如下：1. *Dpal rgwa lo la bstod pa u dum wa ra*; 2. *Dpal la bstod pa gnyis pa*; 3. *Dpal la bstod pa gsum pa*; 4. *Dpal la bstod pa gsum pa*。参见 Lama Zhang Yudrakpa Tsondru Drakpa, *Dpal ldan tshal pa bka' brgyud kyi bstan pa'i mnga' bdag zhang g.yu brag pa brtson 'grus grags pa'i gsung 'bum rin po che*, vol. 1, 68–80。

③ Zhang g.Yu brag pa brtson' grus grags pa, *Dpal chen rgwa lo'i rnam thar*, 181. “野摩塘”的更多介绍参见谢光典：《野摩塘（dByar mo thang）为大夏川补证》，收入沈卫荣主编《西域历史语言研究集刊》（第七辑），社会科学文献出版社2014年版。

④ 其父名为噶智慧积（Rgwa Shes rab brtsegs）。维塔利提出噶译师的族名“噶”来自藏文“Mi nyag 'ga'/gha”一词，表明他来自西夏地区。见 Roberto Vitali, “In the Presence of the ‘Diamond Throne’: Tibetans at rDo rje gdan (Last Quarter of the 12th Century to Year 1300),” p.161。

⑤ 后文提到噶译师在印度依止上师无畏生护（Abhayākaragupta）学法，一般认为这位印度班智达约在1125年前后去世，而后文交代噶译师于三十岁时前往印度，如此推算其生年应不晚于1096年。

⑥ A myes zhabs Ngag dbang Kun dga' bsod nams, *dPal rdo rje nag po chen po'i zab mo'i chos skor rnams byung ba'i tshul legs par bsad pa bstan srun chos kun gsal ba'i nyin byed* [*mGon po'i chos 'byung*], lHa sa: Bod ljongs dpe rnying dpe skrun khang, 2012, 134.

相同。但阿美夏的说法似乎也有一定的依据：夏惹瓦的传记中交代噶译师曾与夏饶瓦有教法上的分歧，甚至产生了激烈冲突。①

二、在印度求法和苦行

途经尼泊尔（Bal po），噶译师到达摩揭陀（Magadha）的圣地菩提伽耶（Bodhigaya），在金刚座寺（Vajrāsana，rDo rje gdan）遇到了具车王（Shing rta can）。他建议噶译师向拶弥相加思噶剌思巴（rTsa mi Sangs rgyas grags pa）学习，后者当时担任金刚座和那烂陀寺（Nālandā）住持：

> 国王问道："你在寻找什么？如果你在寻找佛法，在那烂陀寺有许多班智达居住，在他们当中有一位精通五明、成就最为殊胜的学者，名叫拶弥相加思噶剌思巴。你们所有来印度的藏人都去依止他。"噶译师暗自揣度："拶弥是个藏人，我不远万里到印度来，却要向一个藏人学习，这不合常理。但国王的命令又不能违背。"②

根据艾略特·斯伯岭（Elliot Sperling）的研究，拶弥译师并非藏人，而是出身党项贵胄。他为时轮（Kalacakra）和大黑天（Mahākāla）教法等在藏地的传播发挥了重要作用。③见到拶弥译师之后，噶译师内心未升起敬信，仍执意寻觅印度班智达为师。在他人的引荐下，噶译师拜无畏生护（Abhayākaragupta，11 世纪后半叶—1125 年前后）为师，向他献上了一个用七两黄金制作的曼扎（*maṇḍala*）。无畏生护由此成为了他在印度的第一位重要上师。无畏生护与统治印度东北部的波罗王朝国王罗摩波罗（Rāmapāla，约 1084—1126）是

---

① dGe slong Nam mkha' grags, *sDe snod rin chen gsum gyi yon tan gyis thugs rgyud bltam zhing 'phags pa 'jam dpal gyi sprul par grags pa'i dge ba'i bshes gnyen chen po sha ra ba'i sku che ba'i yon tan* [*Sha ra ba'i rnam thar*], in *sNar thang gser 'phreng* [bdr: W2CZ7888], 221r–232v.

② Zhang g.Yu brag pa brtson'grus grags pa, *dPal chen rgwa lo'i rnam thar*, 184.1–4: *rgyal po de'i zhal nas khyod ci 'tshol ba yin gsungs/ chos 'tshol ba yin na dpal nā len dra'i gtsug lag khang na/ paṇ ḍi ta mang po bzhugs te de'i nang nas kyang che ba rigs pa'i gnas lnga la mkhas shing/ tshe'i dngos grub brnyes pa/ tsa mi sangs rgyas grags pa zhes bya ba bzhugs kyis/ khyed bod thams cad kyang der 'bab pa yin pas/ der song zhig zer ba dang/ bla ma'i thugs dgongs la tsa mi ni bod yin la/ nga rgya gar du phyin nas bod cig la chos zhu ba mi rigs te/ 'on kyang rgyal po'i bka' bcag tu mi btubs pas.*

③ Elliot Sperling, "Rtsa-mi lo-tsā-ba Sangs-rgyas grags-pa and the Tangut Background of Early Mongol-Tibetan Relations," in Per Kwaerne ed., *Tibetan Studies, Proceedings of the 6th International Association for Tibetan Studies vol.3*, Oslo: The Institute for Comparative Research in Human Culture, 1994, pp.801–825.

同时代人，据藏文文献记载，他曾担任金刚座寺、超戒寺（Vikramaśilā）、那烂陀寺和奥坦塔普里寺（Otantapurī）的住持。[①] 无畏生护著述、编撰和翻译了多部密教成就法和仪轨文献，保存在《西藏大藏经》中的便有二十四种之多，其中两部曼荼罗仪轨著作《金刚鬘》（*Vajrāvali*）和《究竟瑜伽鬘》（*Niṣpannayogāvali*）对密教图像学研究意义重大，引起了佛教美术研究者的极大关注。[②] 噶译师从无畏生护受灌顶并习得俱生胜乐金刚教法（*Dbang bskur dang Lhan cig skyes pa*）。在此后三年中，他修习"一座食"（*gdan gcig*）苦行，以乞食为生，朝圣印度佛教圣地，如舍卫城（Śrāvastī，Grong khyer mNyan yod）。在 Rig ya go ri[③]，他停留了三日，期间得到佛陀弟子竭夷迦叶（Gayākāśyapa）的钵盂和锡杖的摄受加持，并顶礼其卧处。

在游历印度的过程中，噶译师一直在寻找合适的印度上师。经人指点后，他欲前往乌坚巴班智达语自在（U rgyan pa Paṇḍita Vāgīśvara）处学法，正要出发时，恰逢后者来向拶弥译师请教其所撰的《时轮》注释《瑜伽鬘》（*Yogamālā*，德格 No. 1376）。在藏文文献中，这位来自尼泊尔滂汀（Pham thing）的班智达被称为塘穷巴（Thang chung pa *gcung* Ngag gi dbang phyug）。他是那若巴（Naropa）的弟子，与其兄长无畏名称（Abhayakīrti，'Jigs med grags pa）合称"滂汀巴兄弟"（Pham thing pa sku mched）。二人在胜乐和金刚瑜伽母（Vajrayoginī）教法从印度传播到西藏的过程中扮演了重要角色。[④]《噶译师传》未详细说明噶译师与语自在交往的细节，在帕木竹巴（Phag mo gru pa Rdo rje rgyal po，1100—1170）所传的《慈乌大黑护法修法集》（*Bya rog ma bstan srung bcas kyi chos skor*）中有一篇题为《三毒怙主成就法秘密血滴》（*Dug gsum mgon po'i sgrub thabs khrag thig gsang ba*）的文章，其尾题表明该文本是由语自在（Vāgīśvara）与噶译师合作翻译的，[⑤] 说明二人在教法上有更深入的交流。噶译师在见到语自在也跟随拶弥译师学法后，认识到了在瞻部洲（Jambudvīpa）找不到比拶弥译师更好的上师，遂向拶弥献上了由三十七两黄金制作的曼扎，请求拶弥为他传授教法。拶弥译师教授他通过修习《六支瑜伽》（*Ṣaḍaṅga-yoga, Sbyor ba yan lag drug po*）而生起慈悲空性的要诀。在《噶译师传》中，拶弥译师有时称呼噶译师为"Kumāra"，这是梵语"Kumāraśrī"的缩略形式，对应藏语"Gzhon nu dpal"。

---

① George Roerich trans., *The Blue Annals*, Delhi: Motilal Banarsidas, 1996, pp.669–670.

② 杨清凡:《无畏生护与曼荼罗仪轨在西藏的译传：以〈金刚鬘〉与〈究竟瑜伽鬘〉文本为中心》,《故宫博物院院刊》2018 年第 3 期，第 44—56 页。

③ Rig ya go ri 应为印度地名，未能同定。

④ 有关语自在和胜乐教法传播的关系，参见魏文:《滂汀巴昆仲与上乐教法在藏地和西夏的早期弘传》,《中国藏学》2016 年第 2 期，第 102—110 页。

⑤ 尾题读作："Slob dpon A ba dhu ti pa 写作，班智达语自在和 Kumāraśrī 译。"见 A ba dhu ti pa, *Dug gsum mgon po'i sgrub thabs*, in Phag mo gru pa Rdo rje rgyal po, *Bya rog ma bstan srung bcas kyi chos skor*, vol. 5, 269–283。

挼弥译师和无畏生护是噶译师在印度求法期间最重要的上师。《噶译师传》突出挼弥译师的地位，除了宣称他是金刚座寺和那烂陀寺的寺座（*gdan sa pa*）之外，还提及无畏生护也随其学法。斯伯岭在他对挼弥译师的研究中指出实际情况可能相反，无畏生护才是挼弥译师的上师。他整理了《西藏大藏经》和《大黑天修法与仪轨合集》中挼弥译师独立或与他人合作翻译的文本名目，内容多为时轮和大黑天相关教法，其中有数篇为挼弥与无畏生护合作翻译。[①] 历史上，印度班智达与西藏译师合作翻译了大量的佛教经典，例如我们熟知的迦耶达啰（Gayadhara）与卓弥译师（'Brog mi Shakya ye shes）。印度上师将原本以印度语言写成（Rgya gar skad du）的佛教典籍传给他的藏族弟子并协助其翻译成藏文，这实际上也是传法的过程。噶译师在印度求法多年，精通当地语言，能熟练翻译印度语文本。在《大黑天修法与仪轨合集》中有一篇《红色语之成就法》（*Dmar po gsung gi sgrub thabs*），题记中言明该文本为噶译师在挼弥译师座前翻译并勘定。[②] 北京版《西藏大藏经》中收录的《吉祥鸦面主满足次第》（*dPal mgon po bya rog ma'i bskangs kyi cho ga'i rim pa*，北京版 No. 4960）的题记表明该文本为无畏生护在那烂陀寺所作，由噶译师翻译。[③] 此外，《大黑天修法与仪轨合集》中收录了一篇题为《等虚空续》（*Nam mkha' dang mnyam pa'i rgyud*）的文本，其题记中提到噶译师与无畏生护在超戒寺对吉祥毗卢遮那金刚（Śrī-Vairocanavarja）和定法幢（lDing Chos kyi grags pa）的翻译进行了重新校订。[④] 噶译师不光能翻译印度文本，还能用梵语写作。他著有一篇短小的成就法《自摄受次第要门成就法》，被收入《西藏大藏经》的《丹珠尔》部（德格 No. 1523），其尾题翻译如下："《自摄受次第要门成就法》，瑜伽大自在 Kumāraśrī 在吉祥那烂陀寺以梵语写成（*san kri ta'i skad du mdzad pa*）。" [⑤]

在那烂陀寺外的一个寺院[⑥]里，噶译师闭关修行两年半后，生起了心续清净的征兆（*thugs rgyud 'byong ba'i rtags*）。在闭关的第六年，他得到了度母的授记，欲前往菩提伽耶城外的寒林墓地（Śmaśāna Śītavana，Dur khrod chen po bsil ba'i tshal）苦修。为此，他询问挼

---

① Elliot Sperling, "Rtsa-mi lo-tsā-ba Sangs-rgyas grags-pa and the Tangut Background of Early Mongol–Tibetan Relations," pp.813–818.

② 题记为 "pandita sangs rgyas grags pa'i spyan sngar lo tsa ba gzhon nu dpal gyis brgyur zhing zhus te gtan la phabs pa'o"。转引自 Elliot Sperling, "Rtsa-mi lo-tsā-ba Sangs-rgyas grags-pa and the Tangut Background of Early Mongol–Tibetan Relations," p.817。

③ 题记为 "dpal mgon po bya rog ma'i bskangs kyi cho ga'i rim pa/ bla ma a bha ya kā ras/ dpal nā len dra'i gtsug lag khang du/ rdo sku rang byung gi rtsar mdzad pa'o/ /phyis bla ma chen po dpal rga los rang 'gyur mdzad pa'o"。见 *bsTan 'gyur*(Pe cin), Vol. 86, 46b2。

④ "*Nam mkha' dang mnyam pa'i rgyud*", in Phag mo gru pa Rdo rje rgyal po, *Bya rog ma bstan srung bcas kyi chos skor*, India: Sungrab nyamso gyunphel parkhang, Tibetan Craft Community, 1973–1979, vol. 1, 287–347.

⑤ *Rang byin gyis brlab pa'i man ngag gi sgrub thabs. bsTan 'gyur*(Pe cin), Vol. 52, 95a6–96b5. 题记原文为：Rang byin gyis brlabs pa'i rim pa'i man ngag gi sgrub thabs/ rnal 'byor gyi dbang phyug chen po kumāraśrīs/ dpal na lan da'i gtsug lag khang du/ sankri ta'i skad du mdzad pa rdzogs so//。

⑥ 该寺名为 "Gho sa kra ma"，未能同定。

弥译师和无畏生护的意见，未得到二人支持。再闭关修行了一年零五个月之后，他再次向拶弥译师请求前往寒林修行。拶弥译师同意了，赠予他钺刀和天杖，嘱咐其于晚间前往寒林墓地。《噶译师传》中对寒林墓地的环境有生动的描述：他在寒林墓地中修行处为“菩提树洞窟”（Shing nya gro ta'i phug），周围有罗刹（*srin po*）、阎罗（*gshin rje*）、食尸鬼（*ro langs*）、食肉鬼（*sha za*）和豺狼（*lce spyang*）出没。在做了荟供（*ganacakra, tshogs kyi mkhor lo*）后，他安住于此。在寒林墓地修行之初，噶译师经常受到外界干扰，无法安心修行：

> 此后，他打坐，但仍无法进入禅定状态。离他不远处有一个黑色的、圆鼓鼓的东西，逐渐变大，变得非常可怕。他走到它面前。当他想看清楚的时候，那个黑色的东西腾空而起，发出雷鸣般的吼声。当他抬头看时，像一个巨大而可怕的面具，它遮住了天空。他发出一声惊呼，那黑色的东西向云层飞去。他在心里想，这个令人怖畏之主来自何方，驻于何处？随后，他入于禅定，第二天黎明时分出定时，他发现荟供上的供品和朵玛都消失了，一盏黄油灯出现在面前。他的卡巴拉碗里装满了酒。以前他不能饮酒，但想到他现在已经成为“大吉祥”，他就将酒一饮而尽。此后，他亲见胜乐金刚六十二尊曼陀罗与八大尸陀林墓地。智慧空行母从他的心中显现，为了他未来（的修行），教授他拙火口诀。在亲见胜乐坛城的同时，他瞬间认识到所有现象的极限，净除了身体污垢，取得了许多共通成就，如不沉于水。①

噶译师前往寒林墓地苦行的叙事充满神话色彩，但并非完全空穴来风，而是以当时印度的“尸陀林崇拜”（the Cult of Charnel Ground）为背景。在印度文化中，尸陀林是安置死人的场所，尸体被抛弃于此，毫无遮挡，任由其腐败。虽然它们在功能上与墓地、坟场、火葬场相似，但是尸陀林与这些地点又有所不同，它是行者修习成就法和进行仪轨活动的重要场所。在这里，瑜伽士（*yogin*）、瑜伽女（*yoginī*）、隐士们摒弃社会道德规范，游走在文明的

---

① Zhang g.Yu brag pa brtson'grus grags pa, *Dpal chen rgwa lo'i rnam thar*, 190. 1–191. 2: de nas bsgoms pas ting nge 'dzin ha cang mi gsal zhing/ pha tshad rgyang nge ba na nag po thum thum zhig je che je cher song ba dang/ shin tu 'jigs pa byung bas/ nag po de'i mdun du song ba dang/ der phed lta snyam pa dang nam mkha' la thug/ sgra dang chom sgra chen po bsgrags te/ yar la gzigs pas mgo brnyan 'jigs su rung bas nam mkha' gang nas/la la ni ha zer/ la la ni a la la zer/ la la ni phaṭ phaṭ zer ba dang skyi bung song ngo/ der bsam pa la 'jigs pa de gang nas byung/ 'jigs pa'i bdag po ga na gnas snyam pa dang/ ting nge 'dzin du lhag gis song ste/ tho rangs sengs kyis dengs pa lta bu zhig byung nas thun btang ste gzigs pas/ tshogs dang gtor ma kun mi snang bar mdun na dkar me re ba zhig snang ba dang/ thod pa chang gis bkang ba zhig tu song bas/ de snga phan chang lar mi 'thung ba la/ da ni dpal chen po rang yin dngos grub byin pa yin snyam nas chang de gsol lo/ de nas nam mkha' la dpal 'khor lo bde mchog gi dkyil 'khor lha drug cu rtsa gnyis dur khrod dang bcas pa mngon sum du gzigs/ thugs ka nas ye shes kyi mkha' 'gro ma zhig byon te/ ma 'ongs pa'i ched du gtum mo'i gdams ngag 'di gnang/ dkyil 'khor zhal mthong ba'i skad cig de nyid la dngos po'i mtha' thams cad khong du chud/ der lus kyi zag pa yang zad/ chu la mi byings pa la thun mong gi dngos grub mang du brnyes so/.

边缘地带，选择一种堕罪的生活和修行方式，从尸体上获取食物、衣物、装饰、法器。湿婆教的骷髅派（Kāpālika）是以践行尸陀林崇拜而著称的流派，该教派对佛教无上瑜伽部的母续（Yoginī Tantras）产生了深刻的影响。在无上瑜伽母续的《喜金刚》和《胜乐轮》相关的教法文献中都能看到对尸陀林的描述。[①]

这段叙事开始交代了在尸陀林中，噶译师调服"怖畏之主"（*'jigs pa'i bdag po*），《噶译师传》中并未明确"怖畏之主"的身份，但结合喇嘛祥为噶译师写的两篇赞颂，可以推测这里说的即为慈乌大黑天（鸦面大黑天）。[②] 调服慈乌大黑天与胜乐修行也相关，在胜乐教法体系中，四臂大黑天是胜乐教法最重要的护法，而慈乌大黑天则是四臂大黑天的眷属，二者常相伴出现。这也为传记后来叙述噶译师亲见四臂大黑天和慈乌大黑天做了铺垫。在调服大黑天之后，噶译师在胜乐修行上取得了突破性进展，获得了"大吉祥"（Dpal chen po）称号——胜乐本尊赫鲁伽（Heruka，Khrag 'thung，意为"饮血"）。从修法的角度来看，这里描述的是胜乐修行的生起次第（*utpattikrama*），即行者观想胜乐本尊和坛城，想自己进入圆满生起的坛城之中，成赫鲁伽，升起佛慢，与本尊身、语、意、功德、事业无二无别。胜乐金刚有多种坛城修法，而文中提到噶译师亲见的"胜乐六十二尊坛城"是较为常见的一种，是由印度大成就者鲁伊巴（Lūipa，约 10 世纪）开创的传规。坛城的核心为五轮同心圆，中心是赫鲁伽与明妃金刚亥母（Vajravārāhī）双身合抱，四方有空行母（Ḍākinī）、喇

① 沈卫荣、侯浩然：《疯癫的圣僧：毗瓦巴、密勒日巴与印藏佛教的大成道者传统》，《中国文化》2022 年秋季号第五十六期，第 271—292 页。

② 赞颂一：喇嘛祥为噶译师所作赞颂《大吉祥师赞二》（*Dpal la bstod pa gnyis pa*）提到噶译师在寒林墓地调服的神灵鬼怪中有一位"手持钺刀、托卡巴拉碗、身出火焰、发出'呵呵、帕特'怖畏之声者"，基于图像学的特征可以辨识出此处所说即为一面二臂慈乌大黑天，也符合《噶译师传记》中对"怖畏之主"的描述。《大吉祥师赞二》中的相关段落，九音节为一颂，是赞颂诗（*bstod pa*）形式，笔者在翻译时未保留原作诗体形式，仅将大意翻译如下："在广大的寒林墓地中，当你——具利他之心的大雄——安住时，忿怒与怖畏的刹土神祇，慑于你的威力而恭敬顶礼，住此寒林墓地中的空行母、阎罗、食肉鬼、无一例外，都成为你的眷属仆从！食人血肉、具忿怒凶恶种种形象之骷髅与裸形行者，手持钺刀、托卡巴拉碗、身出火焰、发出'呵呵、帕特'怖畏之声者，食肉持骨杖者等等，据说他们一见了你，便心生恐惧，任你驱使！尸陀林主亦畏惧你、向你寻求庇护！"藏文转写：/dur khrod chen po bsil ba'i tshal gyi dbus/ /nya gro ta yi sdong po'i rtsa drung du/ /gzhan phan thugs kyis dpa' bo khyod bzhugs tshe/ /shin tu gtum zhing 'jigs pa'i zhing skyong rnams/ /khyod kyis byin mi bzod pas gus khyod 'dud/ /dur khrod der gnas ma mo mkha' 'gro dang/ /srin po gshin rje sha za ma lus pa/ /khyod la 'dud cing khyod kyi zhabs 'bring byed/ /gzi brjid chen po rab 'bar khyod la 'dud/ /mi yi sha za khrag 'thung drag shul can/ /sna tshogs gzugs can keng rus gcer bu rnams/ /gri gug thod pa thogs shing me 'bar ba'i/ /ha ha phaT ces 'jigs pa'i sgra sgrog cing/ /sha za rus pa'i dbyug to thogs pa rnams/ /khyod kyi zhal mthong bas ni de dag kun/ /bred pas ci bgyi bka' stsol zhes zer bros/ /dur khrod bdag skrag mdzad la skyabs su mchi/. 见 *Dpal la bstod pa gnyis pa*, in: *Gsol 'debs bstod pa'i skor*, *Dpal ldan tshal pa bka' brgyud kyi bstan pa'i mnga' bdag zhang g.yu brag pa brtson 'grus grags pa'i gsung 'bum rin po che*, vol. 1, 73.5–74.4；赞颂二：《大吉祥师七支赞》（*Dpal la yan lag bdun gyi sgo nas bstod pa*）中也提到："慈乌大黑天、天母、食肉罗刹、护法与守卫皆现身向你作供养！"藏文转写：nag po chen po bya rog gdong/ ma mo gnod sbyin sha za'i tshogs/ chos skyong srung ma'i tshogs rnams kyang/ khyed sku mchod pa'i phyir lhags/. *Dpal la yan lag bdun gyi sgo nas bstod pa*，*ibid.* 85。

嘛（Lāmā）、康达罗哈（Khaṇḍarohā），鲁皮尼（Rūpiṇī）四瑜伽女环绕，此六尊构成坛城中心的大乐轮（*jñānacakra*）；大乐轮为四轮环绕，由内向外为意密轮（*cittacakra*）、语密轮（*vākcakra*）、身密轮（*kāyacakra*）、三昧耶轮（*samayacakra*）；中间三轮各轮有八尊呈双身相的勇父和空行母，各轮十六尊，三轮共四十八尊；最外三昧耶轮在四隅处各立一佛母，共四尊；另坛城四门也各有一兽面空行母把守，共四尊。以上五轮加上四门的尊神共计六十二尊，构成胜乐金刚六十二尊。坛城外围有八大尸陀林环绕。① 艾米·海勒（Amy Heller）曾公布一幅私人藏家收藏的13世纪绘制的蔡巴噶举派的"胜乐金刚六十二尊坛城"唐卡，题记中记载了该坛城修法的传承：自鲁伊巴始经过数位印度成道者和班智达传至无畏生护，后传于噶译师，喇嘛祥从噶译师处获授该教法。② 由此可见，噶译师是"胜乐金刚六十二尊坛城"从印度向西藏传播的关键一环。

在尸陀林苦行是危险的，噶译师的两位上师拶弥译师和无畏生护怀着忐忑不安的心情，带着大批随行人员来探望他。当得知他幸存下来，二人欣喜若狂，对他表示了极大的敬意。从那时起，他的名声传遍了整个印度。传记中在叙述噶译师在寒林的经历时，提到他遇到了一位叫作梅觉色（Me Jo sras）的同乡。后者带着蔑视意味地谑称他为"小噶"（Rgwa chung），放出狂言道如果小噶能在寒林修行，那么他也可以。然而噶译师的这位同乡在入住寒林当夜即暴毙。这个插曲显示了在尸陀林修行的危险性，也反衬出噶译师的神通广大。在梅觉色死后，噶译师继续在寒林修行。他坐在一尊自生湿婆像的头上冥想，受到外道（*mu rtegs pa*）军队的攻击：

> ……沸沸扬扬的声音在天空中滚动。所有的外道都出现了，并带领他们的军队来到噶译师面前，后者进入了禅定状态。他在外道士兵面幻化成三眼赫鲁伽，士兵们吓得四处逃窜。之后，他在菩提树洞窟左边的观世音菩萨像前打坐，亲见观世音菩萨显现，以半跏趺坐的姿势坐着……后又见到摩利支天现身后，他向她请求教法。在大黑天自生石像前，他供奉了朵玛，安坐下来。随后，他亲见天空中显现一面二臂的慈乌大黑天，并为之作赞颂，开头是："Hūṃ! 在大寒林墓地中……"接下来，他把目光投向地上，四臂大黑天显现，并向他请求大黑心咒和成就法……③

---

① 有关胜乐坛城的更多介绍，参见 David B. Gray, *The Cakrasamvara Tantra (the Discourse of Śrī Heruka): A Study and Annotated Translation*, New York: Columbia University, 2007, pp.54–57。

② Amy Heller, "An Early Maṇḍala of Cakrasaṃvara," *Revue d'Etudes Tibétaines, From Khyung lung to Lhasa, A Festschrift for Dan Martin*, 64, 2022, pp.161–170.

③ Zhang g.Yu brag pa brtson' grus grags pa, *Dpal chen rgwa lo'i rnam thar*, 195. 2–196. 2: nam mkha' la 'ur sgra chen po dang/ mu stegs pa'i mi thams cad kyang der byung ste/ bla ma la dmag drangs pa dang/ bla ma ting nge'i 'dzin la bzhugs pas dmag thams cad kyis he ru ka spyan gsum par mthong nas bros so/ /de nas （转下页）

上面引用的这段话让我们看到了寒林墓地的环境。它提到了三尊造像：湿婆、观世音和大黑天自生石像，表明不仅佛教徒在寒林墓地修行，而且还有其他教派的修行者。《噶译师传》映射出当时佛教与外道之间的冲突和矛盾——这里说的外道指向的是湿婆教——在叙事中通常会演变成噶译师与外道之间的法术竞争。在这一情节中，噶译师幻化成三眼赫鲁伽，吓跑了外道军队，这一叙事也有密教背景。在《西藏大藏经》中有一篇噶译师传于帕木竹巴的《吉祥大黑天现证守护遮止成就法》（*Dpal nag po chen po'i dngos grub dang bsrung ba dang bzlog pa'i sgrub thabs*，北京版 No. 4961），即为观想赫鲁伽与大黑天无别，行者想自身成大黑天，心间出赫鲁伽，以修坛城、作替身、抛食子、诵咒、烧施之术遮止消灭怨敌军队的法门。[①] 噶译师专长于慈乌大黑天的修法，该教法在其亲传弟子喇嘛祥手中得以发扬光大。[②] 上述《噶译师传》摘译段落中提及，噶译师在目睹慈乌大黑天之后，特为其撰写了一首赞颂。该赞颂的藏文和汉文版本都出现在黑水城的出土文献中，我们将在本章末尾讨论这首赞颂。

噶译师在寒林墓地修行了九个月，这使得他的名声在印度、藏地和汉地广为传播。喇嘛祥写道："当时印度盛传一言，谓有大成就者，来自'汉地'（Rgya nag po），栖身于寒林墓地之间。而我藏地众人皆言，有朵思麻之士（Sdo smad pa），名曰康巴噶（Khams pa Rgwa），彼乞金赴印，于寒林静修悟道，乃至善知识温塘巴（Dge bshes Dben thang pa）亦曾聆其讲经说法。"[③] 这段话指出了噶译师的身份，他出生于汉藏交界地区，其地域归属本身就有些模糊不清。有趣的是，虽然他出生在朵思麻，但他经常被称呼为康巴噶，可能是因为他后来在康区积极传教。

传记中提到噶译师与印度波罗王朝的统治者罗摩波罗（Rāmapāla）和具车王（Rgyal po Shing rta can）有交往互动。具车王邀请噶译师担任他的应供上师（*mchod gnas*），但遭到了

（接上页）yang nya gro ta'i g.yon phyogs na sangs rgyas pa'i rten 'phags pa spyan ras gzigs yod pa'i drung du bsgoms te spyan ras gzigs phyed skyil du bzhugs pa'i zhal mthong/.../ lha mo 'od zer cad mthong nas gdams ngag zhus/ dpal nag po chen po'i rdo sku rang byon gyi drung du gtor ma mdzad nas bzhugs pas/ nam mkha' la phyag gnyis pa zhal mthong ste/ hum/ bsil ba'i tshal gyi dur khrod nas/ zhes pa'i bstod pa mdzad/ de nas sa la phyag bzhi pa'i zhal gzigs te/ srog snying dang sgrub thabs la sogs pa dngos su zhus/ / phyis bla ma mi nyag gi sgrub thabs snga ma dang/ zhu thug mdzad pas sngags rnams dang mngon rtogs la khyad par ma byung zer/ go rim cag cag po'i nges pa ni ma byung bar 'dug/ /.

① "*Dpal nag po chen po'i dngos grub dang bsrung ba dang bzlog pa'i sgrub thabs*," in *bsTan 'gyur*(Pe cin), Vol. 86, 46b2—48a2.

② 在蔡公堂寺有专供四臂大黑天与慈乌大黑天的护法殿。学者卡尔·山本（Carl Yamamo）指出慈乌大黑天在喇嘛祥一系列带有军事性质的"诛业"（*drag las*）中扮演重要角色。见 Carl Yamamoto, *Vision and Violence: Lama Zhang and the Politics of Charisma in Twelfth Century Tibet*, Leiden, Boston: Brill, 2012, pp.227–228。

③ Zhang g.Yu brag pa brtson' grus grags pa, *Dpal chen rgwa lo'i rnam thar*, 197. 2–4: rgya gar gyi yul du dur khrod chen po bsil ba'i tshal na/ rgya nag po'i mi grub pa thob pa zhig bzhugs zer/ 'o skol bod na re sngon mdo smad pa khams pa rgaw lo bya ba/ 'di nas gser slong zhing rgya gar du 'gro zer ba de da lta grub pa thob nas dur khrod chen po bsil ba'i tshal na bzhugs zer/ dge bshes dben thang pa btsun chung kyang thos zer/.

外道的反对。在国王的见证下，噶译师和湿婆教代表在寒林墓地旁边的湖上进行了一场法术竞赛，最终噶译师盘腿悬浮在水面之上，而对手则沉入水中。噶译师由此得到了国王的青睐，成为了后者的应供上师，被迎请至金刚座寺。他以盥洗之水抛洒皇后和宫殿，又以此水饮喂大象，协助国王击退杜鲁卡（*Du ru ka*）[①]军队。在离开金刚座寺后，他前往灵鹫山（Bya rgod phung po'i ri），并在此地驻锡三个月。期间见到了从尼泊尔前来的朝圣僧侣，在他们面前展示神通：一挥手，飞鸟坠地而亡，又一挥手，飞鸟瞬间复活。他返回那烂陀寺时，当地僧侣和群众夹道欢迎，人们纷纷在他脚下抛洒鲜花，盛况空前。在见到捞弥和无畏生护之后，噶译师在捞弥位于那烂陀寺的三层寝殿（gzim khang）的中层（bar khang）闭关一个月，向上师证明其身已断除习气烦恼等漏（zag pa chad pa），这是一种圆满成就的标志。他的名声传遍了瞻部洲以及六洲，包括金洲（gSer gling）和铜洲（Zangs gling）。当他在 Ghosakrama 寺时，五百名瑜伽士从东印度前来求见，他拒绝露面。当他出发返回西藏时，具车王带着他的随从来为他送行。至于他返藏的原因，在《大黑天教法史》中，阿美夏说噶译师返回藏地是因为捞弥译师建议他向萨迦喇钦（Sa skya pa Bla chen）——萨迦初祖贡嘎宁波（Sa chen Kun dga' snying po, 1092—1158）——求授禅修。[②]

三、返回藏地传法

返回藏地后，噶译师在后藏拉堆（La stod）的格普（dGe phug）居住了三年。在此期间，他降服了残杀众生的、颠倒教法的外道（*chos log pa*）。此后，他去了前藏（Dbus），在吉麦（Skyid smad）收善知识阿生（Dge bshes A seng）为弟子。善知识阿生在《噶译师传》中也被称为康巴阿生（Khams pa A seng）。[③]《青史》（*Deb ther sngon po*）中记载大约在 1130—1140 年间，一世噶玛巴杜松坎巴（Karma pa Dus gsum mkhyen pa，1110—1193）在彭域（'Phan yul）的杰拉康（Rgyal lha khang）从噶译师和阿生学习了《时轮六支瑜伽》（*Sbyor drug*）和《慈乌大黑天》（*Mgon po Bya rog gdong*）的教法。[④] 噶译师在前藏的主要修行处在纳木措湖中的塞莫朵（Se mo do）和扎西朵（Bkra shis do）岛，《青史》中借帕木竹巴之

---

① "Du ru ka" 亦作 "tu/du rush ka"，源自梵文 "turaṣka"，指 12 世纪入侵印度的阿富汗军队。

② A myes zhabs, *mGon po'i chos 'byung*, 135.

③ 善知识阿生在《噶译师传》中也被称为康巴阿生（Khams pa A seng）或喇嘛阿生，全名是阿生旺秋（A seng dbang phyug），除了师从噶译师之外，他还是萨迦初主贡嘎宁波（Sa chen Kun dga' rnying po, 1092—1158）的弟子，在《道果法》（*Lam 'bras*）传承上占据重要的地位。

④ George Roerich trans., *The Blue Annals*, p.475.

口说噶译师在纳木措修行了七年。[①]《纳木措圣迹志》（*Gnam mtsho'i gnas bshad dad pa chu rgyun*）交代了噶译师在纳木措的活动遗迹。[②] 据《噶译师传》记载，在塞莫朵岛修行期间，他应康巴阿生的请求，在其面前示现神通，接待了善知识珠贡巴（dGe bshes Gru dgon pa）和阿阇梨曲帕（Slob dpon Tshul 'phags）来访，他劈开雅鲁藏布江河水穿行至对岸，令二人惊叹不已、心生敬信，向噶译师顶礼，请求结法缘（*chos 'brel*）。在二人完成皈依和发菩提心（*skyab 'gro sems bskyes*）的加行之后，噶译师方为其传法，授予他们禅定灌顶（*Ting nge 'dzin gyi dbang bskur*）和俱生胜乐教法（*Dde mchog lhan skyes*）。噶译师在塞莫朵岛上收了两位本地弟子：一位是 Byang chub sems dpa' Stag ston，另一位是 Rme 'dor ba Bla ma Pho sgom。《青史》还记载了噶译师在赛莫朵岛上与冈波巴（sGam po pa）的弟子沃卡哇却雍（'Ol kha ba Chos g.yung，1103—1199）进行的一场瑜伽士之间的较量。沃卡哇施展了"迁识"（*grong 'jug*）法术，噶译师为之折服，遂向他请教中阴教法。[③]

离开纳木措之后，噶译师前往拉堆，途经果尔宗的扎科（'Gor rdzong gi brag），到达降地方的拔戎（Byang gi 'Ba 'brom），停留了一年。随后来到朵甘思（Mdo khams）的康波岗（Skam po sgang），在此地住了七年。在康波岗，他调服康波金刚积（Skam po Rdo rje dpal brtsegs），后者供养给他一片山林作为静修处，成为他在当地最重要的支持者。在这期间，他曾重返朵思麻，回到故里后，惊悉父母已双双去世。他为曾为他授戒的堪布旺敦灌顶和传授教诫。在朵思麻不到十天，收到了汉地皇帝（Rgya nag gi rgyal po）的迎请，他未接受邀请，匆匆返回朵甘思。此时，在朵甘思的惹东查拉康（Rab stong tshar lha khang）有恶人（*mi nag po*）毁灭王国的正法（*rgyal khams gyi dam pa'i chos*），摧毁寺院，强迫僧侣还俗，处死拒绝还俗的僧人，使整个地方陷入黑暗之中。他调服异端，修复所有被毁的寺院，使一切回归正道。大约在 1145 年，他来到那曲的索地（Sog），在这里遇到了前来求法的喇嘛祥。[④] 当地一位名叫拉桑（Lha bzang）的施主供养给噶译师许多黄金。在索地，他不仅施展法术降雨，为当地解除了干旱之困，还插手调解了权贵家族尚论色沃（Zhang blon Se bo）的子嗣偷吃寺院酥油引起的争端。在喇嘛祥的陪同下，噶译师从那曲河下游（Nags shod）的扎卡尔（Brab mkhar）的江玛（Gyang dmar）渐次来到果尔宗的扎科，当地因降雪冰冻而导致粮

---

① George Roerich trans., *The Blue Annals*, p.614.

② 有关《纳木措圣迹志》中记载的噶译师在塞莫朵和扎西朵岛上遗留的手印、脚印、修行洞窟、舍利、佛塔等圣迹，参见 John Vincent Bellezza, *Divine Dyads: Ancient Civilization in Tibet*. LTWA, 1997, p.221。

③ 根据《青史》记载，在色莫岛噶译师用双手拇指撑起身体，做出一种被称为"*gnyan lcug*"的瑜伽姿势。沃卡哇目睹之后，认为噶译师做这一切是为了降服他，以其人之道还治其人之身，施展了迁识之术。即他将自己的意识转移到死去的大雁身上，大雁围绕湖面游了三圈后回到原处，意识又回到沃卡哇身上，与噶译师讨论教法。见 George Roerich trans., *The Blue Annals*, p.461, 469。

④ 喇嘛祥在自传中着重记述了他第一次见到噶译师时的场景，参见 Carl Yamamoto, *Vision and Violence: Lama Zhang and the Politics of Charisma in Twelfth Century Tibet*, p.107。

食短缺。在此驻锡五个月后，扎科又发生了严重的旱灾，当地人请求噶译师施法降雨：

> 在果尔宗的扎科，当地人恳求他祈雨。起初，他没有答应这个请求。但在他们一再恳求下，他把据说是西夏国王的法鼓赐给了他们，并嘱咐说："无论哪里需要下雨，就在那里敲打这个鼓。去之前要穿上雨衣，如毡衣，因为〔一敲鼓〕雨马上就下来了。"接下来发生的事情与他说的一模一样。①

施法降雨是西藏高僧传记中常见的叙事情节。值得注意的是传记中提到"西夏国王的法鼓"（*me nyag rgyal po'i khrims rnga*），似乎暗示了噶译师与西夏王室之间的某种联系。噶译师出生于汉藏交界的宗喀地区，此地地缘政治复杂。宗喀 11 世纪时处在吐蕃后裔唃厮啰（997—1065）建立的青唐政权统治之下，青唐吐蕃在 12 世纪初为北宋所灭，宗喀在短暂归属北宋统治之后，在 12 世纪 30 年代又被西夏占领。噶译师在朵甘思活跃的时间大概是 12 世纪中期，此时宗喀正处于西夏统治之下，当时的统治者为夏仁宗（1139—1193）。仁宗崇尚藏传佛教，尤其是在其统治后期，大量印施藏传佛教经典，举办大规模的佛事活动，邀请藏地高僧大德前往西夏传法。由此，我们可以推知噶译师在藏东传法七年时间里，应有很多的机会与西夏接触，或也曾收到仁宗的邀请或赠礼。

喇嘛祥在朵甘思从噶译师学法七年，将噶译师作为自己的根本上师。他从噶译师处所受教法主要包括：那若六法、胜乐、时轮、大黑天，而大黑天教法又以慈乌大黑天为主。② 约在 1152 年，在喇嘛祥的陪同下，噶译师途经拉堆羌返回卫藏。到达卫茹（dBu ru）后，他以法力治愈患麻风病的妇女和精神失常之人。在 Kyu ru G.yu 'brang，他在噶当派僧人面前示现悬浮于河面的神迹，使其产生敬信之心。噶译师又前往叶巴（Yer pa），在热岗（Rab sgang）得到一位苯教僧人的供养。在噶译师晚年，以崩白（'Bum dpal）为首的弟子随侍其左右。《噶译师传》没有记载噶译师于何年去世，但对他临终之际及荼毗时的场景作了详细叙述。已知喇嘛祥于 1193 年圆寂，可以推测噶译师的终年应早于此。喇嘛祥在《噶译师传》的末尾罗列了噶译师的心子（*thugs las skyes pa'i sras*），其中康巴阿生居于诸位弟子之首。

以上是对喇嘛祥所著《噶译师传》的初步研究。通过分析可以看出该传记重点记述了噶

---

① Zhang g.Yu brag pa brtson' grus grags pa, *Dpal chen rgwa lo'i rnam thar*, 209. 3–5: 'gor rdzong gi brag la yul mi rnams kyis char dbab par zhu ba phul bas dang po ma gnang nan drag po bskyed pa'o phyi da la/ me nyag rgyal po'i khrims rnga rin zer ba'i rnga zhig bskur nas/ char gar dgos pa'i sa thams cad la rnga 'di brdungs dang char 'babs kyis/ phying pa la sogs pa char khebs gon la song/ de ma thag tu 'babs yin no gsungs pa la de kho na bzhin du byung/.

② Carl Yamamoto, *Vision and Violence: Lama Zhang and the Politics of Charisma in Twelfth Century Tibet*, pp.57–59, 116.

译师在印度求法及其在寒林墓地修行的见闻经历，生动呈现了一位印藏佛教传统中密教瑜伽士的典型形象；传记中讲述他在藏东的传法经历时，提到"西夏国王的法鼓"，暗喻了噶译师与西夏的某种联系。我们对于噶译师的讨论并不止步于此。在黑水城出土大黑天教法的写本和残卷中，我们新近同定出了数篇噶译师所作的文本，更令人惊喜的是，还在其中发现了噶译师在寒林墓地亲见慈乌大黑天时所写的赞颂。噶译师所传的大黑天教法是如何传入西夏的？下面通过对黑水城出土新材料的解读，我们希望能够对噶译师及其所传的大黑天教法在西夏的传播有一个更为深入的认知。

四、噶译师及其大黑天教法传承

喇嘛祥在《噶译师传》中述及，噶译师在寒林墓地修行期间，亲见四臂大黑天和慈乌大黑天，旋即为后者写了赞颂（*bstod pa*）。然而，喇嘛祥在传记中并没有给出这首赞颂的全部内容，只摘录了开头部分。我们有幸从黑水城出土文献中首次找到了这首赞颂的藏文全文，进而同定出它的两种汉文译本。此外，噶译师传的其他几部大黑天文本也在黑水城文献中保存下来。[①] 在藏传佛教传统中，挼弥译师和噶译师被认为是四臂大黑天（Caturbhuja Mahākāla, Mgon po phyag bzhi pa）教法的重要传播者。在《大黑天教法史》（*Mgon po'i chos 'byung*）中，阿美夏简要叙述了四臂大黑天的传承：

> 胜乐的忿怒怙主四臂大黑天，在《大黑本续王》（*Mgon po mngon par 'byung ba*，德格 No. 440）、《吉祥金刚大黑忿怒尊密成就出现本续》（*Mgon po khros pa*，德格 No. 416）和《沸腾血海续》（*Khrag mtsho khol ma'i rgyud*，普扎 No.756）为首的十二部密续中传授，这些密续已被译成藏文，由龙树父子（Nāgārjuna）、莲花金刚（Padmavajra）、金刚铃师（Ghantapa）所传，并由挼弥译师和噶译师带回藏地发扬光大。[②]

根据阿美夏的描述，挼弥译师和噶译师是将四臂大黑天从印度传播到西藏的关键人物。然而，阿美夏未提及无畏生护，这或与藏文史籍中常将无畏生护说成是挼弥译师的弟子有

① Haoran Hou, "Mahākāla Literature Unearthed From Karakhoto," pp.400–429.

② A myes zhabs, *mGon po'i chos 'byung*, 6: bde mchog khros pa mgon po phyag bzhi pa ste/ 'di ni mgon po mngon par 'byung ba dang/ mgon po khros pa dang/ khrag mtsho khol ma'i rgyud sogs bod du 'byung ba'i bcu gnyis tsam nas bstan cing/ klu sgrub yab sras/ padma vajra/ slob dpon rdo rje dril bu pa sogs las brgyud de/ bla ma tsa mi dang/ dpal chen sga lo la sogs pas gangs can gyi ljongs su spyan drangs te dar zhing rgyas par mdzad do/.

关。实际上，在新译密续传统中，大部分四臂大黑天传承都来自无畏生护，由他传给拶弥译师和噶译师，然后由后二者在藏地传播开来。在黑水城出土的汉文大黑天文本 B59 中也著录了大黑天教法的传承次第：

> 彼刹门相袭次弟者，铃杵法师传贤觉师，彼师傅金刚座法师，彼师傅阿灭葛啰啰八怛，草头路替讹，彼师傅大吉祥，彼师傅阿师，彼师傅浪布师，彼师傅阿浪座主，彼师处传矾上师，彼师处净信弟子，授得此法，无信人勿传者。[①]

从 B59 所记载的大黑天传承中我们看到了与阿美夏的说法一致的部分：铃杵法师即金刚铃师，阿灭葛啰啰八怛指无畏生护，草头路替讹就是拶弥译师，大吉祥乃噶译师，阿师或为康巴阿生（Khams pa A seng）。[②] 浪布师、阿浪座主和礬上师尚未同定，可能是朵思麻或西夏僧人。喇嘛祥作为噶译师的重要弟子并未出现在 B59 所列的师承关系中。然而，噶译师的教法传入西夏的路径也并非一种。[③] 新近俄国学者索罗宁（Kirill Solonin）对不列颠博物馆藏西夏文残片 OR 12380/ 533 进行了翻译研究，认为该残片原为一篇上师赞颂文，将其命名为《噶举上师赞》，其上残存四位上师的赞颂，依次为：拶弥译师、噶译师、喇嘛祥、雅砻斯巴（Yar lungs pa），据此索罗宁认为喇嘛祥与雅砻斯巴存在师承关系。[④] 此外，索罗宁指出黑水城出土文献中发现了数十篇雅砻斯巴所传密法仪轨，或与喇嘛祥的传承有关。[⑤] 喇嘛祥的另外一位弟子帝师惹巴（Ti shri Ras pa Shes rab seng ge，1164—1236）在大黑天教法于西夏的传播中扮演着重要的角色，他在西夏最后三十年，活跃在西夏宫廷，施展法术召唤大黑天神在战场上现身驱逐蒙古人和其他入侵者。[⑥] 对于帝师惹巴在西夏传播大黑天教法的更多事迹，我们需辟新章来研究，此不赘述。以上梳理可以明确大黑天教法向西夏传播的可能路径：通过噶译师的弟子康巴阿生与喇嘛祥及二者的再传弟子传入西夏。

---

① 史金波、魏同贤、克恰诺夫编：《俄藏黑水城文献》第六册，第 43 页。

② 曾汉辰：《西夏大黑天传承初探——以黑水城文书〈大黑求修并作法〉为中心》，《中国藏学》2014 年第 1 期，第 151—158 页。

③ 有关西夏传播的那若六法文献，参见喻晓刚：《光明甚深：俄藏黑水城汉藏佛教与俄藏黑水城那若六法 (*Nā ro chos drug*) 类文献——以西夏文〈六法自体要门〉为中心》，中国人民大学 2023 年博士学位论文。

④ 索罗宁、高艺鹏：《西夏藏传佛教传播杂考：西夏噶举派传承》，《中国藏学》2024 年第 3 期，第 108—117 页。

⑤ 索罗宁：《大鹏展翅：藏传佛教新旧译密咒在西夏的传播》，上海古籍出版社 2023 年版，第 133—156 页。

⑥ Elliot Sperling, “Further Remarks Apropos of the ’Ba’ rom pa and the Tanguts,” *Acta Orientalia Academiae Scientiarum Hungaricae* 57.1, 2004, pp.1–26.

五、黑水城出土的噶译师所作《慈乌大黑赞》

慈乌大黑天俗称鸦面大黑天，形象为乌鸦面，一面二臂。在噶传承（Rgwa lugs）中，慈乌大黑天被称为“事业怙主”（Las kyi mgon po），作为四臂大黑天的随侍，与后者一起出现。这篇《慈乌大黑赞》即为噶译师传记中提到的他在寒林墓地所作的赞颂。笔者在藏文长卷 Dx 178 中找到它的藏文全文，又在黑水城文献中同定出两个汉文版本，分别出现在 TK262 和 B59。[①] 汉藏文本的比较表明两种汉文译本均缺失藏文本开头的顶礼偈和结尾题记。藏文本顶礼偈翻译如下：“大吉祥噶译师栖身寒林墓地之时，亲睹金刚大黑天之尊容，旋即作此赞颂之王，颂其威德。”[②] 尾题翻译如下：“大吉祥噶译师在寒林墓地中作此《慈乌大黑赞》。圆满！圆满！”[③] 作者噶译师的信息在汉译本中消失了，只有在藏文文本的帮助下，才能揭晓这首赞颂的作者是噶译师。在黑水城出土的《慈乌大黑赞》两个汉文译本中，B59 中的版本更接近藏文本。以下是 B59 中的《慈乌大黑赞》的录文，脚注为对应的藏文部分，皆从 Dx 178 中录入。[④] TK262 中包含此赞颂的另外一个版本，见附录：

廣大墓地寒林住　令彼怖畏如刼火
赤黑熾熖於彼中　摩訶葛辢鵶頭像[⑤]
吽字中出於大黑　其身肥矬而大肚
出呵呵啈令怖畏　身上莊嚴於毒虵[⑥]
三目晃耀具拙朴　右手鉤刀出猛焰

---

① Haoran Hou, “rGwa Lotsāba gZhon nu dpal and the Spread of the Mahākāla Teachings in the Tangut Empire,” in Chen Jinhua ed., *From Jetavana to Jerusalem: Sacred Biography in Asian Perspectives and Beyond: An International Conference in Honour of Dr. Phyllis Granoff*, World Scholastic, 2022, pp.655–680.

② dur khrod chen po bsil ba yi ’tshal zhes bya ba na| dpal chen po rga lo bzhugs pa’i tshe | {rdo rje} nag po chen po zhal mngon sum du gzigs nas | de nyid kyi tshe bstod pa’i brgyal po ’dis bstod do|

③ |dpal chen po rga los la| |nag po chen po bya rog gi rnying can la bstod pa||dur khrod chen po bsil ba’i mtshal du’ mdzad pa’ | rdzogs so||rdzogs so||

④ 有关 Dx 178 的研究，参见 Alexander Zorin, *Buddiyskie ritualnye teksty. Po tibetskoy rukopisi XIII v.* [Buddhist Ritual Texts Based on a Tibetan Manuscript in the 13th Century], Nauka: Vostochnaya liteatura, 2015。

⑤ |huṃ dur khrod chen po bsil ba’i mtshal| |’jigs su rung ba’i skal pa yi| |me ltar ’bar ba’i klong dkyil na| |ma ha ka la bya rog gdong|

⑥ huṃ la byung ba’i nag po che| thung la sbrom ba’i gsus po che| ha ha zhes sgrogs ’jigs par byed| dug sbrul gdug pas sku la brgyan|

失記句者分段壞　左手掌於血法椀①
青色金剛食心血　頭髮赤黃熾焰竪
以新人頭為瓔珞　施㝵金刚寃魔降②
恒時張口而滴血　繚牙尖利而咬唇
恒常好樂於血肉　寃人命脉而壞之③
虎皮三祐庄嚴繫　身具億日之光明
口誦破記馬囉也　出於吽字發怛啈④
黑龍圍遶捻大黑　若將脚振大地時
一切蟲毒壞為塵　汝変化身歸空界⑤
鵶頭大黑作法行　其觜尖利手紅赤
觜上恒帶於赤血　喫破記句上半身⑥
及嗽臟腹心腰子　兩手至極而滿掬
以此喫令而奔走　伴遶十方食肉者⑦
无有不伏於彼汝　過去未來及現在
如來妙法汝護持　毀滅正教令作壞
大力常持至時分　勿作慢意釘甚橛⑧
口中火盛大海乾　雷啈黑雲而遼乱
□悪龍王大哮吼　發出電光至極啈⑨
天鐵霹靂如降雨　金剛火中而降雹

---

① |gtum po spyan gsum ’bar ba ste| |phyag g.yas ’bar ba’i gri gug phyar| |dam nyams don snying tshal par ’ges| |g.yon nas khrag bkang thob pa ’dzin|

② |{rdo rje} srin po khrag la ’thung| | ral pa ser po gen du ’bar| |myi ’go rlon pa’i ’phring ba can| |{rdo rje} gnod sbyin dgra’ la phob|

③ |kha gdang khrag gi rgyun ’dzag cing| |rno la ’khros pa’i mche ba gtsigs| |rtag du sha dang khrag la dgyes| |dgra’ ’o srog rtsa ’dreg par byed|

④ |stag gi pags pa’i sham thabs can| |nyi ma ’buṃ gi gzi’ brjid can| |zhal nas dam nyams ma ra ya| |huṃ huṃ phaṭ kyi sgra sgrogs pa|

⑤ |klu gdon nag pa’i ’khor gis bskor| |rkang pas sa la brdabs pa ni| |tham cad sgrol zhing rdul du lhogs| |khyod kyis sprul pas bar snang khebs|

⑥ |bya rog gdong can ’phrin las mdzod| |so rnon lag pa dmar ba dang| |mchu ni khrag gis bskus pa ste | |lus phyed dag ni zos pa dang|

⑦ |mkhal ma snying dang nang grol gyis| |snying pa shin du bkang nas ni | |za bzhin du ni rgyug pa yi| |sha za ’bum gi ’khor gis bskor|

⑧ |myi kyis myi ’dul gang yang myed | |bstan pa srung ba zhal gis bzhes | |bstan pa sdang ba phung bar mdzod| |stobs chen thugs dam dus la bab|

⑨ |ma g.yel ma g.yel phur bu thob| |kha na mye ’bar rgya mtsho skems| |’ur ’ur chem chem sprin nag ’khrigs| |ma rungs ’brug sgra de re re|

額上雨出金翅烏　破記句者壞為塵[①]
不敬上師毀秘密　願食破戒血肉等
毀滅正竟妙法人　最大黑像作法行[②]
自已自作自成熟　摩訶葛辢作付作
汝受佛勑令竟念　囑付作行願成就啞底[③]

附录：

《慈乌大黑赞》（TK 262）
廣大寒林墓地中　怖畏熾盛如劫火
彼中大黑烏眼處　吽字中出於大黑
其身肥矬而駘肚　誦喝喝聲啈施怖畏
身上莊嚴於毒地　叕朴具有三目熾
右手熾盛而執鉤　能喫不善之人心
左手執持於法椀　青色金剛食心血
赤髮黃髻熾盛竪　新人頭髮而莊嚴
伴遶排於六箇母　各個張口而飲血
擁護修習具獠牙　恒常愛樂於血肉
寃人命脉而飲之　虎皮三袪庄嚴繫
猶具億日於光明　無記句人恒念殺
語誦吽發大吼啈　黑龍圍遶扵大黑
脚振地時大海混　其水波濤壞為塵
汝之化身滿虛空　遍滿身上塗抹血
喫於寃人之上接　兼喫腹臟及腎等
手執法椀盛滿血　以此喫飲而吐之
伴遶十方食肉者　各個張口而飲血
彼彼尽皆圍繞之　過去未來現在時
諸佛妙法我護持　汝大力者願執持
專心抱持金剛橛　口中火盛大海乾

---

① |myi bzad klog ’od kam kam ’bar| |gnam lcags thog gi bu yug ’tshun ||{rdo rje}mye re ser ba ’bebs| |dpral ba khrung char phob|

② |dam nyams thal ba rdul du lhogs| |bla ma la sdang ┆ ba gas sngags smod| |dam nyams sha zo khrag la thung| |sangs rgyas bstan pa raṃ ma log|

③ |nag po chen po la las la byon| |rang gis las byas rang la smyin| |ma ha ka la ’phrin las mdzod| |sngon gyi thugs dam dgongs mdzod la| |bcol ba’i ’phrin las grub par mdzod|

雷哱黑雲而積聚　一切毒龍皆哮吼
闪電至極如熾火　面向黑雲執天鐵
以金剛火而降雹　不敬上師毀秘密
食肉喫飲破戒血　壞滅正竟妙法人
大黑作法而作之　自作自受而令服

蒙藏文化交流

关于《白史》的书名与前后序

乌云毕力格
中国人民大学国学院

一、《白史》与西藏“伏藏”文献

《白史》是蒙古学研究领域中学者意见分歧最大的文献之一，关于其书名、作者、成书年代、文献性质等问题一直存在着对立分歧，大致说来，有两种对立的观点：第一种意见认为，《白史》成书于13世纪，作者受忽必烈之命而编纂，现有的抄本是16世纪下半叶切尽黄台吉将原《白史》与元代译师必兰纳识里的旧作校勘而得的本子，它是元朝的治国纲领，体现了忽必烈皇帝的“政教并行”的思想；第二种意见认为，《白史》是16世纪后半期的书，是一部托古之作，反映了16世纪俺答汗时期的政教思想。但是，争执双方至今都没有提供令人信服的论据。

笔者一直主张《白史》是一部西藏“伏藏”式的蒙古文献，成书于16世纪后半期，主要作者是切尽黄台吉，参加编写的应该还有不知名的西藏和蒙古的僧侣们。作为作此判断的证据之一，本文将围绕《白史》的书名和前言后语进行讨论，请方家批评指正。

为了说明《白史》的“伏藏”性质，有必要先简单谈谈西藏“伏藏”文献。“伏藏”（Gter ma）是西藏佛教文献的一种。据藏传佛教宁玛派的说法，公元8世纪时，莲花生大师等佛教大德为了避免日后发生不测，西藏佛教面临危机，他们作为“伏藏师”将大量的佛经、法器和佛像埋藏起来，授记将来会有“掘藏师”将这些潜藏的佛教物品发掘出来，使佛教重新发扬光大。公元9世纪30年代末40年代初，吐蕃赞普达磨（史称朗达磨、朗达玛）掀起灭佛运动，不久被刺身亡，吐蕃帝国随之灭亡，西藏四分五裂。据说从松赞干布时期开始的西藏佛教前弘期至此终结，西藏佛教史进入所谓的“灭法时期”，一直延续至10世纪末。为了重振佛法，自11世纪始，西藏各地出现了大批“掘藏师”，他们陆续“发掘”大量“伏藏经典”，也即所谓的“伏藏”文献，为西藏佛教后弘期的到来推波助澜。据记载，自

11 世纪出现西藏历史上第一位掘藏师桑结喇嘛到 19 世纪贡追云丹嘉措编撰《宝藏法》，西藏出现了大掘藏师百余人，小掘藏师三百多人，前后发掘出上千部“伏藏”文献和佛教器物。[①]

“伏藏”文献中的政教典籍，其实质是后弘期的西藏佛教界为重构吐蕃佛教史和王朝史而编纂的书籍，目的是为当下佛教政治树立榜样并建构理论体系。“伏藏”文献中比较著名的有《柱间史》《五部遗教》《玛尼全集》《莲花生大师传》等。这些文献无一例外出现在西藏佛教后弘期，但其作者往往托名松赞干布或莲花生大师，而且一般由阿底峡或类似的著名佛教大德作为掘藏师在某一个地方将其“发掘”出来，然后宣布从那个时期起一直传到公布者手里。比如，根据《柱间史》本身的记载，该书作者为松赞干布，掘藏师是阿底峡，他受到一个被认为是智慧空行母的拉萨“疯婆”的授记，在大昭寺的柱下将其发掘出来。阿底峡将此书传给了旺敦，旺敦往下依次转给了多隆巴、健阿巴、乃邬素尔巴、直贡巴、迦玛巴、热振巴、衮桑、多杰楚辰、我（公布本书之人）。[②]《玛尼全集》的作者也被说成是松赞干布，伏藏师为吞弥·桑布扎和拉隆·多吉贝，掘藏师为智妥欧珠和释迦·桑布，也是在大昭寺发现的。[③] 但是这些书记载的内容包括西藏佛教后弘期初期的许多人物和事件，作者不可能是松赞干布，而只能是掘藏师本人或者其同时代人，成书时间自然也不是公元 7 世纪，而可能是掘藏师“发掘”公布的那个年代。“伏藏”文献的资料来源比较复杂，除一小部分真正从吐蕃时期传下来的珍贵文献外，大多是口传材料和作者编造的内容，而且是本着服务于后弘期时期的政教要求而编纂的。这些文献渲染吐蕃全盛时期的政治原则是佛教与王政的完美结合，把松赞干布、赤松德赞、赤祖德赞等藏王说成是三转轮王，他们推行“十善法”，以佛教学说治理国家，得到了巨大成功。“伏藏”文献出炉的目的，在于通过树立以佛教治理国家的古代圣王的形象，为当时西藏各地逐渐形成的寺庙宗教派系和当地世俗势力相结合的政教合一的割据集团的统治建构理论体系。

以上是西藏“伏藏”文献的梗概。如果我们认真研究蒙古文《白史》，就不难发现，它是现在所知的第一部地道的蒙古“伏藏”文献。

二、《白史》书名

我们首先从《白史》的书名入手。该书的书名就散发着浓烈的“伏藏”气味。

---

① 诺布旺丹：《伏藏传统学术源流考》，《西藏研究》2017 年第 5 期，第 35—46 页。

②《柱间遗嘱》（*Bka' chems bka' khol ma chen mo*），西藏人民出版社 2015 年藏文版，第 204 页。

③ 德吉卓玛：《伏藏遗训〈十万嘛呢宝训集〉述略》，《青海师范大学民族师范学院学报》2017 年第 1 期，第 10—21 页。

目前笔者所掌握的《白史》抄本有二十二种，其书名简繁不一，基本上可以分为两类：第一类称 Sudur（来自梵文，意为经卷）；第二类称 Teüke（历史）。如下文将要论及的，前者是原名，而后者是曲解原书名的基础上给“Tegüge”（即后来的 Teüke）一词赋予新词义的结果。内蒙古社会科学院图书馆藏 1100325 本的书名①、蒙古国甘丹寺藏本的书名②都叫 Sudur，而这两个抄本为学界公认的古本。此外，笔者认为抄于 17 世纪末期的笔者私藏古抄本的书名也是 Sudur③，以 Teüke 命名的抄本则都属于晚期抄本。

那么，《白史》书名到底是什么意思呢？我们从这本书名的基本信息 arban buyan-tu nom-un čaγan tegüge 入手仔细讨论一下。蒙古语 arban 是基数字“十”；buyantu 的 buyan 来自回鹘语，本意为“善”；tu 是蒙古语形容词后缀，作“具有”解；故 arban buyan 即佛法宣称的“十善”。nom-un 意为“教法的、法门的”，此处指佛法的；čaγan 在蒙古语中除了表示“白色”外，还具有“善、正”之意，诸如：čaγan sedkil（善心），čaγan mör（正道），čaγan üiles（善业）等。Tegüge 一词在蒙古语书面材料中出现的时间较晚，大概在《白史》中首次出现。该词字形为 TAKOKA，人们一直读作 tegüke，也没有深究其词源和词义。该词的正确读音其实应为 tegüge（古蒙古语里的发音转写应为 teḥüḥe），源于蒙古语动词 tegü，意为“采集、收集”，ge 是从动词派生名词的后缀，表示该动词所表示的动作的结果，所以 tegüge 的意思就是“收集的东西”“集子”。ge 是柔性后缀，其刚性形式为 γa。下面以 idege（食物）一词为例说明它的音变过程：《元朝秘史》有“亦咥额”“亦咥延”两个词，旁译均为“茶饭”。前者是 ide（吃）+ḥe = ideḥe，后者是 ide（吃）+ ḥen = ideḥen。古蒙古语里的 -ḥan/-ḥen 或 -ḥa/-ḥe 是从动词派生名词的后缀。这里的 ḥ 是与零声母互通的词首 h 辅音在词中的浊化形式。蒙古文词中的 ḥ 在畏吾体蒙古文中以 q、k、m、b 字母表示。随着辅音 h 在蒙古语中的消失，词中 ḥ 开头的音节和前面的音节并成一个长元音④，但在书写形式上仍保留原来表示 ḥ 的 q、k、m、b 字，这就导致了原来的 -ḥan/-ḥen、-ḥa/-ḥe 变成 -qan/-ken、-qa/-ke。又由于辅音 q、k 的弱化，-qan/-ken、-qa/-ke 变成了 -γan/-gen、-γa/-ge，如 idegen/idege 等。Tegüge 的语音变化过程和 idege 完全一样，它的早期形式为 teḥüḥe，在 h 辅音消失后，teḥü 被合并为一个音节 teü，该词发音变为 teü`e（但字形仍为 tegüge）。到后来，tegüge 的字形也跟着发音被写成 teüge，受到元音逆同化和元音弱化的影响，再从 teüge 变音 tüügh/tüükh 了。

再谈谈 tegüge 的词义。现代蒙古语中有 tegübüri 一词，是 tegüge 的同义词。tegü- 是这

---

① Erten-ü boγda sayid-un bayiγuluγsan dörben yeke törö-yin arban buyan-tu nom-un čaγan tegüge neretü sudur orosiba（名曰《古昔圣贤所建四大政体之十善法正集经》）。

② Erten-ü boγda sayid-un bayiγuluγsan dörben yeke törö-yin yoson jüil-i uqaγulqu-yin onisun arban buyantu čaγan teüke neretu sudur（名曰《宣说古昔圣贤所建四大政体礼制之钥匙十善法正集经》）。

③ Nom-un čaγan teüke čedig neretü sudur orosiba（名曰《教法白史经》）。

④ 关于辅音“h”及其变化，请参考亦邻真著，乌云毕力格、乌兰编：《般若至宝：亦邻真教授学术论文集》，上海古籍出版社 2019 年版，第 188—189、335—339 页。

两个词的词根，意为“（把某东西）收集起来”。策博勒编《蒙古语简解词典》对 tegübüri 的解释为：“从各处搜集的东西，收集物”“著作文书等的集子”。因此，《白史》书名中的 tegüge 的含义是“集子”。故此，所谓 čaqan tegüge 就是“善集”“正集”。《白史》全书名的含义也即《十善法正集》，也就是“关于十善法的正善全集”之意。

在《白史》闻名之前，蒙古历史上的类似历史体裁的文献，往往被称作 Tobčiyan、Tuḥuji 等，如 Monḥol-un niquča tobčiyan（《蒙古秘史》）、Sulqarnai-yin tuḥuji（《亚历山大大帝史》）等。《白史》以 Sudur 为名，是受到佛教文献的影响。但有意思的是，在《白史》成书以后，该书名中包含的 Tegüge 逐渐被蒙古文人理解为“历史”。当然，这个新术语的被接受经历了一段过程。比如，1611 年成书的《俺答汗传》的书名为 Sudur，17 世纪 30 至 40 年代成书的小《黄金史》称 Tobči（Tobčiyan 的单数），大致同时成书的《大黄史》的书名称 Tuγuji（>tuḥuji），1662 年的《蒙古源流》和 18 世纪初的罗卜藏丹津《黄金史》都还用 Tobči 作表示“历史”的书名。最早赋予该词以“历史”之意的史家似乎是喀尔喀的善巴，他在《阿萨喇克其史》（这个书名是后人加的）中明确用 Teüge（Tegüge 的口语形式）来指代“历史”，而这是 1677 年的事。蒙古文学语言普遍接受该词作“历史”的时间比较晚，大概是清代中期以后，而且读音从 Teüge 变成了 Teüke（口语形式是 Tuugh/Tuukh。这是因为人们在不了解该词本义的前提下根据字形读出的便于发音的形式）。

那么，《白史》作者所用的 Tegüge 从何而来？这个词当然不是《白史》作者新造的词，是蒙古语原有的一个普通词，如上所说，意为“收集”。《白史》的理论、框架、史源均与藏文文献有着密不可分的关联，书名也不例外。在藏文文献中有一个大类叫作 Bka’ ’bum 或叫 Gsung ’bum，汉语里一般译作“全集”。Bka’ 和 Gsung 都指经卷，前者更具敬意，佛语或赞普言语等可以用此语，而 ’bum 是藏语数字“十万”，此处表示“多”“全”，而不取实数词本意，所以，这里的 Bka’ ’bum 或 Gsung ’bum 就是“经卷集”“著作集”“（著作）全集”。西藏“伏藏”文献中有著名的《玛尼全集》（Ma ni bKa’ ’bum），它就是记载观世音菩萨的功德、佛教学说、松赞干布事迹、佛教故事等诸多经卷的集子。《白史》作者把他的书定位为十善法的正善全集，也就是关于该书中所宣传的十善法政教二道的历史、理论、信条、授记及执行政教二道的机构与制度设置的正确无误的信息之大全。正因为如此，《白史》作者把藏文 Bka’ ’bum 译成蒙古文用在自己的书名里，或许他正好参考过“Ma ni bKa’ ’bum”也未可料定。

总之，所谓“白史”意为政教二道学说的“正善全集”，没有“白色史书”的含义。该书之名仍然是 Sudur，可以理解为政教二道学说的“经”或“书”。书名从 Tegüge（全集）到 Teüke（历史）的含义转变完全是一个阴差阳错的过程。但无论如何，《白史》书名的来历从一个侧面透露出了它的“伏藏”性质。

从历史主义原则看，《白史》这本书的汉语书名简称应有两种：一种是其含 tegüge 的古本，应译为《十善法正集经》；第二种是改作 teüke 的晚近的写本，应译为《十善法白史》。但是，为避免混淆，下文还是通称该书为《白史》。

三、关于《白史》的前后序

体现《白史》“伏藏”性质的另一个明显的印记是该书的前后序。《白史》的前序是这样写的：“愿吉祥！愿摩诃罗阇永世为瞻部洲庄严！圣教法之本法王上师与大国政之尊国主可汗，其正法之政如绫结不可解，其可汗之严政如金轭不可破。这〔本〕无误并行二道之纲《十善法正集》，最先由忽必烈·转轮王·薛禅皇帝造，后忽图黑台·具色藏·歹成·切尽·黄台吉作为掘藏师发现〔它〕，并从松州〔或肃州？〕城掘出，与畏兀儿之必兰纳识里威正国师旧书相合，使之吉祥圆满地相结合，探究而写成。至顺元年作。”①

《白史》的这个序言实在太奇特了。众所周知，蒙古文献自《蒙古秘史》问世以来，至少到近代为止，从来没有出现过如此完整地交代著作成书相关信息的情况。不说遥远 13 世纪的《秘史》，哪怕是清代中后期的蒙古文人们也没有这样做过，所以有不少文献的作者、成书年代和史料来源都有待考证。《白史》的序言一反常态，给出了以下完整的信息：1. 原作者：忽必烈皇帝；2. 掘藏师：切尽黄台吉；3. 二次编修人：切尽黄台吉；4. 编修时的参考文献：必兰纳识里国师的旧书；5. 成书年代：至顺元年；6. 发掘元典（忽必烈著作）的地点：松州（肃州？待研究）。

《白史》序言的目的十分明显，就是要让世人了解并相信，这部书的原作者是元世祖忽必烈薛禅皇帝，续修人物是当时大名鼎鼎的切尽黄台吉，他还参考过元代国师（后任帝师，《白史》作者可能不了解这一点）的大作。忽必烈皇帝钦造的这本御书没有得到流布，虽然没有明言它一直被秘密伏藏，但从“后忽图黑台·具色藏·歹成·切尽黄台吉作为掘藏师发现〔它〕，并从松州〔肃州？〕城掘出”来看，它显然是一部“伏藏”文献，切尽黄台吉则是这部御书的掘藏师。这些如果不是故意的安排，就蒙古修史或造书传统而言，作者不会这样做。还有，托名古代帝王（忽必烈）和著名佛法弘扬者（必兰纳识里）以及掘藏师（切尽黄台吉）在某处（松州？肃州？）发掘圣书的这一“标准”表述和西藏“伏藏”文献有着惊人的相似！

《白史》的跋文也同样透露着作者故意仿古的特别安排。后序（跋）写道：“长生天的气

---

① Erten-ü boγda sayid-un bayiγuluγsan dörben yeke törö-yin arban buyan-tu nom-un čaγan tegüge neretü sudur orosiba（名曰《古昔圣贤所建四大政体之十善法正集经》），内蒙古社会科学出版社手抄本，收藏号：1100325，叶 1。

力里，大福荫护助里，圣成吉思汗的恩赐里。”并叙述“五色四藩”为了政教利益如何建立了制度。[①]这明显是故意模仿元代文献的格式。但是，在元代，“长生天的气力里，大福荫护助里”是圣旨、懿旨、令旨等才可以用的辞令，就连帝师也不得用之，帝师法旨止于“皇帝圣旨里某某帝师法旨”。[②]再者，“长生天的气力里，皇帝的福荫里”这个辞令类似清代皇帝诏书用语“承天奉运皇帝诏曰”一样，只得在文书开头用，在行文中和结语中从不出现。《白史》作者不仅在跋语中滥用了该辞令，而且还用得不规范，在“长生天的气力里，皇帝的福荫里”后面又加了一句“圣成吉思汗的恩赐里”云云。值得注意的是，这段文字在《白史》二十二种抄本中最古老的内蒙古社会科学院图书馆藏 1100325 本中特意用回鹘体蒙古文字体书写，显然是为了让人相信这本书与元代蒙古人有关。

《白史》的序和跋的做法恰恰暴露了这本书的托古性质，而且也从侧面反映出该书作者深受西藏“伏藏”影响和启迪。笔者认为，西藏的“伏藏”文献是吐蕃帝国灭亡、西藏佛教前弘期结束后，应西藏割据时代之需要，为佛教后弘期助力而诞生的。相应地，《白史》是蒙元帝国灭亡，蒙古的佛教衰败后，应蒙古割据政权的需要，为推动佛教在蒙古地区的第二次弘扬而登场的。西藏伏藏文献和《白史》的问世如出一辙，后者是对前者的模仿。

以上我们仅仅讨论了《白史》的书名和序跋的问题。当然，对这些问题的讨论还不足以说明《白史》成书年代。在探讨《白史》的思想来源、史料来源和具体内容时，我们也发现了可佐证其为 16 世纪伏藏文献的诸多线索。这些问题我们将会在今后的文章中继续讨论。

---

① Erten-ü boɣda sayid-un bayiɣuluɣsan dörben yeke törö-yin arban buyan-tu nom-un čaɣan tegüge neretü sudur orosiba（名曰《古昔圣贤所建四大政体之十善法正集经》），叶 12 上下。

② 参见蔡美彪编著：《元代白话碑集录（修订版）》，中国社会科学出版社 2017 年版。西藏自治区档案馆编：《西藏历史档案荟萃》，文物出版社 1995 年版。

初探邬坚巴几部传记间的关系*

孙鹏浩
南京大学历史学院

藏语言文学中以特立独行的瑜伽士为主角的传奇故事汗牛充栋。如果说其中不乏文学创作和演绎，那么邬坚巴·辇真班（U rgyan pa Rin chen dpal，1230—1309）的故事似乎有更多的历史基础。给人这种印象的一个原因是他的交往圈子——当故事中出现的是忽必烈（1215—1294）、八思巴（1235—1280）、桑哥（？—1291）、奥鲁赤（？—1306后）等历史名人时，"传奇"似乎有了更多的历史根基。有关邬坚巴生平的早期文本留存甚多，虽然它们以禅修指导和佛教哲学为主，但是叙事类材料也占据不小的比例。本文选择了邬坚巴传记中的一个朝廷召请的故事，通过对比不同版本，寻找文学改造背后的叙事意图，以便研究经典的传记文本是如何形成的。

一、召请故事的不同版本

获得朝廷召请，是高僧学问和名声的体现，故传记作品对这类事件多有提及。在著名的邬坚巴传《加持之流》[①]中，提及官员姓名的召请共有四次，这些人员分别叫作亦济勒（I ji

---

* 本文写作中得到范德康教授（Prof. Leonard van der Kuijp）在文献方面的指导和格格其在蒙古语方面的帮助，特此致谢。陈庆英先生（1941—2022）曾经受沈卫荣教授委托，连续三个学期（2009/9—2011/1）在中国人民大学国学院西域历史语言研究所讲授《邬坚巴传·加持之流》，包括本文作者在内的许多同学受益匪浅。谨以此文纪念陈庆英老师！

① 关于《邬坚巴传·加持之流》和其他传记材料，见 Brenda Li, "A Critical Study of the Life of the 13th-Century Tibetan Monk U rgyan pa Rin chen dpal Based on his Biographies," Dissertation, University of Oxford, 2011。本文中的《邬坚巴传·加持之流》主要采用甘托克1976年出版的写本影印版，兼参考《藏族史记集成》（青海民族出版社2011年版）第49卷中收录的写本影印版。

lag < ? ）[1]、忽伦赤（Go ron che < *Qurimči? ）、脱帖木儿（Thog du mur < *Tugh temür）和聂古台（Ne gu ta < *Negütei）。其中亦济勒（I ji lag）是派往乌思藏的著名官员，而其他人物的信息尚待发掘。本文主要关注这位名叫脱帖木儿的官员于 13 世纪 70 年代赴藏邀请高僧的故事。我们先看《加持之流》中对此事的简单描述：

mi chen thog the mur zhes bya ba 1 gdan 'dren du byung ba la yang ma byon pas/ mi chen de na re stobs kyis bzung nas 'khyer zer ba la/ rje grub chen rin po che phyag lcag brdebs shing bka' bkyon mdzad pas 'khros nas song/ gong du sleb dus nyes pa la rtugs skad//[2]

名为脱帖木儿的大人来迎请，也没有接受。那位大人说："抓住，带走！"成就者大宝上师（邬坚巴）用手杖击打他，并以言语谴责。〔那位官员〕愤怒地离开了。据说他抵达朝廷之后被治罪了。

在《加持之流》的写本中，对"抓住，带走"一词还有一段很长的注释：

ba ri lu gu bzung la khyer zer bas/ khyod ba ri lu gu na/ nga glang ri lu gu gsungs nas phyag lcag phab bka' skyon byas pas/ res pa thams cad mda' gzhu ston 'thabs grabs su 'dug/ sku 'khor rnams kyis kyang 'thab grabs byas/ 'thab mo chen po 'ong par byung ba la/ drung nas bskrad pa'i sbyor ba mdzad pas/ kho ya pho zhes de kha la rta rgyugs so/ gad ser du dran pa rnyed de/ dpag shi 'jig po zhig 'dug/ kho'i sgrog de man na khos nga bsod par 'dug ces/ bsgom thag la 'khrul 'dug skad/[3]

---

① 关于亦济勒（I ji lag）的身份，目前有两种猜想。卢西亚诺·伯戴克（Luciano Petech）认为他可能是《经世大典》中记载的 1270 年在云南的"立站使臣带木解、亦只里"中的亦只里；见 Luciano Petech, *Central Tibet and the Mongols*. Rome: Instituto italiano per il Medio ed Estremo Oriente, 1990, p.62。但是"亦只里"的"里"更有可能对应蒙古语的 -l 或 -r 尾音而非类似 lag 的音，因此更可能来自蒙古语名 *Ijil，而不是伯戴克重构的 *Ichilig（他似乎受到 I ji lag 的影响）。另有观点认为此人可能是曾担任吐蕃宣慰使的回鹘人叶仙鼐（?—1306），见陈庆英：《元代朵思麻宣慰司的设置年代和名称》，《中国藏学》1997 年第 3 期，第 45—50 页。张云：《元代吐蕃地方行政体制研究》，商务印书馆 2017 年版，第 153 页。这一同定也有语音上的问题，因为八思巴的 *Go pe las rgyas 'bring bsdus gsum bzhengs pa'i mtshon byed* 介绍了叶仙鼐的家族，其中叶仙鼐作 E se na，见 János Szerb, "Glosses on the Oeuvre of Blama 'Phags-pa, I: On the activity of Sa-skya Paṇḍita," in Michael Aris and Aung San Suu Kyi ed., *Tibetan Studies in Honour of Hugh Richardson*, Warminster: Aris and Phillips, 1980, pp.290–300。为何藏文材料中出现了这样相差不小的两种写法，仍然缺乏解释。陈庆英：《帝师八思巴传》（中国藏学出版社 2007 年版，第 82 页）也表示二者是否为同一人需要进一步考订。总之，我们现在无法在其他语言的文献中找到可靠的对应。

② 转写依据甘托克 1976 年影印出版的写本第 161（81a）页；对应《藏族史记集成》第 49 卷，第 348（95b）页。

③ 甘托克 1976 年影印出版的写本 81a。

这段文字令人费解，需要寻找到这段注释的来源，才能对其进行解读。在一部名叫《邬坚巴传·奇异海》（*Ngo mtshar rgya mtsho*）的作品中我们找到了它的来源。[①]下面先尝试解读《奇异海》中对这一故事的呈现：

> yang phyis thog the mur bya ba 1 gdan 'dren la btang byung ba la/ ma byon pas/ khong khros nas/ ba ri gu lu gzung la khyer zer nas/ khyod ba ra lu gu (sic) na/ nga glang ri lu gu gsung nas phyag lcag rgyab/ bka' bkyon byas pas/ kho'i res pa thams cad mda' gzhu bton nas 'thab drabs byas pa la/ sku 'khor phyag phyis kyang lag cha bzung/ 'thab drabs byas shing/ drung nas bskrod pa'i sbyor ba mdzad/ kho ya po zhes te/ khal rta zhon nas/ thams cad khyis kho'i rje la snyogs/ khos gad ser du dran pa rnyed/ sngags kyi rgyu mtshan kun bshad pas/ pag shi 'jigs po 1 'dug/ kho'i sgrog deng min na/ khos nga gsod par 'dug/ ces sgom thag la 'khrul 'dug skad/[②]

> 再后来，派出名脱帖木儿者来迎请，没有前往。他（脱帖木儿）发怒了，说："巴哩鲁古（*ba ri lu gu*），抓住带走！"〔邬坚巴〕说："你巴哩鲁古的话，我就朗哩鲁古！"用手杖击打他，并以言语谴责。他的卫士全部亮出弓箭，准备战斗。随从和仆人也拿起武器，准备战斗。邬坚巴做了遣退瑜伽。他（脱帖木儿）说句"牙卜！[③]"，然后骑上一头驮马跑了，其他人全都追随他。他在盖色（Gad ser）[④]清醒了。众人解释了咒语的情况，他说："真是一个可怕的上师，要不是他戴着镣铐，我就没命了。"那是他误把瑜伽带认成了〔镣铐〕。

从文字可以看出，《邬坚巴传·加持之流》的注释确实来自《邬坚巴传·奇异海》。不过《邬坚巴传·奇异海》因为具有更全的信息，让我们容易看出，这里写作 *ba ri lu gu* 的，应是蒙古官员所讲的内容。此版本比《邬坚巴传·加持之流》明显多出了密宗瑜伽的内容，使整个故事具有十足的传奇色彩。

由邬坚巴的弟子达瓦僧格（Zla ba seng ge）编辑的两部邬坚巴口述材料中的《口述传记

---

① 关于这部文献及其与《邬坚巴传·加持之流》注释的关系，见 Leonard van der Kuijp, "U rgyan pa Rin chen dpal (1230–1309) Part Two: For Emperor Qubilai? His Garland of Tales about Rivers," in Christoph Cüppers ed., *The Relationship between Religion and State (chos srid zung 'brel) in Traditional Tibet*, Lumbini: Lumbini International Research Institute, 2004, pp.299–339。

② *Ngo mtshar rgyal mtsho*（民族宫写本，编号 004804(1)/007005(1)），81b.

③ 此处的藏文 *ya po* 反映的是蒙古语 *yabu*，即"走 / 行"的命令式。

④ Gad ser 或许是指位于江孜西面 Gad ser 山谷（28°54′07.2″N 89°31′48.0″E）。波士顿佛教数字资源中心的穷达先生告知我，他于 2019 年访问该处，当地有一座名为 Gad ser dgon 的寺庙，据说是主巴噶举大师 'Brug chen Padma Dkar po 所建。据说该地有土黄色（ser po）的峡谷（gad pa），故名 Gad ser。

下册》（*Gsung sgros rnam thar chung ba*）[①]最近得以出版，为我们提供了更多关于这个故事的细节和视角。该文本的语言较为朴实，保留了口述的特征。根据《口述传记下册》，可以看出这次召请十分郑重，因为除了负责迎请的蒙古官员脱帖木儿，还有行政中心萨迦来的僧俗官员的代表，以及从贡塘前来的领主邦德衮（'Bum lde mgon，1253—1280）以及某位当地的军官等等。[②]《口述传记下册》接下来对这一故事给出了更为完整的呈现：

> mi chen khong nang par rang la bdan (gdan B) thegs dgos zer/ rin po che pa nga mi 'gro gsung/ de 'dra'i phar lab tshur la (lab B) byed pa'i 'phro la/ rin po che pa thugs rgyal langs nas/ hor la bka' bkyon drag po 1 byon/ der hor tshig pa zos nas/ rgyal po'i nga rgyal gyis phu rung rjes nas/ ba ri gu lu zer nas/ rin po che pa la 'dzing du byung/ de bod skad du sgyur (bsgyur B) na/ bkyigs nas 'khyer zer skad/ der rin po che pas kyang khyod ba ri gu lu na/ nga glang ri gu la (glang ri gul B) gsungs nas/ hor gyi 'dzing rtsa ('jing tsa B) la phyag lcag 3 rtud 1 rgyab/ der hor gyi gor rje thams cad kyis mda' (+dang B) bzhu bton/ rin po che'i bsku rgyab na yod pa'i btsun pa thams cad kyis kyang/ hor gtso gdung par (hor tsa brdung bar B) byas/ der sa skya ba dang/ mnga' bdag dang/ dpon po mo ga la sogs pa thams cad kyis (kyi B) bar byas/ hor tso phyir bton/ btsun pa tso la gros btab/ de ltar phar bun tshur bun gyi 'phrag la/ rin po che rlung sbyor drag po 1 mdzad kyin 'dug pa dang/ res 1 na (nas B) ngas skrad pa'i rlung sbyor 1 byas pa yin te/ nga rgyud 'khrugs pa des en tsam thal la che/ hor ngan pa de la gyod 1 yong gsung/ bzims khang gi sgo thon ma thag (+/ B) dmag byed pa yin zer nas kho par (phar B) la 'khyus pas/ gad ser du sleb pa kho rang gis ma [B9a] tshor 'dug zer/ de'i dus su pag shi de sgrog bcug pa des go cad/ de men ci byed mi shes par 'dug zer skad/ de rin po che pa'i sgom thag la zer bar yod par bda' (gda' B)/[③]

那位大官说："明日即须启程！"大宝上师（邬坚巴）说："我不去！"如此往来数

---

① *Gsung sgros rnam thar chung ba*，收录于《藏族史记集成》（*Bod kyi lo rgyus rnam thar phyogs bsgrigs*），第 49 卷，第 423—454 页。另外一个版本出现在一套邬坚巴文献集合（TBRC W3CN18501）中，JA 函，1–27 叶。本文中将分别以 A、B 标识这两个版本的异文。虽然书名称为"大册"（che ba）和"小册"（chung ba），其实二者篇幅相同，都大约是传统长条书的三十页，所以其实是指上下册，故我们称之为《口述传记上册》和《口述传记下册》。关于《口述传记》所载的元代西藏行政制度重构及其对僧人生活的影响，参见孙鹏浩：《从〈口述传记〉看元代中央政府对西藏的治理》，待刊稿。

② *Gsung sgros rnam thar chung ba* A4b, B7b: bdan 'dren gyi hor thog du mur zer ba'i mi chen nan tar drag po 1 byung/ bdan 'dren gyi (gyis B) 'tsham sbyor la/ sa skya nas bla ma dang/ dpon chen gyi gser yig pa sgor mo btsugs pa'i pag shi 2 kyis (kyi B) ghos (mgos B) byas pa'i gser yig pa mang po dang/ gung thang khab nas mnga' bdag 'bum lde mgon/ dro shod kyi dmag dpon/ (-/ B) dpon mo ga la sogs pa/ rgyal po'i lag rtags btsugs pa bcu gcig sbud bkra'i bzims (gzim B) khang du 'tshogs/

③ *Gsung sgros rnam thar chung ba*, A4b, B7b.

个回合。大宝上师生气了，谴责了蒙古人。蒙古人发怒了，仗着皇帝撑腰，撸起袖子说："巴哩古鲁（*ba ri gu lu*）！"然后就来抓大宝上师。那句话译为藏语是"绑起来带走"。当时，大宝上师说："你巴哩古鲁（*ba ri gu lu*）的话，我就朗哩古鲁（*glang ri gu lu*）！"在蒙古人的脖子[①]上打了三下，踢了一脚。当时，蒙古的弓箭手[②]全部亮出弓箭。邬坚巴身后的僧人也出来殴打蒙古人。萨迦派的人、领主（邦德衮），以及官员木哈等人，都来调停。蒙古人退到了外面。僧人们聚在一起商量，讨论不休之时，邬坚巴做起了威猛的风行（*rlung sbyor*），说："这次我做一个驱散的风行，那个扰乱我心绪之人有点太过分了，那个歹蒙古人会被降罪的！"居室的门刚一打开，〔那蒙古人〕说"发兵！"[③]，然后逃走了。据说他不知不觉地走到了盖色（Gad ser）。他说："当时，那个戴着镣铐的法师很有能力。我也只能如此，别无他法。"他说的〔镣铐〕其实是大宝上师的瑜伽带。

《口述传记下册》描述了蒙古官员的失礼，即语言上的生硬和没有礼貌，这构成了双方冲突的根源。通过文中给出的"巴哩古鲁"的语音和意义，我们可以确定，它来自蒙古语 *bariyul*，是以 *bari-*（"抓、取"）为词根的使动态，意思是"抓住〔他〕！"邬坚巴的回应，表现了噶举瑜伽士的幽默和骄傲。他所说的"巴哩古鲁"和"朗哩古鲁"，利用了跨语种的双关，把蒙古语 *bariyul* 里的 ba 音解作藏文的 *ba*（"母牛"），并自称是 *glang*（"公牛"），于是在传统的性别观念里，自己占据了力量的上风。由此看来，《邬坚巴传·加持之流》的注释中讲的就是这个故事，最终的源头可能就是与《口述传记下册》类似的一个详细的故事版本。可惜经过《邬坚巴传·奇异海》等的层层传抄，《邬坚巴传·加持之流》的注释把蒙古语的发音拼写错了，且语焉不详，造成了阅读障碍。《口述传记下册》不仅仅帮我们解读了这个注释，更是传递出一个完全不同的叙事效果。

于是，我们得到了对同一事件的四种呈现，分别出现在《口述传记下册》《邬坚巴传·加持之流》《邬坚巴传·奇异海》以及带注释的《邬坚巴传·加持之流》中。每种叙事都有不同的修辞重心，给读者带来不同的感受。《口述传记下册》的讲述显然对事件的严肃性给予了最多的尊重，并且较为完整地讲解了前因后果。《邬坚巴传·加持之流》省略了许多情节如斗殴等，简要地复述了事件的框架，似乎有意降低其戏剧性。《邬坚巴传·奇异海》着重于描写邬坚巴与蒙古官员之间的交锋，强调冲突，完全省略了事件的后续。带注释的《邬坚巴传·加持之流》则从形式上与《邬坚巴传·奇异海》构成了一略（《邬坚巴传·加持

---

① 此处的译文根据 B 版本的 *'jing* 译为脖子。

② 这里的藏文 *gor rje* 显然来自蒙古语"弓箭手"（*qorči*）。作者对此没有任何解释，表示这一借词已经进入当地藏语。

③ 这里并没有如《邬坚巴传·奇异海》使用蒙古语 *yabu*，而是用的藏语 *dmag byed pa yin*。这似乎表示《邬坚巴传·奇异海》与《口述传记下册》有不同的资料来源，或者是源于对蒙古语的误解。

之流》正文）一详（《邬坚巴传·奇异海》）的互补效果。

二、传记的层累

那么，是什么造成了这四种叙事之间的差异？为探求这一问题，我们首先尝试厘清这些文本间的关系。从传记整体上来看，《邬坚巴传·奇异海》在大多数时候是基于《邬坚巴传·加持之流》的一种改编，在结构和大部分内容上甚至是直接复制。这一点作者自己也直言不讳，其跋文道：

dpal grub thob rgyal po rgyal ba au rgyan pa'i rnam par thar pa ngo mtshar rgya mtsho zhes bya ba mkhas btsun chen po bsod nams 'od zer zhabs kyis mdzad pa gzhir byas nas bla ma dam pa ri khrod pa zla ba seng ge'i gsung dang/ bla ma kun dga' don grub dang/ bla ma seng ges mdzad pa'i rnam thar rnams mthong zhing/ ya rabs dag las thog pa'i ngo mtshar ba'i mdzad pa rnams mthong nas/ bla ma dam pa ri khrod pa zla ba seng ge'i gsung gis bskul nas/ dgra bcom pas shrī dpal gyi shar phug mngon dgar bkod pa dge'o/

以学问和德行兼具的大士索南维色（Bsod nams 'od zer）所造之传记（即《邬坚巴传·加持之流》）为基础，又听闻了山居者达瓦僧格（Ri khrod pa Zla ba seng ge）的口述，阅览了喇嘛衮噶顿珠（Bla ma Kun dga' don grub）[①]和喇嘛僧格（Bla ma Seng ge）所造的传记，目睹了高尚者的奇异事迹[②]，在上师山居者达瓦僧格的敦促下，由阿罗汉（Dgra bcom pa）在师利〔地方的〕（Shrī）吉祥夏普温噶（Dpal gyi shar phug mngon dga'）写作完毕。[③]

目前，我们仅仅掌握了其中的两个人物的部分作品，即索南维色的《邬坚巴传·加持之流》和几部达瓦僧格（Zla ba seng ge）的口述材料，而喇嘛衮噶顿珠和喇嘛僧格的作品还没有见到。达瓦僧格是一个关键人物，因为他显然与《邬坚巴传·奇异海》作者有许多交往，同时也是《口述传记下册》的部分内容的讲述者。《口述传记下册》的跋文写道：

---

① 他可能是 Snye mdo Kun dga' don grub（1268—？），也是三世噶玛巴的老师之一。奥尔娜·阿尔莫吉（Orna Almogi）提出他可能是蔡巴《丹珠尔》（Tshal pa *Bstan 'gyur*）的负责人，见 Orna Almogi, *Authenticity and Authentication: Glimpses behind the Scenes of the Formation of the Tibetan Buddhist Canon*, Hamburg: Department of Indian and Tibetan Studies, Universität Hamburg, 2020, p.114, n. 16。

② 这句对 ya rabs dag las thog pa'i ngo mtshar ba'i mdzad pa rnams mthong 的翻译存疑。

③ *Ngo mtshar rgyal mtsho* 115a–115b.

stod hwor (hor B) gyi skor (bskor B) gyi zin bris (ris B) dang/ gzhan yang thog du mur gyi (kyis B) skor (bskor B) la sogs pa/ 'di'i skor gyi zin bris phal che ba l bston (ston B) pa dngul chu ba ces pa/ gsol gyi (gyis B) dngul chu 'tshod mkhan bston (ston B) pa brtson byang gis byas pa yin pa bda'// yang 'di tso'i yar lungs skor (bskor B) gyi zin bris rnams/ dpon rin chen seng ge'i gcung po mdo mkhar du bdan (gdan B) 'dren mkhan la phyin pa de yin par snang//[①]

有关西蒙古的笔记和有关脱帖木儿的笔记等，此中的大部分内容的记录者是被称为“顿巴·水银师”（Ston pa Dngul chu ba）的炼造可食汞的炼丹师顿巴·尊强（Ston pa Brtson ['grus] byang [chub]）。此外，这里收录有关雅隆的笔记，似乎是迎请（邬坚巴）前往多卡（Mdo mkhar）[②]者、仁钦僧格大人（*dpon* Rin chen seng ge）的弟弟所收藏的那些笔记。

在一首赞颂词之后，《口述传记下册》后面还有一段记录，似乎是出自该写本的保管者的手笔：

bla ma zla ba seng ge'i drung du/ slob dpon brtson byang gis (sic) slob ma/ chu mig pa rin rgyal gyis zhus pa gsung 'gros kyi rnam thar 'di/ slob dpon brtson byang gi (gis B) zin bris su bda' (gda' B)/ khong dbus pa dang 'bris che bas (读作 'dris che bas)/ yar lungs kyi zin bris 'di tso yang khong gi phyag tu byung nas sgrigs par bda' (gda' B)/ khong gis bdag la btad pa lags so//[③]

这本由阿阇黎尊强（Slob dpon Brtson byang）的弟子曲弥巴·仁杰（Chu mig pa Rin rgyal）向喇嘛达瓦僧格（Zla ba seng ge）所请求之《口述传记》，是阿阇黎尊强的笔记。他（达瓦僧格？尊强？）与乌思人（*dbus pa*，指卫地方人士）十分熟稔，所以雅隆那段故事的笔记也是由他找到并做整理。是他把笔记交给了我。

这两层跋文令人颇为困惑，想要彻底解读还有待更多背景材料。不过，这里涉及的仁钦僧格，在达瓦僧格整理的《口述传记上册》（*Gsung sgros rnam thar che ba*）的跋文中也有提及，相关部分如下：

'od gsal dang rmi lam sgyu lus la sogs pa'i zin bris 'di rnams rin po che mkhar chu ba'i zin bris su gda'/ khong pa la yang rin po che pa rang gi bka' rgya yod pas spel pa'i gnas ma

① *Gsung sgros rnam thar chung ba*, A15b, B25a.
② 可能是今琼结镇以东约 6 公里处的洞嘎。
③ *Gsung sgros rnam thar chung ba*, A16a, B25a.

rnyed par ma spel ba yin skad/ rin po che mkhar chu ba zhi bar gshegs pa'i dus su zin bris rnams nye gnas 1 gi lag na yod pa/ nye gnas des kyang rten rnams kyi drung du mchod yul du bzhag ba/ de nas nye gnas de grongs pa'i dus su ji zhig cig la/ dpon rin chen seng ge zer ba'i thang po che ba'i dpon rgyud/ rin po che pa thang po cher gdan 'dren de'i phyag du byung yod par gda'/ ... khong grongs pa dang/ khong rang gi sras po slob dpon rin chen dpal gyi phyag na yod pa/ khong nged la nan tar dad pa 1 byung bas/ 'di skad gsung/ bdag rin po che pa nyid dang sa skya ru 'jal ba'i dus khyod rin chen seng ge'i bu/ nga can 'jal du yongs pa de nan tar bzang/ khyed dang rgyun 'dal gyi bar byas pa de brtan po byung yang/ da yang nga can yang yang shog gsung ba lags te gzhon pa'i thal thol du song nas/ drung du 'gro ba ma byung/ da rje u rgyan pa'i dod po khyod la re ba yin pas/ khrid dang gdams ngag dang/ chos bka' thams cad thugs la 'dogs par zhu zer nas bkur cha dang bsnyen bkur dang 'bul ba chen po byas/ de dus su chos bdag po la bstod do gsung nas/ gsung 'gros 'di rnams nged la phul ba lags/①

光明、梦幻、幻身等内容的笔记，是大宝上师喀曲哇（Mkhar chu ba）的笔记。据说这些有大宝上师自己的封印，因此不得广布，故未广布。喀曲哇去世后，笔记交给一位侍者，侍者将其放在法器等处前面供养。侍者去世后，因为种种原因，最后落到把大宝上师邀请到唐波齐去的唐波齐贵族家的仁钦僧格大人（*drung* Rin chen seng ge）② 的手里。……仁钦僧格去世后，笔记落入他儿子阿阇黎仁钦白（Slob dpon Rin chen dpal）手中。他是一位对我十分信任的人。他对我说了如下的话："我与大宝上师（即邬坚巴）在萨迦寺见面时，他说：'你是仁钦僧格（Rin chen seng ge）的儿子，你来见我，实在是太好了！我为你们与俊达（Rgyun 'dal）之间所做的调解工作，十分稳固。不过以后你也要时常来看看我！'③ 我年少任性④，没有去拜见。如今能代替法主邬坚巴的，您最有希望。指导、口诀和教育等等，请您放在心上。"说完，给我做了礼物、服侍和大供养。

---

① *Chos kyi rgyal po u rgyan pa'i rnam thar gsung sgros ma che chung gnyis*, in *Grub chen o rgyan pa rin chen dpal gyi gsung sgros dang rnam thar sogs* (W1KG4220), vol. pha, 22a.

② 前文的 *dpon* 和此处的 *drung* 均做尊称处理，统一暂译为"大人"。

③ 在《口述传记下册》正文中有与此内容相似的段落，见 *Gsung sgros rnam thar chung ba* A3a, B5a: de nas dpon rin chen seng ge'i sras po rin chen dpal sa skya na bzhugs pa'i dus su/ rin po che pa yang sa skyar byon/ der khong gis 'jal ('byal B) du byon pas/ khyod dpon rin chen seng ge'i bu mjal ('byal B) du yong pa de nan tar bzang/ nga dang po khyed rang gyi 'dal gyi bar byas pa yin/ de'i chad so btan (brtan B) po bya'am (byung ngam B) gsung/ drung nas thugs la btags mas chad gnod pa ye ma byung lags zhus pas/ 'o de 'dra ba yong ba yin/ gyi 'dal gyi gnod pa da rung yang mi yong gsung// 译文：后来，仁钦僧格大人的儿子仁钦白在萨迦的时候，正好仁波切（邬坚巴）也来到了萨迦，于是（仁钦白）前往拜见。（邬坚巴）说："你是仁钦僧格大人的儿子，来见我很好！我之前为你和俊达调解，此后是否稳固呀？"说："此后再也没有来危害我们。"说："哦，那就对了，俊达以后也不会伤害你们的。"

④ 对 gzhon pa'i thal thol du song 的翻译存疑。

那时，他说了“赞颂法主！”之后，把这些口述笔记交给了我。

这段记述告诉我们，这位保存了许多笔记的仁钦僧格和他的儿子仁钦白，都是曾与邬坚巴有交往的唐波齐（Thang po che，元译汤卜赤）地方的贵族。[①] 文中提到的俊达（Rgyun ’dal，亦作 Gyi ’dal），是一位难以驯服的地方神，在《邬坚巴传 · 加持之流》和《口述传记下册》中都记载了邬坚巴曾经应唐波齐贵族邀请，调解他们与这位地方神之间的矛盾的故事。[②]

在以上这些有限的信息中，我们尚难得出一个确切的文献链条，因为这些人物和故事似乎是当时的圈子内部人士所熟悉的，因此文中未详细讲述。但是，我们仍然可以看出，传记材料原本是若干独立的笔记（*zin bris*），由不同的作者，从不同渠道搜罗，然后再进行编辑的。同时，这一跋文也说明，《口述传记下册》的整理者已经不太清楚具体的材料来源了。其原因可想而知：在弟子和信徒之中保存和流传的早期笔记，极容易产生混乱；而收集和整理工作涉及许多复杂的社会现实，包括人际关系、地缘、个人魅力、密法的保密性质等因素。比起这些朴素而散乱的早期笔记，同为邬坚巴弟子的索南维色所造的《邬坚巴传 · 加持之流》就相对具有更多加工和创作的痕迹。

综上，我们可以重构这几部文献的关系如下：《邬坚巴传 · 加持之流》是《邬坚巴传 · 奇异海》作者的主要参考材料，但是《邬坚巴传 · 奇异海》又补充了许多《邬坚巴传 · 加持之流》没有采用的口头和笔记史料，所以有些地方的内容超越了《邬坚巴传 · 加持之流》。后来又有人利用《邬坚巴传 · 奇异海》为《邬坚巴传 · 加持之流》做了许多注释。[③] 而带注释的版本似乎成为了主流版本，因为现存的五个版本中有四个都附带注释。至于《口述传记下册》，虽然不一定是《邬坚巴传 · 加持之流》和《邬坚巴传 · 奇异海》的直接参考材料，却代表了一种内容更详细、层次更复杂的早期版本，可以帮助我们理解《邬坚巴传 · 加持之流》和《邬坚巴传 · 奇异海》的书写倾向。

三、作为文学作品作者的传记编纂者

以上展示的文本和形象的多样性，给我们这样一点提示：即使是时代较早的文献，其背后的历史已经十分复杂，遑论后来的《青史》（15 世纪）、《贤者喜宴》（16 世纪）等。因此，

① 关于卡曲瓦，见 van der Kuijp, “U rgyan pa,” 306n21。
② 见《邬坚巴传 · 加持之流》甘托克版第 149 页；*Gsung sgros rnam thar chung ba* A1b, B1b。
③ 关于这些注释的来源，见 van der Kuijp: “U rgyan pa,” 305。

当我们欣喜于《邬坚巴传·加持之流》这类文本为元史研究带来的新信息时，也必须同时把它们作为一种文学创作来研究。

邬坚巴传记材料之所以呈现如此复杂的文本层次，既有客观上材料的因素，也有传记作者主观的选择。作者在多大程度上是生硬剪贴，在多大程度上是在改写故事以表达自己的观点，可能随着具体事件的不同而有所不同。就脱帖木儿的召请故事而言，《邬坚巴传·加持之流》为何舍弃了精彩的细节，而选择了以这样枯燥的方式来讲述这一原本十分生动有趣的故事？通过比较《口述传记下册》与《邬坚巴传·加持之流》，我们可以尝试探索它们各自的写作意图和倾向。

从蒙古相关记载的分布来看，在我目前收集到的邬坚巴相关史籍中，《邬坚巴传·加持之流》是最早比较详细地记述了邬坚巴觐见忽必烈一事的文本。而且，这一段故事在其他早期笔记类传记中尚未找到对应的记载。《口述传记下册》则花了许多笔墨记录邬坚巴与察合台汗国（Stod Hor，“西蒙古”）交往的故事，[①] 这些事件在《邬坚巴传·加持之流》中却一字未提。可以猜测，如何呈现元朝和察合台汗国的斗争是《邬坚巴传·加持之流》作者所关注的一个问题。在这一问题意识之下，即使是那些本来十分符合密宗意识形态的故事，也需要予以改造。“巴哩古鲁”这样的跨语种谐音笑话，发生在特立独行的密宗疯圣身上，十分自然。但是从国家臣民的角度来讲，嘲讽政府官员甚至嘲讽他们的语言，本身是极其敏感的。《口述传记下册》中的“巴哩古鲁”故事的后半段，是由上师的强硬手段引发的一场政治危机，好在当地官员与朝廷及时干预，化险为夷，但是密宗大师与世俗权力之间的权威之争还是以一种尴尬的方式收场了。尽管《口述传记下册》也致力于突出上师的能力，但是它并未隐讳这一危机。《邬坚巴传·奇异海》则走向另一个极端，将这一事件彻底轶事化和传奇化。

相比之下，《邬坚巴传·加持之流》并没有把它完全传奇化，也没有保留《口述传记下册》的复杂层次，而是试图在密宗文学和元朝政治这两个世界中寻找平衡。这种寻求平衡的努力在其他段落中也有体现。例如，在讨论忽必烈的身份和地位时，《邬坚巴传·加持之流》记载了邬坚巴既承认忽必烈的“无量资粮”和“无量威德”，却又含蓄地否定忽必烈的菩萨化身的地位。[②] 这即是《邬坚巴传·加持之流》所具有的特殊的矛盾——在努力将元朝皇帝纳入佛教系统时，既要承认皇帝的权力，也要保持上师的威严。这并不是说《口述传记下册》的版本是真实的历史，而是说它对于这一矛盾的敏感度比不上《邬坚巴传·加持之流》的编者。另外，从文中对蒙古语的处理方式也可以看出，《邬坚巴传·加持之流》似乎有意隐藏关涉蒙古身份的内容。除了 *bariγul*，《邬坚巴传·奇异海》还记录了 *yabu*（“走！”），而《口述传记下册》记录了 *qorči*（“弓箭手”），这些表述在《邬坚巴传·加持之流》中都没

---

① 例如 *Gsung sgros rnam thar chung ba*，A7a—A12b。

② 孙鹏浩：《薛禅可汗与文殊菩萨：见于〈邬坚巴传〉中的某一种联系》，载沈卫荣主编《文本中的历史：藏传佛教在西域和中原的传播》，中国藏学出版社 2012 年版，第 591—594 页。

有出现。这一差异或许与二者的读者群有关。《口述传记下册》具有更粗糙、更纯朴的讲述风格，其听众应该限于邬坚巴的师承圈子内部，因此较少因为时政的敏感而隐讳。《邬坚巴传·加持之流》则面向更为普通的读者群，例如，纪年方面，不再采用“某日”或“上师在某处时”这种模糊的需要背景知识才能理解的小圈子内部的时间表征法，而是采用六十年为周期的元素动物纪年法。事实上，《邬坚巴传·加持之流》也确实获得了更广大的读者，成为《贤者喜宴》等后来的史书的主要参考对象，也超越了教派区分，成为14世纪以来宁玛学者的读物。①

综上，我们通过对早期材料中的平行文本和差异叙事的对比，探究了《邬坚巴传·加持之流》如何改造“巴哩古鲁”故事，尤其关注它在哪些环节保持了沉默。从中不仅可以看出不同传记文献之间的交错关系，也可以看出元代藏僧的多重身份带来的复杂的文学形象。

① 孙鹏浩：《〈五部遗教〉与〈邬坚巴传〉之间的文本关联：兼论伏藏文本的知识更新》，《藏学学刊》2022年第1期，第184—198、274页。

西藏民间信仰与仪式

An Enigma of Tibetan *Leu* (*le'u*): Ritual, Ritual Lore, and Divinities of Foetus

Daniel Berounsky

Charles University, Prague

1. Introduction

The following paper attempts to contribute to better understanding the rather enigmatic term *leu* (*le'u*) that figures in Buddhist chronicles, Bonpo literature, and is known locally in the region of eastern Bhutan and in the Minshan mountain range in the northeast of the Tibetan Plateau. It appears as a designation of certain non-Buddhist lore, rituals, texts, and ritual specialists, but it will be argued here that it was commonly associated with certain divinities in early sources.

The first part of the paper reiterates the existing research on the topic published by R. A. Stein, Ngawang Gyatso, and Toni Huber. This is followed by the second part, where examples of mentions of certain *leu* or *legu* (*le gu*) in the Bonpo texts dated mostly from between the 12th and 14th centuries will be presented. The conclusion then offers a hypothesis concerning the connection of *leu* divinities with human foetus and fertility, and identification of them with *nyen* (*gnyan*) and *lu* (*klu*) spirits based on both texts and anthropological data from the north-eastern part of the Tibetan Plateau.

2. Existing research on *leu*

In his monograph devoted to the research of the Gesar epic published in 1959, R. A. Stein refers to the Buddhist historiographical chronicles mentioning the way of ruling in ancient Bod by means of "stories" (*sgrung*), "riddles" (*lde'u*) and "bön" (*bon*) (Stein 1959: 417ff). Being primarily interested in references to the place of oral narrations and the role of bards in Tibetan culture, he points out certain inconsistencies with respect to the second of the terms mentioned as *deu* (*lde'u*). This term is mostly understood as "riddle". However, confusingly, there appear also rare cases scattered in the literature, where instead of expected *deu* another term written as *leu* (*le'u*) appears. This expression would normally mean "chapter" or "division", but this is apparently not the case in such references.

The extract mentioning *leu*, and serving as a point of departure for R. A. Stein, appears in the 14th century Buddhist "treasure revelation" (*gter*) entitled *Rgyal po bka'i thang yig.*① There is a part of this text enumerating various hidden treasures of emperors inside the Rasa Trulnang (Ra sa 'phrul snang) temple, which remains one of the main temples up to the present time Lhasa. The following section speaks about the treasures hidden in the soil inside the temple bellow a stone slab (*g.yam leb*), where also "ancient", or "original" (*thog ma'i*) *Collection of Stories* (*Sgrung 'bum*) and certain *Leu* (*Le'u*) appear. Their antiquity is underlined by connecting them with the mythical inventor of Tibetan script, Thonmi Sambhota:②

> Further, in the middle part [of the space below the] removed [stone] there are two treasure-hollows: the small and the large ones. There are religious books, riches, [text on] Goddess Zugkyi Nyema③ and others there, and in addition to them original Collection of Stories (*Sgrung 'bum*), ***Leu***, oral instructions of the dharmapāla king and other scrolls which are to be known from elsewhere. In their treasure list [it is stated that] these were put in writing by Thumi [Saṃbhota], who passed them to the hands of the king (...)

The term *leu* (*le'u)* designates here apparently scriptures and appears next to the mention of

① This rather well-known text was revealed as a "treasure" by Orgyen Lingpa (O rgyan gling pa) and constitutes a part of the pentalogy entitled Kathang Denga (*Bka' thang sde lnga*). For the text published in a book form, see U rgyan gling pa 1986.

② U rgyan gling pa 1986: 161: gzhan yang bar gags dang ke'u tshang che chung gnyis na/ chos dang nor dang lha mo gzugs kyi snye ma'i sgrung la sogs pa thog ma'i sgrung 'bum dang le'u dang/ chos skyong rgyal po'i zhal gdams la sogs pa yod de shog dril gzhan du shes so/ gter byang 'di dag thu mis yi ger btab nas rgyal po'i phyag tu gtad/(...)

③ It is written as *Lha mo gzugs kyi snye ma*, which is probably related to the reference by Ratna gling pa, who mentions *Bram ze gzungs kyi snye ma'i mdo* to be allegedly translated by Thonmi Sambhota. This text seems to be related to the well-known opera on *Bram ze gzugs kyi nyi ma/snye ma*. For more information see Sørensen 1994: 581, note 2.

Collection of Stories (*sgrung*). This is a fact, which enabled R. A. Stein to think about it in relation to the brief notes left in the Buddhist chronicles mentioning "stories" (*sgrung*) along the "riddles" (*lde'u*) as a means of governance in pre-Buddhist Bod. Although the historical value of this mention is open to dispute, it is still important that the editor or compiler connected them with the dawn of historical Bod and the beginnings of literacy.

R. A. Stein thus assumes the connection with "riddles" (*lde'u*) mentioned in Buddhist chronicles. It is provided mainly through an ancient expression *le'u glon* meaning "to give an answer" (corresponding to *lan 'don* common nowadays) and relates such *le'u* to the alternating songs consisting of questions and answers.

Another reference mentioned by Stein makes the whole matter even more puzzling. Two influential Buddhist chronicles contain enigmatic terms written in various forms as *le'u tshe/ le'u tse/ le'u ke tse*. It is attributed to central China (*rgya'i le'u tshe*, etc.) and is located to the time of Thisong Deutsen's (Khri srong lde'u btsan) rule over Bod, that is, the 8th century CE. This term is allegedly designating nothing less than the ancient non-Buddhist means of rule introduced from Rgya to Bod. Rolf Stein expresses uncertainty regarding the relation of this term with the *le'u / lde'u* analysed, stating that this could be just a Chinese term transcribed. Nevertheless, he at the same time takes this reference seriously and discusses it within the frame of the "riddles" (*lde'u*) and the supposed *leu* (*le'u*) variant examined.

It is part of the story, which appears in "extended" versions of the Bazhe chronicle (*Dba' bzhed zhabs tags ma*) and which is also repeated in the 16th century chronicle *Feast of Scholars* (*Mkhas pa'i dga' ston*). The latter includes the following version of it: ①

> Then, when the king [Thisong Deutsen] came to mature age, seeing a text of ancestors he counselled his zhanglon ministers: "In my text of ancestors it seems to be said that thinking about the well-being of the subjects, they composed the Chinese *leu-tshe* (*le'u tshe*) and gained

---

① Dpa' bo gtsug lag phreng ba 2003, vol. II: 308–9: de nas rgyal po sku nar son pa dang yab mes kyi yi ge gzigs nas zhang blon rnams dang gros mdzad de/ nga'i yab mes kyi yi ge na 'bangs bde ba'i tshis rna'i (rgya'i) le'u tshe dang sbyar na nga'i yab mes kyis rdzu 'phrul brnyes pa 'dra gsungs/ blon po dag na re yab mes kyi le'u tshe de ci 'dra ba zhig bdog zer/ der btsan pos rgya bzang me mgo la gsungs pa/ nga'i yab kyi sku ring la rgya'i gtsug lag le'u ke tse ces bya ba zhig byung zhes grag na de ji lta zhes gsungs pa dang/ me mgos le'u tse ji ltar lags pa yi ge bklags pa dang/ btsan po'i zhal nas gtsug lag de ni te por bzang ngo nga'i yab mes kyis chos lugs bzang po cig sku nyams su bzhes so// da 'jig rten gyi spyod pa bzang po ci 'byung na blta zhes gsungs pa dang sang shis bsam pa/ hwa shang mngon shes can gyis nam rgyal po mu stegs kyi chos gleng ba'i dus su lha chos snyan du gsol shig bya ba de ni 'di yin pa 'dra zhes bsams nas rgya'i lha chos bzang po byung na le'u tse (Dba' bzhed: adds: khang) de dag de'i phru ma'i sgor yang mi tshud do/ ces gsol ba dang/...

supernatural power (*rdzu 'phrul*) then." The ministers said: "What is the contents of this ancestor's *leu-tshe*?" Then the emperor told the Chinese Mego (Rgya bzang me mgo): "It is known that during the life of my father a Chinese 'art' (*gtsug lag*) known as *leu-ke-tse* (*le'u ke tse*) appeared. What is it like?" Mego read the text saying what the leu-tse is. The Emperor said: "This was very good 'art', the good doctrine of my ancestors contributed to their grandeur. See what the good worldly behaviour looks like now!" Sangshi thought that "it looks as if the king was listening to the exposition of heretical teachings and at the same time omniscient Hwashang was asking him to listen to the divine teaching [of Buddhism]." And he said: "If the good divine teaching had appeared, this *leu-tse* would not have entered the palace gates" (...)

This extract appears in the earliest Buddhist chronicle in Bod called *Bazhe*, but is only found in the "extended versions" (*Dba' bzhed zhabs btags ma*) of it, which are considered likely to be the result of inclusion of additions from unknown time.① Similar to the previous mention of *leu*, one cannot rely on it as it is a safe historical source reflecting actual events. But this mention could at the same time reflect not a historical event connected with the king of Thisong Deutsen, but a general situation related to the introduction of Buddhism to Bod seen from both semi-historical and semi-mythical perspective. If the previous mention suggested the importance of *leu* for ancient traditions of Bod, now it suddenly stands for essential means of non-Buddhist governance in Bod. Quite symptomatically, it is called by the ancient term *tsuglag* (*gtsug lag*) designating in Dunhuang documents the ancestral tradition of Tibetan emperors connected with their rule.

It could be added here that a similar expression is to be found in one of the published versions of Gesar Epic, which is not mentioned by Stein. Although it is part of poetic verses, it contrasts Chinese *leucan* (*rgya le'u can*) with Indian Buddhist dharma (*rgya gar chos*). The written form *le'u can* be well taken to have the same meaning as *le'u tsan/tshan*. ②

In a section of the Gesar epic dealing with his travel to China, the similar expression *rgya lis tshe*, or *rgya le'u tshe,* appears again according to Stein. The text speaks about twelve *rgya lis tshe* and Stein suggest that the meaning could be "noble families" or "generations". Nevertheless, Stein

---

① Cf. *Dba' bzhed bzhugs so* 2010: 74–5, 168–169.

② *Gling ge sar rgyal po'i sgrung gdug pa spun bdun*: 214: rigs drug 'dren pa'i bla ma shog/ mun pa sel ba'i sgron me shog/ dbu nag yongs kyi gtsug rgyan shog/ **rgya le'u can** kyi bdag po shog/ rgya gar chos kyi bdag po shog/ bar ras dkris can gyi mnga' bdag shog/...

has not reconstructed the possible Chinese expression.① The main unanswered question remains to be whether the reported Chinese *leu-tse/leu-ke-tse* could be indeed identified with other mentions of *leu,* including those presented below.

Yet, in another section of Epic of Gesar from Ling, the term *le'u* appears again. It is applied for a certain performance following the horse races in this case and Stein refers to it in the following way:②

> The rGyal-po bka'-thaṅ is not the only one to write *le'u*. In the Ling (III 71b), the rites of the horse race (with offerings to the gods and praises of the warrior gods, *dgra-lha*) are celebrated by people capable of making (or telling?) *le'u*. Now we shall soon see that these horse-racing festivities are precisely the occasion for songs about the genealogies of the clans.

In the description of horse races, there is a reference to a certain "performer of *leu*" (*le'u sgrub mkhan*). It is considered possibly "narrator of leu stories" (corrected into *le'u sgrung mkhan*) by Stein (1959: 477, note 14), which shows that he continues to think within the frame of the Buddhist chronicles mentioning "stories" (*sgrung*) and (*lde'u/le'u*) as a means of governance in this case.

In summary, Stein has established clear textual evidence for the existence of certain tradition *le'u* in a pioneering way. He himself considered it to be probably a synonym, or another variant of the expression *deu* (*lde'u*, "riddle"*),* and some uncertain connection with China related to the expression *leu-tse* was pointed out through the sources used by him. He thought about it in the vague context of genealogical narrations and alternate songs.③ With respect to dating one could cite

---

① Following this digression that mentions Chinese lore called *leu-tshe* (*le'u tshe/le'u tse/ le'u ke tse*), Stein focuses on a passage devoted to the enthronement of Gesar. An elder of the land in question appears there. He has a text depicting the origin and genealogy of the Mugpo branch of the Dong clan (*smug ldong*). This text, called variously *ma yig, pha yig*, or *srid pa'i ma yig,* contains besides the myth of origin also prophecies concerning the future. This serves as a clear illustration of the contexts of enigmatic "stories" and "riddles" being part of the ruling methods, but is also curiously called *smug po gdong gi ma yig le tshan*, where *le tshan* means "section/chapter", but is pronounced very similarly to *le'u tshe*.

② Stein 1959: 434: Le *rGyal-po bka'-thaṅ* n'est pas le seul à ecrire le'u. Dans le Ling (III 71b), les rites de la course de chavaux (avec offerandes aux dieux et louanges des dieux guerriers, dgra-lha) sont célébrés par des gens capables de faire (ou de conter?) les le'u. Or nous verrons bientôt que ces fêtes à courses de chevaux sont précisément l'occasion de chants sur les généalogies des clans.

③ Stein also refers to disturbing mentions of *le'u* divinities (*le'u lha*) in ritual texts dedicated mainly to personal protective gods (*'go ba'i lha*) and explained as a "one who protects during the young age" in a Tibetan dictionary (Chos kyi grags pa 1995 [1957]: 867), but the same dictionary then adds another explanation stating that it is a "god who protects through nine generations" (Stein 1959: 434). This again satisfies Stein, as it accommodates such disturbing evidence with his line of research that also pursues genealogical narrations. For such references, see Concluding remarks of this paper.

the following extract by Stein: "*But we should note at once that these occasions for palaver and recitation are attested as early as the 14th century, at least, and are even attributed to the reign of Khri-sroṅ lde-bcan.*" ① Despite the scarcity of sources, it can be stressed here that although the Gesar Epic cited by Stein could provide evidence for the existence of the *le'u* within the folk religion, Buddhist chronicles see it at the same time at the core of non-Buddhist tradition of Tibetan Empire.

Many years passed after the publication of Stein's book in 1959 without much improvement in our understanding of what *leu* could be. The only text known to me that refers to *leu* is not a strictly scholarly text written by Namkhai Norbu entitled *Drung, Deu, and Bön* published in its English version in 1995. The *leu* is discussed only in the note (Norbu 1995: 282, note 24) supplementing a passage dealing with various transgressions, including "practitioners who defy protective divinities (*le'u lha log mkhan*)" cited from the Bonpo historical chronicle composed at the beginning of the 20th century (Dpal ldan tshul khrims 1972: 420). In the note, the term *leu* is suggested to mean "practitioner", but the note also mentions an opinion given by Tenzin Namdak that it could be synonymous with "donor" or "benefactor" of the ritual (*sbyin bdag*). *Le'u lha* is then interpreted as a protective divinity of the individual or community in the context of the performance of rituals by the village priest (*gshen*) ensuring prosperity and fortune. Unlike Stein's focus on genealogical narrations and alternate songs, it sees it more as a lore connected with the rituals of village priests.

Then, again after many years and almost outside the attention of western scholars, a considerably new and abundant information on the problem of *leu* (*le'u*) was made available. First, a Tibetan-medium article by Ngawang Gyatso (Ngag dbang rgya mtsho) appeared in a local journal *Amdo Research* (*Mdo smad zhib 'jug*) in 2005. It brought sensational information about the local ritual tradition of lay priests called *leu* or "ancestor *leu*") (*a myes le'u*) in the Thewo region (The bo) of the Minshan mountain range, the forested north-eastern edge of the Tibetan Plateau on the border between Gansu and Sichuan provinces in China of the present time.② Although Ngawang Gyatso himself comes from this region, where the tradition was present, he did not know about its existence until his adult age. He spent years of collecting manuscripts related to the *leu* from households of this area then.③ Today, this tradition is almost vanished, and what remains are hundreds of cryptic manuscripts difficult to understand, and a few very old individuals having at least some information

① Stein 1959: 434: Mais nous devons noter tout de suite que ces occasions de palabres et de récitations sont déjà attestées dès le XIV siècle, au moins, et sont même attributées au règne de Khri-sroṅ lde-bcan.

② For this text published in Tibetan, see Ngag dbang rgya mtsho 2005, 2016. For an English rendering of it, see Ngawang Gyatso 2016 (translation by Charles Ramble).

③ Personal communication in summer 2017.

on the rituals and their performance from the times predating "the Great Cultural Revolution". Given the fact that the article by Ngawang Gyatso is written in Tibetan and published in Amdo, the new findings on the *leu* tradition also did not spread to western scholarship.

Hundreds of *leu* manuscripts have been collected and published in the last decades. Facsimiles of the texts from Zitsa Degu (Gzi rtsa Sde dgu), Thewo (The bo) and other places were published in 60 volumes in 2003. This large collection contains not only *leu* texts but is a mixture of manuscripts of various provenance including monastic Bon,① but the editors did not recognize that parts of the texts are connected with this specific tradition. Then news about the sensational discovery of ancient texts from Amdo from the Imperial Period appeared in the Chinese media and 30 volumes of texts from the area of Dongtrom (Ldong khrom) to the east of Thewo were also published as facsimile. Confusingly, the title mentions Datshang (Mda' tshang) as its place of origin.②

Ngawang Gyatso's research on the topic resulted in his Chinese language dissertation (submitted in 2011, Sichuan University in Chengdu) and facsimile reproductions of texts belonging to the *leu* tradition collected by him in Thewo (published in 10 volumes in 2016).③ Recently, another discovery of similar texts has been announced from the Drugchu ('Brug chu) area southeast of Thewo, and another 20 volumes containing facsimiles of the manuscripts are in the process of being published.

This discovery of recent decades is apparently of high importance. We now have access to the vast literature connected with specific locally based ritual tradition labelled *leu*, which is still awaiting its research.

On the one hand, while Stein tackled possible traces of *leu* in a few Buddhist chronicles and Gesar epic, he saw it from the perspective of a pan-Tibetan tradition of storytelling focusing on genealogies and containing riddles and elements shared with alternate songs. On the other hand, we have now only locally distributed a large number of fragments of a ritual tradition with the same name predating "the Great Cultural Revolution" in China. It would be naïve to consider it in its form surviving in known manuscripts to exactly the same tradition referred to in much earlier sources mentioned by Stein. But there should be at least some intersection between the two of them. For

---

① *Mdo khams yul gyi bod yig gna' dpe phyogs bsdus mthong ba 'dzum bzhad*. 60 vols.

② Mda' tshang is an attempt to render its Chinese name Tanchang 宕昌 in Tibetan. For Tibetans it is known as Ldong khrom. See *Mdo smad mda' tshang yul gyi gna' dpe phyogs bsdus mthong ba don ldan*, 30 vols. The volumes are poorly edited and do not list the manuscripts they contain. For a list of texts and other *leu* scriptures contained, largely unpublished, see Charles Ramble's website on Bon rituals, *Kalpa Bön*, URL: http://kalpa-bon.com [2020–12–16].

③ *Gna' rabs bon gyi dpe dkon bris ma*, vols. 1–10.

example, Stein's reference from the Gesar epic that speaks about the *leu* practitioner (*le'u sgrub mkhan*) in the context of horse races could be taken as referring to the performer of the *leu* ritual (and not to the "storyteller" as assumed by Stein). At the same time, it attests that the location of such a ritual has not been confined only to the region of the Minshan mountain range, but probably to the wider regions of Amdo and Kham.

In general, it could also not be confirmed that this tradition would specifically focus on genealogies and riddles as has been supposed by Stein. But these elements are still present there, forming parts of myths rendering the origins of the ritual. Most of the manuscripts that could be ascribed to the *leu* rituals (when sorting out those copying monastic Bon scriptures, etc) typically contain series of origin myths (*rabs*, called also *dpe*) on the ritual under the focus, mentioning mostly mythical ancestor figures of various generations known also from surviving myths on origin of the mythical first Tibetan emperor, such as Yabla Deldrug (Yab bla bdal drug), Tagcha Alol (Stag cha 'al 'ol), etc. Another frequently mentioned ancestor figure is prince Thinge (Thing ge), ① who figures as an ancestor of Tibetans in the known myth on origin of Tibetans entitled *Origin of Little Black-Headed Men* (Karmay 1998). In some of the myths the dualistic origin of the world is described oscillating between the good land of existence (Ye, Smon) and vicious land of non-existence (Ngam), which is very typical for the myths surrounding the *juthig* divination performed via knots randomly tied on ropes. Few examples of manuals used for such divination technique even survive among *leu* texts.

These manuscripts were published mainly haphazardly without any additional information pointing to their context. To make some sense of the manuscripts available would certainly require a long-term project. The research on the content of some of the manuscripts has so far been done by Ngawang Gyatso in his PhD dissertation and mostly unpublished texts generously shared with me. Two articles using *leu* texts and pointing to some links with the monastic Bon and even Mongolian rituals have been published by the present author (Berounsky 2019, 2020).

To mention the last significant and very recent source known to me, Toni Huber in his monumental book in two volumes entitled *The Source of Life* (Huber 2021, namely vol. II, 9–20) makes references to the problem of *leu* in the context of his material collected in Bhutan and surrounding regions. He considers that *leu* retains its obvious meaning as "section/division", but in a specific technical sense related to a ritual. The interchangeability between the term for an account

① Rgyal bu thing ge, but written down in number of forms as Rgya'u thing nge, etc. For the myth *Dbu nag mi'u 'dra chags* see Karmay 1998.

from the series of myths of origin (*rabs*) and *leu* among the Gathang Bumpa Stupa texts serves as an example.

It appears in the common term "nine divisions [of rite]" (*le'u dgu, bon la le'u dgu*). This ninefold scheme of ritual is first introduced through a clear explanation contained in the 15th century compendium *Bshad mdzod yid bzhin nor bu*.① This text is not representing the mainstream monastic Bon religion according to Toni Huber. This feature can be seen from the usage of the term "suitable turquoise bon" (*g.yu rung bon*) presented as the subject of the text, which apparently plays with the homophonic name for "eternal bon" (*g.yung drung bon*).

Similar parts appear then in the anonymous manuscript on *sel* rituals entitled *Mi'u rigs bzhi lha sel,* where it is, nevertheless, written down as *leu-gu* (*le'u gu* corrected into *le'u dgu* by Huber). These serve as information on context for local manuscripts from the region studied that specify such ninefold rites labelled *bon la le'u dgu*. Toni Huber thus provides evidence for understanding the *leu* as a specific rite divided into nine parts and known as *leu-gu* (*le'u dgu*) in the south Bod and eastern Bhutan.

We thus have indications of certain *leu* to relate to pan-Tibetan imperial religion provided by centuries later Buddhist chronicles. Other references from the Gesar epic would be seen as testimony of *leu* existing within folk religion. But Toni Huber then brings evidence that a specific tradition of "nine divisions [of rite]" is referred to in an unorthodox source of the 15th century and survives in an area of eastern Bhutan and surrounding regions. Discovery of *leu* texts in the Minshan mountain range area again attests to the existence of *leu* rituals (devoid of understanding itself in the sense of Huber) seen as a specific tradition connected with lay ritualists of this region.

In what follows, I would like to focus on references from Bonpo texts. This is a topic which has already been partially dealt with by Ngawang Gyatso in his published articles (2005, 2016).② He mentions older references about the *leu* within the Bon literature, which was not known and available to Stein at the time of writing his monograph in 1959 and which is also not considered by Toni Huber. Ngawang Gyatso generally understood the *leu* tradition to be that of central Bod in imperial times, which spread to north-eastern Bod with the soldiers garrisoned in eastern Bod at the time of the Tibetan Empire. But it seems to be far from given. Instead of that, I am inclined to see indication that their place was roughly eastern part of the Tibetan Plateau. I would like to bring

---

① Don dam smra ba'i seng ge 1969.

② This appears to some degree in Ngag dbang rgya mtsho 2005 (English version Ngawang Gyatso 2016), but more sources are mentioned by Ngawang Gyatso in his introduction to the 10 volumes of facsimile of the *leu* texts, see Stong 'khor Tshe ring thar and Ngag dbang rgya mtsho 2016: 1—10.

forth several references mentioned also by Ngawang Gyatso here, but mainly to introduce new ones roughly dated to the 12th—14th centuries, which were not considered by him.

3. Bonpo sources (mostly 12th–14th centuries) mentioning *leu*, or *legu*

There are several older Bonpo sources containing mentions of certain *legu* (*le gu*, or rarely *le ku*) or *leu* (*le'u*). These two ways of writing this expression are apparently synonymous and appear within Bonpo sources with roughly a similar frequency. Their identity is corroborated by the existence of similar phrases conveying the same meaning, which nevertheless contain different written forms of *leu* (*le'u*) and *legu* (*le gu*). Although *legu* could be explained as corruption of *leu-gu* (*le'u dgu*, "nine divisions rites") mentioned by Toni Huber, the combination of relatively late dates (15th century the earliest) for the textual sources attesting to the *leu- gu* as a "nine divisions of rites", and persistence in writing *legu* in the earlier Bon sources leads to reservations regarding such an explanation for all the contexts of *leu* and *legu*.①

The absence of any definitive explanation for the names *leu* and *legu* that goes beyond speculation must be acknowledged. It could be hypothetically related to the Chinese *leu-ke-tse* (*le'u ke tse*) mentioned in the "extensive" version of the Bazhe chronicle. This Chinese term could be abbreviated as *legu* (*le gu/ le ku*) in Tibetan. But it is not certain whether this term *leu-tse* is even related to the mentions of *leu* in other sources. Or an explanation of a myth presented below could refer to a form of *lag* (hand / branch), where *legu* would be a diminutive form of it similarly to other cases ("rope" *thag* – "minor rope" *the gu*).② None of these explanations is satisfactory and this question must remain open here.

The following part will focus on some references from texts which could be roughly dated to the 12th—14th centuries. Quite surprisingly, most of the cases speak about *leu* or *legu* divinities (*le'u/le gu lha*). Following the examples of such references, extracts from the texts where the same expression describing a specific tradition *leu/legu* will be presented. Eventually, references to *leu/legu* ritual specialist will be of focus here.

---

① Although it could be so that this is the original meaning which was altered given disappearance of knowledge of such rituals, it could be well also the other way round. Such understanding also apparently does not always fit the context of *le'u* and *le gu* of the extracts from texts earlier than 15th century introduced bellow.

② Cf. Stong 'khor Tshe ring thar and Ngag dbang rgya mtsho 2016: 6.

3.1 *Leu/legu* divinities (*le'u/le gu lha*)

The largest group of references speaks of *leu* (*le'u*) or *legu* (*le gu*) divinities (*lha*). Bonpo sources frequently mention them in the context of unvirtuous conduct in a certain phrase. This has been the same phrase discussed by Namkhai Norbu mentioned above, who, however, cites a chronicle from the 20th century mentioning (Norbu 1995: 282, note 24) "practitioner who defies protective divinities (*le'u lha log mkhan*)". Ngawang Gyatso subjected Norbu's interpretation to critique and understood that such mention should be corrected into *le'u lta log mkhan* ("wrong view of *leu* [ritualist/practitioner]"). However, the following much older mentions of the similar phrase in a similar context reveals that Ngawang Gyatso's critique is untenable.①

One of such early references represents a text, which was revealed as "treasure" (*gter ma*) by Lungton Lhanyen (Lung ston/bon Lha gnyan) living in the 12th century, whose date of birth is given by some sources as 1088. According to tradition, this text was revealed to him in encounter with one of the mythical past sages of Bon named Tsewang Rigdzin (Tshe dbang rig 'dzin) as a Teaching of another past sage Dranpa Namkha.② The title of the text contained in Bonpo Kangyur is the *Agate of Arrangement of Pledges* (*Rnam par bkod pa dam tshig gi mchong*). It lists ten improper things called "ten fields" (*zhing bcu*) among which also *legu* in the phrase similar to the one mentioned by Norbu appears. This time, it reads: "rejection of the entrusted (?) *legu* divinity" (*bcol ba'i le gu lha log*).③

Another such early example that contains the same phrase is to be found in a work attributed to Azha Lodroe Gyaltsen ('A zha Blo gros rgyal mtshan, 1198–1263). The text is entitled *Dromgon Azha Lodroe's Prayer for Knowledge* (*'Gro mgon 'a zha blo gros kyi mkhyen gsol zhe bya ba*). Azha

---

① Ngawang Gyatso (Ngag dbang rgya mtsho 2005, 2016, Ngawang Gyatso 2016) cites a similar passage from *Ziji* (*Gzi brjid*)–a compendium systematising Bon teachings, which was revealed as a "treasure" in the 14th century. It contains the slightly different phrase *bcol ba'i le'u lha log mkhan* according to him. Ngawang Gyatso suggests the spelling *le'u lta log mkhan* (i.e. "*leu*—the one with the wrong view") and understands it as a polemics with respect to the *leu* ritualists. The evidence presented here—and other occurrences in *Ziji* speaking of *leu* as certain gods — show that *leu* divinity is most probably meant here (*le gu*/ *le'u lha*), and not a practitioner or proponent of some tradition (*le'u lta*). I have not been able to locate this passage in Ziji, but it is more likely to mean "the one who rejects the entrusted *leu* divinity."

② For his biography see Karmay 1972: 113–115. For more extensive Tibetan hagiography written by his son see Lung sgom 'khor lo rgyal po 1972: 276–286.

③ *Rnam par bkod pa dam tshig gi mchong*, 623–665. The whole part reads: (...) de la zhing bcu zhes pa/ bla mas lob dpon sku dgra dang/ gshen dam gnyan po 'khrug pa dang/ bstan pa gnyan la 'tshe ba dang/ bslabs pa'i slob ma dam log dang/ bcol ba'i le gu lha log dang/ bka' las 'das shing ldog pa dang/ srog gcod sdig las sna tshogs byed/ bla ma'i gdan 'phrog grib la 'gom/ slob dpon rdzas brku brdzun mchu smra/ bka' khrims dam nyams skyo phra bskyel ba'o/ tshad ni bla ma mkhas pas don dang sbyar la brtag ste/ bcu po de bsgral thabs drag po'i stobs kyis kyang bsgral/(...)

Lodroe Gyaltsen came from a family based in the Azha principality, i.e. from the eastern part of the Tibetan Plateau. In one passage of the text, he lists bad deeds against the doctrine of Bon to be avoided and asks the protectors of the Bon doctrine to destroy those who commit them. It contains the same phrase *bcol ba'i le'u lha log*, now mentioning *leu* divinity instead of *legu* one:①

> (...) Destroying the Bon doctrine; lowering the high position of Shenrab; stealing harvest and property; violation of profound vows; violation of vows by a disciple who is in training; a wife's betrayal of her [husband at] home (?);② rejection of the entrusted (?bcol ba'i) ***leu* divinity**; betrayal of the community of one's patrilineal kin; wrong actions through violation of one's commitments; general enemies of eternal Bon; personal enemies of us, the priests; those in the category of people who are to be "liberated" (i.e. "killed"); speaking ill with one's mouth and dedicating one's hands to non-virtue: may these enemies of Bon not remain for years or months, but may they be "liberated" within days or the duration of a mealtime; without a time being allocated to them for a future life, or without a sign being established for them in the empty sky, may their deeds come to ripening, and may they be uprooted from their source and "liberated" at the very moment! (...)

It is notable that the mention of *leu* divinities appears within the context of family ties in this extract. What precedes the *leu* divinity in the list is "a wife's betrayal of her [husband at] home" and it is followed by "betrayal of the community of one's patrilineal kin". The *leu* divinities are mentioned between these two actions and somehow stand out from the rest of the list, which is either more general or concerned with the doctrine of monastic Bon. This could well indicate that *leu* divinities appear in the proximity of very intimate ties, perceived to be similar to family relationships. However, it remains rather enigmatic what the "entrusted leu divinities" (*bcol ba'i le'u lha*) could be.

These two texts could be early sources for similar passages to be found in numerous later

---

① *'Gro mgon 'a zha blo gros kyi mkhyen gsol*: bon gyi bstan pa bshig pa/ gshen rab dbu phang smad pa/ rnga thog bkor (= dkor) la 'bag pa/ zab mo'i dam la ldog pa/ slob pa'i slob bu dam log/ nyos pa'i chung ma brang log/ bcol ba'i le'u lha log/ rus kyi pha tshan sde log/ dam la 'das pa'i las ngan log/ g.yung drung bon gyi spyi dgra/ gshen po bdag gi dgos (= sgos) dgra/ sgral ba'i zhing du gyur ba/ kha ngan du smra ba/ lag pa sdig tu bsngo ba/ bsam pa ngan du byed pa/ bon dgra dam nyams 'di lo dang zla bar ma bzhag par/ zhag dang za mar myur du sgrol/ tshe phyi ma la dus ma 'debs par/ nam mkha' stong pa la mtshan ma ma 'dzugs par/ las kyi rnam par smin pa la/ khungs ma 'byin par dus da lta nyid du sgrol cig/ (...)

② The meaning is uncertain. Here, the expression *brang* is taken as meaning "home". The *brang log* could also mean "cheating" (lit. "turning the breast away") as well.

Bonpo texts, but also "Buddhist" ones.

What the *leu* divinities might be is further indicated in the following extract. It appears in the large 14th-century compendium *Ziji* (*Gzi brjid*) and narrates the story of a king of a country called Hömo Lingdrug (Hos mo gling drug), whose wife becomes ill. The illness is caused by a *lu* (*klu*) spirit (i.e. an underground spirit). Various diviners and physicians are invited, and a diviner learned in the *jutig* divination (*ju thig*) appears at the court. After several interesting narrations on the origin and details on *jutig* divination, which is based on the use of cords from divine sheep, the story eventually addresses the state of the king and his wife:①

> All the illness of the queen and the epidemics of the kingdom must have appeared because of turning your back on the the ***leu* divinities** who are related to you. Then, from what appeared in the prognosis of divination concerning the "friends" (gnyen)② of ***leu* divinities**, and from what rituals might be performed for straightening the crooked, if the teacher is invited, and confession of misdeeds along with performance of the ritual of remedying faults will be performed, such a ritual would be beneficial, and the diagnosis would be substantially better (...)

Bearing in mind that *lu* (*klu*, underground or serpent spirit) was mentioned as the primary cause of the illness, it follows that the *lu* spirit is considered to be one of the *leu* divinities in this case. The extract also stresses that the bond between the *leu* divinities and the king is similar to family bonds (*rang gnyen le'u lha*).

Another interesting mention of *legu* divinities appears in a tantric text of the Bon Kanjur, entitled *Mkha' klong rab 'byams bskang ba'i 'phyong bzhugs*. However, this text is difficult to date. It is ascribed to a certain master Ma (Rma) of the Dru (Bru) family. Master Ma might be one of the masters otherwise known as Maton (Rma ston—"teacher of the Ma clan"), but there were several people with this name living in the 11th–13th centuries.③ The text is dedicated to the ritual

① *Gzi brjid*, vol. *cha*, p.449: btsun mo'i nad dang rgyal khams kyi yams thams cad/ rang gnyen le'u lha la rgyab kyis phyogs pa las byung bar 'dug go/ da le'u lha'i gnyen phya'i nang nas/ gto phya'i g.yas (yo) bcos kyi nang nas/ ston pa spyan drangs nas nyes ltung gi bshags pa dang/ nyams bskangs kyi cho ga rnams byas na/ gtos phan cing dpyad rtsis ste/ (...)

② This is a category mentioned earlier in the text for which the divination is cast. It resembles *grogs* ("friend") of more common astrological calculations and is the opposite of "enemy" (*dgra*) in both cases.

③ The colophon states that the text was revealed as a "mind treasure" by Bla ma Rma in Khyung rdzong and that it was faithfully copied from old original by Bru btsun Rgyal mtshan 'od zer, who is from the lineage of transmission: (...) gyer gyi bka' gter khyung rdzong la/ dngos slob bla ma rma la bab/ rgyud du bdag la'o/ bru btsun pa rgyal mtshan 'od zer gyis dpe rgan la zhal bshus so/.

of ransom offering (*glud*) and consists of several stories presented in a series of narrations (*rabs*) recited customarily in the old Tibetan rituals. Many of such narrations contained in this larger text are pronounced by or related to Shenrab Miwo, the founding figure of the monastic Bon. The *legu* divinities appear only in one story, which is also specific to the divinities it mentions. These are unknown to other parts of the text. The composite nature of the text leaves us with the question what the source for the following part might have been:①

> Again, there was one named Camdel Thangpo, who was a king of the country. His fortress was high; he was of virtuous conduct and possessed many riches. But he forgot about the gods above to be propitiated. The protective power of the ***legu* divinities** faded away. The [balanced] state of the eight classes [of spirits and divinities] was terminated. [The king] thought of himself as being greater than the *mu*, *dü*, and *tsen* spirits, the three. He thought of himself as being more powerful than the *nyen, lu* and *tö* spirits, the three. The eight classes of spirits and divinities pledged themselves to punish it. The bad omens of the *dü* demons fell upon the people. The malevolent charisma of *mu* spirits caused destruction. The *tsen* spirits released violence. The *nyen* spirits projected the pain.② The harming power of the *dü* demons broke out. Sickness appeared among people; loss befell the cattle. All thinkable trouble came to them and they thought: What is the reason for this? What should be pursued?
>
> A female ritualist named Tingber Shelcag was asked to perform the ritual, and she said:

---

① *Mkha' klong rab 'byams bskang ba'i 'phyong bzhugs pa'i dbu phyogs lags+'o*, 26: yang 'brel lcam dal thang po zhes bya ba/ yul gyi rje byed/ mkhar gyi bzang mtho/ bzangs (bzang) spyod kyi skor (dkor) ldan te/ steng du gsol ba'i lha yang brjed/ le gu lha bsrung kyi mthu rnal/ sde brgyad stabs la bcad/ dmu bdud btsan gsum bas kyang nga che/ gnyan klu gtod gsum bas kyang nga btsan par dgongs pas/ de la lha srin sde brgyad kyis bka' chad dam ste/ mi de la bdud kyi than babs/ dmu'i (dmu yis) byin bsnyil/ btsan gyis khroms 'grol / brnyen (gnyan?) gyis zer 'phros/ bdud kyis byad rdol/ mi la nad byung/ phyugs la god babs/ ci bsam yang char song te/ 'di ci cho ci 'brang snyams nas/ srid pa'i bon mo ting ber shel lcags zhes bya ba la/ gto byas pas bon mo de na re/ 'di phyi ma cis kyang ma len te/ 'go ba'i lha spang/ le gu sles la bor bas nongs/ lha srin sde brgyad stabs la bcad pas nongs/ 'go ba'i lha bas med/ lha srin za lam skyes pas/ da lha la yon 'bul/ bgegs la glud thongs/ mi nor gyi phywa g.yang skyob cig skad do/ der 'bel 'bang rkang phran gribs/ thar bon dang/ klu bon zor gnyer nas/ lha la rten btsug/ bgegs la glud btang/ le gu'i srungs btsugs te/ che bar gser dang g.yu gzi/ spug/ g.yag/ lug/ rta/ dar zab 'bru bang rnams phul/ chung bar sku glud rings (ring?) tshad dang/ gnam bya ri dwags 'phen/ dud 'gros na tshogs rnams/ gzugs dang gsob du byas nas phul bas/ rgyal po de yi mi nad dang/ phyogs nad yams nad chad do/.

② The text mentions *brnyen* (for *brnyan*), "images," and *zer*, "beam of light." However, it is probable that the text talks about *nyen* spirits (*gnyan*) and "pain" (*gzer*). *Gzer* is also a disease listed among those caused by *gnyan* (*gnyan rigs bco brgyad*), but at the same time means "pain."

"This [conduct] should not be adopted by anyone in the future.① The enveloping divinities② were diminished. It was the fault that the ***legu*** [divinities] were left abandoned. It was fault that the power of the balanced state of the eight classes of divinities and spirits was terminated. No one is here except for enveloping divinities.③ The livelihood④ of the divinities and spirits should be produced. Now, present valuable gifts to the divinities. Send ransom offerings to the spirits of obstructions. Protect the good destiny of people and the well-being of cattle!" Thus she said.⑤

The ritualist Tharbon and Lubon Zornyen erected the supports of divinities. They sent the ransom offerings to the spirits of obstruction. They established the protection of ***legu*** [divinities]. They presented large treasures of offerings of gold, turquoise, onyx, coral, yak, sheep, horse, fine silk, and grains. Then ransom offerings of the body of the smaller proportions: birds of the sky and wild ungulates were casted. The bodies of the various animals were stuffed and offered. And the human sickness of the king and the loss of cattle were stopped.

Legu divinities appear in the proximity of so-called "enveloping divinities" (*'go ba'i lha*) and spirits named *lu* (*klu*), *nyen* (*gnyan*) and *tö* (*gtod*). It is namely the mention of *tö* spirits—otherwise very little known in Bod—that indicates its proximity to the tradition of the so-called *Fourfold Collection* ('Bum bzhi) consisting of four parts dedicated to *lu* (*klu*), *nyen* (*gnyan*), *sadak* (*sa bdag*) and *tö* (*gtod*) allegedly revealed at the turn of the 10th and 11th centuries. The volumes dedicated to *sadak* spirits and *nyen* do mention *leu* as well. Although protective divinities known as *'go ba'i lha* are of different kind, remembering that the *lu* spirit was regarded as *leu* divinity by the previous extract, one could reasonably ask whether this group of spirits that represents mainly wild environment of humans would be identical to *leu* divinities? But given the ambiguity of the sources, one must leave such a question open.

The following example is an extract from a text included in Bon Kanjur entitled *Mdo ka ba gling dgu* where the *leu* divinities are mentioned in the opening sections containing just homage

① The translation is only tentative. The expression in Tibetan is so general that it could be rendered in several ways.

② These divinities are considered to reside in the body of individuals and according to the Buddhist sources consist of male-divinity (*pho lha*), female-divinity (*mo lha*), warrior divinity (*dgra lha*), maternal uncle-divinity (*zhang lha*), etc. Older sources of Bon, however, include more divinities. I am translating their designation *'go ba'i lha* here only provisionally as "enveloping divinities." Later Tibetan sources understand that they are attached (*'go ba*) to the individual's body as a shadow.

③ The sentence is strange and gives the impression that some part is missing.

④ Literally "food and path" (*za lam*).

⑤ The next sentence is omitted because its meaning is not clear at all: *der 'bel'bang rkang phran gribs*.

to some divinities. The homage is paid first to the *leu* divinities, then to the divinities of disciples and then to the divinities of donor,① which might indicate that in this case the *leu* divinities are understood to be a divinity of ritual masters.

Yet another example could be taken from a large compendium *Ziji* (*Gzi brjid*, revealed in the 14th century) where *legu* divinities are named in an extract containing advice for kings and listing various contradictory phenomena which are to be put into harmony:②

> Poor ones need donors from the rich ones, non-existing needs "virtues" of the existing,③ rulers and subjects need separation from each other—and all need absence of disapproval. ***Leu* divinities** require the absence of quarrels (*mkhon*). Therefore it is difficult for kings to support all.

It should be stressed here that the term for "quarrel" or "enmity" (*mkhon*) is very often understood in a specific way. It is not just addressing any conflict, but it is listed among the specific and dangerous pollutants as "widowing" (*yug*), "killing a relative" (*dme*), and "incest" (*nal*). As such, it is generally understood to be an "enmity" on the side of spirits or divinities very close to humans. But with this topic, we are getting to the examples where *leu* suddenly designates ritual specialists.

3.2 *Leu* as ritual specialist

The purification of pollution resulting from enmity (*mkhon*) is a topic of large number of myths contained in the existing versions of the *Nyen Collection* (*Gnyan 'bum*). The revelation of this scripture is ascribed to the rather accidental find by hunters in western Bod prior to 1017 by several Bon chronicles. There is an extensive version of it that survives in Bon Kanjur, where *leu* is mentioned just once,④ but there is also a short version of the *Nyen Collection* rediscovered

---

① *Mdo ka ba gling dgu* (vol. ca, 7th chapter, p.76): le'u lha la skyabs su gsol/ slob bu lha la skyabs su gsol/ yon bdag lha la skyabs su gsol/...

② *Gzi brjid*, vol. kha, chap. *Bzang brag rtsa bar rgyal bur dgyes ston bshams*, p.168: dbul la phug gis sbyin pa dgos/ med la yod kyis dge ba dgos/ rgyal 'bangs so sor 'byed pa dgos/ thams cad kun la 'gras med dgos/ le'u lha la 'khon med dgos/ de phyir rgyal gyi zhabs 'degs dka'/(...)

③ The expression "virtue" (*dge ba*) is frequently used in the context of funeral rituals, where it designates merits or some beneficial acts that are believed to be ascribed to the deceased.

④ *Gnyan 'bum*, p.317: (...) *le'u yon bdag* (...) It is also once mentioned in another collection of myths dedicated to sadak spirits, which is believed to be revealed along with collections on *lu* (*Klu 'bum*) and tö spirits (*Gtod 'bum*) in the similar place. See *Sa bdag 'bum*, chap. 11, p.57: (...) *le'u yon bdag 'di dag gis* (...)

by Ponse Khyung Gotsal (b. 1175), where seven mentions of *leu* appear in this relatively short text.[①]

The myths of the *Nyen Collection* typically describe conflicts between the original people connected with the Dong clan (*Ldong*) and the *nyen* spirits, which should then be ritually appeased. Mentioning *leu,* they in most cases clearly designate a ritual specialist narrating the myth and performing the ritual following the ancient example provided by the narration. The following extract could serve as an example:[②]

> By [offering] the three ones (i.e. curd, milk, and butter) and through the pacification by them, the stream of diseases of *sadak, lu*, and *nyen* spirits was interrupted. Because of that, the place of good white light made the pollutions of "incest" and "enmity" melt and purified. The pollution was eliminated. The obstruction was removed. "Enmity" was averted. Viciousness was cleared away. The misfortunes caused by the *nyen* spirits were lifted. The diseases caused by the *nyen* were extinguished. The army of the *nyen* was dissolved. The crookedness of the lame ones was straightened. The deafness was cleared from the ears. The eyes were returned to blindness. Eloquence was given the muteness. *Lu, nyen* and *sadak* spirits got rid of the grudge.
>
> Today, all these ***leu*** purify the "enmity" of *sadak, lu*, and *nyen*. They are lifting the misfortune of their grudge!

Here we have just one example of ritual purification of the pollution from enmity of spirits or divinities. The *leu* are mentioned there as ritualists and that ritualists are meant can be deduced from other mentions in the same text, which appear not merely as *leu*, but as "*leu* and donors" (*le'u yon bdag*).

But one of the mentions probably contains a sign of extension of the meaning from "*leu* divinity" to a ritual specialist who deals with them. In this case, the ritualist is called "owner/master of *leu* divinity" (*le'u lha bdag*). The following extract concludes a description of a ritual during

① See *Nye lam sde bzhi'i gnyan 'bum*.

② *Nye lam sde bzhi'i gnyan 'bum*, fol. 632: dkar gsum gyis zhi ba byas pas sa bdag klu gnyan nad kyi rgyun chad do//de phyir sa 'od dkar yag zhu'i nel mkhon bya byang /mnol ba bsang ngo //'gag pa byang /mkhon pa bsab bo//gdug sems sangs so//gnyan dal bkyag go/gnyan nad chad do//gnyan dmag gyes so//zha bo sgyud (sgur) drang ngo //'on pa snyan sangs so//long ba spyan dang ldan no//lkugs pa kha mkhas so//klu gnyan sa bdag gdug pa las thar ro//de ring le'u 'di kun yi(s)/sa bdag klu gnyan mkhon ni byang /gdug pa'i dal bkyag/.

which various birds "opened" layers of the sky and remedied the "enmity" of *nyen* spirits:[①]

> Today, may these donors be freed to increase in numbers and their cattle multiply! The key was tied to the neck of the red bird. The **owners of *leu* divinities**—those of *sadak, lu*, and *nyen* of the creation of the world—opened the "white veins" of *sadak, lu*, and *nyen*. By freeing their "white vein", the numbers of people may increase, and they come to peace in their minds! May the adversities of the people's livelihood be cleansed by offering the various [birds of] pleasant voices!

This extract calls poetically ritual treatment by birds (who are messengers of the *nyen*) "opening their white vein" (*rtsa dkar po'i sgo phyes*), which alludes to the release of their beneficial influence manifested by the increase of people and cattle in numbers. But what is quite striking is that these ritualists are specified as "owners of *leu* divinities", which are in turn named "*sadak, lu*, and *nyen* spirits of the creation of the world".

Such mentions of "owners of *leu* divinities" appear in other rather early sources as well.[②] The variant of "*leu* and donors" (*le'u yon bdag*) is frequently present in the recently published *leu* texts from Thewo, but in this case the dating of them is rather problematic.

3.3 *Leu/legu* as a ritual tradition and its relationship with Bon

There are also rather early references to *leu* as a kind of ritual tradition. This occurrence appears in an extracanonical text exposing the doctrine of Shenrab Miwo entitled as *Mdo rnam 'grel bar ṭi ka*, which must be dated earlier than the 14th century.[③] The text mentions the "Bon of the *legu* of ten knowledges" (*le gu shes bcu bon*) and it is apparent that this is to be understood as a basis of the doctrine of Bon. Remembering the research by Toni Huber, in this case one could be inclined to see it as a corruption of *le'u dgu shes bcu bon*, which would in such tentative reconstruction mean

---

① *Nye lam sde bzhi'i gnyan 'bum*, fol. 628–9: de ring yon gyi bdag po yi/ mi grangs grol la phyugs tsi spel/ bya dmar po'i mgul du zangs gyi lde mig btag pa/ sa bdag klu gnyan rnams la srid pa'i sa bdag klu gnyan rnams kyi le'u lha bdag rnams kyi(s) rtsa dkar po'i sgo phyes la rtsa dkar grol la mi grangs spel zhi ba sems dang ldan par gyur cig/ sa bdag klu gnyan 'khor dang bcas pa la/ rin chen skad snyan rnam pa sna tshogs 'bul ba ni/ mi yi rkyen 'gal byang bar gyur cig/.

② It appears in the text revealed by the same person living in the 12th century, where it mentions *le'u lha bdag*, see *G.yag ru dgra chos kyi shog dril mde'u kha nyes byed dam nyams srog gshed*, fols. 952–3.

③ This text is cited in *Bon sgo gsal byed*, which is from the fourteenth century; see Mimaki 2000. For the Tibetan text, see *Mdo rnam 'brel (= 'grel) bar ṭi ka*.

"Bon of nine divisions of rites and knowledge, the tenth." Whatever the case, the meaning was expanded again. It is not divinity, nor ritualist, but a specific ritual tradition. This expression appears in the context in which 12 bon(pos) of various points of compass address their questions concerning the practice. The *legu* is mentioned only in the answer to the 12 bon(pos) of the East, which is an interesting detail:[①]

> Again, twelve bon of the East asked the following unanswered questions: "After the demise of the sole father Shenrab Miwo, who will be the teacher of Bon? Who will be the friend of the Doctrine? Who will further expose the arts (*gtsug lag*)? How will the traditions of origin narration be differentiated?" Shenrab said: "Knowledgeable ones will be the teachers. Search for friends among those with a loving attitude. When the **bon of *legu* of ten knowledges** will be enacted to the disciples of body, speech, and mind, great core treatises of arts (*gtsug lag*) will be exposed there. The specific way of recitation will be passed on in each tradition of origin narration. And thus all creation will be understood."

Quite surprisingly, *legu* is presented here as the principal means of continuity of the practice of Bon. However, one must bear in mind that this concerns the twelve bon(pos) of the East. It is also clear that the extract addresses a certain tradition of *legu*, which is called Bon, although it might mean a tradition related to *legu* divinities. The *legu* is described as containing "arts" (*gtsug lag*). The extract also says that *legu* is bound with recitation of myths about original events and specific ways of reciting them.

In general, the indications of *leu* or *legu* as being connected with the mythical origins of the oldest Tibetan religious practices are scarce in the Bon texts and rather dubious. However, they do exist. There is a short passage dealing with the first Tibetan king's descend from sky to earth which appears in the text entitled *G.yung drung bon gyi rgyud 'bum* and this text is considered to be a particular version of the chronicle *Bsgrags pa rin chen gling grags*. The dating of this specific version is uncertain, but other versions of *Bsgrags pa rin chen gling grags* are mentioned

---

① *Mdo rnam 'brel bar ṭi ka*, chap. 30, fols. 108a–108b, *Sangs po 'bum khris ston pa spyin drangs ba bstan pa*: (...) yang shar bon bcu gnyis kyis zhal na re/ ma byung ste 'di skad zhus/ gshen rab yab cig 'das 'og tu/ bon gyi slob dpon su la bya/ bsten pa'i grogs po su la bya/ gtsug lag rgyas par su la bshad/ smrang rgyud dbye ba ji ltar dbye/ gshen rab yab kyi zhal na re/ shes pa can la slob dpon gyis/ brtse gdung can la grogs po tshol/ sku gsung thugs kyi slob bu la/ le gu shes bcu bon byed na/ gtsug lag gzhung chen de la bshad/ gyer thabs re zhing smrang rgyud dang sprad/ 'on tang srid pa kun gyis go/ (...)

to be revealed in 12th century.① These, however, do not contain the extract translated below. The account of the origin of the first mythical emperor Nyathi Tsenpo (Gnya' khri btsan po) is much more detailed in them and differs significantly from the version given here. I am inclined to see this version to be of later provenance. In any case, it seems to be a very isolated narration appearing solely in this particular version. It connects the *legu* with the mythical beginnings of Bod and the rule of the first legendary king Nyatri Tsenpo and the text also attempts to explain the meaning of the term *legu*:②

> The son of Tri Yabla Daldrug was Tri Barla Duntshig. His son was Barla Sime. He was sent to be the lord of the black-headed men for the benefit of the beings and with the blessing of the Teacher. When this lord was proceeding there, bonpos who emanated from the sky and protected his body were there as well. Mubon from the lineage of Theyan manifested as the king Tshemi. Chabon from the lineage of Thelag manifested as Cho priest of White Hands. These two bonpos supported the king's arms from the left and right sides and so they proceeded to the Yarlung Sogka. Thus, it was the first time that the term ***legu*** appeared to be assigned to Bonpos.

Ngawang Gyatso interprets this usage of *legu* as meaning "hand/arm" (*lag–le gu*) in a way similar to other cases in Tibetan (*phag–phe gu, thag–the gu*), which is understood to be related to the role of the priest in supporting the arms of the king. It is a plausible explanation of what this extract wants to say. However, whether this was indeed the meaning of *legu* remains rather dubious and this explanation resembles frequent popular etymologies. Whatever the case, it is clear that this text is rather innovative in the sense that it renders the story through connections unknown to the earliest sources and clearly within the frame of monastic Bon.

Another mention of *legu* is to be found in the Bon chronicle *Bstan byung dar rgyas gsal sgron* composed by Paten (Spa bstan) probably in 1381. In the parts dedicated to "southern treasure texts" (*lho gter*) it speaks of Pel Gonse (Dpal mgon gsas), the father of Shenchen Luga (Gshen chen klu

---

① Cf. Martin1997: 29.

② This was already pointed out by Ngawang Gyatso (Tsering Thar, Ngawang Gyatso 2016, p.6), the text reads (G.yung drung bon gyi rgyud 'bum, p.18): rje yab bla bdal drug gis ras khri bar la bdun tshig lags/ de'i sras bar la srid med de/ mgo nag mi'i rje ru gshegs pa yang ston pas byin gyis brlabs te 'gro don dub tang/ rje de gshegs pa'i dus su sku srung gi bon po nam mkha' las sprul ba ni dmu bon the yan brgyud las 'tshe mi rgyal du sprul/ phywa bon the lag brgyud las gtso gshen phyag dkar sprul te/ bon po de gnyis kyis rje'i phyag g.yas dang g.yon brtan na yar lung sog kar gshegs pas/ bon po la le gu zhes bya ba'i brtan (=gtan) tshig dang po de ltar lags so/.

dga'), one of the first revealers of the fundamental texts used by the present tradition of monastic Bon, whose act of revelation of manuscripts is mostly assigned to the year 1017. It says that his father practised *legu* (*le gu bskyangs bas* ...) of his maternal uncle, who had no descendants. This perhaps might indicate that a ritual tradition named *legu* was passed on to descendants within the family. It is just interesting to note that the tradition connected with *leu* has been so close to this figure and so important for the development of the monastic Bon according to this source.

But if some of the extracts speak about *le'u bon* and could thus be interpreted as suggesting that *leu* could be seen as a part of the monastic Bon, there are also cases where Bon is different from *leu*. In such a sense, the term *leu* appears in the *juthig* (*ju thig*) divination manuals amongst the names of the individual positions within the series of thirteen casts of knot combinations. It concerns the ninth position known as '*maternal uncle leu and a mountain region of paternal uncle bon*' (*le'u zhang po dang khu bo bon gyi gling ri*).① *Leu* apparently forms a pair with *bon* and is therefore considered to be some tradition separate from *bon*, but complementary to it.

4. Concluding remarks

There are clear references even from the oldest sources available to the close bond resembling family ties between the people and *leu/legu* divinities. Then, there are references—again in relatively old sources from the 14th century—speaking about the underground spirit *lu* (*klu*) as being the *leu* divinity itself. Yet other sources mention fourfold spirits *lu* (*klu*), *nyen* (*gnyan*), *sadak* (*sa bdag*), and *tö* (*gtod*) in the proximity of *leu/legu* divinities. One source lists *lu, nyen*, and *sadak* to be the *leu* divinities.

There are a number of texts that list *leu/legu* divinities among the group of protective gods known as "enveloping divinities" (*'go ba'i lha*) and some of them explicitly mention that these divinities "cherish from the young age of childhood" (*le'u lha ni chung ngu'i dus nas bskyang ba'i lha yin*). This mention appears also in the dictionary compiled by Choekyi Dragpa (Chos kyi grags pa 1995 [1957]), which was cited by Rolf Stein in his text and later also by Ngawang Gyatso. But this dictionary entry repeats the verbatim earlier text of Ngawang Tendar (Ngag dbang bstan dar, 1759–1831), whose text says:②

---

① See Ju Mipham 2007: 14.

② Ngag dbang bstan dar 1971: 563: **le'u lha** ni chung ngu'i dus nas bskyang ba'i lha yin zer/ la las le'u zhes pa bon gyi brda' la grangs kyi dgu'i ming yin pas mi rabs dgu brgyud kyi lha yin zer/.

> *Leu* divinities are gods who cherish [people] from the young age. The term *leu* is a Bon term for number nine and thus it is a divinity of nine ancestral generations of people.

But this interpretation seems to be rather odd and isolated. There is no other source known to me that claims *leu* to mean "nine" among Bonpos and no other mention of *leu* divinity as protector of nine generations. The association with number nine is probably connected with a term "nine *leu*" (*le'u dgu*) which has been clearly shown by Toni Huber to designate "nine divisions of rite" and could be in its form *legu* (*le gu*) considered abbreviated from "nine *leu*" in some cases.

But the mention of *leu* divinity to relate to small children does not seem to be altogether odd. It has support in other works. Yet, it is not just children of young age. *Leu* is specified to mean foetus, literally "child of the womb" (*mngal gyi byis pa*). This appears in the work by two 20th century masters, first of them being 6th master Tshetan Zhabdrung Jigme Rigpay Lodroe (Tshe tan zhabs drung 'jigs med rigs pa'i blo gros 1910–1985),① second of them is a 20th-century physician and author of a commentary on medical text of Gyuzhi (Rgyud bzhi) with name Serkhang Trashi (Gser khang bkra shis). According to the first of them this meaning "foetus" is related to the meaning of "*leu* divinity", although the details of their connection are not specified.② *Leu* should not be a divinity of young children, but a divinity somehow connected with foetus.

Now, a digression to the Thewo region, where hundreds of *leu* manuscripts were found, might provide a clue to this fragmented information. *Leu* ritualists are briefly described in recent work included in brief histories of monasteries as taking part in a monastic ritual, and their main rituals are listed. One of their main tasks is to propitiate *lu* and *nyen*, the two kinds of spirits that can be met closely with *leu* divinities in other sources as well:③

> Then, the so-called worldly "owner of *leu* divinities", a village bonpo knowledgeable about divinities (and somewhat similar to tantric masters) has to perform an offering ritual to *lu* and *nyen* spirits, a ritual of "capturing soul" at the main residence of the monastery, and a ritual of providing protection to village fighters.

---

① Tshe tan zhabs drung 'Jigs med rig pa'i blo gros 2013: 206.

② Gser khang bkra shis 1998: 51: **le'u** ni [...] mngal gyi byis pa ste/ phyi ma la **le'u'i lha** zhes pas mtshon/.

③ Dri med 'od zer 1999: 72: yang srid pa'i **le'u lha bdag** ces lha shes grong bon (sngags pa dang cung zad 'dra) zhig gis klu gnyan gsol mchod kyi gto yi cho ga dang/ nang chen la bla blu dang bla 'gug dang/ grong sde'i dmag mi la srung 'dzugs bya dgos/.

During my fieldwork among the surviving *leu* ritualists in Bozo, Thewo county, an old ritual practitioner recollected not only that *lu* and *nyen* were of the main focus of the ritualists but that even the oral performance of the ritual distinguished two main sounds through which the voicing of all the texts was done in the past. These two sounds were that of *lu* (*klu skad*) and *nyen* (*gnyan skad*). This information copes with the older textual sources mentioning *leu/legu* divinity to be *lu* spirit, then mentioning *lu* and *nyen* (together with *sadak* and *tö*) in their proximity, and eventually naming them explicitly as *leu* divinities.

However, an information connecting all this scattered and rather inconsistent information on *leu* divinities is that both *lu* and *nyen* are locally considered to be the divinities who bring children to people. Many people in the area are given names where *nyen* or *lu* figures for that reason. These are frequently: "Child of *Nyen*" (Gnyan phrug), "One Achieved by *Nyen*" (Gnyan grub), "One Protected by *Nyen*" (Gnyan skyab), "One Released by *Nyen*" (Gnyan thar), "Pleasure of *Nyen*" (Gnyan dga'), "Virtue of *Nyen*" (Gnyan dge), "*Nyen-Män*" (Gnyan sman), "One Reared by *Nyen*" (Gnyan 'tsho). Similar names include *lu*. In the event that there is a childless couple, it is customary to perform a ritual asking *nyen* or *lu* to secure the offspring (*gnyan la bu slong ba*).

Thus, these *leu* divinities are securing fertility of human communities and granting continuity of generations. Now, it could be better understood what the first extracts appearing in 12th–13th century works by Lungton Lhanyen and Azha Lodroe Gyaltsen speaking about rejection of the *leu* divinity could mean. *Leu* divinity is called *bcol ba'i le'u lha* in Tibetan there. But in the given context it is a divinity who "gave" life to the individual, who "deposited" (*bcol*) the foetus (*le'u*) in the womb. Thus, it could be read in the list of transgressions as "rejection of a divinity of the foetus who deposited it [in the womb]" (*bcol ba'i le'u lha log*).

Such conclusion connects the diverse information on *leu*. It seems that it was seen primarily as divinities (*le'u lha*) identified with *lu* and *nyen* spirits. The ritualists and the rituals connected with them were probably started to be designated by this term as well. The alternative version of *legu* remains unexplained. I am inclined to see Toni Huber's explanation as "nine divisions [ritual]" (*le'u dgu*) as an attempt to interpret it at certain time and place newly.

However, I am aware of the obvious cracks and flaws in the flow of the argument. Textual sources from between the 12th and 14th centuries were used for the above hypothesis, supplemented by anthropological data from the present day and references to the meaning of *leu* from texts dating back to the 20th century. The question is whether the association of *nyen* and *lu* spirits with bringing people to life can be extended to many centuries ago. The same question touches on the understanding of the term *le'u* as a foetus.

References

Chos kyi grags pa. 1995 [1957]. *Dge bshes chos kyi grags pas brtsams pa'i brda dag ming tshig gsal ba bzhugs so*. Beijing: Mi rigs dpe skrun khang.

Dba' bzhed bzhugs so. Lhasa: Bod ljongs bod yig dpe rnying dpe skrun khang, 2010.

Don dam smra ba'i seng ge. 1969. *A Fifteenth Century Tibetan Compendium of Knowledge: The Bzhad mdzod yid bzhin nor bu by Don-dam-smra-ba'i seńge*. Ed. Lokesh Chandra, New Delhi: Sharada Rani (Śata pitaka series 78).

Dpa' bo gtsug lag phreng ba. 2003. *Chos 'byung mkhas pa'i dga'ston*. 2 vols. Varanasi: Vajra Vidya Library.

Dpal ldan tshul khrims. 1988. *G.yung drung bon gyi bstan 'byung phyogs bsdus*. Lhasa: Bod ljongs mi dmangs dpe skrun khang.

Dri med 'od zer. 1999. *Stod skyang zhes su grags pa a skyid skyang tshang dgon bkra shis g.yung drung dar rgyas gling gi 'byung ba cung zad brjod pa shel dkar me long zhes bya ba bzhugs so*. In: *Mdzod dge'i dgon sde'i lo rgyus*. Mdzod dge rdzong: Srid gros mdzod dge rdzong u yon lhan khang rig gnas lo rgyus dpyad yig khang gis dpe bsgrigs byas.

Gling ge sar rgyal po'i sgrung gdug pa spun bdun. Lhasa: bod ljongs mi dmangs dpe skrun khang, 1993.

Stong 'khor Tshe ring thar and Ngag dbang rgya mtsho (eds.). 2016. *Gna' rabs bon gyi dpe dkon bris ma*, 10 vols. Xining: Mtsho sngon mi rigs dpe skrun khang.

Gnyan 'bum (*Rnam par dag pa'i 'bum bzhi las rin po che gnyan gyi 'bum bzhugs so*), in: Bon Kanjur (1999 edition), vol. 141, p.325.

'A zha Blo gros rgyal mtshan.*'Gro mgon 'A zha blo gros kyi mkhyen gsol zhes bya ba bzhugs pa dge'o*, available from: Zhang bod rig mdzod kun snang khyab pa website URL: http://xxb.qiongbuwang.com/index/category.html?tid=12843 [2019–08–20].

Gser khang bkra shis.1998. *Gso rig rgyud bzhi'i dka' 'grel*. Lhasa, bod ljongs mi dmangs dpe skrun khang.

Dpon gsas khyung rgod rtsal (revealer). *G.yag ru dgra chos kyi shog dril mde'u kha nyes byed dam nyams srog gshed*. New Collection of Bonpo Katen Texts, vol. 087–70.

G.yung drung bon gyi rgyud 'bum. In: *Sources for a History of Bon: A Collection of Rare Manuscripts from Bsam-gling Monastery in Dolpo* (Northwestern Tibet), nos. 1–46. Dolanji: Tibetan Bonpo Monastic Centre, 1972.

Pa sangs tshe ring (ed.). 2000. *Gzi brjid* (*Mdo dri med gzi brjid*), 12 vols. Lhasa: Bod ljongs bod yig dpe snying dpe skrun khang.

Huber, Toni. 2020. *Source of Life: Revitalization Rites and Bon Shamans in Bhutan and Eastern Himalaya*, 2 vols. Vienna: Austrian Academy of Sciences Press.

'Ju mi pham (Mi pham 'jam dbyangs rnam rgyal rgya mtsho). 2007. *Srid pa 'phrul gyi ju thig gi dpyad don snang gsal sgron me bzhugs*. Vol. 30. In *Gsung 'bum: Mi pham rgya mtsho*, 32 vols. Chengdu: Gangs can rigs gzhung dpe rnying myur skyobs lhan tshogs. BDRC: W2DB16631 (https://www.tbrc.org). For Derge print see BDRC: W23468–2019–3–81.

Karmay, S. G. (transl.). *The Treasury of Good Sayings: A Tibetan History of Bon*. London: Oxford University Press 1972.

Karmay, Samten G. 1998. "The Appearance of the Little Black-headed Man." In: Karmay, S. G. *The Arrow and the Spindle: Studies in History, Myths, Rituals and Beliefs in Tibet*. Kathmandu: Mandala Book Point: 245–281 (French version: *Journal Asiatique*, Tome CCLXXIV, 1–2, Paris 1986, 79–138).

Lung sgom 'khor lo rgyal po. 1972. *Lung ston lha gnyan gyi rnam thar*. In: Namdak, T. (ed.), *Sources for a History of Bon: A collection of rare manuscripts from Bsam-gling Monastery of Dolpo*. Fols. 276–286. Dolanji: Tibetan Bonpo Monastic Centre.

Martin, Dan.1997. *Tibetan Histories A Bibliography of Tibetan-language Historical Works*. London: Serindia Publications.

Mdo ka ba gling dgu, vol. ca. In: Bon Kangjur (1999 edition), vol. 50.

Mdo rnam 'brel bar ṭi ka, n.d., published by Venerable Lama Samtin Jansin Lama, Delhi: Berry Art Press, 123 ff.

Mdo rnam 'grel bar ṭi ka. Dolanji: Tibetan Bonpo Monastic Centre, 2012.

'Brug thar (ed.). 2011. *Mdo smad Mda' tshang yul gyi gna' dpe phyogs bsdus mthong ba don ldan*, 30 vols., Lanzhou: Gansu wen hua chu ban she.

Mimaki, K. 2000. "A preliminary comparison of Bonpo and Buddhist cosmology." In: Karmay, Samten G. and Yasuhiko Nagano (eds.), *New Horizons in Bon Studies*. Osaka: National Museum of Ethnology, 89–115.

Bon Kanjur (ed.). 1999. *mKha' klong rab 'byams bskang ba'i 'phyong bzhugs pa'i dbu phyogs lags+'o*. vol. 150, 19–73.

Ngag dbang bstan dar. 1971. *Rdo rje rnam par 'joms pa'i gzungs zhes bya ba'i 'grel pa legs bshad gang ga'i rgyun bzang zhes bya ba bzhugs so. Gsung 'bum*, vol. 1. New Delhi: Lama Guru Deva.

Ngag dbang rgya mtsho. 2005. *Mdo smad kan lho yul du bon bstan dar ba'i lo rgyus rags rim tsam brjod pa*. In: Ting 'dzin bkra shis (ed.), *Mdo smad zhib 'jug*, vol. 1, Beijing: Mi rigs dpe skrun khang, Kan su'u bod kyi shes rig zhib 'jug khang, 174–81.

Ngag dbang rgya mtsho. 2016. *Mdo smad lho rgyud du dar ba'i chab nag srid pa'i bon gyi cho ga spel mkhan lha bdag le'u la cung tsam dpyad pa*. *Bon sgo* 19: 22–35.

Ngawang Gyatso, Ngonzin. 2016. "The Lhadag leu (lha bdag le'u), ritual specialists of the black water Bon of the phenomenal world in Southern Amdo: a brief introduction (translated from Tibetan by Charles Ramble)." *Archiv Orientální* 84(3) (special issue Tibetan Margins): 561–75.

Norbu, Namkhai, 1995. *Drung, Deu and Bön: Narrations, Symbolic languages and the Bön tradition in ancient Tibet*. Dharamsala: Library of Tibetan Works and Archives.

Nye lam sde bzhi'i gnyan 'bum bzhugs pa'i dbus phyogs legs swo. In: *New Collection of Bonpo Katen Texts*, vol. 253, text no. 25, 603–635.

Rnam par bkod pa dam tshig gi mchong. In: *Bon Kanjur*, Vol. 101, 623–665.

Sørensen, Per K. 1994. *The Mirror Illuminating the Royal Genealogies: An Annotated Translation of the XIVth Century Tibetan Chronicle rGyal-rabs Gsal-Ba'i Me-long*. Wiesbaden: Otto Harrassowitz Verlag.

Spa bstan rgyal bzang po.1972. *Bstan byung dar rgyas gsal sgron*. In: *Sources for a History of Bon*. Dolanji: Tibetan Bonpo Monastic Centre, 498–769.

Stein, Rolf A.1959. *Recherchers sur l'épopée et le barde au Tibet*. Paris: Presses universitaires de France.

Tshe tan zhabs drung 'jigs med rig pa'i blo gros. 2013. *Dag yig thon mi'i dgongs rgyan*. Published by Kun dga' rgyal mtshan (place unspecified).

U rgyan gling pa (revealer). 1986. *Bka' thang sde lnga*. Beijing: Mi rigs dpe skrun khang.

文本翻译与跨文化传播

熟悉的经典，陌生的表述

——《金刚经》中的 *paścādbhaktapiṇḍapātapratikrāntaḥ*

萨尔吉
北京大学东方文学研究中心 / 西藏大学文学院

1. 前　　言

《金刚经》是般若经系统中非常流行的一部经典，在东亚佛教，尤其是汉传佛教史上影响巨大，持续至今，历史上对其的汉文注疏也层出不穷。但囿于相关梵文材料的数量，从多语种层面对《金刚经》的研究并不多见。本文主要借助梵文本，辅之以藏汉文材料，从文本比较的角度探讨《金刚经》序分中关于佛陀乞食场景的表述，进而讨论对其中一段表述的不同理解在各文本中的表现，以此说明古代译师在翻译策略方面的考虑，以及《金刚经》在文本流通过程中的嬗变。

2. 程式化的表达还是增广性的表达?

关于《金刚经》梵文本的研究，学者们已经作出了许多重要贡献，早期有缪勒（Friedrich Max Müller）首开其功，[①] 近来有何离巽（Paul Harrison）集其大成。[②] 从写本的来源地而言，

---

① F. Max Müller ed., "Vagra*kkhe*dikâ [= Vajracchedikå]," in *Buddhist Texts From Japan,* Anecdota Oxoniensia, Aryan Series Vol.1, Part 1, Oxford, 1881, pp.15–46.

② Paul Harrison and Shōgo Watanabe, "Vajracchedikā Prajñāpāramitā," in Jens Braarvig, Paul Harrison, Jens-Uwe Hartmann, Kazunobu Matsuda and Lore Sander eds., *Buddhist Manuscripts in the Schøyen Collection*, Oslo: Hermes, 2006, pp.89–132.

《金刚经》梵文本可以大致分为流通本、中亚本、吉尔吉特本、尼泊尔本，以及近年公布的巴米扬本。缪勒的校勘本主要依据的就是流通本，他利用了日本所藏的两部抄自同一写本的抄本，以及两部从中国北京寻获的梵藏对照刻本，它们的年代相对偏晚，大约在 18 世纪。中亚本包括斯坦因在中国新疆丹丹乌里克遗址发现的 14 叶残叶（完整的应为 19 叶），年代大约在公元 5 世纪末至 6 世纪初，以及近年陆续比定的《金刚经》的一些残叶。1931 年吉尔吉特发现的梵文写本中有 7 叶《金刚经》写本，年代大约是公元 6 至 7 世纪。据载尼泊尔保存有数部《金刚经》写本，目前只发现了一部纸本的《金刚经》抄本，抄写年代是 1701 年。近年在斯奎因写本中发现的《金刚经》写本有 21 叶，据信来自阿富汗巴米扬地区，年代大约在公元 6 至 7 世纪。[①]

就我们讨论的问题而言，相关段落出自《金刚经》最开始的序分，我们先来看序分中涉及释迦牟尼外出乞食的段落，该段在缪勒校勘本中的行文为：

> atha khalu bhagavān śrāvastīṃ mahānagarīṃ piṇḍāya caritvā **kṛtabhaktakṛtya** paścādbhaktapiṇḍapātapratikrāntaḥ **pātracīvaraṃ pratiśamaya** pādau prakṣālya nyaṣīdad bhagavān | prajñapta evāsane paryaṃkam ābhujya ṛjuṃ kāyaṃ praṇidhāya pratimukhaṃ smṛtim upasthāpya |

何离巽根据斯奎因写本，将其校勘为：

> atha khalu bhagavān śrāvastīṃ mahānagarīṃ piṇḍāya caritvā paścādbhaktapiṇḍapātapratikrāntaḥ pādau prakṣālya nyaṣīdad bhagavān | prajñapta evāsane paryaṃkam ābhujya ṛjuṃ kāyaṃ praṇidhāya pratimukhaṃ smṛtim upasthāpya

两相比较，我们可以看到，二者最大的差异是缪勒校勘本在“paścādbhaktapiṇḍapātaprati krāntaḥ”前后各加了短语“kṛtabhaktakṛtya”和“pātracīvaraṃ pratiśamaya”（文中黑体部分），而这两处行文在何离巽的校勘本中则付诸阙如。何离巽这样的抉择自有其理由，一是斯奎因写本的年代比缪勒校勘本所用的写本要早得多，二是佛经一般有行文逐渐增广的趋势，三是如此连用的例子不见于巴利语文献，且巴利语文献中最常见的用例与斯奎因写本更为对应。虽然如此，但是我们需要注意，就《金刚经》写本本身而言，上述数种《金刚经》梵文本中涉及当下我们研究的序分的，我们只有缪勒的校勘本和斯奎因写本。其他写本在此处均有残缺，无法利用。换句话说，何离巽的校勘本所依据的只是一个写本，我们无法判断此处是否

---

① 关于这些写本的整理校勘情况，参见 Paul Harrison and Shōgo Watanabe, “Vajracchedikā Prajñāpāramitā” 中的文献综述部分。

有抄手遗漏脱落的现象，还是原来的行文就是如此。

那么缪勒校勘本所加的短语是否是衍文呢？比较《金刚经》的各种译本，我们有理由相信，缪勒校勘本的读法更为流行。理由如下：

1. 西藏藏有《金刚经》梵文写本一部（目前还未公布），从字体判断，大约是 11 世纪以后的写本，其中的读法与缪勒校勘本一致；①

2. 藏语译本同样说明，当时翻译所用底本有这两处短语；

3. 几乎所有的汉译本都有“饭食讫，收衣钵”的说法，应该对应的就是上述两处短语。尤其值得重视的是达摩笈多的译本，其中“作已食作已……器上给衣收摄”的说法与缪勒校勘本严格对应；

4. 于阗语译本亦可证实上述两处短语的存在；②

5. 上述表述似乎是外出乞食的标准流程，在现存的许多梵文本中均有表现，尤其是在说一切有部的文本中（下详）。

除了上述理由外，我们还应注意到斯奎因写本的年代与上述译本译出的时代相差不远，甚至比一些汉译本还要晚一些。因此，考虑到上述文本几乎处于同一个时间段，我们认为缪勒校勘本反映了更通行的读法，上述文句应该是程式化的表达，而非衍文。

3. 如何理解 kṛtabhaktakṛtya paścādbhaktapiṇḍapātapratikrāntaḥ pātracīvaraṃ pratiśamaya

如果我们认可缪勒校勘本的读法，第二个问题就是如何理解这一表述？我们先来看何离巽对这段文句的英译。何离巽虽然在斯奎因写本的校勘本中沿用了写本本身的读法，但是他的英译则反映了通行的读法：

---

① 据《罗炤目录》（未公布），《金刚经》为多种显密经典合为一函的第一部写本，写本原藏夏鲁寺，现藏布达拉宫，写本一共有 14 叶。感谢西藏社科院的欧珠次仁提供了对应部分的照片，使我有机会核对。笔者发现经文始于 2 行，第 1 行写有一首偈颂，初步转写如下：yad asulabham anantakalpakoṭi | pramaramatair api hetuvarjjitānāṃ | bhavantu hi na jinārccarasmibhutaṃ | tad idam ahaṃ pravivakṣur agrayānaṃ。偈颂的大致意思是《金刚经》无量劫中非常难得，但是对抛弃因乘者而言，很难获得，因为其不会成为胜者的光辉，我希望是这最上乘的宣说者。这很可能是抄写者对抄写《金刚经》的说明。写本没有尾跋，因此无从得知抄写者或抄写的年代。

② 科诺对于阗语文本进行了梵语构拟。参见 Sten Konow, “The Vajracchedika: in the Old Khotanese Version of Eastern Turkestan,” in A. F. Rudolf Hoernle, *Manuscript Remains of Buddhist Literature Found in Eastern Turkestan*, Oxford, 1916, Part II, “Khotanese Texts,” p.241。于阗语文本是：“kū khāysna-kīrä yudä yuḍe hvaḍä khāysä kū sce-tä paryeta hamye pāttara cīvarä pajsīryi”，科诺构拟的梵文为：“yadā **bhakta-kāryaṃ kṛtaṃ** eakāra bhukte bhakte yadā kāle pratikrāntaḥ sametaḥ **pātram cīvaram pratyaśāmayat**”（黑体为笔者所加）。

when he had finished the food business, and when he had returned, after eating his food, he put away his bowl and cloak ... ①

“kṛta-bhakta-kṛtya”是一个复合词，字面意思不难理解，应该就是“食事已办”之意②，对应上述英译的“finished the food business”，但单纯从这个复合词看不出来指的是完成了乞食，还是吃完了乞讨而来的食物③。“pātracīvaraṃ pratiśamaya”比较容易理解，“pratiśamaya”有“放好、处理好”的意思，④连起来就是“放好钵具和衣服”，汉译往往翻译为“收衣钵”。

难解的是复合词“paścād-bhakta-piṇḍapāta-pratikrāntaḥ”，该词由四个词组成，单个词的词义也相对比较清楚，即“paścād”有“后来，随后”之意；“bhakta”是动词“√ bhaj”的过去分词，有“食物”之意；“piṇḍapāta”稍微复杂一些，但基本的词义是“乞食”⑤；“pratikrānta”是动词“prati- √ kram”的过去分词，字面含义是“返回”，还有一个意思则是“弃绝”，吐蕃时期编撰的梵藏辞书《翻译名义大集》(*Mahāvyutpatti*)给出了这两个义项。⑥

根据上面何离巽的英译“when he had returned, after eating his food”，他对此复合词的理解是“吃完饭后返回”，这似乎是对这些词汇基本词义的解释，只是将“bhakta”诠解为了“吃”(eating)，但这样的翻译无法看出该复合词的构成。

如果按照《佛教混合梵语词典》的解释，该复合词指的是“下午乞食回来后”⑦，这说明艾哲顿将“paścād-bhakta”理解为了副词，“食后”即下午⑧，“piṇḍapāta-pratikrāntaḥ”构成依主释复合词，前半部分拆解开是从格，即“从乞食返回”，但这样一来，就和前面的“食事

---

① Paul Harrison, “Vajracchedikā Prajñāpāramitā: A New English Translation of the Sanskrit Text Based on Two Manuscripts from Greater Gandhāra,” in Jens Braarvig, Paul Harrison, Jens-Uwe Hartmann, Kazunobu Matsuda & Lore Sander eds., *Buddhist Manuscripts in the Schøyen Collection*, Oslo: Hermes, 2006, p.142.

② Franklin Edgerton, “kṛtya,” *Buddhist Hybrid Sanskrit Dictionary,* New Haven: Yale University Press, 1953, p.190.

③ 汉译一般将“kṛta-kṛtya”译为“所做已办”，参考此种译法，“食事已办”或许对应的是“kṛta-bhakta-kṛtya”。但是“食事已办”的说法仅见于汉译《中阿含经》第88经《求法经》，而且彼处在“食事已办”之前明确写有“食讫”，即“食讫，食事已办”，说明是吃完了乞讨而来的食物。参见《中阿含经》，《大正藏》第1册，经号：第26号，第570页上栏第6行。

④ Franklin Edgerton, “pratiśāmayati,” *Buddhist Hybrid Sanskrit Dictionary,* p.369.

⑤ 该词一般被拆解成“piṇḍa”和“pāta”两部分解释，“pāta”往往和“pātra”混用，有不同的词源学解释，汉译有时也译作“分卫”。

⑥《翻译名义大集》在关于“舍弃”(spangs pa dang ’dor ba la sogs pa’i ming)的词汇条目下给出了这两个义项，参见榊亮三郎：phyir log pa ’am spangs pa,『翻訳名義大集：梵蔵漢和四訳対校』，鈴木学術財団，1962年，第2563条。《翻译名义大集》也收录了该词动词的形式“pratikramati”(第5097条)，彼处给出的义项只有“回还”(phyir ldog pa)，从前后的词语看，这里取的是其基本含义。“pratikramati”在《佛教混合梵语词典》中给出的释义是“弃绝(罪恶)”(abstains [from sin, abl.])，参见Franklin Edgerton, “pratikramati,” *Buddhist Hybrid Sanskrit Dictionary,* p.361。

⑦ Franklin Edgerton, “paścādbhakta,” *Buddhist Hybrid Sanskrit Dictionary,* p.338. 词条中对该复合词的解释是having returned from (collecting) alms-food in the afternoon。

⑧ 需要注意的是，同书“bhakta”词条中只给出了其有“食物”的含义，并未给出其有“吃”(eating)的含义（第404—405页）。

已办”构成冲突，用在这里显得很突兀。看来，我们有必要回到《金刚经》文本的上下文，并且参考相关译本来确定其含义。

我们先来看汉译。在《金刚经》的六个汉译本中，四个译本都有“饭食讫”的说法，很可能对应的就是“kṛta-bhakta-kṛtya”，真谛译本为“饭食事讫”，应该是把该复合词的“kṛtya”（事）翻译了出来，而达摩笈多的译本更能佐证其对应的复合词是“kṛta-bhakta-kṛtya”，即“作已（kṛta）食（bhakta）作已（kṛtya）”。如果我们遵循汉译本对该词的理解，那么显然该复合词应该被解释为吃完了乞讨而来的食物，这样的话，如果再考虑后一个复合词“paścādbhaktapiṇḍapātapratikrāntaḥ”，就和上述《佛教混合梵语词典》的解释构成了冲突。

我们还需注意到，多数汉译本在“饭食讫”之前都有“次第乞已，还至本处”的说法，但是这种表述无论在语序上，还是在行文上都与现存的梵文本有很大的差异，使得我们很难确定其对应的梵语。“次第乞已”中的“次第”或许对应的梵文是“sāvadāna”[①]，但现存《金刚经》写本并未体现如此的读法。如果我们相信这样的翻译与“paścādbhaktapiṇḍapāta-pratikrāntaḥ”相关，一个比较弱的可能性就是该复合词被读成了三组词，即“paścādbhaktaṃ”“piṇḍapātaṃ”“pratikrāntaḥ”，其中“piṇḍapātaṃ”或许被理解为了“*(sāvadāna)-piṇḍapātaṃ”，即“次第乞”的含义。[②]“还至本处”可能对应的是“pratikrāntaḥ”，如前所述，该词本身就有“返回”之意。就“paścādbhaktaṃ”而言，部分汉译并未表现出对该词的翻译，但真谛、玄奘的译本反映出他们将其理解为时间状语，即“下午”（于中后时）或“吃过饭以后”（于食后时）。因此，如果按照汉译的理解，这个流程大致是：晨朝乞食—返回—吃饭—下

---

① 这方面的一个典型例子是《未曾有法门经》（*Adbhutadharmaparyāya*），该经有吉尔吉特梵文本存世，经文中出现了“sāvadānaṃ piṇḍāya caramāṇo”（2 次）和“sāvadānaṃ piṇḍāya caritvā”（1 次）的表述，参见 Yael Bentor, “The Redactions of the *Adbhutadharmaparyāya* from Gilgit,” *Journal of the International Association of Buddhist Studies* 11.2, 1988, pp.21–52。对应的汉译玄奘的译本《甚希有经》翻译为“次第行乞”和“次第乞已”，参见《大正藏》第 16 册，经号：第 689 号。需要注意的是，玄奘《金刚经》译本并没有出现“次第”一词，说明玄奘所依据的梵本中没有“sāvadāna”。

② 玄奘在《瑜伽师地论》关于头陀功德段落的翻译中出现了“次第乞食”的说法（参见《大正藏》第 30 册，经号：第 1759 号，第 442 页上栏第 10 行），对应的梵文是“sāvadāna-piṇḍapātikaḥ”（参见大正大学総合佛教研究所声聞地研究会・密教聖典研究会：『瑜伽論声聞地：サンスクリット語テキストと和訳』，山喜林房佛書林，1998 年，第 274 页，第 5—6 行）。藏译为“mthar gyis slong ba'i bsod snyoms pa”（《甘珠尔》德格版 4036, 63b4。为简便，将《甘珠尔》德格版简称为“D”，下同，各版本对应的缩略语详见文末附录“《甘珠尔》各版本缩略语”）。根据《瑜伽师地论》的说法，头陀行有十二或十三种，其间的差异在于是否将乞食分为两种，一种是“prāpta-piṇḍapātika”，玄奘译为常期乞食或随得乞食，藏译为“rnyed pas chog pa'i bsod snyoms pa”或“rnyed pas chog shes pa'i bsod snyoms pa”，大意是获取食物知道适可而止；一种是“sāvadāna-piṇḍapātika”。参照《翻译名义大集》所列举的十二头陀行，与《瑜伽师地论》的差异在于彼处应该是将上述两个分类合为了一个，即“paiṇḍapātika”（第 1131 条）。这说明“piṇḍapātika”或“paiṇḍapātika”本身就有两种解释维度，以鸠摩罗什为代表的汉译本是否反映了译者对“piṇḍapāta”在头陀行语境下深层含义的思考？这个问题牵涉到早期僧团的饮食问题，非常复杂，此不赘述。

午收拾衣钵。“paścādbhaktaṃ”在此没有特别的含义，而且理解为下午，与早晨出门乞食也很对应。

因此，在理解“paścādbhaktapiṇḍapātapratikrāntaḥ”一词上面，《金刚经》的汉译并不能给我们提供实质性的帮助，如果我们把目光转向藏译，情况就显得更为复杂。就我所知，藏译对“kṛtabhaktakṛtya paścādbhaktapiṇḍapātapratikrāntaḥ”的表述至少有六种不同的翻译，抛开其中细小的差异不论，这六种翻译可以分为四组：

1. A 组：德格版[①]、北京版[②]、朵宫版（Stog Palace）[③]、协噶版（shel dkar）的一种译本[④]，以及英藏敦煌藏文写本（S.t 170）[⑤]。

   bsod snyoms kyi zhal zas mjug tu gsol te | zhal zas kyi bya ba mdzad
2. B 组：普扎版（phug brag）[⑥]、故宫藏康熙元年（1662 年）《金刚经》写本[⑦]。

   zas kyi bya ba mdzad nas | zas phyi ma'i bsod snyoms spangs nas
3. C1 组：拉萨版。[⑧]

   bsod snyoms kyi zhal zas mjug tu gsol te zas kyi bya ba mdzad nas zas phyi ma'i bsod snyoms spangs pas
4. C2 组：乾隆年间北京刊刻的三文对照《金刚经》[⑨]，以及来自库努补（khu nu spu）地区的一部写本。[⑩]

   zhal zas 'jug tu gsol to | zas kyi bya ba mdzad de | zas phyi ma'i bsod snyoms spangs nas

---

① D 16, 121a3-4.

② P 739, 161b6-7.

③ S 20, 232a5-6.

④ L 653, 206a2. 除了这里提到的《金刚经》，协噶写本在收录有《金刚经》的般若部的最后一函的末尾还收录了五部《金刚经》（L 667-671），每部均独立编写页码。具体到我们讨论的问题，五部中有两部相关之处缺失（L 668; 671），其余三部给出了这组词汇的另一种翻译。

⑤ Louis de La Vallée Poussin, *Catalogue of the Tibetan Manuscripts from Tun-huang in the India Office Library, with an Appendix on the Chinese Manuscripts by Kazuo Enoki*, London: Oxford University Press, 1962.

⑥ F 14, 37b6.

⑦ 据故宫博物院马晟楠告知，这套《金刚经》抄本为藏文、蒙古文各 54 函，共计 108 函，抄经的发起者是顺治皇帝，始于顺治十七年（1660 年），后由孝庄皇太后主持完成。

⑧ H 18, 215b1-2.

⑨ 哈佛大学图书馆藏有《御制重译金刚经》，乾隆皇帝在序中说他重译的依据是从西藏得到了《金刚经》的一本旧本 (dbus gtsang nas byung ba'i dpe rnying)，与汉译本各有同异，所以进行重译。如果结合前述康熙元年的抄本，这里的“旧本”的其中一个差异或许指的就是对这句话的不同翻译。

⑩ 参见网站藏传佛教资源中心（TBRC），现更名为“佛教数字资源中心”（BDRC），写本编号为 W3JT13747，网址为 https://www.bdrc.io/。

5. C3 组：协噶版的另一种译本[①]、《经集》(mdo mang)[②]、《陀罗尼集》(gzungs ’dus)[③]，以及一些独立流通的《金刚经》文本。[④]

zhal zas gsol te | zas kyi bya ba mdzad de | zas phyi ma’i bsod snyoms spangs na

6. D 组：1760 年北京刊刻的梵藏对照《金刚经》。[⑤]

zas kyi bya ba mdzad de | zas phyi ma’i bsod snyoms las tshur spyon zhing

从上文来看，藏译对“paścādbhaktapiṇḍapātapratikrāntaḥ”有数种不同的理解，其中 A、B 组代表了《甘珠尔》系统对该复合词的理解，D 组是晚期的基于梵文本的重译，C 组则代表了对《甘珠尔》系统中两种翻译的杂糅的努力。

从 A 组的译文来看，首先是语序与现存梵文不尽一致，藏译将“paścādbhaktapiṇḍapātapratikrāntaḥ”翻译在前，“kṛtabhaktakṛtya”翻译在后[⑥]，整句话的意思是：最终享用(mjug tu gsol ？) 了乞讨的食物，食事已办。虽然“bsod snyoms kyi zhal zas mjug tu gsol”看起来是对“paścādbhaktapiṇḍapātapratikrāntaḥ”的翻译，但是就翻译策略而言，这种处理不仅打乱了该复合词的词序，而且传达的确切含义并不清楚。“bsod snyoms”(乞食) 一般对应梵语“piṇḍapāta”[⑦]，“zhal zas”这里对应的梵语是“bhakta”，“mjug tu”这里应该对应的是“paścād”，这样一来，“gsol”只能对应“pratikrānta”，但“pratikrānta”并没有“享用”的含义。在这样的对照下，我们不仅看不出藏译对这个复合词拆解的逻辑，更关键的是我们不知道“mjug tu gsol”的具体所指。[⑧]

由上可知，德格版的读法并非孤例，其不仅有《甘珠尔》其他版本，还有敦煌藏文文献的支持，另外，这一短语也出现在《神通游戏经》(*Lalitavistara*) 中，彼处藏文翻译与德格

---

① L 667, 2a2; L 669, 2a3; L 670, 1b6–7.

② 笔者利用的是 1971 年印度瓦腊纳西出版的木刻本的复刻本，参见佛教数字资源中心 (BDRC) 网站，编号 W1KG12536，dza 册，第 2 叶正面第 1—2 行。

③ 笔者利用的是 1994 年德里出版的木刻本，参见佛教数字资源中心 (BDRC) 的网站，编号 W1KG5988，je 册，第 2 叶正面第 2—3 行。

④ 比如印度钱德拉搜集品 (Lokesh Chandra’s collection) 中的《金刚经》。参见佛教数字资源中心 (BDRC) 网站，编号 W1KG12670。

⑤ 参见佛教数字资源中心 (BDRC) 的网站，编号 W1GS54752。这应该就是缪勒校勘时利用的刻本之一。

⑥ 这似乎反映了部分汉译的语序，即“还至本处。饭食讫，收衣钵”对应于“pratikrāntaḥ kṛtabhaktakṛtya pātracīvaraṃ pratiśamaya”。如果这样的理解正确，那么《金刚经》汉译本中的“饭食讫”可能对应的就是“kṛtabhaktakṛtya”。但无法解释的是真谛译本的“还至本处，饭食事讫，于中后时”，以及玄奘译本的“出还本处，饭食讫，收衣钵，洗足已，于食后时”。

⑦ 参见榊亮三郎：『翻訳名義大集：梵蔵漢和四訳対校』，第 8671 条。

⑧ 还有一种可能是将“mjug tu gsol”理解为是对“paścādbhakta”的翻译，即藏译的“gsol”对应“bhakta”，但这样一来，我们需要承认藏译不仅没有翻译“pratikrānta”，而且对“bhakta”进行了双重翻译，一次译为“zhal zas”，一次译为“gsol”，这种可能性非常小。

版一致。[①]

我们再来看B组的译文，其大致可以翻译为：食事已办，弃除了后食（zas phyi ma = paścādbhakta？）的乞食。可以看出，普扎写本与上述版本的差异第一是语序，普扎写本的语序与梵文本对应更工整；第二点，也是最重要的一点，就是普扎写本对“paścādbhakta-piṇḍapātapratikrāntaḥ”的翻译与上述版本完全不一样。从翻译策略而言，普扎写本不仅遵循了该复合词的词序，而且采取了直译的方式，但是于我们而言，“zas phyi ma”的具体含义仍然不清楚。[②]

普扎写本的翻译在《甘珠尔》的其他译本中也能发现，例如根本说一切有部的律藏文献《药事》(*Bhaiṣajyavastu*)[③]，以及《破僧事》（*Saṃghabhedavastu*）[④]等，而且既然清代的《金刚经》抄经选取了此种读法，说明这种读法当时应该很流行。[⑤]

上述D组的翻译反映的是清代藏族人士对“paścādbhaktapiṇḍapātapratikrāntaḥ”的理解，与B组的差异在于对“pratikrānta”的理解不一样，清代文本采用了最常见的含义，即“回返”（tshur spyon）。虽然《翻译名义大集》就有此义项，但是我们不清楚此处的翻译是基于译者自身对梵语的理解，还是有别的参考。[⑥]

至此，抛开晚近的D组的翻译不谈，我们可以看出，就“paścādbhaktapiṇḍapāta-pratikrāntaḥ”而言，藏译传统中至少有两种理解和翻译，单纯从藏文看，要准确理解两种译文的所指都有一定的困难。藏族人应该已经注意到了《金刚经》此处翻译的差异，但是无法

---

① D 95, 195b1, “bsod snyoms kyi zhal zas ’jug tu gsol te | zas kyi bya ba byas nas”。两相比较，二者唯一的不同仅在于德格版对“kṛtabhaktakṛtya”采用了敬语，而《神通游戏经》的藏译对此复合词没有采用敬语。今德格版《金刚经》缺载译者，但司徒·曲吉穷乃的目录中则说是由戒自在菩提（Śīlendrabodhi）和意希德（ye shes sde）所译，并经过了厘定（参见司徒·曲吉穷乃：《甘珠尔编纂史·显密文库》（藏文），四川民族出版社2013年版，第4卷，第431页，第2—3行）。《神通游戏经》的翻译团队为胜友（Jinamitra）、施戒（Dānaśīla）、牟尼铠（Munivarman）和意希德。但我们需要注意的是，胜友和意希德也参与了《未曾有法门经》的翻译，彼处对该短语的翻译是“zas kyi bya ba byas nas bsod snyoms kyi zas phyi ma spangs”（D 319, 194a7）。胜友（Jinamitra）和天月（Devacandra）共同翻译了《撰集百缘经》（*Avadānaśataka*），彼处对该短语的翻译是“zan zos nas zas phyis len pa spangs te”（D 343, 122a6, 128a7, 131b7）。这说明不同的译经团体对同一短语有不同的理解，但很难想象同一位译经者对同一短语有不同的理解，因此，要么是这些译经团队的记载有误，要么我们需要重新审视这些经典翻译的流程，考查其中每一位译经者起到的作用，以及不同经典翻译的时间和后世改动的可能性。

② “zas phyi ma”应该对应汉译达摩笈多译本的“后食”，以及玄奘的“食后”，从真谛“于中后时”的翻译看，该词应有时间的含义。

③ D 1, ka, 306b7: “zas kyi bya ba byas nas zas phyi ma’i bsod snyoms las slar log ste”，注意这里“slar log”（pratikrānta）的翻译。

④ D 1, nga, 81b1–2; 160b3.

⑤《未曾有法门经》的藏译将“paścādbhaktapiṇḍapātapratikrāntaḥ”译作“bsod snyoms kyi zas phyi ma spangs”（D 319, 194a7），虽然用词与普扎写本一致，但语序有调整。

⑥ 比如是否受到了汉译“还至本处”的译文的影响。如前所述，何离巽的英译以及《佛教混合梵语词典》都将该词理解为“返回”。

确定孰对孰错，于是有的校勘者采取了一个折中的处理方案，即把两种翻译都列上，把重复部分合在一处，这样的处理方式可见上列的 C 组。C 组细分又有三种情况，一是将 A 组和 B 组简单叠加，这样的处理可见拉萨版（C1 组）。即使抛开背后的梵文不谈，这样简单叠加的翻译不仅无助于解决问题，反而大大增加了理解的困难，因此有的校勘者努力尝试理顺文句，这反映在上述 C2 和 C3 组中。C2 组将 A 组的“bsod snyoms kyi zhal zas mjug tu gsol te”改为“zhal zas mjug tu gsol to”，可能是意识到“bsod snyoms”一词在“zas phyi ma'i bsod snyoms spangs nas”再度出现，显得有一些冗余。C3 组则更进一步，将“zhal zas mjug tu gsol”缩减为“zhal zas gsol”。由此可见，C2 和 C3 组处理的思路与拉萨版一致，不同之处在于校勘者似乎对“bsod snyoms kyi zhal zas mjug tu gsol te”抱有疑问，因此将其缩减，改成了易懂的“进食”（zhal zas gsol te）①。从现有的《金刚经》文本看，似乎 C3 组的读法更为流行。

“paścādbhaktapiṇḍapātapratikrāntaḥ”在《金刚经》以及其他一些梵语佛教文献中虽然是以复合词的形式出现，但是梵语文献中也有将此复合词拆解的用例，比如《大事》(*Mahāvastu*) 中有“paścādbhaktaṃ piṇḍapātapratikrānto”②的读法，《根本说一切有部药事》中有“paścādbhaktapiṇḍapātaṃ pratikrāntaḥ”③的读法。

巴利语文献中只记录了“pacchābhattaṃ piṇḍapātapaṭikkanta”的形式，根据《佛教混合梵语词典》的解释，这是将“paścādbhaktaṃ”理解为副词，即“下午”，整个词的含义是“下午乞食返回”④。如果将“paścādbhakta”理解为“下午”，与之相对的则是上午（pūrvabhakta），这在梵文律藏文献中也能得到证实。比如，在根本说一切有部《别解脱戒经》（*Prātimokṣasūtra*）的一段文句中，同时出现了“pūrvabhaktaṃ”和“paścādbhaktaṃ”，藏文直接将其译作“上午”和“下午”（snga dro dang phyi dro）⑤。

---

① 我们不知道这样的改动依据何在，但确实有矫枉过正之嫌。

② Émil Senart, *Le Mahāvastu*, Sacred Books of the Buddhists series nos. 16–18, Paris: Imprimerie Nationale, 1882–1897, Vol. I, p.329.16.

③ N. Dutt ed., *Gilgit Manuscript*, Calcutta: Srinagar, 1947, vol. III.1, p.256.

④ 参见 Franklin Edgerton, “paścādbhakta,” *Buddhist Hybrid Sanskrit Dictionary,* p.338。彼处给出了三种释义，一是形容词：食后（after eating [the midday meal]）；二是副词：下午（the afternoon, period after eating）；三是我们这里讨论的复合词，指下午乞食返回（having returned from [collecting] alms-food in the afternoon）。

⑤ Anukul Chandra Banerjee ed., *Prātimokṣa-sūtra (Mūlasarvāstivāda)*, Calcutta: 1954, p.28, no. 81: yaḥ punar bhikṣuḥ sabhaktaḥ kule nimantritaḥ pūrvabhaktaṃ paścādbhaktaṃ kuleṣu cāritram āpadyeta santaṃ kulaṃ apratisaṃvedito 'nyatra tadrūpāt pratyayāt pāyantikā. 藏译参见 D 3, 16a7: yang dge slong gang zas dang bcas pa'i khyim du mgron du bos nas snga dro dang phyi dro khyim dag tu rgyu zhing khyim pa 'dug pa la mi bsgo na || de 'dra ba'i rkyen ma gtogs te ltung byed do。

4. 莲花戒《金刚经广注》对“paścādbhaktapiṇḍapātapratikrāntaḥ”的解释

如上所见，藏译本《金刚经》对该复合词有不同的翻译，追本溯源，这样的翻译或许与印度人对此复合词的不同理解有关，而且我们确实找到了相关证据。

印度僧人莲花戒曾经对《金刚经》有过诠释，藏译保存在《丹珠尔》中，其中对上述文句提出了数种解释路径，兹翻译如下：

> “食事已办”（kṛtabhaktakṛtyaḥ）指的是凡是完成饮食等事宜者，就如此称呼。……
>
> 是以何种形相做到食事已办的呢？所以说了“最后”（paścād）等等。得到一切后，最后进食，即“最终享用了乞讨的食物”（paścād-bhakta-piṇḍapāta-pratikrāntaḥ），这是为了使诸声闻进入头陀功德（dhūtaguṇa）而先进行好好地接受（食物）。“享用”（gsol）的词义是“业已享用完毕”（gsol zin）[①]。
>
> 或者，“最后”指的是凡是第二次的获取，就称之为“后食”（zas phyi ma = paścād-bhakta），后食既是“最后食”（zas mjug），也是“乞食”（piṇḍapāta），词汇是（如此）搭配的[②]。
>
> 或者，〔这是对〕凡是所乞讨得来的（piṇḍapāta）、下午所食的食物（phyi dro'i zas）的称谓。
>
> 因此，为了弃除（spangs）具有头陀功德的，以及非时的饮食而说的“享用”的词义是“没有这二者”。

这段话虽然有一些难解之处，但基本脉络清楚。莲花戒认为“食事已办”的字面含义就是进食完毕[③]，“食事已办”的具体表现用“paścādbhaktapiṇḍapātapratikrāntaḥ”来表达，引申的话有先乞后食[④]、不二次食、过午不食等意思。

莲花戒没有专门讨论“pratikrānta”一词，但是他列出了传统上对“paścād-bhakta”的理解，根据他的说法，“paścād-bhakta”至少有三层意思，一是“最后食”，二是“二次食”，三

---

① 从上下文看，“享用”应该对应的是“pratikrāntaḥ”，但显然解释不通。

② tshig rnam par sbyar=vigraha，参见榊亮三郎：『翻訳名義大集：梵蔵漢和四訳対校』，第 4725 条。这里指的是对复合词“paścād-bhakta-piṇḍapāta”的拆解，要将其理解成持业释，即“后食即乞食”。

③ 这与《金刚经》汉译本的“饭食讫”是一个意思。

④ 这可能与《金刚经》汉译本的“次第乞已”有相关性。

是“下午食”。这三层意思或多或少都与头陀功德相关（下详）。从莲花戒的叙述来看，似乎他反对将该复合词从部派佛教的立场出发进行诠释，而是赋予其大乘佛教的内涵，所以最后他说为了弃除具有头陀功德的饮食以及非时的饮食，该复合词要诠解为“最终享用了乞讨的食物”（bsod snyoms kyi zhal zas mjug tu gsol ba ste）[①]。

虽然莲花戒反对从头陀功德的角度理解该复合词，但这也从另一个方面说明该复合词的三层意思确实与头陀功德相关，如果我们循着这一思路前进，就会发现一些很有意思的地方。

《翻译名义大集》收录了十二头陀行，与饮食相关的有：常行乞食（paiṇḍapātika, bsod snyoms pa）、一坐食（aikāsanika, stan gcig pa）、不取后食（khalu paścād-bhaktika, zas phyis mi len pa）[②]。其中“khalu paścād-bhaktika”[③]的构词与我们这里讨论的“paścād-bhakta”非常接近。[④]《瑜伽师地论·声闻地》对该词有一段解释：

什么是不取后食？为（进）食而安坐，知道获取自己维生的所有食物后再进食，并且在这之后知道自己将不再获取超出此（量）的食物，（这样）考虑后，然后开始取食，

① 我们不清楚莲花戒的这种阐释是否有更早的来源，但是可能在当时有一些人接受了他的诠释，有一些则不然，这也就反映在了藏译对该复合词的不同翻译中。

②《翻译名义大集》第1131至1133条。各经论中对头陀行的数量有不同说法，一般为十二种，也有十三种等其他的说法。其中关乎饮食的名目也不尽一致。例如，《二万五千颂般若经》讲到了头陀行，根据鸠摩罗什的译本《摩诃般若波罗蜜经》，有五个条目与饮食相关，除了我们这里讨论的三种，他还加了节量食和次第乞食两种。节量食对应梵文“prasthapiṇḍika”，从玄奘《大般若波罗蜜多经》随得食的翻译看，应该等同于《瑜伽师地论》中的“prāptapiṇḍapātika”，属于乞食的一种。鸠摩罗什的次第乞食在玄奘译本中是随得敷具，从梵文上下文看，应该对应的是“yāthāsaṃstarika”，藏译为“gzhi ji bzhin pa”，该词在《翻译名义大集》属于十二头陀行的最后一个，从顺序上看，应该与行为举止相关，汉译有时候译作“处座如常”，玄奘《瑜伽师地论》译本译作“处如常坐”，说明该词与饮食无关。玄奘《大般若波罗蜜多经》译本中四个条目与饮食相关。玄奘译本《瑜伽师地论》确实出现了“次第乞食”，但对应的梵文是“sāvadāna-piṇḍapātika”，而且文中说这只是对乞食的两种分类中的一种，如果将乞食分为两种，则头陀行有十三种。需要注意的是继鸠摩罗什后来华的求那跋陀罗曾译出《佛说十二头陀经》，其中十二头陀行的顺序虽然与上述鸠摩罗什《摩诃般若波罗蜜经》译本不一致，但内容一样，与饮食相关的条目也是五个。藏译《宣说解脱道中头陀功德经》（D 306）也说头陀行中与饮食相关者有五个。《八千颂般若经》虽然没有明确罗列十二头陀行，但从上下文看，似乎也有十五种，据梵本，与饮食相关者有三个。藏文《丹珠尔》中还收录有一部拜则（dpal brtsegs）编纂的《法门名义备忘》（D 4362），其中也提到了十二头陀行，但认为其中只有两个条目与饮食相关。我们不清楚拜则所用的资料来源，他也参与翻译了《宣说解脱道中头陀功德经》，但彼处的说法与《法门名义备忘》并不一致。

③ 该词在藏译中没有异译，但是汉译对其有不同的翻译。玄奘将其译作“先止后食”，鸠摩罗什译作“午后不得饮浆”。

④《撰集百缘经》（*Avadānaśataka*）中出现的“paścādbhaktapiṇḍapātapratikrānta”在藏译中被译作“zan zos nas zas phyis len pa spangs te”（D 343, 122a6, 128a7, 131b7），“zas phyis len pa spangs”与“zas phyis mi len pa”意同。

这就是不取后食。[①]

《瑜伽师地论·声闻地》强调的重点是饮食知量，但文中看不出对时间以及午后不食任何食物的强调。玄奘将该词翻译为知止后食，似乎与莲花戒“先进行好好地接受（食物）”意思一致，也与《金刚经》藏译“bsod snyoms kyi zhal zas mjug tu gsol”的表述有共通之处。

鸠摩罗什往往将“khalu paścādbhaktika”译作“中后不饮浆”，可以看出其中强调的是过午不食任何东西，求那跋陀罗翻译的《佛说十二头陀经》对此进行了解释。[②]《除盖障菩萨所问经》讲到不取后食的菩萨有十种功德[③]，其中的重点是“中后不饮浆”，虽然汉译本对应之处将“不取后食”译作“一受食”或“不再食”，但其中强调的也是“中后不饮浆”[④]。

---

① 大正大学総合佛教研究所声聞地研究会·密教聖典研究会：『瑜伽論声聞地：サンスクリット語テキストと和訳』，第 276—278 页：“khalu paścādbhaktikatvaṃ katamat | bhojanārthaṃ niṣaṇṇas tāvan na paribhuṃkte | yāvat sarvabhojanaṃ pratīcchati | yāvatā jānāti śakṣyāmi yāpayituṃ | yataś ca punar jānīte na me ata uttari bhojanena kṛtyaṃ bhaviṣyatīti | tataḥ sarvaṃ parihṛtyārabhate paribhoktuṃ | evaṃ khalu paścādbhaktiko bhavati |” D 4036, 64a2–3: “zas phyis mi len pa gang zhe na | zas kyi phyir ’dug nas | ji srid du ji tsam gyis bdag ’tsho bar shes pa’i zas thams cad ma mnos pa de srid du za bar mi byed cing | gang las bdag gi zas kyi bya ba de las lhag pa mi blang ngo snyam du shes par ’gyur ba de’i ’og tu thams cad blangs nas za bar rtsom pa ste | de ltar na zas phyis mi len pa yin no ||”

玄奘译本：“云何名为先止后食？谓为食故，坐如应座，乃至未食先应具受诸所应食，应正了知，我今唯受尔所饮食，当自支持，又正了知，我过于此，定不当食。如是受已，然后方食，如是名为先止后食。”见《瑜伽师地论》，《大正藏》第 30 册，经号：第 1579 号，第 422 页上栏第 23—28 行。

② 参见《佛说十二头陀经》，《大正藏》第 17 册，经号：第 783 号，第 721 页上栏 26 至中栏第 1 行：“节量食后，过中饮浆则心生乐著，求种种浆果浆蜜浆等，求欲无厌，不能一心修习善法；如马不著勒，左右啖草不肯进路。若著辔勒，则啖草意断，随人意去，是故受中后不饮浆法。”

③ D 231, 87a2–6: “rigs kyi bu chos bcu dang ldan na byang chub sems dpa’ zas phyis mi len pa rnams yin no || bcu gang zhe na ’di lta ste mi brkam pa’i rang bzhin can rnams yin | mi chags pa’i rang bzhin can rnams yin | de dag gis nam tshod bzung bar gyur pa de’i tshe nyi tshod yod dam med kyang rung ste | de dag gi lus rton pa’i yo byad ’di lta ste | mar ram | ’bru mar ram | sbrang rtsi ’am | bu ram ’am | rtsa ba’i khu ba’am | sdong po’i khu ba ’am | ’bras bu’i khu ba de lta bu dag bzar mi rung ngo || gzhan za ba mthong na yang khong khro ba’i sems dang | ’jungs pa’i sems kyang mi skyed do || yang gal te zas phyis mi len pa’i byang chub sems dpa’ de ji lta bu’i nad kyis srog gi bar chad du ’gyur ba’am | dge ba’i phyogs kyi bar chad du ’gyur te | nad tshabs chen des ’gyod pa med cing the tsom med par byas la | sman yin par sems nye bar gzhag pas spyad par bya ste | rigs kyi bu de ltar na byang chub sems dpa’ zas phyis mi len pa rnams yin no || rigs kyi bu chos bcu po de dag dang ldan na byang chub sems dpa’ zas phyis mi len pa rnams yin no.”

④ 比如曼陀罗仙的汉译本：“善男子！菩萨复有十法名一受食。何等为十？不贪食，不染著食，以言食足一切不受，苏油、黑石蜜、阿摩勒汁、甘蔗汁及诸果汁，时非时都不饮食，见他饮食而不生恼，常一受食；菩萨设有患苦，若为命难、善法留难，当尔之时，不生疑悔作药想服。善男子！具此十事，是名菩萨一受食法。”参见《大正藏》第 16 册，经号：第 658 号，第 231 页下栏 20—26 行。题名为曼陀罗仙和僧伽婆罗所译的另一汉译本也有：“善男子！菩萨摩诃萨具足十法，持不再食。何者为十？所谓一食之后无所希望、无所染著，劝食不食，是时、非时悉皆不受；脱能治身种种汤药所可食者，所谓若苏、若油、若石蜜、若白蜜、若砂糖、若根、若果，设见他食亦不生瞋、亦不贪乐、亦不悋惜；若菩萨中后不食而病困苦，若以病故，恐失寿命、恐废行道，以无疑心审知是药能治是病，许为受用。善男子！如是，菩萨具是十法，持不再食。”参见《大正藏》第 16 册，经号：第 659 号，第 268 页上栏 11—20 行。

德格版《丹珠尔》保存有题名为吐蕃译师拜则（dpal brtsegs）撰述的《法门名义备忘》，其中也提到了十二头陀功德，并且说与饮食相关的有两条，一是乞食，二是不取后食，对于后者，书中解释说一时取适量的食物，并且不分别饮食好坏，也没有再次获取的想法，这样就是不取后食，可见其中强调的是食后不再进食。①

除了对“khalu paścādbhaktika”常见的上述两种解释外，经论中还有将其解释为不食残食的用例，如保存在藏译中的《八千颂般若经注》说：

> 保持之后不再进食的原则者，是为不取后食。弃除变质残食，是为不取后食。所谓的“khalu”这里是否定的含义，就像不说话（默默地）做和不做一样。在一个时候取一切食物而后食用，吃的是（自己）获取的，不取其他的食物。②

藏译中保存有一部题名为《解脱道中宣说头陀功德》的论书，其中明确提到不取后食的意思是弃除残食。③

从上面的论述可以看出，如果循着莲花戒注疏中头陀行的观念思考，设定“paścād-bhakta-piṇḍapāta-pratikrānta”和“khalu paścādbhaktika”有相关性的话，这一表述在不同的文本中也有不同的强调，其逻辑脉络似乎是从最基本的食后不再进食，进而引申出不饮浆，以及不食残食。即第一层有“先止后食”（玄奘语）之意，似乎也暗含了“次第乞食”；第二层有“日中一食”之意，但可能也有不食残食的意味；第三层有“午后不得饮浆食”之意。《金刚经》藏译中似乎没有体现“下午食”，但部分汉译把其中体现的时间观念翻译了出来。为清楚起见，我们可以列一个表格：

莲花戒	《金刚经》藏译	《金刚经》汉译
最后食（mjug tu gsol）	最后食（mjug tu gsol）	次第乞已……饭食讫
二次食（lan gnyis pa la blangs pa）	后食（zas phyi ma）	—
下午食（phyi dro'i zas）	—	中后时 / 后食 / 食后
—	—	还至本处④

① D 4362, 274b3: “zas kyis 'grangs pa tsam zhig dus gcig tu blangs te zhim pa'i bye brag dbye zhing phyir 'dod cing len pa med par za ba ni zas phyis mi len pa'o.”

② D 3811, 247b4–5: “phyis yang zas mi za ba'i dang tshul can ni zas phyis mi len pa'o || lhag pa'i zas ldog pa de spong bas na zas phyis mi len pa'o || kha lu zhes bya ba'i sgra ni 'dir 'gag pa'i don te | mi smra bar byas pa dang ma byas pa zhes bya ba bzhin du'o || bza' ba thams cad dus gcig nyid du len cing phyis za ba ste | za zhing blangs pa ni za bar byed la bza' ba gzhan ni mi len pa'o.”

③ D 306, 134b4: “zas phyir mi len pa ni zas lhag par spong ba yin no.”

④ “还至本处”在藏译和莲花戒的诠释中均未得到体现。

由上可见，“paścād-bhaktika”最初可能仅仅用来指代时间，即食后、午后，当与“khalu”连用时，便成为指称头陀行的一种，但其中的内涵在不同的经论中有不同的强调；当该词与“piṇḍapāta-pratikrānta”连用时，有采取字面上（传统？）解释的，即“下午乞食返回”，也有将其与头陀行联系起来解释的。而莲花戒似乎不满意上述部派佛教语境的解释，所以另辟蹊径，从大乘佛教的语境对该词进行了重新界定，我们不清楚他的说法的来源，但从藏译的翻译实践看，他的解释并没有被广泛接受。

5. 并非结论的结论

综合以上的讨论，我们首先可以简单总结如下：

第一，从《金刚经》的梵文本以及藏、汉译本来看，序分中“kṛtabhaktakṛtya paścād-bhakta-piṇḍapāta-pratikrāntaḥ pātracīvaraṃ pratiśamaya”这一读法更为流行。当然，从佛教文献发展的大背景看，不能轻易否定斯奎因写本的读法，若排除抄手的失误，斯奎因写本的读法可能代表了《金刚经》的另一种谱系。

第二，从汉译本看不出译者对这句话，尤其是其中的复合词的理解。从现有梵语和巴利语文献看，这个复合词可以被拆解为“paścād-bhaktaṃ piṇḍapāta-pratikrāntaḥ”或“paścād-bhakta-piṇḍapātaṃ pratikrāntaḥ”，其中部分汉译倾向于将“paścād-bhakta”理解为时间状语。

第三，藏译本除了部分译本对这句话的语序有调整外，最大的分歧在于对该复合词的翻译，但藏译《金刚经》最通行的本子却将两种翻译杂糅在一起，形成对同一组复合词的双重翻译，这在藏译佛经的翻译史上并不多见。

第四，对此复合词的不同理解意见在印度已经产生，至少我们从莲花戒的《金刚经》注疏中已经看到不同的解释维度。

第五，“paścād-bhakta”可能最初仅仅是表达时间的一个副词，意为“午后”，但是因为经文中该复合词与乞食相联系，所以可能造成部分诠经者将其与头陀功德中的一个类似词汇“khalu paścādbhaktika”相联系而加以解释，进而在佛陀晨朝乞食的行为中敷衍出头陀功德。但是这中间的发展演变过程还需详细考察。

《金刚经》文本的复杂性似乎可以从藏族的两句谚语中窥见一斑，一是康巴地区流传的谚语“《金刚经》是地狱之锉刀”（rdor gcod dmyal ba'i sag bdar），一是卫藏地区的谚语“门巴校订之《金刚经》”（mon pas rdor gcod zhus dag）。[①] 对这两句谚语有两种解释维度，其一

① 这两句谚语在桑东仁波切撰写的《〈金刚经〉源流及利益》中有提到，参见 Samdhong Rinpoche, *dkon mchog rjes drang gyi mdo dang | shes rab kyi pha rol du phyin pa rdo rdo rje gcod pa'i mdo | rgyal ba'i zhabs brtan/ bstan 'bar ma bcas*, Dharmasala, 1992, pp.14–15。

是说明《金刚经》的功德和流行程度，其不仅能破地狱，而且连蛮荒之地（门隅）的人们也忙于抄写校订。其二则是说明《金刚经》文本的复杂性，尤其是第二个谚语，有时也写作"门隅《金刚经》"（mon yul rdor gcod）。有一个故事与之相联系，大意是过去门隅地区有三部《金刚经》，一些自以为是的人看到三个本子的遣词造句（tshig sbyor）不尽一致后，三本相互比较，其中两本比较接近，另一本则差异较大，于是想当然地认为后一个本子不正确，将其抛入水中，这就犯了颠倒正确和不正确的错误。[①] 如果从文本校勘的角度考虑，"门隅《金刚经》"的故事一方面似乎说明藏族人已经意识到《金刚经》或者说藏译《金刚经》在历史上就有不同的传本，另一方面也提醒我们在进行文本校勘时，不能简单地用"少数服从多数"的原则，而要从多方面考虑，方能得出可靠的结论。

最后，从上述乞食问题出发，联系到过午不食的传统，我们还需要关注《金刚经》与饮食健康、绝食疗病等的关系。据何离巽介绍，斯奎因写本前面抄《药师经》，后面接着抄《金刚经》，吉尔吉特写本首先抄《金刚经》，后接着抄《药师经》，这说明这两个文本有某种联系。而且早期的壁画图像组合中有一种往往是中间画般若佛母，周围画药师佛。[②] 因此，无论是从图像、文本，还是实践上，《金刚经》与《药师经》的关系还需深入探讨。

附录一　论文涉及的《金刚经》相关文句

汉译

1. 鸠摩罗什译本：于其城中，次第乞已，还至本处。饭食讫，收衣钵，洗足已，敷座而坐。

2. 菩提流支译本：于其城中，次第乞食已，还至本处。饭食讫，收衣钵，洗足已，如常敷座。结加趺坐，端身而住，正念不动。

3. 真谛译本：于其国中，次第行已，还至本处，饭食事讫。于中后时，收衣钵，洗足已。如常敷座。跏趺安坐，端身而住，正念现前。

4. 达摩笈多译本：尔时，世尊闻者大城搏为行已，作已食作已，后食搏堕过，器上给衣收摄，两足洗，坐具世尊施设，如是座中，跏趺结直身作，现前念近住。

5. 玄奘译本：时，薄伽梵于其城中行乞食已，出还本处，饭食讫，收衣钵，洗足已，于食后时，敷如常座。结跏趺坐，端身正愿，住对面念。

6. 义净译本：次第乞已，还至本处。饭食讫，收衣钵，洗足已，于先设座。加趺端坐，正念而住。

---

① 《智慧老人信箱（第一辑）》（*shes rab rgan po'i 'bel gtam*），青海民族出版社 1994 年版，第 178—179 页。

② 最近的研究见罗文华、宋伊哲：《大昭寺早期壁画调查报告》，《故宫博物院院刊》2021 年第 9 期，第 4—24 页。尤其是第 8 页提到"般若佛母为主尊，周围环绕药师佛是后弘初期非常传统的组合"。

藏译

1. D 16, 121a3–4: de nas bcom ldan ’das mnyan yod kyi grong khyer chen por bsod snyoms kyi phyir gshegs nas bsod snyoms kyi zhal zas mjug tu gsol te | zhal zas kyi bya ba mdzad | lhung bzed dang chos gos bzhag nas | zhal bsil te | gdan bshams pa la skyil mo krung bcas nas sku drang por bsrang ste | dran pa mngon du bzhag nas bzhugs so ||

2. S 20, 232a5–7: de nas bcom ldan ’das mnyan yod kyi grong khyer chen por bsod snyoms kyi phyir gshegs nas | bsod snyoms kyi zhal zas mjug tu gsol te | zhal zas kyi bya ba mdzad | lhung bzed dang chos gos bzhag nas | zhabs bsil te gdan bshams pa la skyil mo dkrungs bcas nas sku drang por bsrang ste dran pa mngon du bzhag nas bzhugs so ||

3. F 14, 37b5–38a1: de nas bcom ldan ’das mnyan yod kyi grong khyer chen por bsod snyoms kyi phyir gshegs nas || zas kyi bya ba mdzad nas | zas phyi ma’i bsod snyoms spangs nas | lhung bzed dang chos gos bzhag nas zhal bsil te | gdan bshams pa la skyil mo dkrungs bcas nas sku drang por bsrang ste dran pa mngon du bcas nas bzhugs so ||

4. L 653, 206a1–3: de nas bcom ldan ’das mnyan yod kyi grong khyer chen por bsod snyoms kyi phyir gshegs nas bsod snyoms kyi zhal zas mjug tu gsol te | zhal zas kyi bya ba mdzad | lhung bzed dang chos gos bzhag nas | zhabs bsil te | gdan bshams pa la skyil mo dkrungs bcas nas sku drang por bsrang ste | dran pa mngon du bzhag nas bzhugs so ||

5. L 667, 1b5–7: de nas bcom ldan ’das mnyan yod kyi grong khyer chen por bsod snyoms kyi phyir gshegs nas zhal zas gsol nas zas kyi bya ba mdzad de | zas phyi ma’i bsod snyoms spangs pas lhung bzed dang chos gos bzhag nas zhabs bsil te gdan bshams pa la dkyil mo dkrung bcas nas sku drang por srang ste | dran pa mngon du bzhag nas bzhugs so ||

6. L 669, 2a2–5: de nas bcom ldan ’das mnyan yod kyi grong khyer chen por bsod snyoms kyi phyir gshegs nas zhal zas gsol te zas kyi bya ba mdzad | zas phyi ma’i bsod snyoms spangs nas lhung bzed dang chos gos bzhag nas | zhal bsil te gdan bshams pa la skyil mo krung bcas nas sku drang por bsrang ste dran pa mngon du bzhag nas bzhugs so ||

7. L 670, 1b6–8: de nas bcom ldan ’das mnyan yod kyi grong khyer chen por bsod snyoms kyi phyir gshegs nas zhal zas gsol te | zas kyi bya ba mdzad de | zas phyi ma’i bsod snyoms spangs nas lhung bzed dang chos gos bzhag nas | zhal bsil te gdan bshams pa la skyil mo krung bcas nas sku drang por bsrang ste dran pa mngon du bzhag nas bzhugs so ||

8. H 18, 215b1–3: de nas bcom ldan ’das mnyan yod kyi grong khyer chen por bsod snyoms kyi phyir gshegs nas bsod snyoms kyi zhal zas mjug tu gsol te zas kyi bya ba mdzad nas zas phyi ma’i bsod snyoms spangs pas | lhung bzed dang chos gos bzhag nas zhabs bsil te gdan bshams pa la skyil mo krung bcas nas sku drang por bsrang ste dran pa mngon du bzhag nas bzhugs so ||

附录二　莲花戒《金刚经广注》相关段落

D 3817, 207b1–4

zas kyi bya ba byas zhes bya ba ni gang gis[①] zas la sogs pa zas kyi bya ba byas shing bsgrubs pa de la de skad ces brjod do ...

rnam pa ci 'dra bas zas kyi bya ba byas she na | de'i phyir **mjug tu** zhes bya ba la sogs pa smos te | thams cad blangs nas mjug tu zhal zas gang gsol ba de ni **bsod snyoms kyi zhal zas mjug tu gsol ba ste** | de ni nyan thos rnams sbyangs pa'i yon tan la gzud pa'i phyir yang dag par len pa sngon du btang ba yin no || **gsol** zhes bya ba ni gsol zin zhes bya ba'i tha tshig go ||

yang na **mjug tu** zhes bya ba ni lan gnyis pa la blangs pa gang yin pa de la **zas phyi ma** zhes bya ste | zas phyi ma de ni zas mjug kyang yin la **bsod snyoms** kyang yin no zhes bya bar tshig rnam par sbyar ro ||

yang na **phyi dro'i zas** de za ba gang yin pa'i **bsod snyoms** de la de skad ces bya'o ||

de lta bas na sbyangs pa'i yon tan can yin pa dang | dus ma yin pa'i zas spangs pa'i phyir **gsol** zhes bya ba ni de gnyis dang bral lo zhes bya ba'i tha tshig go ||

附录三　部分文本涉及的头陀行

《二万五千颂般若经》所述头陀行

编号	梵　文[②]	藏　译[③]	鸠摩罗什汉译[④]	玄奘汉译[⑤]
1	āraṇyako (bhaviṣyati)	dgon pa pa	一作阿兰若	住阿练若处
2	paiṇḍapātika	bsod snyoms pa	二常乞食	常乞食
3	pāṃśukūlika	phyag dar khrod pa	三纳衣	粪扫衣
4	khalu paścādbhaktika	zas phyis mi len pa	六中后不饮浆	一受食
5	ekāsanika	stan gcig pa	四一坐食	一坐食
6	prasthapiṇḍika	ci thob pa'i bsod snyoms len pa	五节量食	随得食
7	śmāśānika	dur khrod pa	七冢间住	冢间住
8	ābhyavakāśika	bla gab med pa	九露地住	露地住

① gis G N P: gi D.
② Takayasu Kimura ed.:*Pañcaviṃśatisāhasrikā Prajñāpāramitā* IV. Tokyo: Sankibo Busshorin, 1990, p.44.
③ D 9, kha, 258b2–3.
④《摩诃般若波罗蜜经》,《大正藏》第 8 册，经号：第 223 号，第 320 页下栏第 5—9 行。
⑤《大般若波罗蜜多经》,《大正藏》第 7 册，经号：第 220 号，第 218 页下栏第 10—12 行。

续　表

编号	梵　文	藏　译	鸠摩罗什汉译	玄奘汉译
9	vṛkṣamūlika	shing drung pa	八树下住	树下住
10	naiṣadyika	cog pu pa	十常坐不卧	常坐不卧
11	yathāsaṃstarika	gzhi ji bzhin pa	十一次第乞食?	随得敷具
12	traicīvarika	chos gos gsum pa	十二但三衣	但畜三衣

《八千颂般若经》所述头陀行

编号	梵　文①	藏　译②	玄奘汉译③
1	āraṇyaka	dgon pa pa	居阿练若
2	piṇḍapātika	bsod snyoms pa	或常乞食
3	pāṃsukūlika	phyag dar khrod pa	粪扫衣
4	khalu paścādbhaktika	zas phyis mi len pa	受一食
5	ekāsanika	stan gcig pa	一坐食④
6	yāthāsaṃstarika	gzhi ji bzhin pa	如旧敷具
7	traicīvarika	chos gos gsum pa	但三衣
8	śmaśānika	dur khrod pa	居冢间
9	vṛkṣamūlika	shing drung pa	居树下
10	naiṣadyika	cog bu pa	常坐不卧
11	abhyavakāśika	bla gab med pa	居露地
12	nāmantika	phying ba pa	—
13	alpecchaḥ saṃtuṣṭaḥ pravivikta	’dod pa nyung zhing chog shes pa rab tu dben pa	少欲，或喜足，或乐远离⑤
14	apagatapādamrakṣaṇ	rkang pa skud pa dang bral ba	好廉俭不涂其足⑥
15	mṛdubhāṣī alpavāg	’jam por smra zhing tshig nyung ba	好少言，或乐软语

① Rajendralala Mitra ed., *Ashṭasāhasrikā: A Collection of Discourses on the Metaphysics of the Mahāyāna School of the Buddhists*, Calcutta: The Asiatic Society of Bengal, 1888, p.387.

② D 12, 211b4–6.

③《大般若波罗蜜多经》，《大正藏》第7册，经号：第220号，第551卷，第837页中栏第24行至下栏第1行。

④ 玄奘译本此后还有“一钵食”。

⑤ 玄奘译本此后还有“或乐寂定，或具正念，或具妙慧，或不重利养，或不贵名誉”。

⑥ 玄奘译本此后还有“或省睡眠，或离掉举”。

《瑜伽师地论》所述头陀行

编号	梵 文①	藏 译②	玄奘汉译③
1	prāptapiṇḍapātika	rnyed pas chog pa'i bsod snyoms pa	常期乞食 / 随得乞食
2	sāvadāna-piṇḍapātika	mthar gyis slong ba'i bsod snyoms pa	次第乞食
3	ekāsanika	stan gcig pa	但一坐食
4	khalu paścādbhaktika	zas phyis mi len pa	先止后食
5	traicīvarika	chos gos gsum pa	但持三衣
6	nāmatika	phying pa pa	但持毳衣
7	pāṃsukūlika	phyag dar khrod pa	持粪扫衣
8	āraṇyaka	dgon pa pa	住阿练若
9	vṛkṣamūlika	shing drung pa	常居树下
10	ābhyavakāśika	bla gab med pa	常居迥露
11	śmāśānika	dur khrod pa	常住冢间
12	naiṣadyika	cog pu pa	常期端坐
13	yāthāsaṃstarika	gzhi ji bzhin pa	处如常坐

《甘珠尔》各版本缩略语

D 德格版 目录参见宇井伯寿、鈴木宗忠、金倉円照、多田等観編：『西藏大藏経総目録』，東北帝国大学，1934 年（或名著出版社 1970 年重印版）。

F 普扎版 目录参见 Jampa Samten, *A Catalogue of the Phug Brag Manuscript Kanjur*, Dharamsala: Library of Tibetan Works & Archives, 1992。

H 拉萨版 目录参见 Helmut Eimer ed., *The Brief Catalogues to the Narthang and the Lhasa Kanjurs: A Synoptic Edition of the Bka' 'gyur rin po che'i mtshan tho and the Rgyal ba'i bka' 'gyur rin po che'i chos tshan so so'i mtshan byaṅ dkar chag bsdus pa*. Edited by Ernst Steinkellner. vol. 40, Wiener Studien zur Tibetologie und Buddhismuskunde, Wien: Arbeitskreis für Tibetische und Buddhistische Studien, Universität Wien, 1998。

① 大正大学総合佛教研究所声聞地研究会・密教聖典研究会：『瑜伽論声聞地：サンスクリット語テキストと和訳』，第 274 页。

② D 4036, 63b3–5.

③《瑜伽师地论》，《大正藏》第 30 册，经号：第 1579 号，第 442 页上栏第 10—13 行。

L　协噶版　目录参见 Ulrich Pagel and Séan Gaffney, *Location List to the Texts in the Microfiche Edition of the Śel dkar (London) Manuscript bKa' 'gyur (Or. 6724)*, London: The British Library, 1996。

P　北京版　目录参见西藏大藏經研究會編：『影印北京版西藏大藏経——大谷大学図書館藏——總目録，附索引』，鈴木学術財団，1962 年。

S　朵宫版　目录参见 Tadeusz Skorupski, *A Catalogue of the sTog Palace Kanjur*, vol. 4, Bibliographia Philologica Buddhica, Series Maior, Tokyo: The International Institute for Buddhist Studies, 1985。

“阿魏”：一个中古外来词的中国化历程*

陈　明

北京大学东方文学研究中心 / 北京大学外国语学院南亚学系

受佛教东传以及与波斯（和稍晚兴起的阿拉伯）交流的影响，汉魏至隋唐时期出现了大量的外来词。这些词语有音译词、意译词和音义兼训的合璧词，形式多样。有的被吸收到汉语词库中，逐渐褪去了外来色彩，成为了本土词；有的则昙花一现，在历史的长河中无声无息地消失了。不同的中古外来词中国化的历程各不相同，经历了较为不同的相遇、采纳、吸收、同化的过程，值得深入研究，以揭示不同语言的交融特征。本文以中古时期的一种域外药用植物“阿魏”[①]为例，试图梳理该词漫长的中国化历程，为探讨佛经语言中国化提供一个实例分析。

一、阿魏一词的最早出现及其在汉译佛经中的诸多译名

阿魏是一种伞形科植物，其拉丁名为 Assafoetida，学名为 Ferula asafoetida。该药用植物不仅在古代和现代的多种语言中有不同的名称，词形繁多，即便就其相关汉译名而言，由于语源和含义的不同，该词也比一般的外来药名要复杂得多。因此，阿魏一词的中国化进程尤其多变和复杂，只有在多语言、多元文化的语境中进行通盘梳理，才能明晰其变迁与选定的历史脉络。

---

* 本文为教育部人文社会科学重点研究基地（北京大学东方文学研究中心）重大项目《中国与南亚的文学与文化交流研究》（批准号 16JJD750002）的成果之一。

① 为行文简洁，除特别必要，以下“阿魏”不再加引号。

唐贞观三年（629 年），魏徵受命主编《隋书》，至贞观十年（636 年），《隋书》的帝纪、列传部分完工。《隋书》卷八十三《漕国传》中，列出当地的特产“朱砂、青黛、安息、青木等香；石蜜、半蜜、黑盐、阿魏药、白附子”。此后，唐朝李延寿编纂《北史》时，其卷九十七抄录了《隋书》中的上述记载，但写作“阿魏、没药、白附子”。可见，“阿魏”一词至少出现在贞观十年（636 年）之前。唐显庆四年（659 年），苏敬等编纂的《新修本草》记录了阿魏的性能与功用，“阿魏，味辛，平，无毒。主杀诸小虫，去臭气，破症积，下恶气，除邪鬼蛊毒。生西番及昆仑”①。自此该药正式进入中医历代本草著作之中，初步确立了阿魏一词在中国医药学著作中的主导地位。《隋书》《北史》《新修本草》都是唐代官方主持修订的文献，这些与域外物产有关的名词的译语应该来自主要负责对外交际的官方机构鸿胪寺，是由官方的译语人来确定的。

阿魏显然是一个外来语的音译。对阿魏这一汉译名的语源，学界早有考察。劳费尔（Berthold Laufer）在《吐火罗语拾遗三题》（Three Tokharian Bagatelles）一文中的“汉语中的一个吐火罗语借词”部分，就讨论了阿魏的词源。②劳费尔推测阿魏或源于吐火罗语，即吐火罗语 B 方言（龟兹语）ankwaṣ(ḍ) 的音译。作者又于《中国伊朗编》一书中对这一观点进行了详细论述。③道格拉斯 · 亚当斯（Douglas Q. Adams）所编纂的《吐火罗语 B 词典》中，列出阿魏一词在吐火罗语 B 中为 aṅkwaṣ(ṭ)、aṅkwaṣṭä、aṃkwaṣ，对应佛教梵语（或佛教混合梵语）中的 hiṅgu 一词。④此说与劳费尔之说基本相同。漕国位居中亚，即今阿富汗一带，是阿魏出产之地。初唐时期阿富汗地区通行的语言比较复杂，所以阿魏一词是吐火罗语 B 的音译不无可能。费德里科 · 德拉戈尼（Federico Dragoni）新近考察阿魏一词的语源时，得出了如下的推论：

> 因此，阿魏一词的历史可暂时重构如下：古伊朗语（Proto-Iranian）*_angu-ǰatu-_ > * 粟特语（Sogdian）或者帕提亚语？（*Parthian）[*-_ǰ_-> *-_ž_-] → 于阗语 _aṃguṣḍa-_ [*-_žat-_ > -_ṣḍ-_] → 吐火罗语（Tocharian）_aṅ(k)waṣ(ṭ)_ [-_kwaṣṭ_ < -_guṣḍ-_] →汉语和古回鹘语（独立使

---

① 苏敬等撰、尚志钧辑校：《新修本草》（辑复本第二版），安徽科学技术出版社 2005 年版，第 139 页。

② Berthold Laufer, “Three Tokharian Bagatelles,” *T’oung Pao*, second series, vol.16, no.2,1915, pp.272–281.

③ Berthold Laufer, *Sino-Iranica: Chinese Contributions to the History of Civilization in Ancient Iran, with Special Reference to the History of Cultivated Plants and Products,* Chicago: Field Museum of Natural History, 1919. 劳费尔著、林筠因译：《中国伊朗编》（副标题为《中国对古代伊朗文明史的贡献：着重于栽培植物及产品之历史》），商务印书馆 2001 年（重印）版，第 178—189 页。又见杜正胜译、刘崇校订：《中国与伊朗——古代伊朗与中国文化之交流》，台北编译馆 1975 年版。相较而言，后一译本流传未广，影响不大。

④ Douglas Q. Adams, *A Dictionary of Tocharian B: Revised and Greatly Enlarged*, Amsterdam-New York: Rodopi, 2013, p.7.

用）[Chinese and Old Uyghur (independently)]。[①]

因此，德拉戈尼的分析论证了汉语阿魏一词源自吐火罗语的 *aṅ(k)waṣ(ṭ)* 一词，这一结论也印证了劳费尔的推测。

在敦煌出土的梵语于阗语双语写本《耆婆书》（*Jīvaka-pustaka*）和于阗语写本《医理精华》（*Siddhasāra*）中，阿魏的于阗语写法均为 aṃguṣḍa，这说明有伊朗语背景的该词与其吐火罗语 B 语中的词形是同源的。

1：兴渠、兴蕖、兴虞、殑渠

阿魏并不是该药用植物在中古汉语中的最早名称。其最早名称是汉译佛经中的“兴渠”。从中古音韵来看，“阿”为中古影纽、歌韵（上古影纽、歌部），“魏”为中古疑纽、未韵（上古疑纽，微部）；而“兴”为中古晓纽、证韵（上古晓纽、蒸部），“渠”为中古群纽、鱼韵（上古群纽、鱼部）。可见，“阿魏”与“兴渠”二词的中古音分别拟为“ɑ-ŋĭwəi”和“xĭəŋ-gĭo”，二者差异很大[②]，所对应的原语完全不同。

兴渠一词最早见于后秦时期（384—417）北印度三藏弗若多罗与鸠摩罗什共译的《十诵律》。《十诵律》卷二十一等处将兴渠列为五种树胶药之一：“五种树胶药：兴渠（hiṅgu）、萨阇罗萨（梵 sarjarasa、巴 sajjulasa）、谛掖（梵 / 巴 taka）、谛掖提（巴 takapatti）、谛掖婆那（巴 takapaṇṇi），如是等余清净药，是一切盈长得。”[③]《十诵律》卷二十六：“有五种树胶药：兴渠、萨阇罗荼、帝夜、帝夜波罗、帝夜槃那，尽形寿共房宿。”[④]《十诵律》卷四十六：“五种树胶：兴渠胶、萨阇赖胶、底夜胶、底夜和提胶、底夜和那胶。”[⑤]兴渠是梵语 hiṅgu（巴利语亦为 hiṅgu[⑥]）的音译。慧琳《一切经音义》卷六十七引玄应法师音释《阿毗昙毗婆沙论》卷二十七中的“兴渠”一词：“兴渠：此是树汁，西国取之，以置食中。今有阿魏药是也。”[⑦]《一切经音义》卷四十五慧琳同样音释《梵网经卢舍那佛说菩萨心地戒品经》中的“兴渠”一

① Federico Dragoni, “Materia Medica Tocharo-Hvatanica,” *Bulletin of the School of Oriental and African Studies*, 2021, pp.1–25.
② 这四个字的中古音韵情况蒙胡敕瑞兄指点，特此感谢！
③ 高楠顺次郎、渡边海旭、小野玄妙等编：《大正新修大藏经》第 23 册，大正一切经刊行会 1934 年版，第 157 页上栏。
④ 高楠顺次郎、渡边海旭、小野玄妙等编：《大正新修大藏经》第 23 册，第 194 页上栏。
⑤ 高楠顺次郎、渡边海旭、小野玄妙等编：《大正新修大藏经》第 23 册，第 333 页下栏。
⑥ Kenneth G. Zysk, “New Approaches to the Study of Early Buddhist Medicine: Use of Technical Brahmanic Sources in Sanskrit for the Interpretation of Pali Medical Texts,” *The Pacific World: Journal of the Institute of Buddhist Studies*, New series, No.11–12, 1995, pp.143–154. Cf. p.151.
⑦ 高楠顺次郎、渡边海旭、小野玄妙等编：《大正新修大藏经》第 54 册，第 750 页中栏。另见徐时仪校注：《一切经音义三种校本合刊》（修订版），上海古籍出版社 2012 年版，下册，第 1694 页。

词为："兴渠：梵语，阿魏药也。"[①]可见，在盛唐之际，中土佛教学者已经知晓阿魏有两种作用——用作食物佐料和入药。

兴渠，又写作"兴蕖"。可洪《新集藏经音义随函录》卷八解释《请观世音菩萨消伏毒害陁罗尼咒经》中的"兴蕖"为"巨鱼反。阿魏也"。[②]《梵网经》等佛经将其列为五辛之一。[③]慧琳《一切经音义》卷七十二引玄应法师音释《杂阿毗昙心论》卷四的"兴蕖"一词："兴蕖：此言讹也，应言兴虞。兴字宜借音嫣蝇反。出关乌茶婆他那国，彼土人常所食者也。此方相传以为芸薹，非也。嫣音虚延反。"[④]新罗沙门义寂述《菩萨戒本疏》卷下在解释"五辛"时，指出"兴渠者，婆罗门语唤芸台为殑渠，虑西域诸寺不听食也。又云：岭南生兴渠，形似倭韭，气味似蒜。若有病余药不治，或应开之"[⑤]。此处的"殑渠"与"兴渠"一样，都是hiṅgu一词的音译。

2：馨牛

除兴渠外，梵语 hiṅgu 还有其他音译的词形。与《十诵律》翻译时代相近的另一部律典《四分律》（后秦罽宾三藏佛陀耶舍共与竺佛念等共译）中也有阿魏的不同译名。《四分律》卷四十二云："尔时病比丘须阇婆药，佛言：'听用。是中阇婆者，馨牛（hiṅgu）、馨荛婆提（*hiṅgupatrī）、尸婆梨陀步（*śīvaladravya）、梯夜婆提（巴 takapatti）、萨阇罗婆（娑）（梵语 sarjarasa/ 巴 sajjulasa），比丘有病因缘，尽形寿应服。'"[⑥]所谓"阇婆药"（梵语 / 巴 jatu）就是指树胶药。《四分律》此处所列举的五种树胶药，可以与《十诵律》、梵汉本《根本说一切有部毗奈耶药事》（*Bhaiṣajya-vastu*）的相应部分进行对勘[⑦]。几处比较可知，"馨牛"应即梵语 hiṅgu 的音译[⑧]，指的就是阿魏。但从对音的角度来看，"馨牛"与 hiṅgu 的对音有较大的出入，

---

① 高楠顺次郎、渡边海旭、小野玄妙等编：《大正新修大藏经》第 54 册，第 607 页上栏。另见徐时仪校注：《一切经音义三种校本合刊》（修订版），中册，第 1291 页。

② CBETA, K34, no. 1257, p.896, a12.

③《梵网经》卷二："若佛子！不得食五辛：大蒜、革葱、慈葱、兰葱、兴蕖。是五种，一切食中不得食。若故食者，犯轻垢罪。"见《大正新修大藏经》，第 24 册，第 1005 页中栏。

④《大正新修大藏经》，第 54 册，第 777 页下栏。另见徐时仪校注：《一切经音义三种校本合刊》（修订版），下册，第 1781 页。魏查理认为，"乌茶婆他那国"可对应 *Ja-wuda-sthāna，亦称作 Uḍḍiyāna。参见 Charles Willemen, "Remarks about the history of Sarvāstivāda Buddhism," *Rocznik Orientalistyczny* 1, 2014。魏查理还认为乌茶婆他那国实际是指犍陀罗文化区，包括大夏（Bactria）的罽宾。可参见 A. Cunningham, *The Ancient Geography of India*, Delhi: Low Price Publication, 1871, p.81; Li Rongxi trans., *The Great Tang Dynasty Record of the Western Regions*, BDK America, Inc. 1996, Fascicle XII, p.315。

⑤ 高楠顺次郎、渡边海旭、小野玄妙等编：《大正新修大藏经》第 40 册，第 672 页上栏。

⑥ 高楠顺次郎、渡边海旭、小野玄妙等编：《大正新修大藏经》第 22 册，第 867 页中栏。参见 SIK Hin Tak（释衍德）, *Ancient Indian Medicine in Early Buddhist Literature: A Study Based on the Bhesajjakhandhaka and the Parallels in Other Vinaya Canons*, Dissertation of The University of Hong Kong, 2016, p.167, note 88。

⑦ 陈明：《印度梵文医典〈医理精华〉研究》（修订版），商务印书馆 2014 年版，第 195—197 页。

⑧ 屈大成：《四分律药犍度注释》，台北佛陀教育基金会 2019 年版，第 142 页。

特别是"牛"字的对音不符。因此，笔者推测，"馨牛"中的"牛"字或许为西北方音。

3：阿魏

阿魏一词在汉译佛经中出现的次数不超过二十次，主要见于公元7世纪下半叶和8世纪初唐代汉译的佛教戒律和密教经文，具体有唐代义净译的《根本说一切有部毗奈耶药事》《杂事》和《陀罗尼集经》[大唐天竺三藏阿地瞿多永徽五年（654年）译]卷八和卷九、《大佛顶广聚陀罗尼经》卷五、《不空羂索神变真言经》（大唐天竺三藏菩提流志译）卷十一、《观自在菩萨怛嚩多唎随心陀罗尼经》（唐大总持寺沙门智通译）等。目前尚难以判定阿魏一词最早出现在哪一部汉译佛经中，但无疑要晚于《隋书》，甚至晚于《新修本草》。

值得注意的是，汉译佛经中阿魏一词所对应的原语，与《隋书》中的原语显然不同。唐代义净译《根本说一切有部毗奈耶药事》卷一列举了五种黏药，即："五种黏药者，所谓阿魏、乌糠、紫矿、黄蜡、安悉香。阿魏药者，谓阿魏树上出胶。乌糠者，谓娑罗树出胶。紫矿者，树枝上出汁。黄蜡者，谓蜜中残出也。安悉香者，树胶也。"[①]吉尔吉特出土的梵本《根本说一切有部毗奈耶药事》虽然并非义净译本的母本，但其中也有关于五种黏药的部分，即：

> pañca jatūni / hiṅguḥ takastakakaṇīm tadāgataśca /
> tatra hiṅguḥ hiṅgu-vṛkṣasya niyāṃsaḥ (niryāsaḥ) //
> sarjarasaḥ sālavṛkṣasya niryāsaḥ //
> tako lākṣās-taka-karṇī sikthaṃ tadāgatas-tadanyeṣāṃ vṛkṣāṇāṃ niryāsaḥ [②]//

义净译本中的"阿魏药者，谓阿魏树上出胶"恰好可对应梵本中的"tatra hiṅguḥ hiṅgu-vṛkṣasya niyāṃsaḥ (niryāsaḥ)"，这说明"阿魏""阿魏树""胶"，分别为"hiṅguḥ""hiṅgu-vṛkṣasya""niryāsaḥ"的对译，那么阿魏就是hiṅgu的译名。义净在《南海寄归内法传》卷三中也有"西边乃阿魏丰饶"之语[③]。从对音来看，阿魏显然不是hiṅgu一词的直接音译，而且这一译名在唐代以前的文献中几乎没有出现过。和玄奘法师一样，作为有过多年在天竺求法经历的翻译家，义净也喜欢在译本的注释中使用"讹也""略也"之类标记，来纠正前人的音译词。比如，《根本说一切有部尼陀那目得迦》卷七中就有一例："是时聚底色迦旧云树提伽者，讹也长者即于其前。"[④]那么，义净明明知道阿魏不是hiṅgu一词的音译，他为什么要用阿魏来

---

① 高楠顺次郎、渡边海旭、小野玄妙等编：《大正新修大藏经》第24册，第1页中栏。
② Sitansusekhar Bagchi ed., *Mūlasarvāstivādavinayavastu,* 2 vols., Buddhist Sanskrit Text No.16, Darbhanga: The Mithila Institute of Post-graduate Studies and Research in Sanskrit Learning, 1967, p.2.
③ 义净著，王邦维校注：《南海寄归内法传校注》，中华书局2009年版，第153页。
④ 高楠顺次郎、渡边海旭、小野玄妙等编：《大正新修大藏经》第24册，第444页上栏。

对译 hiṅgu 呢？换言之，他选择阿魏这一译语的依据是什么呢？要回答这一问题，需要继续对唐代汉译佛经文献进行梳理。

4：形俣、形俁

大唐天竺三藏菩提流志译的《不空羂索神变真言经》卷二十一《如意阿伽陀药品第四十五》中记载了一个药方，其中含有“形俣（hiṅgu）、钵怛啰（pattra）、荜茇（pippalī）”①。慧琳《一切经音义》卷三十九中有一处对“形俁”的解释，即：“形俁：虞矩反。《毛诗传》曰：俁，容皃大也。”②“形俣”（“形俁”）实乃唐代佛经中对阿魏的一种新音译形式，它也是梵语 hiṅgu 的音译。

二、阿魏在中古时期本土文献中的诸译名

除了汉译佛经之外，阿魏一物在中古时期的本土文献——与佛教相关的典籍、医学典籍、笔记等中，也有如下多种不同的译名。

5：兴瞿

“兴瞿”此名出自玄奘、辩机《大唐西域记》卷十二的“漕矩咤国”条：“宜郁金香，出兴瞿草，草生罗摩印度川（赫尔曼德河）。”③道宣《释迦方志》卷一引之。慧琳《一切经音义》卷六十八释之云：“兴瞿：具俱反。梵语药名。唐云阿魏也。”④可见，“兴瞿”亦即梵语 hiṅgu 的音译。

6：形具

此名亦不见于汉译佛经，而出自赞宁《宋高僧传》卷二十九“唐洛阳罔极寺慧日传”中所引《往生净土集》“别行所书”对五辛的解释：“……兴渠，梵语稍讹，正云形具。余国不见，回至于阗方得见也。根粗如细蔓菁根而白，其臭如蒜。彼国人种取根食也。于时冬天到

---

① 高楠顺次郎、渡边海旭、小野玄妙等编：《大正新修大藏经》第 20 册，第 339 页中栏。

② 高楠顺次郎、渡边海旭、小野玄妙等编：《大正新修大藏经》第 54 册，第 564 页中栏。另见徐时仪校注：《一切经音义三种校本合刊》（修订版），中册，第 1183 页。

③ 玄奘、辩机原著，季羡林等校注：《大唐西域记校注》，中华书局 1985 年版，第 954 页、第 956 页注释 4。

④ 高楠顺次郎、渡边海旭、小野玄妙等编：《大正新修大藏经》第 54 册，第 754 页上栏。另见徐时仪校注：《一切经音义三种校本合刊》（修订版），下册，第 1707 页。

彼，不见枝叶。”这是中原佛教徒首次对于阗出产阿魏的描述，出自慧日法师的亲身观察。慧日由海路去天竺求法十八年，而沿着西北丝绸之路经于阗，于开元七年（719年）返回长安。《往生净土集》（即《净土往生集》）并非慧日所著，他所著的乃《净土慈悲集》（三卷）。“别行所书”这一表述说明这段引文并非《往生净土集》的原文，但察其内容与叙述口吻，当出自慧日无疑。因此，“形具”一名很可能是慧日游学天竺之后，像玄奘、义净那样用中天竺的读音来评判前代译音为讹误的结果，也有可能是慧日记录在于阗当地所听到的该物名称的发音。

7：兴宜（具）

此名出自宋代景德寺僧法云编《翻译名义集》卷三“兴渠”条，“兴渠：讹也。应法师：此云少，正云兴宜。出乌茶婆他那国，彼人常所食也。此方相传为芸台者，非也。此是树汁，似桃胶。西国取之，以置食中，今阿魏是也。慈愍三藏云：根如萝卜，出土辛臭。慈愍冬到彼土，不见其苗”[①]。很显然，法云是将玄应、慧日（慈愍三藏）两人的解释糅合在一起，而又有所增衍，其中的“此云少”和“根如萝卜”乃没有根据的臆改。“兴宜”亦不能视为宋代出现的新译名。从词义来说，“兴渠”与“少”没有关系；从字形来看，玄应最初的观点是“正云兴虞”，因此，很可能“兴宜”的“宜”应是“具”字形误，而“兴具”与“形具”的发音相似。

8：央匱

盛唐时期王焘编纂的《外台秘要方》是中古最重要的医籍之一。其卷十三的“鬼气方”部分，摘录了唐代崔知悌《崔氏纂要方》（约成书于公元7世纪中期）第七卷中的一个“疗鬼气、辟邪恶、阿魏药安息香方”。崔知悌的原文有注释性的说明：“阿魏药，即《涅槃经》云央匱是也。”[②]可见，“央匱”也是梵语 hiṅgu 的又一个音译词。不过，崔知悌是从当时的《大般涅槃经》写本中抄来的“央匱”一词，而传世的《大般涅槃经》诸译本中并无“央匱”这一写法。该词在《大般涅槃经》中对应的写法是什么，还有待查证。

9：浅根、截根、阿魏截根、阿魏煎

“浅根”之名见于大谷1074号药方书断片。浅根，当即截根，也就是唐代杜佑《通典》所载北庭都护府贡品清单“阿魏截根二十斤”中的“阿魏截根”[③]。不过，浅根、截根可能不

---

① 高楠顺次郎、渡边海旭、小野玄妙等编：《大正新修大藏经》第54册，第1107页下栏。

② 王焘：《宋版外台秘要方》，日本东洋医学研究会印制1981年版，第253页。另见王焘撰，高文铸校注：《外台秘要方》，华夏出版社1997年版，第244页。

③《新唐书》卷四十也记载“北庭都护府土贡阴牙角、速霍角、阿魏截根”。见宋祁：《新唐书》，中华书局1975年版，卷四十，第1047页。

是音译词，而是指所截的阿魏根，如同唐慎微《证类本草》卷九“阿魏”条引“唐本注云：苗、叶、根、茎酷似白芷。捣根汁，日煎作饼者为上，截根穿暴干者为次。体性极臭而能止臭，亦为奇物也”[①]。

据《天宝二年（743 年）交河郡市估案》中的大谷 3042 号物价文书：“阿魏煎壹两　上直钱捌文　次柒文　下陆文。”[②] 则当时西域确实有将阿魏“日煎作饼者”，其质量分为三等。这是盛唐时期阿魏的实物在吐鲁番地区被使用的例证。

10：西阿魏

敦煌出土的羽 042R《药方》中，有一个“疗人风冷腰冷不定且有疼痛者”之“索边丸”，该药方中使用了“西阿魏”。其原卷中写作“阿西魏”，但前两个字之间有对调符号，说明其正确的写法是“西阿魏”，应该是指来自西域地区（或者西方的）阿魏。

11：形虞

此名出唐代段成式《酉阳杂俎》前集卷十八的“阿魏”条。段成式记录其为北天竺伽阇那国对阿魏的称呼，即“阿魏，出伽阇那国，即北天竺也。伽阇那呼为形虞。亦出波斯国，波斯国呼为阿虞截”[③]。从当时北天竺的伽阇那（Ghaznin，现阿富汗的伽兹尼 / 加慈尼）来看，阿魏的“形虞”之名亦即梵语词 hiṅgu 的音译[④]。

12：阿虞截

段成式《酉阳杂俎》中还保留了域外人士对阿魏的描述，即“树长八九丈，皮色青黄，三月生叶，叶似鼠耳，无花实。断其枝，汁出如饴，久乃坚凝，名阿魏。拂林国僧弯所说同”[⑤]。可见，段成式请教过不少在长安的域外人士，所谓“拂林国僧弯”应该是一位来自拜占庭帝国的通晓医药和语言的景教僧。而“阿虞截”一名实乃波斯语 Anguzad 的音译。

---

① 唐慎微撰，尚志钧等校点：《证类本草》，华夏出版社 1993 年版，第 253 页。

② 小田义久编：《大谷文书集成》，法藏馆 1990 年，第二册，第 10 页。另见池田温：《中国古代物价初探——关于天宝二年交河郡市估案断片》，收入氏著《唐研究论文选集》，中国社会科学出版社 1999 年版，第 162 页。

③ 段成式撰，许逸民校笺：《酉阳杂俎校笺》（三），中华书局 2015 年版，第 1336 页。Angela Schottenhammer, “Transfer of *Xiangyao* 香药 from Iran and Arabia to China: A Reinvestigation of Entries in the *Youyang zazu*《酉阳杂俎》(863), ” in Ralph Kauz and Harrassowitz Verlag eds., *Aspects of the Maritime Silk Road: From the Persian Gulf to the East China Sea*, East Asian Maritime History 10, Wiesbaden, 2010, pp.117–152. Cf. pp.135–137.

④ 有学者认为“形虞”与“撒阿因”的语音相同，此说不确。

⑤ 段成式撰，许逸民校笺：《酉阳杂俎校笺》（三），第 1336 页。

以上这十几种名称分别指向六朝隋唐乃至宋时期阿魏一物的三种不同语源（吐火罗语B、梵语、波斯语）及其作为药用的不同形态（截根、煎、饼状）。

三、元明时期伊斯兰医籍中的阿魏诸译名

到了元明时期，随着伊斯兰医药的传入，阿魏的新译名亦逐渐出现，可梳理如下：

13：哈昔泥（尼）

该名出自元代忽思慧《饮膳正要》第三卷"料物"部分，云"哈昔泥：味辛温，无毒。主杀诸虫，去臭气，破症瘕，下恶除邪，解蛊毒。即阿魏"①。哈昔泥或写作"哈昔尼"，是波斯语 kasni（或写作 gha-zni）的音译②，对应蒙古语 gajni、波斯语 gha-zni，因阿魏产于阿富汗的伽兹尼（Ghazni）而得名③。在现代蒙古语中，阿魏被称作 šiṅ-gun，此词当来自藏语 šiṅ-kun。

14：稳展

忽思慧《饮膳正要》又云"稳展：味辛温，苦，无毒。主杀虫，去臭，其味与阿魏同。又云即阿魏树根，淹羊肉，香味甚美"④。劳费尔对"稳展"的语源未有定论。《〈饮膳正要〉注释》亦未对之作解释。保罗·布埃尔（Paul D.Buell）在《饮膳正要》的英译本《大汗之汤》（*A Soup for the Qan*）中，直接将"稳展"译作 Anguzhad⑤，与上述"阿虞截"的对音相同。而据马克斯·迈耶霍夫（Max Meyerhof）的论文，阿魏的根在阿拉伯语中叫作 ushturghâz⑥，那么稳展或许是阿拉伯语 ushturghâz（或者是受其影响的蒙古语词）的音译。其语源的真相如何，尚有待高明之士论之。

---

① 忽思慧撰，刘玉书点校：《饮膳正要》，人民卫生出版社 1986 年版，第 151 页。

② Paul D.Buell & Euqene N.Anderson, *A Soup for the Qan*: *Chinese Dietary Medicine of the Mongol Era as Seen in Hu Sihui's Yinshan Zhengyao*, (Sir Henry Wellcome Asian Series), 2 Rev Exp edition, Leiden: E.J.Brill, 2010, pp.551—552.

③ 劳费尔著，林筠因译：《中国伊朗编》，第 411 页。忽思慧著，尚衍斌、孙立慧、林欢注释：《〈饮膳正要〉注释》，中央民族大学出版社 2009 年版，第 352—355 页。

④ 忽思慧撰，刘玉书点校：《饮膳正要》，第 151 页。又，明代陈士元《诸史夷语解义》引《饮膳正要》："哈昔泥，即阿魏也。稳展，即阿魏根也。"

⑤ Paul D.Buell & Euqene N.Anderson, *A Soup for the Qan*, p.552.

⑥ Max Meyerhof, "Ali at-Tabari's 'Paradise of Wisdom', one of the oldest Arabic Compendiums of Medicine," *Isis*, vol.16, no.1,1931, pp.6–54. Cf. p.34.

15:《回回药方》中的阿魏诸译名

元明之际，伊斯兰医学传入中土颇盛于前代，除前述《饮膳正要》之外，《回回药方》更被后世学者推崇为中世波斯—阿拉伯流行的伊斯兰医学知识的百科全书型的汉译本。《回回药方》中不仅有阿魏饼子、阿魏膏子、阿魏丸方、阿魏马准等诸多方剂，也有阿魏的多种译名，至少可以分为以下四组：

（1）撒阿因、撒额因、撒额冰、撒黑因、撒亦因、撒亦冰

宋岘指出，《回回药方》中，阿魏被称作“撒阿因”（Sa ‘yin），此词与形虞音同，其本意或与阿拉伯语词“绵羊”（Ḍa ‘īn，波斯人呼作 Za ‘īn）有关。由此谓“撒阿因”的对音等同于形虞，证据不足，笔者难以苟同。但谓撒阿因的语义与“绵羊”有关，或许不无道理。宋代赵汝适《诸蕃志》卷下“志物”中的“阿魏”条记载了一个神奇的传说：“阿魏出大食木俱兰。……或曰其脂最毒，人不敢近，每采阿魏时，系羊于树下，自远射之，脂之毒着于羊，羊毙，即以羊之腐为阿魏。”[①] 大食木俱兰（Mukrān），即今伊朗莫克兰（Mukulan）省一带。[②] 此传说也以图像形式出现在李时珍《本草纲目》等本草类著作的插图本之中（见图一），与明代宫廷画家绘制的《本草品汇精要》卷十九中的阿魏插图（见图二）形成对比。[③]

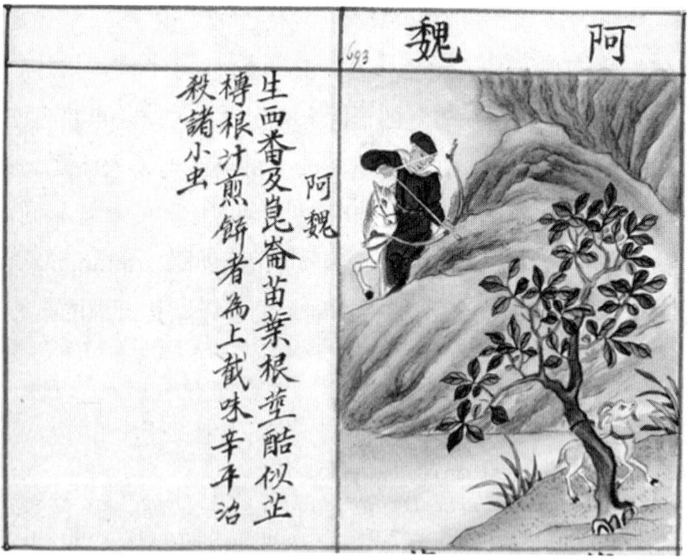

图一 《中国药用本草绘本》（*Traité chinois de botanique médicale*）中的阿魏图

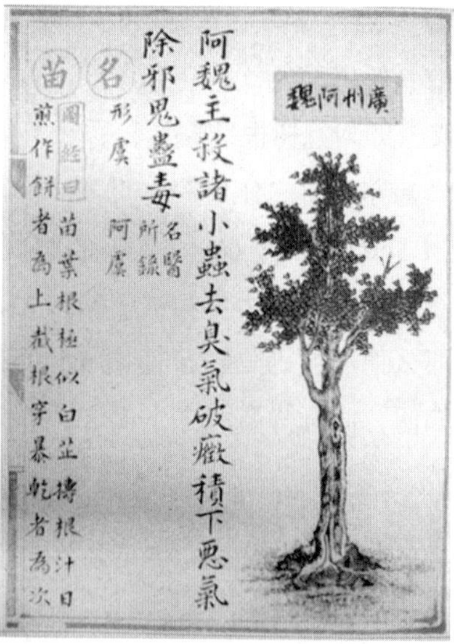

图二 《本草品汇精要》中的阿魏图

① 赵汝适著、杨博文校释：《诸蕃志校释》，中华书局 1996 年版，第 198 页。
② 宋岘：《回回药方考释》，中华书局 2000 年版，第 64—65 页。
③ 有关阿魏传说的图像可参见王家葵等著：《本草纲目图考》，龙门书局 2018 年版，下册，第 1287—1288 页。

宋岘还认为，《回回药方》中的"撒阿因"，即阿维森纳《医典》中的阿魏树胶（Sikbīnaj），撒阿因乃阿魏（Sakb̲īnaj）的别名 Sāghā fyīn 的音译[①]。而撒额冰就是波斯语阿魏树脂（Sakbīnaj）的音译[②]。

《回回药方》中与"撒阿因"类似的译名还有"撒额因""撒额冰""撒黑因""撒亦因""撒亦冰"等。宋岘还指出，"撒额因"的对音为 Ṣaghyīn。这组汉译名的对音均与 Ṣaghyīn 有关。

（2）撒吉别拿失、撒吉别拏只

《回回药方》中的"撒吉别拿失"是阿魏树胶（Sikbīnaj）的另一种称谓[③]。《回回药方》中，该词另写作"撒吉别拏只"，如"哈必撒吉别拏只"[④]。但《回回药方》卷之三十"杂证门"的膏子药方中，有"马竹尼可撒吉别拿只方"，其中的"可撒吉别拿只"（al-Kāsakibīnaj）语义不明，与阿魏似乎无关[⑤]。

（3）安古丹 / 安吉（古）丹、安古当 / 安吉（古）当、安诸丹

《回回药方》中有"安古丹膏子"（Anjudhān）、"古阿里失安吉丹方"（Juwarishn al-Anjudhān，即阿魏化食丹）。安古丹、安古当、安诸丹均为阿拉伯语和波斯语阿魏（Anjudhān）的音译名[⑥]。安吉丹、安吉当中的"吉"乃"古"字的形误。另外，在叙利亚语中阿魏名为"Agdânâ"。

（4）黑黎提提

《回回药方》卷三十中的"马竹尼黑黎提提方"（Ma 'jun al-ḥiltîti），其注解为"即加阿魏合成的膏子药方"，此乃阿魏舐剂。黑黎提提就是阿魏的树脂，是阿拉伯语 ḥiltîti 或 ḥiltît 的音译[⑦]。《回回药方》中的"马竹尼谟八的卢里米咱只方"中就注明了"黑黎提提即是阿魏"。《回回药方》中还有几处如下的注释：

> 黑黎提提（即是阿魏）
> 黑黎提提（即阿魏净者）
> 黑黎提提（即阿魏不香者）
> 墨黎提提（即是阿魏）

---

① 宋岘：《回回药方考释》，第 16—17 页。
② 宋岘：《回回药方考释》，第 19—20 页。
③ 宋岘：《回回药方考释》，第 64—65 页。
④ 宋岘：《回回药方考释》，第 294 页。"哈必"可能是指波斯语 Ghaznī (Ghaznā)，即 Zābulistan 的首府。参见 Berthold Laufer, *Sino-Iranica*, 1919, p.361。Cf. Schottenhammer 前揭文，第 136 页。
⑤ 宋岘：《回回药方考释》，第 80 页。
⑥ 宋岘：《回回药方考释》，第 14 页。
⑦ 宋岘：《回回药方考释》，第 307 页。

很明显，最后的“墨黎提提”应该是“黑黎提提”的形误。

16：昂古则

明代《回回馆杂字》和《回回馆译语》（会同馆本）“花木门”（第 1141 条）记载：“阿魏：昂古则。”“昂古则”是指阿魏的根，本田信实认为该词对应“angūjha”。刘迎胜认为《回回馆译语》中所收的“回回语”是指波斯语，“昂古则”对音应为 anguzha，与唐代“阿虞截”的对音 anguzhad 一脉相承。[①]

阿魏一词在波斯语中的出现时间早于阿拉伯语。《简明牛津英语词典》指出，阿魏的拉丁名 asafoetida 中的 asa 来自波斯语的 aza，意思是“乳香脂”（mastic）。实际上，比波斯语更早的苏美尔语中就有了 as，出现在一个植物名表中的 lasirbitu 一词中，而该词很可能来自表示阿魏的词形 laserpitum[②]。

伊朗《德胡达辞典》（*Loghatnâme*）中收录了阿魏树胶（Anguza），解释如下：

> Anguza：阿魏树胶，又名 anqūza，阿拉伯语作 ḥillīt。是“波斯白芷”或“牛至”（gulpar，此据《波斯语—汉语词典》）枝干上的汁液，通过用刀切割来获取，就像从罂粟（khashakhāsh）中获取鸦片（afiyūn）一样。

这个词还有多个词形上的变化：anqūza, anghūza, angūza, anguzad, anguzhad, anguzha, angūzha。发音相近，均指阿魏。《德胡达辞典》在这些词条下有相似的释义：

> Anguzhad：广义上指树脂，是发出恶臭的树脂。阿拉伯人称其为 ḥillīt。它被叫作 anguzhad 的原因是，它是 angudān 树的树脂，原称 angudān-zhad，在波斯语中 zhad 的意思就是树脂。（引自 *Burhān-i Qāṭi‘*）广义为“树脂”，狭义为“阿魏树胶”，即 angudān。
>
> Anguzha：是 angudān 树的树脂，阿拉伯人称其为 ḥillīt，设拉子人称其为 angusht-ganda（“手指发臭的”）。
>
> Angudān 树：拉丁语为 ferula asa foetida。属伞形花科（tīra-yi chatriyān）草本植物，两年生，在伊朗多数荒野大量生长，高度 2—2.5，根茎直而厚实。又名 abr kabīr，ḥillīt, anjudān。[③]

---

① 刘迎胜：《回回馆杂字与回回馆译语研究》，中国人民大学出版社 2008 年版，第 427—428 页。

② R.Campbell Thompson, “The Migration of Assyrian Plant-Names into the West,” *The Classical Review*, vol.38, no.7/8, 1924, pp.148–149. Cf.p.149.

③ Aliakbar Dehkhodâ, M. Mo’in and J. Shahidi eds., *Loghatnâme (Encyclopedic Dictionary)*, vol.3, Tehran: Tehran University Publications, 1993–1994, p.3083.《波斯语—汉语词典》第 181 页收录的词形为 anqūza（انقوزه）。——以上《德胡达辞典》中的译文以及相关信息，均由北京大学外国语学院西亚系王一丹教授提供，不胜感谢！

《德胡达辞典》中的这些解释可以与《回回药方》中的译名相互印证，从中可以看出阿魏的这些汉语译名分别来自波斯语和阿拉伯语。

四、明代《满剌加国译语》及西域文献中的阿魏

17：莺孤

阿魏主要出产于波斯、印度西北和中亚，不仅通过陆上丝绸之路流传，也通过海上丝绸之路流传。因此，东南亚的语言中也留下了阿魏的身影。明代四夷馆所编的《满剌加国译语》被称作“华人编纂的第一部马来语汉语词典”[①]。尽管该词典的成书时间不明，但有一条线索可以大概估测，即其现存版本为明“嘉靖二十八年（1549年）一月　日通事杨林校正”，这说明该书写成时间至少不晚于1549年。《满剌加国译语》之四的“花木”部分，收录了阿魏的译名，即：

阿魏　asafoetida　莺孤　ying ku　inggu[②]

可见，“莺孤”是马来语阿魏的音译，对应的马来语发音为Inggu。该词的中原音韵读音拟为iəŋ ku[③]。Inggu的源头可能是由梵语Hiṅgu转译为印地语的Ingu。无论如何，该马来语词Inggu体现了16世纪马来地区与印度文化之间的关联。1801年，詹姆斯·豪伊森（James Howison）的《马来亚方言词典》（*A Dictionary of the Malay Tongue*）也收录了Ingo，并将其与阿魏相对应。[④]

18：阿味

明代有关西域的文献中，也不时提及阿魏。最著名的是陈诚的《西域番国志》，据其记

① 孔远志：《〈满剌加国译语〉——华人编纂的第一部马来语汉语词典》，《东南亚研究》1992年第1期，第55—56页。

② E.D.Edwards and C.O.Blagden, “A Chinese Vocabulary of Malacca Malay Words and Phrases Collected between A.D. 1403 and 1511 (?),” *Bulletin of the School of Oriental Studies, University of London*, Vol.6, No.3, 1931, p.724. 汉译文可参见许云樵译：《满剌加国译语注》，《南洋学报》1941年第二卷第一辑，第63—89页。

③ 有关《满剌加译语》的对音，参见林水檺：《满剌加国译语注音》，马来西亚华校教师会总会教育研究中心编印《教育与研究》1994年第1期，第46页。

④ James Howison, *A Dictionary of the Malay Tongue*, London: The Arabic and Persian Press, 1801, p.82.

载，在撒马儿罕之东五百余里的沙鹿海牙，“地生臭草，根株独立，高不尺余，枝叶如盖，春生秋死，臭气迫人，生取其汁熬以成膏，即名阿魏是也”[①]。明代的《西域土地人物略》[②]也记载着当地的一些物产，比如，中亚的亦卜剌城，出产砂糖；亦思城，出产阿味、阿芙蓉；阿即民城，出产阿味；可台城，山下出产西天红花等。其中的“阿味”，有学者认为即指阿魏[③]。《西域土地人物略》所记其出产地与中亚阿魏的实际产地大体相符，阿味与阿魏二者可能为同一物，仅音译有别。

除了上述的这些译名（或正名）外，阿魏还有一些别名，比如，因为味道臭，而被称为臭阿魏。又如五代宋初的陶穀《清异录》卷二中引用唐朝侯宁极的《药谱》，列举了“魏去疾：阿魏”一条[④]。

五、《华夷译语》系列、《西番译语》及藏蒙文等典籍中的阿魏诸名

19：《华夷译语》系列中的阿魏名称：盛棍、悻、英古、阿斯萨弗氏达、代弗勒斯德呵克

明永乐五年（1407年）设立四夷馆，以培养对外交往及翻译的人才，并承袭洪武二十二年（1389年）刊行的翰林院侍讲火源洁等所编订蒙汉合璧的《华夷译语》的做法，陆续编辑了供语言学习及对外交流所用的一批双语词汇集。后世将明清时期的这些官方编纂的“译语”“杂字”“来文”统称为《华夷译语》。据前辈学者们的研究，《华夷译语》系列可分为四种版本，分别为洪武本、永乐本、会同馆本、会同四译馆本。日本学界分别称之为甲种本、乙种本、丙种本、丁种本。《华夷译语》系列中有“香药门”“花木门”等门类，收录了一批常用的名物词。

德国柏林国立图书馆藏的明万历七年（1579年）的《华夷译语》写本[⑤]中，既有《西番

---

① 陈诚著、周连宽校注：《西域行程记　西域番国志》，中华书局1991年版，第92页。

② 作者佚名，收入赵廷瑞修，马理、吕柟纂：《河套西域》，《陕西通志》，三秦出版社2006年版，卷十。

③ 李之勤编：《西域史地三种资料校注》，新疆人民出版社2012年版，第42页。

④ 元末明初陶宗仪的《南村辍耕录》中亦引之。参见陶宗仪：《南村辍耕录》，中华书局2004年版，第200页。类似的用法还见于陈邦俊的《广谐史》（明万历四十三年沈应魁刻本）卷七，他引用了王义山的“甘国老传甘草（集药名）”一文，将药名拟人化而为文，其中“有阿魏者”就是构拟的人物。同卷闵文振的“国老世家甘草集药名”一文中，也有“欲妻以阿魏氏女”这样的拟人说法。见陈邦俊：《广谐史》（明万历四十三年沈应魁刻本），齐鲁书社1995年版，卷七。

⑤ 编号PPN334615730X，共二十四卷。

馆译语》的“香药门”所列的“shing kun：阿魏：盛棍”（见图三）；也有新修《暹罗馆译语》的“花木门”中的“หิง / Hi: ŋ/5 阿魏:悻”（见图四）[①]。阿魏的藏语词形 shing kun 及其泰语词形 Hi: ŋ/5 均源自梵语 Hiṅgu。Hi: ŋ/5 的汉字音译“悻”，比较独特，笔者仅在《暹罗馆译语》和《华夷译语》系列的《暹罗番书》的“香药门”（见图五）中[②]发现了该词，而未在其他文献中见到类似的字形。阿魏不仅是见于中泰双语词典的名物词，也是暹罗（泰国）向明清进贡的物品之一，[③]是当地人熟识并广泛使用的一种物品。

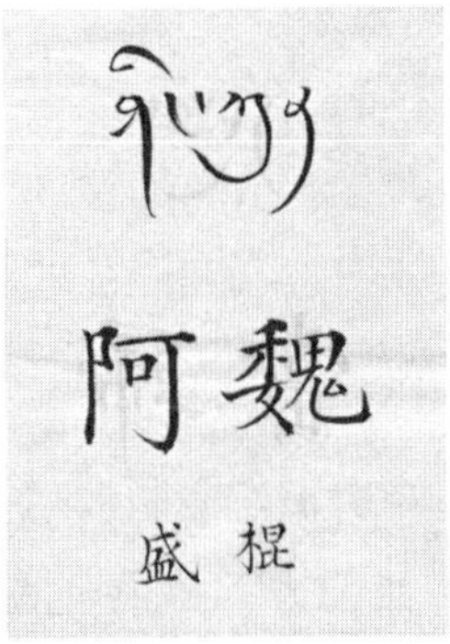

图三 《西番馆译语》中的阿魏

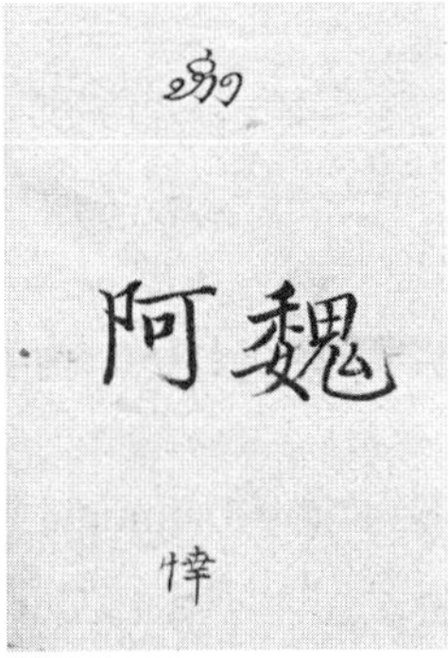

图四 《暹罗馆译语》中的阿魏

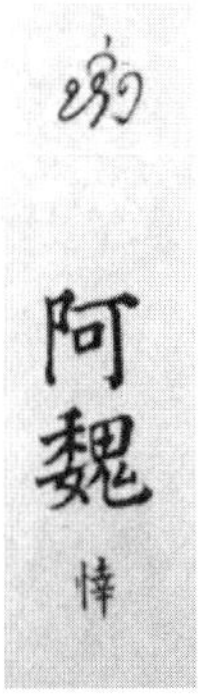

图五 《暹罗番书》中的阿魏

《华夷译语》丁种本是清乾隆十三年（1748 年）按照当时重新审定的《西番译语》的体例进行编辑的、次年完稿的六部汉语—欧洲语言（拉丁、法、意、葡、德、英）的双语词汇集，多出自耶稣会士之手。德国学者福克司（Walter Fuchs）首先在北京故宫发现了这六部著作,并对之简要论述,[④]后逐渐引起了国际学术界的关注[⑤]。这六部中外双语词汇集中均收录了阿魏一词，具体如下：

其一,《嘆咭唎国译语》是汉语与英语（English，“嘆咭唎”）的双语词汇集，共两册。其中的“香药门”收录了:“Ingo 阿魏：英古”（见图六）[⑥]。这个英文词 Ingo 来源于印地语

---

① 感谢北京大学外国语学院东南亚系熊燃博士、程露同学帮助转写阿魏的泰语词形！

② 图五见于《暹罗番书》(第二册)，收入《故宫博物院藏乾隆年编华夷译语》，故宫出版社 2017 年版，第十一卷，第 216 页。

③ 德国柏林国立图书馆所藏《暹罗馆来文》中有二十篇“来文”，所涉及暹罗王的贡物清单中就有阿魏。参见韩一瑾、李英:《〈暹罗馆译语〉新考》,《社会科学》2019 年第 12 期，第 158 页。

④ Walter Fuchs, “Remarks on a new ‘Hua-I-I-Yü’,” *Bulletin of the Catholic University of Peking*, No.8, 1931, pp.91–97. Walter Fuchs, “Das erste deutsch-chinesische Vokabular von P.Florian Bahr,” *Sinica, Sonderausgabe* 1937 I, S. pp.68–72. 感谢李雪涛教授提供福克司的论文与《华夷译语》丁种本的六部文本的资料！

⑤ 李雪涛:《德国汉学家福克司与〈华夷译语〉丁种本之发现》，收入沈国威、奥村佳代子编《文化交渉と言語接触》(内田庆市教授退职纪念论文集)，东方书店 2021 年版，第 179—196 页。有关“不同时代的《华夷译语》及其研究史”概述，见该文第 198—202 页。

⑥《嘆咭唎国译语》(第二册)，收入《故宫博物院藏乾隆年编华夷译语》，第十三卷，第 152 页。

Ingu 的马来语词形 Ingo。显然，在与印度和东南亚接触的早期，英国人便接纳了当地有关阿魏的名称，后来在欧洲近代植物学命名原则下，沿用了阿魏的拉丁语名称。

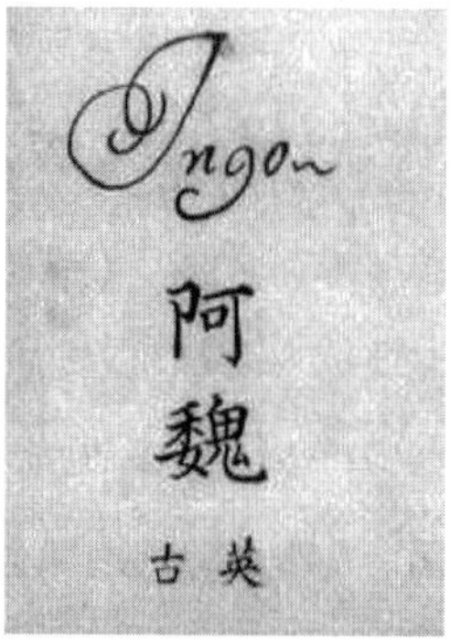

图六 《咦咭唎国译语》中的阿魏

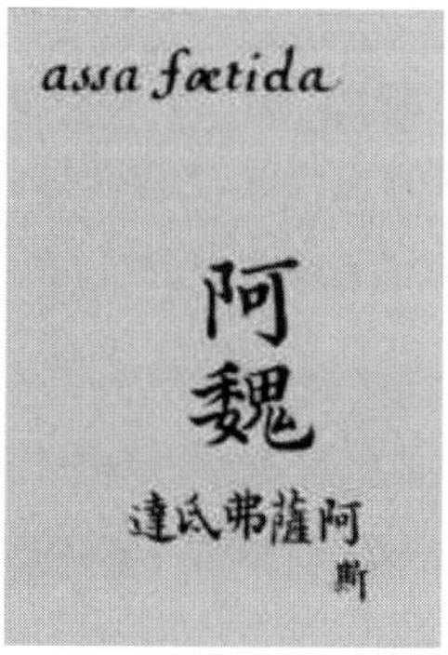

图七 《拉氏诺语》中的阿魏

其二，《拉氏诺语》是汉语与拉丁语（Latinum，“拉氏诺”）的双语词汇集，共五册，收词 2 061 条。其中的“香药门”收录了：“assa faetida 阿魏：阿斯萨弗氏达”（见图七）[①]。Assafaetida 是阿魏的拉丁语名称，也是此后欧洲医学著作中最通用的阿魏名称。

其三，《播都噶礼雅语》是汉语与葡萄牙语（Portugallia，“播都噶礼雅”）的双语词汇集，共五册，收词 2 077 条。其“香药门”中收录了：“Asafetida 阿魏：阿萨弗氏达”（见图八）[②]。很显然，阿魏的名称 Asafetida 源自阿魏的拉丁语名称 Assafaetida。

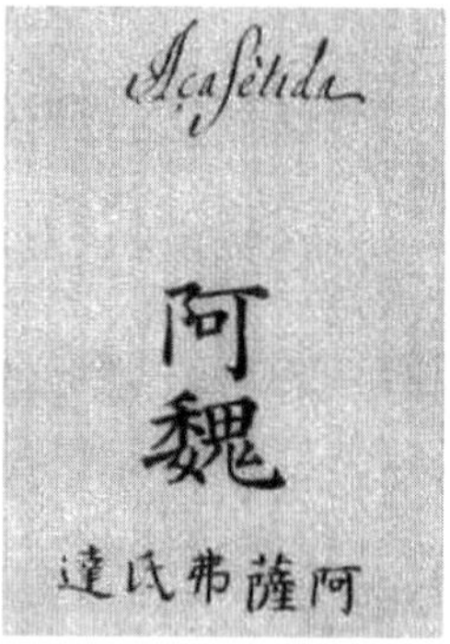

图八 《播都噶礼雅语》中的阿魏

图九 《伊达礼雅语》中的阿魏

其四，《伊达礼雅语》是汉语与意大利语（Italia，“伊达礼雅”）的双语词汇集，共五册，收词 2 070 条。其“香药门”中收录了：“assa fetida 阿魏：阿斯萨佛氏达”（见图九）[③]。同样

① 《拉氏诺语》（第五册），收入《故宫博物院藏乾隆年编华夷译语》，第十八卷，第 447 页。
② 《播都噶礼雅语》（第五册），收入《故宫博物院藏乾隆年编华夷译语》，第十七卷，第 447 页。
③ 《伊达礼雅语》（第五册），收入《故宫博物院藏乾隆年编华夷译语》，第十五卷，第 447 页。

地，阿魏的意大利语名称直接使用了对应的拉丁语之名。

其五，《弗喇安西雅语》是汉语与法语（Francia，“弗喇安西雅”）的双语词汇集，共五册，收词 2 046 条。其“香药门”中收录了：“Larme de Laser 阿魏：拉呼墨德拉塞呼”（见图十）①。Larme de Laser 一词或许与拉丁语 Laser 有关，其意义有待细考。

图十 《弗喇安西雅语》中的阿魏

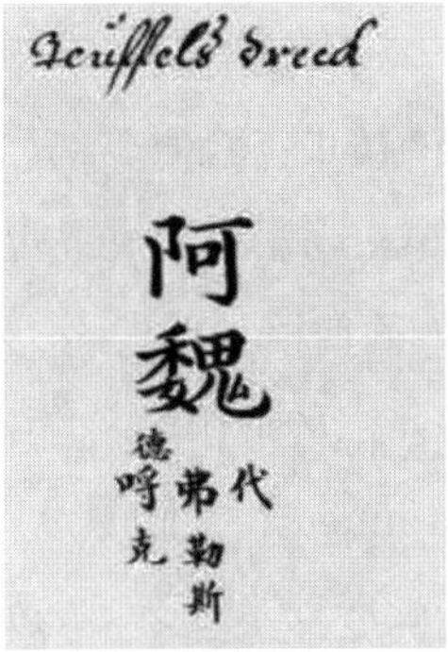

图十一 《额呼马尼雅语》中的阿魏

其六，德籍耶稣会士魏继晋（Florian Bahr，1706—1771）编纂的《额呼马尼雅语》，是一部汉德（Germania，“额呼马尼雅”）双语词汇表，也有五册，共收词 2 071 条，其内容反映了当时清代仍然秉承的“朝贡体系”的观念。② 西洋馆《额呼马尼雅语》的“香药门”中收录了“Teuffels Dreck 阿魏：代弗勒斯德呼克”（见图十一）③。“Teuffels Dreck”意为“魔鬼的污垢”，即“鬼屎”，属于近代中期德语（1650—1800），现代德语词形写作“Teufelsdreck”。可见阿魏的德语名称源自对其特性的描述——“性臭”，即味道极其难闻，而没有使用其对应的拉丁语名称。

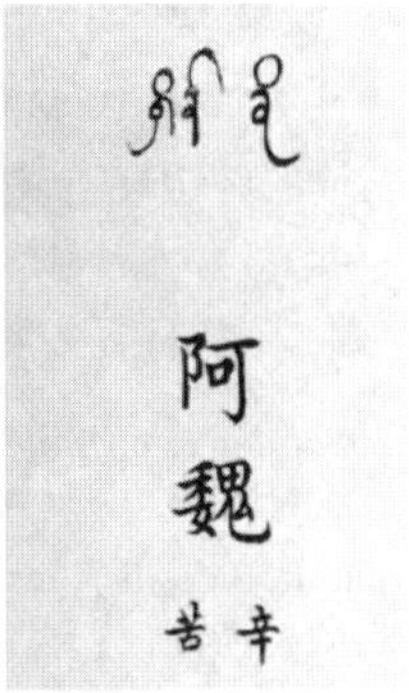

图十二 《缅甸番书》
第四册中的阿魏

图十三 ***A Comparative Vocabulary of the Burma, Malay and Thai Languages*** 中的阿魏名称

---

① 《弗喇安西雅语》（第五册），收入《故宫博物院藏乾隆年编华夷译语》，第十四卷，第 447 页。

② 李雪涛：《〈华夷译语〉丁种本与〈额呼马尼雅语〉之研究》，《中国文化》2021 年第 1 期，第 197—218 页。

③ 魏继晋：《额呼马尼雅语》（第五册），收入《故宫博物院藏乾隆年编华夷译语》，第十六卷，第 447 页。

20：辛苦

故宫博物院所藏乾隆年编《华夷译语》系列中有《缅甸番书》，该书第四册中的“香药门”，列出了“shein kho ：阿魏：辛苦”（见图十二）①。该处的“辛苦”是阿魏缅甸语的音译，读作 çein k‘o，来源于巴利语（或梵语）hiṅgu。因此，切不可依据“辛苦”的字面意来理解该词。阿魏在古缅甸语中写作 hinkiw（对应梵语 hiṅgu），现代缅甸语中写作 rhin:khui②，这说明缅甸阿魏的名称及用法亦来自印度。1810 年的《缅甸语、马来语和泰语比较词汇集》（*A Comparative Vocabulary of the Burma, Malay and Thai Languages*）中，第 540 条为四个语种（缅甸语、马来语、泰语和英语）的阿魏名称（见图十三）③。其中，缅甸语的名称为 çein k‘o④，马来语名称为 Inggu。泰语名称为 mahá-hing，可见该词来源于巴利语（或梵语）mahā-hiṅgu（大阿魏）。1905 年，杰拉德（P.N.Gerrard）的《马来语医学术语词典》（*A Vocabulary of Malay Medical Terms*）收录了“Assafoetida”一词并以“Inggu”注释之⑤，这说明阿魏在马来语中的名称从明代保留了下来，没有新的变化。约翰 · 吉莱特（John D.Gimlette）的《马来亚医学词典》（*A Dictionary of Malayan Medicine*）中解释了阿魏的名称、产地及药用，提到其相关的名称有 hinggu、inggu、Asafoetida 和波斯语 *Anghozeh*。⑥

21：阿咱喳、七（士）姑、阿魏

故宫博物院所藏乾隆年编《华夷译语》系列中有《猓猡译语》五种。《猓猡译语》是云南东川府等地采录的彝汉双语词汇集。其中的“香药门”也列出了阿魏的多种译语。

其一，《猓猡译语》（第二册）的“香药门”中，列出了“a^{33}-dzo^{33}-tʂo^{33} ：阿魏：阿咱喳”（见图十四）⑦。

其二，《猓猡译语》（第三册）的“香药门”，列出了“tshi^{33}-gɔ^{11} ：阿魏：七姑”（见图

---

①《缅甸番书》（第四册），收入《故宫博物院藏乾隆年编华夷译语》，第十二卷，第 291 页。

② Gordon H. Luce, Bo-Hmu Ba Shin and U Tin Oo, *Old Burma: Early Pagan*, Volume Two: *Catalogue of Plates, Indexes*, (Artibus Asiae. Supplementum, Vol.25), 1970, p.36.

③ *A Comparative Vocabulary of the Burma, Malay and Thai Languages,* Serampore: Printed at the Mission Press, 1810, p.38. 感谢北京大学外国语学院东南亚系张哲博士、南亚系吴小红同学帮忙转写阿魏的缅甸语、马来语词形。

④ 张哲认为，该词的发音接近汉语的“央匮”，而它的另外一个缅文发音是 hein go。可见，阿魏的缅甸语词形或源自巴利语或梵语（hiṅgu）。

⑤ P.N.Gerrard, *A Vocabulary of Malay Medical Terms*, Singapore: Kelly & Walsh Limited Printers, Reprinted 1933, p.5.

⑥ John D.Gimlette, *A Dictionary of Malayan Medicine*, edited and completed by H.W.Thomson, London. New York, Toronto: Oxford University Press, 1939, p.82, 85.

⑦《猓猡译语》（第二册），收入《故宫博物院藏乾隆年编华夷译语》，第五卷，第 248 页。

十五）①。笔者怀疑，此处的“七姑”乃“士姑”之误，有可能来自藏语。

图十四 《猓猡译语》（第二册）中的阿魏

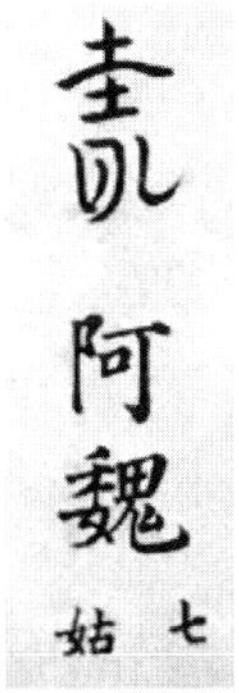

图十五 《猓猡译语》（第三册）中的阿魏

其三，《猓猡译语》（第四册）的“香药门”，列出了“a^{33}-vi^{2}(ve^{33})：阿魏：阿魏”（见图十六）②。

其四，《猓猡译语》（第五册）的“香药门”，列出了“a^{33}-$və^{55}$：阿魏：阿魏”（见图十七）③。后两个彝文词“阿魏”无疑来自汉语。据胡素华教授指点，以上四个彝文词的前两个是意译，后两个是汉语阿魏的音译。第一个词的三个词素的意思分别为“阿”“吃”“畏”。第二个词的两个词素的意思分别为“药”“成熟”，可见“$tshi^{33}$-$gɔ^{11}$”意思或为“成熟的药”。

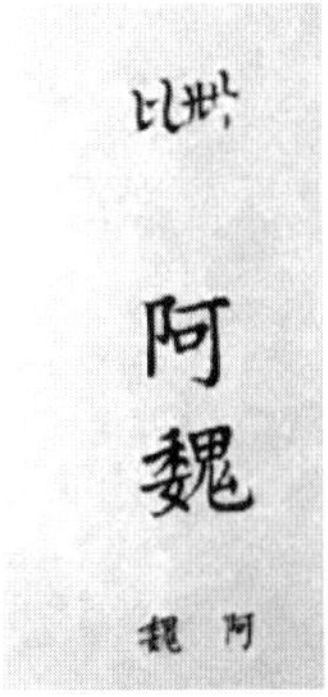

图十六 《猓猡译语》（第四册）中的阿魏

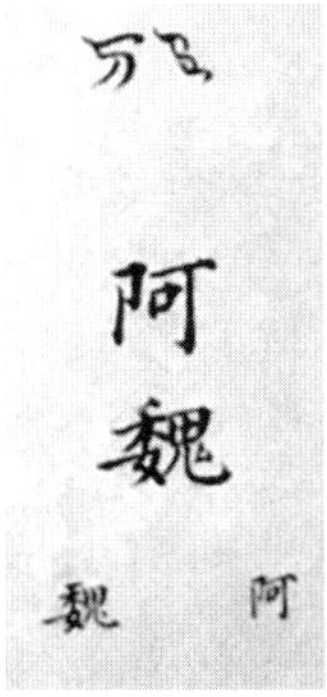

图十七 《猓猡译语》（第五册）中的阿魏

22：盛棍、升官、舍贵、升桂、身股；阿魏里；支达

乾隆十五年（1750 年）西番馆重新编撰刊印的《西番译语》记录了四川西部、北部的

---

①《猓猡译语》（第三册），收入《故宫博物院藏乾隆年编华夷译语》，第五卷，第 458 页。

②《猓猡译语》（第四册），收入《故宫博物院藏乾隆年编华夷译语》，第六卷，第 150 页。

③《猓猡译语》（第五册），收入《故宫博物院藏乾隆年编华夷译语》，第六卷，第 360 页。感谢中央民族大学胡素华教授在猓猡语转写方面提供的帮助！

多种地方方言。聂鸿音、孙伯君编著《〈西番译语〉校录及汇编》一书中的“阿魏”条下列了十种西番语中的读音，抄录如下：

英语释义　asafoetida
松藩　shing kun　盛棍
象鼻高山　’po be red　阿魏里
草地　shing kun　盛棍
木坪　shing kun　升官
打箭炉　shing kun　舍贵
木里　shing kun　盛棍
白马　’o ’od reg　阿魏
多续　kri tan　支达
栗苏　shing kun　升桂
嘉绒　shing kun　身股[①]

这些地方语言中的阿魏，尽管汉译名的用字和读音有所不同，但“盛棍”“升官”“舍贵”“升桂”“身股”等五个词语应是源自通用的藏语词 shing kun（šiṅ-kun），[②] 而该藏语词无疑来自梵语 hiṅgu。白马的“阿魏”一名直接来自汉语，而象鼻高山的“阿魏里”一词或许也是源自汉语。只有多续地区的“支达”一名来源不明。从使用的时间来看，这些译名所对应的地方语词汇远远早于《西番译语》新定本成书时的乾隆年间。

23：施^昂沽^安、陞官

故宫博物院所藏乾隆年修订的《西番译语》本，共有九种。其中的“香药门”所收录的阿魏的藏汉对照词语，与上述聂鸿音、孙伯君编著的《〈西番译语〉校录及汇编》中的十个地区的阿魏名称并不完全相同。现梳理如下：

其一，第一种《西番译语》（第一册）的“香药门”，列出了“shing kun ཤིང་ཀུན: 阿魏：施^昂沽^安”（见图十八）[③]。“施沽”与前述的“盛棍”“升官”“舍贵”“升桂”“身股”所指相同，对应藏语 shing kun。

其二，《西番译语》（第二册），其中的“香药门”列出了“’so be rid འསོ་བེ་རིད: 阿魏：阿魏

① 聂鸿音、孙伯君编著：《〈西番译语〉校录及汇编》，社会科学文献出版社 2010 年版，第 335 页。
② 劳费尔著、林筠因译：《中国伊朗编》，第 188 页。
③《西番译语》（第五册），收入《故宫博物院藏乾隆年编华夷译语》，第一卷，第 354 页。

里"（见图十九）[1]。

图十八 《西番译语》（第五册）中的阿魏

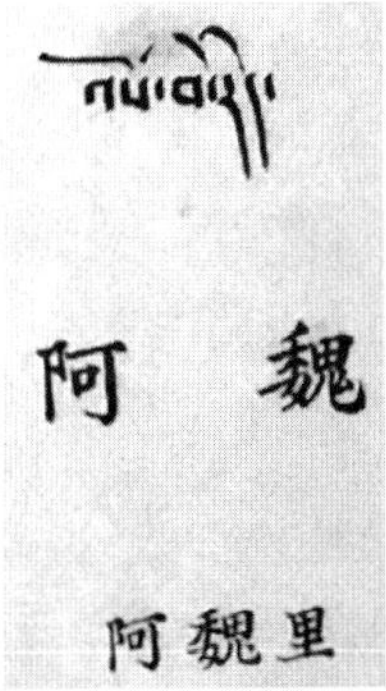

图十九 《西番译语》（第二册）中的阿魏

其三，《西番译语》（第三册），其中的"香药门"列出了"shing kun ཤིང་ཀུན：阿魏：身股"（见图二十）[2]。

其四，《西番译语》（第四册），其中的"香药门"，列出了"'o 'od rig འོ་འོད་རིག：阿魏：阿魏"（见图二十一）[3]。

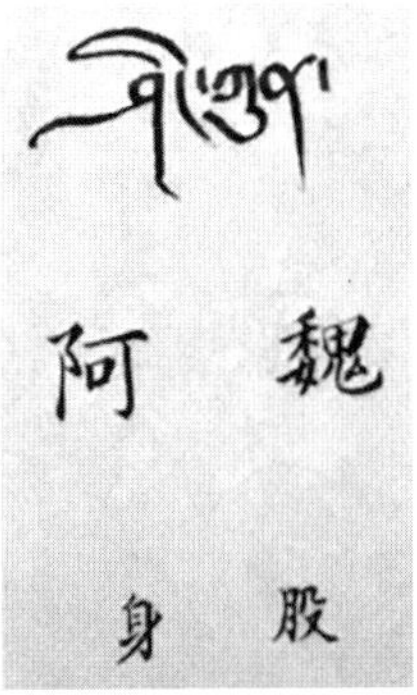

图二十 《西番译语》（第三册）中的阿魏

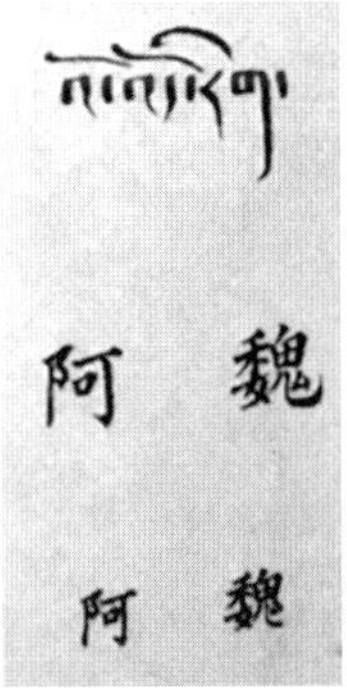

图二十一 《西番译语》（第四册）中的阿魏

其五，《西番译语》（第五册），其中的"香药门"，列出了"shing kun ཤིང་ཀུན：阿魏：升桂"（见图二十二）[4]。

其六，《西番译语》（第六册），其中的"香药门"，列出了"shing kun ཤིང་ཀུན：阿魏：陞官"（见图二十三）[5]。

---

①《西番译语》（第二册），收入《故宫博物院藏乾隆年编华夷译语》，第二卷，第 366 页。
②《西番译语》（第三册），收入《故宫博物院藏乾隆年编华夷译语》，第二卷，第 578 页
③《西番译语》（第四册），收入《故宫博物院藏乾隆年编华夷译语》，第三卷，第 152 页。
④《西番译语》（第五册），收入《故宫博物院藏乾隆年编华夷译语》，第三卷，第 364 页。
⑤《西番译语》（第六册），收入《故宫博物院藏乾隆年编华夷译语》，第三卷，第 576 页。

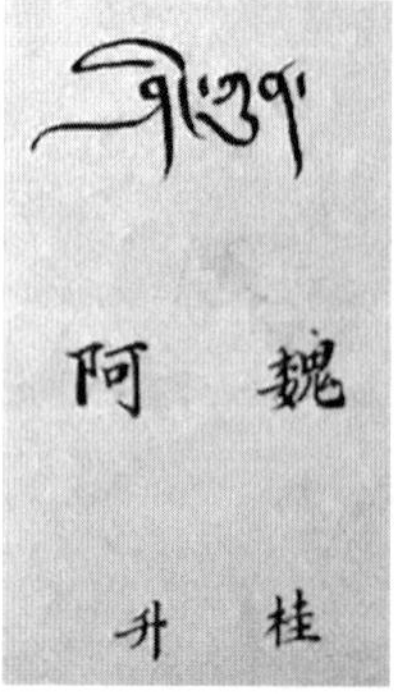

图二十二 《西番译语》（第五册）中的阿魏

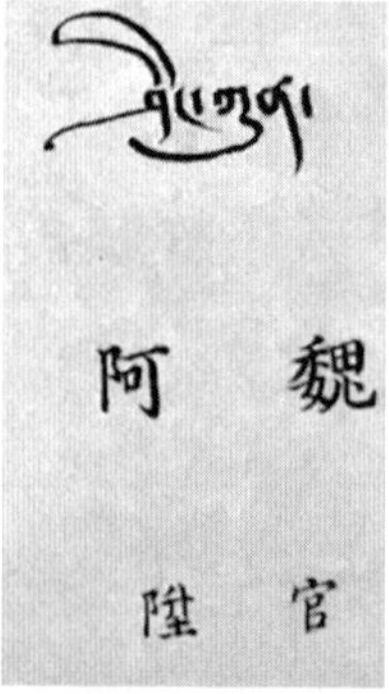

图二十三 《西番译语》（第六册）中的阿魏

其七，打箭炉的《西番译语》（第七册），其中的“香药门”，列出了“shing gun ཤིང་ཀུན：阿魏：舍贵”（见图二十四）[①]。

其八，建昌道《西番译语》（第八册），其中的“香药门”，列出了“kri tan ཀྲི་ཏན：阿魏：支达”（见图二十五）[②]。

其九，建昌道《西番译语》（第九册），其中的“香药门”，列出了“shing gun ཤིང་ཀུན：阿魏：盛棍”（见图二十六）[③]。

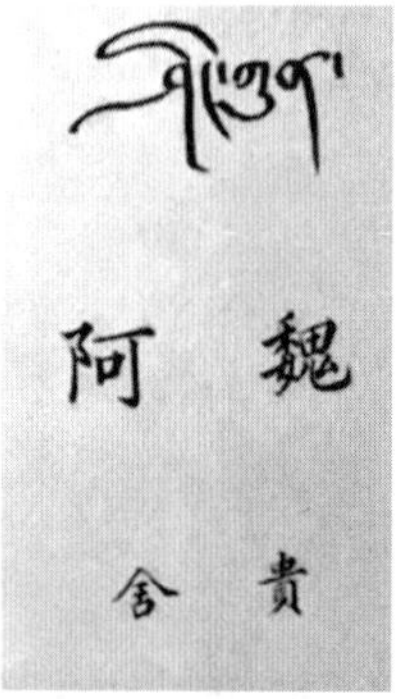

图二十四 《西番译语》（第七册）中的阿魏

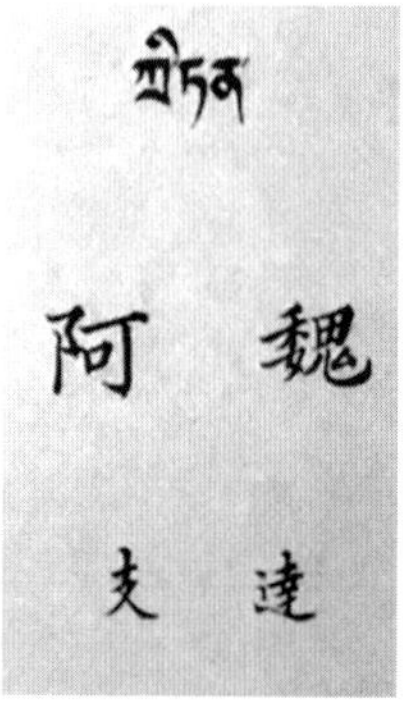

图二十五 《西番译语》（第八册）中的阿魏

图二十六 《西番译语》（第九册）中的阿魏

以上多个地区的《西番译语》的阿魏名称，有不同的词源，其中，“施[昂]沽[安]”“身股”“阿魏”“升桂”“陞官”“舍贵”“盛棍”，来自藏语词 shing kun（shing gun）。而“阿魏里”（'so be rid）、“支达”（kri tan）的词源待考。

---

①《西番译语》（第七册），收入《故宫博物院藏乾隆年编华夷译语》，第四卷，第 154 页。

②《西番译语》（第八册），收入《故宫博物院藏乾隆年编华夷译语》，第四卷，第 366 页。

③《西番译语》（第九册），收入《故宫博物院藏乾隆年编华夷译语》，第四卷，第 578 页。感谢北京大学萨尔吉教授在藏语转写方面提供的帮助！

24：辛固、胜棍

除《西番译语》之外，清代一些藏学文献中也收录了阿魏一词的多种地方读音。萧腾麟于乾隆八年（1743 年）撰成《西藏见闻录》（二卷本），该书卷下有“方语”454 个，其中收录了“阿魏辛固”“牛黄翁布楼”等药名。① 马揭、盛绳祖纂修的《卫藏图识》刊刻于乾隆五十七年（1792 年），所载《蛮语》分为天文等十九类，共收 473 个词语，其中的“香药门”有“阿魏：胜棍 shing kun”和“牛黄：吉望 gi wang”等十二种药名。② 周蔼联（1757—1828）的《竺国纪游》（《西藏纪游》）刊印于嘉庆九年（1804 年），其卷四也采录了“蛮语”，其中包括“阿魏曰胜棍”“牛黄曰吉望”等药名，其内容与《卫藏图识》相同。③ 清代姚莹的《康辖纪行》（原名《康卫纪行》）于 1846 年撰成，其卷五的《番尔雅》条目乃是采录《卫藏图识》中的《蛮语》而成。《番尔雅》亦分十九篇，其中的《释药》收录了十二种药名，包括“胜棍，阿魏也”和“吉望，牛黄也”。④

黄沛翘在光绪十一年（1885 年）纂辑《西藏图考》，其卷六“藏事续考”共有“天时”“地理”“人事”“物产”四类，各类亦有“蛮语附”。其中包括了“阿魏胜棍”和“牛黄吉望”等十数种药名，⑤ 其内容亦与《卫藏图识》《康輶纪行》相同。周懋琦的《西域释名》于光绪十二至十九年（1886—1893）成书，所收药物类名称十二种——朱砂、牛黄、黄丹、白芨、甘草、阿魏、豆蔻、杏仁、冰片、沉香、檀香、藏香，也有“牛黄谓之吉望”“阿魏谓之胜棍”等释义，⑥ 当是来自《卫藏图识》《康辖纪行》等书。

上述诸书中“蛮语附”所列的词语可能来自《西番译语》之类著作。“辛固”“胜棍”与“盛棍”的发音相同，也是藏语 šiṅ-kun（shing kun）的音译形式。

六、日本江户时期兰学文献中的阿魏译名

25：Duivelsdrek、Assafoetida/ 阿魏

在大航海时代之后，来自西洋的物品和知识逐渐流入东方。作为远洋贸易物品之一的阿

---

① 萧腾麟：《西藏见闻录》卷下，中央民族学院图书馆编印 1978 年版，第 15 页。另见王宝红：《清代藏学汉文文献词汇研究》，中国社会科学出版社 2016 年版，第 89—107 页。

② 转引自王宝红：《清代藏学汉文文献词汇研究》，第 107—127 页，其中的“香药门”见第 122—123 页。

③ 周蔼联：《竺国纪游》，文海出版社 1977 年版，第 263 页。

④ 姚莹著、欧阳跃峰整理：《康辖纪行》，中华书局 2014 年版，第 133 页。

⑤ 黄沛翘编：《西藏图考》，文海出版社 1965 年版，第 377 页。

⑥ 周懋琦：《西域释名》，载林圣智主编《“中研院”历史语言研究所傅斯年图书馆藏未刊稿钞本 · 经部 27》，“中研院”史语所 2017 年版，第 437 页。李贞德老师提供该书资料，特此感谢！

魏，其西洋语种的名称也被东西方学者记录下来。江户时代（1603—1867）之前的日本汉语医书中对阿魏的记载，基本上是承袭中国中医本草与医方著作。进入江户时期，以兰医学为代表的很多的欧洲医学知识陆续传入日本。兰学书籍中不时出现阿魏的身影。此时，阿魏之名及其知识不再仅仅与波斯、印度和中国有关，还与远在西洋的欧洲有关。

日本江户时期的几本兰学词典收录了阿魏一词。比如，藤林普山（1781—1836）的《增补改正译键》中有“Duivelsdrek：阿魏”，后来广田宪宽（1818—1888）对之进行补正后仍然有“Duivelsdrek. z.m.：阿魏”一词。桂川国宁（1797—1844）的《兰日对译药物名汇》（*Medicyne stoffe naamen*）中也有“DuiversDrek：阿魏”词条，① 此处的第 1 个“r”字母应该是“l”之笔误。宇田川榕菴（1798—1846）编的《博物语汇》（自笔本）中也收录了“Duivels Drek：阿魏”。这几处收录的都是荷兰语的阿魏名称，即 Duivelsdrek，也写作 Duyvels Drek。《兰疗药解》中列出了“Duyvel Sdrek 阿魏：主效解肉积、杀诸虫也”，但未列出 Duyvel Sdrek 的音译词形。《兰疗药解》是对由荷兰人阿米的尔法编写、广川獬翻译的《兰疗方》中的药物进行解释。可见，阿魏的荷兰语名称在日本同样有不同的写法。

1872 年，中村雄吉的《普英通语对译》收录了四种文字（英文、日耳曼文、汉文、日文）的词语，其中的“通商货类”下列有“Assafoetida，阿魏，Teufelsdreck”②。奥山虎章的《医语类聚》（*A Medical Vocabulary in English and Japanese*）中亦有“Assafoetida，阿魏”③。Assafoetida 本是拉丁语的阿魏名，后成为英语常用的阿魏名。

26：铎乙歇儿牒列吉、铎乙歇儿斯牒列吉、跕乌歇儿斯牒列吉、窋靫夫低达、铎乙歇儿斯私多笼多、鬼屎、窋鹿低多、安底咄、窋靫、因臼、因瓦剌、安宙邓、盎杰荡、盎技窋动、蜡泄儿、泄乙非乌模

就阿魏而言，大槻磐水（大槻玄泽，1757—1827）翻译的《兰畹摘芳》（1790 年抄本）中的记载尤其值得关注。大槻玄泽首先介绍了和（荷）兰船舶上的阿魏：

> 和兰舶上有铎乙歇儿牒列吉（Duivelsdrek/Duyvelsdrek）者，鉴其品性极臭，而能止臭。汉人所谓阿魏是也。彼土古今所说，或木或草，纷纷不一定，盖此以舶来之远物，多伪造者。今考和兰本草及医方诸书，此物亚细亚洲诸地产焉。就中出西利亚国（Syria）者为上好，即采其土产蜡泄儿必丢模（Laserpitium）按白芷、马芹种类之草根，捣烂而榨液汁，日干者也。其脂液者，亚蜡皮亚（Arabia）人谓之窋鹿低多（Altiht,

① 早稻田大学图书馆藏桂川国宁在文化七年（1810 年）的自笔本《兰日对译药物名汇》（*Medicyne stoffe naamen*）上册。

② 中村雄吉：『普英通語対訳』，丸善書店，1872 年，第三十九叶。

③ 奥山虎章：『医語類聚』，名山閣，1872 年，第 20 页。

> 即阿拉伯语 Haltit），又名安底咄（Anjuden?），又名它靫（Assa）也。印度人谓之因白（Ingu，即梵语 hingu），又名因瓦剌（Inguva，即 Bombay 的地方语名称 Hingra）。按：天竺国呼为形虞，《涅槃经》谓之央匮，李氏所录与之音相近。又其滴凝坚固者，土人曰安宙邓（Anjuden），又名盎杰荡（Anjudan），又名盎技它动（Anjoodan）。按：《唐本草》阿魏，又波斯国呼为阿虞。共下略此语尾音者也。犹音译亚卢会呼为芦荟也。和兰国药局谓之它靫夫低达（Assafoetida）。夫低达（Foetida）者，罗甸语（Latin）污臭之义，因其香不可堪闻所名云。又单称它靫（Assa），罗甸名蜡泄儿（Laser），又名泄乙非乌模（Silphium），独乙都国[①]谓之跕乌歇儿斯牒列吉（Teufelsdreck），和兰谓之铎乙歇儿斯私多笼多（Duivels Durt），又名铎乙歇儿斯牒列吉（Duivelsdrek）。共按其名义，鬼屎（Devil's shit / Devil's dung）之义也。是其气味有奇臭故也……[②]

《兰畹摘芳》此段落中出现了阿魏在梵语、阿拉伯语、拉丁语、荷兰语、德语等不同语言中的名称。其中，“铎乙歇儿牒列吉”或“铎乙歇儿斯牒列吉”是阿魏的荷兰语 Duivels Drek 的音译，阿魏的瑞典语名称也是 Dyvelstrack；“跕乌歇儿斯牒列吉”应该是德语 Teuffels Dreck 的音译；“它靫夫低达”则是拉丁文和英文 Assafoetida 的音译。“鬼屎”是阿魏在西方的绰号，因为阿魏具有奇臭的味道。大槻玄泽笔下阿魏的这些音译词基本上由他自己选定，而未能有条件去参考乾隆年间的《华夷译语》丁种本中相关的音译形式。另外，大槻玄泽的按语“天竺国呼为形虞，《涅槃经》谓之央匮”，与明末张自烈的《正字通》中的解说“阿魏，波斯国呼为阿虞，天竺国呼为形虞，《涅槃经》谓之央匮”，基本相似。然而，如前所说，在今本《大般涅槃经》中，“央匮”一词踪迹皆无。经检索中华电子佛典协会（CBETA），“央匮”一词也不见于任何一部汉译佛经。显然，“央匮”要么是误写的词形，要么是一个当时使用而后世消失的词语。

七、晚清前后双语辞书与医籍中的阿魏译名

在鸦片战争之前，由于传教士和商人等欧洲人的陆续进入，为了双方沟通和交流的方便，中国也相继出现了中西双语的辞书。此后，由于战争的影响和商业的作用，中西双语辞书的种类和规模逐渐增加。在这些辞书中，虽然没有像《兰畹摘芳》那样同时出现多语种的

① “独乙都国”或许可对应“Deutsch”“Deutschland”，即德国。

② 大槻玄泽：《兰畹摘芳》，收入肖永芝主编《考事撮要（节选） 兰畹摘芳 本草补》，北京科学技术出版社 2017 年版，第 171—172 页。

阿魏名称，但也有不少西方语言的阿魏名称或者相应的音译名。现将其简要梳理如下：

27：爹部地丁、雅是花利地

不列颠图书馆藏 Or.7428 抄本《华英通用杂话》（*Chinese and English Vocabulary*），是 19 世纪中期用于日常会话与贸易的双语辞书。该抄本中的“入口各项货物门”，列出了“阿魏：爹部地丁、雅是花利地”一条。[①]“爹部地丁”并不是阿魏的英文名称的音译，可能是德文名 Teufelsdreck 的音译。“雅是花利地”则可能是阿魏植物的拉丁文或英文名称 Assafoetida 的音译。

28：哑沙父啲[口遞]

1860 年，子卿原著、福沢谕吉（子囲，1834—1901）译的《增订华英通语》中的“通商货类”收录了“阿魏：哑沙父啲[口遞]、Asafoetida。”[②]“哑沙父啲[口遞]”是阿魏的拉丁语或英语名 Asafoetida 的音译。

29：阿魏非罗拉、真弟司故能阿魏、恒其息

近代中医典籍中很少见到阿魏的有关译语，只有少量汉译西医著作中提到阿魏的译语信息。1887 年，傅兰雅（John Fryer，1839—1928）与赵元益（字静涵，1840—1902）翻译了由英国人来拉（John Forbes Royle，1798—1858）初撰、海得兰（Frederick William Headland，1830—1875）和哈来（John Harley）补充的《西药大成》（*A Manual of Materia Medica and Therapeutics*），其中卷五之二的“阿魏”条体现了航海时代以来西方植物学界、药物学界对该药认知的极大进步。该书中有关阿魏的名称论述如下：

> 古时梵文谓之阿米拉苦萨（Amera Cosha）。……近有植物学家在彼处查此草，谓之西勒非恩他坡西阿（Thapsia silphium）。……阿非色那（Avicenna）云：乌勒弟脱（hulteet）质有两种。……刚伯法（Kaempfer）名曰弟司故能阿魏（Assafoetida Disgunensis）……立尼由司（Linnaeus）名曰阿魏非罗拉（Ferula Asafoetida）。……以上所言之草，余以为必是真弟司故能阿魏（Asafoetida disgunensis），即刚伯法书中所谓恒其息（Hingiseh）。[③]

---

① 内田慶市、沈国威編著：『言語接触とピジン——19 世紀の東アジア（研究と復刻資料）』，白帝社 2009 年版，第 335 页。

② 子卿著、福沢谕吉译：《增订华英通语》，日本早稻田大学图书馆藏快堂藏板万延元年（1860 年）版，第二十七叶。

③ 来拉、海得兰撰，傅兰雅、赵元益译：《西药大成》，江南制造局翻译馆译本，卷五之二，第 106 页。

“阿非色那”（Avicenna）指中古伊斯兰医学家伊本·西那（Ibn Sina）。刚伯法（Engelber Kaempfer，1651—1716）是亲身游历过东方的德国学者，他有一本拉丁文著作《*Amoentitatum Exoticarum*》，音译名为《乞木尼答跕斯》（*Amoentitatum*），意译名称有多种，比如《外国植物书》《海外珍闻录》等，是一部“集录印度、支那、日本等物产书也”。立尼由司”（Linnaeus，即 Carl Linnaeus；Carolus Linnaeus）是指著名植物学家林奈（Carl von Linné），这是他受封为贵族之前的原名。“乌勒弟脱”（hulteet）源自阿拉伯语中阿魏的名称 Haltit、Hiltut，“恒其息”则是阿魏的德语词形 Hingiseh 的音译。此处的“西勒非恩他坡西阿”（Thapsia silphium）乃植物水飞蓟，与阿魏无关。

30：阿虚

1890 年，晚清美国医学传教士洪士提反（S. A. Hunter）编译的《万国药方》卷三中的“Asafoetida 阿魏”条，提到“阿魏，又名阿虚。此药原产印度之阿弗干，取该树之汁制成，酒与水均能提出功力，色红黄而白，味苦而辛，其臭颇烈”①。此处的“阿虚”之名或许就是 assa 的音译。

31：中西双语辞书与医药文献中的阿魏

明末清初以来，随着西人入华逐渐增多，中西语言交流成为新的趋势，中西双语辞书的编纂也成为必然。就阿魏一词的出现情况而言，值得注意的是，这些双语辞书基本上是采用了“阿魏”这一词语形式，而较少有其他的汉语音译形式。现将目前笔者能查阅到的相关辞书与医药文献中的阿魏词条，梳理如下：

1822 年，马礼逊（Robert Morrison，1782—1834）的《华英字典》（*A Dictionary of the Chinese Language: in three parts*），有“Asafoetida, 阿魏，o kwei”。②1828 年，马礼逊《广东省土话字汇》（*Vocabulary of the Canton Dialect*）中也有“Assafoetida: 阿魏，o gei”一条。③ 1865 年，马礼逊《五车韵府》云：“阿魏，O wei, assafoetida。”④

1831 年，葡籍汉学家江沙维神父（Joaquim Affonso Goncalves，1781—1841）在澳门出版了《洋汉合字汇》（*Diccionario Portuguez-China*），该书中有词条“Assa Fetida: 阿魏”，此处列出了葡萄牙语的阿魏名称为 Assa Fetida。⑤

---

① 洪士提反：《万国药方》，光绪二十四年（1898 年）上海美华书局第三次重镌本，卷三，第 106 页。

② R.Morrison, *A Dictionary of the Chinese Language: in three parts*, Part III. London, 1822, p.30.

③ Robert Morrison, *Vocabulary of the Canton Dialect*, Macao, China: The Honorable East India Company's Press, 1828.

④ Robert Morrison, *A Dictionary of the Chinese Language* (《五车韵府》), Vol.2, Shanghae: London Mission Press. London: Trubner & Co., 1865, p.107.

⑤ Joaquim Affonso Goncalves, *Diccionario Portuguez-China* (《洋汉合字汇》), Macao, 1831, p.73.

1841年，美国来华新教传教士裨治文（E.C.Bridgman, 1801—1861）的《广东方言汇编》（*A Chinese Chrestomathy in the Canton Dialect*）或《广东方言撮要》中有一句话："Asafoetida is brought from Persian. 阿魏出波斯国。O ngai chut Po csz' kwok。" ① 与阿魏对应的也是Asafoetida。

1844年，卫三畏（Samuel Wells Williams, 1812—1884）在澳门出版的第二版《中国商业指南》（*A Chinese Commercial Guide*）中记载的中国进口商品目录（按字母顺序排列）的第一种就是"Assafoetida, 阿魏 *o wei*"。②

1847—1848年，麦都思（Walter Henry Medhurst, 1796—1857）的《英华字典》（或称《英汉字典》, *English and Chinese Dictionary*）有"Asafoetida, 阿魏 o wei" ③, 其相应的手抄本则有"Asafoetida：阿魏" ④。

1858年，英国入华传教士合信（Benjamin Hobson，1816—1873）的《医学英华字释》（*A Medical Vocabulary in English and Chinese*）的"药品目录"中列出了"Assafoetida 阿魏" ⑤。

1859年，英国入华传教士湛约翰（John Chalmers，1825—1899）编纂的《英粤字典》（*An English and Cantoese Pocket Dictionary*）中，收录了"Asafætida 阿魏 *oh*-ngai`" ⑥ 这一词条。

1866年，罗存德（Wilhelm Lobscheid, 1822—1893）的《英华字典》（*English and Chinese Dictionary with the Punti and Mandarin Pronunciation*）第一册也记载有"Asafoetida 阿魏 o ngai. O wei"和"Assafoetida, see Asafoetida" ⑦。

1871年，司登得（George Carter Stent, 1833—1884）的《汉英合璧相连字汇》（*A Chinese and English Vocabulary in the Pekinese Dialect*）收录了"a^1 wei^4 阿魏：Assafoetida" ⑧。

1872年，卢公明（Justus Doolittle, 1824—1880）的《英华萃林韵府》（*Vocabulary and Hand-book of the Chinese Language*）也有三个词条："Asafaedita，阿魏 a wei"，"Pill of assafoetida, 阿魏丸 o wei wan"和"Assafoetida Tincture, 阿魏酒 o wei chiu" ⑨。

---

① E.C.Bridgman, *A Chinese Chrestomathy in the Canton Dialect,* Macao: S. Wells Williams, 1841, p.200.

② Samuel Wells Williams, *A Chinese Commercial Guide*, Second Edition, Macao, 1844, p.152.

③ Walter Henry Medhurst, *English and Chinese Dictionary*, Shanghae: Printed at the Mission Press, 1847-1848, p.75.

④ 早稻田大学图书馆藏日本学者中村敬宇1865年的手抄本《英汉字典》（请求记号：文库08 C1021）第一册中有"Asafoetida：阿魏"。

⑤ Benjamin Hobson, *A Medical Vocabulary in English and Chinese*, Shanghae Mission Press, 1858, p.59.

⑥ John Chalmers, *An English and Cantoese Pocket Dictionary,* Hong Kong: Printed at the London Missionary Society's Press, 1859, p.7.

⑦ Wilhelm Lobscheid, *English and Chinese Dictionary with the Punti and Mandarin Pronunciation*, Part I, Hong Kong: The Daily press office, 1866, p.92, 96.

⑧ George Carter Stent, *A Chinese and English Vocabulary in the Pekinese Dialect*, Shanghai: Printed and Published at the Customs Press, 1871, p.1.

⑨ Justus Doolittle, *Vocabulary and Hand-book of the Chinese Language*, Vol.I, Foochow: Rozario, Marcal and Company, p.23, 360, 494.

1873 年，英国苏格兰长老会传教士杜嘉德（Carstairs Douglas, 1830—1877）的《厦英大辞典》（*Chinese-English Dictionary of the Vernacular of Spoken Language of Amoy*）中的“厦门口语词典”（Dictionary of the Amoy Colloquial Language）部分也有“a-gui, asafoetida”①一词，a-gui 就是阿魏的厦门语音。

1882 年，荷兰汉学家和田野博物学家施古德（G.Schlegel，1840—1903）主编的《荷华文语类参》（*Nederlandsch- Chineesch Woordenboek*）收录了“Duivelsdrek (Asafoetida) 阿魏香，o guī”②这一词条。

1883 年，麦高文（J.Macgowan, 1835—1922）编纂的《厦门方言英汉字典》（*English and Chinese Dictionary of the Amoy Dialect*）收录了“Asafoetida 阿魏，a-gūi”③这一词条。

1899 年，邝其照（1836—1891）《华英字典集成》（*An English and Chinese Dictionary*, 原名《字典集成》，有 1868 年、1875 年和 1887 年三个版本）也有“Asafoetida：阿魏”。该字典附录的“药材名目”部分中，还有“阿魏：Assafaetida”④。

1901 年，上海基督教方言学会编纂的《英汉上海方言词典》（新版名《晚清民初沪语英汉词典》）中，也有“Asafoetida，阿魏：ah-we^{0}”⑤一词。

1903 年，法国传教士路易·奥巴扎克（L.Aubazac, 1871—1919）编著出版的《法粤字典》（新版改名《晚清民初粤语法汉词典》）收录了“Assa-foetida: 阿魏，o^{1} ngai$_{3}$”⑥。

1908 年，颜惠庆（1877—1950）《英华大辞典》（*An English and Chinese Standard Dictionary*）中收录了有关阿魏的三个词条，分别为“Asafoetida, Asafetida, (as-a-fet'-e-da) n. A fetid inspissated sap from India, used in medicine. 阿魏，西药（用之以止抽筋者）”，“Devil's-dirt, (dev'ls-dirt) n. Asafoetida, 阿魏”和“Sagapenum,（sag-a-pe-num）n. A Persian gum-resin of service in medicine.（药）阿魏类，波斯树汁，波斯树胶，萨格比奴末树汁，镇痉剂用之药材”。⑦

1911 年，卫礼贤（Richard Wilhelm, 1877—1950）的《德英华文科学字典》（*Deutsch-Englisch-Chinesisches Fachwörterbuch*）有两个词条：“Ferula scorodosma f. (Steckenkraut)，阿魏”和“Teufelsdreck m. asafoetida：阿魏”。⑧

---

① Carstairs Douglas, *Chinese-English Dictionary of the Vernacular of Spoken Language of Amoy*, London, 1899, p.1.

② G.Schlegel, *Nederlandsch- Chineesch Woordenboek*（《荷华文语类参》）, Deel: I, Leiden: E.J.Brill, 1886, p.1036.

③ J.Macgowan, *English and Chinese Dictionary of the Amoy Dialect*, London: Trubner & Co., 1893, p.22.

④ 邝其照：《华英字典集成》，循环日报 1899 年版，第 22、606 页。

⑤ 上海基督教方言学会等编：《晚清民初沪语英汉词典》，上海译文出版社 2018 年版，第 52 页。

⑥ 路易·奥巴扎克编：《晚清民初粤语法汉词典》，上海译文出版社 2018 年版，第 70 页。

⑦ 颜惠庆：《英华大辞典》，上海商务印书馆 1908 年版，第 112、600、1965 页。

⑧ Richard Wilhelm, *Deutsch-Englisch-Chinesisches Fachwörterbuch*, Tsingtau: Deutsch-Chinesischen Hochschule, 1911, p.152, 540.

1912 年，翟理斯（Herbert Allen Giles，1845—1935）的《华英字典》(*Chinese–English Dictionary*）有“阿魏：asafoetida”。[①]

1913 年，商务印书馆编译所的《英华新字典》(*English and Chinese Pronouncing Condensed Dictionary*)：“Asafoetida. Asafetida, (as-a-fet'-e-da)n.（西药）阿魏。”[②]

1916 年，赫美玲（Karl Ernst Georg Hemeling, 1878—1925）的《官话》(*English–Chinese Dictionary of the Standard Chinese Spoken Language*（官话）*and Handbook for Translators*）一书中收录了五个有关阿魏的词条：“Asafoetida, n., (devil's dung or food of the gods or narthex), 阿魏。部定。a wei, 阿虞 a yü”，“Tincture of–(tincture asafetidae), 阿魏酒。部定。a wei chiu”，“Devil's dung (narthex or food of the gods), 阿魏 *o wei*”，“Food of the gods, 阿魏。部定。O wei”，以及“Narthex, n., (asafetida, devil's dung or food of the gods), 阿魏。部定。o wei”。[③]

在以上汉译的西洋药物或植物学著作，乃至晚清的各类中外双语词典中，我们搜寻了阿魏一词的相关痕迹，主要涉及了阿魏在英、德、法、葡萄牙、荷兰语等多种欧洲语言中的名称，以及该词在多个地方（广东、厦门、上海等地）方言中的发音。汉语基本上以“阿魏”为主，仅仅赫美玲的《官话》多列了“阿虞”一名。可以说，在中外双语辞书中，“阿魏”一名已经占据了绝对位置，未再被其他汉译名所动摇。

可以说，“阿魏”一词是西方现代植物学知识传入中国的一个缩影。虽然《西药大成》或《万国药方》乃至《德英华文科学字典》等文献中，均未像日本兰学著作《兰畹摘芳》那样提供诸多阿魏在西方的称呼，但是综合来看，鸦片战争前后的汉文文献论及阿魏在不同语言、地方方言中的诸多译名，仍为我们了解当时中西文化交流潮流的复杂情况提供了一个较为丰富的知识图景。

八、汉籍中对阿魏词义的误读

不论是唐代，还是明清时期。中国学者引述或修改前代著述中有关阿魏的知识时，也会出现一些误释或误读的现象。慧琳《一切经音义》中就有误释之处，该书卷三十九的“毕唎

① Herbert Allen Giles, *Chinese–English Dictionary,* Shanghai: Kelly & Walsh; London: B. Quaritch. Second edition, 1912, p.1.

② 商务印书馆编译所：《英华新字典》，上海商务印书馆 1913 年版，第 28 页。

③ Karl Ernst Georg Hemeling, *English-Chinese Dictionary of the Standard Chinese Spoken Language*（官话）*and Handbook for Translators,* Shanghai: Statistical Department of the Inspectorate General of Customs, 1916, p.75, 378, 547, 915.

祦俣”条云：“祦，音羊两反。下音隅。梵语药名，古云阿魏也。”[①]“毕唎祦俣”，另译“毕履阳愚药”等，是梵语词 priyaṅgu 的音译[②]，断非阿魏。二者绝非一物，因此慧琳的判定有误。有学者在讨论阿魏时，仅据此就认为“毕唎样俣”是指草本阿魏[③]，而并未辨析二者所对应的梵语原词，故其说难以令人信从。

明代李中立《本草原始》（1612 年）卷四对“阿魏”之名别有新解：“阿曰呢，魏曰哒，西番语也。一云：阿，我也；魏，畏也。此物极臭，阿之所畏也。《唐本草》谓之薰渠，古人谓之哈昔泥。”李中立这样拆字释名，完全是望文生义，令人不知所云。类似的，清代沈穆（字石匏）的《本草洞荃》（1661 年）中亦将“阿魏”条释为“夷人自称曰‘阿’，此物极臭，阿之所畏也”。这也是对阿魏一词的极大误读。

清代浦士贞汇辑《夕庵读本草快编》（1697 年）卷五阿魏条，虽未列举所引书名，但大部分内容抄录前人之著述，如“刘纯有云：‘阿魏无真却有真，臭而止臭乃为珍，信矣’”[④]，又如“西域人自称曰‘阿’。此物极臭，阿之所谓也”[⑤]。这样不知所云的解读，乃是袭用了沈穆《本草洞荃》中的错误，其背后或许体现了这些学者对年代久远的域外风物已不再明了却又强作解人的心态。

类似的还有《同治太湖县志》卷四十五，其中“阿魏则方音读遏”下注文字为：“阿魏出天山及博克达山，生有定期。每三年而一出。根如莱菔，取其自凝之汁，名肉阿魏，杂伪者名草阿魏，塞外呼阿魏曰遏魏。盖阿有遏音，与阿曲之阿音有别。”这一解释基本上是从汉字“阿”入手，而与该词所对应的域外词语无关，因此，所有的这些解释只能被视作臆想，显然与原词的正确含义背道而驰。

此外，由于受到波斯医学文化的影响，我国新疆维吾尔族使用阿魏较为常见。维吾尔语中的阿魏名称来自波斯语和阿拉伯语，而不是梵语或汉语。维吾尔族的医学著作《注医典》《白色宫殿》《拜地依药书》等均记载了阿魏的药性、药效。[⑥]其中，《拜地依药书》指出，“阿魏分为两种，一种气味较强，称之为‘依里特提蒙谈’；另一种气味较弱，称之为‘依里特提提依比’”。这样的分类无疑是沿袭了波斯医学的说法，但“依里特提蒙谈”和“依里特提提依比”是现代汉语中的阿魏译名，不属于古代范畴，因此本文不予讨论。

---

① 高楠顺次郎、渡边海旭、小野玄妙等编：《大正新修大藏经》第 54 册，第 560 页下栏。

② 陈明：《汉译佛经中的天竺药名札记》（四），《中医药文化》2018 年第 4 期，第 48—55 页。

③ 李曌华、王育林：《“菴罗”“紫铆”“阿魏”考释》，《中华医史杂志》2015 年第 1 期，第 7—11 页。

④ 浦士贞汇辑，贾晓君点校：《夕庵读本草快编》，收入郑金生主编《海外回归中医善本古籍丛书》，人民卫生出版社 2003 年版，第十册，第 653—654 页。

⑤ 浦士贞汇辑，贾晓君点校：《夕庵读本草快编》，收入郑金生主编《海外回归中医善本古籍丛书》，人民卫生出版社 2003 年版，第十册，第 654 页。

⑥《维吾尔药志》对阿魏的用法有详细的解释，参见刘勇民等编：《维吾尔药志》，新疆人民出版社 1986 年版。

九、藏蒙等少数民族医籍中的阿魏名称

19 世纪上半叶，蒙古族医学家占布拉道尔吉（Jam-dpal-rdo-rje, 1792—1855）用藏语撰写的《蒙药正典》（又名《美丽目饰》）中记录了阿魏，其主要内容如下：

阿魏：用大蒜修制而成的说法是有误的。《时轮大释》中云：“为宝嘎的树分泌的树脂，涂于白线可使其变蓝色。”实际此物状如萝卜，其根一半露于地上，有汁液流出，制成膏剂，黄白色，如干燥的脑髓状。气味极大，不易混淆。《历算日月轮》中云：“阿魏性重热，生巴达干。”又，《言教三十章》中云：“阿魏消化后味辛，开胃。驱虫，驱寒，清心赫依。”

【注解】阿魏：蒙古名为“乌木黑-达布日海”。为伞形科植物新疆阿魏（Ferula sinkiangensis K.M.Shen）或阜康阿魏（Ferula fukanensis K.M.Shen）的树脂。《内蒙古药材标准》收载。①

此处的“乌木黑-达布日海”，应该是阿魏在蒙古语中的现代名称。《蒙药正典》共载药六百余种，并有药图五百多幅，每种药物名称均用四种语言（蒙古、藏、满、汉）记录。其中的阿魏图形旁注有藏语和汉语“阿魏”之名（见图二十七、图二十八、图二十九）。

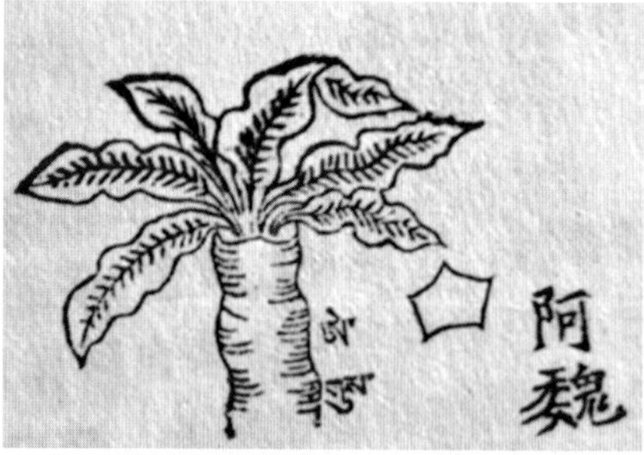

图二十七　《蒙药正典》中的阿魏图

图二十八　中国国家图书馆藏《蒙药正典》中的阿魏图

① 包哈申主编：《占布拉道尔吉与〈蒙药正典〉研究》，内蒙古教育出版社 2012 年版，第 168—169 页。

图二十九 《蒙药正典》中的阿魏（套色彩图）

上述《蒙药正典》有关阿魏的内容多来自藏语医药典籍，如帝玛尔·丹增彭措在1736年刊印的《晶珠本草》（又名《药物学广论》），该书下部《甘露药物味性功效名称广论》第二编“各类药物性能分论”第五章“树木类药物”第七节“树脂类药物”之下，列出了阿魏的内容：

阿魏，šiṅ-kun，Ferula assafoetida L.

阿魏杀虫治寒病，并且治疗心隆症。

《计算日月之轮》（*rtsis nyi zla vkhor lo*）中说：“阿魏性重、热，生培根，治疗重急隆病有良效。”《明释三十章》（*sum cu pa*）中说：“阿魏化味辛，开胃，治培隆并病，止痛，生赤巴。”巴保（dpav bo）说：“阿魏治隆病，培根病，止痛，生赤巴；化味辛，开胃，效轻；生阳化食。”让穹多吉（rang byung pa/*sman ming rgya mtsho*《药名海》）说：“阿魏治一切隆病。”本品之名有：孜吾切（rtsi bo che）、兴更 (hing gu ma)、保尔（bo kka na）、稚青（dri chen）、相苟玛（shing ku ma）。梵语（rgya nag, 汉语）中称为阿苟西尔（a ghu shir）。高昌语（khrom）中称为赫都塔（hel tu la tha）。隐语 (gab, 秘密语，黑话) 中称为孜尼（rtsi gnyis, 二汁）、脑金刚玛尔（gnod sbyin rkang mar, 药叉骨髓）。

本品分为原品和制品两种。原品，《时轮大释》中说：“阿魏原品为保嘎嘎树的树脂，可以将白线染成青色。”状如干脑，气味非常浓烈，不易搞错。或者说，阿魏是在保嘎嘎树的木皮之间，放上一块人肉，由于人肉的效力，吸收树汁，熬膏而成。也有人说，在该树的割口中，涂上人的脑髓，吸收树脂而成阿魏。制品，由蒜等烧存性，配上岩羊脑浆发酵而成，黄色或青色，气味比前者差。①

① 帝玛尔·丹增彭措著，毛继祖等译：《晶珠本草》，上海科学技术出版社2012年版，第123—124页。

《晶珠本草》中有关阿魏的记载比《蒙药正典》要复杂，但二者相关内容基本上吻合。《晶珠本草》中记载了阿魏的九种名称，即藏语五种（孜吾切、兴更、保尔、稚青、相苟玛）、梵语一种（阿苟西尔）、高昌语一种（赫都塔）、隐语二种（孜尼、脑金刚玛尔）。尽管说其中的“阿苟西尔”是梵语，但笔者推测该词更像是波斯语“阿虞截”（Anguzad）的转读。当然，这些名称的语源确定需要进一步的探求。阿魏早就传入吐蕃地区，其使用方式见于公元8世纪末期宇妥·元丹衮波编纂的《医学四续》（《四部医典》）等早期藏医学典籍，如“阿魏，功效是驱虫，医治寒性疾病、心隆病”①。在象雄语中，阿魏的名字是Shing:gun，与藏语阿魏 šiṅ-kun /shing kun 基本相同。②

十、讨论与结语

阿魏一物的名称在汉语文献中均为音译，自始至终没有出现一个意译名。经初步梳理（详见附录“阿魏的历代译名一览表”），阿魏至少有五十七个不同的译名，代表了不同时期、不同语言的传译情况。

如前所述，阿魏一物最早的汉译名并不是“阿魏”，而是“兴瞿”。阿魏之名最初应该是通过唐代的国家外事接待机构鸿胪寺中的译语人之手而传入的。官方译语人笔下的阿魏之名并不像唐代佛经那样多源自梵文本，而是来自中亚语言，它所对应的原语是吐火罗语B的 *aṅ(k)waṣ(ṭ)*。从唐初开始，“阿魏”之名才出现在汉译佛经中，多见于密教经文和义净译的律典。但在佛教语境中，“阿魏”译名对应的是梵语 hiṅgu 一词。就此而言，官方机构的译名与佛教译场的译名之间出现了交互，其间的复杂关系值得进一步厘清。就佛经译者而言，南北朝时期多用 hiṅgu 一词的音译“兴瞿”等词形，唐代玄奘法师也用“兴瞿”，该类来自梵语 hiṅgu 的音译词形，绝大部分出现在佛教语境的文献之中。

梳理上述阿魏的历代汉译名，可以得出下列四种印象：

其一，这些语词不是散乱无关的，可以看出其中有一个若隐若现的语言网络，这些不同的名称就如同遍布在网络上的节点，这些语言包括中古时期的吐火罗语B、梵语、波斯语、于阗语，以及元明时代的阿拉伯语、波斯语、藏语、蒙古语，地域上不仅涵盖西南少数民族（彝族等）地区的语言，还有东南亚的马来语、缅甸语、暹罗语（泰语）等，甚至涉及六

① 宇妥·元丹衮波著，毛继祖、马世林、罗达尚、毛韶玲译注：《医学四续》，上海科学技术出版社2012年版，第40页。

② 罗秉芬、刘英华：《象雄医学文献I.O.755试析》，收入黄福开主编《藏医药研究文集：纪念北京藏医院建院十周年》，中国藏学出版社2003年版，第239页。

种欧洲语言（英、拉丁、葡萄牙、意大利、法、德）。阿魏在这些语言中的名称相互之间存在着密切的关联。在波斯本土语言中，阿魏就有许多不同的名称，[①]这也是导致其汉译名复杂繁多的原因之一。因此，只有从纵向和横向两个层面去观察，才能形成较为完整的印象。一方面，我们既要看到在中古以来的本草著作和方剂书中，"阿魏"一名占据主导的地位，特别是到了明清之际，其他的那些汉译名基本上成了仅仅用于"博物"介绍的知识，而医疗活动中的实际使用大为减少，即便是《回回药方》中的诸多名称中也没有再现其身影；另一方面，我们也要看到在西南和西北这些非汉语族群中，该药名透过前代的语言词汇（如藏语等），将域外的背景隐藏起来加以使用。这些所谓少数民族的药物知识谱系中，也不乏与域外文化的联系，而这恰恰是以往的研究所忽略的地方。

其二，阿魏的称呼是多样的，既包括了对其叶、根、树脂和整株植物的称呼，也译介了阿魏的一些别称；中土文人还根据阿魏的药用特性，给它取了本土的绰号。这样就逐渐丰富了对阿魏这一药物的称谓，并且使其积累了更多的文化色彩。类似贯休和尚《桐江闲居》一诗咏及的"静室焚檀印，深炉烧铁瓶。茶和阿魏暖，火种柏根馨"，提升了阿魏在文人情怀中的意象之美。而五代后蜀王衍时期流行的童谣，所谓"我有一帖药，其名曰阿魏，卖与十八子"[②]，则以预告和调侃地方政治时局的方式，迅速在当地民众中加深了对阿魏药物的共同记忆。

其三，有关阿魏的这些词语的记录与传播的方式也是多样的，既有域外佛教徒的面授和翻译，如译经僧和《酉阳杂俎》中所记的摩揭陀国僧提婆（Deva）等的传授，也有对前代文献的抄录或归纳。我们要特别注意到这些词语所出现的文献涵盖了汉译佛经、中土佛教徒的著作（求法、异域地理、佛经音义、佛教辞书等）、笔记，也包括了医著（本草、方书集）、域外医书译本或编译本（《兰畹摘芳》《西药大成》《万国药方》等）、官方编撰的语言交流手册（《回回馆译语》《西番译语》《满剌加国译语》等）、西方传教士编撰的中外双语辞书等，也就是说，阿魏及其相关词语不仅出现于单纯的医学著作（本草、药方集、医学字典等），而且也在宗教、语言手册、译本、辞书等多元的语境中被记忆、使用和流通。阿魏不同译名的出现场域，也与不同地区、不同时代的文化和习俗等有密切的关系。

其四，阿魏一词在中国（甚至东亚）流传近 1 500 年，可谓岁月绵长。在漫长的时光中，其域外词源在不同时段经历了多次变化。首先，在中古以佛教为中印交流媒介的时期，阿魏一词多与天竺的梵语 hiṅgu 一词有关，依托佛经和印度、中亚的医学知识而流传。其次，在元代，随着亚洲海上丝绸之路的日渐繁盛以及伊斯兰教的传播，阿魏一词与波斯

---

① Peyman Matin, "Apotropaic plants in the Persian Folk culture," *Iran and the Caucasus*, vol.16, no.2, 2012, pp.189—200.

② 宋代吴处厚《青箱杂记》卷七对此童谣的含义有所解释："衍在蜀时，童谣曰：'我有一帖药，其名为阿魏，卖与十八子。'其后，衍兄宗弼果卖国归唐。而宗弼乃王建养子，本姓魏氏，此其应也。"见吴处厚著，李裕民注解：《青箱杂记》，中华书局 1985 年版，第 70 页。

语（anguzha、anguzhad 等）、阿拉伯语（ḥillīt）之间的关系日益密切，集中体现在《回回药方》之中。阿魏的相关词语也进入到中国少数民族的文化语境之中，并且呈现多元的格局。再次，随着地理大发现和大航海时代的来临，原本发源于西亚、南亚以及中亚部分地区的阿魏知识在传入欧洲之后，又返传至中国和东亚。此时，阿魏的拉丁语（Ferula Assafoetida/Assafaetida）、荷兰语（Duivelsdrek）、葡萄牙语（Assa Fetida/Asafetida）、德语（Teuffels Dreck/Teufelsdreck/Hingisch）、法语（Assa-foetida/Larme de Laser）、意大利语（assa fẹtida）、英语（Ingo/Assafoetida）等欧洲语种的名称，开始以新的面貌出现在东亚的文献之中。而到了19世纪中期鸦片战争前后，依托英国的强大国力，英语在世界各地广泛流通，阿魏的英语名称Assafoetida逐渐占据中心位置，"阿魏"也作为唯一汉语名称被确定下来，而其他数十种音译词则消失在历史的风云之中，对后世再无影响。

从唐初的"阿魏"（aṅkwaṣ〔ṭ〕）到晚清的"阿魏"（Assafoetida），这一看似简单的转变，背后实际上隐藏了长时段的、复杂的世界文化的传播与流变过程。"阿魏"被最终确定为此物的固定汉语名称，完成其中国化的历程，其原因并不是单一的。

一方面，比起其他的汉译名，"阿魏"一开始就占有优势。这既是唐代官方译语人确立的译名，更是对此外来药物的第一个命名。从官方译语人到佛经译场的译者，"阿魏"一词的确立有自上而下的效果。义净等佛经翻译者对印度文化与医学有更多了解，知道 hiṅgu 与"阿魏"之间的对应关系，再加上选择已经在社会上有一定流行度的"阿魏"一词来描述此外来物品，更便于一般读者接受。而"兴瞿"虽最早出现在佛教戒律译本之中，但戒律文本属于僧团的内部读物，基本不向非出家人开放，所以该词的受众范围较为有限。此外，从唐官方组织编撰的《新修本草》开始，历代的本草与医方集也基本使用"阿魏"一名，更从实用的层面进一步奠定了该词的主导地位。

另一方面，就音译词的结构而言，"阿魏"的"阿"字并不是任意添加的前缀，而是原语 *aṅ(k)waṣ(ṭ)* 一词的前缀对音。比起"兴瞿"系列及其他相关的波斯语音译词来看，"阿魏"的构词形式符合外来语的名词前加"阿"字的用法（或惯例），更符合汉语词汇的样式，切合民众心理，其流行度和使用度自然更广。

此外，在汉语文献中，"阿魏"一词的选择与固定，也与中医著作对它的频繁使用有密切的关系。无论是在本草、医方，还是与医药相关的笔记条目中，学人们使用最多的就是"阿魏"，而不是该物的其他译名。再加上阿魏具有"奇臭"的特性以及"黄金（或黄芩）无假、阿魏无真"这一民间谚语在不同文体（如禅宗语录、蒙书、类书、辞典等）中的广泛流传，① 更强化了"阿魏"一词作为社会语言流通的优势，并且最终定于一尊。

---

① William Scarborough trans. and ed., *A Collection of Chinese Proverbs*（《谚语丛话》）, Shanghai: American Presbyterian Mission Press, 1875, p.270.

概言之，作为中古以来的域外药名翻译浪潮中的一朵小浪花，阿魏一词的知识图景、译名转换及其用法在古代亚欧的流传之旅，[①] 恰好是人类知识互动与健康维护的历史反映。前辈所谓“一滴水中看到大海”“凡解释一字即是作一部文化史”（陈寅恪语），此亦其例也。

（本文初稿曾以《历代译名及其词义流变：阿魏的文化史之一》为名，发表于《欧亚学刊》新8辑，商务印书馆2018年版，第143—157页。今做大幅度的增订，并改为现名。）

① Angela K. C. Leung and Ming Chen, “The Itinerary of hing/awei/asafetida across Eurasia, 400-1800,” in Pamela H. Smith ed., *Entangled Itineraries: Materials, Practices, and Knowledge across Eurasia*, The University of Pittsburgh Press, 2019, pp.141-164.

附录：阿魏的历代译名一览表

序号	译名	出　处	时　代	作者 / 译者	对应的词语	翻译的地点	备　　注
1	兴渠	《十诵律》	后秦（384—417）	弗若多罗、鸠摩罗什	梵语 hiṅgu	长安	可能是该物最早的汉译名
2	馨牛	《四分律》	后秦（384—417）	佛陀耶舍、竺佛念	梵语 hiṅgu	长安	“牛”字或为西北方音
3	阿魏	《隋书·漕国传》	唐贞观十年（636 年）	魏徵	Tocharian *aṅ(k)waṣ(ṭ)*	长安	出自鸿胪寺的译语人之手
		《陀罗尼集经》	永徽五年（654 年）	阿地瞿多	梵语 hiṅgu	长安	—
		《根本说一切有部毗奈耶药事》	大周证圣元年至大唐景云二年（695—711）	义净	梵语 hiṅgu	长安 / 洛阳	有梵本《药事》（*Bhaiṣajya-vastu*）可证
4	兴瞿	《大唐西域记》	唐贞观十年（636 年）	玄奘、辩机	梵语 hiṅgu	长安	—
5	形俱	《不空羂索神变真言经》	神龙三年（707 年）	菩提流志	梵语 hiṅgu	长安	—
6	央匮	《外台秘要方》	唐天宝十一年（752 年）	王焘	梵语 hiṅgu	长安	引自《涅槃经》
7	阿魏截根	《通典》	唐贞元十七年（801 年）	杜佑	—	长安	不是音译词，而是指所截的阿魏根
8	形虞	《酉阳杂俎》	公元 9 世纪上半叶	段成式（约 803—863）	梵语 hiṅgu	长安	“伽阇那呼为形虞”
9	阿虞截				波斯语 Anguzad		“拂林国僧弯所说同”
10	西阿魏	羽 042R《药方》	唐末（或五代）	—	—	敦煌	敦煌出土残卷
11	形具	《宋高僧传》	北宋端拱元年（988 年）	赞宁	梵语 hiṅgu	于阗	或许与于阗当地的称呼有关
12	兴宜	《翻译名义集》	南宋绍兴二十七年（1157 年）	法云	梵语 hiṅgu	平江（苏州）	“宜”应是“具”字形误

续 表

序号	译名	出 处	时 代	作者 / 译者	对应的词语	翻译的地点	备 注
13	哈昔泥	《饮膳正要》	元天历三年（1330年）	忽思慧	波斯语 kasni，对应蒙古语 gajni，波斯语 gha-zni	大都	或写作“哈昔尼”
14	稳展				阿拉伯语 ushturghâz		阿魏的根
15	撒阿因	《回回药方》	元明之交	—	阿拉伯语 Sa ‘yin	大都	阿魏（Sakb̲īnaj）的别名 Sāghā fyīn 的音译
16	撒额因				波斯语 Ṣaghyīn		—
17	撒额冰				波斯语 Sakbīnaj		阿魏树脂
18	撒黑因				阿拉伯语 Sa ‘yin		—
19	撒亦因				阿拉伯语 Sa ‘yin		—
20	撒亦冰				阿拉伯语 Sa ‘yin		—
21	撒吉别拿失	《回回药方》	元明之交	—	波斯语 Sikbīnaj	大都	阿魏树脂
22	撒吉别拏只				波斯语 Sikbīnaj		阿魏树脂
23	安古丹	《回回药方》	元明之交	—	阿拉伯语、波斯语 Anjudhān	大都	阿拉伯语和波斯语阿魏（Anjudhān）的音译名。“吉”是“古”之误。
	安吉丹						
24	安古当						
	安吉当						
25	安诸丹						

续　表

序号	译名	出　处	时　代	作者 / 译者	对应的词语	翻译的地点	备　注
26	黑黎提提	《回回药方》	元明之交	—	阿拉伯语 ḥiltîti	大都	黑黎提提的注释有："即是阿魏""即阿魏净者""即阿魏不香者"
27	墨黎提提						"墨"是"黑"的形误
28	昂古则	《回回馆杂字》	明永乐年间（1403—1424）	明代四夷馆所编	波斯语 anguzha	—	《回回馆译语》同。
29	阿味	《西域土地人物略》	明宣德十年（1435 年）或成化十年（1474 年）之后	作者佚名	—	中国西北、中亚	指"阿魏"。收入明代马理编纂的嘉靖《陕西通志》卷十
30	莺孤	《满剌加国译语》	明嘉靖二十八年（1549 年）	明代四夷馆所编	马来语 inggu	北京	通事杨林校正。此词源自印地语 Ingu
31	盛棍	《西番馆译语》	明万历七年（1579 年）	明代四夷馆所编	藏语 shing kun	川西	明万历七年（1579 年）《华夷译语》写本
32	悻	《暹罗馆译语》	明万历七年（1579 年）	明代四夷馆所编	泰语 หิง / Hi: ŋ/^{5}	北京	另见《暹罗番书》，源自梵语 Hiṅgu
33	英古	《嘆咭唎国译语》	清乾隆十四年（1749 年）	耶稣会士	英语 Ingo	北京	来自源于印地语 Ingu 的马来语词形 Ingo
34	阿斯萨弗氏达	《拉氏诺语》	清乾隆十四年（1749 年）	耶稣会士	拉丁语 assa faetida	北京	欧洲医学著作中最通用的阿魏名称
35	阿萨弗氏达	《播都噶礼雅语》	清乾隆十四年（1749 年）	耶稣会士	葡萄牙语 Asafetida	北京	源自阿魏的拉丁语名称 Assafaetida
36	阿斯萨佛氏达	《伊达礼雅语》	清乾隆十四年（1749 年）	耶稣会士	意大利语 assa fetida	北京	直接使用了对应的拉丁语名称

续　表

序号	译名	出　处	时　代	作者 / 译者	对应的词语	翻译的地点	备　　注
37	拉^{呼}墨德拉塞^{呼}	《弗^{喇安}西雅语》	清乾隆十四年（1749 年）	耶稣会士	法语 Larme de Laser	北京	或许与拉丁语 Laser 有关
38	代弗勒斯德呼克	《额^{呼}马尼雅语》	清乾隆十四年（1749 年）	德籍耶稣会士魏继晋	近代中期德语 Teuffels Dreck	北京	意为"鬼屎"。现代德语词形写作 Teufelsdreck
39	辛苦	《缅甸番书》	清乾隆十五年（1750 年）前后	会同四译馆	缅甸语 shein kho	北京	来源于巴利语（或梵语）hiṅgu。
40	阿咱喳	《猓猡译语》（第二册）	清乾隆十五年（1750 年）前后	会同四译馆	彝语 a^{33}-dzo^{33}-tʂo^{33}	西昌	三个词素分别意为"阿""吃""畏 / 魏"。此词意即"吃阿魏"。
41	七姑	《猓猡译语》（第三册）			彝语 tshi^{33}-gɔ^{11}	叙永	"七姑"乃"士姑"之误。"tshi^{33}-gɔ^{11}"意思为"成熟的药"。
3	阿魏	《猓猡译语》（第四册）			彝语 a^{33}-vi^{2}(ve^{33})	—	汉语"阿魏"的音译。译语采集地点不明。
		《猓猡译语》（第五册）			彝语 a^{33}-vɚ^{55}	—	
42	施^{昂}沽^{安}	《西番译语》（第五册）		会同四译馆	藏语 shing kun	川西	—
43	阿魏里	《西番译语》（第二册）		会同四译馆	藏语 'so be rid / 'po be red	松潘	象鼻高山
44	身股	《西番译语》（第三册）		会同四译馆	藏语 shing kun	松潘	嘉绒
3	阿魏	《西番译语》（第四册）		会同四译馆	藏语 'o 'od rig / 'o 'od reg	松潘	白马

续 表

序号	译名	出　处	时　代	作者 / 译者	对应的词语	翻译的地点	备　　注
45	升桂	《西番译语》（第五册）	清乾隆十五年（1750年）前后	会同四译馆	藏语 shing kun	建昌道	栗苏
46	陞官	《西番译语》（第六册）		会同四译馆	藏语 shing kun	川西	木坪
47	舍贵	《西番译语》（第七册）		会同四译馆	藏语 shing gun	打箭炉	建昌道
48	支达	《西番译语》（第八册）		会同四译馆	藏语 kri tan	建昌道	多续
31	盛棍	《西番译语》（第一册、第八册）		会同四译馆	藏语 shing gun	建昌道	松藩、草地、木里
49	辛固	《西藏见闻录》	乾隆八年（1743 年）	萧腾麟	藏语 shing kun	西藏	—
50	胜棍	《卫藏图识》	乾隆五十七年（1792年）刊刻	马少云、盛梅溪	藏语 shing kun	卫藏	—
51	爹部地丁	*Chinese and English Vocabulary*	19 世纪中期		德语 Teufelsdreck	广州（？）	不列颠图书馆藏 Or.7428 抄本
52	雅是花利地				拉丁文或英文 Assafoetida		
53	哑沙父哷噠	《增订华英通语》	19 世纪中后期	子卿原著、福沢谕吉译	拉丁文或英文 Assafoetida	广东	—
54	阿魏非罗拉	《西药大成》	1887 年	来拉、海得兰、哈来著，傅兰雅、赵元益译	拉丁文 Ferula Asafoetida	上海	江南制造局翻译馆译本
55	真弟司故能阿魏				拉丁文 Asafoetida disgunensis		
56	恒其息				德文 Hingiseh		

续 表

序号	译名	出 处	时 代	作者 / 译者	对应的词语	翻译的地点	备 注
57	阿虚	《万国药方》	1890 年	洪士提反	assa	上海	—
3	阿魏	《华英字典》	1822 年	马礼逊	英文 Asafoetida	广东	—
		《洋汉合字汇》	1831 年	江沙维	葡萄牙语 Assa Fetida	澳门	—
		《荷华文语类参》	1882 年	施古德	荷兰语 Duivelsdrek	福建	—
3	阿魏	《法粤字典》	1903 年	路易·奥巴扎克	法语 Assa-foetida	广东	来源拉丁语 Assafoetida
		《德英华文科学字典》	1911 年	卫礼贤	德语 Teufelsdreck	山东	—

A lag sha Ngag dbang bstan dar (1759–August 1, 1840) on some Chinese Lexemes and the Chinese Language, Part Two*

Leonard W.J. van der Kuijp
Harvard University

I recounted the little that we know about Ngag dbang bstan dar's life in Part One of this essay that was published in the volume that honors the work of my old comrade in studies, Franz-Karl Ehrhard.① There, I began my exposition of his references to Chinese, and the present contribution continues in the same vein and constitutes the second and last part of the essay.

As far as Ngag dbang bstan dar's scholarship in general is concerned, he is especially known for his vignette-like glosses on several important texts, for his relatively short tracts dealing with the knowledge-domain of language (*sgra'i rig gnas*), which includes grammar, poetics and lexicography, with logic and epistemology, as well as for a number of commentaries on shorter works. Several of these he never completed and we must be grateful to the unknown editor(s) of his "complete" works for nonetheless including these fragments in his *gsung 'bum*. Not the usual traditional scholar, he was also interested in more practical matters as is indicated in his fascinating study of the weights,

---

* This paper was first presented on October 16, 2021 at the *International Symposium on Eurasian and Buddhist Philology in Memoriam of Professor Tschen Yin-Koh* that was held at Tsinghua University on October 15–17, 2021. My gratitude goes out to Profs. Shen Weirong and Wu Juan, and to Drs. Hou Haoran and Yao Shuang for their kind invitation and correspondence. As in Part One, I should like to thank my friend Christoph Cüppers for having read an earlier incarnation of this essay and for pointing out some infelicities and errors.

① See van der Kuijp 2019. There, in connection with tea and tea drinking in the Tibetan area, I was unaware of the excellent dissertation on the subject in Booz 2011, and the fine master's thesis of Li 2013 to which we may now add Sun 2021. And I was equally unaware of Choĝtu [=(Čoγtu) 1999–the bibliographical entry in Ujeed 2009: 228 drew my attention to this work—and the biographical sketch of Ngag dbang bstan dar's life in Powers 2016: 118–121.

measures, and currencies of Indian, Sinitic, and Tibetan regions and their relative valuations in the past as well as in the present, a work that should prove of interest to someone studying aspects of Tibetan economic history.① Further details about this work are given below and in the Appendix.

Over the years, several studies of his more philosophical writings were published in the secondary literature, and they will be duly signaled in my essay on his examination of Dignāga's (6th c.) **Hetucakraḍamaru* that is currently under preparation. One of the interesting features of his oeuvre as a whole is his obvious sensitivity to philological and text-critical issues, and he frequently points out variant readings in the texts that he cites. His works show furthermore that he was a discerning critic and that he did not shy away from setting things straight that, in his opinion, had gone awry.

An example of this may be taken from his tract on weights and measures, currencies, and their respective values in the context of what constitutes the infraction of stealing, "to take what is not given" (*ma byin gyi len pa, adattādāna*), according to *vinaya*-canon law and how much of value needs to be stolen to warrant the perpetrator's excommunication or expulsion (or near-expulsion) from the Buddhist community. Depending on the value of what has been taken when it was not given such an act may or may not constitute a *pārājika-pham pa* violation, one for which, in its most severe case, a monk will be "excommunicated" from the assembly.② The problem of course was how to calculate value, especially diachronically and under different social circumstances and geographical regions! In the course of his deliberations, Ngag dbang bstan dar addresses a problem with an alleged canonical source that he found cited in the Tibetan literature; he writes③:

> *... gzhan yang 'grel pa shes rab 'byed pa'i lung yig cha rnams su drangs pa yod cing / sde dge'i bstan 'gyur khrod na 'grel pa shes rab 'byed pa zer ba e mi bzhugs shing / 'grel pa prajndza ka ra zer ba gcig mchis pa 'grel pa shes rab 'byed pa la ngos 'dzin dgos pa 'dra na'ang yig cha rnams su drangs pa'i lung tshig der mi rnyed pas / des na so thar 'grel pa glang po che chu 'thung zhes pa sngon khri srong lde btsan gyi dus su yod par / dran dbang sang rgyas rgya mtshos g.ya sel du gsungs kyang deng sang mi bzhugs pa bzhin 'di yang de dang 'dra ba yin nam dpyad par 'tshal /*

---

① This is his *Ma byin len gyi pham pa'i rin thang gi tshad bshad pa 'khrul spong mkhas pa'i dgyes byed mchod yon rnam dag*, for which see NGAG1[1], 730–755, and NGAG2, 433–448, and below in the Appendix.

② For an excellent study of this offense and the various legal issues that are implied by it, without going into any detail about the values of the material goods that may be stolen, see Kieffer-Pülz 2011.

③ NGAG1[1], 748–749, and NGAG2, 444. Truth be told, there is something that is not quite fluent with the syntax of this passage, and I have made certain adjustments without, I hope, violating its meaning.

> ... furthermore, there is a scriptural source from the *Shes rab 'byed pa* (**Prajñāvibhāga*) commentary that is cited in monastic text-books and the so-called *Shes rab 'byed pa* commentary is not at all contained in the Sde dge *Bstan 'gyur* collection① And even if it may be necessary to identify the commentary titled *Prajñākara*② (*Shes rab byed pa*) as the *Shes rab 'byed pa*, we do not find therein the wording of what is quoted in the text-books. Hence, although the powerful scholar③ Sangs rgyas rgya mtsho (1653–1705) has stated in the *G.ya sel* that there existed a **Pratimokṣa* [*sūtra*] commentary [sub]titled *Glang po che chu 'thung ba* in earlier times during the era of king Khri srong lde btsan (c. 742–800)④ — it is also likewise not extant today—, one should inquire whether also this [*Shes rab 'byed pa*] is similar to that.

There is also no question that Ngag dbang bstan dar had the courage of his own ideas and that he often waxed quite brilliantly in his philosophical works. Some years ago, Jampa Panglung suggested that he was not averse even to take Dalai Lama V Ngag dbang blo bzang rgya mtsho (1617–1682) in the cross hairs, in this case, apropos of the origins of the *tsha gsur/bsur* ritual complex. This ritual or ceremony involves the burning of food in a pot of clay so as to feed those who are in the intermediate state between death and rebirth (*bar do ba*) with the smell of food, since these disembodied entities are of course unable to eat a solid meal! Jampa Panglung was of the opinion that he had criticized Dalai Lama V in his *Tsha gsur la dogs gcod pa'i 'khrul spong*

---

① We can add here that this work is also not listed in the *vinaya* section of the other *Bstan 'gyur* xylographs, for which see BSTAN, vols. 84–93. But he refers to a work with this title in NGAG1[1], 743, and NGAG2, 440, as if this is the title that is cited in Dalai Lama I Dge 'dun grub's (1391–1474) study of the *vinaya*. It is not! Both available xylographs have *Shes rab byed pa*!; see Dalai Lama I 1978–1981: 191 and No date: 253. For reasons that remain to be investigated, the Lhasa Zhol printing blocks for Dalai Lama I's *'Dul ṭīk rin chen phreng ba*, were only prepared as late as 1896 under the aegis of Dalai Lama XIII Ngag dbang blo bzang thub bstan rgya mtsho (1876–1933).

② For this work, the *Vinayasūtravyākhyāna* that was written by Prajñākara, see BSTAN, vol. 92, 3–773.

③ My rendition of *dran dbang* is based on the entry for this term in Btsan lha 1997: 340.

④ Sde srid 1976: I, 269. No work by this name is listed in the *Lhan dkar ma* or the *'Phang thang ma*, the earliest extant catalogs of translated scripture. Ngag dbang bstan dar also mentions this work in his undated *So thar sdom pa 'bogs chog gi lhan thabs legs bshad gser thur*, a study of the liturgy of the transmission of the *pratimokṣa* vows—see NGAG1[1], 701, and NGAG2, 416–where he cites the *Las ṭik*, that is, Bu ston Rin chen grub's (1290–1361) 1357 commentary on Guṇaprabha's (7th c.) *Ekottarakarmaśataka*; see Bu ston 1971a: 844. Gser mdog Paṇ chen Shākya mchog ldan (1428–1507) cites the same passage from Bu ston in his 1472 exegesis of the text—see Gser mdog Paṇ chen 2013: 288. Some Tibetan scholars seem to have held that Vinītadeva (8th c.) had written the *Ekottarakarmaśataka*, but such commentators as Bu ston and Gser mdog Paṇ chen never wavered in their view that its author was Guṇaprabha.

dgongs pa rab gsal,① an undated work that, in his view, was quite explicitly written against Dalai Lama V's *Bsur chog gi rim pa yid bzhin 'dod 'jo* - we should include here also Dalai Lama V's *Dkar cha bzhi'i dga' ston phan bde'i 'dod 'jo*.② Ngag dbang bstan dar cites both works and it is true that in both, the Dalai Lama had argued that, firstly, no canonical texts, not even those belonging to the literature of the Old School (Rnying ma pa), contain any mention of such a ritual and that, secondly, in any event, no one in the intermediate state can be nourished or gain enjoyment from such "food" . Ngag dbang bstan dar tells us what had motivated him to write his work on the topic at hand. A Qalqa Mongol anchorite in Ulan Batar had wondered why the *Gsur*-singed ritual practice that had been so widespread among the Qalqa had ever fewer virtuosi of this ritual, and this had led Ngag dbang bstan dar to look for reasons. He first cites the misgivings that the Dalai Lama had voiced in these two little texts. However, contrary to Panglung's view that Ngag dbang bstan dar had rejected the Dalai Lama's claims out right, a closer reading reveals that he really did not do so. Thus, Ngag dbang bstan dar writes after his citations from the two relevant texts of the Dalai Lama that③:

> *lnga pa chen pos kyang rang lugs la tsha gsur khungs med du bzhed pa ma yin par / rgyud sde bzhi'i nyer spyod kyi mchod pa'i nang gi bdug spos phul ba'i tshig ji snyed pa dang/ 'dod yon lnga'i dri phul ba'i tshig ji snyed byung ba thams cad dang bsangs kyi cho ga rnams de'i khungs su bzhed par gsal te ...*

> It not being the case that the Great Fifth (Dalai Lama V), too, claimed for his own position that *tsha gsur* had no authentic source, it is clear that he claimed as its authentic source [1] all of the entire wording of the offering of incense among the offering rituals of the practice of the four tantra classes, [2] all of the entire wording for offering fragrance of the five objects that engender cupidity-attachment,④ and [3] the rituals associated with *bsangs*-

---

① NGAG1[2], 710–729, and NGAG2, 848–859, and Panglung 1985.

② Dalai Lama V 2009a and 2009b. Both are undated. The first actually comprises two different texts of which the first is the *Bsur chog gi rim pa yid bzhin 'dod 'jo* that was written at the behest of Dbu mdzad Blo bzang yon tan, Brag sna Chos rje Blo bzang ngag dbang, and Ri khrod pa Blo bzang chos 'phel, while he wrote the second, untitled work for Sde pa Blo bzang mthu stobs, his right-hand man, who acted as his *sde srid*, his secular but subordinate counterpart, from 1669 to 1774. He wrote the second, the *Dkar cha bzhi'i dga' ston phan bde'i 'dod 'jo*, for his relative Ldum po ba Nor bu dar rgyas.

③ NGAG1[2], 710–729, and NGAG2, 848–859.

④ I am not entirely sure what this may mean, but I opted for the *'dod pa'i yon tan lnga* entry in Nor brang 2008: 1110, where the five are: beautiful color-shape, mellifluous sound, fragrant smell, sweet taste, and soft to the touch.

smoke offerings.①

Indeed, the Dalai Lama himself had said in his *Bsur chog gi rim pa yid bzhin 'dod 'jo* that even if there were no explicit literary source for this ritual, there is nonetheless some benefit that can be derived from it (*'on kyang 'di la phan yon cung zad 'byung*), and he follows this up by detailing these very kinds of benefit.②

Panglung closed his essay by concluding that this ritual "must be sought in pre-Buddhist beliefs" of the Tibetans and indeed points to a Bon po text from Dunhuang, Pelliot tibétain 1042, in which the term *gsur*, "singed, something slightly burned," occurs. This manuscript, which was of course not available to either Dalai Lama V or Ngag dbang bstan dar, was *inter alia* studied by M. Lalou, R.A. Stein, and Chu Junjie.③

As was shown in Part One of this essay, Ngag dbang bstan dar had some competence in Chinese, a competence that he had probably picked up, first, in his native land, and then especially during his stay in Beijing. The present paper further opens the aperture on this theme and is thus a continuation of an assessment of his use or mention of the Chinese language as well as its conclusion.

In addition to the Chinese words that I referenced in Part One, he mentions three more in the tract on traditional weights, measures, types of currency and their relative values that I mentioned earlier.④ This fascinating treatise bears a full and careful study. It will be readily noticed that, in

---

① NGAG1[2], 714, and NGAG2, 849. This statement will probably not dispel the widespread view that the burning of *bsangs*, juniper, has no Indian Buddhist precedent, even though Ngag dbang bstan dar has written in NGAG1[2], 717, and NGAG2, 851, that: "Those who say that putting together *bsangs*-smoke offerings and the receptacles (statues) of worldly deities belong to the eternal Bon tradition and not to the Buddhist tradition of the Indians is the meaningless chatter of not having been able to trace their scriptural sources ..." (*bsangs mchod dang 'jig rten pa'i lha rten btsugs pa dag ni g.yung drung bon gyi lugs yin gyi rgya gar pa'i chos lugs min zhes smra ba rnams lung khungs rtsad ma chod pa'i 'chal gtam yin/ ...*), at which point he indicates the sources for the *bsangs*-offering that he had adduced earlier and also adds a number of sources for constructing statuary for the so-called worldly deities. A valuable collection of different *bsang* offering rituals is Chab 'gag 2006.

② Dalai Lama V 2009a: 456.

③ See Lalou 1952, Stein 1970, and Chu 1991. For the occurrence and notion[s] of *bon* in the Tibetan Dunhuang corpus, see the dossier compiled by and studied in van Schaik 2013a.

④ This is his *Ma byin len gyi pham pa'i rin thang gi tshad bshad pa 'khrul spong mkhas pa'i dgyes byed mchod yon rnam dag*, for which see above n. 2. A similarly difficult work is the Sde srid's replies to several questions about weights, measures, and values posed to him by Bstan srung rnam rgyal (?1646–after 1699), then king of Sikkim, for which see the text in Spen pa lha mo 2014: 296 ff. and its Chinese translation in Spen pa lha mo 2014: 127 ff. My thanks to my student Mr. Sun Penghao for providing me with a copy of this volume. These questions were prompted by the Sde srid's 1681 work on administrative law; see Sde srid 1989. For （转下页）

some places, I have not been very successful in fully understanding the terminologies used therein and I am sure that a future study of this work can improve on what I have written here. Its core title indicates that it deals with the amount/measure (*tshad*) of value (*rin thang*) for the transgression of taking what has not been given, that is, theft. For its structure and Ngag dbang bstan dar's Tibetan sources, see the Appendix to this paper. A full topical outline is given in the Appendix, but for now it will suffice to note that it falls into the following three main parts:

1. An explanation of the measure of a *zho* and a *srang*
   (*zho srang gi tshad bshad pa*)
   NGAG1[1], 732–740, and NGAG2, 433–438
2. An explanation of the measure of value
   (*rin thang gi tshad bshad pa*)
   NGAG1[1], 740–749, and NGAG2, 438–444
3. An Exposition of my own position
   (*rang gi lugs rnam par gzhag pa*)
   NGAG1[1], 749–755, and NGAG2, 444–448

Right or wrong, Ngag dbang bstan dar begins his narrative by writing that there is no agreement among the learned about the measure of value. And since Indic and Tibetan scholars did not explain the measure of the *zho* (*karṣa/kārṣa*) and *srang* (*pala*), he will first take up this topic. He writes that Indians and Tibetans used grain (*sran ma*), rosary peas (*dmar ru mgo nag*), barley (*nas*), rice (*'bras bu*) and the like as substances (*rdzas*) to measure goods, whereas broomcorn millet (*khre'am drus ma*) was used in China. For a survey of the Indic terminology, he cites *Amarakoṣa*, II: 9: 85d–86a,①

（接上页）useful but still incomplete surveys of Tibetan weights, measurements, valuations, etc., see the German language Wikipedia article *Tibetische Maßeinheiten* and D. Martin's blog Tiblical/measurements/numbers. For Tibetan currencies, see Boulnois 1983, Xiao (1987) and Bertsch (2002), which is the standard work on the subject in English, and D. Schuh's article "Gold und Goldmünzen" in (primarily) his tibet-encyclopaedia.de/gold-goldmuenzen.htm; the Wikipedia article "Historical Money of Tibet" is also quite useful. For all of these weights, measurements, and valuations in the Indian subcontinent, see the monumental synchronic study of Wilson 1855 and the ever so useful work of Sircar 1968. Titled *The Power of Wealth–Economy and Social Status in Pre-Modern Tibetan Communities*, the issue of *Revue d'Etudes Tibétaines* 57 (2021) has much to offer about various economic activities, but not in terms of methods of measurement and relative valuations of currencies. Last but not least, the lengthy and highly informative Wikipedia article "Qing dynasty coins" illustrates the numismatic complexities of the period.

① For the reference to the *Amarakoṣa*, see Amarasiṃha 1940: 87; for some Tibetan references, see, （转下页）

for additional terms like *guñja* (rosary pea) and *māśaka* (bean) that were used for measurements, Guṇaprabha's *Vinayasūtra* for the valuation that four *ka ka ni* (*kākiṇī*) make up one *ma sha ka* (*māśaka*), and the latter's **Svavyākhyāna*-commentary for the idea that one *ma sha ka* make up eight *se ba*.① Of course, the problem with these and other Indic sources that may be marshalled for shedding light on the subject is that there is no hard evidence that any universal standards existed in the entire subcontinent for weights, measures, and currencies, either synchronically or diachronically. And we need to apply this caveat for the Tibetan area as well as is made quite clear in some of the passages that he cites and that are cited below. Aside from primarily religious sources that deal with the sociology of the monastery and the punishments that are meted out for such transgressions by the clergy as theft, it is obvious that Tibetan legal, that is, secular texts will have much to say about weights, relative valuations, and currencies. For example, a number of passages of the Gtsang pa Sde srid legal code that was issued by Karma bstan skyong dbang po (1606–1642) are potentially quite rewarding in this respect.②

Having cited some Indic sources, Ngag dbang bstan dar then quotes at length Dalai Lama V's study of aspects of *vinaya*-canon law, which he completed in 1679.③ The passage that he cites belongs to the section on theft and begins with distinguishing between two types of *kar ṣa pa ṇa*

（接上页）BSTAN, vol. 110, 473, and BSTAN, vol. 110, 634. In these, the text reads: *ma* [*tu* sic!] *ru lnga sogs mā sha ka / de rnams bcu drug zho gnyis te //*, rather than Ngag dbang bstan dar's citation: *kuñja* (read: *guñja*) *lnga sogs ma sha ka / de dag bcu drug zho gnyis te //*, both of which should correspond to Sanskrit: ... *guñjaḥ pañcādhyamāṣaka // te ṣodaśākśaḥ* ... For the various editions and translations of the Tibetan text of the *Amarakoṣa* [and Subhūticandra's commentary] see the somewhat editorially mangled text of van der Kuijp 2009a and now also Deokar 2020 and the literature cited therein, including her meticulous study of the first portion of this work. 'Jam dbyangs bzhad pa'i rdo rje II Dkon mchog 'jigs med dbang po's (1728–1791) edition of the Tibetan text of the bilingual edition of the *Amarakoṣa* that his predecessor 'Jam dbyangs bzhad pa'i rdo rje I Ngag dbang brtson 'grus (1648–1721/22) had prepared in *circa* 1715/16 has: *ma ru lnga sogs mā sha ka / de rnams bcu drug karṣaḥ ste //*; see 'Jam dbyangs bzhad pa'i rdo rje I 1972–1974: 701. On the other hand, Si tu Paṇ chen has in his bilingual edition: *ma ru lnga sogs sran khre'u'i tshad // de bcu drug zho zho tshad ni //*; see Si tu Paṇ chen 1990: 150, who evidently also read ... *karśaḥ*, but *karśa* and *akṣa* are synonyms for the Terminalia Bellirica known for its bedda nuts.

① For the *Vinayasūtra* and the **Svavyākhyāna* references, see BSTAN, vol. 88, 871, and BSTAN, vol. 89, 83; see also Nakagawa 1996.

② For the Tibetan text and its Chinese translation, see Spen pa lha mo 2014: 217–219, 228–231 and 2014: 66–68, 74–76. Of great interest is that Karma bstan skyong dbang po cites older official documents/codes (*khrims yig rnying pa*) and the official document/code (*khrims yig*) of the Tshal pa, which I take to refer to Tshal pa myriarchy that was established in the 13th century when Dbus gtsang and Mnga' ris skor gsum were under Mongol rule and occupation. Ehrhard 2015 is a study of the introductory matter of this code.

③ For what follows, see Dalai Lama V 2009c: 64–65.

(< *kar/kārṣāpaṇa*), a real one (*mtshan nyid pa*)① and a nominal one (*btags pa ba*) that have the same value (*rin* [*thang*]). The actual one is forged from precious metals, whereas the nominal one is made from such things as cowrie shells (*mgron/'gron bu*), etc. Dalai lama V cites a reply of Zhwa lu Lo tsā ba Rin chen chos skyong bzang po (1441–1527) to a query on theft in which the latter had stated that one-fourth (*bzhi cha*) of a *kārṣāpaṇa* is equal to a pair of golden *se ba* (*gser se ba do*).②

Having laid down some terminological groundwork, Ngag dbang bstan dar then discusses the meaning and valuations of *guñja, kākaṇī*, and *se ba*. It is in connection with his discussion of *se ba*③ that he explicitly mentions a Chinese lexeme; he writes④:

> *se ba zhes pa ni dmar ru la sogs pas gzhal bar bya ba'i lcid tshad zhig gi ming yin gyi dmar ru sogs las logs su med do // de yang se ba gcig gi tshad ni dmar rus gzhal na dmar ru che shos gcig gam chung tshad gnyis kyi tshad dang mnyam / nas 'bras gzhal na nas 'bru gsum sam bzhi'i tshad dang mnyam / 'bras 'brus gzhal na 'bras 'bru drug yan gyi tshad dang mnyam pa zhig yin no // de ltar se ba gang gi tshad dmar ru gnyis kyi tshad la byas pa 'di 'thad par sems te / baidūr g.ya sel du'ang /*

---

① Dalai Lama V refers to the famous commentary on the *Vinayasūtra* by Mtsho sna ba Shes rab bzang po (13th–14th c.) where it is written that a real *kārṣāpaṇa* is made from silver and has the shape and design of a *dong tse*, "a coin"; see Mtsho sna ba 1993: 271–272. Mtsho sna ba cites the *Zhu 'grel*—this is the incomplete canonical *'Dul ba lung bla ma'i bye brag lung zhu ba'i 'grel pa* as his source for *dong tse*; —and that it was "made" by Dpal legs gtam/bltams; see BSTAN, vol. 88, 624. In his 1335 catalog of the Zhwa lu *Bstan 'gyur*, Bu ston notes that this work was authored by a Dge ba'i bshes gnyen (*Kalyāṇamitra, or a spiritual friend [*dge ba'i bshes gnyen*]), an exponent of the sutras, and that the text was incomplete at the beginning and at the end; see Bu ston 1971b: 613. "Dge ba'i bshes gnyen" appears to be a carving error for "Dge legs bshes gnyen" (*Kalyāṇamitra), the name of an author of numerous works on the *vinaya*. Laufer 1916: 506–507, no. 218, already pointed out that *dong tse* derives from Chinese *tongzi* 銅子. However, Tibetan *dong tse* (*rtse*) also translates Sanskrit *dīnāra* as in the *Abhidharmakoṣabhāṣya* where the Chinese equivalent is *jinqian* 金錢; see Hirakawa et al. 1973: 182. Now that a number of earlier Tibetan studies commentaries on the *vinaya* have become available, it is incumbent on future research to make full use of these.

② For more on the gold or silver *kārṣāpaṇa* and their values, see NGAG1[1], 740–741, and NGAG2, 438–439.

③ The word *se ba* by itself can also refer to the red-winged rose for which De'u dmar Dge bshes Bstan 'dzin phun tshogs (1672–?), the great physician from Sde dge, appears to have *se ba'i me tog* in his *Dri med shel sgong/Dri med shel phreng* pharmacopeia of 1727; see De'u dmar Dge bshes 1986: 226. pp.211, 212, and 248 of the latter work contain entries for *se yab*, flowering quince, *se 'bru*, pomegranate, and *se rgod*, rosa sertata. He writes anent the latter that it is called *ha tsi ki* and *kha 'bar ba*; in Chinese: *zur pa ting dang* and *gha kul*; and in the Mi nyag (= ?Xixia / Tangut or the language used in Khams Mi nyag) language: *to hi tis, phrom gyis*, and *kas bya*. The usual Chinese name for the *se rgod* is *qiangwei* 薔薇. On the other hand, the Mongol physician Jambaldorǰ (< Tib. 'Jam dpal rdo rje) (?1792–?1855) gives the Chinese equivalent of *yeciwei* 野刺薇 in his *materia medica;* see 'Jam dpal rdo rje 1971: 120 (= Dge bsnyen 'Jam dpal rdo rje 2008: 108).

④ NGAG1[1], 734, and NGAG2, 434–435.

dmar ru'am ka ka ni gnyis la se ba / de nyi shu la zho / zho brgyad la srang gang ...

zhes gsungs pa dang shin tu mthun pa'i phyir / de lta bu se ba gang gi tshad rgya thur la 'degs[a] *na rgya'i hphun gang gi phyed longs par myong bas grub pas / des na dmar ru bzhi'i lcid tshad la se ba do dang / se ba do la rgya nag gi hphun gang dang bod kyi skar ma gang yod ces kho bos smras pa yin no //*

[a] NGAG1[1]: *gdegs*.

se ba is a term for a weight that is measured in rosary peas, etc., but it does no exist apart from rosary peas, etc. Moreover, the measure of one *se ba*, when it is measured in rosary peas, is equal to a measure of the largest rosary bead or to two small ones. When a *se ba* is measured in barley, it is equal to three or four grains (*nas 'bru*). If it is measured in rice grains (*'bras 'bru*), then it is equal to up to six rice grains. So, we think that to take the measure of a single (*gang*)① *se ba* to be the measure of two rosary peas is correct, because it is quite consistent with what is also stated in the *Baidūr g.ya sel*②:

> Two rosary peas or *ka ka ni*, a *se ba*; twenty of these, a bedda nut (*zho*), eight bedda nuts, a single *srang*.

Accordingly, since it is established by experience that, when such a single *se ba* is weighed on a Chinese scale (*rgya thur*),③ it amounts to half of a single Chinese *hphun* (< *fen* 分), we therefore say that the weight of four rosary peas involves a pair of *se ba* and that a pair of *se ba* involves a single Chinese *fen* and a single Tibetan *skar ma*.

① Tibetan *gang* has the sense of "a single."

② Sde srid 1976: I, 563: *ma ru'am ka ka ni gnyis la se ba / de nyi shu la zho / zho brgyad la gser srang*... Without textual support, he states that these valuations held for the period of the Tibetan religious kings (7th–9th c.).

③ The term *rgya thur* suggests a *thur* of Chinese origin; see Laufer 1916: 522. Weights and measurements are of great importance for the preparation of medicines, and it is thus not surprising that De'u dmar Dge bshes should devote a reasonable amount of space to their discussion in De'u dmar Dge bshes 2007a: 832–834. There he appears to distinguish between two kinds of scales (or steelyard balances), a "black stick from China" (*rgya nag nas 'byung thur nag*) and a "large white bone stick" (*rus pa'i thur dkar che ba*). While I am not sure of this, NGAG1[1], 737, and NGAG2, 436, appear to distinguish between a *rgya'i thur* and a *rgya nag gi thur*, that is, an Indian and a Chinese scale?

If these relative values were not sufficiently confusing, we now enter a virtual morass of relative weights/measures and values. Turning to the Tibetan area proper, Ngag dbang bstan dar begins by stating that Tibetan is terminologically quite rich where *zho* and *srang* are concerned, and he writes that a golden *zho* has [a weight of] thirty-two *se ba* (*gser zho zhes pa se ba so gnyis can*) and that a *byes zho* of Lhasa weighs thirty-six *se ba*. Well aware of the possibility of adulterated coinage–he cites Dalai Lama II who wrote that some had suggested that a *kārṣāpaṇa* is made from unadulterated silver (*dngul lhag med)* and that the *byes zho* of early Lhasa had a measure of sixty-six *se ba* (*sngar gyi lha sa'i byes zho se ba so drug gi tshad dang ldan pa yin*).① Ngag dbang bstan dar gives additional valuations for different *zho* and his source for this was evidently the work by De'u dmar Dge bshes that is titled *Lag len gcig bsdus*; he cites it as follows:

/ sa shed bzang ngan snyoms pa'i nas kyi 'bru /
/ drug la se ba gang gang de nyi shu /
/ nas 'bru brgyad [*read: brgya*] *dang nyi shu byung ba de /*
/ 'degs zho gang zhes yongs la grags pa'o /
/ se ba nyer bzhi mgur zho gang du bzhed /
/ se ba nyer lnga gzhung zho gang zhes pa /
/ de gsum snga bar phyi ma'i lugs gsum yin /

A work with the title of *Lag len gcig bsdus* is not found among De'u dmar Dge bshes' published writings. But these lines of verse bear great similarity with, even if they are not identical to, a passage that we find in a compendium titled the *Lag len gces rigs btus pa sman kun bcud du sgrub pa'i las kyi cho ga kun gsal snang mdzod*, which De'u dmar Dge bshes had written at the behest of a certain *sprul sku* Ba zal Padma dbang rgyal.② In fact, the readings are sufficiently close to allow for the conjecture that Ngag dbang bstan dar's *Lag len gcig bsdus* is none other than another manuscript

① See Dalai Lama II 2006: 238 with slight variations. For what follows, see NGAG1[1], 738–739, and NGAG2, 437–438.

② Written posterior to his more famous *Dri med shel phreng* of 1727, which it cites, the passage in question of this rewarding work is found in De'u dmar Dge bshes 1957: 57a–b. The 1957 printing blocks of this Lcags po ri xylograph of his study is based on four manuscripts (*ma dpe*) that were in part edited by Mkhyen rab nor bu (1883–1962); see also De'u dmar Dge bshes 2007: 833–834. The variant readings in brackets are those of the 2007 publication. De'u dmar Dge bshes' considerations occur in the section (pp.832–834) that is concerned with measures (*gshor tshad*) and weights (*'degs tshad*). Also known as *'jal tshad*, the first has two parts, the first dealing with measures in the medical tradition (*sman lugs*) and the second with measures that are in common use (*spyi lugs, 'jig rten spyi lugs*).

of this work; there we read the following:

/ sa shed bzang ngan snyoms pa'i nas kyi 'bru /
/ che ba gsum la ra ti zhes su bshad [*smra*] */*
/ ra ti gnyis te nas drug se ba gang /
/ se ba nyi shu [*shur*] *ra ti bzhi bcu ste /*
/ nas 'bru brgya dang nyi shu 'byung ba der /
/ 'degs zho gang zhes yongs la grags pa'o /
/ se ba nyer bzhir 'gur[a] [*bzhi mgur*] *zho gang du bzhed /*
/ se ba nyer lngar[b] [*lnga*] *gzhung zho gang byed pa /*
/ de gsum snga bar phyi ma'i lugs gsum yin /

[a] Sublinear note: *nas 'bru brgya dang bzhi bcu rtsa bzhi* [*zhe bzhi*].
[b] Sublinear note: *nas 150* [*nas 'bru brgya dang lnga bcu*].

Three large barley grains of a good, bad or even ?fertile soil (*sa shed*),
Are called a *ra ti*.①
Two *ra ti*, that is, six barley grains or a single *se ba*;
Twenty *se ba*, forty *ra ti*;
The occurrence of a hundred and twenty barley grains
Is universally known as a *'degs zho*.
Twenty-four *se ba* are claimed to be a single *mgur zho*.
Twenty-five make a single *gzhung zho*.
These three are the early, middle, and later [measurement] traditions.

Aside from the otherwise little known *ra ti* unit of measurement, this passage thus isolates three different kinds of *zho*:

1. one [?pre-]weighed *zho* (*'degs zho*)= twenty *se ba*
2. one market place *zho* (*mgur zho*)= twenty-four *se ba*
3. and a government *zho* (*gzhung zho*) = twenty-five *se ba*

① On the *ratī* (not *rati*), see Wilson 1855: 440 and Sircar 1968: *passim*.

Continuing with his quotation from what is ostensibly De'u dmar Dge bshes' work, Ngag dbang bstan dar writes:

/ rgya nag nas rgya thur che ba dang /
/ tshong 'dus mgur mo'i zho la khyad par med /
/ 'degs zho bcu la srang gang de la ni /
/ bod 'gar spor gang zhes pa'i tha snyad byed /
/ srang bzhi nyag gang de lnga khyor ba gang /
/ de bzhi khal gcig gam ni rgya [*ma*] *gang bya /*

There is no difference between a large *rgya thur*
From China[①] and the *zho* of the Mgur mo market.
Ten *'degs zho* is a single *srang*,
In some Tibet[areas], [a *srang*] is called a single *spor*.
Four *srang*, a single *nyag* (or: *nya ga*);[②] five of these, a single handful.
Four of these are said to be a *khal* or a single *rgya* [*ma*].

Earlier, De'u dmar Dge bshes had noted another *zho*, the so-called *gshor zho*, and he writes[③]:

/ ... ...phul bzhi la /
/ bre gang zhes bya bre bzhi gshor zho yin /

---

① I do not quite know what to make of this, but here *rgya thur che ba* does not appear mean "a large scale." Rather, it must refer to a value. See also below.

② De'u dmar Dge bshes 2007: 834 has an interesting gloss in which differences are noted between a Dbus and a Gtsang *nyag*, and between the Khyung po, Chab mdo, Lha thog *rgya ma*, etc. I leave these terms untranslated, since it is far from clear (to me) what exactly is indicated.

③ De'u dmar Dge bshes 2007a: 832. This passage occurs in a paraphrase of passages that he cites from the fifth chapter of the *Aṣṭāṅgahṛdayasaṃhitā* (BSTAN, vol. 111, 627–628), and Candranandana's (?10th c.) commentary on it (BSTAN, vol. 114, 217), and from an unidentified passage of Śālihotra's *Aśvāyurveda*; for the latter treatise, see Blondeau (1972: 37–110). He refers to the same sources, as well as to this work, in his later study of technology and the manufacture of various items and substances; see De'u dmar Dge bshes 2007b: 217–218—there he cites A bo (pho) Lnga 'Dzoms, a high-ranking person who is also referred to in Dmu dge Bsam gtan rgya mtsho's (1914–1993) narrative of the precipitous decline of Dalai Lama VI Tshang dbyangs rgya mtsho's (1683–1706) status as Dalai Lama; see Dmu dge Bsam gtan 1997: 190–191. Undated, De'u dmar Dge bshes' work was written at the behest of a number of individuals including the aforementioned Ba zal Padma dbang rgyal.

/ gshor zho bzhi la gro na zhes bya ste /
/ gshor zho lnga la gshor khal gic tu 'dod /
… … … … … … … … … … … … … … .four *phul*,
Are said to be one *bre*; four *bre* is a *gshor zho*.
Four *gshor zho* are said to be a *gro na*.
Five *gshor zho* are claimed to be one *khal*.

Ngag dbang bstan dar wrote immediately after he cited De'u dmar Dge bshes' line "Four of these are said to be either a *khal* or a whole *rgya*," that the majority of Tibetan intellectuals appear to have used fractions of a *zho* (*zho cha*) that were apparently common in the Mgur mo market and that according to De'u dmar Dge bshes the measure of its *zho* (*de'i zho tshad*), that is, the *zho* of the Mgur mo market.

A propos of the Mgur mo market, Dpa' boII Gtsug lag phreng ba (1504—1566) remarked in his well-known chronicle that during the lifetime of Lo ston Rdo rje dbang phyug (10th c.) this market (*tshong 'dus*) was called the Rab kha market, and Ngag dbang bstan dar echoes this.① The Mgur mo market is located in Ru lag, to the southwest of Shigatse. It so happens that the well-known lover of lexemes A kyā [阿嘉] Yongs 'dzin Blo bzang don grub (1740—1827), alias Dbyangs can dga' ba'i rdo rje, had also something to say about this in connection with his gloss of *ma byin len gyi rin thang* where he wrote the following②:

bu ston rin po ches / tshong 'dus kyi mgur mo bzhin gsungs pa'i mgur mo ji lta bu yin zhes pa ni / dris tshig nor ba ste / tshong 'dus mgur mo'i bzhi nam zhes pa yin / de ni sngon dus gtsang gi phyogs bu ston rin po che'i gdan sa zha lu'i nye 'dabs su nyo tshong byed pa'i gnas shig byung ba la / ming tshong 'dus mgur mo zhes chags / de'i bzhi nam zhes pa tshong 'dus de'i gser zho gang gi bzhi cha yin par sems / zho srang gi tshad ni / nas gnyis la ma ru gcig / ma ru gsum la palla gcig / palla brgyad la dha ra ṇa gcig / dha ra ṇa gnyis la tshong 'dus mgur mo'i zho gang du brtsi bar bshad do // des na ma ru bzhi bcu zhe brgyad kyi lcid dang mnyam pa'i gser ni gser zho gang yin pas / de'i bzhi cha ma ru bcu gnyis kyi lcid dang mnyam pa'i gser se ba drug la bya'o // ma ru ni bal po'i sran ma dmar po nag thigs can de yin par bshad / ma byin len gyi rin thang gi tshad yig cha rnams su mkhas pa'i bzhed tshul sna tshogs bkod la

① See, respectively, Dpa' bo II 1986: 473 and NGAG1[1], 739, and NGAG2, 437. Tshong 'dus Mgur mo is located in Ru lag, to the southwest of Shigatse.
② A kyā Yongs 'dzin 1971a: 119—120.

/ rdzas kyi rin thang dang / zho srang gi tshad sogs kyang yul dus kyi dbang gis 'gyur bas nges pa med phyir / mkhas pa mang pos / dngul zho gang ngam gser se ba gsum brkus na pham pa 'byung ba yul dus kun tu nges pa yin gsung ngo // se ba ni phal cher ma ru gnyis kyi lcid mnyam la bshad / 'ga' zhig tu ma ru gcig gi lcid mnyam la zer ba'ang 'dug ste / yul dus kyis zho srang ga brtsi gzhi mi 'dra ba'i khyad du snang ngo //

To ask what is a *mgur mo* in the precious Bu ston's statement "like (*bzhin*) the *mgur mo* of a market" is a wrongly worded question, that is, "is it four (*bzhi*) of the Mgur mo market? (*nam*)" ① In early times, the Mgur mo was a place for buying and selling in the Gtsang region, close to Zhwa lu, the see of the precious Bu ston, and it was called the Mgur mo market, and I think that the phrase "is it four of that?" means one quarter of a single golden *zho* of the Mgur mo market. The *zho* and *srang* are weight measures: It has been explained that for two barley grains, one rosary bead; for three rosary beads, one *pala*②; for eight *pala*, one *dharaṇa*; one *dharaṇa* is reckoned as a single *zho* of the Mgur mo market. Hence, in as much as gold that is equal in weight to forty-eight rosary peas (*ma ru* = *dmar ru*) is a single golden *zho*, one quarter should be six golden *se ba* which are equal in weight to twelve rosary peas. A *ma ru* is explained to be a red Nepalese bean with a black spot③. Various claims of the learned have been recorded in textbooks about the measures of the values of taking what is not given. But because the value of substances and the measure of the *zho* and *srang*, etc. are uncertain due to the changes in regions and time periods, many scholars have said that it is certain that one would have incurred a *pārājika-pham pa* violation in every region and at all time periods were one to steal a single silver *zho* or three golden *se ba*. A *se ba* is for the most part explained to be equal in weight to two rosary peas. In some sources, it is also suggested that it is equal in weight to one rosary pea; due to region and time period, there appears to be a difference on what basis a *zho* and a *srang* are calculated.

Ngag dbang bstan dar then cites A kyā II Blo bzang bstan pa'i rgyal mtshan's (1708–1768)

① I have not found the source for this statement, neither in the relevant section of Bu ston's commentary on the *Ekottarakarmaśataka*–see Bu ston 1971a: 921–nor in that of his 1356 commentary on Guṇaprabha's *Vinayasūtra*–see Bu ston 1971d: 314–315.

② The Tibetan equivalent of *pala/palla* is *srang*.

③ Blo bzang rin chen (1810–1907), alias Sumatiratna, has this very line in his great Tibetan-Mongol lexicon: *ma ru ni bal po'i srin ma dmar po nag thigs can de yin par bshad*; see Sumatiratna 1959: II, 392. Chi Galsang 1982: 440 registers Mongol *ulaɣan burča*, "red pea/bean," and even *körüsü sirui*, "topsoil," for Tibetan *ma ru*.

miscellaneous writings (*gsung thor*), to wit, his *Rtsis kyi skor sna tshogs*,① a wonderful miscellany on the calendar, *skar rtsis*-astronomy, *nag rtsis*-astrology, and, and the chronology of the historical Buddha's life, to the effect that②:

> *nas gnyis la dmar* [*ma*] *ru gcig / dmar* [*ma*] *ru gsum la pa la* [*palla*] *gcig / palla brgyad la dha ra ṇa gcig / dha ra ṇa gcig la mgur mo'i zho gang du brtsi'o //*

And this may of course have been the very source tapped by A kyā Yong 'dzin we met in his work that I just cited, since he was the tutor of A kyā III Ye shes bskal bzang rgya mtsho (1817–1869).

Just before this citation, Ngag dbang bstan dar then refers once again to De'u dmar Dge bshes and writes③:

> *nas 'bru drug la se ba gang du byas pa'i se ba nyer bzhi'i tshad dang ldan zhing rgya nag gi rgya thur che ba dang mnyam zer kyang / de ltar brtsi na se ba nyer bzhi la nas 'bru brgya zhe bzhi thob cing / de chēn* [NGAG2, 438: *chen*] *lung rgyal po'i ring gi shī phing* [NGAG2, 438: *la shi thing*] *zer ba rgya thur che ba dang bsdur na zho gang skar lnga yan longs pas na rgya thur dang tshad mi mnyam par gsal /*
>
> Although it is alleged that what has the measure of twenty-four *se ba*, where a single *se ba* is made up of six barley grains, is equal to a Chinese *rgya thur che ba*, if calculated accordingly, twenty-four *se ba* would obtain one hundred and forty-four barley grains and if one compares

---

① Undated, the *Mahā tsi na'i byang mtha' rgyal khab chen po pé kying gtso bor gyur pa'i byang phyogs kyi yul 'khor la 'os pa'i dus sbyor gyi rnam bzhag padmo'i tshal rab 'byed pa'i* ***nyi*** *ma* ***gzhon*** *nu* is but the first work of this miscellany (pp.1055–1064) and ends with a colophon–it consists of five folios to which is added a table that is tellingly titled *Dus sbyor* ***nyi gzhon*** *ma*! Not every work in this collection was by A kyā II. On pp.1071–1075 (fols. 9a–11a), there is a short piece written by an Oirat Mongol who is referred to as Hu bil gān (< Mo. *qubilγan* = Tib. *sprul pa*[*'i sku*]) Rab 'byams pa [gün] Paṇḍita. His tract on Buddhist chronology on pp.1075–1104 (11a–25b) is dated 1760, but none of the others are. Portions of this miscellany were studied in Lobsang Yongdan 2018–2019.

② NGAG1[1], 739, and NGAG2, 438, citing A kyā II No date: 1164 (fol. 55b)–the variants of the latter are in square brackets. A kyā II's texts continues: *palla bcu bzhi la dha ṭa ka gcig ste / 'dir ma ru gsum la se ba phyed dor byed pas ma ru gnyis la se ba gang ngo // yang ma ru lnga la taṃ ma gcig / taṃ ma bcu drug la zho gang / zho bzhi la srang gang du brtsi bar snang bas / ma ru brgyad bcu la zho gang du byas pa'o // yang zur rtsis zhig la / se ba bco brgyad zho yi bcu cha dgu / zhes dang / se ba bcu drug zho yi lnga cha bzhi / zhes pa ltar na se ba nyi shu la zho gang du byas pa'o // yang nas*$_2$ *ma ru*$_1$ *gser se ba*$_1$ *rnams lcid mnyam zhing / bal taṃ la se ba nyer bzhi'i lcid yod zer ba'ang snang //.*

③ NGAG1[1], 739, and NGAG2, 437–438.

the so-called *shi thing/phing* of Qianlong's reign (1735–1796) with a large *rgya thur*, then it is clear that, insofar as a single *zho* exceeds five *skar*, it is not equal to a *rgya thur*.①

And he uses the terms *dong tse* and *dong tse tā chen* (< 銅子？大錢) in connection with their respective valuations, and he refers to the relevant passages in what he calls the "three Indian commentaries." ②

Ngag dbang bstan dar quotes a passage from Sum pa Mkhan po Ye shes dpal 'byor's (1704–1788) *Dris lan rab dkar pa sangs* in which the latter points to the relativity of weights, measures and monetary valuations that exist in different regions and for different time periods. The implication that can be drawn from his remarks and those of Sum pa Mkhan po and A Kyā Yongs 'dzin is that this relativity creates problems for an assessment of how much needs to be stolen before it becomes a major infraction according to Buddhist canon law.③ But it is especially in the third and last main portion of his work that Ngag dbang bstan dar draws repeated attention to this very relativity and from which we learn that he and other members of the Tibetan Buddhist clergy were ever so well aware, as they should be, of the importance of the maintenance of the rule of law in the land (*rgyal khrims*) and the degree to which its maintenance is a precondition for the maintenance of the clergy's

---

① My colleague Prof. Zhang Changhong of Sichuan University kindly suggested to read *shi ding* 十錠, "ten ingots," for Tibetan *shi thing/phing* but I am unclear how this might fit the narrative. Further, I am not at all sure what to do with a "large *rgya thur*".

② NGAG1[1], 749, and NGAG2, 444. As is indicated in NGAG1[1], 742, and NGAG2, 439–440, these are Kamalaśīla's (8th c.) *Don brgyad ma* (*Dge sbyong gi kā ri kā lnga bcu pa mdo tsam du bshad pa*, BSTAN, vol. 93, 733–799), *Shes rab byed pa* (Prajñākara's *Vinayasūtravyākhyāna*, BSTAN, vol. 92, 3–733), and the *'Grel chung yon tan 'od ma* (*Vinayasūtravṛtti*, BSTAN, vol. 92, 737–1682). In his Zhwa lu *Bstan 'gyur* catalog of 1335, Bu ston 1971b: 612 suggests that the third may have been of Tibetan origin (*bod ma*). However, twenty-two years later, in his survey of the *vinaya* and its literature of 1357, he wonders whether the second and third might have been Tibetan lecture notes (*bod kyi zin bris*); see Bu ston 1971c: 113. Two of the passages cited occur in BSTAN, vol. 93, 769; vol. 92, 872, but I have not been able to verify this statement in what is allegedly Prajñākara's work.

③ NGAG1[1], 744, and NGAG2, 441, citing Sum pa Mkhan po 1975: 325–326. The latter reference occurs in the eleventh question of a series of some twenty-seven questions on a wide range of subjects, from religious practice to astronomy and Sanskrit-Tibetan prosody, posed to him by a certain Ngag dbang nyi ma on pp.310–347. Sum pa Mkhan po's astute remarks deserve a separate study. Dngul chu Dharmabhadra (1772–1851) expresses a similar sentiment in his brief statement about theft in his many replies to equally many questions that were posed to him over time; see Dngul chu 1973–1981: 424–425. Recently, Dorji Wangchuk drew attention to a passage in the late Dung dkar Blo bzang 'phrin las' (1927–1997) encyclopedic dictionary in which the author opines that the so-called third "great decree" (*bkas bcad chen po*) issued during the reign of Khri gtsug lde btsan (r. 815/818–836/838), alias Ral pa can, was concerned with achieving parity between Magadha-Indian and Tibetan weights and measures; see Wangchuk 2020: 950–951.

proper behavior, one that is in accordance with canon law (*chos khrims*) and other norms.[①] And what is more, they were also cognisant of the fact that scarcity of goods, as for example during a famine, creates an upward pressure on prices and impacts the stability of monetary values. We can expect that the strength of the rule of law and its application will have a bearing on the prevalence of infractions, theft among them, within the community of the clergy. The degrees to which local, regional law (*yul khrims*) or customary law (*'bangs khrims*) may have played a role in these determinations are of course questions that need further study. Here, my translations of *yul khrims* and *'bangs khrims* are tentative. The first occurs in a version of the *Bka' chems ka khol ma*, where we read that "Srong btsan sgam po created the good *yul khrims*"[②]. Here, *yul khrims* may also be an abbreviation or short for *yul gyi khrims*, "law of the land," in the sense of the law in the country under his domain. The *Blon po bka'i thang yig* of U rgyan gling pa (1323–?) enumerates in one breath *rgyal khrims, chos khrims*, and *'bangs khrims*, suggesting thereby a distinction between the first and the last.[③] Commenting on the final five-hundred year period of the five thousand year duration of the Buddha's teaching, when all is about to go to hell, U rgyan gling pa's *Rgyal po bka'i thang yig* uses the phrase *'bangs kyi mi chos*, which I submit is a phrase that is closely associated with the term *'bangs khrims*[④]:

/ rab tu 'byung ba'i mkhan slob yul gzhi stongs /
/ rgyal po'i bka khrims nyi ma lta bu rgas /
/ 'bangs kyi mi chos sog ma'i phon thag gcod /
/ bla mchod chos khrims dar mdud lta bu grol /

The world has been emptied of renunciate abbots and masters[⑤].
The king's laws have weakened like the sun.[⑥]
The popular religion of the people has the straw rope cut.[⑦]

---

① See, for example, the passage in NGAG1[1], 750, and NGAG2, 444–445, in which Mtsho sna ba 1993: 270, 271 is cited.

② Smon lam rgya mtsho 1989: 315.

③ U rgyan gling pa 1986: 520. U rgyan gling pa 1986: 446 contains a narrative in which all four notions of *khrims* find a place.

④ U rgyan gling pa 1986: 108.

⑤ It is possible to read *slob* as *slob dpon*, the master who aids in the ordination ceremony, or as *slob ma*, the student who is to be ordained.

⑥ I can only understand *rgas* in the sense that the sun's heat has grown weaker towards the end of the year.

⑦ The straw rope (*sog ma'i phon thag*) motif also occurs in connection with the idea of *'bangs khrims* in U rgyan gling pa 1986: 446: */ 'bangs khrims sog ma'i phon thag mang yang 'dus /*.

The religious law of the court chaplains becomes loose like
a silk knot.

Referring to Chinese lexemes as *rgya skad* or *rgya nag gi skad*, Ngag dbang bstan dar also made several references to Chinese in the *Gangs can gyi brda' gsar rnying las brtsams pa'i brda' yig blo gsal mgrin rgyan*, his important, undated study of archaisms (*brda rnying*) and their updates (*brda gsar*), a literary genre of which M. Taube has given an impressive, if now somewhat dated, survey①; he writes②:

1. *khyogs ni mi chen sogs 'degs byed de / rgya'i skad du kyo zer ba de yin zhing......*

A *khyogs* is that which carries important persons; in Chinese, it is called *kyo* [*jiao* 轎, sedan chair].③

2. *dan kong ni 'jim pa las byas pa'i ril bu skam po 'phen pa'i gzhu'o 'di rgya nag gi skad yin /*

A *dan kong* is the slingshot that shoots a dry globe made of clay; this is Chinese [*dan gong* 彈弓].

3. *phrag rdang gi khur ni shing ring po'i phan tshun snye la khres*[a] *po dpyang ste phrag pas khur ba'o // rgya'i skad du thi'o dan zer ro //*

[a] NGAG2, 655: *khris*.

A *phrag rdang gi khur* is a load that dangles on the mutual support of a long pole, and it is carried on the shoulders. In Chinese, it is called *tiaodan* 挑擔 .

① Taube 1978.

② NGAG1[2], 317, 355, 367 [2x], 401 [2x], 406, and NGAG2, 626, 648, 655 [2x], 674 [2x], 677.

③ The word *khyogs* is glossed by *kyā'o* (*jiao* 轎) in his commentary on Mkhas grub Dge legs dpal bzang po's (1385–1438) praise of his teacher Tsong kha pa, his famous *Bstod pa dad pa'i rol mtsho*, in NGAG1[2], 33, and NGAG2, 467.

4. *phyags ma ni sdud byed dang dag byed / rgya'i skad du swo kyo'u /*

A *phyags ma*-broom is what gathers and cleans; in Chinese *saozhou* 掃帚.

5. *sho gam ni rgya'i skad du shu'u / sog skad du ha'i li zer /*

sho gam-tax in Chinese is called *shui* 税 and in Mongol *γaili*.

6. *shod thabs ni brtsi grangs brtsis pa'i thabs te rgya nag gi skad du swa phan dang bod kyi brtsi gzhong dang sa gzhong lta bu'o //*

A *shod thabs*-abacus is a means for calculating numbers; it is *suanpan* 算盤 in Chinese and it is like the Tibetan *brtsi gzhong* and *sa gzhong*.①

7. *slo ma ni zhib ma ste de yang glang ma dang smyug ma sogs las bzos pa'i snod sgor mo ste rgya nag gi skad du pha'o lū zer /*

A *slo ma*-basket is a *zhib ma*. Further, a round container/basket that is made from willow reed and/or bamboo; in Chinese, it is called *beilou* 背簍.

In his undated and fragmentary *Yi ge'i mtha' dpyod ma dag pa'i dri ma 'khrud pa'i chab gtsang*, Ngag dbang bstan dar deals with a number of orthographic ambiguities and mistakes that he culled from a host of orthographic dictionaries (*dag yig*) and xylographs.② Even if some Tibetan authors have suggested that several earlier works belonged to the Tibetan literary genre of the *dag yig*, the expression first seems to have made its appearance in an actual title as late as the 13th century with Snye thang Grags pa seng ge's *Dag yig ganggā'i chu rgyun*—this work has not (yet) come down to us, but it is mentioned in various later specimen that belong to the *dag yig* genre. True, Ngag dbang bstan dar refers to a *dag yig* tract by Rngog Lo tsā ba Blo ldan shes rab (ca.1059–1109), which can only be the *Dag yig nyer mkho bsdus pa*, but the jury is still out on whether it was correctly

---

① For the abacus and its use in Tibetan cultural area, see Schuh 2012: xxxvi ff. and 2012a: 694–697.

② NGAG1[2], 585–610, and NGAG2, 781–795.

attributed to him.① I personally doubt this very much, since it contains the disparaging expression *hor 'dra*, "Mongol-like", which only gained currency during the Mongol occupation of Dbus gtsang (1240–1368) and was unknown prior to this time.② Tax-collectors were often called *hor 'dra*. Among the many Tibetan authors who wrote *dag yig* works, Ngag dbang bstan dar cites three of the better-known representatives of the genre several times. In addition, he also cites a piece on correct orthography that Dalai Lama VII Skal bzang rgya mtsho (1708–1757) had written in response to some philological queries that the translator Tā bla ma Kau shrī Shes rab rgya mtsho had sent him from Beijing.③ In the course of his deliberations in the *Yi ge'i mtha' dpyod ma dag pa'i dri ma 'khrud pa'i chab gtsang*, Ngag dbang bstan dar refers to Chinese on the two occasions,④ of which only the first is relevant here:

> *spa dbyug ces pa dang sba dbyug ces pa sde tshan bzhi pa'i dang po dang gsum pa / gnyis yod pa ltar gnyis ka 'thad de / byams pa gling pa'i smra rgyan du /*
>
> */ spa dang spa ma'i nags su sdod /*
>
> *ces gsungs pas spa ma'i nags yod na spa shing yod par grub cing / spa shing yod na spa dbyug kyang grub la / der ma zad za ma tog tu /*
>
> / sprang[a] *po'i spar mor spa dbyug 'chang /*

---

① He refers to it in NGAG1[2], 590, and NGAG2, 782. Gser tog Blo bzang tshul khrims rgya mtsho (1845–1915) quotes a passage from what is *allegedly* Rngog Lo tsā ba's work in his 1891 study of Tibetan grammer; see Gser tog 2005: 86b *ad* Rngog Lo tsā ba 2006: 2b–3a [96–97], and it was studied in Miller 1976: 72. A kyā Yongs 'dzin cites another passage, Rngog Lo tsā ba 2006: 3a [97], in his undated work on Tibetan grammer; see A kya Yongs 'dzin 1971a: 432. Miller 1976: 78–80 also studied a passage from what turns out to be Ngag dbang bstan dar's *Sum cu pa dang rtags 'jug gi don go sla bar bsdus pa'i bshad pa skal ldan yid kyi pad ma 'byed pa'i snang mdzod*, for which see NGAG1[2],160 and NGAG2, 540.

② Rngog Lo tsā ba 2006: 4b [100]. Mr. Sun Penghao is in the process of completing a study of these enigmatic officers of various bureaucracies.

③ NGAG1[2], 592, and NGAG2, 784; the possibly incomplete work in question is Dalai Lama VII 1975, and the cited passage occurs therein on p.122.

④ NGAG1[2], 586–588, 593, and NGAG2, 781, 784. The second has to do with the old Tibetan expression *rgya nag stong khun, tong kun*, etc. for which see the illuminating article in van Schaik 2013b. One slight correction can be made, the Rol pa'i rdo rje mentioned therein is not Karma pa IV, but Lcang skyā III (1717–1786); see van der Kuijp 2010: 125, n. 104.

[a] NGAG1[2], 587, and NGAG2, 781: *spyang*.

zhes dang / ngag sgron du /

/ sprang po'i spar mor spa dbyug sprad /

ces byung bas spa dbyug yod pa gdon mi za'o // sba dbyug ces pa'ang yod pa yin te / ngag sgron du /

/ sbyag tshe lus sbrid sba 'khar sbom /

zhes pa'i sba 'khar de sba dbyug las 'os med cing / smra rgyan du /

/ da dung sbyag na sba dbyug bsten /

ces gsal por byung bas sba dbyug kyang grub bo // des na rnam thar sogs su bshad pa'i sba dbyug ni rgya nag gi skad du theng tse zer zhing rgya'i yul du lcag yu byas pa de yin snyam zhing / spa shing gi ngos 'dzin ma mthong yang gong du drangs pa'i dag yig rnams kyi lung so sor yod pa bzhin shing gi rigs kyang so so ba e yin snyam /

As there are both words *spa dbyug*, "bamboo walking stick", and *sba dbyug*, "rattan stick", with the first and the third of the fourth category of the Tibetan alpha syllables/graphs, both are correct; since the phrase

"Bamboo and staying in a bamboo forest ..."

is stated in Byams pa gling pa Paṇ chen Bsod nams rgyal ba'i sde's (1400–1475) *Smra rgyan*,① it is established that when there is a bamboo forest, there is bamboo and that when there is bamboo, there is also a bamboo walking stick. And not only that, since

① Byams gling Paṇ chen 2014: 355. The *Smra rgyan* dates from 1419 and was thus written when the author was a teenager!

"A bamboo walking stick is held in the hand of the beggar."

occurs in Zhwa lu Lo tsā ba's *Za ma tog*[①] of 1514 and since,

"Giving a bamboo walking stick in the beggar's hand."

occurs in Dpal khang Lo tsā ba Ngag dbang chos kyi rgya mtsho's (16th c.) *Ngag sgron* of 1538,[②] the expression "a bamboo walking stick," too, exists without a doubt.

There is also the word *sba sbyug*. There is no possibility that the *sba 'khar* ("bamboo/ rattan cane") that is stated in the *Ngag sgron*[③]:

"Frail, numb, cane, corpulent."

---

① Zhwa lu Lo tsā ba No date: fol. 31a; 2002: 82–83; and 2014: 70; Zhwa lu Lo tsā ba's work was partly studied in Laufer 1898 where, however, this line was not translated; see now also R. Kaschewsky's study of the bilingual Tibetan-Mongol text of this dictionary where we read this line in Kaschewsky 2017: 120: "[in Tibetan] *spyang po'i spar mor spa sbyug 'chang.* [in Mongol:] *kersegüü-yi-yin adqun-dur spa beriy-e barimu.* [in German:] klug. Wanderstab in der Hand halten." He noted the variant *sprang po'i* for *spyang po'i*–we find the same in No date: 31a where *spyang po* is given a Sanskrit equivalent!–and that Tibetan *spa* was not given a Mongol translation. The bilingual Tibetan-Mongol xylograph of this work was published in Zhwa lu Lo tsā ba 1981, where the line is found on fol. 38b [5890]. The Tibetan carver of the blocks, the Mongol translator, and the editor[s] mistook the correct Tibetan *sprang po'i* for *spyang po'i* and then misread *spyang po'i* for *sbyang po'i* so that the Mongol translation would read *kersegüü-yi-yin*, "intelligent." To be sure, the Mongol equivalent of *sprang po*, "beggar," is *γuilinči*. The basic text dates from 1514 and was completed at Grwa thang monastery. The manuscript replete with many Sanskrit glosses on which the undated xylograph (with Tibetan and Chinese pagination) is based dates from a text that was completed in Bsam grub bde chen, in 1526.

② Dpal khang Lo tsā ba 2014a: 19. The year of his birth is sometimes given as 1456, but, as far as I am aware, there is no evidence for this. Dpal khang Lo tsā ba is also known as Karma 'phrin las pa II, as if he were the reembodiment of Karma 'phrin las pa I (1456–1539). This is not the case. A collection of his letters, poetic admonitions, and other ephemera contains *inter alia* a long, undated letter to Karma 'phrin las pa I; see Dpal khang Lo tsā ba No date: 16a–19a. The *Bod kyi brda'i bye brag gsal bar byed pa'i bstan bcos tshig le'ur byas pa mkhas pa'i ngag gi sgron ma'i 'grel pa bdud rtsi'i dga' ston* on occasion parades as an autocommentary on the *Ngag sgron*. Contained in Dpal khang Lo tsā ba 2014, its table of contents states that Dpal khang Lo tsā ba was its author. The colophon (pp.189–190) clearly disputes this claim and in fact its author turns out to be a certain *bkṣu* (*sic*!) *sum* (*sic*!) *ti gu ṇa* (*bhikṣu* Blo bzang yon tan), who completed this work in 1848 in Bshad sgrub dga' tshal in Bde mo thang, Amdo. Once again using *bi kṣu su ma ti gu ṇa* as his name, he is without doubt also the author of the 1837 biography of Blo bzang 'jam dbyangs phyogs las rnam rgyal, alias Tshangs sras sgeg pa'i rdo rje (1789–1808), for which see Blo bzang yon tan No date. Indications are that Tshangs sras sgeg pa'i rdo rje was a precious and a precocious talent, who passed away way too young.

③ Dpal khang Lo tsā ba 2014a: 21, where we read *mkhar* instead of *'khar*.

is other than the *sba sbyug*, and *sba dbyug* is moreover established, since the *Smra rgyan* has clearly stated①:

"Nowadays, if you lose weight, you rely on a cane."

Hence, the *sba dbyug* that is mentioned in biographies, etc. is called *tengzi* 藤子 in Chinese and I think that it is called whip-handle (*lcag* [*gi*] *yu* [*ba*]) in China. Although I have not seen identifications of the *spa shing*, "*spa* tree," I wonder whether just as there are a variety passages of the orthographic dictionaries that were cited above, there would also not be several species of trees.②

Finally, aside from the aforementioned lexemes, he makes one pertinent, if elementary, remark a propos of the Chinese language that is spoken in northern China in his undated study of the Tibetan language titled *Yi ge'i bshad pa mkhas pa'i kha rgyan*. Contrasting Chinese with Sanskrit, Tibetan, and Mongol, he writes③:

rgya gar dang bod dang sog po gsum la rnam dbye brgyad med mi rung zhing[a] *rgya nag la rnam dbye gtan nas mi dgos par / tshig gong 'og brje ba'i khyad par tsam las ming thams cad brjod par 'dod cing / rnam dbye'i tshab tu phing / nang / chus / bzhu'u zhes pa bzhi 'dod cing / de yang dbyangs sam nga ro yin par mngon pas / phing zhes pa dbugs cha snyom pa'i shugs kyis thon pa dang / shang*[b] *zhes pa dbugs gyen du btegs pa'i shugs kyis thon pa dang / chus zhes pas dbugs thad kar phyir 'phul ba'i shugs kyis thon pa dang / bzhu'u zhes pa dbugs thur du phyung ba'i shugs kyis thon pa dang / ming gang brjod kyang brjod tshul bzhi po 'di las ma 'das zer ro //*

[a] NGAG1[2], 246, adds /.[b] NGAG2, 587: *nang*.

Case endings in Sanskrit, Tibetan and Mongol are indispensable and while Chinese never

① Byams gling Paṇ chen 2014: 360.

② A kyā Yongs 'dzin 1971a: 120–121 has something similar to say about *sba smyug* and *sba dbyug* and does not set store by the *spa/sba* variant, which he says seem to be based on synonymy (*don gcig pa 'dra*).

③ NGAG1[2], 246–247, and NGAG2, 587. It is interesting that he shows a broad appreciation of language as such. This is not the case with Sum pa Mkhan po, his senior contemporary and as well ethnically a Mongol, whose works on orthography and on what may be called the language arts (*sgra rig*) focuses solely on Tibetan and Sanskrit.

had a need for a case ending, it is asserted that all characters (ming) are expressed based on the mere difference in the interchange of their word order. And as a substitute for a case ending, it asserts the four [tones] of level (*phing* < Ch. *ping* 平), rising (*shang* < Ch. *shang* 上), departing (*chus* < Ch. *qu* 去), and entering (*bzhu'u* < Ch. *ru* 入). Further, since it is obvious that these involve voice (dbyangs) and pitch (nga ro),[a] the level tone is articulated with the force of an even exhalation, the rising tone is articulated with the force of an upwardly raised exhalation, the departing tone is articulated with the force of a pulled back and straight forward exhalation, and the entering tone is articulated with the force of a downward exhalation. And it is alleged that no matter what word is spoken, it does not go beyond these four manners of articulation.

In addition to writing on Tibetan grammar② and the Tibetan alpha-syllabary and orthotactics, Ngag dbang bstan dar also authored a Mongol grammar, the *Kelen-ü čimeg* or *Language Ornament* of 1794, which was studied by Taube and others, and a Tibetan-Mongol dictionary.③ These were not included in the Tibetan editions of his oeuvre.

Postscript One: Many years ago, I surmised that the deep engagement with spelling and the study of language and grammer that we witness in such learned men as Ngag dbang bstan dar and A kyā Yongs 'dzin-we can add the names of Si tu Paṇ chen and Sum pa Mkhan po-, may have been in part a reflex of the Qing dynasty's philological concerns, its *hanxue* 漢學. Both men lived in the Sino-Tibetan marches and at least Ngag dbang bstan dar had also worked in Beijing—there is evidence that Ngag dbang bstan dar was familiar with A kyā Yongs 'dzin, for he refers to one of his lexicographic glosses in his 1834 commentary on Candragomin's (5th c.) *Śiṣyalekha*.④ But I now believe that this impression of mine was too hastily formed and, in fact, was quite wrong, so that I now wish to distance myself from it. Instead, I would suggest that their interest in grammar and lexicography had to do with them living at the end of an intellectual environment in the formation of which they were late participants. This environment was characterized by the printing (and publication) of large-

① I follow here the 1624 commentary of A mes zhabs Ngag dbang kun dga' bsod nams (1597—1659) on Sa skya Paṇḍita Kun dga' rgyal mtshan's (1182—1251) *Rol mo'i bstan bcos*, his essay on music; see A mes zhabs 2012: 146, 149. I read a portion of this work with my student Mr. Ma Zhouyang whose insights enabled us to disentangle some difficult passages.

② See his *Sum ca pa dang rtags 'jug gi don go sla bar bsdus pa'i bshad pa skal bzang yid kyi pad ma 'byed pa'i snang ba'i mdzod* in NGAG1[2], 115—214, and NGAG2, 538—569, and the brief remark in Tillemans 2007: 54—55.

③ See, respectively, Taube 1961 and A lag sha Ngag dbang bstan dar 1982.

④ NGAG1[1], 636, and NGAG2, 379, where he refers to A kyā Yongs 'dzin glossing *bya gar* with *bya gag*; see A kyā Yongs 'dzin 1971c: 208.

scale literary collections such as the canon, Kanjur and Tanjur, and a good number of editions of the collected oeuvre of many leading Tibetan scholars, past and present, and as well the scholarly milieu that contributed to this. There is no question that the great Si tu Paṇ chen also fits very well in this milieu. He was not only deeply concerned with both Sanskrit and Tibetan grammar and lexicography but was also engaged in editing the Kanjur portion of the Tibetan Buddhist canon. Working on editing the canon went in tandem with the inception of a specific genre of Tibetan lexicography that the earliest treatise in which what were considered to be lexical archaisms (*brda rnying*) were given their updated equivalents (*brda gsar*). I am thinking here of the little text that came from the pen of Dbus pa Blo gsal, whose nickname was Rtsod pa'i seng ge (ca.1270–ca.1355).① We find a brief mention of the notion of an archaic or dated lexeme plus three examples in Sa skya Paṇḍita's celebrated treatise on what a person who aspires to scholarship should know.② But there seems to be little room to doubt that, contrary to Sa skya Paṇḍita's brief mention, Dbus pa Blo gsal's work should be viewed by bearing in mind that he was *inter alia* the editor-compiler of the Snar thang Tanjur manuscript of the 1310s.

Postscript Two: In Part One of this essay—van der Kuijp 2019: 288, n. 5 -, I mentioned Se cen Mgon po skyabs' bilingual Tibetan-Chinese materia medica, at least this was how the author of this work was identified. I had forgotten that L. Chandra had reproduced a xylograph of this work titled *Sman ming bod dang rgya'i skad shan sbyar ba*, the accompanying Chinese and Mongol titles of which are *Fan han yaoming* 番漢藥名 and *Em-ün ner-e töbed kitad qadamal üge*.③ Also published by Chandra, the so-called *Sman sna tshogs kyi per chad* is nothing but a somewhat incomplete manuscript copy of the *Sman ming bod dang rgya'i skad shan sbyar ba*.④ The introductory note, the section headings, and the concluding remarks plus the printer's colophon are given in both Tibetan and Mongol; the printer's colophon reads:

---

① First published in Mimaki 1990, which is based on Dbus pa Blo gsal 1983. For similar texts with different titles that are ascribed to Dbus pa Blo gsal, see van der Kuijp 2009b:128, n. 2. A somewhat different manuscript of this work has now become available, for which see Dbus pa Blo gsal No date. The latter has been wrongly included in a collection of several works by his namesake. This person must have flourished in the 15th and 16th century, since, in some of the writings contained in this collection, the author mentions his teacher Rdo ring Kun spangs pa, who must certainly be identified as Kun bzang chos kyi nyi ma (1449–1524).

② Sa skya Paṇḍita Kun dga' rgyal mtshan 2007: 15.

③ Se cen Mgon po skyabs 1980a. Laufer 1916: 440–441 reacted quite vehemently, but rightly, against Hübotter 1913 for the many mistakes he had made in his book that was based on Se cen's work. A revised edition appeared in Hübotter 1957. On F. Hübotter (1881–1967) and his contributions, see the interesting capsule scientific biography in Schnorrenberger 2010: 157–159.

④ Se cen Mgon po skyabs 1980b.

... slar yang yung ceng gi gnam lo bcu gnyis pa shing stag dbyar zla 'bring po'i tshes bzang la spar 'di skyar brkos byas pa yin no // dge'o //

... again, the blocks were carved once more on Yongzheng twelve, the wood-tiger year, the "good day" ① of the intermediate-summer month.

Thus, the xylograph probably dates from printing blocks that were prepared on June 11, 1734.

Appendix

The Structure of the *Ma byin len gyi pham pa'i rin thang gi tshad bshad pa 'khrul spong mkhas pa'i dgyes byed mchod yon rnam dag*②

Ngag dbang bstan dar begins his work with the usual statement of homage and verses of obeisance. Just prior to the main body of his text, he ends his preamble with two verses. Waxing poetic, he states in the first that earlier generations of scholars, who were not able to drink the muddy water of how to go about valuating things, neglected to deal with this in a comprehensive fashion. But help is on the way, and he writes in the second verse:

bdag gi rnam dpyod nor bu ke ta kas //
rnyog ma gang de legs par bgrungs byas nas //
legs par bshad pa'i mchod yon gtsang ma'i chab //
deng 'dir sbreng ngo mkhas rnams 'dir 'dus shig //

Having appropriately strained whatever impurities there were,
With the Ke ta ka gem③ of my intellect,
The pure water, a gift that is well-articulated,
Is now decanted in this treatise; may the learned gather here!

---

① Not specified which *bzang po* day of the month, I, rightly or wrongly, take it to be the first one which is equivalent to the second day of the first week of the month.

② For the text, see above n. 2.

③ This mythical "purificatory" gem is of Indic origin and is already found mentioned in the * *Āryamūla-sarvāstivādaśramaṇerakārikā*, in BSTAN, vol. 93, 168, that is attributed to Śākyaprabha.

The Indian Buddhist literature on canon law was quite explicit that theft is a significant infraction for the mores of the Buddhist monastic community, but it was not always clear on how much of value needed to be stolen that would result in the culprit's expulsion or ex-communication from the community, that is to say, when it would constitute an actual transgression or downfall. At the same time, what in fact constitutes theft, intentional or otherwise, was also a much-debated issue. Standards of measurements and valuation and their terminologies no doubt varied from region to region in the Indian subcontinent, never mind the variations that would occur during the passage of more than a thousand years of the Indian Buddhist literature that was then ultimately translated wholesale into Tibetan. In addition, we can be sure that measurements and valuations also fluctuated in the Tibetan area. This made things exceedingly complicated. Undeterred and without historicizing his sources, Ngag dbang bstan dar valiantly tackled the subject of value and currencies in the following three main sections and a number of subsections:

1. An explanation of the measure of a *zho* and a *srang*
   NGAG1[1], 732–740, and NGAG2, 433–438
   1a. A general explanation of *zho* and *srang*
       NGAG1[1], 732–734, and NGAG2, 433–438
   1b. The value of *zho* (**karṣa*) and *srang* (**pala*) of the Holy Land [India]
       NGAG1[1], 734–738, and NGAG2, 433–437
   1c. The value of *zho* and *srang* of Tibet
       NGAG1[1], 738–740, and NGAG2, 437–438
2. An explanation of the measurement of value
   NGAG1[1], 740–749, and NGAG2, 438–444
   2a. Inquiry into the things that form the basis of value
       NGAG1[1], 740–741, and NGAG2, 438–439
   2b. How these are stated by Indian scholars
       NGAG1[1], 741–743, and NGAG2, 439–440
   2c. How they are commented on by Tibetan scholars
       NGAG1[1], 741–743, and NGAG2, 440–442
   2d. Inquiry into what and what is not correct about these ways
       NGAG1[1], 743–749, and NGAG2, 442–444
3. An exposition of my own position
   NGAG1[1], 749–755, and NGAG2, 444–448

What now follows is a listing of Ngag dbang bstan dar's citations of Tibetan authors and their works in the order in which they are cited for the first time (multiple citations are not registered and the dates of authors already given in the main body of my paper or in the footnotes are not repeated here):

1. Dalai Lama V Ngag dbang blo bzang rgya mtsho
   Las mchog gser mdog rnam rgyal
   1a. Cites: Zhwa lu Lo tsā ba Chos skyong bzang po
       Dris lan
2. Sde srid Sangs rgyas rgya mtsho
   Baidūr g.ya sel
3. Skyed tshal Mkhan po Kun dga' chos bzang (1433–1503)
   'Dul ba spyi don lung rigs gter mdzod
4. Rgyal ba Dge 'dun rgya mtsho
   Bslab bya lag len gsal ba'i sgron me
5. [De'u dmar Dge bshes] Bstan 'dzin phun tshogs
   Lag len gcig bsdus
6. Gtsang gi Lo ston Rdo rje dbang phyug (?10th c.)
7. A kyā II Blo bzang bstan pa'i rgyal mtshan
   Gsung thor bu (*Rtsis skor sna tshogs*)
8. Lo chen Chos skyong bzang po (Zhwa lu Lo tsā ba)
9. Thams cad mkhyen pa Skal bzang rgya mtsho (1708–1757)
   Dris lan dpyod ldan yid kyi shing rta
10. Kun mkhyen Mtsho sna ba [Shes rab bzang po]
    Legs bshad nyi ma'i od zer
11. Mkhas pa Dmar ston (?–?)
12. 'Dul 'dzin Grags pa dpal ldan, *alias* 'Dul 'dzin Blo gros bas pa (1400–1475)
    Ka ri ka'i ṭīk chen legs bshad chu rgyun
13. Sum pa Mkhan po Ye shes dpal 'byor
    Dris lan rab dkar pa sangs
14. Rgyal ba Dge 'dun grub
    'Dul ṭīk rin chen phreng ba
15. [Rgyal ba] Dge 'dun rgya mtsho
    Bslab bya lag len gsal ba'i sgron me

16. Paṇ chen Bsod nams grags pa (1478–1554)

    'Dul ba lung rigs kyi nyi ma

    16a. Cites: *Gtsang ṭīk rin chen phreng ba'i dgongs pa rmad du byung ba*

17. Dkyil khang pa Blo gros legs bzang (?–?)

    'Dul ba rin chen phreng ba'i dgongs rgyan

18. Kun mkhyen 'Jam dbyangs bzhad pa I

    'Dul ba skal bzang re ba kun skong

19. Kun mkhyen 'Jam dbyangs bzhad pa I

    'Dul ba'i mtha' dpyod

20. Yongs 'dzin Ye shes rgyal mtshan

    Bslab bya 'od ldan snying po

21. Rgya 'Dul 'dzin pa [?Dbang phyug tshul khrims (11th c.)]
22. Sbal ti Brtson 'grus dbang phyug (1129–1215)
23. Red mda' ba Gzhon nu blo gros (1349–1413)
24. Spyan snga Blo gros rgyal mtshan

    Bslab bya 'od phreng

    Bslab bya gzhan phan snying po

25. A kyā II Blo bzang bstan pa'i rgyal mtshan

    'Dul ba rgya mtsho'i snying po'i rnam bshad 'phags nor rin chen 'dren pa'i gru gzings

Abbreviations

BSTAN Krung go'i bod rig pa zhib 'jug lte gnas kyi bka' bstan dpe sdur khang (ed.), *Bstan 'gyur [dpe bsdur ma]*. Beijing: Krung go'i bod rig pa dpe skrun khang, 1994–2008. 120 vols.

NGAG1[1,2] *Collected Gsung 'bum of Bstan dar lha ram of A lag sha*. 2 vols. New Delhi: Lama Guru Deva, 1971.

NGAG2 Ser gtsug nang bstan dpe rnying 'tshol bsdu phyogs sgrig khang (ed.), *Bstan dar lha rams pa'i gsung 'bum*. Lhasa: Bod ljongs mi dmangs dpe skrun khang, 2008.

References

Tibetan Sources

A kyā III Blo bzang bstan pa'i rgyal mtshan. No date. *Rtsis skor sna tshogs*. In: *Collected Works*. Part A. *Sku 'bum* xylograph. Manuscript: 1055–1166 (fols. 56). bdrc.org W30533.

A kyā Yongs 'dzin Blo bzang don grub. 1971a. *Dris pa'i lan brjod pa mkhas pa'i dga' ston*. In: *Collected Works*. Vol. 2. New Delhi: Lama Guru Deva: 89–121.

A kyā Yongs 'dzin Blo bzang don grub. 1971b. *Rtags kyi 'jug pa'i dgongs 'grel rab gsal snang ba*. In: *Collected Works*. Vol. 2. New Delhi: Lama Guru Deva: 399–433.

A kyā Yongs 'dzin Blo bzang don grub. 1971c. *Be'u bum sngon po'i ming brda go dka' ba 'ga' zhig bshad pa som nyi'i mun sel*. In: *Collected Works*. Vol. 1. New Delhi: Lama Guru Deva: 200–228.

A lag sha Ngag dbang bstan dar. 1982. *Brda' yig ming don gsal bar byed pa'i zla ba'i 'od snang*. In: L. Chandra (ed.), *Four Tibetan-Mongolian Dictionaries*. Vol. 1. Delhi: Sharadi Rani: 208–420.

A mes zhabs Ngag dbang kun dga' bsod nams. 2012. *Rig pa'i gnas lnga las bzo rig pa'i bye brag rol mo'i bstan bcos kyi rnam par bshad pa 'jam dbyangs bla ma dges pa'i snyan pa'i sgra dbyangs blo gsal yid 'phrog 'phrin las yongs khyab*. In: Si khron bod yig dpe rnying myur skyob 'tshol sgrig khang (ed.), *Collected Works*. Vol. 9. Lhasa: Bod ljongs dpe rnying dpe skrun khang: 135–193.

Blo bzang yon tan. No date. *Mkhan chen sprul pa'i sku tshangs sras sgeg pa'i rdo rje'i rnam thar skal bzang yid 'phrog*. Manuscript (fols. 123). bdrc.org W1KG12170.

'Brom ston Rgyal ba'i 'byung gnas. 1993. [*'Brom ston pa rgyal ba'i 'byung gnas kyis mdzad pa'i*] *Jo bo rje'i rnam thar lam yig chos kyi 'byung gnas*. In: Mkha' 'gro tshe ring (ed.), *Jo bo rje dpal ldan a ti sha'i rnam thar bka' gdams pha chos*. Xining: Mtsho sngon mi rigs dpe skrun khang: 229–298.

Btsan lha Ngag dbang tshul khrims. 1997. *Brda dkrol gser gyi me long*. Beijing: Mi rigs dpe skrun khang.

Bu ston Rin chen grub. 1971a. *Las brgya rtsa gcig gi rnam par bshad pa cho ga'i gsal byed*. In: L. Chandra (ed.), *Collected Works*, Part 21 (Zha). New Delhi: International Academy of Indian Culture: 731–979.

Bu ston Rin chen grub. 1971b. *Bstan 'gyur gyi dkar chag yid bzhin nor bu dbang gi rgyal po'i phreng ba*. In: L. Chandra (ed.), *Collected Works*. Part 26 (La). New Delhi: International Academy of Indian Culture: 401–644.

Bu ston Rin chen grub. 1971c. *'Dul ba spyi'i rnam par gzhag pa 'dul ba rin po che'i mdzes rgyan*. In: L. Chandra (ed.), *Collected Works*. Part 26 (La). New Delhi: International Academy of Indian Culture: 1–139.

Bu ston Rin chen grub. 1971d. *'Dul ba mdo'i rnam par 'byed pa 'dul ba rgya mtsho'i snying *po rab tu gsal bar byed pa*. In: L. Chandra (ed.), *Collected Works*. Part 21 (Zha). New Delhi: International Academy of Indian Culture: 141–730.

Byams gling Paṇ chen Bsod nams rgyal ba'i sde. 2014. *Brda'i bye brag rnam par phye ba'i tshig le'ur byas pa smra ba'i rgyan*. In: Khroṃ thar 'Jam blo et al. (eds.), *Bod kyi brda sprod phyogs sgrigs*. Vol. 19. Chengdu: Si khron dus deb tshogs pa / Si khron mi rigs dpe skrun khang: 313–387.

Chab 'gag Rdo rje tshe ring (ed.). 2006. *Bsang mchod*. In *Mtsho lho'i dmangs khrod kyi rig gnas dpe tshogs*. Lanzhou: Kan su'u mi rigs dpe skrun khang.

Chi Galsang. 1982. *Bod sog gso rig brda yig/Töbed mongγol emnelge-yin toli*. Hohhot: Öber mongγol-un arad-un kebel-Uun qoriy-a.

Dalai Lama I Dge 'dun grub pa. 1978–1981. *Legs par gsungs pa'i dam pa'i chos 'dul ba mtha' dag gi snying po'i don legs par bshad pa rin po che'i 'phreng ba* (Lhasa Zhol xylograph). In: *Collected Works*. Vol. 1. New Delhi: Dodrup Lama Sangye.

Dalai Lama I Dge 'dun grub pa. No date. *Legs par gsungs pa'i dam pa'i chos 'dul ba mtha' dag gi snying po'i don legs par bshad pa rin po che'i 'phreng ba* (Bkra shis lhun po xylograph). In: *Collected Works*. Vol. 3. bdrc.org W24769.

Dalai Lama II Dge 'dun rgya mtsho. 2006. *Dge slong gi bslab bya lag len gsal ba'i sgron ma 'dul ba bsdus pa'i snying po*. In: *Collected Works*. Vol. 5. Dharamsala: Library of Tibetan Works and Archives: 215–366.

Dalai Lama V Ngag dbang blo bzang rgya mtsho. 2009a. *Bsur* [read: *Gsur*] *chog gi rim pa yid bzhin 'dod 'jo*. In: Ser gtsug nang bstan dpe rnying 'tshol bsdu khang (ed.), *Collected Works*. Vol. 14. Beijing: Krung go'i bod rig pa dpe skrun khang: 455–459.

Dalai Lama V Ngag dbang blo bzang rgya mtsho. 2009b. *Dkar cha bzhi'i dga' ston phan bde'i 'dod 'jo*. In: Ser gtsug nang bstan dpe rnying 'tshol bsdu khang (ed.), *Collected Works*. Vol. 14. Beijing: Krung go'i bod rig pa dpe skrun khang: 499–504.

Dalai Lama V Ngag dbang blo bzang rgya mtsho. 2009c. *Bstan pa'i rtsa ba rab byung dang khyim pa la phan gdags pa'i cho ga mtha' dpyod dang bcas pa 'khrul spong rnam rgyal gser mdog*. In: Ser gtsug nang bstan dpe rnying 'tshol bsdu khang(ed.), *Collected Works*. Vol. 17. Beijing: Krung go'i bod rig pa dpe skrun khang: 1–363.

Dalai Lama VII Skal bzang rgya mtsho. 1975. *Tā bla ma kau shrī shes rab rgya mtshos dag yig dang brda gsar rnying gi brda chad 'ga' zhig gi dris lan*. In: *Rgya hor bod kyi mchog dman bar pa la stsal ba'i 'phrin yig gi rim pa phyogs gcig tu bkod pa dpyod ldan yid kyi shing rta*. In: *Collected Works*. Vol. 3. Gangtok: Dodrup Sangey: 110–128.

Dbus pa Blo gsal. 1983. *Brda gsar rnying gyi rnam par dbye ba*. Otani University Manuscript,

Tome 986, no. 13987: Manuscript: fols. 5. bdrc.org W1KG12170.

Dbus pa Blo gsal Sangs rgyas ’bum. No date. *Brda’ gsar rnying gyi rnam par dbye ba.* Manuscript: fols. 9. bdrc.org W2PD17527.

De’u dmar Dge bshes Bstan ’dzin phun tshogs. 1957. *Lag len gces rigs btus pa sman kun bcud du sgrub pa’i las kyi cho ga kun gsal snang mdzod.* Lcags po ri xylograph: fols. 64. bdrc.org W4CZ22138.

De’u dmar Dge bshes Bstan ’dzin phun tshogs.1986. Rdo rje rgyal po (ed.), *Shel gong shel phreng*. Beijing: Mi rigs dpe skrun khang.

De’u dmar Dge bshes Bstan ’dzin phun tshogs. 2007a. Mtsho sngon zhing chen bod kyi gso rig zhib ’jug khang (ed.), *Lag len gces rigs btsus pa sman kun bcud du sgrub pa’i las kyi cho ga kun gsal snang mdzod.* In: *De’u dmar gso rig gces btus rin chen phreng ba.* Smad cha. Arura 044. Beijing: Mi rigs dpe skrun khang: 760–843.

De’u dmar Dge bshes Bstan ’dzin phun tshogs. 2007b. *Rig pa bzo yi gnas kyi las tshogs phran tshegs ’dod dgur bsgyur ba phra phab ’od kyi snang brnyan.* In: Mtsho sngon zhing chen bod kyi gso rig zhib ’jug khang (ed.), *De’u dmar gso rig gces btus rin chen phreng ba.* Smad cha. Arura 044. Beijing: Mi rigs dpe skrun khang: 154–230.

Dge bsnyen ’Jam dpal rdo rje. 2008. *Gso byed mdzes mtshar mig rgyan*, Arura 065. Beijing: Mi rigs dpe skrun khang.

Dmu dge Bsam gtan rgya mtsho. 1997. *Bod spyi’i lo rgyus bshad pa.* In: Padma rdo rje (ed.), *Collected Works*. Vol. 3. Xining: Mtsho sngon mi rigs dpe skrun khang: 1–383.

Dngul chu Dharmabhadra. 1973–1981. *Dris lan gyi rim pa phyogs gcig tu bsgrigs pa.* In: *Collected Works*, vol. 4. New Delhi: The Tibet House: 223–516.

Dpa’ bo II Gtsug lag phreng ba. 1986. Rdo rje rgyal po (ed.), *Chos ’byung mkhas pa’i dga’ ston.* Stod cha. Beijing: Mi rigs dpe skrun khang.

Dpal khang/sgang Lo tsā ba Ngag dbang chos kyi rgya mtsho (dbyangs can snyems pa’i sde). 2014. *Bod kyi brda’i bye brag gsal bar byed pa’i bstan bcos tshig le’ur byas pa mkhas pa’i ngag gi sgron ma.* In: Khroṃ thar ’Jam blo et al. (eds.), *Bod kyi brda sprod phyogs sgrigs*. Vol. 20. Chengdu: Si khron dus deb tshogs pa / Si khron mi rigs dpe skrun khang: 1–34.

Dpal khang/sgang Lo tsā ba Ngag dbang chos kyi rgya mtsho (dbyangs can snyems pa’i sde). No date. In: *Mkhas pa’i dbang po karma ’phrin las pa gnyis pa’i gsung shog gi skor legs par bshad pa rin po che’i ’phreng ba.* Manuscript: fols. 296. bdrc.org W8LS37364.

Gser mdog Paṇ chen Shākya mchog ldan. 2013. *Las brgya rtsa gcig gi dka’ gnas so so’i don gsal bar byed pa’i bstan bcos zla ba’i shing rta.* In: Tshangs po (ed.), *Collected Works*. Vol. 22.

Beijing: Krung go'i bod rig pa dpe skrun khang: 233–399.

Gser tog Blo bzang tshul khrims rgya mtsho. 2005. *Bod kyi brda' sprod pa sum cu pa dang rtags kyi 'jug pa'i mchan 'grel mdor bsdus te brjod pa ngo mtshar 'phrul gyi lde mig*. In: *Collected Works*. Vol. 6. Sku 'bum xylograph: fols. 115; bdrc.org W29702.

'Jam dbyangs bzhad pa'i rdo rje I. 1972–1974. *Mngon brjod kyi bstan bcos 'chi med mdzod*. In: *Collected Works*. Vol. 15. Delhi: Ngawang Gelek Demo: 567–791.

'Jam dpal rdo rje. 1971. L. Chandra (ed.), *An Illustrated Tibeto-Mongolian Material Medica of Āyurveda*. New Delhi: International Academy of Indian Culture.

Mtsho sna ba Shes rab bzang po. 1993. Rdo rje rgyal po (ed.), *'Dul ṭīk nyi ma'i 'od zer legs bshad lung gi rgya mtsho*. Beijing: Krung go'i bod kyi shes rig dpe skrun khang.

Nor brang O rgyan. 2008. *Chos rnams kun btus*. Stod cha. Beijing: Krung go'i bod rig pa dpe skrun khang.

Rgyal ba Dge 'dun grub. 1999. Bstan 'dzin phun tshogs (ed.), *'Dul ṭīk rin chen phreng ba*. Beijing: Mi rigs dpe skrun khang.

Rngog Lo tsā ba Blo ldan shes rab. 2006. Dpal brtsegs bod yig dpe rnying zhib 'jug khang (ed.), *Dag yig nyer mkho bsdus pa*. In *Bka' gdams gsung 'bum phyogs bsgrigs*. Vol. 1. Chengdu: Si khron dpe skrun tshogs pa/Si khron mi rigs dpe skrun khang: 93–109.

Sa skya Paṇḍita Kun dga' rgyal mtshan. 2007. Dpal brtsegs bod yig dpe rnying zhib 'jug khang (ed.), *Mkhas pa rnams la 'jug pa'i sgo*. In: *Collected Works* [*Dpe sdur ma*]. Vol. 4. Beijing: krung go'i bod rig pa dpe skrun khang: 15–135.

Sde srid Sangs rgyas rgya mtsho. 1976. *Bstan bcos baiḍūr dkar po las dris lan 'khrul snang g.ya' sel don gyi bzhin ras ston byed* (Sde dge xylograph). Vols. I and II. Dehra Dun: Tan Po Sakya Centre.

Sde srid Sangs rgyas rgya mtsho. 1989. *Blang dor gsal bar ston pa'i drang thigs dwangs shel me long*. In: Yig dpe rnying dpe skrun khang (ed.), *Bod kyi snga rabs khrims srol yig cha bdams bsgrigs*. *Gangs can rig mdzod* 7. Lhasa: Bod ljongs mi dmangs dpe skrun khang: 198–274.

Se cen Mgon po skyabs. 1980a. *Sman ming bod dang rgya'i skad shan sbyar*. In: L. Chandra (ed.), *Multi-Lingual Buddhist Texts in Sanskrit, Chinese, Tibetan, Mongolian and Manchu*. Vol. 7. New Delhi: International Academy of Indian Culture: 2209–2235.

Se cen Mgon po skyabs. 1980b. *Sman sna tshogs kyi per cha*. In: L. Chandra (ed.), *Multi-Lingual Buddhist Texts in Sanskrit, Chinese, Tibetan, Mongolian and Manchu*. Vol. 6. New Delhi: International Academy of Indian Culture: 1991–1995.

Si tu Paṇ chen Chos kyi 'byung gnas. 1990. *Ming dang rtags rjes su bstan pa'i bstan bcos 'chi med mdzod ces bya ba'i gzhung skad gnyis shan sbyar*. In: *Collected Works* (Dpal spungs xylograph). Vol. 4. Sansal: Palpung sungrab nyamso khang: 1–241.

Smon lam rdo rje(ed.). 1989. *Bka' chems ka khol ma*. Lanzhou: Gan su 'u mi rigs dpe skrun khang.

Spen pa lha mo(ed.). 2014. Rdo bis Tshe ring rdo rje *et al.* (transl.). *Bod kyi snga rabs khrims srol bdams bsgrigs / Jiu xizang fagui xuanji gu* 舊西藏法規選輯. Lhasa: Bod ljongs mi dmangs dpe skrun khang.

Sum pa Mkhan po Ye shes dpal 'byor. 1975. *Nang don tha snyad rig gnas kyi gzhung gi ngogs gnas 'ga' zhig dris pa'i lan phyogs gcig tu bris pa rab dkar pa sangs*. In: L. Chandra (ed.), *Collected Works*. Vol. 8. New Delhi: International Academy of Indian Culture: 171–369.

Sumatiratna. 1959. *Bod hor hyi brda yig ming tshig don gsum gsal bar byed pa mun sel sgron me*. Vols. I–II. In: Rinchen (ed.), *Corpus Scriptorum Mongolorum*. Tomus VII. Ulaanbaatar: Ulsün Khevlel.

U rgyan gling pa. 1986. Rdo rje rgyal po (ed.). *Bka' thang sde lnga*. Beijing: Mi rigs dpe skrun khang.

Zhwa lu Lo tsā Rin chen chos skyong bzang po. No date. *Bod kyi brda'i bstan bcos legs par bshad pa rin po che'i za ma tog bkod pa*. Xylograph: fols. 37; bdrc.org W1NLM525.

Zhwa lu Lo tsā Rin chen chos skyong bzang po. 1981. *Legs par bshad pa rin po che'i za ma tog bkod pa*. In: L. Chandra (ed.), *Multi-Lingual Buddhist Texts in Sanskrit, Chinese, Tibetan, Mongolian and Manchu*. Vol. 12. New Delhi: International Academy of Indian Culture: 5854–5901.

Zhwa lu Lo tsā Rin chen chos skyong bzang po. 2002. *Bod kyi brda'i bstan bcos legs par bshad pa rin po che'i za ma tog bkod pa*. In: *Dag yig phyogs bsgrigs mu tig tshom bu*(edited on the basis of the Sde dge xylograph). Xining: Mtsho sngon minzu chubanshe: 39–92.

Zhwa lu Lo tsā Rin chen chos skyong bzang po. 2014. *Bod kyi brda'i bstan bcos legs par bshad pa rin po che'i za ma tog bkod pa*. In: Khroṃ thar 'Jam blo et al. (eds.), *Bod kyi brda sprod phyogs sgrigs*. Vol. 19. Chengdu: Si khron dus deb tshogs pa / Si khron mi rigs dpe skrun khang: 34–77.

Non-Tibetan Sources

Amarasiṃha. 1940. "*Amarakośa*, edited by Sardesai, N.G. and D.G. Padhye." In: *Poona Oriental Series* No. 69. Poona: Oriental Book Agency.

Bertsch, W. 2002. *The Currency of Tibet. A Sourcebook for the Study of Tibetan Coins, Paper Money and other Forms of Currency*. Dharamsala: Library of Tibetan Works and Archives.

Blondeau, A.-M. 1972. *Matériaux pour l'étude de l'hippologie et de l'hippiatrie tibétaines (à partir des mansucrits de Touen-houang)*. Centre de recherches d'histoire et de philologie de la IVe section de l'École pratique des Hautes Études, Hautes Études orientales 2. Genève-Paris, Librairie Droz.

Boulnois, Lucette. 1983. *Poudre d'or et monnaies d'argent au Tibet*. Paris: Éditions du Centre National de la Recherche Scientifique.

Choġtu (ed.). 1999. *Aġwangdandar-un sudulġan-u ögülel-ün chiġulġan* (*Papers on the Study of Agwangdandar*). Khailar: Öbür Mongġul-un soyul-un keblel-ün khoriy-a.

Chu Junjie 褚俊杰. 1991. "A Study of Bon-po Funeral Ritual in Ancient Tibet: Deciphering the Pelliot Tibetan Mss (*sic*) 1042." In: Hu Tan (ed.), *Theses on Tibetology in China*. Beijing: China Tibetology Publishing House: 91–158.

Deokar, Lata Mahesh. 2020. "The Transmission of Subhūticandra's *Kavikāmadhenu* Commentary in Tibet." *Zeitschrift der Deutschen Morgenländischen Gesellschaft* 170: 425–444.

Ehrhard, F.-K. 2015. "'A Thousand-spoke Golden Wheel of Secular Law': The Preamble to the Law Code of the Kings of gTsang." In: D. Schuh. (ed.), *Secular Law and Order in the Tibetan Highland: Contributions to a Workshop Organized by the Tibet Institute in Andiast (Switzerland) on the Occasion of the 65th Birthday of Christoph Cüppers from the 8th of June to the 12th of June 2014*. Andiast: International Institute for Tibetan and Buddhist Studies: 105–125.

Galli, Lucia, Kalsang Norbu Gurung, Jean-Luc Achard Lucia. 2021. *The Power of Wealth–Economy and Social Status in Pre-Modern Tibetan Communities*. In: *Revue d'Etudes Tibétains* 57.

Hirakawa Akira et al. 1973. *Index to the Abhidharmakośabhāṣya (P. Pradhan Edition), Part One: Sanskrit-Tibetan and Chinese*. Tokyo: Daizo Shuppan Kabushikikaisha.

Hübotter, F. 1913. *Beiträge zur Kenntnis der chinesischen sowie der tibetisch-mongolischen Pharmakologie*. Berlin and Wien: Urban &. Schwarzenberg: 49–147.

Ishihama, Yumiko and Fukuda, Yoichi. 1989. *A New Critical Edition of the Mahāvyutpatti. Sanskrit-Tibetan-Mongolian Dictionary of Buddhist Terminology*. Studia Tibetica No. 16. Tokyo: The Toyo Bunko.

Kaschewsky, R. 2017. "Zweite Nachlese zur Berthold Laufers *Za ma tog* unter Berücksichtigung des Mongolischen." *Zentralasiatische Studien* 46: 75–148.

Kieffer-Pülz, P. 2011. "The Law of Theft: Regulations in the Theravāda Vinaya and the Law Commentaries." *Journal of the Pali Text Society* XXXI: 1–54.

van der Kuijp, L.W.J. 2009a. "On the Vicissitudes of Subhūticandra's *Kāmadhenu* Commentary on the *Amarakoṣa* in Tibet." *Journal of the International Association of Tibetan Studies* 5: 1–105.

van der Kuijp, L.W.J. 2009b. "Some remarks on the Meaning and Use of the Tibetan Word *bam po*." *Zangxue xuekan* 藏學學刊 / *Bod rig pa'i dus deb* བོད་རིག་པའི་དུས་དེབ་ /*Journal of Tibetology* 5: 114–132.

van der Kuijp, L.W.J. 2010. "The Tibetan Expression '*bod* wooden door' (*bod shing sgo*) and its Probable Mongol Antecedent." In: Shen Weirong (ed.), *Xiyu lishi yuyan yanjiu jikan* 西域歷史語言研究集刊 / *Historical and Philological Studies of China's Western Regions* (Wang Yao Festschrift). Vol. 3. Beijing: Science Press: 89–134.

van der Kuijp, L.W.J. 2019. "A lag sha Ngag dbang bstan dar (1759–after August 1, 1840) on some Chinese Lexemes and the Chinese Language, Part One." In: V. Caumanns, M. Sernesi, and N. Solmsdorf (eds.), *Unearthing Himalayan Treasures. Festschrift for Franz-Karl Ehrhard.* Indica et Tibetica, Band 59. Marburg: Indica et Tibetica Verlag: 287–298.

Lalou, M. 1952. "Rituel Bon-po des funérailles royales (fonds Pelliot-tibétain 1042)." *Journal asiatique* CCXL:339–361.

Laufer, B. 1898. "Studien zur Sprachwissenschaft der Tibeter. *Zamatog*." In: *Sitzungsberichte der philosophisch-philologischen und der historische Classe der k.b. Akademie der Wissenschaften zu München*. Erster Band. München: Verlag der Akademie der Wissenschaften: 519–594.

Laufer, B. 1916. "Loanwords in Tibetan." *T'oung Pao* 17: 403–552.

Li Zhiying 李志英. 2013. Yishi chuanshuo gongcha: Chaji de renleixue yanjiu 儀式　傳說　供茶：茶祭的人類學研究 [*Ritual, Legend and Tea Offering Rituals: An Anthropological Study*]. Sichuan University MA Thesis, Chengdu.

Lobsang Yongdan. 2018–2019. "An Exploration of a Tibetan lama's study of the Pythagorean theorem in the mid-18th century." *Études mongoles et sibériennes, centrasiatiques et tibétaines* 49: 1–16.

Martin, D., blog Tiblical/measurements/numbers.

Miller, R.A. 1976. "Some Minor Tibetan Grammatical Fragments." In: *Studies in the Grammatical Tradition of Tibet*. Amsterdam: John Benjamins B.V., 71–84.

Mimaki Katsumi. 1990. "Dbus pa blo gsal no '*Shin kyū goi shu'- kōteibon shokō* (The *Brda gsar rnying gi rnam par dbye ba* of Dbus pa Blo gsal–a First Attempt at a Critical Edition)." In: *Asian Languages and General Linguistics. Festschrift for Professor Tatsuo Nishida on the Occasion of His 60th Birthday*. Tokyo: Sanseidō, 17–54.

Nakagawa Masanori. 1996. "The Text of the *Adattādāna-pārājikam* in the *Vinayasūtravṛtti*." *Journal of the Chikushi Jogakuen Junior College* 31: 19–25.

Panglung, Jampa L. 1985. "On the origin of the *Tsha-gsur* ceremony." In: B.N. Aziz and M. Kapstein (eds.), *Soundings in Tibetan Civilization*. New Delhi: Manohar Publications, 268–271.

Powers, J. 2016. "Ngawang Dendar's Commentary. Philosophy through Doxography." In: D. Duckworth, M.D. Eckel, J. Garfield, J. Powers, Yeshes Thabkhas, and Sonam Thakchoe (eds.), *Dignāga's Investigation of the Precept. A Philosophical Legacy in India and Tibet(China)*. New York: Oxford University Press, 118–130.

van Schaik, S. 2013a. "The naming of Tibetan religion: Bon and Chos in the Tibetan imperial period." *Journal of the International Association for Bon Research* 1: 227–257.

van Schaik, S. 2013b. "Ruler of the East, or Eastern Capital: What lies behind the name Tong kun?" In: I. Galambos (ed.), *Studies in Chinese Manuscripts: From the Warring States to the Twentieth Century*. Budapest: Eötvös Loránd University, 211–223.

Schnorrenberger, C.C. 2010. "Zur Entwicklung der chinesischen Medizin im Westen–Teil 1." *Schweizerische Zeitschrift für Ganzheitsmedizin* 22: 157–165.

Schuh, D. 2012. "Einleitung (German) *Rtsis rig la 'jug pa'i byis pa mgu ba'i gtam*." In: D. Schuh (ed.), *Contributions to the History of Tibetan Mathematics, Tibetan Astronomy, Tibetan Time Calculation (Calendar) and Sino-Tibetan Divination*. Vol. 1. Andiast: International Institute of Tibetan and Buddhist Studies, ix–cxlix.

Schuh, D. 2012. 2012a. "Studien zur Geschichte der Mathematik und Astronomie in Tibet, Teil 1, Elementare Arithmetik." In: D. Schuh (ed.), *Contributions to the History of Tibetan Mathematics, Tibetan Astronomy, Tibetan Time Calculation (Calendar) and Sino-Tibetan Divination*. Vol. 2. Andiast: International Institute of Tibetan and Buddhist Studies, 689–788.

Sircar, D.C. 1968. *Studies in Indian Coins*. Delhi: Motilal Banarasidass.

Stein, R.A. 1970. "Un document ancient relative aux rites funéraires des Bon-po tibétaines." *Journal asiatique* CCLVIII: 155–185.

Sun Penghao. 2021. "To the Place where Tea come from: Gyi-ljang's Trip to China." In: Ester Bianchi and Weirong Shen (eds.), *Sino-Tibetan Buddhism across the Ages*. Leiden, Brill, 90–110.

Taube, M. 1961. "Das *Kelen-ü čimeg* des Ṅag-dbaṅ-bstan-dar: Ein Beitrag zur einheimischen mongolischen Grammatik (In memoriam Eduard Erkes)." *Wissenschaftliche Zeitschrift der Karl Marx Universität* 10: 147–155.

Taube, M. 1978. "Zu einigen Texten der tibetischen *brda-gsar-rñiṅ*-Literatur." In: E. Richter and M. Taube (eds.), *Asienwissenschaftliche Beiträge, Johannes Schubert in memoriam*. Berlin: Akademie-Verlag: 169–201.

Tillemans, T.J.F. 2007. "Transitivity, Intransitivity, and *tha dad pa* verbs in Traditional Tibetan Grammar." *Pacific World* 9 (Third series): 49–62.

Ujeed, Uranchimeg Borjigin. 2009. *Indigenous Efforts and Dimensions of Mongolian*

Buddhism–Exemplified by the Mergen Tradition. Ph.D. dissertation. London: School of Oriental and African Studies.

Wangchuk, Dorji. 2020. "The Three Royal Decrees (*bka' bcad gsum*) in the History of Tibetan Buddhism." In: V. Tournier, V. Eltschinger, and M. Sernesi (eds.), *Archaeologies of the Written: Indian, Tibetan, and Buddhist Studies in Honour of Cristina Scherrer-Schaub*. Napoli: Unior Press, 943–975.

Wilson, H.H. 1855. *A glossary of judicial and revenue terms and of useful words occurring in official documents relating to the administration of the government of British India from the Arabic, Persian, Hindustání, Sanskrit* .... London: W.H. Allen and Co.

Xiao Huaiyuan 肖懷遠. 1987. *Xizang difang huobi shi* 西藏地方貨幣史 [*History of Local Tibetan Currency*]. Beijing: Minzu chubanshe.

缅怀陈寅恪先生

陈寅恪与佛教和西域语文学研究

沈卫荣
清华大学人文学院中文系

一

1923年，还在欧洲留学的陈寅恪（1890—1969）写信给他妹妹说：

西藏文藏经，多龙树马鸣著作而中国未译者。即已译者，亦可对勘异同。我今学藏文甚有兴趣，因藏文与中文，系同一系文字。如梵文之与希腊拉丁及英俄德法等之同属一系。以此之故，音韵训诂上，大有发明。因藏文数千年已用梵音字母拼写，其变迁源流，较中文为明显。如以西洋语言科学之法，为中藏文比较之学，则成效当较乾嘉诸老，更上一层。然此非我所注意也。我所注意者有二：一历史，唐史西夏西藏即吐蕃，藏文之关系不待言。一佛教，大乘经典，印度极少，新疆出土者亦零碎。及小乘律之类，与佛教史有关者多。中国所译，又颇难解。我偶取金刚经对勘一过，其注解自晋唐起至俞曲园止，其间数十百家，误解不知其数。我以为除印度西域外国人外，中国人则晋朝唐朝和尚能通梵文，当能得正确之解，其余多是望文生义，不足道也。①

这封史无前例的《与妹书》位列陈寅恪著作目录之榜首，② 亦可算作他发表的最早的一篇学术作品。于此，陈寅恪首先对梵、藏、汉文佛教比较语文学研究的学术意义发表了超越时

---

① 陈寅恪：《与妹书》，《学衡》第20期，1923年8月。后收入陈寅恪：《金明馆丛稿二编》，生活·读书·新知三联书店2015年版，第355—356页。

② 蒋天枢：《陈寅恪先生论著编年目录》，收入氏著《陈寅恪先生编年事辑》（增订本），上海古籍出版社1997年版，第193页。

代的远见卓识。他认为勘汉、藏文佛经之异同，必将使汉语“音韵训诂上，大有发明”，“如以西洋语言科学之法，为中藏文比较之学”，则可超越以乾嘉诸老为代表的中国传统学术之成就。接着，陈寅恪对其今后的学术方向做了规划，明确历史和佛教将是他学术研究的重点；历史研究以吐蕃、唐和西夏历史为主，佛教研究则以对印度、西域和汉地大乘佛典的比较研究和佛教史为重点，尤其重视梵、藏、汉文佛经的对勘，以此纠正汉译佛典及其注疏中因译著者不擅梵文、望文生义而产生的各种错误。

陈寅恪于欧美留学期间，主修梵文、巴利文和印度学，同时还接受了很好的中亚语文学（Central Asian Philology, Sprach- und Kulturwissenschaft Zentralasiens）训练，曾学过藏文、蒙古文、满文、古回鹘文、西夏文、波斯文等中亚（西域）语文，是一位十分难得的优秀东方语文学家（Oriental Philologist）。所以，在回国之前他立志要以佛教和中亚（西域）语文学研究为其未来学术研究之重点，以期在中国开创佛教和西域语文学研究的学术新风尚。尽管陈寅恪现今成为了全民膜拜的学术偶像，被奉为一代文化的托命之人，他的佛教研究和吐蕃、蒙古、西夏等西域地区的历史和文化研究却少有人称道，言者大多对他的中国中古史和中国古典文学作品研究推崇备至。他脍炙人口的著作有《隋唐制度渊源略论稿》（1940）、《唐代政治史述论稿》（1941）、《论再生缘》（1953）、《柳如是别传》（1954）等，其中没有一部与佛教和西域研究直接相关。今天的陈寅恪是一位伟大的历史学家、文学家，甚至是一位杰出的哲学家、思想家，是民族和国家之学术、传统、气节和情怀的象征，可唯独少有人记得陈寅恪还是一位训练有素且有卓越成就的东方语文学家。

其实，不论是从陈寅恪留学欧美时的求学经历，还是从他回国之后的近十年间在清华国学院和中文、历史二系的教学和科研成绩来看，陈寅恪首先是一位专业的东方语文学家，他对佛教语文学和中亚（西域）语文学在中国学界的引进和发展，作出了无与伦比的学术贡献，而且他具有极大的影响力，可以说是中国现代蒙古学、西藏学、西夏学、满学、突厥学研究的开创者。由于陈寅恪学贯中西，兼擅中国传统汉学和中亚（西域）语文学（“虏学”），故傅斯年（1896—1950）于中央研究院建立历史语言研究所，努力建构和实践中国“民族语文学”（National Philology），并由此培育出中国传统人文学术现代化时代最博学和最理想的人文学者。[①]

笔者此前曾就陈寅恪与语文学的关系做过一个总体性的论述，[②]于此谨就他于佛教语文学

---

① Perry Johansson, “Cross-Cultural Epistemology: How European Sinology Became the Bridge to China’s Modern Humanities,” in Rens Bod, Jaap Maat and Thijs Weststeijn eds., *The Making of the Humanities*, Volume III: *The Modern Humanities*, Amsterdam: Amsterdam University Press, 2014, pp.449–464. Markus Messling, “Representation and Power: Jean-Pierre Abel-Remusat’s Critical Chinese Philology,” *Journal of Oriental Studies*, Vol. 44, No. 1&2, 2011, pp.1–23.

② 沈卫荣：《陈寅恪与语文学》，《北京大学学报》（哲学社会科学版）2020 年第 4 期，第 97—107 页。

和藏学、蒙古学等语文学在现代中国所作的开创性贡献和成就，做一些具体的叙述和讨论，以就教于方家。

二

1919年至1921年，陈寅恪于哈佛大学印度语文学系（the Department of Indic Philology）随兰曼（Charles Rockwell Lanman，1850—1941）教授学习梵文；自1921年至1925年，陈寅恪入德国柏林大学随古代印度语言和文献学教授路得施（Heinrich Lüders，1869—1943）"治东方古文字学"（Oriental Philology），主要学习梵文、巴利文，长近五年之久。[①] 众所周知，陈寅恪海外留学深造不以获取学位为目的，论其留学时主修的科目类别，无疑以梵文和印度语文学研究为主。但学成归国后的陈寅恪并没有选择像他的两位导师一样，做一名职业的梵文和印度学家，专门从事梵文、巴利文文献的语文学研究。路得施本人以及他的弟子林冶教授（Ernst Waldschmidt，1897—1985，他曾是陈寅恪在柏林大学的同学，也是季羡林先生后来于德国哥廷根大学求学时的导师），对印度学和佛教研究的最大贡献是对当时中亚（西域）新出土的梵文佛教文献残本进行了细致整理和深度研究。[②] 然而，陈寅恪并没有走上和他们同样的学术道路。

据曾经与陈寅恪二度于哈佛和柏林同学的俞大维（1897—1993）先生回忆："他的梵文和巴利文都特精。但他的兴趣是研究佛教对我国一般社会和思想的一般影响。至于印度的因明学及辩证学，他的兴趣就比较淡薄了。"[③] 同样，陈寅恪自己也曾坦言："寅恪昔年略治佛道二家之学，然于道教仅取以供史事之补正，于佛教亦止比较原文与诸译本字句之异同，至于微言大义之所在，则未能言之也。"[④] 可见，陈寅恪用心学习梵文、巴利文并不是要当一名职业的梵文和印度学家，而主要是为了研究中国的佛教。即学好梵文、藏文是为了读懂汉文佛典，通过梵文、藏文和汉文佛经的对勘，纠正汉译佛典及其注疏中因为译著者不擅梵文、望

---

① 值得说明的是，陈寅恪曾先后两次入学的柏林大学，实际上指的是今天的洪堡大学，这所大学创建于1810年，起初称"柏林大学"，1828年改称为"柏林弗里德里希-威廉皇家大学"（Königliche Friedrich-Wilhelms-Universität zu Berlin），1948年改称"柏林洪堡大学"（Humboldt-Universität zu Berlin），以此与1948年建立的西柏林自由大学（Freie Universität Berlin）相区分。此外，陈寅恪当年于哈佛留学时的"印度语文学系"后于1951年改名为"梵文和印度研究系"（Department of Sanskrit and Indian Studies），进入21世纪后，它又改名为"南亚研究系"（Department of South Asian Studies）。

② J. W. De Jong, *A Brief History of Buddhist Studies in Europe and America*, Bharat-Bharati: Oriental Publishers & Book Sellers, 1976, p.49.

③ 俞大维：《怀念陈寅恪先生》。转引自蒋天枢：《陈寅恪先生编年事辑》（增订本），第49页。

④ 陈寅恪：《论许地山先生宗教史之学》，收入氏著《金明馆丛稿二编》，第360页。

文生义而产生的各种错误，进而考察由佛教的传播而带来的中印文化互动、交流的历史，研究佛教对中国社会和文化的深刻影响。

至 20 世纪 20 年代初期，世界治梵文和佛教学的学者们已开始认识到藏语文和藏文佛教文献对梵文和印度佛教研究的重要意义，至今主导世界佛学研究的印藏佛学研究（Indo-Tibetan Buddhist Studies）传统正在形成和发展之中。但是，当时还很少有人注意到梵、藏语文和梵、藏文佛教文本对汉藏语言的比较研究、汉藏语系的构建和汉传佛教研究同样具有十分重要的意义，也还没有人做梵、藏、汉文三种佛教文本的比较研究，以此纠正汉译佛典中出现的种种错误，达到正确理解汉文佛教文献的目的，并进而探索大乘佛典自印度经西域至中国形成和发展的历史。就当时的中国学界而言，还没有一位学者能真正读懂梵文、巴利文文献，陈寅恪是第一位在海外主修梵文、印度学，并在中国的大学开设梵文文法和佛经翻译课程的中国教授。由于陈寅恪是一位天才的汉学家，本来就十分熟悉汉传佛典，故他在欧美接受了梵文和印藏佛教研究的训练之后，率先注意到了对梵、藏、汉文佛教文本进行对勘和比较研究的重要学术意义，开创了一条非常有创意的梵藏 / 汉藏佛教语文学的学术道路。

值得一提的是，比陈寅恪更早开始在梵、藏、汉佛教语文学这个领域探索，并作出了很大学术贡献的是当年流亡中国的爱沙尼亚男爵、印度学和佛教学家钢和泰（Baron Alexander von Staël-Holstein，1877—1937）先生。他是一位于德国哈勒大学取得印度学博士学位的梵文 / 印度学研究专家，早年也曾随路得施教授学习过梵文，毕业后曾在英国牛津大学、俄国圣彼得堡大学从事印度学的教学和研究工作。1917 年俄国革命爆发，当时正在中国访问的钢和泰从此开始了他在北京近二十年的流亡生涯。他曾作为特聘的客座讲师和教授，多年在国立北京大学传授梵文、印度宗教、历史等课程。1927 年，在哈佛燕京学社等欧美学术机构的帮助下，钢和泰在北京创建了中印研究所（Sino-Indian Institute），专门从事梵、藏文教学和以梵、藏、汉文佛教文献对勘为主的印、藏、汉三种佛教传统的比较研究工作。自此，他开始对梵文佛典与相应的汉文佛典进行对勘，尝试以汉文佛典中对梵文咒语的音译来研究中国古代音韵，得到了当时中国著名学者梁启超（1873—1929）、丁文江（1887—1936）和胡适（1891—1962）等的赏识和热情支持。钢和泰长期专注于《大宝积经》之梵、藏、汉文本的对勘。1926 年，他在上海商务印书馆出版了英文著作《大宝积经迦叶品梵藏汉六种合刊》（*The Kāçyapaparivarta: a Mahāyānasūtra of the Ratnakūṭa class*/edited in the original Sanskrit, in Tibetan and in Chinese）。[①] 这是世界佛教研究史上第一部梵、藏、汉文佛典对勘的佛教语文学著作。1923 年，钢和泰在《国学季刊》创刊号上发表了由胡适亲自翻译的《音译梵书与中国古音》（*The Phonetic Transcription of Sanskrit Works and Ancient Chinese*

① 钢和泰在上海商务印书馆出版这部著作前后花了四年时间，历经曲折和辛酸。他的私人档案中保留了大量他与商务印书馆就该书的出版和校改进行沟通的往来信件。

Pronunciation）一文，尝试用西方历史比较语言学的方法，用汉文佛典中的音译梵文咒字来研究中国古代音韵，曾在中国学界引起了巨大的反响。

前述陈寅恪对于梵、藏、汉佛教语文学的学术兴趣和设想，显然与这位流亡中的爱沙尼亚男爵不谋而合、殊途同归。陈寅恪回国后即在清华国学院开设“佛经翻译文学”和“梵文文法”等课程，北京大学也曾特邀他去讲授“佛经翻译”课，显然有意在中国开拓梵、藏、汉佛教语文学的研究。可惜这样的学问离当时中国学者们的学术关注太过遥远，曲高和寡，不管是陈寅恪还是钢和泰，都没有能够成功地在此前从未受过任何语文学训练的清华和北大学生中找到他们的学术知音，故并未能在中国开创出梵、藏、汉佛教语文学的学术传统。在此期间，陈寅恪一直热心参与钢和泰主持的私塾型读书班（privatissimum），与他一起对勘和校读梵、藏、汉文本的《大宝积经》《妙法莲华经》等佛经。那些年间，先后参与这个每周六在钢和泰位于东交民巷的私宅内举行的四小时读书班的学者，除了钢和泰的中国弟子于道泉（1901—1992）、林藜光（1902—1945）等人外，还曾有一众后来名闻天下的欧美梵文/印度学家、佛教学者、汉学家等，如雷兴（Ferdinand Dietrich Lessing, 1882—1961，美国加州大学伯克利校区汉学教授）、弗里德里希·维勒（Friedrich Weller, 1889—1980，德国莱比锡大学印度语文学、汉学和东亚宗教史教授）、李华德（Walter Liebenthal, 1886—1982，德国图宾根大学汉学、佛教学荣誉教授）、顾立雅（Herrlee Glessner Creel, 1905—1994，美国芝加哥大学汉学教授）等。[①]这些学者都是兼通梵、藏、汉文的佛教学者，是梵、藏、汉佛教语文学研究的先驱。他们在钢和泰组建的中印研究所的旗帜下，组成了一个十分豪华的国际性的佛教语文学学术团队。可惜，这样一个高水准的国际学术合作因为钢和泰于1937年英年早逝，以及全民族抗日战争的爆发，很快就偃旗息鼓。而陈寅恪于1937年11月离开北京，开始了在南方诸省多年的颠沛流离的生活，从此再没有机会专心从事梵、藏、汉佛教语文学的研究工作。这实在是中国学术的一大遗憾。

毋庸讳言，陈寅恪并没有在和钢和泰共同设计和开创的这条学术道路上继续前行，也没有发表过他从事梵、藏、汉文佛教文本的对勘和比较研究的学术作品。钢和泰和陈寅恪在北京开创的这个梵、藏、汉佛教语文学研究的传统，长期以来都没有在中国开花结果。近几十年来，中国学者多有借助梵、藏、汉文佛经的比较研究，来做中国古代音韵训诂类的研究，特别是借助这种方法研究古代汉语音韵和语法，取得了令人瞩目的成绩。但以这种方法做佛教语文学研究、研究佛学本身的十分少见。最好地实践、发展并实现了钢和泰、陈寅恪将近一百年前提出的这个学术理想的或是不久前英年早逝的当代最优秀的佛教语文学家（文献学家）之一、日本创价大学教授辛岛静志（1957—2019）。辛岛先生为佛教语文学学术贡献了

---

① 王启龙：《陈寅恪与钢和泰学术交谊注记》，《西藏民族学院学报》（哲学社会科学版）2014年第1期，第1—9、153页。

一生，其最大成就是通过对见于梵、汉、藏文佛教经典中的大量佛教语词进行逐字逐句的比照和校勘研究，还原了大乘佛典从印度经西域到中国的形成和发展的历史，并就汉传佛教经典的语言、概念和传统的确定和演变的历史过程提出了很多具有颠覆性的真知灼见。[①]或可以说，辛岛静志正是钢和泰、陈寅恪最体己的学术知音和最具格的衣钵传人，他们之间的学术血脉传承超越时空。

三

如前所述，陈寅恪于《与妹书》中自称他并非特别注意“成效当较乾嘉诸老更上一层”的汉藏语言比较研究，而对历史和佛教研究更感兴趣。然而，从他早年的研究作品来看，他对历史和佛教的研究其实从未脱离印藏佛教学者所擅长的语文学方法，对语言（术语）和文本的比较研究始终是他的学术研究的最大特色，凸显了其作为语文学家的学术本色。与他同时受聘为清华国学院导师的赵元任（1892—1982）曾经在回忆陈寅恪的文章中说：“第二年到了清华，四个研究教授当中除了梁任公注意政治方面一点，其他王静安、寅恪跟我都喜欢搞音韵训诂之类问题。寅恪总说你不把基本的材料弄清楚，就急着要论微言大义，所得的结论还是不可靠的。”[②]这从侧面证明陈寅恪对佛教的研究以语文学研究为出发点，而不以对宗教义理和思想的研究为重点。

陈寅恪归国最初几年发表的学术论文基本上是关于佛教文本的，特别是对当时敦煌新出土的汉文佛教文本的研究，其中有《大乘稻芉经随听疏跋》（1927）、《有相夫人生天因缘曲跋》（1927）、《童受喻鬘论梵文残本跋》（1927）、《忏悔灭罪金光明经冥报传跋》（1298）、《须达起精舍因缘曲跋》（1928）、《敦煌本十诵比丘尼波罗提木叉跋》（1929）、《大乘义章书后》（1930）、《敦煌本维摩诘经文殊师利问疾品演义跋》（1930）、《敦煌本唐梵翻对字般若波罗蜜多心经跋》（1930）、《莲花色尼出家因缘跋》（1932）、《西夏文佛母大孔雀明王经夏梵藏汉合璧校释序》（1932）、《斯坦因所获西夏文大般若经残卷跋》（1932）等等。[③]由此可见，他早期发表的这些学术文章主要是其佛教语文学研究的成果。

上列这些文章的篇幅大部分很短小，都是陈寅恪对当年新见的敦煌和黑水城出土汉文

---

① 辛岛静志著，裘云青、吴蔚琳译：《佛典语言及传承》，中西书局2016年版。除了辛岛静志外，海外还有那体慧（Jan Nattier）、左冠明（Stefano Zacchetti, 1968—2020）等著名学者从事早期汉语佛教文献的研究，也注重梵、汉和藏、汉佛典的比较研究，参见那体慧著，纪赟译：《汉文佛教文献研究》，广西师范大学出版社2018年版。

② 转引自蒋天枢：《陈寅恪先生编年事辑》（增订本），第62页。

③ 蒋天枢：《陈寅恪先生论著编年目录》，收入氏著《陈寅恪先生编年事辑》（增订本），第193—195页。

和西夏文佛教文本的简单介绍和说明。[1] 文章的内容大致有以下三个类型：一是同定这些新见的、残缺的敦煌佛教文本，即通过比对与这一文本相对应的梵、藏文本，并参考海外学者对这些文本所做的最新的整理和研究成果，来辨明它们的来历、传承和内容。其学术意义在于通过对多语言文本的比较研究、对文本之形成背景的分析（语境化和历史化），重构佛教传承的历史。二是通过追溯某些特殊词汇、概念的翻译和流播过程，观察与之相关的思想、观念和习俗的流变。例如，他在《大乘义章书后》一文中分析汉文佛典对“悉檀”（Siddhānta）、“菩提”（bodhi）等词汇的误读是如何产生的，以及汉文中的“道”“末伽”等词与梵文的“Mārga”一词的渊源关系等；又在《斯坦因所获西夏文大般若经残卷跋》一文中讨论西夏文语词“有情”“众生”和“无上”等词汇的来历，辨明它们与梵、藏、汉文相应词汇之间的关系，试图从考察一个词汇（术语）的形成和流播出发勾勒出一段思想和观念的历史。三是对佛教经典文本对于汉语文学作品的影响有特别独到的研究。如他在《敦煌本维摩诘经文殊师利问疾品演义跋》一文中以《维摩诘经文殊师利问疾品演义》中的具体事例来解释“由佛经演变之文学”的过程，即将“此篇与鸠摩罗什译维摩诘所说经原文互勘之，亦可推见演义小说文体原始之形式，及其嬗变之流别，故为中国文学史绝佳资料”[2]。陈寅恪对佛教文献中的故事、母题和叙事的形成和传播，以及它们对中国文学作品从体裁到内容的影响有许多十分精到的发现和研究，如对《贤愚经》成书的分析，对《西游记》中孙行者、猪八戒、沙僧三个人物之原型的溯源，对华佗故事的探究等。

20 世纪 20 年代初，瓦尔特·本雅明（Walter Benjamin, 1892—1940）曾说：“我不将语文学定义为语言的科学或者历史，在它最深的层面，语文学是术语的历史（Geschichte der Terminologie）。”[3] 他认为语文学的一个最独到的本领就是能从多个视角、多个层面，即从多种语言、文本、文化传统出发，来看待历史和变化。在这一点上，与其同时代的陈寅恪无疑是本雅明最好的学术知音。他前期的学术作品都是从多语种文本、多元文化的视角出发，通过对一些佛教词汇（术语）、概念、叙事的比较研究，来重构不同民族、宗教和文化之间互动和交流的历史。

不管是梵文 / 印度学研究，还是佛学研究，在陈寅恪学术养成的那个年代，从事的都是一种文本语文学（textual philology）的研究。换言之，所有梵文 / 印度学家和佛学家首先都应该是语文学家，他们的研究工作常常围绕着一个具体文本的校读和译注展开。而这种来自欧陆的文本语文学学术传统无疑与中国学者们熟悉的传统学术方法相距甚远，很难把它原封

① 对陈寅恪利用和研究敦煌文献的总体介绍，参见荣新江：《不负国宝，襄进学术——陈寅恪对敦煌文献的利用与阐发》，《文汇学人》2020 年 1 月 17 日，第 5—6 版。

② 陈寅恪：《金明馆丛稿二编》，第 203 页。

③ Haruko Momma, *From Philology to English Studies, Language and Culture in the Nineteenth Century*, Cambridge: Cambridge University Press, 2013, p.7. 语文学众多的定义中有一种是“对言语（单词、词汇）的历史的研究”（the study of words historically），这与本雅明所说的“语文学是术语的历史”有共通之处。

不动地引进中国，有必要对它进行中国化的改变，以适应并进而改革中国的学术传统。陈寅恪整个学术生涯都没有发表过任何梵文或者藏文佛教文本的精校本之类的狭义语文学学术作品，但这并不表明他完全忽略了他曾长期浸淫于其间的这种十分高精尖的文本语文学传统。相反，他比同时代的大部分中国学者更重视他所研究的汉语文本的版本和流传的历史，也曾花费大量时间对他所研究的文本进行十分细致的校读和考订。他将梵文 / 印度学传统中的精校文本的学术方法运用到了汉学研究领域，并把东方文本语文学的文本精校（critical edition）和文本批评（textual criticism）方法与中国传统的训诂、对勘和考据等方法结合在一起。可以说，在语文学这个层面上，陈寅恪将中西学术传统完美地整合到了一起。

按其弟子蒋天枢的说法，陈寅恪“自归国任教清华后，逐渐开展对中译本佛经之研究，尤其在迁居清华西院三十六号后，用力尤勤。惜所校订有关佛经之书，今仅存《高僧传》一至四集及《弘明集》《广弘明集》各书而已”[①]。“先生治学方法，用思之细密极于毫芒。虽沿袭清人治经途术，实汇中西治学方法而一之。”“先生于此书，时用密点、圈以识其要。书眉、行间，批注几满，细字密行，字细小处，几难辨识。就字迹、墨色观之，先后校读非只一二次，具见用力之勤劬。而行间、书眉所注者，间杂有巴利文、梵文、藏文等，以参证古代译语，皆枢所不识，不敢赞一辞也。”[②]

由此可见，陈寅恪校订汉文佛教文书的工作量甚至超过了西方文本语文学中的“精校本”制作之所需，除了文本的厘定和语文、词语的订正外，还加入大量注疏、史事考订和他自己的研究心得等内容。可惜这些经他校订过后的汉语佛教文本从未得到整理出版，有的可能早已遗失，这是中国佛教语文学学术的重大损失。显然，精心校读文本是陈寅恪治学之根本，他不但不遗余力地校订汉语佛教文献，而且对他所研究的文学和历史文献同样也是如此。据说他曾对《世说新语》做过非常精细的校读和批注，特别是对其中与佛教相关的内容做过很认真的文本研究。他还仔细地批注过《新五代史》，可惜它们都已于 1938 年丢失。[③] 于颠沛流离于南方诸省之际，陈寅恪还曾三度精校《新唐书》（1939 年 9 月、1940 年 12 月、1942 年 4 月）[④]，其唐史研究之所以为人称道，无疑是建立在他对《新唐书》等文本的精心校读的基础之上。傅斯年说“史学即史料学”“史学语学全不能分”，此即是说，历史研究的基础首先是对史料进行语境化和历史化的处理，当用语文学的方法对史料进行正确处理，历史也就跃然于纸上了。所以，语文学家同时也是历史学家，陈寅恪便是这样一个生动的例子。

---

① 蒋天枢：《陈寅恪先生编年事辑》（增订本），第 85 页。
② 蒋天枢：《陈寅恪先生编年事辑》（增订本），第 89、91 页。
③ 据传当年陈寅恪转道去昆明时随身所携的两箱书籍被窃，其中有他批注的《世说新语》和《新五代史》，自此从未复得。参见蒋天枢：《陈寅恪先生编年事辑》（增订本），第 160 页。
④ 蔡鸿生：《仰望陈寅恪》，中华书局 2004 年版，第 5 页。

四

陈寅恪第二次入柏林大学留学的近五年间，除了主修的梵文、巴利文和印度学以外，他还同时接受了全面的中亚（西域）语文学的训练。这个时代正好是柏林中亚语文学研究的黄金时代。德国的几次吐鲁番探险带回了大量梵文、藏文、古回鹘文、蒙古文等中亚语文和汉文文献，对它们的解读和研究给柏林的东方学、中亚语文学研究带来了前所未有的勃勃生机。如前所述，陈寅恪的梵文、巴利文导师路得施教授携其弟子林冶等专门从事吐鲁番出土梵文佛教文献残本的研究，而著名的古回鹘文专家、德国民俗博物馆的研究员马克斯·缪勒（Friedrich Max Müller，1863—1930）则负责整理吐鲁番出土的古代回鹘文佛教文献，与他合作的还有著名突厥学家、中亚探险家阿尔伯特·冯·勒柯克（Albert von Le coq, 1860—1930）。与此同时，德国当时最著名的汉学家、柏林大学汉学教授奥托·福兰阁（Otto Franke, 1863—1946）组织了一个专门解读清代四体碑刻的读书班，参加者有后来成为福兰阁继承人的汉学家、蒙古学家、满学家埃里希·海涅士（Erich Haenisch, 1880—1966）教授和满学家埃里希·豪尔（Erich Hauer, 1878—1936）教授等学者，他们分别负责对清四体碑刻的蒙古文和满文的解读。柏林也是当时欧洲藏学研究的一个重镇。陈寅恪在柏林大学留学时恰逢一批有名的藏学家在柏林从事藏语文的教学和研究。柏林大学第一位藏学教授奥古斯特·赫尔曼·弗兰克（August Hermann Francke, 1870—1930）正是在陈寅恪留学柏林大学期间完成了教授升等论文，渐次担任私人讲师和教授职位。在他之前，在柏林大学教授藏语文的是宗教学教授赫尔曼·贝克（Hermann Beckh, 1875—1937）。而同时期在柏林从事藏学研究的藏学大家至少还有考古学家、印藏学家阿尔伯特·格伦威德尔（Albert Grünwedel, 1856—1935），汉学家、佛教学家雷兴，汉学家、语言学家西门·华德（Walter Simon, 1893—1981），藏学家、蒙古学家约翰内斯·舒伯特（Johannes Schubert, 1896—1976），等等，可谓群星璀璨。[①] 甚至连西欧最初解读西夏文《法华经》的汉学家安娜·贝恩哈特（Anna Bernhardi, 1868—1944）当年也在柏林民俗博物馆工作。今天我们无法一一确定陈寅恪是否和上述这些中亚语文学领域内的精英学者们有过直接的学术联系，但可以肯定的是，当时柏林这种浓郁的中亚语文学学术氛围给陈寅恪的学术成长带来了巨大的影响。上述这些学者都是身怀多种绝技、跨越多个学术领域的语文学家，为当时在柏林同时学习梵文、藏文、古回鹘文、蒙古文、满文和西夏文等多种语文的陈寅恪提供了极其肥沃的学术土

① 有关柏林大学藏学和中亚语文学研究的历史概况，参见 Toni Huber and Tina Niermann, “Tibetan Studies at the Berlin University: An Institutional History”, in Petra Maurer und Peter Schwieger eds., *Tibetstudien: Festschrift für Dieter Schuh zum 65. Geburtstag*, Bonn: Bier’sche Verlagsanstalt, 2005, pp.95–122。

壤，在这种学术氛围下，他得以最终成为跨越多个学术领域的中亚语文学家也是顺理成章的事情。

陈寅恪在西方学习了多种东方和中亚古代语文，能够相对便利地利用当时新出土的和已被解读了的敦煌出土古藏文历史文书和新疆吐鲁番出土的梵文、古回鹘语文资料，以及新近被欧洲东方学家翻译、研究过的藏文和蒙古文历史文献等，再加上他对有关西域史地的汉文历史资料本就非常熟悉，故研究古代突厥、吐蕃、回鹘、蒙古、满洲等“塞表殊族之史事”，对他来说或是一种非常自然的学术选择。回国前，他急切地要求妹妹为他购买“总价约万金”的图书资料，其中“最要者即西藏文正续藏两部”，“又蒙古满洲回文书，我皆欲得”。[①] 可见，除了佛教研究之外，他对西域语文和历史研究，特别是西藏、蒙古、满洲和突厥等的历史和宗教研究都曾有过很大的热情。在他归国的头几年，西域语文和历史也是他研究工作的重心之一。1930 年起，他担任中央研究院历史语言研究所历史组的组长，参与部署所内之西域史地的研究规划；1931 年，他“又兼任故宫博物院理事、清代档案委员会委员。得遍阅故宫满文老档”。[②] 陈寅恪为现代中国藏学、蒙古学、突厥学、西夏学和满学等学术领域的开创都作出了不可磨灭的巨大贡献。

1927 年至 1931 年间，除了前述多种佛教语文学研究作品外，陈寅恪还发表了多篇研究西域语文和历史的学术文章，包括《元代汉人译名考》（1929）、《灵州宁夏榆林三城译名考》（蒙古源流研究之一，1930）、《吐蕃彝泰赞普名号年代考》（蒙古源流研究之二，1930）、《彰所知论与蒙古源流》（蒙古源流研究之三，1931）、《蒙古源流作者世系考》（蒙古源流研究之四，1931）、《几何原本满文译本跋》（1931）等。上列这几篇学术论文，几乎是迄今所见陈寅恪学术生涯中发表的中亚（西域）语文学研究的全部作品，看似寥寥可数，但它们却是中国最早的、具有国际水准的现代西藏学和蒙古学（蒙元史）研究的优秀成果，不但开创了中国西域研究的新风气，而且为中国传统汉学研究注入了“虏学”（西域学）的新养分。

严格说来，陈寅恪并不是一名专业的藏学家、蒙古学家、西夏学家或者满学家。在他活跃的那个年代，一名专业的藏学家会选择从事梵、藏文佛教文献的文本研究，或者会做敦煌、吐鲁番出土古藏文文献和吐蕃金石碑刻、简牍的翻译和解读工作；而蒙古学家则会专注于对诸如《元朝秘史》《蒙古源流》等古代蒙古文历史文献的收集、整理、翻译和研究工作。而陈寅恪没有直接做藏、蒙古文文本译注的文本语文学研究，他所从事的更多是语文学中的“文本批评”（textual criticism）或者“高等批评”（higher criticism）之类的工作，确切地说是对这些文本的作者、来历、成书和传播过程进行细致的考据，并通过多语种文本的比较厘清文本中出现的各种名物制度的语言和历史含义，以构建历史（history through textual

① 陈寅恪：《与妹书》，收入氏著《金明馆丛稿二编》，第 355—356 页。
② 蒋天枢：《陈寅恪先生编年事辑》（增订本），第 77 页。

criticism)。陈寅恪对清代汉译《蒙古源流》的研究就充分反映了这一学术特点。

表面看来，陈寅恪最擅长的无非是对多语种文本中记载的人名、氏族名、地名、职官名和年代，及它们之间的嬗变关系的细致考证，可正是这样的研究使他超越了乾嘉诸老等传统中国学术大家在西域史地这个领域内所取得的学术成就，并使中国学者摆脱了因不通“虏学”而在西北舆地之学研究上所遭遇的巨大困境。韩儒林曾经说过，对蒙古学研究而言，波斯文、阿拉伯文文献非常重要，而中国的前辈学者“为时代所限，对穆斯林史料不甚熟悉，本人又不能直接阅读西人论述，所用外国材料全是从欧洲译本重译的穆斯林史料。早期欧洲蒙古史学家，多不懂汉文，不能互相比勘，译音用字规律不严，人名地名随意译读，根据这种水平不高的西方译本请人译成汉文，自然是错上加错，结果贻误了我们的老前辈”[①]。而陈寅恪将他于欧美所受的这一套中亚语文学训练十分完美地运用到了他对藏学和蒙古学的研究之中，为中国的西北舆地之学开创了兼通中西的现代学术新风。

近日，刘迎胜称“蒙元〔史〕研究是历史学家陈寅恪先生所开创，吸纳了欧洲东方学元素，学人群起而相从的现代中国史学研究领域之一”[②]，这是他在重读陈寅恪发表于1929年的《元代汉人译名考》一文之后得出的深刻体会。陈寅恪这篇文章讨论的是元末笔记陶宗仪《南村辍耕录》中所载“汉人八种”之名目。此前，钱大昕（1728—1804）、箭内亘（1875—1926）等中外知名学者都曾怀疑此中既不见“汉人”，也没有“南人”的所谓“汉人八种”当属舛误，而陈寅恪却认为其中必有“待发之覆”，故“今为考证当日汉人之名，其译语本为何字，兼采近年外国成说，覆以蒙古旧史之文，以其界说之变迁及含义之广狭，立一假定之说，以解释之”。他通过对《元史》《华夷译语》《元朝秘史》《蒙古源流》《史集》《史贯》等当时最重要的汉、蒙古、波斯文历史文献中出现的各种与“汉”“汉人”“汉军”相关的名称进行细致的排查、比较和分析，大致弄清了“汉人八种”之名目的来历和含义，从而为人们认识宋、辽、金、元时代中国北方错综复杂的民族关系，理解当时民族认同之复杂性提供了巨大的帮助。正如他自己所总结的那样，“盖一时代之名词，有一时代之界说。其含义之广狭，随政治社会之变迁而不同，往往巨大之纠纷伪谬，即因兹细故而起，此尤为治史学者所宜审慎也”。[③]

陈寅恪的另一篇与蒙元史研究相关的论文《灵州宁夏榆林三城译名考》同样是中亚语文学研究的一篇经典之作。地名，标志着一个地方的地理位置和地理环境，对于历史和历史研究的重要意义自不待言，但“历史上往往有地名因其距离不远，事实相关，复经数种民族之

---

① 韩儒林:《穹庐集——元史及西北民族史研究》，上海人民出版社1982年版，自序第2页。

② 刘迎胜:《“汉人八种”新解——读陈寅恪〈元代汉人译名考〉》，《西北民族研究》2020年第1期，第45页。对陈寅恪之蒙元史研究的评价，也可参见蔡美彪:《陈寅恪对蒙古学的贡献及其治学方法》，《历史研究》1988年第6期，第58—61页。

③ 陈寅恪:《元代汉人译名考》，收入氏著《金明馆丛稿二编》，第99—105页。

语言辗转移译，以致名称淆混，虽治史学之专家，亦不能不为其所误者，如蒙古源流之灵州宁夏榆林等地名，是其一例”[①]。《蒙古源流》中出现了“Turmegei”“Temegetu”和“Irghai”三个地理位置相近的地名，早在《蒙古源流》的蒙古、满、汉三种语言版本的对译中，这三个地名就已出现混乱，而在《元朝秘史》《史集》《圣武亲征录》《马可波罗游记》和《元史》等各种历史文献中，它们也以不同语言和不同形式的名称出现；前辈学人如《蒙古源流》的辑校者和德文译者施密特（Isaac Jacob Schmidt, 1779—1847）、《圣武亲征录》的校注者王国维、《马可波罗游记》的编注者亨利·玉儿（Sir Henry Yule, 1820—1889），还有《蒙兀儿史记》的作者屠寄（1856—1921）、《多桑蒙古史》的作者多桑（Abraham Constantin Mouradgea d'Ohsson, 1779—1851）等人，他们对这些地名的认知各有各的说法，也各有各的错误。在那个年代，汉学家不懂蒙古文、波斯文，蒙古学家也不懂汉文，双方对这些名称的确认和译写都不得要领。陈寅恪通过对以上文本中出现的这些地名及与它们相关的历史事件的仔细比照和考证，最后考定其译名，确认“Turmegei”即灵州，“Irghai”为宁夏，“Temegetu”是榆林。

需要补充的是，无论是解释《南村辍耕录》中出现的含有多个非汉语名称的“汉人八种”之名目，还是确认蒙古、满、汉三种语言文本的《蒙古源流》中出现的这三个地名之确切指向，这一类问题是无法通过乾嘉旧学的方法解决的，因为仅仅依赖汉文文献的内部对勘是不够的，而必须借助蒙元时代的蒙古语和波斯文文献，运用比较语言学的方法，对不同语种文本中出现的相关名称进行细致的对比研究，才有可能使它们一一名从主人。而每一个名称演变的背后，都有着一段曲折的历史，若能把这些名称放回到它们实际所处的那个时代的历史中去考察，对其变化中的历史含义给出符合时代的界说，则将有助于揭示这一段政治和社会发展的历史。傅斯年主张历史研究要“上穷碧落下黄泉、动手动脚找东西”，还要“以汉还汉、以唐还唐”，这种语文学家和历史学家必须具备的学术精神在陈寅恪这篇文章中得到了完美的体现。

能将一个“汉人”问题的研究，和元代与西夏相关的几个地名的研究，放在如此广阔的多民族、多语种的历史背景中来考察，能把一个汉学和蒙古学的问题放进一个如此国际化的多元和高端的学术环境中来进行对话，这在近百年之后的今天依然还是我们正在努力的一个学术方向。所以，说陈寅恪是现代中国蒙元史研究的学术开创者是恰如其分的。他既熟悉东西方蒙古学、蒙古史研究的最新成就，又能直接利用蒙古文、波斯文文献来研究蒙元史，远远超越了洪钧（1839—1893,《元史译文证补》）、柯劭忞（1848—1933,《新元史》）、屠寄（1856—1921,《蒙兀儿史记》）、王国维（1877—1927,《圣武亲征录校注》）等前辈中国学者

① 陈寅恪：《灵州宁夏榆林三城译名考》，收入氏著《金明馆丛稿二编》，第108页。

在这一领域的研究成就。[①] 尽管陈寅恪关于蒙元史研究的论述不多，但就其学术方法和水准而言，或可与世界汉学第一人保罗・伯希和（Paul Pelliot，1878—1945）做比较，也可与兼擅蒙古学、满学的德国汉学教授海涅士相仿佛，而后者可能就是陈寅恪在柏林读书时的蒙古文和满文老师。

五

尽管陈寅恪不是一位职业的藏学家、藏学教授，但他同样可以被认为是现代中国藏学研究的开创者。1925 年，德国柏林大学任命奥古斯特・赫尔曼・弗兰克为该校历史上第一任藏学教授，同一年，或曾随其学习藏文的陈寅恪离开了柏林大学，后被清华大学国学院聘为导师，他或是中国历史上第一位可以称得上是现代藏学家的大学教授。

我们通常将于道泉（1901—1992）誉为现代中国藏学研究的开创者。与陈寅恪相比，于道泉的确是一位更职业的藏学家，曾为新中国藏学研究的形成和发展作出巨大贡献。于先生对中国藏学研究作出的主要贡献，当是他于 20 世纪 50 年代初在中央民族学院建立起中国大学中第一个从事西藏语文教学的学术机构，并培养出新中国第一批藏学研究的核心人才。然而，当陈寅恪发表《大乘稻芊经随听疏跋》《吐蕃彝泰赞普名号年代考》《彰所知论与蒙古源流》等学术文章时，于道泉还正在雍和宫跟随喇嘛们学习藏语文。于道泉也可算是陈寅恪的弟子，他曾随钢和泰、陈寅恪一起学习梵语文、对勘《大宝积经》，后来也是在陈寅恪的推荐下进入中央研究院历史语言研究所担任助理研究员，并在他指导下专门从事藏学研究的。在这个意义上，陈寅恪无疑远早于于道泉接受了现代藏学的学术训练，并率先发表了具有国际一流学术水准的藏学论文，于中国学界开创了现代藏学研究之先河。[②]

《大乘稻芊经随听疏跋》应该是陈寅恪正式发表的第一篇学术论文，时年已三十七岁。这篇论文不但标志着他厚积薄发的学术著述生涯的开始，而且是中国藏学研究史上的一个重要的里程碑。当时敦煌出土古藏文佛教文献研究尚处于草创阶段，陈寅恪在伯希和、羽田亨（1882—1955）和石滨纯太郎（1888—1968）等人前期研究的基础上，确认了不见于汉地佛教载记的吐蕃译师法成的身份、活动年代及主要译著，还在《西藏文大藏经》中进一步确认了法成所译的唐玄奘弟子圆测造《解深密经疏》之藏文译本，并探究了法成造《大乘稻芊经

① 对于陈寅恪于蒙元史研究学术史中的位置，俞大维于《怀念陈寅恪先生》一文中有十分精到的叙述，参见蒋天枢:《陈寅恪先生编年事辑》（增订本），第 49—51 页。

② 王尧:《陈寅恪先生对我国藏学研究的贡献》，收入纪念陈寅恪教授国际学术讨论会秘书组编《纪念陈寅恪教授国际学术讨论会文集》，中山大学出版社 1989 年版，第 582—588 页。

随听疏》于藏文佛典中的可能的文本源头，提出“今日所见中文经论注疏凡号为法成所撰集者，实皆译自藏文”的观点。陈寅恪最后指出“夫成公之于吐蕃，亦犹慈恩之于震旦”，“同为沟通东西学术，一代文化所托命之人”①。这样精彩的断语，今天听来依然振聋发聩，而近百年来世界敦煌古藏文佛教文献研究的成果充分证明陈寅恪当年言之有理，他的远见卓识迄今依然令人钦佩。②

陈寅恪另外的与藏学研究相关的论著是他专门研究《蒙古源流》后所作的系列论文中的《吐蕃彝泰赞普名号年代考》《彰所知论与蒙古源流》两篇。《蒙古源流》自清代被译成满文和汉文后，一直是研究蒙古历史，特别是蒙藏关系史的重要文献。但是，对于不能同时利用其蒙古、满、汉三种语言版本的学者来说，要读懂和使用这份历史资料还是有很大困难的。因为《蒙古源流》多采藏文历史著作中的资料，经过多种文字的传译之后，其中各种名称存在许多讹误，难以辨明和解读。陈寅恪曾经有一个将蒙古文《蒙古源流》与清代的满文、汉文译本进行比较研究的远大规划，他要对读这三种文字的文本，参照当时施密特的蒙文校译本和德文译本，并借助藏文历史文本的译著本，来订正《蒙古源流》各种文本中出现的“千年旧史之误书，异地译音之伪读”，以还其历史的本来面目。③

陈寅恪研究《蒙古源流》率先做的工作是对书中所见的吐蕃赞普名号和年代记载的订正。由于《蒙古源流》对于吐蕃赞普之名号、年代和历史的记载大多辗转传自吐蕃古史，本就多有舛误；翻译成满文、汉文时，又增加了更多的错误，是故“综校诸书所载名号年代既多伪误，又复互相违异，无所适从”④。于是，陈寅恪将它们与新、旧《唐书》等汉文史籍中所载吐蕃赞普资料进行比照，复引当时德国佛教和西藏学者埃米尔·施拉津特维特（Emil Schlagintweit，1835—1904）已经刊布和翻译的《吐蕃王统记》（《拉达克王统记》，即藏文中所谓的“嘉喇卜经 [Rgyal rabs]”）中有关吐蕃赞普王统的记载，来厘清吐蕃赞普之名号和年代，依次校正蒙、满、汉文的《蒙古源流》中的各种文本错漏。⑤尤其可贵的是，陈寅恪利用了北大所藏缪氏艺风堂“拉萨长庆唐蕃会盟碑”拓本，于其碑阴吐蕃文（藏文）列赞普名号中发现了与汉文古籍中所称“吐蕃彝泰赞普”相应的吐蕃赞普的藏文名

① 陈寅恪：《大乘稻芉经随听疏跋》，收入氏著《金明馆丛稿二编》，第 287—289 页。

② 高山杉：《陈寅恪的第一篇学术文章》，《读书》2002 年第 7 期，第 23—28 页。对法成及其译著的研究近百年来持续不断，常有新的发现，代表作品有上山大峻：《大蕃国大德三藏法师沙门法成的研究（上、下）》，《东方学报》（京都）第 38、39 期，1967—1968 年。任小波：《吐蕃时期藏译汉传佛典〈善恶因果经〉对勘与研究，收入氏著中国藏学出版社 2016 年版。

③ 陈寅恪研究《蒙古源流》时参照的德文译本即是施密特的《东蒙古及其侯王们的历史》，即 Isaak Jakob Schmidt, *Geschichte der Ost-Mongolen und ihres Fürstenhauses verfasst von Ssanang Ssetsen Chungtaidschi der Ordus*, St. Petersburg/Leipzig, 1829。

④ 陈寅恪：《吐蕃彝泰赞普名号年代考》，收入氏著《金明馆丛稿二编》，第 121 页。

⑤ 陈寅恪这里参照的施拉津特维特的著作应该是 Emil Schlahintweit, *Die Könige von Tibet von der Entstehung königlicher Macht in Yarlung bis zum Erlöschen in Ladak*, München: Verlag der k. Akademie, 1866。

号“Khri gtsug lde brtsan”，即《新唐书》中的“可黎可足”，与其年号“彝泰”相应的藏文为“skyid rtag”，于是，由于古今不同语种文本辗转传译而造成的有关吐蕃赞普名号和年代的种种违误和争议便迎刃而解了，《蒙古源流》所载吐蕃赞普的历史从此变成了有确切名号和年代依据的信史。①

陈寅恪《彰所知论与蒙古源流》一文，则以元帝师八思巴所作的《彰所知论》“与蒙古民族以历史之新观念及方法，其影响至深且久”为出发点，认定《蒙古源流》“其书之基本观念及编制体裁，实取之于《彰所知论》”。②他的这篇文章即通过分析以《蒙古源流》为代表的蒙古旧史如何受到《彰所知论》的影响，遂于蒙古族族源“与其本来近于夫余鲜卑等民族之感生说，及其所受于高车突厥诸民族之神话”之上，“更增建天竺吐蕃二重新建筑，采取并行独立之材料，列为直贯一系之事迹。换言之，即糅合数民族之神话，以为一民族之历史”。③陈寅恪通过对《彰所知论》和《蒙古源流》的比较研究，考察了西藏历史叙事传统对蒙古著史传统所产生的深刻影响，成功地厘清了蒙古人一层层地建构其祖先和民族历史的过程。与此同时，他还借助藏文《吐蕃王统记》的记载，对汉译本的《彰所知论》和《蒙古源流》中所列的吐蕃赞普及蒙古王族之名号一一做了校正，并对《吐蕃彝泰赞普名号年代考》一文做了更进一步的补充。

像这样类型和水准的藏学研究在当时的中国学界是绝无仅有的，这种能将汉、藏、蒙古、满语文宗教和历史文本研究熔于一炉，以小见大的藏学、蒙古学研究，于当时的中国恐怕只有陈寅恪一个人能够做到。值得一提的是，陈寅恪上述几篇与藏学相关的学术文章所讨论的问题的论域其实是汉学或者蒙古学研究，像考定吐蕃彝泰赞普的名号和年代，订正蒙、满、汉文本《蒙古源流》中赞普名号等，其学术意义主要在于解决了汉学和蒙古学研究中的难题。所以，陈寅恪所做的这种类型的藏学、蒙古学研究，都与汉学研究相关，或更应该归类于中亚语文学（“虏学”）的范畴。这样的研究对学者的语文能力和语文学水准比仅从事专业的藏学或者蒙古学的学者们有更高的要求。这样的研究在海外汉学家中也只有像伯希和、海涅士这样兼通多种中亚（西域）语文的学者才能把它做好，而陈寅恪是少数几位可以和伯希和、海涅士比肩的兼擅汉学和中亚语文学的杰出学者。

---

① 傅斯年在他所著的《史学方法导论》中引陈寅恪的《吐蕃彝泰赞普名号年代考》一文作为“纯粹史学的考定”的一篇范文，并称赞道：“我的朋友陈寅恪先生，在汉学上的素养不下钱晓徵，更能通习西方古今语言若干种，尤精梵藏经典。近著《吐蕃彝泰赞普名号年代考》一文，以长庆唐蕃会盟碑为根据。‘千年旧史之误书，异国译音之讹读，皆赖以订。’此种异国古文之史料至不多，而能使用此项史料者更属至少，苟其有之，诚学术中之快事也。”见欧阳哲生主编：《傅斯年全集》（第二卷），湖南教育出版社2003年版，第321页。

② 陈寅恪：《彰所知论与蒙古源流》，收入氏著《陈寅恪史学论文选集》，上海古籍出版社1992年版，第76页。

③ 陈寅恪：《彰所知论与蒙古源流》，收入氏著《陈寅恪史学论文选集》，第76页。

六

令人遗憾的是，陈寅恪很快就不再涉足中亚（西域）语文学的研究，特别是进入20世纪40年代后，他很少再做有关西域诸民族语文和史地的研究，自称"凡塞表殊族之史事，不复敢上下议论于其间"。究其原因或有很多，其中之一当如其所谓："寅恪平生治学，不敢逐队随人，而为牛后。"①他当年从事中亚语文学研究时的学术参照和对话对象，都是当时世界一流的学术人物及其一流研究成果，如荷兰蒙古学家、藏学家施密特，德国藏学家、佛教学者施拉津特维特，德国古回鹘语文研究专家缪勒，日本西域、满蒙研究专家白鸟库吉、箭内亘，俄国突厥学、蒙古学家瓦西里·巴托尔德（1869—1930），德国梵文/印度学家路德施，法国汉学、中亚语文学家伯希和，等等。陈寅恪所撰写的有关多语种佛教文献和西域史地的研究文章很多都与回应、补充或者订正前列世界一流学者们的相关著述有关。而这样的学术条件，在他归国多年之后已不复存在。他不但再难及时获得西方新发布的学术资料和学术著作，而且就连原来在欧洲时购集的西文学术著作也已经丢失不少，故从来不甘为牛后的陈寅恪只好放弃他曾用力最多的对敦煌出土多语种佛教文献和西域史地的研究。

虽然陈寅恪本人于20世纪40年代初已不再专门从事蒙古、西藏、西夏研究，但他作为中国现代西域语文学研究的开创者，已经对现代中国的西藏学、蒙古学、西夏学和佛教语文学研究的形成和发展作出了无可替代的重要贡献。而且，值得庆幸的是，他所开创的这几个西域语文学研究领域于中国已经后继有人，一度出现相当喜人的进步。中国新一代杰出的语文学、历史学学者如韩儒林、王静如和林藜光等人，也步陈寅恪之后尘，在西方特别是在巴黎，亲随伯希和等优秀的中亚语文学家接受了严格的语文学训练，他们自20世纪30年代中后期开始陆续发表的一系列研究成果，显然比陈寅恪的上述学术论文更专业、成熟和精致，很快超越了陈寅恪在这些领域内的学术成就。

中国学者中直接继承和发展陈寅恪的蒙古学（蒙元史）、藏学和突厥学研究传统的是中国蒙元史学术大家、南京大学历史系教授韩儒林（1903—1983）。韩先生曾是伯希和的入室弟子，随伯希和接受了中亚语文学的训练，亦曾在陈寅恪留学过的柏林大学亚洲研究院深造。1936年学成归国后，他即成为了继陈寅恪之后的中国现代蒙元史研究最重要的开创者，他以"审音勘同"为特色的历史语言学方法运用于对中国西北民族史地的研究，并在这一领域取得了超越陈寅恪的出色成就。②例如，他发表于1940年的《成吉思汗十三翼考》和《蒙

① 陈寅恪：《朱延丰突厥通考序》，收入氏著《陈寅恪史学论文选集》，第513页。

② 陈得芝：《韩儒林的元史研究》，马光采编，2018年10月24日于海交史发布。本文链接：https://haijiaoshi.com/archives/3611[2021-10-15]。

古氏族札记二则》等文章从学术选题到史学方法上，都与陈寅恪的《元代汉人译名考》和《灵州宁夏榆林三城译名考》等文章有明显的共性，但显然更专业、更深入。[①] 同样，在藏学研究领域，韩儒林也继承和发扬了陈寅恪所开创的学术风气，他的《吐蕃之王族与宦族》一文与陈寅恪研究吐蕃赞普名号的学术方法一脉相承，是陈寅恪《吐蕃彝泰赞普名号年代考》发表十年之后，最能代表中国藏学研究成就的优秀作品。[②] 还有，韩儒林于1936年完成的《突厥文阙特勤碑译注》《突厥文芘伽可汗碑译注》《突厥文日欲谷碑译文》三篇文章也是最早专业地将西方突厥学研究成果介绍给中国学术同行们的重要著作。[③] 如前所述，陈寅恪曾于柏林开始学习西夏文，但自称"于西夏文未能通解"[④]，但是他回国后第一时间在中国倡导并发起了现代西夏语文研究。严格说来，他所做的西夏学研究都是与他曾经指导过的清华大学国学研究院学生王静如（1903—1990）合作研究的成果。他们师徒曾经一起尝试读解西夏文佛教文本，并合作编写见藏于中国的西夏文文献目录。尽管陈寅恪后来未能像他原先设想的那样在西夏语文和历史研究这一领域内有更多的耕耘和收获，但王静如却成了那个时代世界范围内最杰出的西夏学家之一，更是中国"使西夏研究直上科学道路的首创者"。1932年至1933年间，中央研究院历史语言研究所出版了王静如编著的《西夏研究》一至三辑，奠定了他在国际西夏学研究领域的学术领先地位。1933年，王静如赴欧洲留学，也受业于伯希和等西方汉学和中亚语文学大家。1936年，王静如以其三卷本的《西夏研究》获得了被人称为世界汉学研究之诺贝尔奖的儒莲奖，他在西夏研究领域所取得的优秀成果得到了国际学术同行们的承认。[⑤] 同样，进入20世纪40年代后，在梵文和佛教语文学领域，陈寅恪也再没有新的著作问世，然而他在这一领域所开创的事业并没有中断。曾为钢和泰弟子并在汉印研究所学习、工作多年的林藜光先生，于1933年赴法国深造，长期从事《诸法集要经》(《正法念处经》)之梵、藏、汉文本的对勘、校订、翻译和注释工作，其先后出版的《诸法集要经研究》四卷成为了这一领域内的经典著作。[⑥] 林藜光于佛教语文学领域的学术成就和国际影响力无疑超越了包括陈寅恪在内的任何现代中国学术同行们。

最后，或有必要指出的是，尽管陈寅恪是群星璀璨的现代中国人文学术史上最耀眼的一位伟人，是中国现代学术的一名超级英雄，而且，迄今为止他依然还是受世人膜拜和难以超

---

① 韩儒林：《成吉思汗十三翼考》《蒙古氏族札记二则》，收入氏著《穹庐集——元史及西北民族史研究》，第1—17、50—60页。

② 韩儒林：《吐蕃之王族与宦族》，收入氏著《穹庐集——元史及西北民族史研究》，第383—389页。

③ 这三篇文章分别发表于：《北平研究院院务汇报》第6卷6期，1936年；《禹贡》第6卷6期，1936年；《禹贡》第6卷7期，1936年。

④ 陈寅恪：《西夏文佛母大孔雀明王经夏梵藏汉合璧校释序》，收入氏著《金明馆丛稿二编》，第224页。

⑤ 王静如著、史金波编：《序言》，《王静如文集》，社会科学文献出版社2015年版，第5页。

⑥ 林藜光：《林藜光集：梵文写本〈诸法集要经〉校订研究》，中西书局2014年版；参见徐文堪：《林藜光先生的生平与学术贡献》，《文汇学人》2014年12月19日版。

越的学术偶像；但是，毋庸讳言，陈寅恪的学术影响力基本局限于中国，他并不是一位世界性的学术大师。陈寅恪于现代中国学术之最伟大的贡献在于他把西方中亚（西域）语文学的学术方法和成果引进了中国，使汉学或者说中国传统人文学术得以进入一个更大、更广阔的学术空间，变成一个更加专业、规范和现代的学科，并真正成为世界学术的一个有机组成部分。但是，尽管陈寅恪是一位优秀的中亚语文学家，可他所从事的学术研究主要以汉学和对汉文文献的研究为中心，在学术风格上和他同时代大部分专业的西方中亚语文学学术同行们有明显的差别，故很难与他们进行直接的学术对话，也很难对他们的学术成就做公平的学术比较。而且，陈寅恪从来没有用汉文以外的文字发表过任何有关佛教和西域语文学研究的作品，迄今所见他的英文论文仅有发表在《哈佛亚洲研究杂志》上的两篇由编者翻译的短文，分别讨论“韩愈和唐代小说”和“《顺宗实录》与《续玄怪录》”，它们既不代表他当年所从事学术的重点，也不足以典型地反映他的学术成就。①

与陈寅恪同时代的那些西方中亚语文学学术大家，绝大部分是专精于某一个学术领域的文本语文学权威。如路得施、钢和泰、林冶是印度学、印藏佛教语文的专家，以整理和解读梵文、藏文佛教文献为毕生志业，而缪勒则是解读吐鲁番出土古回鹘文佛教文献的开创者和学术权威，同样以文本语文学的卓越成就著称于世。在陈寅恪活跃的那个时代，欧洲各国都出现了不少顶级的藏学家，除了或曾是陈寅恪藏文老师的奥古斯特·赫尔曼·弗兰克以外，还有如英国的托马斯（F. W. Thomas，1867—1956）、法国的雅克·巴科（Jacques Bacot，1877—1965）、玛尔赛勒·拉露（Marcelle Lalou，1890—1967）和意大利的朱塞佩·图齐（Giuseppe Tucci, 1894—1984）等人。他们无疑都是比陈寅恪更专业的西藏语文学家，其学术事业以整理、解读新疆和敦煌出土古藏文文献，和研究藏传佛教文献、历史和艺术为主。由于陈寅恪基本没有直接从事过对梵文、藏文、蒙古文、满文等西域语文文献的整理、精校和研究工作，所以，陈寅恪的学术作品虽然优秀，却很难与上述这些中亚语文学大家的学术成就进行直接比较。与陈寅恪的学术路径最为接近的应该是西方那些同样对中亚语文学有极大兴趣的汉学大家们，如德国的海涅士、雷兴（战后成为美国加州大学伯克利校区东方语言系的教授）和法国的戴密微（Paul Demiéville，1894—1979）等等，他们都曾与陈寅恪有过相对紧密的学术联系。若以纯粹的传统汉学而言，相信陈寅恪的学术水准当在这几位学术大家之上；然若从“虏学”的角度来评判，则他们的西域语文学水准或胜于陈寅恪。海涅士虽然是一名汉学教授，但他同时也是一位杰出的蒙古学和满学研究专家，其杰出的学术成就表现在他对《蒙古秘史》的研究、对满语文法的构建和对满文历史文献的收集和整理等方面。②

---

① Tschen Yin-koh, “Han Yu and the Tang Novel,” *Harvard Journal of Asiatic Studies*, I, 1936, pp.39–43; “The Shun-Tsung Shih-Lu and The Hsu Hsuan-Kuai-Lu,” *Harvard Journal of Asiatic Studies*, III, 1938, pp.9–16.

② Erich Haenisch, *Die Geheime Geschichte der Mongolen*, Leipzig: Otto Harrassowitz, 1948, 2nd Edition, XVIII, p.196; *Mandschu-Grammatik. Mit Lesestücken und 23 Texttafeln*, (Manchu Grammar)Hardcover, 1961.

而雷兴虽然也是一位汉学教授，但他对藏学、蒙古学，特别是藏传佛教的研究也是他那个时代的佼佼者，他的学术成就主要集中在对雍和宫的藏学、佛学和佛教图像学研究，以及对藏传佛教格鲁派祖师宗喀巴大师的弟子克主杰所作的《密宗道次第论》的翻译和注释。此外，他甚至还编写、出版了一部蒙古文—英文字典。① 而戴密微的传世之作是《吐蕃僧诤记》，他是世界上第一位利用敦煌出土汉文佛教文献对藏传佛教史上一个十分重要的历史事件——“吐蕃僧诤”做出了精湛研究的汉学大家和佛教学者，对藏学和藏传佛教研究的进步有着十分重要的推动作用。②

当然，陈寅恪所走的将汉学和中亚语文学紧密结合在一起的学术道路，显然与被公认为世界汉学第一人的伯希和最为相像。伯希和虽以汉学大师名世，他于法兰西学院之教授讲席却被标记为“中亚语言、历史和考古”，此即是说，伯希和在中亚语文学领域的学术成就丝毫不逊色于他的汉学研究。美国著名汉学家薛爱华（Edward H. Schafer，1913—1991）教授曾经对伯希和之汉学研究的卓越做过如下总结，他说伯希和的学术“方法的一个典型特色是，追随雷慕沙的榜样，充分发掘和利用大量不同种的东方语言文献，包括属于闪含语、印度伊朗语、阿尔泰语和汉语等不同语系的许多种语言。他有能力以一种史无前例的程度达到了对早期汉语文献的完全的理解，这些文献都程度不等地带上了受亚洲其他高等文化的语言和文献影响的烙印。他不把中国看成是一种自我封闭的、被孤立的文明，而是一种在整个亚洲的语境中形成的文明”；“伯希和的著作还有另一个特点，就是他对书目文献（bibliography，版本目录学）的十分细致和一丝不苟的态度，这在欧洲文化的人文研究中是习以为常的事情，而在东方研究，尤其是汉学研究中却是很少见的。在他之前，一部汉文古籍的任何版本，哪怕是一部千年古书的劣质的木活字刻印本，其中充满了讹误和脱衍，都会被大部分研究者不加批评（校勘）地利用。伯希和为汉文资料的研究引进了一种有理有据的精确性，使得那种粗枝大叶的票友性质的学术遭人唾弃”。③

简单说来，伯希和最大的学术贡献就是凭借他出色的语文能力，借助汉语以外的东西方各种不同语种的文献资料，力图彻底理解和读懂古代汉文文献，并由此把汉学研究放在整个亚洲文明，甚至整个世界文明的语境中进行考察和研究，从此使汉学成为世界学术的一个有机组成部分。与此同时，伯希和还将欧洲现代人文学术的科学、理性的语文学学术方法、规

---

① Ferdinand D. Lessing, *Yung-ho-kung: an iconography of the Lamaist Cathedral in Peking; with notes on Lamaist mythology and cult* Vol. 1, Stockholm, 1942. Ferdinand D. Lessing and Alex Wayman eds. and trs., *Mkhas-grub rje's Fundamentals of the Buddhist Tantras: Rgyud sde spyihi rnam par gźag pa rgyas par brjod*, Indo-Iranian Monographs, Vol. VIII, The Hague, Paris: Mouton, 1968, Guilders 64.

② Paul Demiéville, *Le Concile de Lhasa: Une controverse sur la quiétisme entre bouddhistes de l'inde et de le Chine au* VIII *ème siècle* (The Council of Lhasa: A controversy on quietism between Buddhists of India and China in the 8th century), Paris: Bibliothèque de l'Institut des Hautes Études chinoises, 1952.

③ Edward H. Schafer, "What and How is Sinology?" *Tang Studies*, 8–9, 1990–91, p.33.

范和评判标准，最大程度地运用到汉学研究的实践之中，使汉学成为一门可与欧洲其他人文学术研究领域并驾齐驱的现代人文学科。尽管在以上这两个方面，陈寅恪的学术或略逊色于伯希和，但陈寅恪的学术实践和成就对于中国现代人文科学之形成和发展的学术贡献，却完全可以与伯希和对于汉学的进步和汉学的世界化所作出的巨大贡献相媲美。

中英文摘要

Divisions and Chapter Titles of the *Lotus Sūtra* in Central Asia

Peter Zieme

Berlin-Brandenburg Academy of Sciences and Humanities

Abstract: In Old Uyghur Buddhism, the *Saddharmapuṇḍarīkasūtra (Lotus Sūtra)* is richly attested, mainly its chapter 25. All Uyghur fragments seem to be translated from Kumārajīva's Chinese version. The *Lotus Sūtra* is known in Old Uyghur Buddhism from the 10th century to the end of the Yuan Dynasty. Among the Uyghur block-printed books of the Turfan collection in Berlin there are so far only two pieces of a booklet which are related to the *Lotus Sūtra*. These two fragments of the Berlin Turfan Collection testify to a special concertina book: U 4780 (TM 31) and Mainz 490 (T III D). The booklet is a kind of guide in the form of an overview of the *Saddharmapuṇḍarīkasūtra*. The names of the chapters from the 11th to the 20th have been preserved. Perhaps the work served as a bibliographical medium to arrange Buddhist scriptures, because with the listing of chapter names and distinctive sentences it was possible to get a quick overview. In comparison with similar Chinese texts the fragments are here edited and explained.

Keywords: the *Lotus Sūtra*; Berlin Turfan collection; Old Uyghur Buddhism; Central Asia

中亚出土回鹘文《法华经》之章节划分与章题

皮特·茨默

柏林勃兰登堡科学与人文科学院

摘　要：在回鹘佛教中，有丰富的证据表明《法华经》(Saddharmapuṇḍarīkasūtra) 流传广布，尤其是该经的第二十五章。迄今所发现的回鹘文残片，均源自鸠摩罗什 (Kumārajīva) 的汉译本。自 10 世纪至元末，《法华经》在回鹘佛教界享有极高的知名度。在柏林吐鲁番藏品中所见回鹘文木刻本中，至今已发现有两件与《法华经》有关的残片，编号为：U 4780 (TM 31)、Mainz 490 (T III D)。这两件残片同属一部经折装小册子，纂辑《法华经》之要旨，犹如经文概览，其中保留了《法华经》第十一至二十章的名称。据此推测，这部小册子原本可能是编纂佛经之书目媒介，罗列诸章之名、摘录每章之特色经文，以便览者速晓佛经之概略。本文参照《法华经》的汉译本，对这两个残片进行校订和译注。

关键词：《法华经》；柏林吐鲁番藏品；回鹘佛教；中亚

New Traces of Aśvaghoṣa on the Silk Road

Jens-Uwe Hartmann
Munich University

Abstract: Aśvaghoṣa was one of the most famous Buddhist poets of ancient India. Unsurprisingly, his works have also left vestiges in the literature of the Buddhist cultures along the Silk Road. One of them, the play about the conversion of Śāriputra and Maudgalyāyana, is only known from there. The recently initiated study of the *Tridaṇḍamālā*, a compendium of texts for recitation in certain rituals containing about 1500 poetic verses, has brought to light further remarkable traces of Aśvaghoṣa in Central Asia.

Keywords: Aśvaghoṣa; Central Asia; *Tridaṇḍamālā*

马鸣在丝绸之路上的新踪迹

延斯–乌维·哈特曼
慕尼黑大学

摘　要：马鸣是古印度最负盛名的佛教诗人之一。毫不意外地，他的著作在丝绸之路沿线的佛教文学作品中也留下了印记。其中，一部关于舍利弗和摩诃迦叶皈依佛陀的戏剧，唯在此地流传，为人所熟知。最近开始的对《三启集》（Tridaṇḍamālā）的研究则进一步彰显了马鸣在中亚地区遗留的踪迹，此集约含一千五百个诗节，为在某些仪式中诵读的文本汇编。

关键词：马鸣；中亚地区；《三启集》

Reading between the Characters: Notes on the *Dhūta-sūtra* and Its Reception

Chen Ruixuan 陈瑞翾
School of Foreign Languages, Peking University

Abstract: This paper examines the Chinese Buddhist apocryphal text *Dhūta-sūtra* (佛爲心王菩薩説頭陀經), tracing its textual history, stylistic features, and cross-cultural reception. Rediscovered in Dunhuang and Turfan manuscripts, the text offers insights into early medieval Buddhist practices influenced by Tathāgatagarbha thought. The study highlights the unique Chinese hermeneutical methods applied to key concepts like *dhūta* through syllable-based analysis, reflecting the interplay of indigenous linguistic traditions and Buddhist doctrinal innovation. The paper also situates the text within the broader cultural and intellectual milieu of mid-Tang literati, as discussed by Chen Yinke, and investigates its reach beyond China, particularly into Sogdian and Tibetan contexts.

Keywords: the *Dhūta-sūtra*; Dunhuang and Turfan manuscripts; the Chinese hermeneutical methods; Sogdian and Tibetan contexts

字里行间探微意:《头陀经》及其流传述略

陈瑞翾
北京大学外国语学院

摘　要：本文探讨了中国佛教疑伪经《佛为心王菩萨说头陀经》的文本历史、风格特征及跨文化传播。通过对敦煌与吐鲁番出土写本进行研究，本文揭示了此经受如来藏思想影响的中古早期禅修实践背景，并分析其对“头陀”等关键概念进行的逐字训释方法，展现了中国本土解经传统与佛教教义创新的互动。文章还结合陈寅恪对中唐文人的研究，将此经置于特定的文化史与知识史语境中，并探讨其在粟特语与藏语世界中的传播与影响。

关键词：《头陀经》；敦煌与吐鲁番写本；中国本土解经传统；粟特语和藏语世界

Three *Nayatraya* Texts: Path Hierarchization within Indian Buddhism

Kazuo Kano

Komazawa University

Abstract: In the field of Indian Buddhism, there have been persistent efforts to gain a comprehensive understanding of the Buddhist tradition. However, as Esoteric Buddhism gained prominence and became firmly established, there was a conscious effort to integrate it into the broader doctrinal and practical framework. This led to the emergence of a body of work from the 9th century onwards that focused primarily on the concept of *nayatraya*. *Nayatraya* encompasses a scholastic and practical system of knowledge concerning the "paths" of doctrine and practice and is divided into three categories: Śrāvakanaya (representing Hīnayāna), Pāramitānaya (representing Mahāyāna), and Mantranaya (representing Esoteric Buddhism).

Among these works centered on *nayatraya*, a key text is the *Nayatrayapradīpa* ("Lamp of Nayatraya") by Trivikrama, dating back to the 9th to 10th century, followed by various texts, including those found in the Derge Tanjur (such as Tōhoku Nos. 3710–3720). Until recently, these works were mainly known through Tibetan translations. In recent years, however, their Sanskrit manuscripts have come to light. These include the *Nayatrayapradīpa* by Trivikrama, the *Nayatrayabheda* by Kuśalaśrī, and the *Nayatrayahṛdaya* by an unknown author. All of these are included in a collection of miscellaneous tantric texts, a manuscript of which is currently preserved in Potala palace. This paper gives an overview of these works, their historical background, and their significance in the development of Indian Buddhist doctrine.

The paper also examines the relationship between *nayatraya* and *saṃvaratraya* (the Three Sets of Restraints), the latter being a triple group of guidelines for the lives of all monks, consisting of the *prātimokṣasaṃvara*, the *bodhisattvasaṃvara*, and the *vajrasattvasaṃvara*. Furthermore, it discusses a possible correspondence between the three groups and the three titles of Buddhit: *śākyabhikṣu*, *mahāyānānuyāyin*, and *mantranayānuyāyin* found in colophons of Sanskrit manuscripts and inscriptions.

Keywords: Indian Buddhism; *Nayatraya*; Path Hierarchization; Sanskrit Manuscripts

印度佛教修证道路的层级化研究：以三篇“三理趣”文本为中心

加纳和雄
驹泽大学

摘　要：在印度佛教领域，人们一直在努力全面理解佛教传统。然而，随着密教兴起和牢固确立其地位，人们开始有意识地尝试将其融入更广泛的教义和实践框架中。这一趋势促使自公元 9 世纪始，一系列著作应运而生，这些著作的核心聚焦于“三理趣”（nayatraya）这一概念。“三理趣”涵盖了一套关于教义和修行之“道”的学术和实践知识体系，细分为三类：声闻乘（Śrāvakanaya，代表小乘佛教）、菩萨乘（Pāramitānaya，代表大乘佛教）和陀罗尼乘（Mantranaya，代表密教）。

在这些以“三理趣”为核心的著作中，有一部至关重要的文本，即特里维克拉玛（Trivikrama）所著的《三理趣明灯》（Nayatrayapradīpa），其历史可追溯到 9 至 10 世纪。此后，又涌现了诸多相关文本，包括德格版《丹珠尔》中编号为 3710 至 3720 号的文本。长久以来，人们主要通过藏文译本了解这些作品。然而，近年来，这些著作的梵文写本相继面世。这些写本中，除了特里维克拉玛的《三理趣明灯》外，还有库萨拉西（Kuśalaśrī）的《三理趣分别》（Nayatrayabheda）以及一位佚名作者的《三理趣心髓》（Nayatrayahṛdaya）。这些珍贵的写本均被收录在杂密文集中，现珍藏于布达拉宫。本文将对这些著作、它们的历史背景以及它们在印度佛教教义发展中的重要性进行概述。

本文还探讨了“三理趣”与三戒（saṃvaratraya，即三种约束）之间的关系。三戒作为所有僧侣必须遵循的三重生活准则，包括别解脱戒（prātimokṣasaṃvara）、菩萨戒（bodhisattvasaṃvara）以及金刚乘戒（vajrasattvasaṃvara）。此外，本文还讨论了三戒与在梵文写本和碑铭的题跋中发现的三种佛弟子称号——释迦比丘（śākyabhikṣu）、大乘随行弟子（mahāyānānuyāyin）和陀罗尼乘随行弟子（mantranayānuyāyin）——之间可能存在的对应关系。

关键词：印度佛教；“三理趣”；修证道路层级化；梵文写本

Buddhist Narrative and Non-Narrative Sources on the Salvation of the Patricidal King Ajātaśatru

Wu Juan 吴 娟
Department of Chinese Language and Literature, School of Humanities, Tsinghua University

Abstract: The salvation of the patricidal king Ajātaśatru is a recurring theme in Indian Buddhist traditions. The present article provides a survey of both narrative and non-narrative sources related to this theme. In terms of narrative sources, there are at least five groups of stories illustrating the repentance and/or salvation of Ajātaśatru in Indian Buddhist literature. Among them, prophecies of his future buddhahood or pratyekabuddhahood are the most significant, which demonstrate the temporary nature of karmic obstacles to spiritual growth, the salvific power of the Buddha (or the bodhisattva Mañjuśrī), the efficacy of the Buddhist Dharma, and the overwhelmingly positive nature of Buddhist soteriology. In terms of non-narrative (or more precisely, scholastic or expository) sources, the *Abhidharma-mahāvibhāṣā*, the *Sarvāstivādavinayavibhāṣā*, the *Karmavibhaṅga*, the *Tarkajvālā* and *Sūtrālaṃkāra-vṛttibhāṣya* all speak about the mitigation or elimination of Ajātaśatru's punishment in hell. These non-narrative sources suggest that some Buddhist philosophers in ancient India took the salvation of Ajātaśatru seriously and exploited this theme in diverse ways for the sake of scholastic argumentation.

Keywords: Ajātaśatru; patricide; narrative sources; non-narrative sources; Indian Buddhist soteriology

弑父罪犯阿阇世王救赎主题的佛教叙事性与非叙事性文献

吴 娟
清华大学人文学院中文系

摘 要： 弑父者阿阇世王的救赎是印度佛教传统中反复出现的主题。本文对与这一主题相关的叙事性和非叙事性文献进行了调查。就叙事性文献而言，印度佛教文献中至少有五组故事说明了阿阇世王的忏悔和/或救赎。其中，关于阿阇世王未来成佛或成独觉佛的预言最为重要，这些预言表明了对宗教修行造成阻碍的业障的暂时性、佛陀（或文殊菩萨）的救赎力量、佛法的功效以及佛教救赎论的压倒性积极性质。就非叙事性（或更确切地说，佛教哲学论著）文献而言，《阿毗达摩大毗婆沙》（Abhidharma-mahāvibhāṣā）、《萨婆多毗婆沙》（Sarvāstivādavinayavibhāṣā）、《业分别》（Karmavibhaṅga）、《思择焰》（Tarkajvālā）和《大乘庄严经论》（Sūtrālaṃkāravṛttibhāṣya）都提到了减轻或消除阿阇世王在地狱中的惩罚。这些非叙事性文献表明，古印度的一些佛教哲学家认真对待阿阇世王的救赎，并以不同的方式利用这一主题进行学术论证。

关键词： 阿阇世王；弑父；叙事性文献；非叙事性文献；印度佛教救赎论

Retrieving the *Oral-Tradition Gems*

Iain Sinclair
The University of Queensland

Abstract: A previously unstudied anthology of quotations with the title *Zhal lung rin po che'i snying po'i phreng ba* or *Mukhāgamaratnasārāvalī* has been transmitted as a Sanskrit-Tibetan bitext (Q5096). The thirty-seven verses in the anthology, the *Oral-Tradition Gems*, were uttered by the famous 15th-century *paṇḍita* Vanaratna to his student Bsod nams rgya mtsho, who transcribed and translated them. This paper traces thirty of these verses to their sources in tantric and non-tantric Mahāyāna Buddhist works. Many relate to the literate Vajrayoginī praxis tradition going to back to Śabarapāda, as elaborated by Advayavajra, Raviśrī, Munidatta and others. The Hevajra tradition is also represented. Much of the anthology was not, therefore, transmitted exclusively in spoken form. Nonetheless, some verses have features suggestive of oral transmission, such as misattribution and impromptu conflation, and their translations are mostly novel; but they also have errors originating in written transmission. The contents of the *Oral-Tradition Gems* are also found to be echoed in the Nepalese manuscript corpus of the 15th century. This paper provides a work-in-progress edition of the Sanskrit verses, a philological commentary, Tibetan-Sanskrit lexica and an English translation.

Keywords: *Mukhāgamaratnasārāvalī*; Sanskrit-Tibetan bitext; *paṇḍita* Vanaratna

重拾《口传宝鬘》

伊恩·辛克莱尔
昆士兰大学

摘　要:《西藏大藏经》中保存了一部梵藏双语的语录选集——《口传宝鬘》(*Zhal lung rin po che'i snying po'i phreng ba*, Mukhāgamaratnasārāvalī) (Q5096)，然而遗憾的是，该选集长久以来一直未引起学术界的足够关注。《口传宝鬘》汇编了三十七首诗篇，皆出自 15 世纪印度著名班智达森宝 (paṇḍita Vanaratna) 之口，由他亲自向藏族弟子福海 (Bsod nams rgya mtsho) 口授。福海不仅将这些诗篇的梵文原音以藏文字母转录，还将将其内容意译成藏文。本文追溯了其中三十首诗在密宗和非密宗大乘佛教作品中的渊源。研究发现，其中多首与金刚瑜伽母修习的文献传统有关，可以追溯到沙巴拉帕达 (Śabarapāda)，并经由不二金刚 (Advayavajra)、拉维希里 (Raviśrī)、穆尼达塔 (Munidatta) 和其他人进一步阐发。同时，喜金刚传统在其中亦有体现。因此，选集的大部分内容并非仅依赖口头形式传播。尽管如此，一些诗句具有口头传播的特征，如文本来源的误传或不同文本之间的即兴混用，这些诗句的译文也大多风格独特；但是，这其中也夹杂着一些源于书面传承的错误。此外，本文还发现《口传宝鬘》的内容与 15 世纪的尼泊尔写本存在呼应之处。本文提供了《口传宝鬘》梵文诗篇的初步校订版、语文学评析、藏梵对照词汇表以及英文译文。

关键词:《口传宝鬘》；梵藏双语文本；班智达森宝

藏译疑伪经《北斗七星经》再探

才　让

西北民族大学铸牢中华民族共同体意识研究院

摘　要： 藏文本《北斗七星经》的第二位译者贡噶多杰即蔡巴万户长，赴元廷觐见期间，有机会学习了蒙古语，并了解朝廷重视星辰崇拜习俗，并将此经带入西藏。从藏译本之跋文看，此经翻译的顺序是回鹘文、蒙古文、藏文，后来藏文本又译为蒙古文。通过比对，发现间接翻译过来的藏文本与汉文原本之间有较大的差异，某些部分只能说主旨、大意存焉。翻译本身就是对跨文化文本的理解，在这种过程中出现的某些"走样"，可能是与本土文化对接的创造性阐释，《北斗七星经》藏译本与原本间存在的明显差异造就了一种新的文本。研究者曾认为《北斗七星经》在藏地影响不大，但该经收入《陀罗尼集》等众多文献集中，说明此经在翻译成藏文后一直在流通，尤其受到民间的重视。藏传佛教界的两位学者曾对该经有所评述。《北斗七星经》在流传过程中，出现了藏传佛教式的祭祀仪轨，遵循了藏传佛教同类仪轨的撰写模式，使《北斗七星经》进一步实现了藏传佛教化。而且这一仪轨的制定，是以阙失星符的藏译本为基础的，可视为对藏译本之一种诠释，解决或明确了如何实现本经功能的途径或方法。又在密教的语境下，进一步强化、延伸或扩展了经典的功能。

关键词：《北斗七星经》；贡噶多杰；密教化；翻译语境

A Re-exploration of the Tibetan Translation of the Suspected Pseudo-Sutra *Big Dipper Seven Star Sutra*

Cairang
Northwest Minzu University

Abstract: Kun dga' rdo rje, the second translator of the Tibetan version of the *Big Dipper Seven Star Sutra*, also known as Tshal pa, the head of the ten thousand households, had the opportunity to learn Mongolian during his visit to the Yuan court. He learned Yuan's emphasis on the worship of stars, and brought this sutra to Xizang. According to the postscript of this sutra's Tibetan version, it can be seen that the sutra was translated from Uyghur and Mongolian first, then in Tibetan. Later on, the Tibetan text was re-translated into Mongolian. A comparative analysis reveals significant differences between the Tibetan version and the original Chinese text, with some sections only retaining the general theme or gist. Translation itself represents a cross-cultural interpretation of texts, and the discrepancies arising in this process may reflect creative reinterpretations to align with local cultural contexts. The notable differences between the Tibetan translation and the original have resulted in a new text. Researchers previously believed that *Big Dipper Seven Star Sutra* had limited influence in Xizang. However, its inclusion in numerous collections such as the *Dhāraṇī Compendium* indicates that the text continued to circulate in its Tibetan form and was especially valued among the general populace. Two scholars within the Tibetan Buddhist tradition have commented on this scripture. During the dissemination of the *Big Dipper Seven Star Sutra*, a Tibetan Buddhist-style ritual was developed around the scripture, following the similar writing model of Tibetan Buddhist rituals. This adaptation further integrated this Sutra into Tibetan Buddhist practices. Moreover, the ritual was based on the Tibetan translation, which lacks certain star symbols, and can be seen as an illustration of the Tibetan version. It clarified or established methods for realizing this Sutra functions. Within the tantric Buddhist context, the Sutra was further enhanced and expanded the scripture's functions.

Keywords: *Big Dipper Seven Star Sutra*; Kun dga' rdo rje; Tantricization; Translation Context

从《吐蕃大事纪年》看吐蕃巡守制度

黄维忠
中国人民大学国学院

摘　要：目前学界未关注到吐蕃礼仪制度中的巡守制度问题，文章根据敦煌藏文文献对吐蕃巡守制度做初步探讨。在敦煌藏文文献中，与赞普巡守有关的专用词汇为གཤེགས（gshegs）。文章对《吐蕃大事纪年》中出现的གཤེགས一词进行了统计与分类，指出该词总体而言有三种意思，最多的与赞普巡狩有关。根据《吐蕃大事纪年》，吐蕃多位赞普在任期间，外出巡狩共计二十九次，巡狩范围所及可分狩猎、政事巡狩、避寒三种；其中政事巡狩的情况相对复杂，又可细分为四种。文章认为，吐蕃巡守制度是探究吐蕃礼仪制度的重要门径之一，值得学界持续关注。

关键词：吐蕃；礼仪制度；《吐蕃大事纪年》；巡守制度；政事巡狩

The Tibetan Patrol System from the *Tibetan Chronicles*

Huang Weizhong
School of Chinese Classics, Renmin University of China

Abstract: At present, the academic community has not paid attention to the issue of the patrol system in the Tibetan etiquette system. This article makes a preliminary exploration of the Tibetan patrol system based on the Dunhuang Tibetan documents. In the Tibetan documents in Dunhuang, the special vocabulary related to the patrol of the king is "གཤེགས" (gshegs). This article conducted a statistical and classification analysis of the word "གཤེགས" appearing in the *Tibetan Chronicles*, and pointed out that the word generally has three meanings, with the most related to the inspection tours of the Tibetan kings. According to the *Tibetan Chronicles*, during their tenure, several Tibetan kings made a total of twenty-nine expeditions. These expeditions could be categorized into three types: hunting expeditions, political expeditions, and expeditions to escape the cold; The situation of political affairs patrol is relatively complex, and can be subdivided into four types. The article maintains that the Tibetan patrol system is one of the significant avenues for exploring the etiquette system of Tubo, meriting continued academic attention.

Keywords: Tubo; etiquette system; *Tibetan Chronicles*; patrol system; political patrol

曹议金东征甘州回鹘史事证补

——浙敦114号《肃州府主致沙州令公书状》译释

任小波

复旦大学历史地理研究中心

摘　要： 本文对浙敦114号《肃州府主致沙州令公书状》(928—930)做了译释。这件写本所涉史事，当在曹议金任归义军节度使期间(914—935)。基于这件写本以及相关文献，可以揭示924—925年曹议金东征甘州回鹘的一些新证据。根据这件写本，东征之役胜利以后，肃州官民、龙家部族皆向曹议金宣誓效忠，并以北方护国祐方之神多闻天王证盟。

关键词： 曹议金；甘州回鹘；肃州府主；龙家；多闻天王

New Evidence on the History of Cao Yijin's Conquest of Ganzhou Uighurs:

A Study on Tibetan Manuscript Zhejiang 114 from Dunhuang, the *Official Letter from Suzhou Fuzhu to Shazhou Linggong*

Ren Xiaobo

Research Center for Historical Geography, Fudan University

Abstract: This article provides an interpretation of Tibetan manuscript Zhejiang 114 from Dunhung, the *Official Letter from Suzhou Fuzhu* 肃州府主 *to Shazhou Linggong* 沙州令公 written in 928–930 AD. The historical events mentioned in this manuscript must be in the period of Cao

Yijin 曹议金 (rg. 914–935 AD), the Linggong (Tib.: leng kong) of Return-to-allegiance Army 归义军. Based on this manuscript and related documents, we could discover some new evidence on the history of Cao Yijin's conquest of Ganzhou Uighurs (Tib.: hor) 甘州回鹘 in 924–925 AD. According to this manuscript, a pledge of allegiance to Cao Yijin was taken by the Fuzhu (Tib.: dbang po), Chinese inhabitants and Long tribal group (Tib.: lung 'bangs) 龙家 of Suzhou after the conquest, and meanwhile an oath-taking ceremony was held in front of the image of Vaiśramaṇa (Tib.: rnam thos sras, 毗沙门), who was regarded as a great divine power to preserve peace in the Hexi Corridor region of northwestern China.

Keywords: Cao Yijin; Ganzhou Uighurs; Suzhou Fuzhu; Long tribal group; Vaiśramaṇa

国之神祇

——一篇来自敦煌的9世纪 Tridaṇḍaka 祈祷文（rGyud chags gsum）

波恩大学　刘易斯·唐尼　著
中国人民大学　扎　西　译

摘　要：本文对近期发现的一篇藏文祈祷文做了具体分析，该祈祷文发现于莫高窟17号窟，可追溯至9世纪。这一 Tridaṇḍaka 祈祷文最初或为吐蕃时期（约600—842年）所书写、翻译或编辑。文中的某些短语与公元8世纪所写之“桑耶寺钟铭文”相对应，另一些则指示了本文与《净治一切恶趣续》和《顶髻尊胜总持经》之间的相似性。分析这篇祈祷文的内容有助于评估早期藏传佛教的赞颂文献及其与当时印度和汉传佛教的联系，此外亦能将吐蕃时期的文献与后来藏传佛教的历史编纂联系起来。

关键词：吐蕃；敦煌文献；祈祷文

Imperial Gods:

A 9th-Century *Tridaṇḍaka* Prayer (*rGyud chags gsum*) from Dunhuang

Lewis Doney
University of Bonn

Abstract: This article offers some more details on a Tibetan prayer dating from the 9th century and recently discovered in Mogao Cave 17. This Tridaṇḍaka prayer was perhaps first written, translated or compiled in the the late Tibetan imperial period (circa 600–842). Some phrases in the prayer correspond to the bSam yas Bell Inscription written during the 8th century, and others point towards similarities between this prayer and *the Sarvadurgatipariśodhana tantra* and the closely connected *Uṣṇīṣavijaya dhāraṇī sūtra*. Analysing the content of this prayer helps to assess early Tibetan Buddhist praise literature and its connections with contemporaneous Indic and Chinese Buddhism. It also links Tibetan imperial literature to later Tibetan Buddhist historiography in Tibet.

Keywords: Tubo; Dunhuang documents; Prayer

经典、文本、写本

——佛教文献的三个层次

圣　凯

清华大学人文学院哲学系

摘　要：本文从经典、文本与写本三个方面，探讨佛教文献的形成与传播过程及其深层意义。经典作为佛陀教义的核心记录，蕴含神圣性和思想价值，是佛教信仰与智慧的根本载体；文本通过翻译、注释等语言与观念的具体表达，展现了佛教文化的适应力与创新性；写本则作为经典传播的物质媒介，不仅具有历史记录功能，还体现了佛教思想的社会化与地域化特征。在此过程中，时间、语言和价值成为贯穿写本、文本与经典三者的核心维度，共同建构出佛教文献的多维观念世界。

关键词：佛教文献；经典；文本；写本

Scripture, Text, and Manuscript:

Three Dimensions of Buddhist Literature

Sheng Kai

Department of Philosophy, School of Humanities, Tsinghua University

Abstract: This paper explores the formation and dissemination of Buddhist literature through three key dimensions: scripture, text, and manuscript, highlighting their deeper significance. Scriptures, as the core records of the Buddha’s teachings, embody sacredness and intellectual value, serving as the fundamental carriers of Buddhist faith and wisdom. Texts, realized through translation, commentary, and interpretation, provide linguistic and conceptual expressions of scriptures, reflecting the adaptability and innovation of Buddhist culture. Manuscripts, as the material medium for scripture transmission, function not only as historical records but also as tools for illustrating the socialization and localization of Buddhist thought. Time, language, and value emerge as the central dimensions connecting manuscripts, texts, and scriptures, collectively constructing the multidimensional conceptual world of Buddhist literature.

Keywords: Buddhist Literature; Scripture; Text; Manuscript

从胜迹志文献理解寺庙艺术：以多罗那他的平措林寺为例

姚　霜
中国人民大学文学院

摘　要：围绕圣地的艺术与文学塑造是喜马拉雅地区一个重要的文化主题。在西藏历史中，藏人对于诸多自然景观与人文艺术建筑都有属于自己的文化诠释与观览方式，而这些知识以文本的形式流传了下来，形成了独立的文献体裁。本文以圣地文化中的"胜迹志"（*gnas bshad*）为出发点，在西藏文化语境下探讨胜迹志整体的创作目的与叙事结构，并重点以出自17世纪下半叶著名的藏地祖师觉囊·多罗那他（Tāranātha, 1575—1634）全集中的《甘丹平措林胜迹志》（*Dga' ldan phun tshogs gling gi gnas bshad*）为例，在文本叙事的脉络里探寻平措林寺艺术空间的历史塑造过程，于文化语境之下开辟解读寺庙艺术的新路径与可能性。

关键词：胜迹志文献；寺庙艺术；多罗那他；平措林寺

Understanding Temple Art through *Gnas Bshad* Literature: A Case Study of Tāranātha's Phun Tshogs Gling

Yao Shuang
School of Liberal Arts, Renmin University of China

Abstract: In the literary and artistic landscape of the Himalayan region, the construction of sacred sites (*gnas*) is a significant theme for historical and cultural studies. Various literary genres, including site guidebooks (*gnas bshad*), itineraries (*lam yig*), and travelogues (*gnas yig*), document the formation of both large and small *gnas*. Among these, *gnas bshad* is distinctive for its focus on the builder's vision rather than the visitor's perspective. This viewpoint is essential for art-historical research aimed at reconstructing the context of temple art. This paper addresses the interpretation of *gnas bshad* text, particularly its narratives, which encompass myths, prophecies, tenets, "histories," icons, and other elements. How can these texts help us contextualize the historical construction of temples or a monastic complex? As a case study, this paper will conduct a textual analysis of *Dga' ldan phun tshogs gling gi gnas bshad*, the central *gnas bshad* text attributed to Tāranātha (1575–1634). This analysis will illuminate the establishment of the Phun Tshogs Gling Monastery, the last monument of the Jonang tradition in Central Xizang.

Keywords: Gnas Bshad Literature; Temple Art; Tāranātha; the Phun Tshogs Gling Monastery

黑水城的藏传佛教量论之钥：俄藏黑水城文献 912 号研究

马洲洋
奥地利科学院

摘　要： 在诸多现藏于俄罗斯科学院东方所的西夏文写本中，有一部题名为《正理空幢要门解锁》（𗅋𗏁𗖵𗂸𗏹𗠁𗤀𗉔，Tśhja wo ŋa dźjow tshji ŋwu̱ wjij phie, 第 912 号）的短小残片。这部简洁的论著几乎可称得上一部辞典。它为佛教量论中的关键概念诸如四种现量等提供了精辟的解释。这一文本的结构和其中的一些辞句似乎反映了桑浦内邬托寺（Gsang phu ne'u thog）论师的著作中的那些辞句。本文考察了这些特点，并且探究了西夏佛教徒获取藏传量论知识的智识环境。

关键词： 黑水城出土文献；量论；桑浦内邬托寺；西夏佛教

A Tangut Key to the Lock of Tibetan Buddhist Epistemology: A Study of Khara-Khoto Manuscript Inv. 912

Ma Zhouyang
Austrian Academy of Sciences

Abstract: Among the many Tangut manuscripts housed in the Institute of Oriental Manuscripts, Russian Academy of Sciences, a short fragment is entitled *Unlocking the Instruction of Empty Victory Banner on Buddhist Epistemology* (𗅋𗏁𗖵𗂸𗏹𗠁𗤀𗉔, *Tśhja wo ŋa dźjow tshji ŋwu̱ wjij* *phie*, Inv. 912). This concise treatise, almost a dictionary, provides pithy explanations for essential concepts in Buddhist epistemology, such as the four types of direct perception. The structure and some words and phrases of the text seem to reflect those in the works of Gsang phu ne'u thog masters. This paper examines these features and explores the intellectual environment in which Tangut Buddhists acquired Tibetan expertise in Buddhist epistemology.

Keywords: Kharakhoto documents; Buddhist epistemology; Gsang phu ne'u thog; Tangut Buddhism

噶译师软奴班与大黑天教法在西夏之流传

侯浩然
浙江大学历史学院

摘　要：本文旨在深入探究 12 世纪藏传佛教高僧噶译师软奴班（1105—？）之生平事迹。彼出生于汉藏交界宗喀之地，三十岁时，孤身跋涉天竺，拜谒诸名师，潜心修习佛法，历经十三载春秋。归雪域后，途经乌斯藏，渐至藏东之壤。复以七年之功，于朵甘思广布法音，教化众生。近来，学者于黑水城出土文献之中，发现多种大黑天教法之典籍，兼以汉藏双语载录，其年代横跨 12 至 14 世纪。其中，不乏噶译师所传扬之教法。本文拟稽考其藏文传记，并研析黑水城所出之相关写本残卷，以期明晰噶译师软奴班于天竺求法以及在朵甘思传法之见闻和经历，进一步揭示其对大黑天教法在西夏（1038—1227）弘传之贡献与影响。

关键词：藏传佛教；高僧传；西夏；大黑天信仰

rGwa Lotsāwa gZhon nu dpal and the Spread of the Mahākāla Teachings in the Tangut Empire

Hou Haoran
School of History, Zhejiang University

Abstract: This paper presents a study of the 12th-century Tibetan Buddhist master rGwa Lotsāwa gZhon nu dpal (1105–before 1193). He was born in the Tsong kha area. At the age of thirty, he embarked on a solitary journey to India. There, he took refuge under esteemed masters of his time, immersing himself in the study and practice of Buddhism for more than thirteen years. On his return to the Snow Land, he passed through dBus tshang and arrived at sDo Khams, where he spent seven years collecting disciples and preaching the Buddhist doctrines and practices. Recently, scholars have recovered a significant number of fragments and manuscripts of the Mahākāla literature from Kharakhoto. The textual materials, dating from between the 12th and 14th centuries, are written primarily in two languages, Tibetan and Chinese. Among them, a number are attributed to rGwa Lotsāwa gZhon nu dpal. Based on his biography and the excavated documents from Kharakhoto, this paper aims to examine the life story of rGwa Lotsāwa gZhon nu dpal, focusing on his experiences in India and sDo Khams, and to clarify his influence on the spread of the Mahākala teachings in the Tangut Empire (1038–1227).

Keywords: Tibetan Buddhisn; Buddhist Hagiography; the Tangut Empire; the Cult of Mahākala

关于《白史》的书名与前后序

乌云毕力格
中国人民大学国学院

摘　要：《白史》是蒙古学研究领域中学者意见分歧最大的文献之一，人们对这本书的书名有不同的理解。

《白史》是蒙古语 čaγan teüke 的对译。čaγan 在蒙古语中除了表示“白色”外，还具有“善、正”之意。Teüke 从 tegüge（古蒙古语里的发音为 teḥüḥe）变化而来，其词根为 tegü，意为“（把某东西）收集起来”。《白史》书名中的 tegüge 的含义是“集子”。故所谓《十善法白史》全书名的含义即《十善法正集》。

《白史》的这一书名与西藏“伏藏”文献有关。《白史》作者把他的书定位为关于十善法政教二道的历史、理论、信条、授记及执行政教二道的机构与制度设置的正确无误的信息大全。正因为如此，《白史》作者把藏文 *Bka' 'bum* 译成蒙古文用在自己的书名里，或许他正好参考过 *Ma ni bka' 'bum* 也未可料定。总之，所谓“白史”意为政教二道学说的“正善全集”，没有“白色史书”的含义。

《白史》的序言不符蒙古史书的一贯传统，给出了这本书的作者、二次编修人、参考文献、成书年代、掘藏师、发掘地点等所有信息，实际上就是按照西藏“伏藏”文献的做法编写的。《白史》的跋文的用语和字体也同样透露着作者故意仿古的特别安排，也是为了让人相信这本书的文字与元代蒙古人有关。

关键词：《白史》；蒙藏文化交流

On theTitle, Preface, and Postscript of *Čayan teüke (The White History)*

Oyunbilig Borjigidai
School of Chinese Classics, Renmin University of China

Abstract: *Čayan teüke*, or known as the *White History*, is one of the most controversial texts among scholars in the field of Mongolian studies, and the title of the book has been interpreted in different ways. "White History" is a word-for-word translation of the Mongolian phrase *čayan teüke*. In addition to "white", *čayan* also means "noble, righteous" in Mongolian. *Teüke* is transformed from *tegüge* (pronounced as *teḥüḥe* in ancient Mongolian), whose root is *tegü*, meaning "to gather (something) together". The meaning of *tegüge* in the title of the *White History* is "a collection of texts". Therefore, its full title *Arban buyantu nom-un čayan teüke*, or the *White History of Ten Virtuous Dharma*, needs to be understood as the "Noble Collection of Ten Virtuous Dharma". The title of this book is related to the Tibetan *terma* literature. The author of the *White History* defined his book as a compendium about the history, theories, tenets, teachings of the two paths—politics and religion—of Ten Virtuous Dharma and the institutional and systematic setup for their implementation. It is for this reason that the author translated the Tibetan word *bka' 'bum* into Mongolian and put it in the title of his book. It is possible that he happened to have referred to the *Ma ni bka' 'bum*. In any case, the so-called "White History" stands for the "noble and virtuous full collection" of the two paths of politics and religion, and has no meaning as "a white book of history". The preface to the *White History*, which is not in keeping with the traditions of Mongolian annals, gives all the information about its author, its secondary editor, the references, the date of completion, its discoverer (*gter ston*), the place of its discovery, etc. In fact, the organization of its preface exactly follows the practice of the Tibetan *terma* literature. The wording and font of the postscript of the *White History* likewise reveal the author's intention to imitate texts of the past and to give credence to the idea that the literature is related to the Mongols of the Yuan dynasty.

Keywords: *Čayan teüke* (the *White History*) ; Cultural exchange between Mongolia and Xizang

初探邬坚巴几部传记间的关系

孙鹏浩
南京大学历史学院

摘　要：围绕着元代乌思藏僧人邬坚巴辇真班（1230—1309）丰富的一生，不同的作者创作了大量藏文作品。从一则朝廷召请故事入手，通过分析不同作品的不同版本，包括《加持之流》《奇异海》和《口述传记下册》等，我们可以揭示细节呈现上的差异，并由此探索这些文本之间的关系。传记材料原本是若干独立的笔记（*zin bris*），由不同的编辑，从不同渠道搜罗和编辑。在弟子和信徒之中保存和流转的早期笔记，极容易产生混乱；而收集和整理工作涉及许多今天难以探寻的复杂因素。不过，我们可以看出这些传记之间的差异反映了传记作者在处理宗教与政治关系时的矛盾心理，也从不同的角度折射出元朝前期的西藏历史。

关键词：藏文传记；元代西番僧；乌思藏地方史

Exploring the Layers of the Biographies of U rgyan pa Rin chen dpal

Sun Penghao
School of History, Nanjing University

Abstract: A substantial corpus of Tibetan texts has been devoted to the life of U rgyan pa Rin chen dpal (1230–1309), a prominent monk from Dbus-Gtsang during the Yuan dynasty. This study focuses on a specific episode from his biographies—his encounter with a Mongol official named Tugh Temür—analyzing its various renditions in biographical works such as *Byin rlabs kyi chu rgyun*, *Ngo mtshar rgya mtsho*, and *Gsung sgros rnam thar*. These biographical accounts originally stemmed from a collection of independent notes (*zin bris*), compiled and edited by different individuals. These notes were preserved and circulated within U rgyan pa's discipleship, with their compilation shaped by intricate social dynamics that are now difficult to reconstruct in their entirety. Nonetheless, the divergences among these biographies reflect the compilers' differing perspectives on the interplay between religious and political concerns.

Keywords: Tibetan biographies; Tibetan monks during the Yuan Dynasty; Local history of Ü-Tsang

An Enigma of Tibetan *Leu* (*le'u*): Ritual, Ritual Lore, and Divinities of Foetus

Daniel Berounsky
Charles University, Prague

Abstract: This paper deals with the enigmatic Tibetan term *leu* (*le'u* or *le gu*). Already R. A. Stein, in a 1959 publication, noted the occurrence of this term in various contexts and assumed that it was somehow related to oral narratives and another term, *lde'u* ("riddles"). In contrast, a recent publication by Toni Huber interprets the term as "nine divisions (of ritual)" (*bon la le'u dgu*). The article following this introduction provides a number of references from mainly texts of the religious tradition of Bon dating between the 12th and 14th centuries. These show that far more often the term refers to specific deities (*le'u lha*) and only secondarily to ritualists or ritual tradition. Some fragments of texts indicate that these deities are meant to be *klu* and *gnyan* spirits. By the mid-20th century, a ritual tradition called *leu* was widespread in the Minshan region. Fragments of information from old ritualists in the area then reveal that these spirits *klu* and *gnyan* were worshipped for bringing forth offspring. This fact is then accompanied by information from some medical texts that interpret the term *le'u* to mean "fetus." From this information gathered, the hypothesis is then that the common term *le'u lha* referred to deities of human fertility, especially *klu* and *gnyan*, and by extension to the ritualists and ritual tradition related to them.

Keywords: *le'u/le gu*; the Bon rituals; the Minshan region

藏语“勒乌”（le'u）之谜：仪式、仪式传说和胎儿之神

丹尼尔·贝伦斯基
查理大学

摘　要：本文探讨了神秘的藏语术语“勒乌”（le'u或le gu）的含义。石泰安（R. A. Stein）在1959年发表的一篇文章中注意到该术语在各种语境中频繁出现，并推测它与口头叙事和另一个术语“lde'u”（“谜语”）之间存在着某种联系。而托尼·胡贝尔（Toni Huber）则在其新近出版的专著中对“勒乌”一词提出新解，将之阐释为“仪式的九个部分”（bon la le'u dgu）。在回顾前人成果之后，本文引用了大量源自12世纪至14世纪的苯教传统的文献资料。这些资料显示，“勒乌”一词更多时候指的是特定的神灵（le'u lha），其次指仪式师或仪式传统。一些文本片段进一步揭示，这些被称为le'u lha的神灵应该是“鲁”（klu）和“念”（gnyan）。时至20世纪中叶，一种名为“勒乌”的仪式传统在岷山地区广泛流传。根据当地年迈的仪式师提供的零散信息，人们敬奉“鲁”和“念”这两位神灵，祈求他们赐予后代。一些医学文献中的记载也印证了这一点，这些文献将“勒乌”（le'u）一词解释为“胎儿”。综合上述信息，我们可以合理推测，常见的术语le'u lha指的是主管人类生育的神灵，特别是“鲁”和“念”，而这一称谓也延伸到与他们相关的仪式师和仪式传统上。

关键词：勒乌；苯教仪轨；岷山地区

熟悉的经典，陌生的表述

——《金刚经》中的 *paścādbhaktapiṇḍapātapratikrāntaḥ*

萨尔吉

北京大学东方文学研究中心 / 西藏大学文学院

摘　要：文章以《金刚经》序分中 *paścādbhaktapiṇḍapātapratikrāntaḥ* 这一复合词入手，首先从校勘层面探讨梵文写本中与此复合词相关的前后语词的取舍；进而借助《金刚经》的多个汉藏译本，从文献学角度讨论该复合词在上下文中的语境，以及由该复合词引发的《金刚经》藏译本的编校问题，说明藏族人——无论是译者还是编校者——对《金刚经》不同传本的认识。文章参考莲花戒的《金刚经注疏》，说明对这一复合词的不同理解在印度学者中已经产生。文章旨在通过对《金刚经》不同写本和译本的探讨，揭示出文本生成、翻译、流通，直至再接受的复杂过程，以及语文学在理解这一过程中的独特功效。

关键词：《金刚经》；*paścādbhaktapiṇḍapātapratikrāntaḥ*；莲花戒；《金刚经注疏》

Familiar Scripture, Enigmatic Phrasing:

Paścādbhaktapiṇḍapātapratikrāntaḥ in the *Vajracchedikā-prajñāpāramitā-sūtra*

SAERJI

Research Center of Eastern Literature, Peking University

School of Humanities, Tibet University

Abstract: The article begins with the compound “paścādbhaktapiṇḍapātapratikrāntaḥ” in the prologue of the *Diamond Sutra* (the *Vajracchedikā-prajñāpāramitā-sūtra*) in Sanskrit, initially examining the word group surrounding the compound in Sanskrit manuscripts from a perspective of textual criticism. Subsequently, by utilizing multiple Chinese and Tibetan translations of the *Diamond Sutra*, the article digs into the contextual meaning of this compound from a philological standpoint. It also explores the editing challenges posed by this compound in Tibetan translations of the *Diamond Sutra*, thereby illustrating Tibetans', either translators' or editors' awareness for various understandings of this compound in the *Diamond Sutra*. The article refers to *the Commentary of Diamond Sutra* (the **Prajñāpāramitā-vajracchedikā-ṭīkā*) by Kamalaśīla, highlighting the emergence of diverse interpretations of this compound among Indian scholars. The aim of the article is to unveil the intricate process of text generation, translation, circulation, and re-acceptance by exploring different Sanskrit manuscripts and translations of the *Diamond Sutra*. Additionally, it underscores the distinctive role of philology in comprehending this dynamic process.

Keyword: *The Diamond Sutra*; *Paścādbhaktapiṇḍapātapratikrāntaḥ*; Kamalaśīla; *the Commentary of Diamond Sutra*

“阿魏”：一个中古外来词的中国化历程

陈　明

北京大学东方文学研究中心 / 北京大学外国语学院南亚学系

摘　要： 受佛教东传以及与西亚文化交流的影响，汉唐时期出现了大量的形式多样的外来词。这些词语有的被吸收到汉语词库中，逐渐褪去了外来色彩，成为本土词；有的则消失了。不同外来词的中国化的历程也各不相同，其不同的相遇、采纳、吸收、同化的情形值得深入研究，以揭示不同语言的交融特征。本文以中古时期的域外药用植物“阿魏”为例，试图梳理该词从魏晋到晚清民国时期漫长的中国化历程，揭示该词在不同时期所对应的不同域外语言形态，不仅为探讨佛经词语的中国化提供了一个实例分析，更为深化中外医学与文化交流史的认识做出了新的尝试。

关键词： 阿魏；外来词；佛经词语；中国化；文化交流

The Sinicization of a Foreign Word in the Medieval Period

—Taking Awei 阿魏 (Asafoetida) as an Example

Chen Ming

Research Center of Eastern Literature, Peking University

Department of South Asian Studies, School of Foreign Language, Peking University

Abstract: The Han to Tang periods (2nd to 10th centuries) witnessed a significant influx of foreign terms influenced by the spread of Buddhism from the Western regions and interactions with Persia (and the later emerging Arab influence). Some of these terms assimilated into the Chinese lexicon, gradually shedding their foreign connotations to become localized expressions, while others faded into obscurity. The Sinicization processes of these diverse foreign terms varied, presenting unique encounters of adoption, absorption, and localization, warranting in-depth investigation to unveil the merging characteristics of different languages. This study examines the foreign medicinal plant "awei 阿魏" (Asafoetida) during the medieval period. It traces its extensive Sinicization process from the Wei-Jin period to the late Qing and Republic of China era. The aim is to delineate the various linguistic forms corresponding to this term in different periods and across regions and languages, serving not only as an illustrative analysis for exploring the Sinicization of Buddhist textual language but also as a novel attempt to deepen our understanding of the history of medical and cultural exchange between Sinic and non-Sinic regions.

Keywords: awei (Asafoetida); Foreign Terms; Buddhist Terminology; Localization; Cultural Fusion and Exchange

A lag sha Ngag dbang bstan dar (1759–August 1, 1840) on some Chinese Lexemes and the Chinese Language, Part Two

Leonard W.J. van der Kuijp
Harvard University

Abstract: I recounted the little that we know about Ngag dbang bstan dar's life in the first part of this essay that was published in the volume that honors the work of my old comrade in studies, Franz-Karl Ehrhard. As far as Ngag dbang bstan dar's scholarship in general is concerned, he is especially known for his vignette-like glosses on several important texts, for his relatively short tracts dealing with the knowledge-domain of language (*sgra'i rig gnas*), which includes grammar, poetics and lexicography, with logic and epistemology, as well as for a number of commentaries on shorter works. Several of these he never completed and we must be grateful to the unknown editor(s) of his "complete" works for nonetheless including these fragments in his *gsung 'bum*. Not the usual traditional scholar, he was also interested in more practical matters as is indicated in his fascinating study of the weights, measures, and currencies of Indian, Sinitic and Tibetan regions and their relative valuations in the past as well as in the present, a work that should prove of interest to someone studying aspects of Xizang's economic history. Further details about this work are given below and in the Appendix.

Keywords: A lag sha Ngag dbang bstan dar; Xizang's economic history; Asian Cultural Exchange

阿拉善·阿旺丹达尔（A lag sha Ngag dbang bstan dar, 1759—1840 年 8 月 1 日）关于汉语词汇和语言的研究（第二部分）

范德康
哈佛大学

摘　要：在本文的第一部分，我已简要介绍了我们目前对阿旺丹达尔生平的有限了解。那篇文章有幸刊载于纪念我的老同学佛朗茨–卡尔·艾哈特（Franz-Karl Ehrhard）为藏学研究所作贡献的文集之中。谈及阿旺丹达尔的学术成就，他尤以对几部重要典籍所撰写的小品式注释而著称。他的这些作品篇幅虽短，但却涵盖了语言知识领域（*sgra'i rig gnas*）的多个方面，包括语法学、诗学、词典学，以及逻辑学和认识论。此外，他还发表了许多针对短篇作品的评论。值得一提的是，其中有几部作品他并未完成，我们应感激那些整理其“全集”、未署名姓的编撰者，正是他们将阿旺丹达尔的这些未竟遗作收录进他的文集之中。阿旺丹达尔并非一位拘泥于传统的学者，他对更为实际的问题也抱有浓厚的兴趣。这一点，从他对于印度、汉地和藏地的度量衡和货币单位，以及它们在历史变迁中的相对估值所做的引人入胜的研究中，便窥见一斑。他的这项研究，无疑将引起研究西藏经济史方面的学者们的极大兴趣。关于该研究的更多详细内容，请参见下文及附录。

关键词：阿旺丹达尔；西藏经济史；亚洲文化交流

陈寅恪与佛教和西域语文学研究

沈卫荣
清华大学人文学院中文系

摘　要： 在欧美接受过严格中亚语文学训练的陈寅恪，在归国前即以佛教和中亚（西域）语文学研究为其未来学术研究的重点，归国后便潜心梵、藏、汉佛教语文学以及敦煌汉文佛教文本的研究工作，并创造性地将东方文本语文学的文本精校和文本批评方法与中国传统的训诂、对勘和考据等方法完美结合在一起，使东西方学术传统熔于一炉。陈氏关于中亚（西域）语文学的文章寥寥数篇，却别开生面，成为中国最早的、具有国际一流水准的现代西藏学和蒙古学（蒙元史）研究成果，不但开创了佛教和西域语文学研究的学术新风，而且也为中国传统汉学研究注入了“虏学”（西域学）的新养分。

关键词： 陈寅恪；佛教语文学；蒙古学；藏学

Chen Yinke and His Studies of Buddhist and Central Asian Philology

Shen Weirong
Department of Chinese Language and Literature, School of Humanities, Tsinghua University

Abstract: Among studies of the intellectual history of modern China, few scholars have touched upon the philological perspectives found within Prof. Chen Yinke (1890–1969, also known as Tschen Yin-koh)'s corpus of scholarly output. What Chen retained from his Western academic background was his research focus on Central Asian and Buddhist philology. His philological approaches to the Dunhuang texts and Buddhist scriptures opened the doors of modern textual criticism in China; furthermore, his application of comparative philology to Chinese literature through a multilingual perspective was a pioneering work of modern Tibetan and Mongol-Yuan studies, and served to extend traditional Sinology to historical studies on the vast western regions of China.

Keywords: Chen Yinke; Buddhist philology; Mongolian Studies; Tibetology

编　后　记

侯浩然

随着此部《不古不今不中不西之学：纪念陈寅恪西域与佛教语文学研究文集》的编纂完成并付梓出版，我们似乎看到了陈寅恪先生那深邃而睿智的目光再次照亮西域与佛教语文学研究的道路。

说起这部文集的问世，其缘起可追溯至2022年10月，恰逢清华大学人文学院成立十周年，由沈卫荣教授策划，成功召开了“纪念陈寅恪西域与佛教语文学国际研讨会”。此次会议以线上与线下结合的方式进行，学者阵容鼎盛，线下群英荟萃，汇聚了国内众多杰出学者；线上更是跨越国界，吸引了来自欧美、日本、澳大利亚等世界各地名校的顶尖学者共襄盛举，可谓群贤毕至，高朋盈门。会议不设门槛，向全球听众开放，吸引了海内外众多学者的热烈参与，为当时颇为低迷的国内外学术交流注入了一股新的活力，堪称一场意义非凡的学术盛宴。

陈寅恪先生与清华大学有不解之缘，自欧美负笈归国后，他首先任教于清华大学国学院，受聘为四大导师之一，后又在中文系、历史系开设“佛经翻译文学”“梵文”等课程，矢志在中国开拓佛教语文学研究的新天地。作为一位训练有素的东方语文学家，陈寅恪先生兼收并蓄，不仅深谙传统学问之精髓，更汲取了欧洲现代语文学的先进方法和规范，将其巧妙地融入自己的研究之中。在佛教语文学及中亚（西域）语文学领域，他以独到的学术见解和深厚的学识底蕴，为中国学界带来了全新的研究视角和方法论，开启了学术研究的新篇章。

然而，陈先生的研究旨趣在当时显得曲高和寡，未能立即得到同辈学者的共鸣与响应，且他的学术重心随后转向了中古史领域，但他在西域和佛教语文学研究所留下的深刻烙印，却跨越了时空的界限，对中国现代印度学、蒙古学、西藏学、西夏学、满学、突厥学等诸多学科的产生和发展起到了开创性的作用。“念念不忘，必有回响。”而今，这部文集的出版，不仅是一部会议论文的集合，更是对陈寅恪先生在西域和佛教语文学领域卓越学术贡献的深情缅怀，对他在清华大学任教生涯的崇高致敬。

在入职浙江大学历史学院之前，我有幸在清华大学中文系从事了为期两年的博士后研究，期间参与了此次会议的筹备与组织工作。会议圆满结束后，我又承担了论文的收集和编辑工作。作为主编，我深知肩负重任。文集中所收录的每一篇论文，都是作者心血与智慧的结晶，凝聚着他们的学术探索与研究热忱。论文主题广泛而深入，涵盖了印度佛教、汉藏佛教、佛教在中亚（西域）的传播和影响、跨文化交流传播、西藏民间宗教以及吐蕃与归义军的历史等。在研究材料上，论文作者们博采众长，广泛涉猎。他们深入挖掘了敦煌文献宝藏，解读梵文贝叶经，梳理了中亚出土的多语种佛教文献和残卷，研究了黑水城出土文献，发掘了汉、藏文大藏经的宝库，还关注了佛教艺术、医方文献、民间文献等多种材料。这些丰富多样的研究材料，为论文的撰写提供了坚实的基础和广阔的视野。更加难能可贵的是，作者们普遍能够熟练运用西域语言进行研究，如梵文、巴利文、藏文、回鹘文、西夏文、蒙古文、粟特文等。这些研究成果，秉持着语文学的严谨方法，将语言和文本作为研究的核心特色，不仅极大地丰富了我们对西域与佛教语文学的认知和理解，还为我们提供了新的研究思路和方法论启示。

在阅读这些论文时，我无不深感敬佩、赞叹与鼓舞。敬佩于前辈学者们的卓越成就与深厚学识，他们以其深邃的洞察力和不懈的探索精神，筚路蓝缕、披荆斩棘，为西域与佛教语文学研究开疆拓土、奠定基石；赞叹于同辈学者的国际化视野与创新精神，他们勇于挑战传统束缚，敢于提出独到新见，不断拓展研究的边界，为这一领域注入了新的活力。而西域与佛教语文学研究领域的广阔前景与无限可能，更是让我倍感鼓舞，充满了对未来的期待与憧憬。

这部文集的出版，不仅是对过去研究成果的总结与展示，更是对未来研究的激励与召唤。我相信，它将激励更多的青年学者投身于这一领域的研究之中，共同为推动西域与佛教语文学研究的繁荣与发展贡献自己的力量。在此，我要向所有参与此文集的撰写、编纂与出版的学者与工作人员表示最诚挚的感谢。是你们的辛勤付出与无私奉献，使得这部文集得以顺利问世，为学界增添了一份宝贵的财富。愿这部文集成为连接过去与未来的学术桥梁，让陈寅恪先生“独立之精神、自由之思想”的学术理念得以薪火相传，生生不息！